THE OTHER SIDE OF THE WIRE VOLUME 4

With the XIV Reserve Corps to the Bitter End, September 1917–11 November 1918

Ralph J. Whitehead

Hardback edition produced in a strictly limited printing of 750 individually numbered and signed copies

This copy is 003 of 750

Ralph J Whitehead

THE OTHER SIDE OF THE WIRE VOLUME 4

With the XIV Reserve Corps to the Bitter End, September 1917–11 November 1918

Ralph J. Whitehead

Helion & Company

Helion & Company Limited
Unit 8 Amherst Business Centre
Budbrooke Road
Warwick
CV34 5WE
England
Tel. 01926 499 619
Email: info@helion.co.uk
Website: www.helion.co.uk
Twitter: @helionbooks
Visit our blog at blog.helion.co.uk

Published by Helion & Company 2024
Designed and typeset by Mach 3 Solutions (www.mach3solutions.co.uk)
Cover designed by Paul Hewitt, Battlefield Design (www.battlefield-design.co.uk)

ISBN 978-1-912390-88-5

British Library Cataloguing-in-Publication Data.
A catalogue record for this book is available from the British Library.

Preface

The creation of the third and fourth volumes of my series of volumes on the XIV Reserve Corps has been the most difficult of the entire project. These volumes took far longer to complete than I had expected, in part due to the need to accumulate and then translate all of the materials that were necessary for the narrative, in part due to unexpected outside factors that are beyond our control. Finally, after a great deal of time and effort I have finally reached the point where I am pleased with the results of my writing. I feel that the last book has remained true to my original efforts to restore the humanity of the people behind the historic facts and not just to provide places and dates and troop movements.

Perhaps this approach is appropriate now that every veteran of the Great War has passed away from old age and there is no one left to provide a personal experience of the war. Without books that preserve the information we have today, what will become of it all in the future? I am reminded daily of just how little people respect the study of the past, whether ancient time periods or events that happened even a few decades ago. This lack of interest was evident in the recent political campaign for the presidency of the United States and the final outcome of this event. I have been watching events and listening to rhetoric that remind me all too much of the actions of certain world leaders from the 1930s with mounting concerns. The most frightening aspect of it all is how few people appear to see the same thing as I do and simply ignore the possibility of history becoming repeated.

When I look at my grandchildren, five at present count, Clara, Owen, Eliza, Sophie and Alice, I hope that they will have an interest in history or at the very least have an understanding of the events that shaped the world in which they live. In my point of view I see most if not all modern world events having their roots in the Great War.

The Second World War is a direct extension of the Great War, as is the Ba'ath Party in the Middle East that grew out of the events of the Second World War. The turmoil that faced the world by 1918 was directly involved in the formation of the Communist Party, the Cold War, the Iron Curtain, conflicts throughout Asia, Africa and the Middle East can all be traced to events and decisions made during and after the Great War. In the Middle East the Sykes-Picot Agreement and the rise of Arab nationalism shaped that region of the world and set the stage for what we are experiencing today. If so many of today's problems can be traced back to a war that ended over a century ago, perhaps we should have a better understanding of the war and the actions that followed so we know why certain events occurred and perhaps be able to predict the general course of future occurrences. Who knows if my point of view is correct or just my odd way of thinking?

In either case, I am pleased to have the chance to have my efforts published and I would like to thank the foresight of Helion & Co. Limited in general and my publisher Duncan Rogers in particular, for taking on an unknown author with a subject that has a limited readership in the overall scheme of things.

Acknowledgments

As I had originally planned on producing a single volume about the XIV Reserve Corps from the period of late September 1914 through 30 June 1916 I was not adequately prepared to expand this single volume into what would eventually become four volumes that would cover the XIV Reserve Corps through the end of the war and in the decades that followed.

Much of the time was spent in translating the hundreds of pages of German documents needed to complete the book and reviewing thousands of original records from various national archives for any mention of the XIV Reserve Corps. Fortunately, I had the required books in my collection as well as having unprecedented access to on-line archive materials, something that has only increased in scope since I started the first volume.

It seems that with the publication of each volume I receive more and more inquiries from fellow enthusiasts as well as people with family connections to the men of the XIV Reserve Corps. In this last category, I am extremely grateful to everyone who has shared their family history with me and who have a similar interest in history, especially when it involves the XIV Reserve Corps. I would like to thank Rod Otey of London, England in particular for his support, his family history and his enthusiasm. It seems that with each volume I have relied upon a good friend and fellow enthusiast Felix Fregin from the Netherlands. Despite having the responsibilities of a growing family, Felix has been very helpful in providing support in obtaining photos from his superb collection and most of all translations of Sütterlin script from various letters. I would also like to mention Major Jason Coad who shared his personal story about his great-grandfather who had been a member of RIR 109.

This increased level of interest and the current celebrations of the 100th Anniversary of the war have had a detrimental effect on my personal collecting habits. While once it was not very difficult to locate and obtain period postcards and other memorabilia related to the XIV Reserve Corps, the prices and the competition have increased dramatically. More often than not I have lost out on numerous items listed on on-line auctions making it that much harder to obtain the illustrations that could be used to enhance the written narrative with photographs of the actual men who are mentioned.

German Army Organization and Rank Comparison

In order for the reader to better understand the military terms and ranks mentioned in this volume, I have prepared a basic breakdown of the formation of the German army and the comparison of ranks between the German Army and the British Army. The German Army consisted of several parts including Active regiments, Reserve regiments, *Landwehr* regiments and *Landsturm* units. All qualified German males would be required to serve 2 years in the Active Army starting at age 20. 4-5 years in the Reserve, 11 years in the Landwehr and 7 years in the *Landsturm* 2nd Ban followed this.

The basic infantry regiment consisted of three battalions of infantry, designated I, II and III. Each battalion consisted of four companies (1-4, 5-8 and 9-12 respectively) that were further broken down into three platoons (*Zug*) and then into sections or *Gruppe* that consisted of 1 Non-Commissioned Officer and 8 men. Each soldier in a reserve regiment would have been armed with the M98 Mauser rifle or the M88 rifle. Each regiment would normally contain one Machine Gun Company armed with six MG08 heavy machine guns and one spare gun. The average strength of the regiment would have been 83 officers and 3,204 men.

The XIV Reserve Corps that was presented in Volume 2 has been restored to include the two original divisions, the 26th (Württemberg) and 28th (Baden) Reserve Divisions. The different divisions contained men from one active regiment as well as reserve regiments. The men who fought on the German side could range in age from their late teens to a few in their 50s and 60s. The field artillery was normally established into three sections or *Abteilung*. The I and II *Abteilung* consisted of 3 batteries each of M96 7.7cm field guns while the III *Abteilung* consisted of 3 batteries of M98.09 10.5cm light field howitzers.

As in most cases there were always exceptions to the rules. RIR 99 was one of the regiments in the army that had 4 battalions (I, II, III, IV) instead of the normal 3 and therefore had 16 companies of infantry at the start of the war. The 27th RFAR assigned to the 28th Reserve Division consisted of two *Abteilung* (I and II) and was not equipped with the light field howitzers, something not uncommon in reserve units.

Abbreviations used to designate the different military units found in this book.

RIR 99	Reserve Infantry Regiment Nr. 99
IR 180	Infantry Regiment Nr. 180
II/RFAR 26	II *Abteilung* Reserve Field Artillery Regiment Nr. 26
4/R109	4th Company Reserve Infantry Regiment Nr. 109
III/R111	III Battalion Reserve Infantry Regiment Nr. 111
9/180	9th Company Infantry Regiment Nr. 180
III(F)/FAR 12	III *Abteilung*, (howitzers), Field Artillery Regiment Nr. 12
1R/*Pionier* Bn 13	1st Reserve Company 13th *Pionier* Battalion

Rank Comparison

Grenadier *Musketier* *Füsilier* *Jäger* *Wehrmann* *Landsturmmann* *Landsturmpflichtiger* *Reservist* *Infanterist* *Soldat* *Ersatz-Reservist*	Ranks equivalent to a Private Soldier. The different terms were due to the type of unit the soldier belonged to, the military class of the soldier or from tradition.
Schütze}	(Normally associated with Machine Gun troops)
Einjährig Freiwilliger	One Year Volunteer
Kriegsfreiwilliger	War Volunteer
Kanonier	Gunner
Radfahrer	Cyclist
Pionier	Sapper
Fahrer	Driver
Hornist	Trumpeter
Tambour	Drummer
Krankenträger	Stretcher-bearer
Gefreiter	Lance Corporal
Oberjäger	Corporal (*Jäger* units)
Unteroffizier	Corporal
Sergeant	Sergeant
Vizefeldwebel	Staff Sergeant
Vizewachtmeister	Staff Sergeant (Cavalry, artillery, train)

Feldwebel	Sergeant Major
Wachtmeister	Sergeant Major (Cavalry, artillery)
Fähnrich	Officer Cadet
Offizier Stellvertreter	Acting officer
Feldwebelleutnant	Sergeant Major Lieutenant
Leutnant	Second Lieutenant
Oberleutnant	Lieutenant
Rittmeister	Captain (Mounted unit, Transport)
Hauptmann	Captain
Major	Major
Oberstleutnant	Lieutenant Colonel
Oberst	Colonel
Generalmajor	Major General
Generalleutnant	Lieutenant General
General der Artillerie	General of Artillery
General der Infanterie	General of Infantry
General der Kavallerie	General of Cavalry

Medical Staff

Sanitäter	Medical Assistant
Assistentzarzt	Second Lieutenant
Oberarzt	Lieutenant
Stabsarzt	Captain
Oberstabsarzt	Major or higher

Chaplains

Pfarrer	Padre

One final point regarding terminology used in the Great War. The reader will note the use of terms such as shrapnel and shellfire. These represent two different types of ammunition used during the war. High explosive shells formed fragments or splinters when exploding and were set off by impact fuzes. Shrapnel shells were basically large shotgun shells. Each shrapnel shell was filled with numerous lead balls that were expelled by an explosive charge inside the shell casing. This was accomplished with the use of a time fuze so that the shell would burst at an appropriate height above enemy troops scattering the lead balls over a wide area. The term shrapnel only applies to the latter type of shell and should not be confused with the modern version of this term.

Introduction

It was a warm night in the summer of 1956 as a small group of elderly men sat around a table at a restaurant in Stuttgart, enjoying cigars and cigarettes while finishing their beer and coffee. They looked like any other group of friends who were sharing a pleasant evening together.

The average onlooker would never tell that so much had happened in the lives of these men; the turmoil of the First World War, the collapse of the German monarchy and the civil unrest that followed. The terrible times with the restrictions placed on Germany from the Versailles Treaty to the crippling effect of hyper-inflation that was rampant during the Great Depression only to be followed by the rise of the National Socialist Party, the Nazi Party under Adolf Hitler and the horrendous six-year war that followed. Then, the Cold War, with the partition of Berlin and Germany as Communists assumed control of Eastern Europe.

Now, while in the midst of the Cold War, the older men sitting around the table were not concerned about any of these recent problems, instead they were reminiscing about the time they had spent in the 26th Reserve Division during the Great War. They

Veterans of the 26th Reserve Division, 1956. (Author's collection)

talked about old, almost forgotten friends and the events they had experienced in the war. Time had tempered many of the stories and memories of these men; however what they had undergone their minds were as sharp as they had been so many years earlier. It was a time of great sacrifice and loss for these old soldiers and the bonds that had formed during their shared experiences in the war would last until they had all died from old age.

In looking at these old men, it would be difficult to see them in their youth, full of life and hopes for the future. They had survived all that history had thrown at them, and what they looked back upon with such pride was formed in a time when the world was a very different place. With the last of these men having died of old age, their memories would of the time of the Great War would eventually be lost if it were not for current historians, professionals as well as amateurs, who have taken the time to preserve their history.

What follows is an account of the events that took place in the last year of the war until the Armistice in November 1918 and a brief look at the decades that followed the Great War. Hopefully the information provided will give the readers a small idea of the events that helped shape the history of the modern world and keep the memory of the men on all sides of the first great conflict of the 20th Century alive for future generations.

1

The 28th Reserve Division

August–December 1917
Aisne Sector. 3rd Army, Group Dormoise, XXVI Reserve Corps, 56th Reserve Infantry Brigade, Sector K (R109), LL (R110), M (R111)

Following the recent fighting by Verdun, the men of the 28th Reserve Division were not being given any time to even catch their breath. After arriving in the Aisne sector, the I/R109 was reviewed on 29 August 1917 by the Brigade Commander, *Generalmajor* Rogge. Following the review, the battalion sent out an advance party to the new sector by motor lorries on 30 August 1917. On the same evening the I/R109 was moved to Ardeuil, from where the battalion marched to the new position, arriving at 12 midnight. In the early morning hours of 31 August 1917 the I/R109 relieved the III/91 in the right sectors K1 and K2 and in the same night the II/R109 relieved the II/91 in the left sectors K3 and K4. The command of the sectors was taken over by the regimental staff at 8 a.m. on 1 September 1917.

The position located on the *Kanonenberg* was already familiar to the men of RIR 109 from the summer of 1916. This time, the sectors held by each regiment were far wider than the earlier occupation. Now, two battalions were placed in the forward position, one next to the other, each with two companies in the battle trench. One readiness company was on the right in the *Herzberg Stollen*, one the left in the *Pionier Stollen* and one readiness company acted as the security garrison on the right in the strongpoints *Zoo*, *Halle*, *Magdeburg* and *Berlin*, northwest of Cernay, and on the left in the strongpoint *Altmark*.

The position was well constructed, with an extensive tunnel system that allowed the reserves to be quickly brought up from the rear. This was critical as the position lacked any real depth and the reserves needed to be kept in a safe location in order to remain intact when needed at the front. The distance to the enemy trenches varied greatly in the new position. In the right sector, the forward enemy trench was only 60 to 80 meters distant; on the left it was considerably further, up to 900 meters distant.

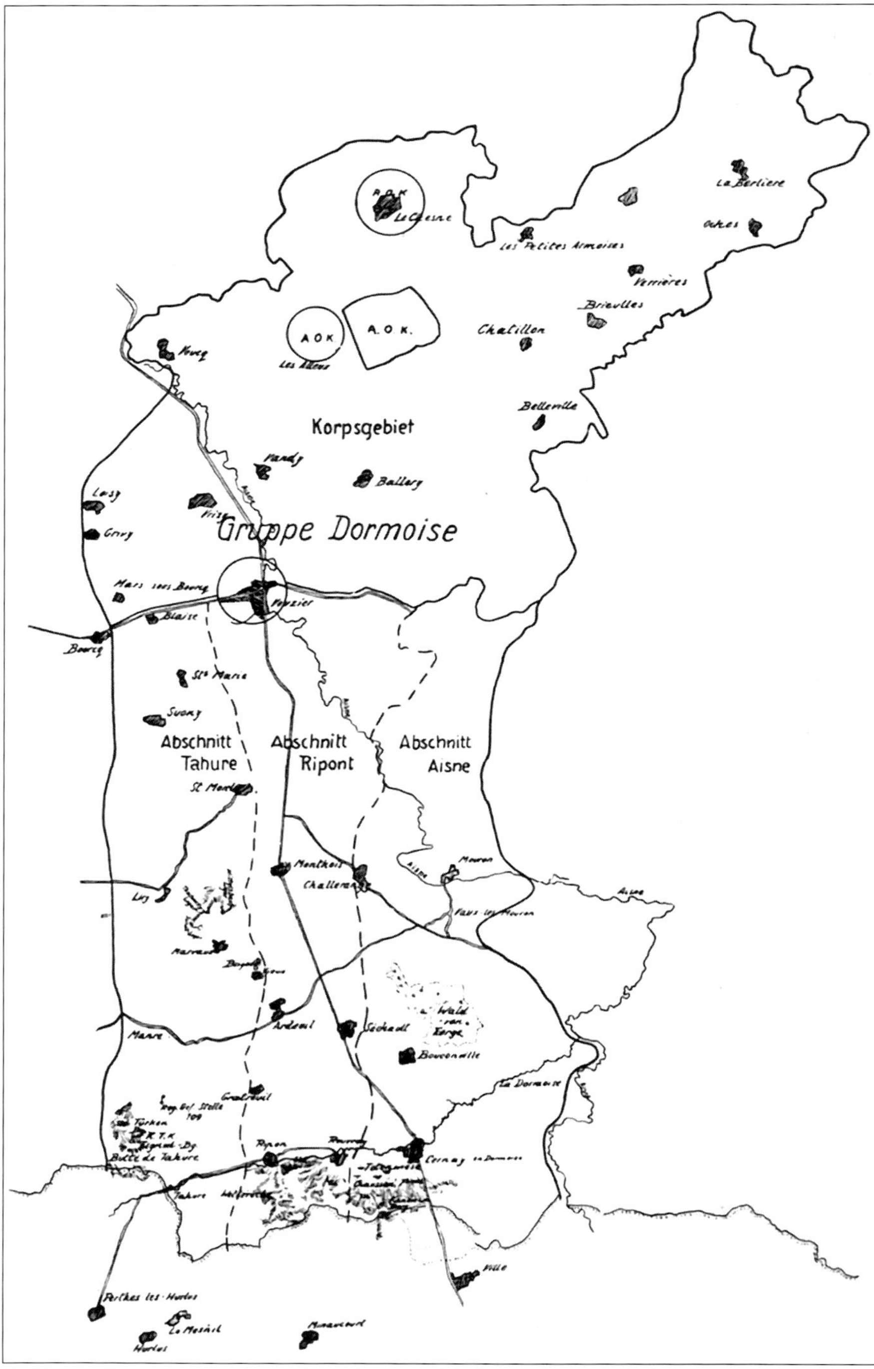

Gruppe Dormoise.

RIR 110 was inserted on the right of RIR 109; RIR 111 was inserted on the left. The position was relatively quiet with an occasional burst of fire from the enemy artillery or mine throwers. However, a revolver cannon located in front of the left battalion sector made itself quite disagreeable, causing a number of losses with its annoying fire. Among the losses was *Leutnant of der Reserve* Schönthal, leader of the 1/R109; he was killed by French shell fire on 4 September 1917. He had only belonged to the regiment since July 1916 following the opening of the Battle of the Somme. He was considered a brave soldier who was respected by his commanders and loved by his subordinates. His loss was considered to be particularly painful for the regiment.

The majority of men of RIR 110 were housed in barracks. There, the men were deloused, rested and restored their uniforms and equipment. An advance detachment of the I/R110 consisting of the Battalion staff and three company leaders was transported by motor lorries to the new position at 2.00 a.m. on 30 August 1917. *Leutnant* Eggert, 4/R110, then led the battalion forward on the same evening; RIR 110 was going to be deployed in the Bois de Ville.

The I/R110 relieved the II/74 in Sector M Right. In the night from 31 August to 1 September 1917 the II/R110 relieved the I/74 in Sector M Left without incident. The companies were transported by train to a nearby location and then marched on foot to the position. The III/R110 remained in rest in the *Saalburg Lager*.

The position taken over by RIR 110 was described as 'quiet' and that was extremely appreciated by the men who were literally exhausted from the recent fighting by Verdun. Relaxation was needed for the men to recover their physical and mental strength and the quiet position would be enjoyed for as long as they occupied it. No heavy tasks were expected of them other than normal trench routine.

The right wing regiment of the division, RIR 109, occupied the position on the right flank of RIR 110, where the *Kanonenberg*, a mound of churned up chalk towered above the position with a steep slope to the east and more level slope to the north. The battalion staff of the III/R110 lived in a comfortably furnished concrete dugout in the Bois de Ville, also called the *Stadtwald*. The battalion battle headquarters in a good position, near the railway and close to the reserve company. The regimental battle headquarters lay in the Pappel copse. Generally, the line was good. The weakest point of the division sector was considered to be the left wing of the position held by RIR 110. Great effort was made to ensure that this part of the line was reinforced as much as possible.

When RIR 110 arrived at the *Stadtwald* the trees were still in full foliage. Over time, the forest would gradually turn to bright fall colors and finally became bare and bleak in the winter months. The forest was passed through with glades and trenches; it accommodated infantry, machine guns, *Minenwerfer* and artillery and kept the position kitchens hidden from enemy observation. A German cemetery lay in the middle of the former Bois de Ville Farm. Here rested the numerous fallen from the Champagne fighting in 1915.

The men discovered strange, almost mysterious trenches that cut through the wood where there were no fire trenches. The mystery of these odd trenches would soon become solved when with the onset of the rainy season the concrete shelters became full of water. These mysterious trenches were artificially created open drainage facilities, which

Souvenir postcard, RIR 110. (Author's collection)

Souvenir postcard, RIR 110. (Author's collection)

diverted the excess water and made the accommodations of the troops in the *Stadtwald* habitable during the winter months.

> On 2 September 1917, healed from my wounds again, in accordance with my orders by the 28th Reserve Division in Mouron an der Aisne I reported for new front line duty. I asked about the new situation there. I was assigned to RIR 110 and entrusted with the command of the 7th Coy, which at the time was in the front in the Bois de Ville in the valley which lay between the Argonne and the Champagne. On the way there I asked a *Landser* who was coming back how the position was: 'It is very green, like a summer fresh Rhein' was the jolly reply. The man had not exaggerated much. The position actually moved through what the front soldiers at first considered immensely peaceful and graceful and had moreover contained uncommon comforts. The mutual exchange of shells was temporal and the quantity was regulated, as one was soon informed. A velocipede arranged the traffic to the front and was on almost every connection to the forward trench. Warm bath tubs were installed in the second trench line. Anybody that paid homage to the sport of hunting, found opportunities at the sea of Ville a Tourbe in front of the first line and found game ducks to shoot or sport fishing to make use of; there also the French made use of this hunting territory, a certain reciprocal consideration was necessary, which also became practiced with pleasure. The regiment came out of the Hell of Verdun, and so it was understandable that this became relatively felt like a paradise.
>
> *Leutnant der Reserve* Fritz Schmitt, RIR 110.[1]

Railway lines also existed in the *Stadtwald*, which were used for transporting men, materials and food to the front much to the great delight of the regimental transport. Now only one man was required to operate the engine to deliver all of the supplies and material that was needed at the front each night. The railway station equipment also served one other purpose than simply transporting men and supplies; bathtubs had been installed by the kitchens of the left battalion sector, even one located in the second line. The large kettles of the bath facilities required hot water, which became heated with the railway engine overflow.

The foreground consisted of the swampy valley of the Tourbe. It was generally passable, particularly when the *pioniers* erected a dam by Chapelle Farm and elevated the level of the Tourbe over a meter. The area was safe from enemy observation because of the high reeds and clusters of bushes that blocked the enemy's view. Fortunately, the French were quite far off; and little could be seen of him. The wood of Hauzy contained the mysteries of the French position, just as the *Stadtwald* concealed the German positions. The hills of Vienne la Ville, Malmy, Virginy and Massige rose up south of the Tourbe valley, the places where the enemy had positioned his artillery.

On the opposite side, where the Aisne flowed, lay the town of Servon, and while it was once a pleasant place to live, now it was only ruins in which *Landwehr* troops were housed in shelters. To the east and south one could see the dark woods of the Argonne forest that was so hotly fought over several years earlier, and where silence now prevailed.

Regimental Headquarters, RIR 110 in the *Stadtwald*. (*Reserve-Infanterie-Regiment Nr. 110 im Weltkrieg 1914-1918*)

The enemy activity had been reduced to modest disturbance fire, which mostly lay on the right wing of Sector M-Right and on the Brigade Copse. At night the men could hear a couple of sentry shots, maybe one time the rattle of a machine gun. The pilot activity on both sides was low, something very appreciated by the troops. Individual patrols were sent out nightly, which were mostly uneventful. Enemy patrols that came up against the German sentries in the outpost zone were repulsed with little effort.

The rail journey from Chauvency le Château by way of Charleville-Vouziers brought RIR 111 into the Champagne again, into the zone of the 3rd Army. The battalions were unloaded on 26 and 27 August 1917 in Sugny south of Vouziers and received billets in the Army camp Mont St. Martin, located by the village of the same name, three kilometers south of Sugny, where the men were not begrudged a few days of rest in comfortable barracks. The area was well known to the veterans of RIR 111 from the period July-October 1916 when the regiment was at Ripont.

On 30 and 31 August 1917 the I and III/R111 were conveyed up to the ruins of Ardeuil on the same field-railway route the regiment had used in 1916 and relieved IR 78 on the left of trenches the regiment had previously occupied in a sector south of Cernay en Dormois.

The main position consisted of two lines running from the *Kanonenberg*, which RIR 109 had previously occupied, in an easterly direction via the *Kreuzberg* and ended about 1 kilometer east of the Cernay-Ville sur Tourbe Road, where RIR 110 was inserted, holding the front line up to the Aisne. The large road formed the border between the battalion sectors. Something new had been added to the defenses since the regiment had

More and more resources were being applied to anti-aircraft duties, RIR 111. (Author's collection)

been on the *Kanonenberg*. In order to prevent the approach of enemy tanks along the roadway, it was equipped with a deep cut across the road that served as a tank trap, and four light machine guns equipped with armour piercing K-Ammunition were distributed on both sides of the cut to act as a tank defense.

The position battalions had two companies each in the forward line placed next to one another. The regimental machine guns were deeply partitioned, distributed between and behind the lines; one machine gun platoon was specifically assigned for anti-aircraft duties. The position was well developed in general and offered sufficient numbers of shell proof housing. In the right sector the first and second lines were connected through a tunnel leading under the *Kreuzberg*, which had six entrances and exits and in which a garrison of approximately 300 men could find accommodations. The tunnel also held the reserve company and the battalion staff. However, the stay in the tunnel was considered to be unpleasant due to the prevailing dampness inside the mountain.

The left sector had a tunnel-barracks on the northern hillside which sloped down to Cernay, which took on the descriptive name '*Rattenburg*.' Subsequently to the east were further dugouts in a third line, the *Albrechtsburg*, in which the battalion staff had its command post. One company lay in the strongpoint *Thuringen* which was on the road leading out of Cernay in an easterly direction to Conde lez Autry. Kitchens were constructed at numerous places in the position, so that the men could be provided with warm food at any location of the sector.

The First Line Transport of RIR 111 was in Vaux, where the rest quarters of the regimental staff were located. The Construction Company lay by the railway station Autry south of Vaux des Mouron; alongside the work on concrete structures in the position, the largest part of the company was occupied with the creation of the 2nd battle zone in the vicinity of Bouconville.

There were unique dangers associated with the position, as some of the veterans remembered the horrific disaster at the *Winterberg Stollen.* On 27 September 1917 a barrel of benzene standing at one of the entrances of the *Kreuzberg Stollen* was ignited by a direct hit and a small fire broke out. The fire could have quickly spread to a nearby barracks in the tunnel, instead, the barracks were quickly blocked off and the fire was extinguished. The disaster of the *Winterberg Stollen* was not going to be allowed to be repeated. Despite the dampness and potential dangers, the companies were able to maintain their strength and were able to work on the extension of the position, especially the construction of concrete dugouts, and perhaps best of all, they also had time and opportunities for the education of the replacement troops in trench warfare.

The main position on this portion of the front was about 1,500 meters distant from the French, and as such it was a very quiet front. Apart from the occasional enemy artillery fire there was no fighting action taking place. Fortunately, the bombardments did not cause very much damage.

> I took over my sector in the best spirits on the left wing of the regiment [RIR 110] by the destroyed Chapelle Farm that was crowned by a heavy machine gun, called '*Ratte*', and moved into my above ground dugout with windows found in the immediate vicinity. Already on the next day I nearly suffered a bad shock in my opinion of the 'quiet' position. So about 5 p.m. the French artillery, entirely opposite the otherwise normal program threw a placement of four shots on the remains of the farm and placed this drama about me, which in the opinion of the Other Ranks was viewed as the equivalent of a broken treaty. The joy was of short duration, because almost in the same moment the air pressure from a short shot blew all of the window panes in my face, while behind me my den comrade who was holding his body, groaning and filled with pain, jumping from one leg to the other. It lasted a long time, until it was possible for me to open my eyes further and my pocket-mirror showed me a blood smeared face peppered with small glass splinters. Otherwise everything was in good order. The feared projectiles also injured my suffering comrade with a stomach blow from a fist sized stone. So I came away in the truest sense of the word with one blue eye, the other with a bruise. Quite slender results for the French, whose fun cost a couple of hundred shells. It was by the way unfair; one wanted the frog to be fully and completely shoved into the same shoes of this malignant raid. The *Ratte* at the farm was responsible first of all and out of shear malice had fired on a French pilot flying by, who then was so spiteful he hounded us with his artillery. No further disturbance occurred of the idyll.
>
> In the remaining therefore this position was not free from blemishes. It was the sign of the water. The high ground water in this terrain forced most to use the installation of concrete blocks as dugouts. Anyone who moved in this water could experience once that when one awakened in the morning and the entire furnishings

on the floor floated around on waves about the dweller. There was no lack of water rats and mice despite the presence of dogs and cats. Of particular note it brought the numerous amphibians like frogs, toads and lizards in the same accustomed monotony. Unfortunately my small racing hound Bubi, whose attack spirit was normally not lacking, took an opposite, friendly attitude towards these pests.

Leutnant der Reserve Fritz Schmitt, RIR 110.[2]

In sharp contrast to the main position with the large distance between the opposing sides were the experiences of the garrison holding a brick works situated in a clay-mine, which had been given the name *Briqueterie Stellung.* This position was in constant close battle contact with the enemy. This outpost line extended out from the *Kanonenberg* to the south and ran parallel to the enemy front in a length of 2,300 meters until to the Sea of Ville. The distance to the French position decreased west of the Cernay-Ville sur Tourbe Road until the opposing sides were 30 to 40 meters apart. Between the lines here was a tangle of old trenches, wire entanglements and large mine craters. The position consisted of two rather crumbling trenches lying one behind the other.

These trenches had been abandoned as a battle position because the enemy could easily observe every movement made inside them. Also, the unfavorable high ground water situation prevented the construction of deep mined tunnels. One company from RIR 111 served as the garrison of this position, which was relieved every ten days, alternating with the right or the left battalion. In order to be able to adequately secure the long sentry line, the company was reinforced through one platoon from the reserve company and two captured French machine guns. Only two Groups remained as rear support, which were with the company leader on *Schwerins Höhe,* located halfway to the main position.

The task of the company in the *Briqueterie Stellung* was difficult. It had to hold the front line against any small enemy attacks despite its poor defensive facilities. Faced with any large attacks, the sentries were directed to evade to *Schwerins Höhe,* where preferably longer opposition could be afforded. The terrain at *Schwerins Höhe* offered a favorable position however it still remained an open question, if the position could successfully withstand the impetus of a powerful enemy attack.

The sentries and the light shelters used by the relief troops inside the trench offered little protection against the enemy close combat methods. Also, the old facilities required a great deal of work, in order to ensure the routes used by the counterattack troops were always passable. In order to safeguard the *Briqueterie* Company, all enemy movements had to become recognized in a timely manner. This meant that patrols were sent out nightly, which occasionally clashed with enemy patrols.

In order to reach the front line the men of RIR 111 were required to march for three hours from the *Grunewald* rest camp, located in a forested hollow east of Vaux les Mouron. There were several other options available to transport some of the replacements to the front; one using a small field railway, another transporting the men with motor Lorries up until Cernay. However the field railway was primarily used to bring up food and other supplies and therefore could only carry a limited number of troops at any one time.

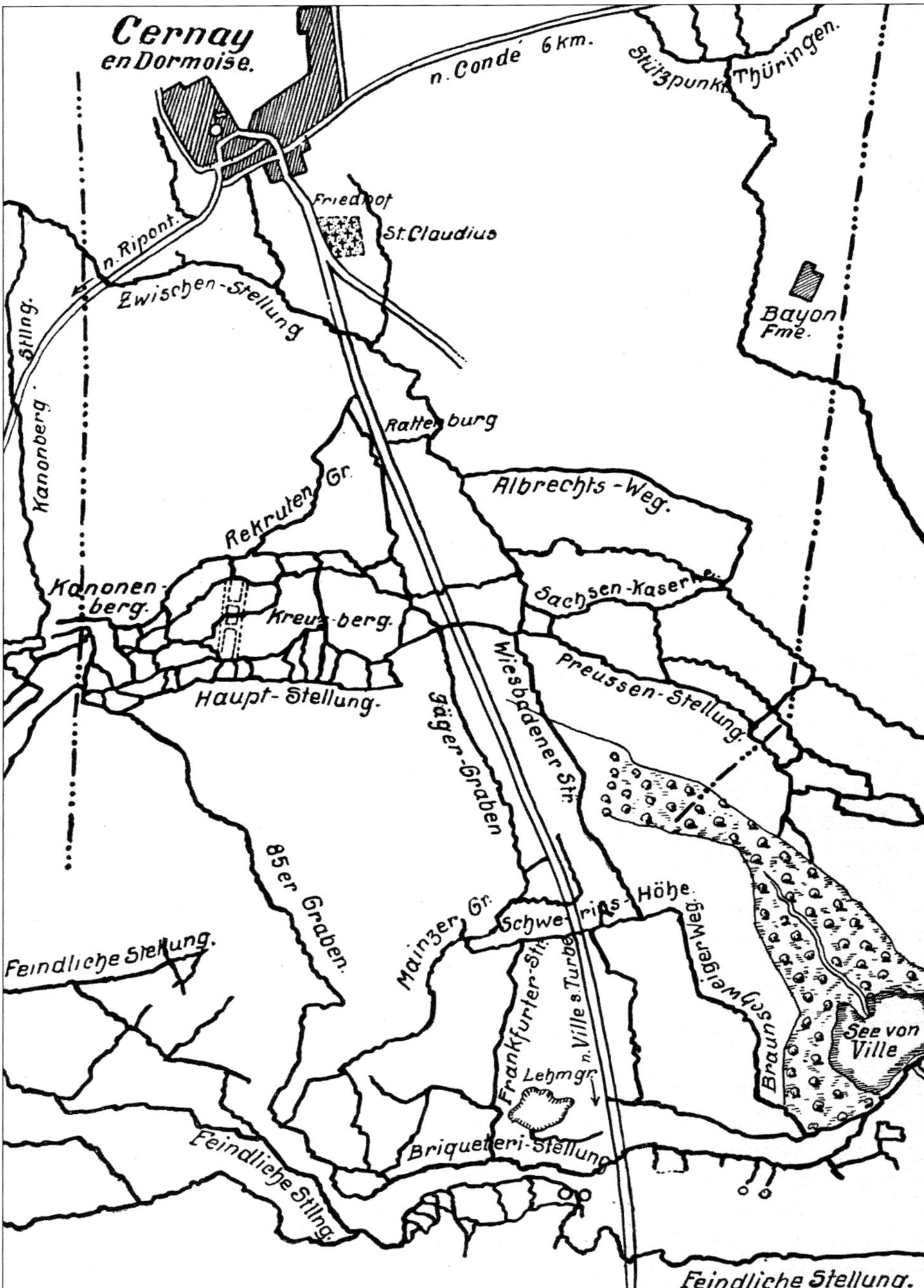

Trenches held by RIR 111.

The billets in the camp barracks were tidy and comfortable and generally safe from enemy shell fire. Because of these circumstances there was ample time for training; which was of special meaning at this time. The newest techniques developed for the defensive battle, were being introduced to the men; the mobile or fluid defense where the troops would no longer rigidly hold a fixed line.

An especially useful weapon for this new type of defense was the light MG 08/15 machine gun, of which each company was now allotted three guns. Training on the new weapons was pursued eagerly by the men who recognized the benefits of the increased firepower. There were also special training courses for the under-leaders furnished at the field recruit depot in Brientres in the latest tactics employed at the front. The significance of reliable battlefield communications became increasingly important in the regiments. A *Nachrichten* Company, (Communication Company), was set up in RIR 111; it was divided into four platoons, one for the regimental staff and one each for the battalions, which were to develop the secure connections from the battle line to the command post and maintain it at all times.

The main task that existed, besides the protection of the sector through sentries and patrols, was in the extension of the position. For this purpose a Construction Company was formed in RIR 110 again on 21 September 1917 out of the tradesmen from the three battalions and placed under the command of *Leutnant der Reserve* Zwanziger. This company was assigned to construct the concrete dugouts, the extension of the position on Hill 148 and the creation of the regimental battle headquarters in the Brigade Copse. At the end of October the Construction Company started the extension of a second battle zone for the regiment. Even with a specialized construction company there was

Nachrichten troops, RIR 111. (Author's collection)

7.6cm Light Minenwerfer training course, RIR 111. (Author's collection}

still more than enough work for the infantry companies in reinforcing the wire obstacles, the extension of the trenches and the all-important drainage facilities.

The rest battalion of RIR 109 was positioned in Vaux les Mouron on the Aisne in good billets. The rest time in RIR 109 also became used for exercises and drilling on a large training field established nearby. There had been a fundamental change in what now constituted 'training'. Instead of the companies using the pre-war drill regulations, the recently introduced 'Training Rules for the Infantry' was promoted. The new regulations were more in line with the realities facing the men at the front, especially in consideration of the new weapons and tactics being introduced. There were special courses given to the *Stosstrupps*, the crews of the MG 08/15 light machine gun as well as the *Minenwerfer*.

While two battalions occupied the front line sectors, the battle strength of RIR 109 was extraordinarily low through the heavy losses suffered on Hill 344 and was barely enough to be able to garrison the large sector. Over the next six weeks, RIR 109 received multiple drafts of new men that were a welcome addition to the undersized regiment.

In the period from 12 August to 26 August 1917 RIR 109 had lost 97 officers and men killed, 229 officers and men missing, as well as 89 men who were known to be prisoners of war. 385 officers and men wounded and 202 officers and men sick for a total of 1,002 officers and men. The trench strength of the regiment on the 19th was 27 officers, 11 *Offizier Stellvertreter*, 170 *Unteroffiziere* and 1,412 Other Ranks for a total of 1,620 officers and men (this number includes the regimental reserve and carrying troops).

On 31 August 1917: 12 *Unteroffiziere* and 300 men arrived from the Field Recruit Depot. On 9 September: 14 *Unteroffiziere*, 245 men arrived from Germany. On 15 September: 201 men arrived from Germany, amongst them were many returning wounded who had previously belonged to the regiment. On 26 September 1917: 129 men arrived. On 2 October: 21 men arrived from the Recruit Depot. On 12 October: 21 Bandsmen and 56 Machine Gun *Schützen* arrived.

With the addition of these men, by mid-October the regiment had the ration strength of 45 officers, 12 *Offizier Stellvertreter*, 2,289 men, 236 horses. The battle strength was 29 officers, eight *Offizier Stellvertreter*, 1,864 men, 28 MG 08 heavy machine guns and seven MG 08/15 light machine guns. The number of light machine guns was still far below the amount needed. As new supplies were received the companies would gradually receive the number of guns required under the newest guidelines. The low number of officers eventually became supplemented with several promotions and the arrival of an additional 16 officers and four *Offizier Stellvertreter*, part of which came from Germany, part came from other units who were transferred to the regiment.

The companies and battalions in RIR 110 were also gradually brought to full fighting strength once again. The companies received a stream of replacements, the vacant officer positions became newly filled; the machine gun companies received replacements for the guns lost in front of Verdun and the ammunition supplies were replenished. Three light MG 08/15 machine guns became assigned to each company. The *Minenwerfer* of the three battalions became combined to form one *Minenwerfer Abteilung* under the command of the *Minenwerfer* officer *Leutnant der Reserve* Linde and was immediately placed under the control of the regimental staff.

The quiet situation also allowed large numbers of officers, *Unteroffizieren* and Other Ranks being sent to company leader, machine gun, *Minenwerfer*, and *Stosstrupp* leader courses. During the rest period in the *Saalburg Lager* the companies and battalions had the time to properly train the new men, so that the troops were gradually restored to their old fighting strength once again.

Of course, not everything in the rear areas revolved around drills and training.

Gewehr Zollinger, RIR 110. (*Reserve-Infanterie-Regiment Nr. 110 im Weltkrieg 1914-1918*)

7.6cm Light *Minenwerfer* stand in the Bois de Ville. (*Reserve-Infanterie-Regiment Nr. 110 im Weltkrieg 1914-1918*)

There was still time for rest and relaxation. Concerts were given by the regimental band for amusement of the men. The church concerts by the regimental band offered a pleasant diversion for the troops. Movies were offered every evening in one of the field cinemas that had been taken over by the regiment and opportunities for bathing in the Aisne were a frequent occurrence and appreciated by the men, both for the ability to become clean on a regular basis as well as helping with the summer heat.

Advertising of and buying of war bonds became eagerly pursued in RIR 109. One officer was assigned as the advertising officer in each battalion, and the companies in each battalion held a competition in the amount reached in the purchase of war bonds by the men.

Whilst large portions of the new sector were quite distant from the enemy line, the portions of the line that projected within close proximity of the French trenches such as the *Briqueterie Stellung*, quickly became quite active following the arrival of the division. On the early morning of 1 September 1917, immediately after the *Briqueterie Stellung* was taken over by the 1/R111, enemy artillery fire was placed on *Schwerins Höhe* and the access-routes, while the sentry line was covered with rifle grenades and machine gun fire. At 6.00 a.m. two enemy assault detachments attempted to penetrate the German trench.

The company leader, *Leutnant* Winterer, had already sent a *Stosstrupp* toward the position from *Schwerins Höhe* at the commencement of the enemy fire-raid. The French had attacked the German line after blowing up the wire entanglements, aided through the dense fog, and at one spot captured a portion of the main trench. The sentry located here, who had raised the first alarm received support from nearby troops as well as the *Stosstrupp* sent by *Leutnant* Winterer and they immediately threw the French out of the position. At a second location the sentry was able to repulse the enemy in front of his position with support from his relief.

Such surprise raids were repeated over and over. So each *Briqueterie* company had a fully exhausting time behind them, when they were replaced after ten days in the position and then occupied an intermediate position south of Cernay. The regiment soon raised the question if the strain on the regimental strength outweighed the perception of the benefits of holding this portion of the line. The answer was no and on the corresponding recommendations by the regiment the sentry line in the forward most trenches became abandoned in the middle of September. The empty trenches became filled with wire obstacles and the protection of this portion of the line was taken on by patrols with advanced double sentry posts, behind which were four pickets, distributed in the few usable dugouts.

The defensive strength of the men located on *Schwerins Höhe* was considered to be quite effective, but the situation still facing the pickets remained threatening. The pickets were too far distant from one another to be able to provide mutual support, and the rest of the company on *Schwerins Höhe* could barely reach the position in a timely manner in the event of a sudden enemy raid.

This unfavorable situation of the position by *Schwerins Höhe* was soon discovered by the French, most likely from the betrayal of a deserter according to the regimental history of RIR 111. On the night of 30 September to 1 October 1917, 12 to 15 Frenchmen sneaked through the misty valley unnoticed and managed to reach the rear of the pickets at the left wing. Then blocking artillery fire fell with a sudden blow around the picket position and when the garrison exited the mined dugout, the French already stood in front of the entrance. Despite the element of surprise the French were quickly expelled.

Meanwhile, the sentry in the first trench at the left wing discovered that the captured French machine gun located there had been overrun by the enemy raiding party. The men who had been on guard had been surprised from behind and had put up an energetic defense; two of them, *Wehrmann* Tröndle, 3/R111, and *Musketier* Seitz, 1/R111, were killed through pistol shots to the head. Before the supports could interfere in the fighting, the enemy was gone, taking three prisoners with them.

Following this raid there was no more doubt that the outpost line with the small garrison was still not adequately secure. On 11 October 1917 the complete evacuation of the *Briqueterie* position was ordered. All fighting material and dugout furnishings considered to be useful were brought to the rear and the sentry line became moved back to *Schwerins Höhe*. The *Kanonenberg* and the sector on the left towards the Sea of Ville were all protected by pickets, which also had to preserve the connection to the neighboring regiments.

Patrols, which were formed from a special command, were committed to wiring and blocking off the foreground. They succeeded in deceiving the enemy about the occupation of the *Briqueterie* through eager firing with rifles, machine guns, *Granatwerfer*, as well as through frequent firing of light rockets so that at the end of November the enemy still continued to bombard the old picket positions with rifle grenades. All the while *Schwerins Höhe* continued to become reinforced entrenching. *Minenwerfer* were brought into position at *Schwerins Höhe*, which took the enemy trench lying opposite the *Briqueterie* under fire. RIR 111 constructed an elevated observation position for close surveillance of the adversary, which was occupied by *Offizier Stellvertreter* Schempp.

The *Briqueterie Stellung* then became the starting point for numerous operations held by RIR 111. Patrols went out across the tumbled down trenches and craters against enemy sentries. Patrols lurked in the intermediate terrain, waiting for opposing enemy patrols. However the French were very alert, and the heavily wired works hindered the mobility of the men, so that they did not succeed in bringing in any prisoners. On the lighter side, copies of the Gazette of the Ardennes occasionally became thrown into the enemy trench to let the French know that the Germans still controlled no man's land.

Proven patrol leaders at this time, filled with fresh attack spirit were: *Leutnants* Bender, Frey, Germer, Geng, Höfler and Trilling; *Offizier Stellvertreter* Wurth; Vizefeldwebel Joes 2/R111, Weimer 9/R111, Bauer 10/R111, Sälzler 12/R111; Sergeant Ziegler 3/R111; *Unteroffiziere* Kaiser 1/R111, Probst, Bischler 3/R111, Birke, Schienle 4/R111, Fabian, Grimm 5/R111, Schneider, Holland, Duffner 7/R111, Heid, Bitsch, Fegler, Küpper 9/R111, Wolfer 10/R111, Wessing 11/R111, Baas, Riegger, Schuhmann 12/R111; *Gefreiter* Buri, Oetzel 1/R111, Becker 3/R111, Dörsam, Dunke, Grimm 9/R111, Wüst 3MG/R111.

The reports of the numerous patrols provided a clear picture of the enemy sentry arrangements that were constantly shifting position. The forward enemy trenches were wired throughout, and advance French sentries were protected by especially strong, square shaped portable wire obstacles. Numerous machine gun positions were established throughout the French lines. Based upon the reconnaissance reports an operation was organized on the early morning of 10 September 1917. After a short period of preparation fire from artillery and *Minenwerfer*, the *Stosstrupp* of a *Sturmbataillon* reached a large crater between the lines west of the Cernay-Ville Road through an alley that an explosive tube had torn in the enemy wire entanglements.

However, the troops immediately received severe hand grenade fire from the opposite edge, which wounded several men, so that the leader gave the command to retreat. The sentries of the II/R111 then repulsed a French patrol, which wanted to follow after through the alley in the wire, with machine guns and hand grenades.

In another attempted raid, *Unteroffizier* Kaiser along with 10 men of the 1/R111 and six *pioniers* exited the German lines east of the Cernay-Ville Road at 3.45 a.m. The artillery and *Minenwerfer* remained silent; and after arduously crawling forward, by 4.30 a.m. Kaiser and his men were exploring the enemy line through an alley in the French wire obstacles, about 200 meters distant from the road. The *pioniers* cleared a second lane about 10 meters to the left of it with an explosive tube, then, breaking forth from two sides, they hoped to be able to capture an annoying enemy machine gun.

However, the sound of dragging the explosive tube apparently alerted the enemy sentries and before it could become detonated the patrol came under machine gun fire and hand grenades bursting all around; all attempts to break-in had to be given up. The raiding party was back in the German trench again at 5.00 a.m. without losses.

On the evening of 2 November 1917 the I/R111 staged an attack on a nearby French position as a distraction from a large operation by RIR 109. Five *Minenwerfer* fired effectively on a position west of the large road, and two *Flammenwerfer* directed their flaming spray on two projecting corners of the French position. Despite the diversion the French responded to the attack by the I/R111 with powerful defensive fire, which resulted in two slightly wounded men in the 2/R111.

The 'quiet' position was also being taken advantage of by RIR 109 through lively patrol activity. The position companies, especially in the left sector, sent out patrols almost every night into no man's land that explored the condition of the enemy obstacles and made detailed notes on the location of the enemy sentry posts and machine guns.

On 8 September 1917 patrol Operation 'Heiter' was attempted by RIR 109 with the participation of a *Stosstrupp* from *Sturmbataillon* 2 against *Blau Punkt 157*. Because of imprudent actions made by some of the men who were very noisy, the patrol was discovered by the enemy and repulsed through rifle and hand grenade fire.

At 11.45 p.m. on 7 October 1917, a patrol in the strength of two *Unteroffiziere* and 15 men, under the leadership of *Unteroffizier* Bürkle from the 2/R109, went forth from *Punkt 866* against the enemy position. They penetrated *Blau Punkt 157* by surprise, and rolled up the French trench to the left and attacked an enemy double sentry post and the French coming forth out of the dugouts with hand grenades. The patrol returned back to the exit position with two prisoners and without any German losses. *Unteroffizier* Bürkle was recognized with the Iron Cross I Class, *Unteroffizier* Hauger was promoted to *Vizefeldwebel*. The other participants were in part awarded with the Iron Cross II Class, in part promoted to *Gefreiten* or *Unteroffizieren*. All participants received 11 days furlough that was considered well earned. Another patrol from the 7/R109 advanced against the same point on 27 October 1917 but came upon an alert enemy and was repulsed with losses.

RIR 110 wanted to ensure that the attack spirit had not been lost following the days of heavy fighting by Verdun by holding regular patrols. *Unteroffiziers* Holzer and Kruse and *Musketier* Krause of the 7/R110 had firmly established the location of an enemy sentry post through careful observation by day and at night. The three men had also explored the terrain, the wire obstacles and the exact location of the sentry on four previous patrols. In the night from 8 to 9 October, at 10 p.m., the patrol left with nine additional volunteers from the 6th, 7th and 8/R110 who were assigned the duty of patrol security.

Nine wire obstacles, all very strong, and thick, were crossed in the course of three hours; the enemy had not noticed anything out of the ordinary. A pitch black night in streaming rain and strong winds provided extra protection for the operation. After overcoming the last obstacle the patrol discovered it was in front of a screen that was woven out of reeds and wire; it became cut through in a width of two meters. In the trench behind the screen the patrol came upon two telephone wires that were immediately destroyed. The patrol continued further, leaving behind three men as the security garrison. The patrol fell upon the enemy double sentry post and overpowered it. At 2.00 a.m. the participants returned to their own trench again on the same route with prisoners and without any German losses. The two prisoners belonged to the 6th Company, *Territorial Régiment d'Infanterie 131*.

Division, Brigade and Regimental headquarters spoke of their recognition to all of the participants for their dashing behavior. The division commander awarded *Unteroffizier* Holzer with the Iron Cross I Class, *Musketiers* Reister, Wagner and Denkler of the 7th Coy the Iron Cross II Class, *Unteroffizier* Kruse was promoted to *Vizefeldwebel*, *Musketier* Charles Rösch was promoted to *Gefreiten* because of bravery in front of the enemy.

> In the course of the week the friendly neighborly relationship to the frog was also first spoiled. However, one could not quite even suffer for the duration. There was, for example, the sandbag-castle in front of our left wing that we had annexed with pleasure: also taunting with numerous patrols, moreover the terrain that was covered with numerous groups of trees that strongly aided these operations. As such *Vizefeldwebel* Kruse together with his inseparable friend, *Unteroffizier* Holzer, probably two of the most audacious, most dashing patrol members of the regiment, brought a French sentry in full equipment to me at night in my dugout, who in a straight forward exquisite manner, had been dug out without noise and blood being shed. The chap was still so shocked that he could barely speak. Regiment and brigade contributed considerable praise. Also two German officers from Infantry Regiment 256 and Guard Alexander escaped out of a French prison camp and a few days later were rescued in our lines.
>
> *Leutnant der Reserve* Fritz Schmitt, RIR 110.[3]

Awards and promotions given for bravery in front of the enemy had always been considered a boost to the morale of the entire regiment and it was no different in the new sector. On 5 September 1917 *Leutnants der Reserve* Straub and Biegelmaier, *Leutnant der Landwehr* Sattlers and *Vizefeldwebel* Leidig, RIR 109, were awarded with the Iron Cross I Class. Then, a particular honor was extended on 30 September 1917 when the *Leutnants der Reserve* Markwitz and Franz Ganter were bestowed with the Knight's Cross of the Military Charles Friedrich Merit Order for the action on 13 August 1917 by Verdun.

Another occasion of special note occurred on 14 October 1917 for the III/R109. In accordance with a decree, a writ from the Supreme Commander, the III/R109 became bestowed with the *Garde Litzen* in recognition of its outstanding bravery in the defense of Hill 344. *Hauptmann von* Wolff, whose prudent and worthy leadership was responsible for the successes achieved by Verdun, received the order *Pour le Mé*rite on 30 November 1917. The regiment was proud that it had one of its leaders in its ranks who earned this highest war honor. The joy expressed by the Grenadiers in the III/R109 was especially great as everyone in the battalion looked upon their commander with respect and admiration.

Not every patrol was successful. The patrol operation of the III/R110 did not fare well. *Leutnant* Recklies along with five volunteers of the 10/R110 and *Leutnant* Glombiza with two volunteers from the 12/R110 left the *Steinbruch Graben* at 3.00 a.m. on 20 October 1917 in front of Chapelle Farm. The raiding party went over the Tourbe Bridge, then along the southern arm of the Tourbe, continuing further to Sap 11; this

One of the lucky men who escaped from the French. (*Reserve-Infanterie-Regiment Nr. 110 im Weltkrieg 1914-1918*)

was deserted. The patrol went further on the southern shore of the Tourbe, therefore in the enemy line as far as Pappel Copse. It was soon 6.45 a.m., however the terrain was covered with dense fog and the men remained hidden from view.

The members of the patrol suddenly saw an enemy dugout about 10 meters distant on the opposite, northern shore of the Tourbe. Six men stood in front of the dugout, three sentries stood northwest of it. The enemy had discovered the patrol at the same time and opened fire. *Leutnant* Glombitza and *Unteroffizier* Haug were wounded and both fell together. *Leutnant* Recklies immediately sprang through the Tourbe upon the three enemy sentries, shot one down and took the other two prisoners after a lengthy and vicious fight. *Musketier* Leyk followed behind immediately and supported *Leutnant* Recklies, who then crossed back over the Tourbe and reached *Gefreiter* Hornig who was located on the southern shore and helped bring the prisoners across the river to safety. The security patrol that was still located on the southern bank of the Tourbe, one *Unteroffizier* and three men, had meanwhile moved closer to the fighting and kept the French troops in the Pappel Copse occupied, allowing *Leutnant* Recklies to successfully transport the prisoners back through the Copse. The security patrol then moved further northeast over the Tourbe, back to the German position.

The two prisoners belonged to *Territorial Régiment d'Infanterie 131*. Although *Leutnant* Glombitza and *Unteroffizier* Haug were wounded and remained in enemy hands, all of the participants were given the highest recognition by the high command because of their boldness and bravery. The division commander invested *Unteroffizier* Forschbach,

Musketiers Lenk, Huber and Blester from the 10/R110 and *Gefreiten* Hornig from the 12/R110 with the Iron Cross II Class. Furthermore the regiment promoted *Gefreiten* Hornig and *Musketier* Mack to *Unteroffizieren* for bravery in front of the enemy.

In the night from 26 to 27 October 1917 an operation was executed by RIR 109, which was recorded in Regimental Order No. II:

> In the night from 26/27 October 1917, during a reconnaissance taking place for a well prepared patrol by the 7th Company under the leadership of *Leutnant* Friedrich, came close to the obstacles in front of the occupied enemy trench by *Punkt 157* in a dashing advance. The goal, to penetrate into the trench and take prisoners could not be completed by the patrol, although already a part of the enemy obstacles had been cut through by it, because they must withdraw due to the fire from the strongly occupied enemy trench. Here *Grenadier* Hildebrandt found the heroes death. He was severely wounded and died while he was being carried back by his comrades, the *Unteroffiziers* Albert Ratzel and Riexinger, as well as the *Krankenträger* Erne.
>
> *Grenadier* Hildebrandt was born on 23 November 1896 at Wetter am Ruhr, since 1 August 1916 was in the field and since 19 September 1917 with the regiment. He was a beloved comrade and a brave faithful soldier up to his death. Honor his memory! All participants of the patrol, especially the leaders and the under leaders, I speak of their dashing and intrepid advance, the *Unteroffizieren* Ratzel and Riexinger and the *Krankenträger* Erne for their comradely behavior, through my complete special acknowledgment.
>
> I have seen that all participants, of which many came out of the regiment, desire fresh operations and have courageous decision power inherent in them, whereby they have an exemplary effect on their comrades. I speak to all leaders and participants of the patrol my full acknowledgment. *von* Baumbach
>
> Distribution I, II, III Battalions
> M.G. O. b/St.
> Regiment 2.[4]

A short time after the disastrous operation of 27 October 1917, another large scale raid was to take place. The undertaking '*Kommando nach Beverloo* (*Herbstanfang*)' was thoroughly prepared on the practice works at Mouron under the guidance of *Leutnants* Biegelmaier and Gushurst and *Vizefeldwebel* Leidig. It was scheduled to take place on 1 November 1917, at 6.20 p.m. with a raiding party in the strength of 100 men. The goal was to capture enemy prisoners from a double sentry post by *Punkt 99*.

The raid was thoroughly rehearsed in the days before the 1st and it appeared that the confident mood of the leaders and the Other Ranks was almost a guarantee for success as was reflected in the after action report:

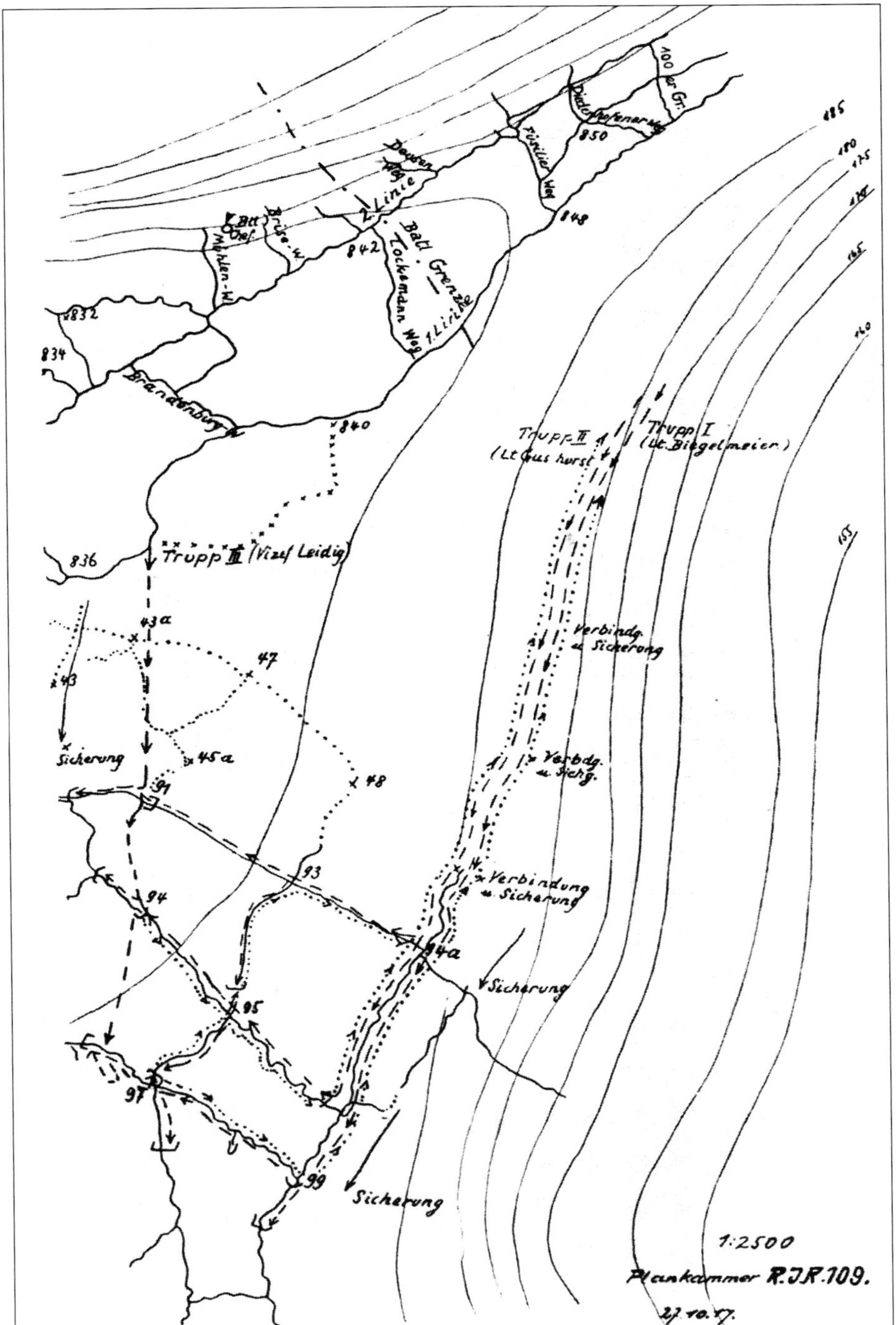

Plan of attack for *Herbstanfang*, 1 November 1917

Res. Inf. Reg. 109
I. Nr. I. 2070 R. St. Qu. 5th November 1917.

Report on Operation 'Herbstanfang' on 1 November 1917.
(gem. Div. Bef. v. 22nd October 1917 I Nr. 6031.)
Purpose: Identification of the opposite enemy troop formation.

Break-in-area: The trenches 49 until 99, 94 until 93, 99a until 95, 99 until 97 were chosen as break-in-area-locations, because it was to have accepted that the enemy at that distance from the German position didn't expect an attack and the readiness position and the approach of the *Stosstrupps* in an old trench leading to Point 49 was possibly covered.

It especially came into consideration in the area that could be inspected that every man who was in the enemy trench system could become shown the return route that the registration fire was possible with ground observation, and that the troops were protected against fire from the west through the terrain.

On later orders a *Stosstrupp* further west became placed on the hill to advance out of the area *Rote Punkt 836* through the wired enemy foreground via *Punkt* 91 and 94a (the break-in-position could not be observed).

Preparations: For the execution: three *Stosstrupp* became composed and formed from volunteers under *Leutnant* Biegelmaier. (Leader of the II and III *Stosstrupp Leutnant* Gushurst and *Vizefeldwebel* Leidig). Furthermore, 5 *pioniers* each with *Trupp* I and III. In the preceding days the participants became educated about the terrain in the position, break-in-positions so and so forth.

The bombardment of the artillery and *Minenwerfer* took place in the afternoon in the time from 24 October until 1 November 1917. Simultaneously destructive bombardments took place upon individual points of the break-in-area, e.g. destroying the obstacles at *Punkt* 94.

The results of the bombardments, the works and the sentry lineup of the adversary would be recorded daily through patrols and the *Lux* Service. (22nd October until 1st November of 1917: 25 patrols.)

It was determined that the bombardment should be very strong, also that the resulting destruction could be recognizable by the eye, however the wiring of the trench (between Points 49 and 94) had not suffered, and that the French attempted to repair the obstacles again in the quickest time. The French were extremely alert. The sentries at Point 99 were repeatedly determined, otherwise only sentries at times at Points 95 and 45.

Mütze, no shoulder tabs, pistol on cord about the neck, 32 cartridges, knives, electric torch, light compass, belt without cartridge pouches and without bayonet, handle and egg hand grenades in two draped sandbags, every second man a wire cutter, empty pockets, if possible compression bandages.

On the afternoon of 1 November the troops were conveyed to the position in motorized lorries.

Housing of the patrols in the vicinity of the exit points (*Stosstrupp* I and II in the *Präskestollen* II, *Stosstrupp* III in the *Pionier Stollen*). Both tunnels became connected with the regimental command post in the Kanonenberg by telephone.

To ease the return of the men who would probably be dispersed, alleys were previously cut in the obstacle posts positioned with lamps with blinker apparatus.

In each sector a special Collection service was furnished and provided with nominal lists, in order to be able to immediately determine respectively, about which men came back and which were missing.

Execution: The *Stosstrupps* I and II under the leadership of *Leutnants* Biegelmaier and Gushurst left at 6.20 p.m. in detachments of 10 men in the first line and at 7.20 p.m. were ready at the exit point in the old trench north of *Punkt* 49. Everything was carried out unnoticed by the adversary.

The preparation fire started suddenly at 7.55 o'clock in the afternoon. Transferring the fire further back first took place at 7.59 o'clock. Therefore, breaking forth started two minutes later, as planned. The advance of the troops in the trench through entanglement and barricades was made difficult.

The leader of *Trupp* I, *Leutnant* Biegelmaier, pushed forth outside the trench of *Punkt* 49 to *Punkt* 99, where he discovered a sentry post. He surprised the double sentries in a shelter situated in the immediate proximity, compelled them out through pistol shots and took them captive.

A further advance to the end goal via *Punkt* 97 became made impossible through our own strong blocking fire that still lay on this point and west of it, as well as through the splinter effect from projectiles from our own artillery that smashed in the immediate vicinity.

Therefore, at 8.09 p.m. *Leutnant* Biegelmaier gave the red green signal for the return. Meanwhile *Leutnant* Gushurst behind *Trupp* I on the planned route, had reached *Punkt* 95, however mostly outside the trench. He had pressed forward over it, when the signal from the leader appeared, and furthermore our own fire lying on *Punkt* 97, set a goal for a further advance.

The troops of both officers went back in the planned manner via 49. Meanwhile, the pioniers had widened the alleys in the obstacles and laid down tape for the return between 49 and 94l. The enemy artillery fire that began at 7.58 p.m. lay mainly as disruption and response fire in the area of our obstacles and the first and second lines.

Going back further became accommodated. Fire pauses and the fire dying down became taken advantage of for the return. *Leutnant* Gushurst followed at the end with 20 men.

From both troops there were ten men slight and moderately severely wounded, two men were missing. The corpse of the one that had fallen through an A.G. direct hit, would be brought in on the following night, the other was buried and returned back in the fourth night.

Stosstrupp III under *Vizefeldwebel* Leidig had left their trench at 7.57 p.m., had penetrated into the enemy position at *Punkt* 43a and reached *Punkt* 91 via *Punkt* 45. The very strong obstacles were not destroyed here. An exploration was quickly accomplished that there were also no alleys on the right and the left. Nevertheless Leidig now attempted to penetrate with wire cutters and so on and so forth. However, in the meantime the signal to return became given.

For the protection of the right flank of the troops a machine gun became moved forward up to a hollow south of *Punkt* 43.

Strong enemy fire also hindered this party from immediately going back. *Vizefeldwebel* Leidig remained lying in shell craters between *Punkt* 45 and *Punkt* 43 until the fire died down.

All of the troops returned back. 1 *Unteroffizier* (died in the military hospital during an operation) had a medium wound.

Artillery and *Minenwerfer*: It consisted of: 1st and 7/RFAR 29, 6th Bavarian *Landwehr* FAR, 3rd and 1/FAR 18 and *Minenwerfer* (8 heavy, 7 medium and 30 light). The blocking off and the holding down of the numerous flanking machine guns on the southern situated hills was successful in the most perfect manner. The hereby called forth destruction was, how it appeared to the eyes on the following day, extraordinary.

Losses: Fallen: 3 (1 *Unteroffizier*, 1 man from the *Stosstrupps* and 1 man from the *Minenwerfer* through a bore explosion); wounded: 14 (4 from the *Minenwerfer*).

The capture of the double sentry post and the brave and dashing behavior of all participants justified the trust the regimental commander placed in the officers, *Unteroffiziere* and Other Ranks most handsomely. The troops have rendered honour to the regiment and proved to be a valuable service for the Army leadership. *Oberst von* Baumbach spoke of his special acknowledgment of the intrepid leaders, *Leutnant* Biegelmaier, *Unteroffizier* Burkhardt, 1/R109 and *Gefreiter* Strauss and that through resolve and lack of concern of the fire, succeeded in advancing and taking the double sentry post into their hands.

The sense of duty and cooperation of the *pionier* troops with the infantry also deserved special mention; likewise the behavior of the *Minenwerfer* detachment, who in conjunction with the detachments of RIR 110 and RIR 111, irrespective of the enemy's fire executed preparation and blocking fire in an immaculate manner. Therefore, the pretense operation in the area of RIR 111 (*Herbstanfang*), which drew part of the enemy's artillery fire there, has supported the operation exquisitely. The foregone dashing executed patrols of the II and III Battalions that brought important information, has essentially contributed to the success in the entirety

Unfortunately losses were also not avoided here. The best was *Unteroffizier* Heinrich Schädel, 8/R109. He was the right hand of the leader of *Stosstrupp* 3 and was always with him. He was moderately severely wounded by a shell splinter on the thigh; he came into the military hospital at Senne. There he contracted blood poisoning, and he died during the necessary operation. Another good man, *Grenadier* Nagel, 6/R109, fell on the return route in the enemy's barrage fire through a direct hit. The faithful *Grenadier* Wilhelm Renner, 8/R109, fell at his *Minenwerfer* in his strong sense of duty, in result of a burst in the bore. Honor his memory!

Awards made – several Iron Crosses I and II Class. 7 *Gefreiter* promoted to *Unteroffizier*. 11 *Grenadiers* promoted to *Gefreiter*.[5]

The men of Operation *Herbstanfang*. (*Das Reserve-Infanterie-Regiment Nr. 109 im Weltkrieg 1914 bis 1918*)

The patrol of 1 November 1917 by RIR 109 was supported by 48 men from RIR 110 under the command of *Leutnant der Reserve* Stetefeld and *Unteroffizier* Kühn with eleven 7.6cm Light *Minenwerfer*. About 1,500 shells were fired off at French positions in disturbance and blocking fire. Despite the strong enemy retaliatory fire in the vicinity of the thrower stands at the northern slope of the *Kanonenberg* no one in RIR 110 was injured and they had effectively contributed to the success of the operation by RIR 109.

On the evening of 2 November 1917 the III/R110 relieved the II/18 in the Sector *Arturhang Links*: the 11th and 12/R110 were in the front line, the 10/R110 in readiness and the 9/R110 in reserve. In the night from 3-4 November 1917 the 3rd MG/R110 was also inserted into the line. The companies immediately started improving the position that was in very poor condition by clearing up the dugouts and tunnels and wiring the position. The artillery and mine fire was quite active on both sides of the line and each night patrols were sent out into the foreground.

A patrol of the 11/R110 under *Unteroffizier* Immenkamp with 13 men and one light machine gun decided to attack the French wiring parties. The patrol surprised the enemy outside by the wire obstacles, opened fire on the wiring party with the light machine gun and caused a number of losses. Unfortunately no prisoners could become taken, because the enemy still had strong obstacles in front of them. *Musketier* Reich particularly stood out in this raid. The patrol suffered two men slightly wounded.

On 7 November 1917 a patrol of the II/R110 under the command of *Unteroffizier* Holzer of the 7/R110 and *Unteroffizier* Heim of the 5/R110 pressed forth against the destroyed houses opposite the battalion border, in the enemy position. The *Stosstrupp* also reached the enemy trench, however it came to a fierce fight with the enemy supports rushing here from all sides. Finally the patrol was forced to move back, so it would not become isolated. *Musketier* Hopp, who received a shot through the left thigh, could be taken back with them. The proven, brave patrol leader *Unteroffizier* Holzer, holder of the Iron Cross I Class, unfortunately remained wounded in the hands of the enemy. *Unteroffizier* Heim, *Musketier* Hopp, *Musketier* Reinschmidt and *Gefreiter* Winkels received the Iron Cross II Class:

> However, all of the glad memories became overshadowed by a dark incident. In the night to 8 November the brave *Unteroffizier* Holzer was fatally wounded, who a few weeks before had been awarded with the Iron Cross I Class, and who fell into the hands of the enemy during a patrol undertaking. He was a heavy blow, not only for my company. One of the best in the regiments was taken from us. Almost four months we lay in the Bois de Ville. In this time attached the first bonds of strong trust, that I and my dear 7th Company became joined in true comradeship, a comradeship, that in the coming heavy hours would prove to be magnificent.
> *Leutnant der Reserve* Fritz Schmitt, RIR 110.[6]

Following the most recent raid, work was focused on the extension of the 2nd battle zone in the Dormoise plain, for which the security garrison was used for mined dugout construction. On 2 November 1917 His Royal Highness *Grossherzog von* Baden reviewed the I/R109, the rest battalion from RIR 111 and a delegation from RFAR 29, on the parade ground north of Mouron where he praised them for the fighting by Samogneux and on Hill 344.

As the end of the year approached the number of raids began to decrease and life took on a normal routine and other than the rotation of battalions, little else took place. This norm was disrupted slightly when the II/R111 under Major Höhne was ordered to take over a sector south of Ripont by the right neighboring division, the 41st Infantry Division, from 2 to 13 November 1917. It was a part of the position that the regiment had occupied in the summer of 1916, which however was a far more favorable situation, because the dominating enemy positions on *Strassen* hill by Champagne Farm had been taken by German troops. The 5th and 6/R111 were in a crater position east of the hollow until close to the hotly contested farm. The 7th Company was the readiness company in the *Hahn Graben*, named after the commander of the 28th Reserve Division; the 8/R111 lay in the 2nd Line by Fontaine. The battle activity in the new position was very lively, and the II/R111 had ten exhausting days behind it, when it was relieved on the night of 12/13 November 1917 by a battalion from IR 170 and moved into the *Grunewald Lager*.

On 21 November 1917 His Royal Highness *Grossherzog von* Baden visited the 28th Reserve Division once again, this time visiting RIR 110, and brought greetings from home. He later spent time with RIR 111 where he greeted the III/R111 under *Hauptmann* Coester at a training place by Mouron.

On the 22nd RIR 111 was supposed to hand over the sector by Cernay to a regiment from the 51st Reserve Division. The transfer to the new division however had to be postponed, as there were different indications that the enemy might attack. The French trenches showed signs of increased activity and noise. In order to face this possible threat elevated battle readiness was ordered, and the rest battalion, the III/R111, was moved to the reserve positions in the strongpoint Thuringen as well as in the mined dugouts and cellars of Cernay.

The major problem facing RIR 111 was that no provisions had been made for the large number of men in the reserve positions. Fortunately, the French artillery opposite the regimental sector behaved quietly, because part of the reserve troops were housed in

Grossherzog von Baden distributing awards to the men of RIR 110. (*Reserve-Infanterie-Regiment Nr. 110 im Weltkrieg 1914-1918*)

poorly constructed shelters that were not shell proof by any means. On the afternoon of 24 November 1917 the battle readiness of the regiment was increased, still without any sign of the suspected enemy attack.

RIR 109 had also ordered heightened battle readiness due to the enemy restlessness in the time from 23/24 November 1917, which came to nothing. The rest battalion was moved forward for support; however it was moved back to Mouron again on the 24th. On the same day *Leutnant* Gushurst took over command of the 9/R109 in place of *Hauptmann* Becker who had been sent to Karlsruhe.

On orders from the 28th Reserve Division dated 28 November 1917 all Other Ranks within each regiment involved in communication duties, telephonists, signalers, earth telegraph, in a strength of 160 men must become combined into a single Communication Company. In RIR 110 the new *Nachrichten* Company would be commanded by *Leutnant der Reserve* Hölzer. In RIR 109 the Other Ranks of the regiment who were used for communication duties became formed into a *Nachrichten* Company, under the command of *Offizier Stellvertreter* Metzner.

Whilst raids on both sides of the wire had reduced in numbers there were still occasional attempts being made to take enemy prisoners. At 6.00 p.m. on 29 November 1917, *Leutnant* Happel with 17 men of the 12/R110 attempted to penetrate the enemy trench opposite the *Feldstellung* and take prisoners. Before Happel and his men were able to enter the French trench two enemy patrols appeared and attacked the raiding party. It quickly turned into a hand grenade fight, which finally forced Happel and his men to return to the German trenches without any prisoners.

The 28th Reserve Division was scheduled to be relieved in the time from 7 until 12 December 1917 when the 11th Infantry Division would take over the sector. The men were not happy that they were being moved once more as the evidence supporting the concept of a quiet sector could be clearly seen in the losses reported by RIR 110 in the period from 30 October to 7 December: two Other Ranks killed; one officer, 26 Other Ranks wounded and one Other Rank missing. It clearly was a 'quiet' sector.

RIR 109 regiment handed over the position to its successor, Reserve Infantry Regiment 51, and provided it with substantial memorandum, clear maps and sketches of the sector. The III/R109 was transported on 9 December 1917 from Grandpré and arrived in Sedan on the 10th, and then marched to St. Menges, the II/R09 followed on the evening of the same day. On 11 December 1917 the I/R109 travelled to Bad Zeilles and marched to Floing, where regimental staff, the Construction and *Nachrichten* Companies were also billeted. The three machine gun companies would not be relieved until the 12th and eventually received quarters in Floing, St. Menges and Illy.

During the rest period, the 28th Reserve Division was in the association of the Crown Prince's Army Group. At this time the three machine gun detachments in RIR 109 were placed under the command of *Leutnant* Rothfelder while a single *Minenwerfer* Company, composed of three *Abteilungen*, now stood directly under regimental control. The ration strength of RIR 109 on 19 December 1917 was an impressive: 61 officers, 21 *Offizier Stellvertreter*, 2,909 men, 236 horses. Battle strength: 42 officers, 16 *Offizier Stellvertreter*, 2,326 men, 1,904 rifles, 36 heavy and 38 light machine guns. This was a substantial number of men for an infantry regiment in late 1917. But, if you looked closely at the men and not simply the numbers you would have seen a large portion of the troops were untrained and physically unfit for front line duty.

Recognition for bravery continued to be a source of pride to the men. While behind the lines, a number of troops in RIR 109 were awarded with medals for their actions at the front. *Vizefeldwebel* Kaucher was awarded the Iron Cross I Class for bravery in front of the enemy; furthermore a large number of Iron Cross II Class and Baden Military Merit medals were awarded to men in the regiment.

From 7 to 9 December 1917 Grenadier Regiment 10 took over the sector by Cernay. The men of RIR 111 welcomed the relief but were concerned about where they were being sent. The division was being relieved but not for service at another front, it was instead being moved to the vicinity of Sedan, where it would become the army reserve. There was a change in command at this time as well, when *Generalmajor von* Geyso was replaced by *Generalmajor von* Held. RIR 111 embarked in Grandpré and in Savigny and was transported to Doucy, eight kilometers southeast of Sedan.

The Construction Company that had been a part of RIR 111 for the last three years was being disbanded. This company had provided indispensable support for the extension of the different sectors, and in providing supplies for the regiment during the days of heavy fighting. Now the veterans in the Construction Company were needed to reinforce the battle strength of the fighting troops. *Oberleutnant* Lantelme, who had been in command of the Construction Company since its formation in Martinpuich, now became the leader of the 4/R111.

Much of what was to take place in the 28th Reserve Division was directly related to the upcoming offensives as the prelude for the immense task that lay ahead of the German Army, to prepare to shatter the allied front in 1918. The time spent by Sedan was to be utilized for the serious work of increasing the fighting value of the troops. All of the troops must become trained in the new forms of the attack battle, as they had developed out of the experiences of the war, according to proven principles and starting with the commencement of individual training.

The senior commanders needed to be convinced that the regiments of the 28th Reserve Division were tactically and technically prepared to meet all of the requirements that would be required for an offensive action. These requirements included practices in large associations; the satisfactory cooperation by all of the different branches of the service and weapons, and finally that they could fully rely upon the spirit of the troops. The German Army, which had originally expected a victorious early end of the war, had been fighting for more than three years. The army that existed in late 1917 was admittedly different than the enthusiastic group of men that had marched off in August 1914.

Few of the veterans of 1914 were still in the ranks of the companies at the end of 1917. The replacements received during the last year or more consistently lacked the necessary training needed for an active term of service. The three years of exhausting position warfare had not been without consequences. The hardships experienced at home were also felt by the soldiers in the field. Despite all of these hurdles, RIR 111 eventually became recognized as one of the regiments that had demonstrated the inner strength needed by experienced battle troops; men who were determined to give their best in the approaching decisive battle, and on which the higher leadership could place their full confidence.

It was at this time that the men of RIR 111 heard a miraculous story of how one of their own had managed to escape from a French prisoner of war camp and manage to return to his family and eventually to the regiment after going missing near Craonne on 4 May 1917:

Escape from captivity

The desolation on 4 May 1917 by Craonne in French captivity and escape on 19 November 1917 with two comrades from the prison camp in Abbéville.

Preparations

The summer was long past. The cold autumn days had begun. I still felt hard feelings about my fate. Also came the dread of winter in captivity. I could endure it no longer: these disparaging injustices, this forced activity, how I have experienced in the half year as a prisoner. The desire for freedom moved in me as strongly as ever with the longing after my wife and children. So thoughts of escape came to me again.

It was on the fair Sunday. My comrade Löffler and I talked; we spoke of home and our fate here. There we wished the other to be home and remarked that the Christmas festivities here will be especially sad. I found the only response: 'By Christmas I want to be at home!'

With it the desire to escape was firmly in me. My comrade Brändlin also had similar thoughts. We mutually trusted one another and were determined to jointly implement the plan. To be sure one told himself generally that an escape from out of here would be very difficult. However we two did not allow ourselves to be discouraged thereby with our thought, we even found a third fellow in Comrade Böhne. We met secretly and carefully made our preparations. We prepared confidentially, so that everyone was responsible for himself, and that no others could be accused of anything because of his future fate. As the execution day we had chosen the last day of our daily shift. For supplies each man had finally saved 2 pounds of bread and purchased a half pound of fat for themselves.

Our escape out of the camp

The great day had arrived. We worked as normal until 7.00 p.m. Before the night meal we hauled fresh washing again. We packed the things together that we wanted to bring and concealed them in the yard. After the nightly meal we must peel potatoes for the following day. This opportunity occurred in a dining room where we were directed. At first all three helped with it; then one after the other vanished. We arrived in the yard, got our precious possessions and waited for the moment when our door to freedom opened because the door to our freedom, a small doorway next to the kitchen, was only to be used by the officers and sentries. We knew specifically that at this time the sentries were at the nightly meal and the sentries were allowed behind this door, also going in the kitchen next door. This was the moment we anticipated. The sentries had barely gone into the kitchen, so we scurried out, first went Brändlin. He was hardly outside, when an officer came. I already believed that he had seen him, because he curved off to the right, while Brändlin had gone to the left. Now followed Böhne, then I. That was an event of a couple of seconds. It had hardly happened when the sentry stood at his place in front of the gates again. Straight before us stood a single house, in it was a dog that apparently heard us had and made a tremendous noise.

Towards the unknown

Now we stood in the middle of a field, there was no time for hesitation, we had to act. We quickly arranged our packs, so that they were not a hindrance to us on the march. Then I took my compass that I had managed to save through all searches, and firmly set the direction. To smudge our tracks, we first went towards the west. After approximately one hour we reached a marsh. Our path took a far route, so that it would make a pursuit with police dogs impossible. Afterward we slowly curved back by way of the north to the east, always across country through woods and meadows. If we came on a road, we would listen, if the air was clear, we crossed over it at a run. We let the greatest precaution prevail everywhere. We listened at every sound. The most that alarmed us initially were the partridges, until we had become accustomed to them. Once we ran into an English camp. Fortunately we timely heard how one sentry called to the other, and we could disappear. We circumvented villages and towns as far as possible. In this manner we came a good piece forward on the first night.

Dangerous hiding place

When the morning approached, we thought about looking for a hiding place for the entire day. One of the many that appeared suitable to us was a straw stack sitting in the middle of the field. However for over an hour we attempted to reach it in vain. We decided therefore to look for a place in the nearby wood. We ran in deep, then crawled in a thicket and covered ourselves with foliage. Gradually it became light. All around us was silence. Only now and then the sound of barking dogs penetrated our hiding place, whence I presumed that we were in the proximity of a village. When it was finally quite bright we saw to our horror that we were lying only 10 to 15 meters distant from the other side of the wood edge, where a road led past. Immediately we also saw already a mounted *Gendarme* with 2 dogs coming forward on the road. We became properly warm, however he had noticed nothing. Afterward it started to rain. That was good for us, because we thought now nobody would come into the wood.

Towards midday it ceased again. Although we were wet through and through, we continued to remain lying still. Later we heard some children. They had almost discovered us during the wood gathering. When they were gone, I said: 'We cannot remain here, they might come again!' Therefore we crawled further in the wood and we concealed ourselves in a fox or badger burrow with several entrances. Here we were somewhat warm however in spite of our wet clothes and therefore remained until it became dark.

First hardships and a breezy hiding place

After the onset of darkness the journey went further. However we only came slowly onward; there the terrain was difficult and very wet, and we were tired. However we don't give in. Our route led by way of a few permanent paths. About midnight we felt a fierce thirst. Nowhere was drinking water to be found, although we all scanned the meadows for water. Therefore our comrade Brändlin practiced his occupation and milked one of the grazing cows. Everyone drank 2 cups of milk, so that we had something in our stomach again.

Tired and wet from the rain, we wanted to look very early for a hiding place. After a long search we found a place protected from the wind in a hollow with dense thorn-hedges. Here we crawled under, however frozen like wet dogs. When it became day, we saw that we were in a real wilderness and we felt safe. Towards midday we heard a hunter in the vicinity hunting. My senses did not deceive me. Shortly after, he approached our hedge with his dogs and suddenly stood close in front of us. His dogs were sniffing out our tracks. However he went further, without having discovered us. They were long seconds! We had not taken a breath, and once he had been past, we could not speak from excitement. We left prematurely, although it was still not quite dark.

Disagreeable encounters and obstacles: Undisturbed quarters

So now it went again diagonally across fields, on a straight path upon a wood. In the middle of the fields we saw a farmer digging up turnips. We therefore curved off to the right, but he had already observed us. A piece further we bumped upon a farmer plowing. Both stood there and looked after us. However we continued to walk as if we also had the fullest right. Afterward we almost allowed ourselves to fall into the hands of two farmers again, who came out of the wood. At the last moment we could still avoid them in the wood. There we placed ourselves approximately one hour in the shrubbery and looked out, to see whether one didn't pursue us. However there was nothing to hear. Therefore we took to the road again. We nursed our thirst with rain water, which stood in small puddles on the fields, and hunger with white turnips, which were still in quite large number in the fields. After marching about three hours a white strip emerged in front of us, which we considered to be a road. When we reached it, it was a quite wide river that we were not able to cross over without a rowboat or bridge. After about half an hour pause we went on again, went along the river and after an hour came to a house with a garden, in which horses still stood idly about. Lights still burned in the house. Also beyond the river life still prevailed. After a few minutes a bridge appeared in front of us. Naturally we would first check it out, and as no sentries stood there, we then scurried across like lightning and immediately vanished over there again in the undergrowth.

Now our route led for hours through a marsh with numerous disagreeable obstacles. Finally we came on a château with a large park. Avoiding it was impossible. We therefore, although grudgingly, climbed over the high fence and through the park, in which numerous owls made a terrifying noise. It now went toward morning. There, as we were wet except for the skin and already for three days slept without our eyes fully shut, we took hold of the plan, to look for a farm and there we would creep into it. After a long search we discovered a house in a group of trees at the wood edge. I initially considered it to be a chapel. When I then got there I saw a half ruined empty house. Here we accommodated ourselves on the last, approximately one and a half cubic meter large, remnant of the broken down ceiling. In this sparse corner we laid down, one next to another. Naturally we could hardly move, otherwise we would fall down; it also called for caution, because a wood cutter was nearby. Because our socks were entirely soaked, we took them off and placed them on our naked bodies to dry. We remained here undisturbed the entire day and could rest. The excitement did not allow us to quite fall asleep. In spite of everything this rest was good for us. At the onset of darkness we continued to march further. With it we discovered in the area of the house a fully laden apple tree. We could not allow ourselves to avoid it. We collected the apples; we ate them and still filled our bread bags.

Quarters in the stall

Our hope on the success of the plan became larger each day, which was reinforced with our courage and our perseverance. They accompanied us in the fourth night. Again we marched through fields and crossed over numerous obstacles. We even went past an English rifle range this night. Where we were actually, we didn't have any notion.

Since until now we had been lucky, we obtained more and more courage and became cheeky. Towards morning we went past by a village, in order to find a house by the village edge, in which we could creep into the day over. However there were dogs everywhere, which sung out barking at any approach. Finally we came to a house without dogs, in which already lights burned. At the rear side of the house we found a small storeroom that we forcibly opened. I reached in and obtained a turnip in the hand. In the assumption it was a turnip cellar; Brändlin crawled in, lit a match and firmly determined that it was a stall, in it a cow, a roof was placed on a few crosswise joined pieces of wood, on which small oat straw bundles lay that appeared to give us a hiding place. We therefore employed a stick and climbed up. Overhead we directed ourselves so that half of the bundles hid us and with the other half to cover us. We had barely laid down when the stall door opened up and a woman came for feeding and milking. She worked almost the entire day under us in the barn, also a large number of people came into the stall now and then. We lived in constant fear against discovery. Our boldness had almost betrayed us. However, this day went past well for us. By the evening we already climbed down about 5.30 p.m. on the same road, on which we had come. It was not dark, but we succeeded.

The position area is reached!

Through different fenced in pastures we came again to the open fields. There we allowed ourselves to lie down at the first straw stack and before marching further ate a piece of bread and a turnip. Already in the previous night we had heard the first cannon thunder again. Today however we heard it clearly. It sounded like a friendly greeting to us and for us was a sign that we had come into the vicinity of the front. After we had first passed an English airfield, we bumped upon English troop camps that we always duly recognized and could safely avoid. Finally we came on a small rise, from which light balls rose up on the horizon and we could see the fire of the gun flashes. That was a joy! We rejoiced loudly upon this sweet sight. There in front of us lay our goal, our comrades, our home with our loved ones! We knew now where we had to go. Our hopes, our courage and our confidence grew considerably.

However, the difficult part was still ahead of us; the passage through the enemy position. Already after a few hundred meters we reached the first trench, apparently an old English reserve position. As morning approached, we searched for protection in an old dugout for the next day. At the last moment we noticed, that it was occupied, and could still timely vanish unseen. It seemed more advisable, to lie in an open trench and take cover. Therefore we looked together for some old grass. When I wanted to lie there among this pile however, I saw a skeleton lying amongst it. That also put us off this plan, and we went further. Finally we discovered a half destroyed dugout. There we crawled in and remained undisturbed inside the entire day.

In the tangle of the reserve position

In the now following night we believed we could reach up to the enemy artillery position. However we only moved forward slowly in this confusion of trenches. The weather was favorable, then it rained in streams and a terrible storm raged. We had to give up the attempt, to sneak through an English troop camp. We could circumvent the obstacles only with effort. Meanwhile the night came to an end and we must again look for a dugout to hide in for the day. This time we found an old German dugout. Here we had particular luck. Under a pile of empty tin cans we discovered a full can of English meat, whose content we consumed without bread. Therefore we remained unnoticed in this hiding place.

Through the artillery position

We definitely hoped to reach our goal in this night and therefore broke quite early on. Soon we saw the launching of bright lights. We came upon a mass of telephone wires in the terrain, field railways and more of the same, therefore the only thing that indicated that we could not be far from the artillery position. We also saw and heard the unending vehicle columns on the road there, moving here. A few time we had to across over such roads. There each time it required a gap in the wagon train to detect and to take advantage of this to scurry across lightning fast.

This spurred everyone on over and over, to endure and to strive forward! 'Only forward! There lay the goal! There waved freedom and deliverance!' It shouted spontaneously in our hearts. It was not light. The danger grew from step to step. Double caution was necessary in this area. We did not allow it to be lacking. We used all of our attention. As soon as we saw a shape anywhere we lay in a shell hole or crawled further on the ground. So we worked slowly, however surely to the front. With great effort we succeeded, soon crawling like snakes, soon by jumping or upon the knees, to come through between the batteries planted on open fields. Here by we also came past a dugout, into which all of the different wires lying together disappeared, on which we had run into in our advance. In any case this was the headquarters of a senior staff. We already believed to be through here, when we were suddenly in the middle of a battery, standing between the guns. There was no going back. So we simply went boldly right through in rapid steps. A few hundred meters further we placed ourselves in a shell hole, in order to recover from the excitement of this risky business. An approximately 10 meter wide wire obstacle, on which we thrust during our advance, was not overcome without great effort. With it we had the artillery position behind us.

In the infantry battle position

We went forward carefully. A white streak in the chalk ground already betrayed the next trench to us from a long distance. When we reached it, we saw that it was still being worked on. Only after a long time were able to come over it. The following trench was already neatly arranged, however still unoccupied. We went over it without effort. Only making it through the obstacles was difficult. With increased caution we approached the third trench. Directly in front of us we saw a sentry beside a machine gun post, who was wrapped up in a raincoat until it was over the ears. We now crawled more to the right and looked for a position, at which no sentry stood. There I slid into the trench, with both others immediately after, and on the other side we raised ourselves up mutually. Then we rolled from shell hole to shell hole until to the obstacles. Fortunately a shell had torn a gap in this so that we could easily come through. Again now followed trench upon trench. A piece further we came into a communication trench, however we then left it again and we crawled forward further. Still two more times must we go through over occupied trenches and under obstacles. We also needed a very long time and became wet up to the skin.

Unfortunately, we could not reach the German lines before daybreak. It became light quickly, we therefore crawled quickly into a shell crater and covered ourselves with earth and grass and remained lying still. We were only approximately 20 meters distant from the closest English trench and could hear every individual Englishman walking. When it became full day, the German artillery began to fire. Most of the fire now lay upon the area of our hiding place. It was no small thing, to lie here with shell splinters and fuzes whistling slightly away above us, and having clods of earth flying across on us. We could not even stir, otherwise the pilots would notice us, which in spite of the severe cold and occasional rain showers were above. With time we could no longer feel our limbs from the cold. Nevertheless we allowed ourselves to have a cigarette, so that we could at least feel some warmth. The day passed very slowly. We were profoundly excited, because our reserves were simply strained. In the course of the day we determined to get the wire rolls that were lying in proximity and so laden walk boldly through the trenches despite our German uniforms.

At the onset of darkness an active life began with the Englishmen. Roughly 150 meters distant from us was namely the unloading place for food and construction materials, also about a company worked on the approach route to this place. We were now neatly pinned in their grip and could not get very far, especially as today the moon ends up standing in the heavens. About 6.00 p.m. however we risked it, given however the plan with the wire roles and crawled somewhat covered through the quite high grass until to the next trench. This was perchance not very wide. In a suitable moment we could cross over it between two traverses, where now no sentry stood. The wire barrier on the other hand was quite strong, and we needed two to three hours, until we were underneath it. With it rattled the machine guns behind and in front of us, and mines flew away above us. However we did not allow ourselves to lose our composure. Under similar difficulties we crawled further to the next trench. Here we hesitated a long time, because we found no suitable point for the crossing. Finally however we collected our courage, although the English double sentry with a machine gun lay only four to five meters distant, and we succeeded. Over there we first placed ourselves in a shell hole for a few minutes. Then we went forward to the wire entanglements. This was exceptionally strong and wide. We were also at the mercy of English fire from machine guns, and German projectiles colliding on the wire. Simultaneously *Minenwerfer* were active on both sides, and we clearly heard, how here, how there the mines burst with a crash in close proximity – it was the Scarpe. After more than three hours of great effort we were finally successful however, to come out of the wire. Meanwhile the moon had risen further and shone considerably bright through the clouds. Therefore at first we wanted not to go further, but remain lying in a shell hole, until it became darker. Then however this seemed too dangerous, because too easily an English patrol could come, and we were so close to the goal to be lost now.

At the goal!

How far it was still up to the German trench and if we had already had the last English trench behind us, we did not know and also could not determine it, because no light balls were fired. Without any visible signs, instead however with complete confidence in our hearts, we made a guess about our goal. We suddenly came upon a wire obstacle, without that we had run up against a trench. 'That is German!' came simultaneously to the lips of the three of us. With all joy we remained quiet and conserved so much caution, that we first once again precisely examined it. However we had not deceived ourselves, a pair of wire rolls lying in the vicinity gave us the proof. We were at the goal! No, not yet completely, we still had to get through the obstacles. However, that did not go any further without more. Now we were determined to look for a sentry and to allow him to recognize us. We probably searched over one hour and we could not locate one anywhere, because we could not dare to come too close up against the wire. Finally, behind the wire, I discovered a black spot, which moved back and forth. I quickly called Brändlin, and both of us now observed the spot. Finally we were confident that this must be a German steel helmet. Now I collected my courage and cried aloud: "Sentry! Sentry! There it already sounded back: 'Yes'. To eliminate any doubts, we three quickly jumped up and allowed us to be recognized as Germans. However both brave sentries – they were namely a sap post – did not trust us, and everyone grasped a hand grenade. However before they could still pull the string, we stood in the trench.

We were at our goal! Indescribable joy shook us. Everything past is forgotten. We can hardly contain our happiness. It was as if we were born again. Hot tears poured down the cheeks and over and over we embraced the sentries. However we cannot be allowed to remain here. We must go back, however, the sentry also wanted to know how it looked on the other side. We only tell both people where the enemy sentry stood, then we go back to the company leader of the Saxon regiment.

They greeted us fully of joy and sent us with two orderlies to the battalion commander. Now every Saxon wanted to go with us, because everyone burned with curiosity. The adjutant greeted us at the Battalion battle headquarters, and following even the battalion commander also stood in front of us. He immediately gave us a glass of schnapps and wine, and for the first time after seven months we again enjoyed a drop of alcohol, which properly warmed us up. Then he gave us something for the stomach. Here we also briefly told what we experienced and what noteworthy things we had seen with the adversary.

About 6 a.m. we came to the regimental headquarters, which had already allowed coffee to be prepared for us. Our stay here was very short, because a car soon came from the division to collect us. With it we were entertained again. Amongst which came all the different officers. Everyone gave us words of acknowledgment, also they did let us lack something to smoke that we had missed for so long. The division doctor, who saw us in our pitiful constitution, asked the division commander that we first of all be sent to a hospital for a few days. He brought us in a closed car to a military hospital. Here we could immediately bathe ourselves and received new laundry. We were there so long our stomachs were not too small. Major Schmieder from Durlach in Baden looked after us like a father and provided us with entirely new clothes. From out of the military hospital I could now tell my loved ones at home of my return and have a quick reunion. Afterward we still went to the Army *Oberkommando*, where we must remain a few days. During this time we were quartered in a hotel and we could relax very well.

Back home!

Finally on 4 December we three comrades must separate, who through common necessity and danger have welded together as friends for life. Each returned first back to his regiment again and to his company, where the joy over the successful escape was no less great. A longer furlough was first of all the thanks for our deeds. So I could celebrate Christmas again with my loving wife and my loving children, how I had wished it once in the sorrowful days in the Grand Nation, the 'Guardian of culture.'

Unteroffizier Wilhelm Menzer, 7/R111 (Menzer died in 1934).[7]

From 7 to 9 December 1917 RIR 110 was relieved by Fusilier Regiment 38 from the 11th Infantry Division. The regiment was then transported by train to an area where it became part of the Army Group Reserve and was quartered in villages south of the gloomy Ardennes forest.

While in the new quarters, winter set in. There was sunshine during the day; however it was very cold, particularly at night. The men were quite content with the billets they had been given in the local villages; the only real difficulty was the procurement of adequate firewood for keeping warm. Wood cutting detachments were sent to the Ardennes forest daily; however, the fresh wood smoked a great deal when used, and while it smelled good when burning it still did not keep the quarters very warm. Other than that small issue, the quarters were seen as being more beautiful and agreeable than the most delightful dugout.

The only real complaint made by the men at this time was that the division had not been fully extracted out of the battle front. Now, the main task for battalions and companies of the three regiments during the rest time was the completion of training. The usefulness and effectiveness of the machine gun was recognized more and more. As each draft of Other Ranks replacements arrived with little or no training, more of the riflemen were being replaced with machine gun squads.

RIR 110 issued a detailed regimental order that regulated the training of all officers, *Unteroffiziere* and preferably as many Other Ranks as possible on all aspects of the heavy and light machine gun. There were daily lessons, firing and drills with both weapons and the men became fully familiar with the operation of the guns and especially how to recognize and clear any jam. On 18 December 1917 the regimental commander observed the newly trained machine gun troops and was quite satisfied with the results.

In addition to the general training of the men, RIR 110 had been assigned a special task to perform during the rest period. It was designated as the Training Regiment for the leadership course located in Sedan. A large exercise field was positioned between Escombre and Messincourt and the leaders of all ranks could watch the training presentations from a large spectator platform, which were led by General Staff officers. The I and III/R110, reinforced with companies of the II/R110, formed the training troops. A company from *Sturmbataillon* 5 and the 1st and 8/RFAR 29 were also there to demonstrate the close cooperation between the two branches of the army. No longer would the artillery be a separate entity, firing from positions further in the rear of the main battle line. The new tactics called for close cooperation between the units, with the artillery accompanying the infantry as close support weapons.

The training provided to the leadership dealt most importantly with two tasks: first, the attack by a French or British battalion, the break-in into the German position and the German counterattack by the battle reserve; second, a more organized German counterattack. The new tactics that had developed in the course of the war, using all means of modern fighting, was systematically demonstrated on the training field.

One particularly new tactic was the advance by *Stosstrupps* with *Flammenwerfer*, smoke bombs and hand grenades. The training included the new type of infantry advance utilizing several loose waves of infantry, the use of all possible means of communication, furnishing captured trenches for defense and the fight against machine gun nests. Toward the end of December there was an official presentation for the higher commands. The presentation became carefully rehearsed for several days, so that everything went smoothly on 19 and 20 December 1917 when the senior commanders of the army viewed a demonstration of the new tactics.

The fourth Christmas of the war was rapidly approaching. The festive feelings and hopes for a quick end to the fighting had all but disappeared in the years of fighting and the holiday, while still celebrated, would be more subdued than ever. For the first time since the outbreak of the war the regiments of the 28th Reserve Division were granted the privilege of being completely intact and in rest quarters in time for the celebration of the Christmas festivities.

A large number of gifts had arrived from the *Ersatz* Battalion RIR 109 in Karlsruhe, from the War Committee of the Red Cross in Heidelberg, from the Red Cross branch in Sigmaringen, from the Fatherland Women's Association Sigmaringen and from many others sources, so that everyone belonging to RIR 109 could become presented with a gift.

On 20 December 1917 the regimental commander of RIR 110, Major *von* Schmeling, had invited all officers of the regiment to the Château Messempré for a Christmas celebration. It was the first time during the entire war that the entire officer corps of the regiment was assembled in one place. Naturally the regiment must preserve this important moment and the officers were assembled for a group photograph.

The festive occasion was tempered when the discussion turned to remembering all of the good, true comrades, who had shared good times and bad with the officers and

Nachrichten troops, RIR 111. (Author's collection)

Entire officer corps of RIR 110 at Château Messempré, Christmas 1917. (*Reserve-Infanterie-Regiment Nr. 110 im Weltkrieg 1914-1918*)

who were now gone. The celebration was plain and simple, not unexpected as it was the fourth celebration of war. A lighted tree and a row of candles placed in empty bottles gave the room a somewhat solemn, Christmas feeling. The repast was very simple: rice and the inevitable canned meat. 'In a wistful mood we think of the loved ones at home and the comrades in front of the enemy.'

Companies held their own Christmas celebrations in the afternoon of the 24th, in their quarters. Christmas trees lit with candles burned everywhere; everyone received Christmas gifts that were mostly small practical articles. The large Christmas packages from loved ones at home had also arrived, therefore gifts in the form of cigars and cigarettes were distributed all around, naturally also free beer was given out and mulled wine. 'Out of the houses sounded the old, lovely Christmas songs, sung from rough soldier's throats. It was almost, almost like at home!' The following week brought the New Year's celebration. The Line of Communication troops set off a pyrotechnic display, as if they were being attacked by the enemy. White, red, green and yellow light balls provided the necessary fireworks.

In RIR 111 the fourth war Christmas was spent in a quiet manner. The companies joined together for celebrations, and good food as well as the regimental band contributed to the gaiety of the festivities. Overshadowing the festivities were the memories of lost friends and comrades as well as the hardships their families were experiencing at home. The concerns about the health and safety of the soldier's families weighed heavily on their minds. In the idea that the war had been thrust upon Germany and that the men were fighting to protect the Fatherland the men were proud that in the more than three years of fighting the enemy had not been able to take any German territory with the exception of a small corner in Alsace. The army looked back on this achievement with pride.

At the same time, the immense effort required to achieve these results was gradually exhausting the men. Also, while Germany was isolated the Allies could rely upon the help of the United States, whose immense resources in men and materials were of great importance, probably no more so than in the coming year. Many men in the division realized that 1918 had to bring the final decision and firmly believed that it would favor Germany.

With regard to this last statement there had been a great deal of speculation among the men of the 28th Reserve Division about what 1918 would bring. Many suspected that the war should have been brought to a conclusion following the defeat of Russia, which freed up a large number of men. Perhaps 1918 would be the year in which the long desired end would come. The conviction of the men in RIR 110 was 'rock solid' that the New Year would be the year of decision:

> A monstrous artillery preparation would allow the infantrymen to spring up and breakthrough the enemy lines in a brilliant storm. New, fresh offensive spirit filled the troops. Our people were rested and had even practiced the new attack procedure in the collaboration with all weapons; it could not go wrong, the blow must succeed. Admittedly the spirit of August 1914 did not exist anymore. Three years of hard warfare had made the Other Ranks mute and hard. The replacements were not of equal value as before anymore. They existed out of men, which came out of the Convalescent Companies, and from youngsters. The straining of the Line of Communication Other Ranks therefore soon brought the reality that the life in the Line of Communications or in the home better suited them than that in the fire trench. However all in all, the company leaders were satisfied; obedience and the sense of duty and the expectation of a successful decision would animate the troops.[8]

Much of the recent training the men had been given was focused on a war of movement. Most of the veterans of 1914 had almost forgotten about marching and the attack battle after the long position war. Now, all available time was used to educate the companies in the attack, in the thorough use of the terrain. Under the watchful eyes of the battalion commanders the companies practiced in the diverse terrain found in the area of the billets.

Night exercises were also held, something quite unfamiliar to almost every man in the division. Practices in larger formations occurred that at times included the Communication and *Minenwerfer* troops, as well as supporting artillery. On 26 December 1917 RIR 110 conducted a realistic skirmish along with the 1/RFAR 29 west of Messincourt, with the brigade commander being present.

The New German assault troops. (Lehrer im Krieg)

The final large brigade practice formation under the direction of the brigade commander, *Generalmajor* Rogge, occurred on 30 December 1917. All available forces had to participate; even the First Line Transport took part. A large terrain exercise by the full division took place by Froncheval in the Maas valley, where a small example was provided to demonstrate the offensive tactics that were to be used in the following year.

The exercise involved one of the three infantry regiments, the III/RFAR 29, 1/*Ersatz Pionier* 16 and one platoon from Telephone Detachment 428. At 8.00 a.m. the battalions moved out of their quarters, became fed from the field kitchens, and the troops did not return to their billets until 6.00 p.m. in the evening. A second demonstration of the new leader course took place on 17 January 1918 at the training works. Among the spectators were the commanders of the 7th Army, *General der Infanterie von* Boehn, Prince Eitel Friedrich *von* Prussia, Prince Franz *von* Bavaria and 18 division commanders.

Notes

1. Greiner & Vulpius, *Reserve-Infanterie-Regiment Nr. 110 im Weltkrieg 1914-1918*, pp. 211-212.
2. Greiner & Vulpius, op. cit., pp. 212-213.
3. Greiner & Vulpius, op. cit., p. 213.
4. G. Frisch, *Das Reserve Infanterie Regiment Nr. 109 im Weltkrieg 1914 bis 1918*, pp. 228-229.
5. Frisch, op. cit., pp. 232-235.
6. Greiner & Vulpius, op. cit., p. 213.
7. Bachelin, Major Eduard, *Das Reserve-Infanterie-Regiment Nr. 111 im Weltkrieg 1914 bis 1918*, pp. 335-343.
8. Greiner & Vulpius, op. cit., pp. 221-222.

2

26th Reserve Division

Flanders

Following a period of heavy fighting during the Arras offensive and in front of Bullecourt the men of the 26th Reserve Division were about to become involved in the latest British attack. When the news came that the 26th Reserve Division was being sent to another part of the front, everyone in the division was extremely curious about where they were going. On 10 and 11 August 1917 the division was transported by trains in a northerly direction toward Douai and Lille and into Belgium and finally to Sweveghem and Courtrai approximately five kilometers east of Kortrijk where the men and equipment were unloaded. The 26th Reserve Division was going to Flanders where the endless swampy terrain made position warfare extremely unpleasant. The division was now part of Group Wytschaete of the 4th Army and was the battle reserve of Army Group *Kronprinz* Rupprecht *von Bayern*.

The Württembergers were faced with an entirely different landscape than what they were used to. It consisted of a wide, vast plain with extended avenues, canals, hedges, gardens and meadows with scattered farms edged by splendid spinneys and church steeples that towered into the sky from the seemingly countless villages. There was rarely even a gentle ground swell to break the monotony of the landscape. Accommodations for the men were neat and clean but also very cramped; still, it was a wonderful place to be quartered when compared to what the men had experienced just a short time earlier.

With all of the recent changes in the new defensive methods the training of the men could not be neglected in the new sector. The companies continued to be made familiar with the MG 08/15 light machine gun, the light 7.6cm *Minenwerfer* and small signaling equipment (Lamp Signal apparatus) and instructed in their use. While the army was concentrating on the new style of warfare, the old ways were still being preserved. Riding courses were provided for the officers; which in IR 180 was taught by *Vizewachtmeister* Schmid of the Baggage Section of the Train who was a riding teacher in peacetime.

Aside from the normal infantry training that took place there were also some radical changes in the basic infantry structure. Small, intricate fighting units were gradually being formed from the traditional infantry companies. The new units were composed

Relaxing before deployment while under enemy fire? Or possibly fishing with explosives. (*Das Württembergische Reserve-Infanterie-Regiment Nr. 119 im Weltkrieg 1914-1918*)

of many different specialized weapons so that soon the actual rifleman in the companies was being reduced to only a small handful of men.

The three *Minenwerfer Abteilung* of IR 180, which had been distributed among the three battalions of the regiment, were combined once more into a larger organization for the purpose of greater fire and control direction and began training as a *Minenwerfer* Company under the leadership of *Leutnant* Anton Kromer. This was considered to be the best manner to deploy these important weapons.

For the most part the men were kept busy training and attending courses on tactics, specialty weapons and exercises. Still, there was also time for the men to hike in the afternoon to nearby Kortrijk, and view the sights offered by the historic area. However, Kortrijk also contained the higher commands and was a regular target of British bombers. In most instances the perceived threat was worse than reality, as most bombs fell with little accuracy. On one such raid, at 10.00 p.m. on 16 August, enemy bombers dropped four large bombs on the city but did not cause any damage or casualties. Still, these attacks could not be taken lightly as there was the occasional time when men were killed or wounded from these raids.

The troops were also warned that spies were reported to be lurking everywhere. While the local populace appeared to get along with the men, it was suspected that many of them carried a secret hatred of the invaders in their hearts and were working for the enemy. Behind the lines the men were housed in wooden barracks or in summer huts and in the houses of the local populace. At the front men built sandbag walls, barricades or utilized hedges or barriers made from reeds and other materials to mask the positions from enemy observers. Trenches could not be constructed in the same manner as on the Somme due to the high water table.

Above ground trench. (Author's collection)

All of these efforts proved to be sufficient protection at the moment because the enemy artillery could not easily direct its fire against specific targets without the help of observation aircraft and aerial activity along the front line on both sides was often very low. There was also the problem facing the opposing sides, a shortage of ammunition which meant that the artillery could only fire in the featureless and flat terrain with great difficulty and only if it was considered absolutely necessary.

When the regiments arrived by the river Yser there were no familiar deep mined dugouts because of the high water table and swampy terrain. Instead, there were numerous concrete blockhouses that were provided for the men. Most of these were well constructed and offered adequate protection against light caliber shells. A few were even sturdier and could protect against medium caliber shells. However everything changed when this front became drawn into the great Flanders Battle. Systematic bombardments of guns of all calibers made many of the concrete blockhouses unusable. New ones could not be built under the constant rain of shells and the sandbag walls as well as the barricades offered no real protection for the troops. The men in the front line were primarily dependent on a crater position, in which foot traffic by day was almost impossible.

It was under these circumstances that the front line was partitioned for a defense in depth. The machine guns were distributed in a checkered pattern inside specially constructed machine gun nests that were spread throughout the entire zone. The readiness battalions were distributed in shell craters, the few usable concrete blockhouses or ruined houses and the reserve or rest battalion preferably looked for areas where there was little or no enemy fire.

The 26th Reserve Division had been ordered north into the Flanders battle which had started at the beginning of the month with the attacks by the French and British. On 17 August 1917 the 26th Reserve Division, as the army reserve, was placed between Tourhut and Staden and on 18 August 1917 the infantry and artillery would be placed behind the right wing of Group Ypern (Headquarters III Bavarian Army Corps, *Generalleutnant Frhr. von* Stein), by Schaap-Balie and Ondank on both sides of the Staden-Langemarck railway line; the division headquarters was in Gits.

The situation facing the division in the middle of August was the result of two days of uninterrupted enemy attacks, staring from 31 July 1917. The enemy had advanced 1 kilometer into the German positions despite heavy resistance and had captured several towns and villages but had not managed to break through the German lines as had been hoped. The failure of the Allied armies in breaking through the German line was credited to the new defense in depth and the tenacity of the German defenders.

The rumors and stories of the intense fighting and heavy losses that had spread through the regiments were not encouraging news when the men prepared to move toward the fighting. There were divided feelings among the men as the regiments prepared to march off on the evening of 17 August 1917 and the early morning hours of 18 August 1917; some of the less experienced men were looking forward to their first time in combat, while older veterans knew all too well what was in store for them.

After a long delay, the orders finally came and at 2.30 p.m. the troops were transported to Staden, from where they marched to Schaap-Balie on the Staden–Langemarck

Eingreiftruppen, 26th Reserve Division, in the church of Gits. (*Die 26. Reserve Division 1914-1918*)

Concrete shelter by Ondank. (*Die 26. Reserve Division 1914-1918*)

Road. Once there, IR 180 received billets in a barracks camp, while the regimental staff went to the brigade battle Headquarters in Veldhoek and was given a briefing on the situation at the front. On 18 August 1917, RIR 121 moved forward to Staden where it would act as a *Stoss Regiment,* a thrust regiment that would be used for an immediate counterattack wherever it was needed. RIR 121 was positioned behind the 204th Infantry Division.

On 18 August 1917 RIR 119 marched to Houthulst Wood where the 26th Reserve Division was located in the wood pieces on the left and right of the *Rogge Strasse.* 19 August 1917 was also the last day the regiments would receive warm food for the foreseeable future. Only cold food came up to the line with the food carriers and there was no possibility of heating it up without giving away the positions to the enemy.

However food was one of the least problems facing the men of the 26th Reserve Division. A few concrete dugouts offered meager protection for a small number of troops while most of the men lay in shell craters and shallow holes scraped into the ground, looking for protection against the enemy artillery fire that fell on the roads and the forest. Under these conditions RIR 119 relieved Bavarian *Ersatz* Regiment 3 in the position located on the Broenbach on 19/20 August 1917.

With the entire 26th Reserve Division being considered an *Eingreif Division*, the men waited for orders to join the battle. They could clearly hear the terrible sounds of the battle raging in the front. Hours passed without any orders arriving for a counterattack; the men simply passed the time as best they could.

The company leaders of RIR 119 commanded the men while in the crater field of the front line, something very different than the fighting in the Artois. In Flanders there were no communication trenches, no well-built position with deep dugouts. Here the men only found a strongly shot up area. The roads and runner paths stood under destructive artillery fire and they were avoided at all cost. The Württemberg troops were not used to moving in the open and felt defenseless against the enemy fire.

The troops quickly began to understand the style of warfare they had been thrown into. If enemy planes fired at any foot traffic in the *Eisenbetonlager* it meant that fire from heavy caliber guns would soon follow, forcing the men to seek cover in the shell craters. The few shallow dugouts that existed were quickly shattered in the heavy fire. As the garrison in the front lines had no real means of protection against the enemy fire, the tactic of avoidance was used. The crater garrison skillfully jumped sideways, backwards but mostly forward of the areas being shelled in order not to become buried in their shallow holes.

However, constantly changing positions proved to be a great strain on the men who were quickly becoming extremely tired, and despite all precautions, losses could not be avoided. Once the British recognized the new protective measure of avoidance was being utilized, they came up with a solution. In addition to heavy shells falling on the garrison, lighter high explosive shells with a strong splintering effect or shrapnel shells were fired across the front in order to catch the men trying to avoid the heavier shells as they moved in the open.

There could be no thought of sleep or rest while in the front line and this resulted in rotating the battalions every three days. The only protection against rain, wind and cold

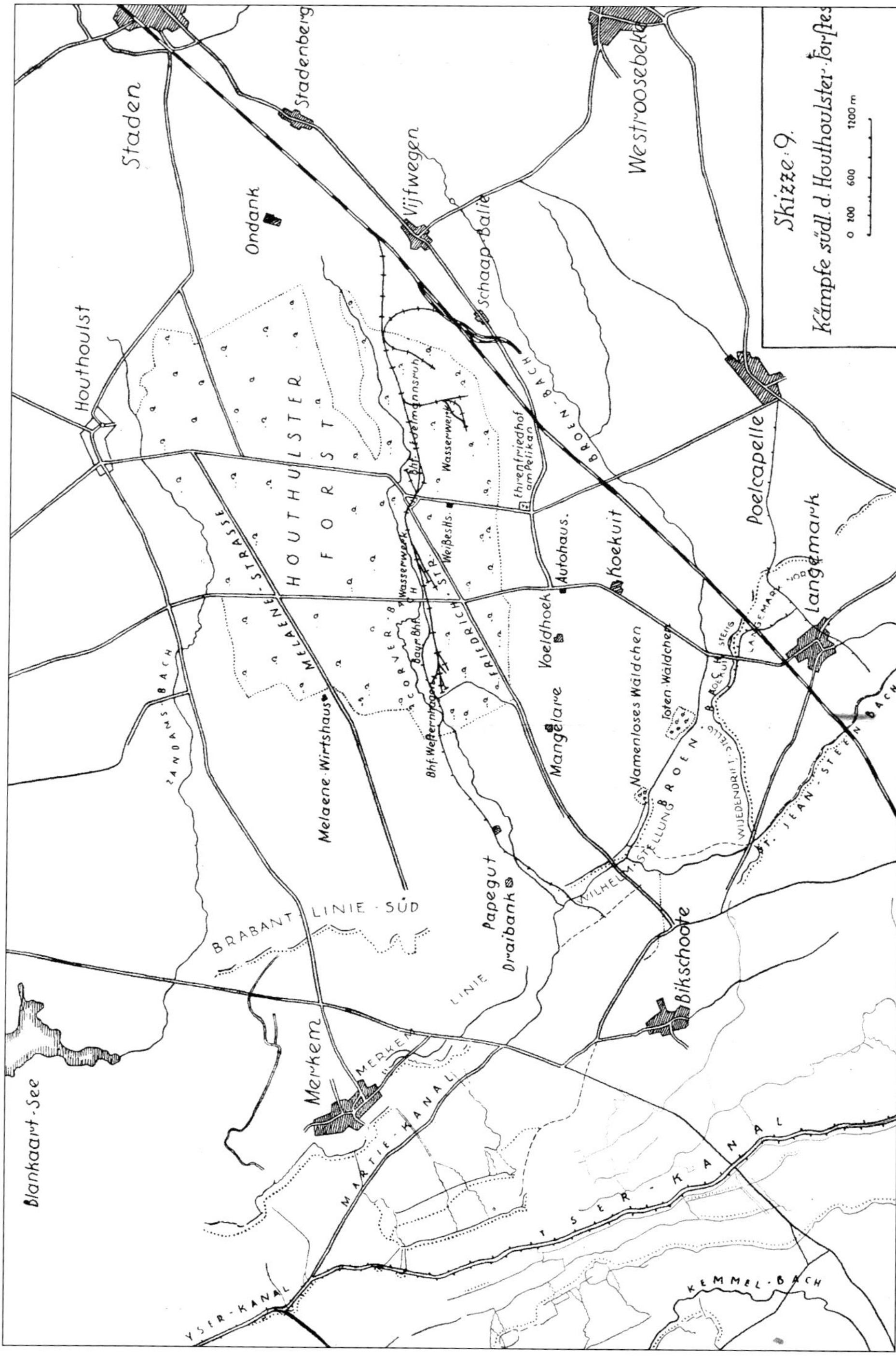

Houthulst Wood and surrounding sectors

was the overcoat and tent cloth. The numbers of men reporting sick increased from day to day and slowly destroyed the strength of the regiment without any actual fighting taking place.

The *Krankenträger* had it even worse than the infantry. They performed their difficult work in terrible conditions and were exposed to constant enemy fire but still managed to accomplish their task and saved many lives in the process. The dressing stations were generally in the front, as the transport of a wounded man through the crater field many times lasted 3-4 hours, an eternity of torment for the wounded as well as for the *Krankenträger*.

There were numerous acts of kindness and devotion to duty that often went unnoticed in the confusion of the time. One such act took place on 22 August 1917 when *Krankenträger* Scherrer, 11/R119, was thrown out of his crater into a pasture from the nearby impact of a heavy shell during a period of intense drum fire. He suffered a badly crushed shoulder from the concussion of the shell. Despite his painful injury, he continued to carry back seriously wounded men with help from a comrade, all the while in great agony. Unfortunately, during one trip to the rear with a wounded man a shrapnel ball struck and killed him instantly.

As the regiments took up their new positions, they faced new challenges at almost every move. When the I/180 was to relieve the reserve battalion of Bavarian RIR 11 by the *Pferdetränke* at the southwest corner of Houthulst Wood in the night from 19/20 August, a location that the battalion commander had previously explored, his battalion was not where it was supposed to be when the battalion commander arrived. Instead, the I/180 was found at the railway station Westernhagen. The Bavarian battalion commander sent a message that the I/180 would not be able to occupy the original designated sector because numerous German batteries stood by the *Pferdetränke,* which was continuously under strong enemy artillery fire. Instead, the I/180 was placed at the ready at the *Bayernbahnhof*, where the regimental headquarters had acknowledged that it was far safer and the companies of the I/180 then camped in the wood piece by the *Bayernbahnhof*.

However they now stood just southeast of several other batteries, 500-600 meters southeast of the *Bayernbahnhof*, which on the next day received strong enemy artillery fire starting at 9.00 a.m., from which the shell splinters reached the vicinity of the battalion billets. One heavy shell actually hit the camp of the 1/180 and the 1MG/180 and caused losses of seven dead and 12 wounded. At 3.45 p.m. the I/180 was finally forced to move camp in a northerly direction because of the enemy bombardment.

The enemy counter-battery fire falling on the unfortunate batteries grew stronger and longer in duration and the move was necessary in order to prevent larger losses among the troops. In addition to the losses mentioned above, four additional men had been wounded from shell splinters that had travelled at least 1,000 meters from the point of impact. After the British fire on the battery had died down the I/180 moved several hundred meters north of the *Bayernbahnhof* where a few concrete dugouts provided some protection against shell splinters and shrapnel balls and where barracks offered some protection against the wet ground.

The days that followed were the stuff bad dreams are made from. The enemy directed all of his fire, day and night, in uninterrupted lively destructive fire from guns of all

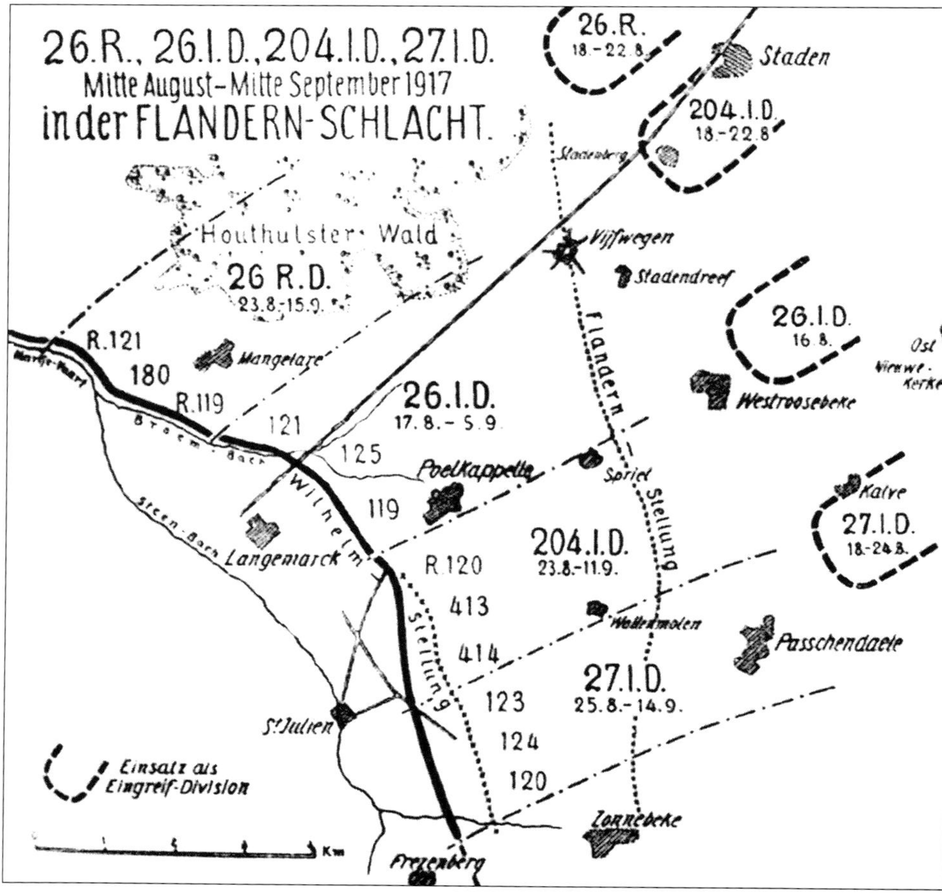

Flanders Battle from the middle of August to the middle of September 1917.

calibers on the crater position and the rear terrain. By daybreak and after the onset of darkness searching machine gun fire also spread across the entire position trying to catch anyone out in the open.

Losses under such circumstances were inevitable and no one was immune from the constant fire. On 20 August 1917, a direct hit close to the crater occupied by the commander, adjutant and orderly officer of the III/180 buried and slightly wounded all three men. The leadership of the III/180 was then taken over by *Oberleutnant* Teuffel, company commander of the 12/180. Miraculously, on 23 August 1917 another battalion of the regiment arrived at the front without suffering a single loss.

In the evening of 19 August 1917 the 26th Reserve Division had relieved the 214th Infantry Division, and became mingled together with parts of the 9th Bavarian Reserve Division, behind the Broenbach and from the *Friedrich Strasse* leading through Houthulst Wood until to the Langemarck-Staden railway line. The 119th Infantry Division was on the right of the division; the 26th Infantry Division was on the left. IR 180 occupied the right division sector and RIR 119 occupied the left sector. RIR 121 remained behind with an *Abteilung* of field artillery as a *Stoss Regiment* by Pelikan and Schaap-Balie. French forces were opposite the right division sector, British troops opposite the left division sector and enemy light machine gun posts stood along the Broenbach.

The 204th Württemberg Infantry Division stood behind the 26th Reserve Division and then the 10th *Ersatz* Division further to the rear. The 26th Reserve Division took over a very important artillery position, the largest part being massed in the four square kilometers of Houthulst Wood. Enemy pilots were always searching for these batteries, as were light ranging troops and sound ranging troops.

Enemy artillery fire fell throughout the forest in an attempt to destroy the German batteries and it was proving very difficult to bring ammunition up to the guns, many of which had just arrived. Fifteen ammunition columns were required to supply all of the guns, and all roads and paths through the wood were under constant fire and the routes were badly shot up making each trip extremely difficult.

The artillery batteries in Houthulst Wood were divided into close combat and long range combat battle groups. One Group was designated to fire at the second enemy wave and one special heavy group under the control of the AOK to be used against longer range targets. With the close combat under groups, between the Broenbach and Houthulst Wood were also *Fuss Artillerie* batteries. The long range groups stood in the Houthulst Wood and the Second Wave Group was found in the area of the *Eingreif Division*, also north and east of the wood. One platoon of field artillery had also been assigned to every infantry battalion in reserve.

The artillery observation positions were quite good. The Stadenberg south of Staden provided a good overview of the enemy lines and numerous observation posts were located near the front line in Houthulst Wood. While there was no shortage of good observation posts in the front lines, at times, observation was very difficult in the rainy weather, which many times made it impossible.

The light *Minenwerfer* were now concentrated in a single company in each infantry regiment, and two *Minenwerfer* companies were placed close to the front line to provide effective bombardments and close infantry support. The division was no longer in position warfare; it was now open field warfare. Something the men had to get used to after so many years of trench fighting. There was a thin sentry line with small detachments on foot who would be the first to meet the enemy and provide a weak defense to slow them down. Behind them were the *Stoss* Companies and further back, positioned wide and deep were the *Stoss* Battalions.

The enemy artillery was very maneuverable. They took everything under fire that was not protected against shells or against being seen and they systematically destroyed one concrete dugout after another. The support companies were also forced to practice avoidance in order to evade the enemy artillery fire. The infantry suffered badly under the heavy pressure on their nerves in the forward battle zone as well as in the rear areas, particularly suffering from constant movement and from fatigue through lack of sleep.

The artillerymen were no better off. They lived in the open or in light huts that were not even splinter proof, or that offered any protection even against the rain. Gun positions were exposed to enemy aircraft as the protective cover of trees was becoming destroyed from the constant artillery fire. Even if the guns remained silent they would become individually targeted during the day or at night, mostly with heavy caliber shells, and eventually damaged or destroyed. Whenever there was a fire pause the entire gun crew would have to carry ammunition up to the battery positions and this too prevented the artillerymen from having time to sleep.

The *pioniers* carried construction materials to the front under great difficulty, as well as helping to move 21cm mortars out of the support zone further to the rear. The unpleasant rainy weather during this time turned the crater terrain of Flanders into a sea of mud and made living here a nerve shattering misery. On 19 and 20 August 1917 strong enemy artillery fire from all calibers, particularly long range medium and large caliber flat trajectory guns, and railroad guns, lay upon the battle zone, and particularly on the support and artillery zone, as well as on the billets and reserve battalions.

RIR 121 also came under powerful drum fire on 19 August 1917 and could hear the sounds of heavy fighting in the distance. This continued on 20 August 1917 but the fighting was further to the south and the regiment did not become involved. On 21 August 1917 the enemy artillery fire grew to the heaviest level. While an attack was expected to follow, a large gas bombardment came instead on 22 August 1917. Mass enemy attacks did take place on 22 August 1917, however they fell against the 26th Infantry Division and further to the south, during which the 26th Reserve Division provided support with flanking fire.

Day after day the heavy British fire would swell up in strength and then almost as quickly, die down. Between 12.15 and 1.30 p.m. on 23 August 1917 the shelling reached the level of drum fire and suddenly, light waves of British skirmishers advanced on both sides of the Langemarck –Koekut Road before crossing the Broenbach. The men of RIR 119 in the front line opened fire with rifles and machine guns; however the enemy continued to send forth new waves.

The heavy fire from the men of RIR 119 forced the British infantry to stop and remain in the British barrage fire zone as well as coming under the accurate barrage fire directed at them from the German batteries. Finally, the friendly fire became so powerful and so destructive, the British troops who had crossed over the Broenbach realized they were without support and were forced to withdraw. Many of the wounded men were lost during the attack, as they drowned in the mud filled craters.

On 23/24 August 1917RIR 119 was relieved and the III/R119 then took over the left part of the sector of IR 180 on the Broenbach between *Granaten* and *Totenwäldchen*. The new position only differed slightly from the others the men had occupied. Here the garrison of the forward zone was spared somewhat as the enemy artillery fire mostly overshot the front line and it was far worse in the readiness position which received almost all of the fire of the British guns.

The men of RIR 121 were moved forward, and then brought back to the rear several times in the first days of the deployment. On the nights of 23/24 August and 24/25 August 1917 the regiment moved forward and relieved IR 46. On the night of the 25th and the following morning the enemy artillery fire lessened somewhat and the men finally had a chance to view the new position. In the weeks of heavy shelling the

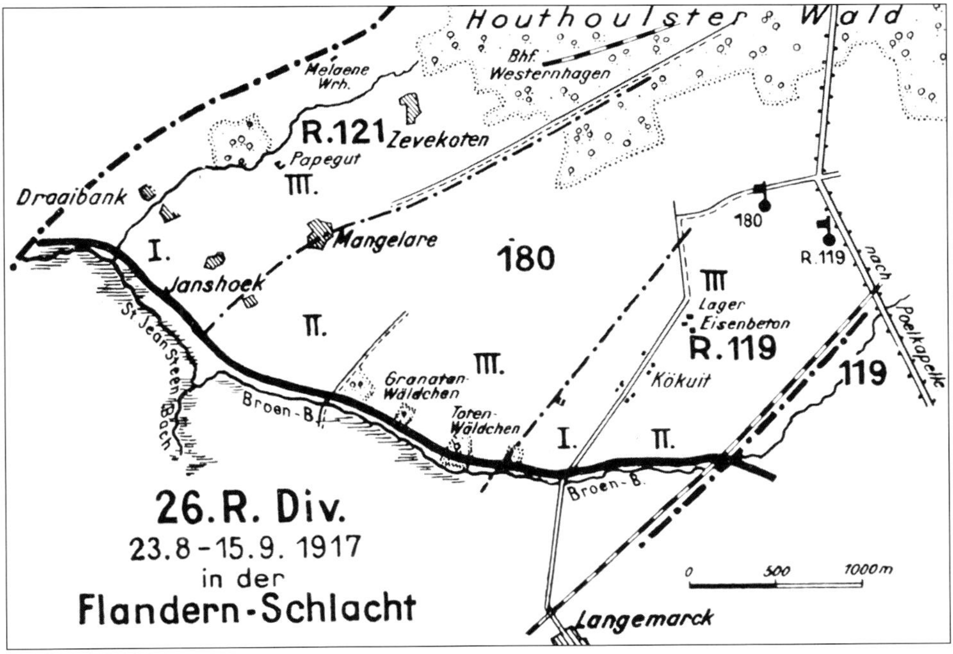

The 26th Reserve Division in the Flanders Battle 23 August t0 15 September 1917.

landscape looked like the surface of the moon, pockmarked with large and small craters. The only difference between Flanders and the moon was that the craters here were occupied by the men and were also filled with water.

The concrete structures found in the sector still carried the names of the farmsteads, in which they originally lay: Draaibank, Janshoek, Melaene Wirtshaus, Zevokotem, Papegut (KTK), Mangelare, Bahnhof Westernhagen (BTK). Before the front flowed the Steenbach, its swampy banks forming a modest obstacle. This area faced the French who were fighting alongside the British. It was suspected that a few French divisions had been inserted between the British divisions, because the large losses suffered in the recent British attacks could not be replenished.

Despite the natural obstacle formed by the Steenbach, several Frenchmen stumbled into the German lines in the proximity of the outpost positions. Both times the men were apparently lost as there was no well-formed front line on either side. Among those who had lost their way and who were taken prisoner was a French chaplain. Other than the occasional patrol or lost soldier, the battle activity was limited on both sides to artillery duels and bombardments of the concrete dugouts which teetered and swayed with each shell that impacted the area, because of the wet subsoil.

The constant dampness and rain continued to have a detrimental effect among the men. The numbers of officers and men who reported sick continued to grow on a daily basis. There was already a shortage of officers in the 26th Reserve Division and it was not uncommon for officers to be transferred from one unit to another. At 3.00 a.m. on

25 August 1917 a battalion from IR 180 was relieved by the I/R119 and became the rest battalion in the prisoner camp by Vijfwegen. Once in the rear *Hauptmann* Schneider, RIR 121, took over the leadership of the III/180 from *Oberleutnant* Teuffel.

On 26 August 1917 the 26th Reserve Division was handed over to the command of Group Dixmuiden. The division sector on the left of RIR 119 was turned over to the 26th Infantry Division, while the left sector of the 119th Infantry Division was taken over by the 26th Reserve Division. The division sector ran from the area southwest of Draajbank until the area southwest of Gruyterszale. The sector was divided into three zones, RIR 121 on the right, part of IR 180 in the middle, RIR 119 on the left. The forward sentry line stood along the Broenbach with the enemy close by on the opposite bank. There were no changes in the artillery dispositions in the rear with the new division sectors.

The enemy forces in front of the division were, from north to south: 51st French Division, 1st French Division and the British Guards Division. The border between the British and French troops, according to reliable reports, was approximately west of the regimental border between IR 180 and RIR 119.

On the afternoon and evening of 27 August 1917 the British attacked the front on the left of the 26th Reserve Division, against the 26th Infantry Division, 204th Infantry Division and 27th Infantry Division. The attack took place after a period of powerful drum fire with high explosive, gas and smoke shells, supported by numerous low flying aircraft in the sky and by numerous tanks on the ground by Poelkappelle and St. Julien. The enemy attacked two separate times using all of their forces, however they were unable to capture any ground and they finally had to withdraw.

The fighting along the front continued on 27 August 1917 when the enemy shelled and then attacked the left neighboring sector occupied by IR 125; they were eventually thrown back. The day was considered a day of honor for Württemberg troops, whose bravery and determination was the basis for the successful results, along with the combined efforts of the supporting artillery. While the 26th Reserve Division was not directly attacked, the division provided critical support with flanking artillery fire and the commander of AOK 4 sent a telegram to the King of Württemberg advising him of the bravery of his division.

The following day, 28 August 1917, was comparatively quiet. Then, on 30 August 1917 the 26th Reserve Division provided critical flanking fire again with heavy artillery fire when the Herenthage Park was attacked by enemy troops with flamethrowers. The division also fired upon Ypres out of Boesinghe along with supporting Marine Artillery.

At 5.00 a.m. on 31 August 1917 a strong enemy skirmish line advanced against the 8/R119 but were repulsed in the heavy defensive fire. Once the attack was over, a patrol under *Leutnant der Reserve* Fluck and *Vizefeldwebel* Huber, 7/R119, went out on reconnaissance and found a hastily constructed bridge thrown across the stream. While they were inspecting the makeshift bridge, they were seen by British sentries who fired at them, severely wounding *Unteroffizier* Bauer. Despite being quite a distance from the British sentries, the patrol members threw hand grenades toward the British sentries wounding several of them.

Other enemy groups had also advanced across the stream in front of companies of the II/R119; in front of the 8/R119 the British nested into a small wooded piece. The

Concrete shelter on the Broenbach. (*Die 26. Reserve Division 1914-1918*)

German sentries observed two sturdy foot bridges that led to the position over the 1 1/2 meter deep Broenbach.

The defensive crater line ran along the edge of the trees, or actually the remains of trees, while the enemy post lay 50 meters deep in the woods. The British troops that had crossed the Broenbach had been stopped by a concrete blockhouse located at the southwestern edge of the former forest. Plans were then drawn up to expel the enemy foothold on the German side of the Broenbach and on the night of 2/3 September 1917 a *Stosstrupp* from the 4/R119 which had relieved the 8/R119, threw the enemy back over the stream after a short hand grenade battle. Afterward, *pioniers* blew up the foot bridges in order to prevent any further enemy advances.

The enemy shelling of the command zone only mildly distressed the staff that simply called the shell fire 'Paper drum fire.' By 3 September 1917 the low level of enemy fire convinced the division staff, the brigade staff, regimental staff and artillery group staff that no attack appeared to be planned against the division. As such, part of the division was sent to the rear to rest, after being replaced by a regiment from the current *Eingreif Division*; RIR 371 from the 10th *Ersatz* Division. Once out of the front line, the men were taken to the area of Hooge-Schnur.

The rotation of the battalions continued to take place every three days due to the strain of holding the front line on top of the increasing sick list. It would not be too long until the entire division would need to be relieved and taken from the front line despite not having been involved in any serious fighting. The loss of men was being offset to some degree with the introduction of increased firepower being provided to each company in the 26th Reserve Division. This was possible with the increased number of light machine guns being available, the MG 08/15. Now each company had three or more light machine guns assigned to it.

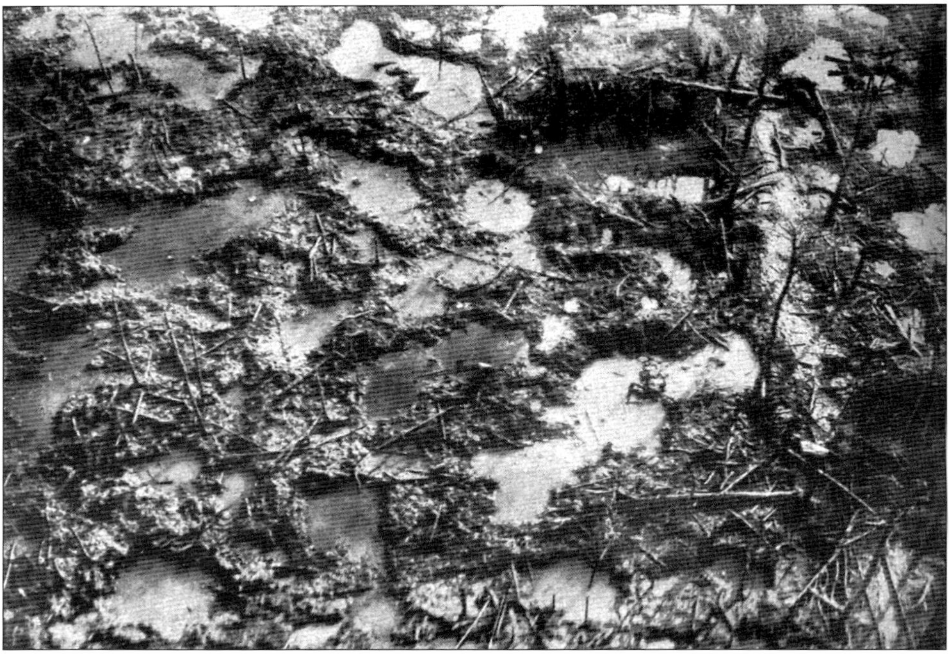

'Our position' in Houthulst Wood, taken by an observation aircraft. (*Die 26. Reserve Division 1914-1918*)

On 5 and 6 September 1917, RIR 119 exchanged positions once again and took over the sector on the northeastern bank of the St. Jean Steenbach north of Langemarck from RIR 121. Two thirds of the garrison was in concrete shelters, one third was in craters, many filled with water and mud. It was a poor position, only narrow routes along the edge of the stream provided any dry place for the defenders. The enemy held a concrete blockhouse upon a small hill opposite the regiment. The swampy Steenbach formed the line between the opposing sides and all foot bridges and larger bridges across the stream had been blown up.

It was a quiet area where the German guns would fire during the day according to the supply of ammunition at hand. The enemy infantry, the French, also behaved quietly. It was probably fortunate that this sector was designated as a quiet area as the II/R119 numbered only 192 rifles on 10 September 1917 while manning a firing line of 1,100 meters. Considering the situation, it was decided to place the small number of men into concentrated groups. This would mean that large parts of the front line were unoccupied and could easily be penetrated by the enemy, but there was nothing else to be done with so few troops at hand.

The sector of the battle battalion being held by the II/R119 was narrow and significantly deeper than the one previously held. The left wing lay in the vicinity of the Staden-Langemarck railway, where the German line moved along the Broenbach, on this side of the stream were two small, well preserved pieces of woods, the *Totenwäldchen* and the

RIR 119 MG 08/15 machine gun team (Author's collection)

Namenlose Wäldchen. Further to the rear, about one kilometer, was slightly ascending cover-free terrain, then again some hedges and wall remnants, in which machine gun nests were installed and then again two kilometers of open terrain until Houthulst Wood.

The strongpoints located in the position were called: Koekuit, Veldhoek, Autohaus (KTK), Brigade Haus, Pelikan, *Weissen Haus* (BTK). The garrison of these positions formed no coherent line, only individual scattered strongpoints lying in the terrain with machine gun nests. Any traffic from the KTK to the front by day was impossible and in the dark nights could be found only if you took hold of the telephone wire lying on the ground and used it as a guide. At least one hour was required to make the 3 kilometer long journey through the crater field.

The Broenbach lying along before the front formed the border between the opposing positions and offered some protection against surprise attacks. However it soon became evident that enemy sentries and pickets, in this instance British, were in the *Totenwäldchen* and the *Namenlose Wäldchen* at night. Aerial photographs provided clear evidence to the leadership that the enemy had been able to establish strong nests on the northern Broenbach bank in both woods.

These nests formed a constant danger for RIR 119 and therefore they would have to be cleared from the enemy. Unfortunately the battle battalion was not allowed any time for the preparation of this task as it would not be an easy thing to throw the British back across the stream. The skirmishing continued about these wooded pieces until the relief of RIR 119 on 16 September 1917. The removal of these enemy positions was fully acknowledged by senior commands and operations were ordered using the II/R121, supported by parts of the III/R119, *Stosstrupps* from a *Sturmbataillon* and supporting artillery that would eliminate the enemy threat.

When the men received the orders there was little joy in the ranks at the prospect of being involved in such an attack. At this time RIR 121 was on the right wing of the division, IR 180 was in the middle and RIR 119 on the left wing where the main enemy pressure was concentrated. Connecting on the left of the division since the beginning of September was the Württemberg 26th Infantry Division. The exchange of positions between the badly frayed RIR 119 and RIR 121 began on the night of 6/7 September 1917 in preparation for the attack. The I/R119 became the battle battalion, the III/R119 became the readiness battalion at the *Weissen Haus* and II/R119 became the brigade reserve in Hooge.

Oberleutnant der Reserve Metz. (*Das Württembergisches Reserve-Feldartillerie-Regiment Nr. 26 im Weltkrieg 1914-1918*

In order to accomplish the task of clearing the enemy posts, two companies of 100 men each were quickly formed and on the evening of 12 September 1917 travelled forward to the old position. At 11:45 a.m. the *Sturmtrupp* arrived and now the company leaders first found out about the exact plan of attack. Using a shell crater where a tent square had been stretched across the top, the *Stosstrupp* leader informed the officers of RIR 119 and RIR 121 of the plan using the light of an electric torch.

By 2.00 a.m. all preparations were completed, however it was so dark that no one could become oriented in the terrain. A few minutes before 3.00 a.m. the fire raid began on the *Namenlose Wäldchen* and *Totenwäldchen*, however several shells fell short and exploded among the right hand company that was placed by *Namenlose Wäldchen*. The Groups were scattered in the fire and the men were bewildered. The leader who knew the area was missing, the *Sturmabteilung* assigned to the company became lost in the darkness and so this part of the attack fell flat.

The company advancing against the *Totenwäldchen* had better luck under *Leutnant der Reserve* Renz. A *Stosstrupp* of 20 men went along the edge of the wood against the stream, bumped into the British in a strong point and threw hand grenades at them and the surviving enemy troops surrendered. Now the *Sturmtrupp* turned toward the stream and grabbed the next strong point from the rear, drove the garrison out, pursued them to the third crater, closed off the bridge over the stream and overwhelmed the garrison with assistance from the men of RIR 121. One officer and 25 Other Ranks were taken prisoner during the attack.

At the same time *Unteroffiziers* Reiff and Staiger from the 12/R119, each with eight men, broke in the *Totenwäldchen*, attacked the concrete blockhouse found at the southeast corner and with RIR 121 men overwhelmed the enemy strongpoint in hard fought close combat and took one officer and 20 Other Ranks prisoner. At 10.30

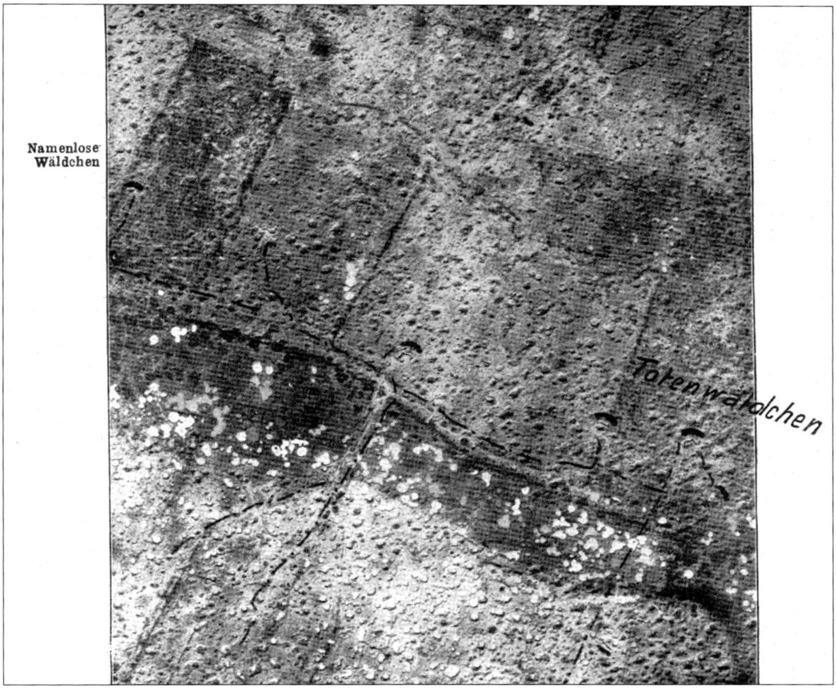

Aerial photograph of *Namenlose Wäldchen* and *Totenwäldchen*. (*Das Württembergische Reserve-Infanterie-Regiment Nr. 119 im Weltkrieg 1914-1918*)

a.m. the *Sturmtruppen* returned back to camp after the successful attack. The last act was to make sure that every foot bridge across the stream was completely destroyed and this was finally accomplished by the *pioniers*. The Irish Guards who had held the positions had suffered heavy losses during the fighting and in addition to the men killed or wounded, they left 1 officer, 65 men and 6 machine guns in German hands. The losses in RIR 121 in this position amounted to: 35 killed among which were *Leutnants der Reserve* Leiberich, Mauer, Schülen, *Feldwebel Leutnant* Wöltje, and 145 men wounded.

The fighting about these wooded pieces continued until the relief of the regiment on 16 September 1917. The experiences on this front were quite different than the officers and men had experienced in previous fighting. During the Flanders battle, the younger officers stood out especially, leading their men by example and encouraging them under very difficult conditions. Instead of fighting from fixed defenses, the officers were just as exposed as their men. The officers stayed in front of the troops when attacking enemy sentries who were usually equipped with machine guns, even when they did not know where the enemy was positioned or how strong they were. That was quite a deed under the circumstances of that time. It was somewhat different than fighting on the defensive and almost contrary to the natural inborn instinct of self-preservation. It also resulted in higher than average losses among the officers in the regiments.

Prisoners (Irish Guards?) captured by RIR 121 in the counterattack against the Totenwäldchen. (*Die 26. Reserve Division 1914-1918*)

In the days following the attack the enemy artillery fire started up again and at times it increased to drum fire, mixed with gas and artificial fog. This fire did not cause many losses among the small, scattered garrison lying in the terrain, probably as the men were spaced so far apart and made small targets. Enemy attacks took place only further to the south, so that this time RIR 121remained spared, however not every danger facing the men came from the enemy.

While in the position, the left wing company of the battle battalion of RIR 121 suffered a very disagreeable experience. The company received continuous fire from one of the German batteries further to the rear. Although all commands up to army headquarters were advised of this friendly fire they only succeeded in discovering the identity of the battery after eight days had passed; it was located many kilometers further south and fired along the front. The position held by RIR 121 formed a corner in the line, and the friendly shells struck the position because of a small inaccuracy in the maps being used to show the position. The error was corrected and the fire finally stopped.

Communication was very difficult in the especially large, deep defensive zone. Six methods were utilized by the *Kampf-Truppen-Kommandeur* (KTK) for secure reporting methods: the telephone, wireless, earth-telegraph, dog messengers, carrier pigeons and when all else failed the runner with a system of intermediate runner posts running the length of the zone. The telephone wires were mostly shot up; by day they could not be repaired in the front. Wireless and earth-telegraph were so numerous on this particular fighting front that they were continuously interrupting one another and little could be done to prevent the confusion this caused. Dogs and messenger pigeons worked well and were reliable; however, both went only to a specific location station. All that remained as the most reliable and most thorough method was man. These runners performed magnificently, they often went on their dangerous journeys without a murmur, knowing that they would not have been sent if it had not been necessary.

The duty of the carrying troops was likewise difficult. The regimental transport of RIR 121 lay in and by St. Joseph north of Staden, however it was also established further forward in the vicinity of the reserve battalion by Ondank, where the food become carried forward from the kitchens to the front line. It was a route of about 8 kilometers, of which 3 kilometers was a crater field.

Four weeks in the shell craters and damp woods under continuous strong bombardments from the enemy had severely weakened the health of the men. The number of troops reporting sick was very high. Lying around in the wet earth and eating cold food because of transportation difficulties, led too frequent colds and intestinal-illness. The state of the men's spirits had also suffered, and in part they had become completely apathetic. It was considered critical that the troops became extracted out of the battle zone and received quarters where they could recuperate, rest and regain their strength.

The 26th Reserve Division was relieved by the 18th Infantry Division in the days between 15-18 September 1917 and were sent to the area of Gits where the men boarded trains and travelled to Bohain, northeast of Cambrai where they joined Group Caudrey. The new commander was *General der Infanterie. Frhr. von* Watter, and the division would support the XIII Army Corps. Von Watter greeted each regiment in the first days after their arrival and welcomed the battle proven regiments into his Group. Despite the strain on the nerves and health of the men while in Flanders, they were quickly restored to health by good quarters and adequate food. The rest time was unfortunately disturbed by enemy bomber squadrons, from which IR 180 suffered a number of losses. Still, the division was fully content to remain behind this quiet front for as long as possible.

The period of rest was long overdue. Despite being on the Flanders front for a considerable period of time and at the fringe of the massive battle taking place nearby, the division did not become embroiled in a direct attack. Instead it assisted the divisions further south with artillery and machine gun fire. Still, through physical and nervous exhaustion, sickness and small sorties the division strength fell even when new replacement troops had been received. Until this period of time the battle losses to the 26th Reserve Division amounted to 1,084 men while the number of men reporting sick was 898. The battalions were now reduced to an average of 580 men each.

During the time spent in Flanders the regimental doctor in RIR 121, *Stabsarzt* Dr. Böss, had set up a sick room in the church of St. Joseph that was quite busy. Dr. Böss was in the unique situation where he could observe the differences in human nature when people were under great stress. On one hand he saw sick men, who very well had the right to report sick, yet they remained in the position with their comrades. On the other hand there are also men who took advantage of any situation in order to avoid frontline service. These men employed marginal malaise to elude the dangers and hardships of position warfare. In view of these circumstances, the lightly sick in St. Joseph became given the opportunity to support the men who were still fighting by employing their labor usefully with the potato and oat harvest for their comrades under the watchful eye of the Supply Officer.

Once in the rear, the men were deloused, bathed and straightened up their equipment. Then there were the inevitable parades, inspection of arms, integrating the replacements that arrived from home and on Sundays, regular church services were held in the local churches where the Field clergymen of the division provided the sermons. Field exercises, schools of marksmanship and *Stosstrupp* training then followed and in the afternoon, gymnastic exercises in each company.

There was a machine gun instruction course in each battalion for officers and an MG 08/15 instruction course in each regiment that consisted of four *Unteroffiziere* and 24 men. There was the officer's riding school, which in IR 180, the new leader of the First Line

Transport, *Vizewachtmeister* Strauss, was the instructor. The Instructional Officer of the regiment, *Leutnant der Reserve* Griesinger, held talks with every battalion on numerous subjects.

Finally, since the mobilization in late 1914, the 26th Reserve Division was happy that it had three weeks in the zone of communication without being subjected to battle alarms. The regiments were broken down into smaller units; the men, horses and equipment were all placed into good condition; then, practices and exercises were held in the pleasant terrain. Exciting schools were held in battalion and regimental associations, along with the artillery regiments. New, formerly unknown battle formations were created to take advantage of every branch of the service working in conjunction with each other. They trained by Groups, platoons, companies and battalions and worked on the close cooperation between the infantry and artillery and the air service.

The men continued to train on numerous specialized infantry weapons; particularly the heavy and light machine guns, light *Minenwerfer* and various forms of communications equipment. Courses were held and the troops were schooled in combat methods that were unique for the Flanders battle. Smaller courses were held in the companies on new methods of trench warfare using live hand grenades, *Granatwerfer* and *Minenwerfer*.

Even with all of the intense training there was still sufficient time for relaxation, sports and visits to the cinema in nearby Bohain. The battalions held sports festivals, of which a great deal was quite merry and not just another means of training. With the beautiful fall weather, good food, to which the Line of Communication cows unwillingly provided milk, and by the neat and clean housing, the men in the division recovered swiftly from the efforts of the last months and the regiment only grudgingly separated from the beautiful, quiet area after three weeks.

Even positioned far from the effective range of the enemy artillery, there was always the threat of air attacks. During one such raid, on a sunny day at 3.00 p.m. on 30 September 1917 15 French pilots flew over Fresnoy le Grand where IR 180 was billeted and they dropped about 25 medium bombs on the quarters of the II and III/180. Both battalions suffered heavy losses from this attack; the II/180 had four men killed, one officer and 12 men wounded. The III/180 had seven men killed, six seriously and 11 slightly wounded. A further aerial attack followed between 10.00 p.m. and 11.00 p.m.

October arrived and some of the regiments had to say goodbye to officers that they had known since the start of the war. On 7 October 1917 *Hauptmann* Heyberger left IR 180; he had been with the regiment since August 1914, first as the leader of the Machine Gun Company, then as the commander of the I/180 and now he went to a new post as the adjutant of the 54th Reserve Division. *Hauptmann* Schneider took his place, and other than a short time when he was wounded, he led the I/180 to the end of the war.

The Intelligence officers had now begun to receive information on major operations scheduled for the future while they were in Germany on training courses. The men behind the front were having a good time during physical training and competitions, where the comradeship between men and officers grew closer as rumors began to spread of the prospect of a large offensive that was going to take place. All of the training the men were undergoing appeared to be devoted to what was going to be expected of the men in the future. Much of the training and emphasis on the new tactics now made sense.

At the beginning of October the regiments practiced in larger formations, with battle training in half battalions, battalions and also as full regiments. So while the regiments trained, the health and spirit of the men improved until it was time for the division to be sent back to Flanders once more.

The 26th Reserve Division was sent to Flanders between 11 and 13 October 1917 when the regiments were sent north to the railway center Lichtervelde and from there in a westerly direction to Gits by rail. Once there, the division relieved the 26th Infantry Division from Group Staden in the 4th Army and into their old sector where they exchanged places with the 27th Infantry Division as the *Eingreif* and *Kampf Division* for Group Dixmuide in the position in front of Houthulst Wood.

On 12 October 1917 the 26th Reserve Division was the *Eingreif Division* under the newly formed Group Staden, Headquarters Guard Reserve Corps, *General der Kavallerie Frhr.* Marschall, in three locations in the area of Staden-Lichtervelde, the latter often becoming the uncomfortable bombing target of enemy aircraft. The division headquarters was in Gits with the 27th Infantry Division.

RIR 119 arrived in the position on 14 October 1917 and the men marched in rainy weather and mud and ended up heading toward Schaap Balie, where the wet and tired men were placed in cramped and poor quarters. While the division had rested and the men had been restored the enemy had not been idle and had captured Poelkapelle and pressed back the former front line of the division. The enemy now attacked in smaller areas following overpowering artillery preparation instead of his old plan of a mass breakthrough on a large battle front.

After days of artillery preparation, using high explosives, gas and fog bombs, the enemy infantry attacked in several waves with tanks. The advancing enemy forces were protected by indirect machine gun fire and a rolling artillery barrage 500 meters deep. The enemy pushed forward slowly, destroying everything in the artillery fire zone. A deep fire barrier then protected the captured ground against any German counterattacks for an hour until the fire wall moved forward to the next goal of the attack. Low flying aircraft supported the infantry, dropping bombs and firing machine guns.

The German defenders quickly adapted to these new tactics and the weakly held foreground was reinforced with additional light machine guns that the enemy had to clear before continuing to advance. In the newly established main opposition line the enemy assault troops ended up in the German barrage fire that they formerly had been able to run through but the poor condition of the ground prevented any movement beyond a walk. All defensive lines were now equipped with numerous machine guns and light *Minenwerfer*. In addition there was a 1,000 meter deep destructive fire zone and very effective gas bombardments of the enemy batteries.

On the morning of 15 October 1917 the I and III/R119 were alarmed and moved to Hooge where a British attack was expected, however it did not take place. So the battalions marched back to Lichtervelde where they were joined by the II/R119. In six days they alternated between being the *Eingreif Division* and a position division.

The situation found by the men of the 26th Reserve Division had changed a great deal since the first time the division had occupied this sector. On 20 September 1917 the third Flanders battle had begun and the enemy had pressed forward to the edge of Houthulst

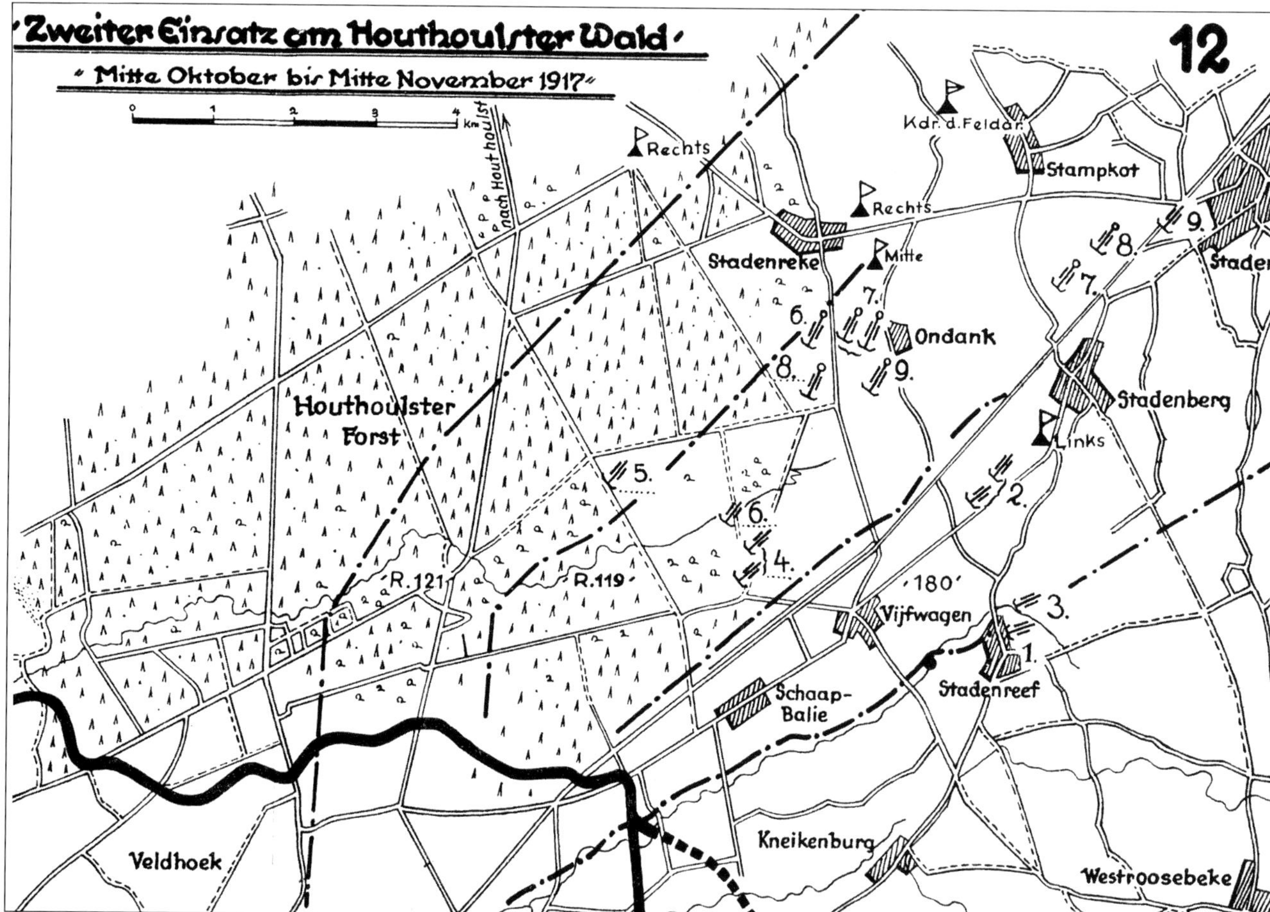

26th Reserve Division artillery positions in Houthulst Wood.

Wood on 10 October 1917. The forward line of the 27th Division now ran along the southern edge of the wood, closely in front of the *Weissen Haus*. The former sector of the battle battalions of the division had been lost during the absence of the division.

After being unloaded, the battalions of RIR 121 were given quarters in Luithoek and Scherminkelmolen and on 14 October 1917 the regiment was inserted by the 27th Infantry Division where there were frequent alarms and preparations for counterattacks, however no attack ever followed.

IR 180 was provided with poor and cramped quarters upon its return to the front. As Column B of the *Eingreif Division* the regiment had to be held ready to march at any time. On 15 October 1917 IR 180 also took over the Readiness position by Lindeken, southeast of Staden, however no insertion of the front occurred here as well.

While the 26th Reserve Division was in Prémont-Fresnoy le Grand the British had continued to push forward in the direction of Staden and in successive attacks had reached the line north of Draibank-*Ehrenfriedhof* Mangelare-Brigade House. South of the railway he pressed forward via Poelkapelle in the direction of Schaap-Balie.

On 16 October 1917 the artillery commander of the 26th Reserve Division took over the command of the artillery in the sector of the 27th Infantry Division. He now controlled 24 field artillery batteries and 18 heavy batteries in the positions that were positioned between Houthulst Wood and Staden. On the night of 17/18 October 1917 the two divisions, the 27th and the 26th Reserve, traded positions.

The regiments quickly assimilated all local knowledge of the sector from the troops being relieved; however the actual relief was still quite difficult because of the artillery fire in the badly destroyed wood. Furthermore the entire wood was being gassed, so that at times during the march toward the front gas masks had to be worn. The artillery fire was particularly strong at night and was directed mainly on the front line and the rearward connections. Wherever the long-range enemy guns could not reach, enemy aircraft took over using bombs. Under these difficult circumstances the battalions exchanged places every two days with one another.

This was the situation when the 26th Reserve Division became a battle division on 17 October 1917 and relieved the 27th Infantry Division. IR 180 took over the left sector, formerly occupied by IR 124, with RIR 119 on the right and Marine Infantry Regiment 1 was on the left. The forward line crossed the intersection of the railway line with the Staden–Langemarck Road; it was approximately 600 meters wide and only a crater position. The I/180 was the battle battalion, the II/180 the readiness battalion and the III/180 the rest battalion in Stampkot; the regimental staff was in Stadenberg. Twelve machine guns from a Machine Gun Marksman detachment were located in the regimental sector as well as one company from Marine Infantry Regiment 1 as the border command on the left. In RIR 121 the II/R121 became the battle battalion by the *Weissen Haus*.

On 18 October 1917 the 26th Reserve Division took over the eastern part of the sector of the 27th Infantry Division from east of the Langemarck–Pierkenshoek Road until east of the Schaap-Balie (Langemarck)-Staden road. RIR 121 was on both sides of the Poelkapelle–Houthulst Road, IR 180 on the left on both sides of the road and Langemarck–Staden railway, RIR 119 was in the middle. After the recent rest period, all the regiments in the division had a battalion strength averaging 600 men that made

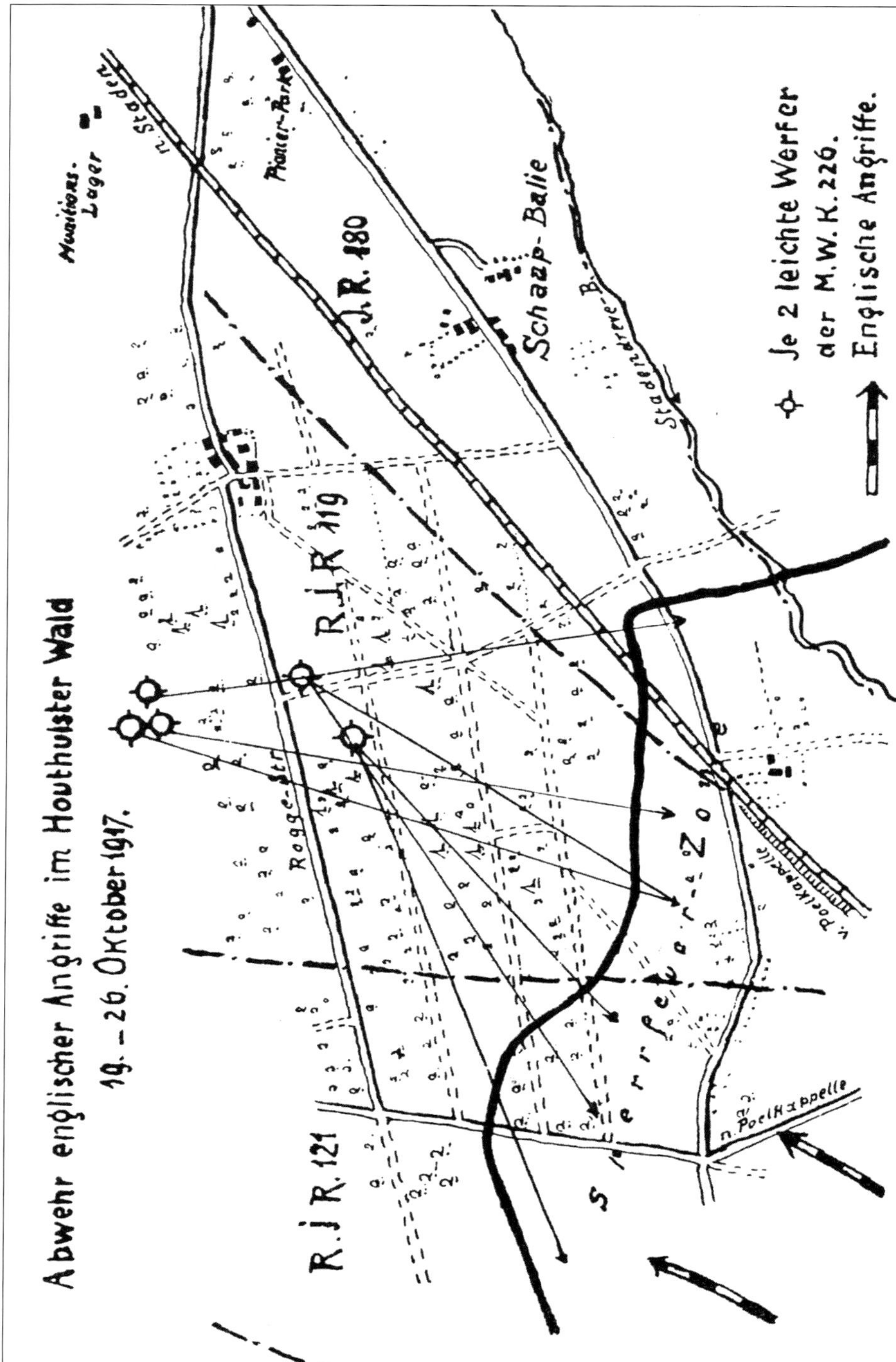

Light 7.6cm *Minenwerfer* positions, *Minenwerfer* Coy 226.

Rademacher
Leutnant d. R. im Inf.-Regt. 180,
gefallen bei Schaap Baillie
am 18. Oktober 1917

Paret
Leutnant d. R. im Inf.-Regt. 180,
gefallen bei Schaap Baillie
am 19. Oktober 1917

Left: *Leutnant der Reserve* Rademacher, IR 180, KIA 18 October 1917.
Right: *Leutnant der Reserve* Paret, IR 180, KIA 19 October 1917 (*Kriegstagbuch aus Schwaben*)

occupying the large sectors a little easier. The western part of the sector formerly occupied by the 27th Infantry Division was taken over by the reorganization of the artillery of the 58th Infantry Division, which the 26th Reserve Division supported. The left neighboring division was the 3rd Marine Division.

The main defensive line that ran approximately along the southern edge of Houthulst Wood, was a tangle of completely shot up and impenetrable undergrowth. An actual foreground had to first be created. As a result of the constant fighting about the main opposition line this did not happen. The main force of artillery stood in the area of Pierkenshoek-Stadenreke-Vijfwege-Manneken farm on the *Friedrich Strasse*, and still in the devastated area that was once known as Houthulst Wood.

On the night of 18/19 October 1917 the battle battalion of IR 180 received strong artillery fire from heavy caliber guns. A direct hit struck the second line where the 2/180 was positioned inside a cellar and caused the loss of 14 men killed and 17 men wounded. As a result of this, the 2/180 was given a platoon from the readiness battalion for support. On 18 and 19 October 1917 *Leutnants der Reserve* Rademacher and Paret were also killed.

On 20 October 1917 the enemy fire increased in volume which continued for the rest of the day and into the night. The seriousness of the situation dictated that on 20 October 1917 a change of the battalions was already needed; in addition to the change the 2nd Company of Machine Gun Marksman Detachment 74 was also inserted into the sector of the battle battalion, the II/180.

British prisoners captured 21 October 1917. (*Das Württembergische Reserve-Infanterie-Regiment Nr. 119 im Weltkrieg 1914-1918*)

RIR 119 was positioned at the southern edge of Houthulst Wood, north of the Staden-Boesinghe rail line, and consisted of a line of shell craters with a few scattered concrete blockhouses. The wedge the British had driven into the German position threatened Houthulst Wood from the south. British searching fire and German bombardments were a daily occurrence. On 20 October 1917 the artillery fire reached the level of drum fire and at 4.45 a.m. British forces advanced from the railway embankment against the 2nd and 3/R119. Quickly deployed defensive barrage fire drove the enemy back; then destructive fire continued for the rest of the day on 21 October 1917.

On 20 October 1917 a strong enemy patrol advanced in three waves against the middle of the II/180 and was repulsed by rapidly deployed barrage fire as well as infantry and machine gun fire. On the same day a direct hit destroyed a concrete dugout occupied by the 6/180 and resulted in losses of 14 men killed and two men severely wounded. Another battalion rotation was needed once more on 21 October 1917 and the II/180 was relieved as battle battalion by the III/180 on the night of 21/22 October 1917.

On 21 October 1917 the enemy fire reached the strongest levels and in the evening and during the night waves of drum fire lay upon the entire division sector. On the afternoon of the same day pilots reported seeing the assembly of strong enemy forces in the crater position in front of the entire division sector. Following this report, the German guns opened annihilation fire on the enemy infantry. Infantry patrols sent out at night also found white linen tape pointing toward the German position which had already been discovered three days before, presumably to serve as a direction line for advancing enemy skirmishers. After these findings, an enemy attack must be expected.

The artillery fire falling on the entire division sector increased to the greatest strength on the afternoon of 21 October 1917 as well as in the night from 21/22 October 1917.

At 6.30 a.m. on 22 October 1917, after the overwhelming fire on the forward battle zone, the enemy advanced behind the fog and smoke caused by a wave of rolling fire. The Allied attack, supported by infantry pilots, was directed against the 116th Infantry Brigade, 26th Reserve Division and 3rd Marine Division. According to a captured map the narrow attack goal was the short stretch of line from the *Friedrich Strasse* to the railway line.

Several enemy waves penetrated the positions of the 116th Infantry Brigade at its wing, part of which were from the 1st French Division, and the brigade was unable to throw them back completely into the exit position. After a period of close fighting at several locations in the 26th Reserve Division sector the division regained full possession of its entire line by the late afternoon. The forces opposite the division were parts of the 35th and 34th British divisions. The support by the artillery was particularly good and the numerous machine guns had performed very well in the intense fighting. The 3rd Marine Division had also held its position.

The losses on both sides were considerable. The British left three officers, 95 men and 10 Lewis Guns in the hands of the 26th Reserve Division. The consumption of the reserves in the counterattacks, as well as filling the gaps in the garrison and the connection units had used up all available support troops of the 26th Reserve Division. Parts of the 27th Infantry Division had to be moved forward to the Houthulst and Stadenrecke but they were not deployed. Strong rain that followed on 23 October 1917 apparently dampened the enemy artillery fire and the desire for further attacks.

At 6.35 a.m. on 22 October 1917 strong drum fire fell on the entire line held by IR 180, which was concentrated in the front line, as well as being particularly directed against the 9/180, the *Stoss Kompagnie*. The embankment between Schaap-Balie and Stadenberg as well as the battery positions in the rear also received very strong fire.

At 6.40 a.m. the first attack waves of the enemy were observed, and immediately the barrage fire signals went up high along the entire line, also by the right and left neighboring divisions, and well placed barrage fire quickly came down across the front. After a short time all telephone wires to the rear were broken, light signal connections did not work because of the dense fog. The only communication system still in operation was the wireless connections between the KTK and the regimental headquarters. At 9.00 a.m. the telephone connection was restored due to the diligence of the telephone repair troops who worked in the open among the falling shells.

Despite very heavy losses from the German barrage fire as well as infantry and machine gun fire the enemy advanced against the regimental position in deep partitioned waves and overran the left wing, which was forced to move back 150 meters. When this movement was reported the KTK ordered the 3/180 located by Vijfwegen, to counterattack. The 3/180, together with a similar counterthrust by a company of the Marine Infantry, brought the enemy to a stop and the situation was restored once more.

Assuming that the 9/180 had already counterattacked independently, the 4/180 located at the Westroosebeke railway station was placed in movement by the KTK, in order to support the right wing of the regiment. The regiment placed the 1st and 2/180

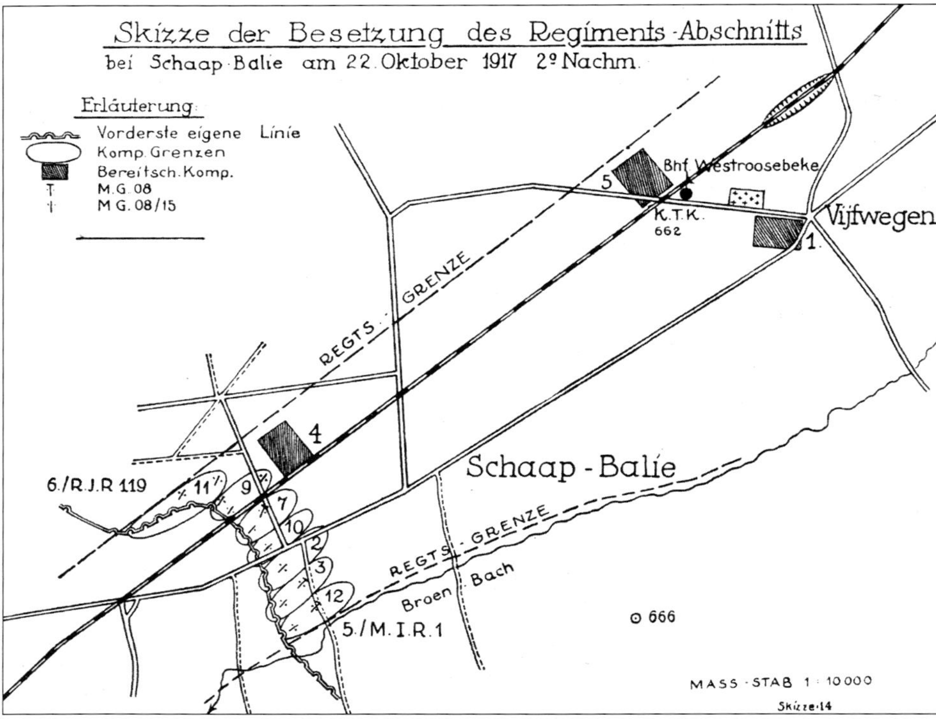

Positions of RIR 119 by Schaap Balie 22 October 1917.

as the readiness companies to the disposal of the KTK, which now occupied the former positions held by the 3rd and 4/180. The different companies tried to hold onto the crater position in bitter close fighting, however they also finally became pressed back in the middle and on the right wing about 150 meters, especially as the line at the right neighboring regiment had also been taken back somewhat.

The 9/180 and the 4/180 were both involved in the counterattacks; with the companies attempting to advance through the enemy blocking fire. The two companies suffered a number of losses in the heavy fire and were unable to make any real headway until 10.00 a.m., when the enemy artillery fire lessened somewhat and the companies were able to advance. The 2/180 was then placed at the railway station Westroosebeke by the KTK and ordered to take a position in the front line approximately 500 meters behind the middle of the regimental sector to act as support and the 5/180 was sent forward to occupy the newly vacant position.

The enemy artillery fire gradually reduced in strength, and the infantry battle that had lasted until about 11.00 a.m., finally came to a conclusion. At 2.00 p.m. the garrison was distributed as follows:

> In the Front Line were: The right wing until the railway line: 11/180 with two MG 08/15 and the 9/180 with three MG 08/15. In the middle: the 7/180 with the rest

> of the 10th and 2/180; with two MG 08/15 and two MG 08. On the left wing: 3/180 with the rest of the 12/180; with two MG 08/15 and two MG 08. The 4/180 lay about 300 meters behind the right wing in echelon. A connection on the right to the 6/R119 and on the left with the 5/Marine IR 1 was established. The 5/180 was the readiness company at the Westroosebeke railway station and the 1/180 by Vijfwegen.[1]

Once the enemy fire had died down almost completely a new distribution of the troops was ordered so that there was a clear division of the different sectors and the command structure could be regulated in the front line in an attempt to restore a semblance of order from the confusion caused by the recent fighting.

In the course of the night patrols were sent forward that firmly established that the outpost area was only occupied by weak enemy forces, and so the companies were able to drive these sentries back and once again occupied their old positions. Despite the strong enemy attacks not a single foot of ground had been lost. In addition two enemy officers and 45 men were taken prisoner on this day. According to statements from prisoners the enemy had suffered heavy losses, particularly through machine gun fire and the well placed artillery fire.

Haspel
Leutnant d. R. im Inf.-Regt. 180,
gefallen bei Schaap Baillie
am 22. Oktober 1917

Leutnant der Reserve Kaspel, IR 180, KIA 22 October 1917. (*Kriegstagbuch aus Schwaben*)

The losses suffered by IR 180 were: four officers (*Leutnants der Reserve* Haspel, Waldmann, Freudenmann and Brenz) and 16 men killed; two officers and 83 men wounded and six men missing. The spirit of the troops was described as being excellent and this was reflected in the successful defense of a major enemy attack.

Starting from midnight on 22 October 1917 the enemy artillery fire increased more and more by RIR 121 and at 6.30 a.m. drum fire fell with a blow, which was followed by an infantry attack. The enemy was only able to penetrate the weakly occupied outpost zone. He was thrown back further at the left wing, in the middle he became firmly situated in the ruins of the *Weissen Haus*, which was recaptured in the evening through a counterattack by the 3rd and 7/R121, so that the entire position was occupied by RIR 121 again. Another smaller British advance took place early on 23 October 1917, however it too was repulsed.

At 4.30 a.m. on 22 October 1917 there was drum fire on the positions of RIR 121 that eventually died down after 30 minutes. The German batteries that had responded to the fire had also stopped firing when suddenly, at 5.30 a.m. a fire storm of unheard of strength suddenly fell on the German positions, rending the badly churned up ground and splintering the few remaining trees in the sector, all the while strong fog lay over the battlefield. The entire front of the 26th Reserve Division experienced this destructive fire.

Within moments, red light balls could be seen climbing into the sky from the right division sector held by RIR 121; where the railway embankment, illuminated by the flares, could be seen through the fog. The sector of RIR 119 and IR 180 also sent up barrage fire signals into the dark sky and toward 6.00 a.m. a storm of fire from the German guns fell along the entire division front. The enemy fire was transferred to the German rear to block off the battle front and then the attack took place. The main enemy thrust went to the north against the *Weissen Haus* and to the northeast along the avenue towards the middle of the 8/R119 and along the Boesinghe-Staden rail line.

The British successfully penetrated the German lines at the *Weissen Haus* held by RIR 121 so that the right wing of the 8/R119 was now in the air. The platoon from the 8/R119 lying at the right wing also suffered considerably from short shots from the German guns and many men became buried. The survivors could no longer stand firm against the extensive enemy attack and friendly fire. The situation was made even worse when every machine gun with the 8/R119 were destroyed, buried or made unserviceable. The remnants of the brave company fought back as best they could, but the superior enemy strength continued to force the small company back more and more. The withdrawal did not stop until the men were by the dugout of the company leader, *Leutnant der Reserve* Siegle. Once here two operable machine guns protected the exposed flank.

The crater garrison sentries, who had tenaciously stuck to individual crater positions, fell in close combat. The right wing platoon of the 7/R119 was also forced to retreat. The leader, *Leutnant der Reserve* Dürr, succeeded in stopping his men from yielding and the company leader, *Leutnant der Reserve* Grossmann, bent back his wing so that the danger of the flank being encompassed was reduced. The British were now seated firmly in the crater terrain and continued to bring up fresh reserves.

The reserves of RIR 119 had also been placed on alert when the wounded brought back wild stories of the fighting at the front, stating that most of the men had been killed or captured and that all was lost. *Hauptmann der Reserve* Künlen Decided to move forward to the *Rotes Haus* with the 1st and 2/R119 in order to prevent the enemy from breaking through the line. The men hurried through the fire zone and found the 4/R119 already occupied the *Rotes Haus.*

The 3/R119 also moved toward the front line from the rear, while the 9th and 10/R119 took the place of the companies that had moved forward. The reserve company, the 5/R119 was unable to form any clear picture of the situation because of the bizarre reports still being spread by the returning wounded and finally sent patrols to the battle line in order to personally assess the situation.

Leutnant der Reserve Schmidt, 5/R119, finally had some clarity about the situation at 6.45 a.m. Then, the rest of the 8/R119 formed a *Stosstrupp* under *Vizefeldwebel* Pressmar along with a light machine gun and prepared for a counterattack. The *Stosstrupp* was positioned with a group from the 5/R119 as reinforcements. *Leutnant* Schmidt advanced with his men and they were pushed into the gap that had formed between the 7th and 8/R119 as a result of a counterattack. The men advanced rapidly against the British who

Zur frommen Erinnerung
im hl. Gebete
an unsern lieben Bruder und Schwager
Michael Engler
Gefreiter im Res.-Inf. Regt. 119, 5. Komp.
Inhaber des Eisernen Kreuzes und der silbernen Verdienstmedaille,
geboren am 11. Nov. 1894,
gefallen am 22. Oktober 1917 in Flandern
Allmächtiger, barmherziger Gott, der Du in Deiner anbetungswürdigen Vorsehung uns den Augenblick des Todes bestimmt hast, wir bitten Dich aus vertrauensvollem und ergebenem Herzen: siehe gnädig auf die Seele dieses gefallenen Kriegers, nimm den in treuer Pflichterfüllung erlittenen Tod als vollgültige Buße an und führe sie nach den Schrecknissen des Krieges in Deinen ewigen Frieden! Amen.

Gefreiter Michael Engler, 5/R119, KIA 22 October 1917. (Author's collection)

had no time to become fixed in the captured ground and who then became overrun in the swift counterattack, pushed from crater to crater until they finally had to retreat.

Now the entire 7/R119 joined the attack under *Leutnant* Grossmann and forced the British back to their exit positions, during which they had to move through the German barrage fire one more time and suffered heavy losses as a result. At 7.45 a.m. the entire sector was cleared of the enemy.

Leutnant Schmidt however made the decision to also expel the enemy who had penetrated by the neighboring regiment and stormed the *Weissen Haus* in order to restore the connection with RIR 121. Schmidt and his men soon received heavy fire from a British nest lying further in the rear and his men were forced to withdraw after Schmidt had become severely wounded. Schmidt was recovered from the open ground under great effort under the protection of a Red Cross flag, which the British honored, and brought safely to the rear.

In all of the confusion and fighting the 6/R119 had not become attacked; however the left wing platoon of the company had taken the attackers advancing against IR 180 north of the embankment under effective fire and inflicted heavy losses in the British ranks. A second enemy attack suffered the same fate and the British troops who were avoiding the counter thrust by the 5th, 7th and 8/R119 also ended up in the flanking fire of the 6/R119. The company leader, *Leutnant der Reserve* Fluck, fell in the enemy fire during the fighting while encouraging his men. 25 prisoners from the 35th British Division were brought in as well as nine Lewis Guns and 50 rifles by the II/

R119. However, the losses in the battalion had been very severe and there was a critical shortage of hand grenades and rifle ammunition.

During this same time, RIR 121 also attempted to recapture the *Weissen Haus* on the *Rogge Strasse*; the counterattack failed and the situation facing RIR 119 was still considered to be very dangerous. The 26th Reserve Division then ordered that the regimental reserves, the 9th and 10/R119 would attack along the road against the *Weissen Haus* and the 11th and 12/R119 would also advance in support.

However, the companies lacked close combat means and when they arrived at the threatened position shortly after midday the men were distributed along the crater line. Then, a counter-order arrived in which the companies were ordered back to the rear. Finally, the troops were in position and the planned attack finally took place. The fog that had blanketed the area had dispersed during this time and the weather became clear. The persistent artillery fire had almost completely ceased, and a pause in the fighting allowed the garrison to take a breath.

When the enemy trenches became filled once more toward 2.00 p.m. German light signals were sent up which unleashed new destructive fire from the artillery. Then, there was something not seen too often. German infantry pilots roared down from the clear sky and attacked the British trenches with bombs and machine guns.

Shortly after 4.00 p.m. the strongest enemy drum fire broke upon the entire front, and an attack on the *Weissen Haus* was in full course. While the 9th and 10/R119 advanced on both sides of the road, RIR 121 pushed there from a northeasterly direction. The British were thrown back in heavy fighting. At 6.00 p.m. the *Weissen Haus* was German once again and the British attack had failed under heavy losses for the enemy. The completely exhausted companies of RIR 119 were relieved and replaced by others that had suffered less; as the regiment had lost more than half of its total number, including two dead, five severely wounded and two slightly wounded officers.

Despite their recent losses, the British were still acting very aggressively. Later the same night a large enemy patrol broke into the crater position of the 5/R119, overran a forward shoved sentry post, which was occupied by stout patrol participants. The sentries were attacked in the darkness from the rear, and after a short period of hand to hand fighting were overwhelmed. Three men were taken prisoner and a light machine gun was carried off. Two men of the small garrison managed to escape in the darkness and reported about the enemy attack. A quickly formed counterattack by other parts of the 5/R119 brought in two British prisoners.

On 24 October 1917 the 26th Reserve Division and 27th Infantry Division were to exchange positions. On the evening of 23 October 1917 RIR 119 was relieved by Grenadier Regiment 123. Even now, while marching toward the rear, the companies were continuously harassed by long range enemy artillery fire and aircraft bombs. On 23/24 October 1917 RIR 121 was relieved by IR 120. The regiment marched to the area of Gits. Once there, they were harassed many times by aircraft and during one bombing attack in Lichtervelde there were losses in the regiment. Following the fighting IR 180 was relieved. On the night of 23/24 October 1917 the regiment was relieved by IR 124, assembled in the rear near Staden and marched to their individual billets.

The *Weissen Haus*. (*Die 26. Reserve Division 1914-1918*)

On 26 October 1917 the enemy attacked the position again after strong drum fire. There was a chance that the readiness groups of the 26th Reserve Division would be required and the men were placed on alert. Fortunately the attack was repulsed without the need of any assistance by the division. In the next days the rest of the regiments were greatly impaired through repeated alarms and movements to Stadenberg. On 27 October 1917 St. Joseph and Luikhoek were shelled from heavy flat trajectory guns and a change of quarters was planned for IR 180 with exception of the I/180, with the regimental staff moving to Gits, which was soon followed by the staff of the II/180 and eventually the III/180.

After a few days of rest, it was back to the Ypres front for the third time on 29 October 1917. The terrain was in even worse condition from the constant shelling and rain. Destroyed trees were scattered about everywhere, they crisscrossed the land forming effective barriers to observation and movement and it was almost impossible to observe the enemy at all during the day. The nights were very dark and if you fell into one of the numerous, large, water filled craters made by the heavy shells then you were most likely lost unless your comrades were close at hand and could pull you free. German artillery fire varied in strength during the day and German gas bombardments did provide some relief from enemy activity.

On 29/30 October 1917 RIR 121 was moved forward again and relieved IR 120. In the night there was further heavy artillery fire, and from 6.45 a.m. drum-fire fell upon the position. The troops in the front line immediately called for defensive barrage fire and it was suspected that the British attack was prevented by the rapidly deployed German artillery fire. On 29 October 1917 IR 180 was placed in its former position again and there relieved IR 124 from 5.30 p.m. on. With the very small battle strength of the companies, 30-40 men each, it meant that all four companies of the battle battalion had to be placed in the front line.

Strong enemy artillery fire of every caliber lay upon the regimental position the entire night and in particular on the left neighboring division that since 6.00 a.m. had increased to drum fire. When movements by the enemy in the area of the line keeper's house were observed, defensive barrage fire was requested that fell quickly on the target areas, and the enemy's development became nipped in the bud with help from German machine gun fire.

On 30 October 1917 the division returned to being a position division and it occupied approximately the same sector it had given up a few days earlier. The right neighbor was the 58th Reserve Division; the left neighbor was the 239th Infantry Division. The former would shortly be replaced by the 35th Infantry Division and the latter by the 3rd Marine Division. Due to the physical conditions and heavy losses the divisions were being rotated out of the line in only a few days. Of course, the use of words such as division, regiment or battalion to describe the German units was deceiving when you consider that an average battalion in the 26th Reserve Division consisted of 150-160 men and an average company between 30-40 men at best.

On 30 October 1917 the positions of the division lay under strong fire as before, however no attack occurred. Instead, the enemy attacked further south. Through the capture of some prisoners it was determined that the British 57th and 50th divisions were opposite 26th Reserve Division. Mainly, the enemy placed his attacks with limited goals further to the south. The position of the 26th Reserve Division in Houthulst Wood, from where the division artillery could provide effective flanking fire to the divisions southeast and further south in the past also provided excellent flanking fire in the latest enemy attack. Finally, the attacks seemed to come to an end when Passchendaele finally came into the possession of the enemy.

On the evening of 31 October 1917 the battalions of IR 180 exchanged positions, and likewise on 2 November 1917. The enemy infantry remained quiescent, only the hostile artillery remained active by scheduled, accurate shooting with medium and heavy caliber guns against the concrete dugouts of which one was completely demolished.

On 31 October 1917 the 8/R119 reported lively activity in the enemy trenches on its front and this resulted in annihilation fire from the batteries. Towards 6 a.m. they saw a 500-600 meter wide skirmish line break forth from the enemy line. The 8/R119 was ready for action in a moment and drove back the attackers with rifle and machine gun fire. When the II/R119 was being relieved by the I/R119 in the evening, a 25 man strong British patrol attempted to overrun the 1/R119, however they were met with machine gun fire and driven away.

In November the fighting in Flanders died down. The enemy breakthrough had been stopped and he was prevented from capturing any important U-boat harbors. While the major fighting had ended there was still times when skirmishes took place across the division front. One adventure was experienced on All Saint's Day by *Gefreiter* Dubs and *Landsturmmann* Seiz, 2/R119 as they moved along a road opposite the company. This thoroughfare became a routine site for standing patrols:

> Dubs and Seiz wanted to move from their post in the darkness and when Seiz was 10 meters behind Dubs 'like a rat's tail', three Englishmen came out of the darkness who were strolling through the terrain which later turned out to be prohibited. Two of the three were similar, however Dubs did not give it a moment's thought. He was so skillful that he never fell into the hands of the British.
>
> Instead of simply shooting down the enemy as he had the right to do, Dubs hurled himself at the two tall chaps, grabbed them by the wrists and booted them because he could not speak English, and in this *Swabian* manner he directed them to go with him. The enemy, terrified to death, allowed their weapons to fall and meekly yielded to their fate. However, the other man was not of a similar mind and he came at Dubs. Now Seiz did not tolerate this and jumped on the Englishman with furious blows. Now he was also startled by this. He threw his rifle away, raised his hands high and gave himself up. Both valiant men triumphantly moved back with their prisoners from the British 50th Division.[2]

Between 4-5 November 1917 RIR 119 was relieved, after the 12/R119 had driven off an enemy patrol observed advancing against its position. RIR 121 remained in the position until 4 November 1917 with fluctuating artillery fire that did not reach the powerful level of the previous days again. Instead the men had to endure dank, foggy weather with strong downpours. The ground loosened from the projectiles became like mashed clay, the shell craters and shelters were all filled with water, the soldiers and their weapons were covered with a crust of clay, the machine gun belts were swollen from the wetness. The machine gun locks were filthy so that many of the guns had become unusable.

The enemy dead lay around everywhere that could not be buried; while the corpses of their comrades were naturally brought to the rear under great danger, in order to bury them in the churchyard by St. Joseph. However, since the level of fighting had died down and as no one wished to risk their lives needlessly fewer fallen comrades were being recovered from the crater field.

On the night of 4/5 November 1917 RIR 121 once more exchanged places with IR 120 and became an *Eingreiftruppe* behind the 27th Infantry Division. The Flanders battle raged further south and in the nights the entire ground shook from the impacts of the thousands of shells. When orders arrived on 7 November 1917 relieving the division, everyone breathed a sigh of relief.

The time spent by Houthulst Wood was costly for RIR 121. 79 men were dead, 365 were wounded and 36 men were missing. Among the dead were *Oberleutnant* Hegelmaier and *Leutnant der Landwehr* Brauch. Among the wounded were: *Oberleutnant der Reserve* Burtscher (gas sick), *Leutnants der Reserve* Matthas (gas sick) Chr. Honold, Stutz, Würz, Klink, Zieher, Birkenmaier, Graf, and one officer was missing: *Leutnant der Reserve* Hirsch. The men of the regiment had felt a special pride that it had held its position and had not lost a foot of ground. It should also be said that the regiment had not faced the full enemy onslaught in the Flanders battle and had fought at the left flank of the enemy advance. Losses would have been far higher had the men of RIR 121 stood further to the south.

On 4 November 1917 IR 180 was relieved by IR 124 and moved back to Lichtervelde, where it occupied the former billets of IR 120. The quarters were very cramped, there was a shortage of stoves and there were no cellars for protection against aerial attacks like the ones during the previous rest time upon the railway station and city of Lichtervelde. The nights were clear and bright and therefore enemy aircraft came in the night from 6/7 November 1917, dropped bombs by the railway station and fired on the streets with machine guns, however without causing any losses to the regiment.

Leutnant der Reserve Haller. (*Das Württembergisches Reserve-Feldartillerie-Regiment Nr. 26 im Weltkrieg 1914-1918*

On 5 November 1917 the 26th Reserve Division became an *Eingreif Division* again and on 9 November 1917 was replaced by the 41st Infantry Division. Then the 26th Reserve Division relieved the 19th *Landwehr* Division by Group Dixmuiden, Headquarters XVIII Army Corps, and from 16 November 1917 Headquarters X Reserve Corps, under *General der Infanterie von* Eberhardt.

RIR 121 had suffered the most casualties in the division in the latest time in Flanders. In total, 35 officers, 1,241 men had been lost; in addition the number of sick in the same period was 479 men. After receiving 497 replacements the company strength only amounted to about 50 men each.

The stay in Lichtervelde by IR 180 did not last very long, because already at 11.00 a.m. on 8 November 1917 the battalions marched off in the direction of Thourout with spacing of 45 minutes between the battalions as a precaution against artillery fire and the constant aerial attacks. From there the men marched to their new quarters between Thourout and Ostende. The regiment was now very close to the North Sea and everyone hoped to have the opportunity to view the sea and to enjoy the city of Ostende, both of which would be extensively visited by the men of the division.

The 26th Reserve Division had now been sent to a quiet front in the flooded area of the Yser located between Dixmuide and Nieuport and this was greeted with joy by the men, to finally be far away from the horrors of the Flanders battlefield. The rumor mill had come up with the story that the High command had expected large enemy attacks on the Yser Canal, and they were replacing the *Landwehr* divisions holding this portion of the front line with battle proven divisions. On 8 November 1917 the companies of RIR 121 marched north and arrived at the new billets. The next day the regiment relieved the 19th *Landwehr* Division in the Yser position.

Yser Canal. (*Die 26. Reserve Division 1914-1918*)

The initial housing provided to the men was generally poor, as the largest part of the available quarters were still occupied by men from LIR 383. There was some comfort with the knowledge that the stay in these quarters was only temporary and the situation would improve.

IR 180 was in the middle of the division sector on the Yser, west of Keyem and north of Dixmuide where the regiment relieved part of LIR 383. The relief began on 10 November 1917 and the companies were distributed across the new position. The housing was adequate, mostly in concrete dugouts. The rest battalion would remain nearby in Moere. In the following days the battle battalion took its position on the left bank of the Yser.

The new home of RIR 119 was no different than that of IR 180. On 11/12 November 1917 the regiment relieved part of LIR 383 on the Yser Canal. The new position was quite different than experienced by the men until then. It was a bottomless Flanders landscape where only a narrow paved embankment provided any firm soil, while on the right and left, man or horse would sink knee deep into the muddy swamp and water. On 11/12 November 1917 the I/R121 relieved the battle battalion of LIR 285, while the other two battalions remained in rest and received new replacements.

The new position of the division was just to the north of Dixmuiden, on a small section of the Yser canal. Marine Division 2 was to the north, whose sector reached to the sea; to the south stood the 54th Württemberg Reserve Division. Artillery fire was almost non-existent, and Belgian troops lay opposite the division, the first time the men had faced this opponent. Because of the expanse of water, large operations could not take place. In part, small actions using boats and by crossing small streams were held by both sides. Because it was a quiet zone, the length of the division front was extended and still the men had a complete sense of security.

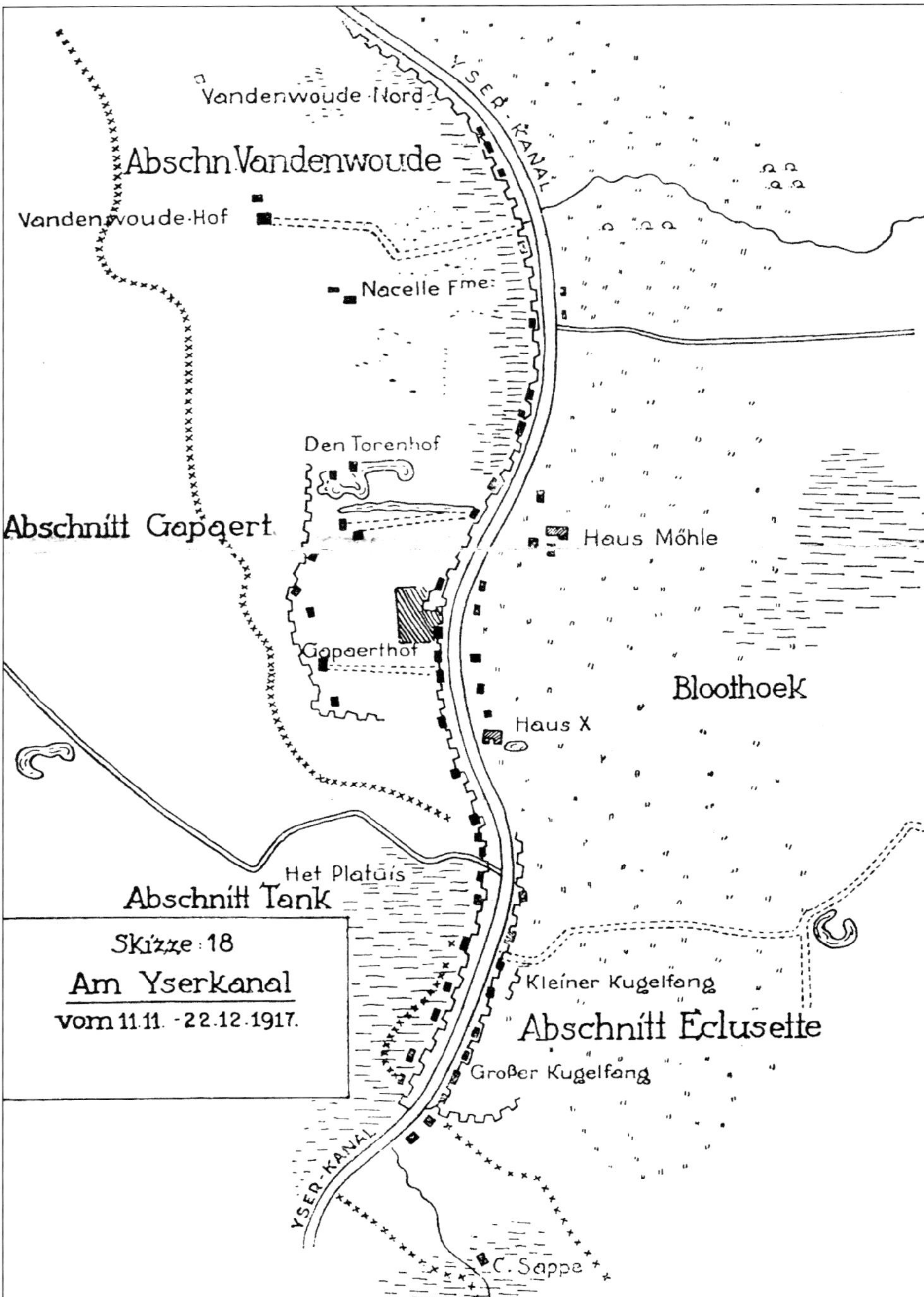

The Yser Canal, November and December 1917.

The Kerem–Beerst Road denoted the boundary with firm land. Water was the dominant element in the new position. The dams which prevented the low lying areas from flooding were destroyed in 1914, resulting in the entire are being inundated. Large bodies of water separated both sides, only narrow strips of dry land existed. Wood bridges and wooden walkways were found everywhere, with many of the walkways raised above the water.

Even in these conditions there was an outpost line and main opposition line. Each regiment was responsible for 3-4 sectors, which contained scattered strongpoints and concrete dugouts throughout the sectors. *Gapaert Hof* was one of these strongpoints which during the previous week had been attacked by the Belgians who captured the occupants and blew up the emplacement.

The fighting activity was very low in the new sector. The enemy, the Belgian Army, could only be seen along the Schoorbakke–Pervijze Road otherwise the thick reeds masked the view. The Belgians however could see into the German positions at several locations, and the men had to be careful that they were not observed at these places. In the remaining parts of the sector the Belgians could only reach the German position with artillery and the enemy fired on the pickets at the farmyards mostly towards evening, which however had good, shellproof concrete dugouts.

Here the regiments found an entirely new, unfamiliar situation in front of them. The area along the Yser Canal was entirely flat, with countless ditches and water courses running through it. All of the properties were enclosed with hedges or ditches because of the rural economy that was prevalent there. The property borders and roads were lined with very tall trees such as poplars, silver-poplars, with numerous pastures, flat planes, etc. The villages were mostly small, in part they only consisted of a church, a mayor's office, school house, small industries and otherwise a few buildings, while most of the citizens live on the individual farms that dotted the landscape.

Many times these farmyards were surrounded by a wide ditch. These ditches originated because of the high groundwater situation and because of the annual flooding, the farm buildings had to be highly placed. Where there was no natural rise, the buildings were surrounded with a 5-6 meter wide trench that had been dug out and the earth spoil was used to fill in the building site. In this manner, the local populace received a dry farmyard and simultaneously the farmyard was protected against the outside world because the trench was filled with groundwater in every season.

The sectors were given names taken from a particular location or feature. The sector named 'Tank' received the name from a tanker ship and was protected by a swamp. Sector 'Eclusette' contained Sap C, a 400 meter long sap, in part under water on an existing dam located in a swamp, one-two meters deep. Fascines protected men against observation as well as forming the support for the observation post. The earth thrown up while preparing the strongpoint, also known as a '*Kugelfang*' or bullet-trap protected men from most enemy projectiles. Here the enemy was holding a slightly higher position and could see far into the German rear.

Great care had been taken to provide safe, shell-proof facilities for the men and especially for command posts. At 8.30 p.m. on 11 November 1917 the headquarters staff of IR 180 took over the battle headquarters east of Keyem at Fonteyn Farm and subsequently the command over the sector. The accommodations provided here were far

Abschnitt Tank. (*Das Württembergische Reserve-Infanterie-Regiment Nr. 119 im Weltkrieg*, 1914-1918)

better than those in the village of Mokker, because the large concrete dugout contained several rooms. Daylight was allowed in to the shelter through window openings and it was comfortably furnished. Externally it had a neat tile roof and it was completely painted to look like a barn that belonged to the closely situated residential farm house. In addition, it was still surrounded with high trees and because of this camouflage it was not deemed to be a threat by the enemy pilots and therefore it was ignored.

All of the supplies for the troops were transported by boats or barges. They became unloaded at a designated location on the right bank and from there brought to the individual sectors by smaller boats. As such, there was very active boat traffic on the waterways and the expert rowing men of the different companies contended to demonstrate their skills for their comrades. If the barge came to shallow position and became stuck, the occupants would disembark and push the barge until it was free once more. Motor boats from the Navy also operated on the canal and were used for towing the barges filled with materials. All this was necessary as the terrain behind the main position was only passable on the raised roads in the wet season.

The newly occupied Yser positions were proving far better than anyone could have hoped for. Giant flocks of water birds of all types could be seen covering the surface of the water, including fisher herons, seagulls, all types of game ducks, water-hens, peewits, etc. The wonderful views of the countryside, especially at sunrise or sunset, became unforgettable to everyone that was there.

The thousands of game ducks that stopped there also naturally enticed the men to acquire a tasty roast duck to supplement their rations as well as the plentiful supply of fish found in the flooded areas. When, on one morning, at sunrise, after the brigade commander arrived in the position, he later grumbled to the regiment that he had found no one in the position. The entire battalion including the battalion commander had apparently been on a duck hunt. This was not really considered to be a problem due to the current circumstances, there was no real danger that the enemy could have approached the position and attacked without being observed. However the shooting of game became forbidden as complaints came from all sides, and from the neighboring regiment that someone had become wounded through a stray bullet which had been fired at a duck. Despite orders to the contrary the men frequently heard rifle shots in the reeds and away over the water during the day and in the bright nights. Most of this fire was still being directed against the numerous game ducks that swam through the reeds, it was simply too tempting.

The flat land with its scattered farmsteads, the long rows of trees and numerous hedges, the fertile fields and lush meadows, between numerous small water trenches or brooks, which ran through the black earth, individual groups of trees, small pieces of woods or parks, under a blue or light cloudy sky and the background mingled with the sky in a soft mist provided an insight into the paintings produced by the artists of the old school. It was a wonderful place to rest, recuperate and restore the spirits of the men. Coffee could be obtained at Moere, music played in the afternoon on the main road and if a man was lucky, he could get a pass to Ostende to see the sights and the sea. The scene was very romantic but the constant dampness brought on complaints of rheumatism by many of the older men.

Usually this peaceful idyll was not disturbed through artillery fire; the only sign that the enemy was nearby came in the form of moderate searching fire on the rear terrain. Now and then the dam and sluices regulating the water height of the Yser and holding back some of the flood waters became damaged. Special *pionier* detachments supervised these facilities and operated the sluices to regulate the depth of the water. They would also make any necessary repairs to the damaged areas. Many times the long footbridges were damaged by the enemy shell fire. Until the repairs could be made by the Footbridge Construction Detachment the traffic in the sector was maintained using barges.

The connection between the different regiments was only possible using patrols, which had to travel through the swampy ground each day and night. Dugouts made of wooden boards and corrugated iron gave some protection against shell splinters and the wet weather. Most of the dugouts and concrete shelters were partly filled with water and the men were constantly standing in wet ground or water. Sentries had a terrible time, standing for hours, often in water knee deep.

Even in these unfavorable conditions, raids were held on both sides to identify opposing units. On 24 November 1917, the Belgians participated in an operation in front of "Tank", occupied by the 3/R119. The Belgians were eventually driven off by machine gun fire. On 27 November 1917 a patrol from the 10/R119 was attacked by an enemy force four times larger. After heavy fighting and the leader of 10/R119 becoming wounded, the men were driven out of the strongpoint to the main line but the enemy was unable to follow due to the heavy defensive fire coming from the main position.

Several weeks later, on the morning of 8 December 1917 a patrol from the II/R119 under *Leutnant* Wenstler held a small operation against the farm *Feindlich Gapaert*. The raid resulted an unknown number of enemy casualties and one prisoner of the 4th *Jäger* Regiment; without sany losses on the German side. With this prisoner, the Belgian 3rd Infantry Division was identified as opposite the 26th Reserve Division. *Leutnant der Reserve* Dürr, RIR 119, was also very active at this time, spending entire nights exploring the enemy sentries and their schedules and locations.

While Flanders had been quite different than the positions normally occupied by the men of the 26th Reserve Division, the position along the Yser was even more so. The companies were protected by pickets, which were positioned in the farms that dotted the landscape, which were lying in front of the main position and surrounded by water. These positions were connected to the companies by foot bridges as there was no other way to reach them other than by boat; some of the walkways reached a length of two kilometers. The situation on the enemy side of the line was just the same. Patrol activity was only possible on barges and as such almost entirely impossible. The only land connection with the enemy was at the left wing where there was a tenuous connection.

Many wooden bridges and foot bridges connected both banks of the Yser, furthermore rowboats and rafts were available in the event the bridges became impassable through shelling. The left bank was furnished as the main opposition line for the defense and included large numbers of concrete residential areas for the troops. The KTK had its concrete dugout on the right bank. The villages of Zande and Moere lying 6 kilometer behind the position were still well preserved, while the villages lying close behind the front had become completely destroyed by the British and Belgians during the Flanders battle.

At the beginning of December 1917 a new distribution of troops in the division sector was also implemented. The regiments would now have two battle battalions in the forward position, one next to the other. One company from each of these battalions was placed in the readiness position. The Rest battalions remained in Zande. It was at this time that a light frost started to appear and the Yser and the flooded area began to freeze over. This caused great excitement among the men who feared that the Belgians could advance across the ice. However, it had not become so cold that the ice could bear the weight of fully armed men and in the meantime relief orders came for the division and the beautiful 'winter-freshness' on the Yser was unfortunately coming to an end.

At the start of December IR 180 moved to Zedelghem that was approximately halfway between Thourout and Brugge, with the exception of 3MG/180 that temporarily remained in Moere until the barracks construction in Zedelghem had been completed. It was supposed to be 20 days of rest and training time beginning on 7 December 1917. However this would all depend upon the behavior of the enemy. When IR 180 arrived in Zedelghem the accommodations provided were reasonably good; however there were numerous repairs and other work needed to get them into good condition. The main problem was the lack of adequate sleeping quarters; too many men were packed into very small spaces.

While in Zedelghem the exercise and training duties continued once more, with training courses being held for all troops in the mornings on the machine gun and the *Granatwerfer* along with specialized training for the *Nachrichten* Company and the *Minenwerfer* Company. The training involved the newest tactics as well as live fire situations that included the artillery. A three week long course was held on the MG 08/15 of which each company received three additional guns. The men now learned about indirect fire and barrage fire using the new weapons.

In the afternoons the companies started holding gymnastic games, organized singing groups and then, more training. *Leutnant der Reserve* Griesinger, the Instruction Officer of the regiment, held tactical discussions with the men but he became even more well-known by his considerable musical talents. Griesinger was the driving force behind the formation of creating a choir composed from men in the different battalions, in conjunction with part of the regimental band. Choir rehearsals were held in the local church that soon resulted in an excellent singing group. The singing hour left all of the participants with pleasant memories of the stay in Zedelghem. As the rest time never lasted very long the singing rehearsals had to suffer long interruptions over and over again in order to fit in all of the other specialized training courses.

While at rest the battalions could be deloused in large facilities located in Brugge. At the same time the men also had the opportunity to tour the city that for 500 years was the richest trading place in Flanders, if not of all northern Europe. Even if the city had declined in importance it was still filled with splendid buildings with tall spires, gables, pointed bow windows, arcades, galleries and stairways, all of which gave evidence of the wealth and pageantry of the past.

The city held the paintings of the Masters of the old school in Flanders such as Jan van Eyck, Hugo van der Goes, Roger van der Weyden, Gerard David. Hans Memling, was particularly pointed out as a Master, probably because he was originally German who later became Flemish. The works of the Masters were housed in an old, unadorned museum and especially in the ancient Johannes Hospital.

The city streets were always filled with soldiers and gave the impression of being a major military facility, especially through its significance as a base for U-Boat warfare. The U-Boats would travel down the canal to Zeebrügge and then out into the open sea, to wage war against enemy shipping. In addition to the numerous men from the army there was a large contingent of the Imperial Navy present.

Some men were fortunate in being able to travel down the canal to Zeebrügge on navy steamers, where they could visit this important naval port. The long pier at the opening of the harbor allowed the men to watch the torpedo boats sitting at anchor, or observe the naval seaplanes being swung out over the water on cranes, then slicing through the water and gradually rising out over the sea. For many of the men the sea was an unfamiliar place that they had only seen in photographs. Now they could look out over the open water and watch sentry ships, or possibly a U-boat approaching the port on a return journey. The sleek submarines sliced through the water in a short arc around the light tower and navigated in the quiet waterway of the harbor.

The remaining time in the position was only filled with work activities, through which the housing was vastly improved – unfortunately all of the hard work would be enjoyed by the next division to occupy the position as the 26th Reserve Division was about to move once again.

The relatively quiet days in Zedelghem passed quickly under the different activities assigned to the men. The barracks construction was finally complete and the I/180 with one machine gun company was scheduled to move on 17 December 1917 from Moere to Zedelghem. The move was suddenly cancelled when orders arrived by telegraph that the division might be returning to an active front. No further details were known and this caused a great deal of uneasiness among the men. This was especially disconcerting as the Christmas holiday was quickly approaching and everyone in IR 180 was looking

Concrete shelter with men from RIR 119. (Author's collection)

forward to celebrating Christmas in Zedelghem; now it appeared that all of their hopes were vanishing.

The men still wondered about their final destination. Shortly before Christmas, on 22 December 1917 the 26th Reserve Division was going to relieve the 8th Bavarian Reserve Division in Sector Q of Group Dixmuide. The sector was further south of the southern Blankaart Sea almost up to Houthulst Wood, where the division would be inserted between the 187th Infantry Division on the right and the 35 Infantry Division on the left.

The troops breathed a sigh of relief as this sector was considered a quiet part of the front. While not as quiet or enjoyable as the Yser Sector, it was not actively involved in any fighting. The new sector was just west of Houthulst Wood, and IR 180 was assigned to the left sector that was very narrow and with its left wing resting close to Houthulst Wood. The regiment replaced Bavarian RIR 22 while the right sector was assigned to RIR 121, which relieved Bavarian RIR 19 in an area just north of Houthulst Wood on the night of 20/21 December 1917. In the following night, 21/22 December 1917, the I/R121 moved into the line in support in Ammersvelde and the II/R121 remained in Handzaeme in reserve. The battalions would rotate their positions every three days. The regimental staff and First Line Transport were accommodated in and near Handzaeme.

The 26th Reserve Division had been assigned to occupy the gap between Blankaartsee and Houthulst Wood. This was the northernmost end of the battlefields of the Flanders Battle and as such the German line here had also become pressed back in the course of the summer fighting. When the men took over the new sector no actual position existed, it consisted only of individual concrete dugouts scattered in the crater field. The border between the two opposing lines formed a modest obstacle, at least to the eyes and in order to make this border recognizable to the artillery observers, large red and white painted signboards were put up there.

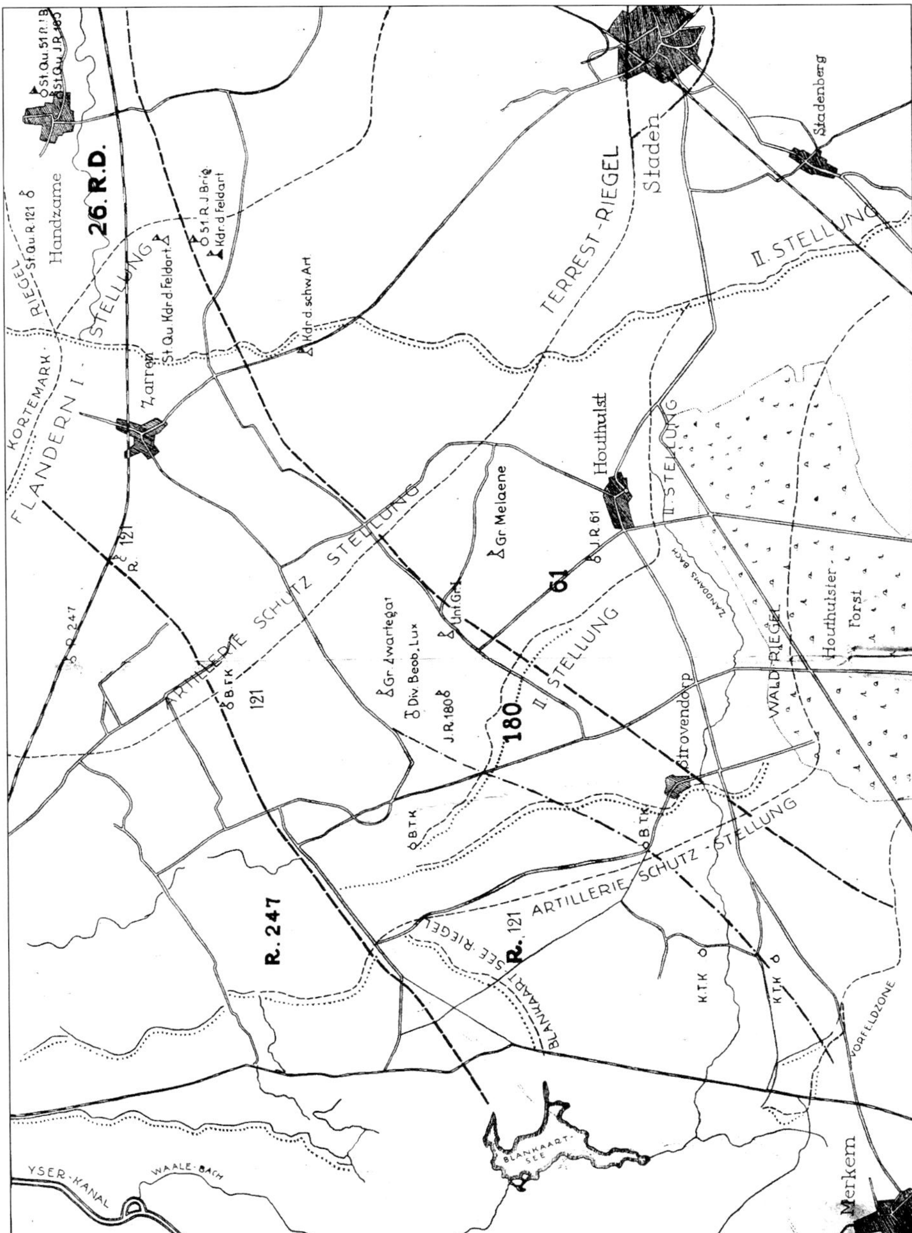

The 26th Reserve Division by Handzame.

The identification boards had already been in use since the Somme battle. However they did not always prevent batteries from other divisions occasionally firing into the positions of the 26th Reserve Division. However, it was generally considered to be poor quality ammunition that was responsible for this friendly fire and not poor gunnery skills.

The new sector was considered to be quite unpleasant. The foreground and main opposition line had been involved in the heavy fighting in October, and consisted of a Flanders crater position, mostly without concrete bunkers. The garrison lay in 'doghouses' only protected from the rain in the shallow dugouts that were protected by thin corrugated iron. There was no protection against shell splinters or the cold. The housing locations in the rear areas had been destroyed for the greatest part and were insufficient to house all of the men and their equipment.

On 18 December 1917 IR 180 departed from Zedelghem and the battalions marched to the quarters situated in the rear of the new sector and were accommodated in Handzaeme and Kortemark. The quarters were a great disappointment when the men arrived, they were in terrible condition and there were no stoves or beds. The men struggled to keep warm in the intensely cold December weather. On 19 December 1917 the positions became occupied: the III/180 as the Battle battalion, the II/180 as the support battalion, the I/180 as the rest battalion located in Handzaeme.

From 18 to 20 December 1917 RIR 121 was also relieved by Bavarian RIR 22 and the regiment was transported to Handzaeme where it joined IR 180. RIR 119 became relieved from this sector from 19 to 22 December 1917 as part of the division move and traded places with RIR 23 in the position further south of Jonkershove.

The position consisted out of the outpost and the main opposition lines. The outposts were positioned far apart and consisted of wood and corrugated iron dugouts that in part were built in shell craters that were filled with water and that hardly offered any protection against shell splinters. Each sector in the main opposition line possessed a concrete dugout. The large numbers of the garrison also lay here in corrugated iron and wood huts, which were considered even worse than dog kennels and the situation by the support battalion was similar. At this time the weather was turning very cold and did not warm up much even during the day.

Now there was considerable pressure to work on improving the quarters in Handzaeme and Zarren and also to create better housing possibilities in the front. Fortunately the enemy infantry behaved quietly in general, the Belgian artillery disturbance fire varied in strength and on drizzly days was very weak. On 20 December 1917 the First Line transport and baggage section of the train arrived in Handzaeme and remained there.

Starting from the middle of December it was very cold and windy and in the early morning of 19 December 1917 the Yser was frozen solid. The food barges could not travel through the thick ice and all food and supplies had to be brought up by carrying troops. In a short time the marshy outpost zone was so firm that it could easily be walked on. Matters were made worse with a blanket of dense fog that lay over the canal countryside, requiring heightened alertness by the sentries.

At least the new sector was quiet, apart from random searching fire and patrolling enterprises from both sides. As usual, a clear picture of the enemy forces and dispositions had to be obtained through the capture of prisoners despite the horrible weather conditions.

Foot bridges on the Yser. (*Das Württembergische Reserve-Infanterie-Regiment Nr. 121 im Weltkrieg 1914-1918*)

The divisional artillery in part was relieved from the position at the Yser Canal from 16-19 December 1917 and placed into positions in Houthulst wood. From 27-30 December 1917 the I/RFAR 26, followed by the II/RFAR 26, and finally the rest of the regiment were equipped with the new Krupp field gun Model 16 that was equipped with a longer barrel for greater range.[3]

From past tours of duty in Houthulst wood the artillerymen were already well aware that Houthulst wood was no longer considered a wood except for a reference on a map. All that was left of the once thick wood were twisted and splintered trees and a mass of tangled branches and tree trunks which made any movement almost impossible. 'The enemy's bombardment of the wood had performed destructive work fit for Satan.' With the trees gone there was no longer any protection against being observed by the enemy.

However, there was a silver lining in the massive destruction of the forest. The numerous fallen trees that littered the forest floor in large tangled masses prevented hundreds if not thousands of wounds or fatalities by shrapnel balls and shell splinters from the enemy fire as these natural obstacles absorbed the deadly missiles. Still, the air was filled with the terrible odor of death from the numerous decomposing bodies, of both men and horses, from which noxious gasses formed and filled the air.

The recent rest time enjoyed by the division was fortunate as the tasks it now faced were tripled. First, the entire sector including the rearward positions and supply facilities had to be furnished for defense. Second, the entire sector also had to be prepared for the possibility of a large attack upon Dixmuiden and the connecting positions. Advance roads, masking screens, depots of all types, *Minenwerfer* and battery positions all marked out from prepared plans. Third, the division had to become prepared for an attack of great importance that involved educating the men in new tactics; this was just another sign of the planned offensives set for early 1918. Truly a huge task was ahead of the 26th Reserve Division. The work was performed as well as could be expected under the circumstances, especially with the reduced strength of the division in late 1917.

The battle activity on both sides was limited to artillery fire. The Belgian infantry who were opposite the division were very quiet. Still, it was not wise to be seen in the front line during daylight. On one morning a battalion commander and his adjutant walked forward into the front line under the protection of the early morning fog. The two officers became observed by the Belgians in the fog, probably silhouetted from the sunrise behind them, and were greeted with a salvo from four-five rifles. Fortunately the Belgian's aim was bad and the officers found protection in a nearby crater and then began the return journey by crawling on all fours. They were not taking any further chances that the enemy's aim might improve.

It was safer on the left wing of the division sector where there was a concrete dugout which could be safely reached even during the day. On one day even the Commanding officer, General von Eberhard, visited the front and whilst there he distributed a backpack full of gifts for the men.

The battalions holding the front lines were relieved after only a few days in the position. This was done in part because of the cold weather and in part so that the men could celebrate the Christmas holiday in the safety of the rear in Handzaeme. However, with the fourth Christmas in the field since the start of the war there was even less festivity than in the previous years. The regiments had been through some very difficult time in the past year. The average company strength had withered down to 40-50 men; the survivors were simply exhausted. The housing in Handzaeme was bad, far worse in the position, with the men partly in earthen holes that were barely protected against the effects of the weather, which was dank and misty for weeks at a time. All of this had a detrimental effect on the mental and physical health of the men.

Despite this depressing landscape, the war weary men celebrated Christmas as best they could. Christmas songs, including the well-loved Silent Night could be heard coming from nearly every structure in Handzaeme. The men continued to set up small fir trees adorned with simple ornaments and lighted candles. The division clergy provided sermons to the men with devout prayers for a victorious end to the wear. All of the grieving mothers, widows and orphans, who have lost their loved ones in the war were especially remembered in the prayers of the men.

The I/180 celebrated Christmas in Handzaeme with a church service for both denominations in the village church and then later by each company in an unpretentious manner. The two other battalions of the regiment celebrated the Holy day as good as the situation allowed, undisturbed by the enemy, who behaved absolutely quiet from 5.00 p.m. on and apparently only worked on the extension of his position.

The war returned with a vengeance on 26 December 1917 when fierce drum fire raged from Dixmuiden southward, while the sector occupied by the 26th Reserve Division remained quiet, much to the relief of everyone. The support troops suffered the most under the weight of the enemy fire. They looked for protection in the badly damaged village of Jonkershove, but soon had to abandon the village and find safer locations as a result of the destructive fire falling all about the area.

Once the heavy fire died down, life at the front returned to normal. The battalions took turns relieving each other in a regular sequence and 1917 came to an end without any further incidents. The New Year had arrived and the regiments held celebrations according to which position was being occupied at the time. The III/180 held a New Year's celebration in the church of Handzaeme, followed afterward by a roast for the Other Ranks, along with a salad and mulled wine. The battalions at the front celebrated the end of the year in a far less joyous manner other than another quiet holiday where enemy activity was almost non-existent.

Notes

1. A. Vischer, *Das 10. Württembergische Infanterie-Regiment Nr. 180 im Weltkrieg 1914-1918,* p. 98
2. M. Gerster, *Das Württemberg Reserve Infanterie Regiment No. 119 im Weltkrieg, 1914-1918*, pp. 97-98.
3. The newer model field guns had one major difference than the older M96 field guns. The Model 16 did not use fixed ammunition, where the shell was attached to a shell casing and could be loaded as a single unit. The newer model used separate shells and propellants making it far more difficult to interchange the ammunition between the old and newer model field guns.

3

1918
Year of Decision

26th Reserve Division
Michael and Mars Offensives

The New Year had arrived, the fourth since the start of the war. The skies were cold and grey and the wet earth made life at the front a miserable experience. Houthulst Forest, which was at the northern edge of the division sector, had taken on a gruesome appearance. The shells had uprooted mighty trees, ripped apart enormous tree trunks leaving nothing behind but inextricably tangled splinters and matted undergrowth. Heavy shells had torn enormous craters into the old, dense forest that were filled with water up to the very edge. The New Year also began with the usual artillery fire, especially heavy along the front line. Enemy pilots also participated in the New Year celebrations by dropping bombs on Handzaeme, fortunately without causing any losses.

Following the 'New Year' fireworks display from the enemy artillery the opposing artillery directed only moderate disturbance fire on the German positions, usually in the rear terrain and against the nearby batteries. Only now and then did the enemy guns direct their fire against the front line. Therefore the front remained quiet for the most part and losses were very low from enemy action. However, the effort required to maintain the position and to keep vigilant against enemy raids or attacks used up the regimental strength little by little.

There were few clear days in January; most were dull, rainy and often accompanied by drifting snow and blustery winds. This was followed by the arrival of frost and then a thaw, and finally prolonged rain. While uncomfortable when outside, the poor weather gave the men time to accomplish a great deal of work on the defenses. A large part of the concrete dugouts and almost all of the corrugated iron huts required constant maintenance in order to make them even moderately inhabitable. The hard work made it necessary to exchange the battle battalion and support battalions every three days, while the rest battalion remained six days at rest.

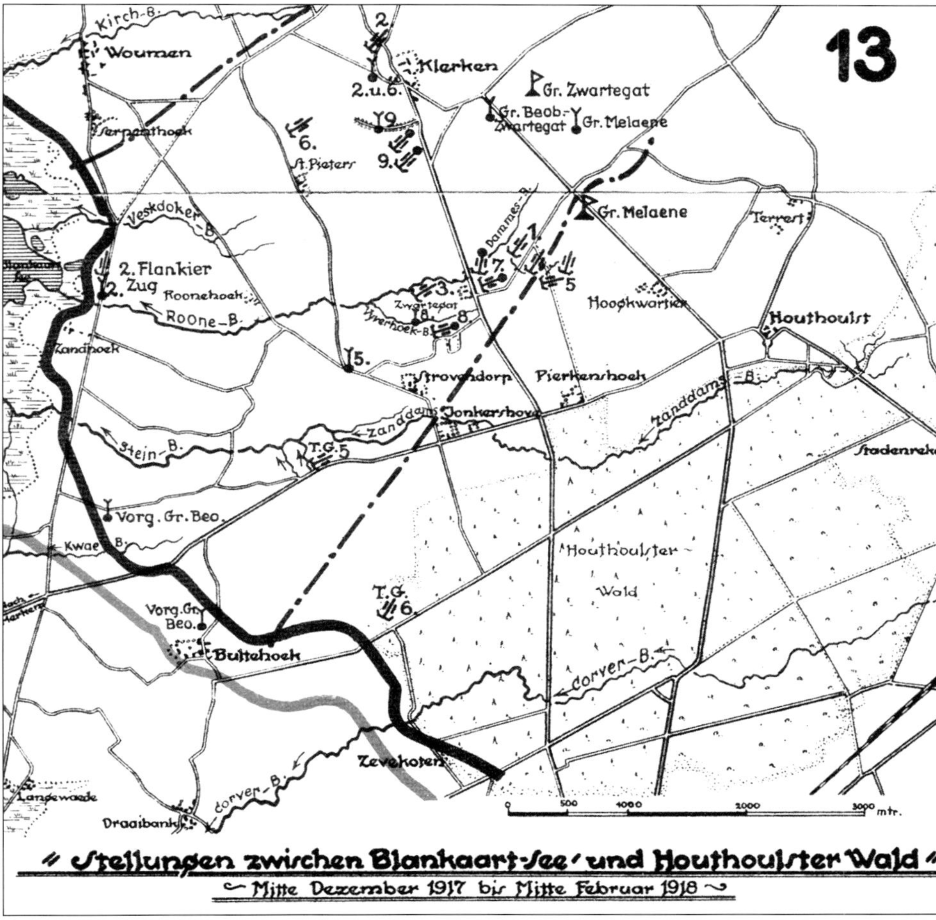

RFAR 26 positions between Blankaart See and Houthulster Wald.

During the month of January entire regiments of the 26th Reserve Division were rotated out of the line and given a chance to rest and refit. This meant that while one regiment was resting, the other two had to shift their positions in order to cover the entire division sector with only two regiments.

The hard work, an increase of illnesses among the men and the constant need for carrying parties caused the battle strength of the companies at the front to become very weak. The large amounts of building materials required a constant stream of carrying troops that made the difficult journey to and from the *pionier* parks in the rear. In IR 180 it finally became necessary for the battle battalion to put an additional company into the front line and for the support battalion to move men closer toward the front.

Carrying troops had a difficult time as they meandered through the devastated terrain filled with mud and water with their heavy loads. If an individual strayed from the path,

Regimental band, IR 180. (Source: Author's collection)

he was certainly lost if he fell into a deep pool of mud and water. If his companions were not nearby, the man would quickly become sucked down into the muddy water and lost. At least the food could always be carried up to the front line still completely hot out of the conveniently located position kitchens through carrying parties equipped with specialized thermos containers. Kitchens were also installed in the ruins of the Château Blankaart, whereby it became even easier to make hot meals for the men. The hot food was very appreciated by the cold, wet men sitting in the front line.

The enemy behaved very quietly during this time and almost all of his activity was limited to weak patrols moving through the foreground. There were also numerous German patrols into no man's land and a few larger operations that were held in order to identify the opposing units and to keep the enemy troops off balance.

The weather remained cold for the rest of the month and soon everything was covered with a coating of ice. The troops were almost completely exposed to the elements in the small holes and 'dog kennels', where they literally froze. The sentries were also positioned too far apart and were always in constant danger, especially on the left wing, from enemy patrols skulking along and becoming overpowered before help could arrive. The main fighting of the nightly patrols played out on the road on the eastern shore of the Blankaartsee that lead from Dixmuiden to Woumen, which cut through both battle lines.

The time spent resting in the rear front of Jonkershove made the same demands upon the men as in a single day of heavy fighting; because the support position located in the ruins of Jonkershove was held in constant tension from the British heavy long-distance fire which forced continuous changes of location. Despite shifting positions there were inevitable losses such as on 2 January 1918 when a direct hit on a house killed five men and wounded six others of the 10/180.

Much effort was also placed on the extension and improvement of the quarters in Handzaeme, which gradually made the situation there more bearable, so that the rest battalion could actually find rest and relaxation. The regimental band of IR 180 played in the afternoons at the church plaza and these concerts were well attended by the Other Ranks. The men of IR 180 were very proud of their band and appreciated the performances. This pride became evident when shortly before the relief of the regiment in Handzaeme a different regimental band was playing and in the opinion of the men from IR 180, it fell far short of their own musicians.

While in the rear, the *Zahlmeister* were untiring in their efforts to ensure that everything the men could possibly want or need was available to them in the regimental canteens. When IR 180 was relieved and the new regiment took over the sector the men were quite pleased and surprised to find such a well-stocked canteen at their disposal.

The *Zahlmeister* knew that their efforts could moderately alleviate the harshness of the war, even if only for a short time. They also spent a great deal of time ensuring that the food provided to the men was of sufficient quantity and the highest quality possible. Actually, the men had become so used to smaller rations and poor quality food, many of the companies competed in trying to economize as much as possible in regard to the rations they consumed even when supplies were adequate for their needs.

One of the biggest problems facing the troops was the scarcity of vegetable at this time. The supply officers looked for all possible substitutes to improve the nutritional value of the food. One solution was in the use of stinging nettles as a substitute vegetable, which was seen as a great success. At Staden there were large quantities of potatoes still in the fields. The desire for fresh potatoes even surpassed the threat from random enemy artillery fire. The men simply ignored the bursting shells until the last potatoes became taken out of the ground.

One *Verpflegungs Offizier* had been successful with pig breeding and his efforts had brought a delightful variety in the menu of the companies. Unfortunately the pork being supplied to the men had to come to an end when fodder became scarce and the frequent change of quarters made transporting the pigs difficult, especially as the number of horses and wagons in each company were being reduced more and more. How much the food was appreciated overall could best be observed when Other Ranks of different units, especially Prussian regiments, mentioned just how pleased they were when allowed to join in the meals prepared by the Württemberg troops.

The Blankaartsee was also filled with fish and the company lying in the Château Blankaart augmented their menu with fish caught using hand grenades. This method of fishing was forbidden, and the men had specifically been warned not to use close combat methods simply to catch fish. However the officers who had decreed this ban were far away from the front and apparently the fish caught in such a manner tasted best of all.

Vizewachtmeister Schmid, the former leader of the baggage section of the train in IR 180 who was an excellent riding teacher and a stall master in civilian life, was born in Berlin. He was considered a master when making do with the limited quantities and quality of many of the food supplies. In situations where even he could not make the food supplies stretch too far he often said to his men: 'Children, children, you cannot believe how good you have it. Not even the Kempinski in Berlin has it as good as you today!'[1]

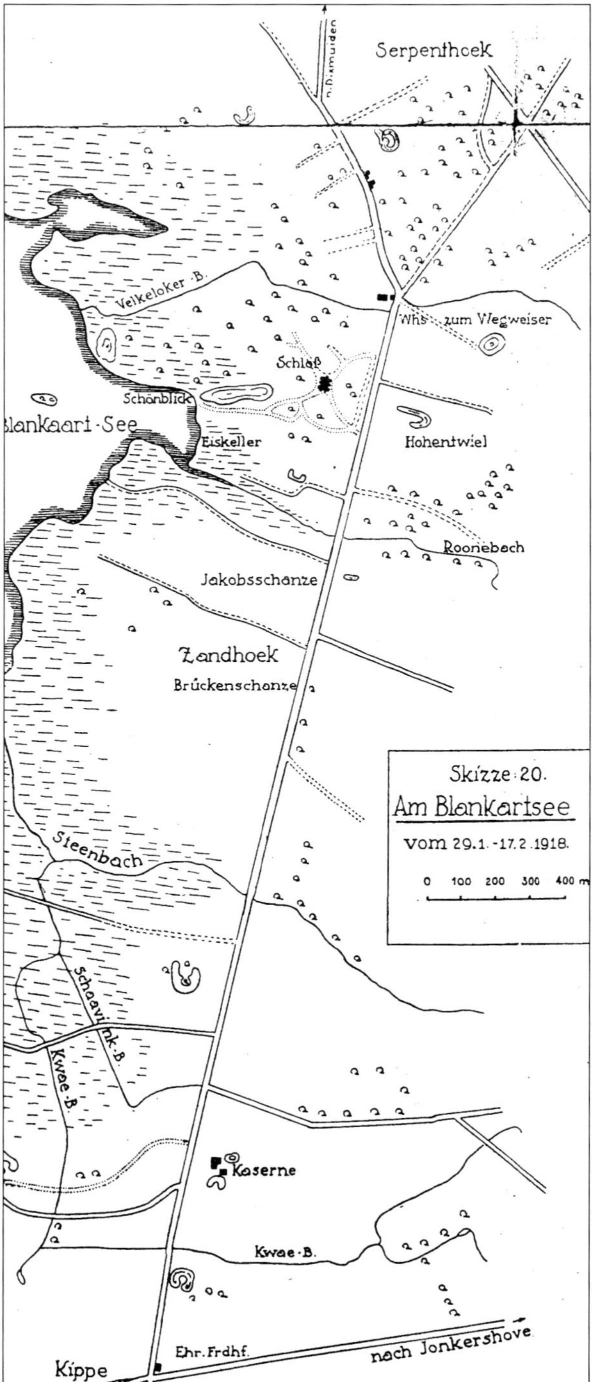

Blankaaer See.

On 8 January 1918 the sector garrison was considerably weakened when RIR 119 was sent to Torhout for rest and refitting. The two remaining regiments stretched further to the left to cover the division sector. RIR 119 found rest and relaxation in comfortable quarters in Torhout and once there, began the preparations for the great attack battle, which would hopefully bring the end of the war.

On 15 January 1918 the 26th Reserve Division became stretched even further when the right neighboring division, the 187th Infantry Division, was removed from the front. The 26th Reserve Division now had to take over almost two additional regimental sectors to the northeastern corner of the Blankaartsee. It was fortunate that the level of enemy activity at this portion of the front was so low at this time. The overstretched division was eventually provided with some relief when the 35th Infantry Division arrived and allowed the regiments of the 26th Reserve Division to occupy smaller sectors.

The troops sent to the rear found Torhout to be a small provincial city without any particular attractions. It was located in the Line of Communications zone, and had a provisions office, Field hospital, and large bath facilities, delousing facilities, cinemas, a theater at times, bookstores, small industries and canteens of all types where the men could obtain much needed items from writing paper to food.

There was an active military life in the city, with columns of vehicles and troops marching through the streets at all hours. Toward midday the regimental band played at the market place and the younger men enjoyed their time in the duty free hours drinking Belgian coffee. It was the first time in 3 1/2 years of war that the men had the opportunity to learn about life behind the front.

While the men of RIR 121 were awaiting their turn to be relieved the regimental commander, Major Schmidt, was reassigned on 11 January 1918 to command *Landwehr* Regiment 124. *Oberstleutnant Frhr.* Varnbüler *von und zu* Hemmingen became the new regimental commander. Once again, the time spent in the rear had come to an end, all too soon in the opinion of the men. After a period of three weeks of training RIR 119 was returned to Flanders on 29 January 1918, and relieved RIR 121 on the Blankaartsee and on 30 January 1918 RIR 121 was transferred to Torhout as the Group reserve. RIR 121 was accommodated together in one place while in Torhout. This opportunity was used for a rare opportunity where all of the officers could meet together at the same time, something that remained in their memories for many years to come.

Much of the time spent in Torhout was filled with hard work and practice drills as well as in company and battalion battle formations. Parades and smaller exercises were held in the afternoon, and whenever possible the uniforms became restored and weapons and equipment brought into order. After a short time the companies of RIR 121 looked impeccable, like peace time companies before an inspection.

In addition to playing in the market place the regimental band under its talented music leader Heckmann entertained the regiment with a number of good artists in a well-received church concert in Spital church, in which Minister Dr. Lempp held an especially good sermon, all of which was designed to reach the heart and minds of his listeners and to restore the soul of the men.

Christliches Andenken
im hl. Gebete
an unsern unvergeßlichen lieben Sohn
und Bruder, Jüngling
Josef Dopfer
Schreinermeisterssohn von Holzleuten.
Gefreit. d. Landwehr Württ. Inf.-Regt. 180.
Geboren den 14. März 1886.
Gefallen am 13. Febr. 1918 in Flandern.

Im heissen Kampf im Feindesland
Traf Dich die Todeswunde;
Die Lieben Dein im Heimatland
Traf schwer die bittre Kunde;
Den Heldentod fürs Vaterland
Bist, Bester, Du gestorben,
Hast mutig Dir mit tapf'rer Hand
Den Himmelslohn erworben.
O Herr, gib ihm die ewige Ruhe!

Death notice for Gefreiter der Landwehr Josef Dopfer, IR 180. (Source: Felix Fregin)

The harsh realities of war were soon experienced by the men from RIR 119 after returning to the front lines. On 1 February 1918 the Belgians infiltrated through the chain of sentries at 10.00 a.m. in dense fog and attacked a dugout with hand grenades. On a dark, stormy night on 9 February 1918, *Musketiers* Gauss, Koch and Wankmüller, RIR 119, who were on sentry duty, were suddenly attacked by a larger enemy force. Gauss fell into a water filled shell hole during the hand grenade fighting and when he regained consciousness he found his two comrades dead beside him.

On the left wing on 15 February 1918 a reconnaissance detachment of the II/R119 under *Leutnant* der Reserve Kurtz was able to capture a soldier from the 14th Belgian Regiment from an enemy dugout. However, this important reconnaissance raid for the establishment of the opposing enemy unit came with a high price, the death of *Leutnant* Kurtz. While on the return route from the raid he was killed by enemy fire.

While the left wing of the battle sector was considered dangerous, the middle and right wing of the sector were quiet and pleasant. In front of the middle sector lay the marshy shores of the Schaavinek and Steenebaches that joined with the Blankaartsee. The size of the sea protected the right wing against any enemy approach where the opposing side could be seen using a stereo periscope and only during clear weather.

Then, in the middle of February the entire division suddenly became extracted out of the position and transported to the area southwest of Antwerp. RIR 121 became embarked on 16 February 1918 in Erneghem and travelled in four trains via Gent to St. Nikolas, 18 kilometers southwest of Antwerp.

On 17 February 1918 the regiments of the 26th Reserve Division were relieved by the 35th Infantry Division. RIR 119 was extracted out of the battle front, embarked in Erneghem, and transported to St. Niklaas and received billets in Hamme. This move was seen as necessary of the 26th Reserve Division was to be prepared for the breakthrough battle that would take place before too long.

Zur frommen Erinnerung im Gebete
an
Anton Haas
von **Waiblingen-Fachsenfeld**
Ers.-Reservist im Res.-Inf.-Reg. 121,
Inhaber des Eisernen Kreuzes 2. Klasse
und der Silb. Verdienstmedaille
geboren den 10. August 1891,
gestorben den 16. Februar 1918
im Reserve-Lazarett in Gmünd.

Gebet.

O Gott, Du Vater der Barmherzigkeit erbarme Dich der Seele Deines Dieners Anton, und führe sie ein in die himmlischen Freuden Deiner Glorie, damit sie dort Fürbitterin sei für die Ihrigen. Durch Christum unsern Herrn. Amen.
Vater unser.

O Jesus, sanftmütig und demütig von Herzen, bilde mein Herz nach Deinem Herzen.

Anton Haas †

In der schönsten Lebensblüte
Brach mir an der letzte Tag.
Lebet wohl ihr meine Lieben,
Ich entrann der Erdenplag;
Blicket nach des Himmels Höh'n
Dort gibt es ein Wiederseh'n!

Death notice for Ersatz Reservist Anton Haas, RIR 121. (Source: Author's collection)

Early in the morning of 17 February 1918 IR 180 was relieved by IR 61 following which the battalions marched via Handzaeme to Edewalle and surrounding area where the men received temporary quarters. On the next day the regiment marched to the embarkation railway station at Cerneghem, from where they departed. The railway journey went via Ostende-Brugge-Gent-Lockeren to St. Niklaas west of Antwerp and from 20 February 1918 the regiment was accommodated in St. Niklaas and Temsche, southeast of St. Niklaas, on the Schelde. The housing in general was very good, only the 2/180 had to be accommodated in the local barracks, the rest of the men were billeted in the homes of the local citizens while the men of RIR 119 received billets in Hamme.

While in the recent positions, the division had lost four officers and 213 men killed, wounded or missing. The sick list while in the positions amounted to three officers and 1,123 men, indicating just how badly the division had suffered from the poor weather. It was not only men that were in short supply, the availability of horses had also decreased substantially and as the majority of army relied upon horses to move everything from heavy artillery to mounted orderlies, this would present a problem. The artillery was going through reorganization and due to the shortage of horses wagons that once had teams of four horses would now be pulled by two horses, only increasing the pace at which the horses became completely worn out.

Once in the rear the men from RIR 121 were housed in St. Paul and Sinay on the Dutch border. Until now these villages had avoided the war to some degree, only a few

1st Machine Gun Coy, RIR 119, February 1918. (Author's collection)

German soldiers ever being quartered there. The sudden flood of troops did not suit the local people. There were many incidents until the populace was forced to face the inevitable that their lives were going to be disrupted and they now had to share their home with German soldiers. After the people had accepted the situation, the relationship between both sides gradually improved, and a very friendly relationship soon existed between the soldiers and the residents, particularly the females. The area was the typical Flemish, with the hedges and high trees, the windmills and clean small houses. The male population was employed in age old traditions of working the land and with clog carving. Three men always worked together and could produce a pair of clogs in an hour.

The first days in the rear were set aside for rest and making the quarters as homely as possible. While the men rested the staff was kept busy looking for practice locations, exploring the terrain, picking out firing ranges, and taking time to prepare safeguards for the defense of the border towards Holland. It had not been ruled out that the British could still land in Holland and fall on the rear of the German army. Once these initial duties were completed then military discipline was enforced once more through inspections and cleaning; hair and beards were clipped, uniforms mended or exchanged and weapons were restored and cleaned. The men once more took on the look of a German soldier with their spit and polish appearance.

The severely depleted regiments of the 26th Reserve Division were in desperate need of replacement troops after the fighting in Flanders. New drafts of men began to arrive at this time and were quickly divided among the different battalions and in a short time the companies returned to normal battle strength for this time of the war, still a far cry of what they had been in 1914. While the numbers had increased, the lack of experience by many of the new men would take time to remedy. Other replacements were returning wounded, who in many instances had not fully recovered from their injuries and were not at full strength, physically or mentally. Others were inadequately trained new recruits or older men combed from the air service, Line of Communications and rear echelon units. In total, the 26th Reserve Division received 1,750 replacement troops during this period of time.

While in Temsche and St. Niklaas intensive training began once again for all parts of the service. It proved to be the final preparations for the breakthrough battle that was planned for early spring. At first the men were trained in small groups, gradually increasing too larger and larger units. The 26th Reserve was fortunate to have a spacious practice field near Waasmünster that could be used by all three regiments simultaneously. The practices in the battalion and in the regimental associations were mainly directed for attacks and the penetration of the enemy line.

There was a welcome break in the training schedule on 25 February 1918 as it was the birthday of His Majesty the King. The day was celebrated with a parade at the market place in St. Niklaas, in which the brigade commander reminded the men and the elderly village occupants of the meaning of the day. Afterward the regimental commanders awarded Württemberg medals and awards in a ceremonial presentation to the officers, *Unteroffiziere* and Other Ranks as well as holding small banquets. The rest of the day remained duty free in commemoration of the country's leader and the Swabian homeland.

Hauptmann von dem Holtz gave the following speech in front of the I/R121 and an *Abteilung* of RFAR 26 at the market place in St Paul:

> His Majesty the King celebrates his birthday today for the fourth time in the war. All wishes that are sent to him today from all sides sound out in this one word: 'peace.' We also wish peace for our King. However, it cannot be made with wishes alone. It is on us soldiers, to worry about it that this wish is also fulfilled. However, so long as we have not overcome our opponents, so long as we have not brought them to awareness with force … so long we have not received any peace, at least not such as we need it. Germany makes ready now as before, to deliver a great blow. We will also be part of it. Because we want every individual one of us, in his full and complete place and everyone, if it must be, to risk his life for success and a good end. We vow that His Majesty on the present day, in which we shout: His Majesty our King and *Kriegsherr* – Hurra![2]

It was believed that if all Germans were fully behind this desire for a decisive end to the war then there was the possibility of obtaining a just peace. However, there was also the possibility existing that the serious will required for such a peace was lacking. There were already signs that victory was beyond their reach.

The future held great promise as well as great danger but there were always distractions that would take the men's minds off the of the uncertainty of the times. During this period in the rear, anyone who could, made use of any opportunity to travel to Gent or Antwerp, where they could sightsee in these beautiful cities and forget about the war for a short time. Both cities were filled with magnificent buildings with a rich heritage of artists, music, shipping, museums, and other sights.

The III/180 was quite comfortable being billeted in Temsche, where the men had received excellent accommodations. One of the popular activities when off duty was to visit the Schelde River the men were reminded of the nearby seaport, because the ebb and flood of the tides were still clearly noticeable there and there was frequent steamboat traffic that connected Temsche with Antwerp.

With the quarters in the homes of the local civilians, the Swabians soon established closer relationships with the population much as had the men from RIR 121. Apart from a few exceptions, relations were friendly and pleasant. Many of the inhabitants of the villages who were apprehensive at first were now very welcoming to the men. In the afternoons or evenings the soldiers and local civilians would sit together in the cinema and attempted to bring the Flemish language in harmony with the Swabian dialect, with great fun on both sides.

Afterward, military duties started once again. Fortunately, once the hard work on the training field was over, the men immediately went in search of everything agreeable and entertaining. They could listen to the regimental bands playing in the afternoon in the spacious town hall. Not unexpectedly, the female members of the population possessed considerable magnetism to the men.

The women proved to be very fond of dancing and in the evenings the companies would hold dances. Music from player pianos and gramophones could be heard coming from every pub and café in the towns, playing waltzes and polkas during which many rough soldiers and respectable fathers danced in circles with the young ladies and took part in the Polonaise with great enjoyment. It was an odd sight when the heavy Swabian ammunition boots pranced about the wooden floors which the dainty stiletto heeled shoe of the slim Belgian women between them. It was often described as being like an outdoor festival.

The officers made every attempt to balance the needs of the military with the needs of the men, and even though training was held daily it was never allowed to degenerate into military over eagerness, and as such made little impact on the men's enjoyment. Still, everything was being done to create strong attack troops out of the battalions that until now were only practiced in the defense.

In the short time available before the start of the attack battle, the men had to be transformed from a mindset of being defensive troops to being effective offensive troops; something the majority of the men in the 26th Reserve Division had no experience in. There were too few men left who remembered the early offensive fighting in 1914 and even if they did, the tactics had changed so much that the earlier training would be of little use in 1918.

The practice fields at Waasmünster were one kilometer wide, filled with fire trenches and wire obstacles, where the men practiced attacks at the company, battalion, regimental and finally at the brigade level. The men needed to practice silently assembling and manning their own trench system and breaking forth in attack waves in the dark nights, while running through the enemy barrage fire while in open formations. Then, once the attack goal had been reached, the men had to quickly manufacture the necessary defense in depth and prepare against the inevitable enemy counterattacks.

All the experiences that until now had made the men successful defenders had to be utilized in the role of the attacker. While this proved to be a great deal of work for the leaders and the men, it proved to be interesting work. The idea of going on the offensive

Regimental band, RIR 119. (Source: Author's collection)

with the possibility of obtaining peace at the end was a goal that filled everyone with a joyful mood.

In between training sessions, great emphasis was placed on repairing and restoring the equipment of the men and horses. Horse carts and Russian carts were collected to transport ammunition supplies. Feed allowances were increased so that the old, long serving transport horses that had suffered greatly in 1917 from a scarcity of food were now visibly heavier and stronger.

So, in a fairly short time the defensive regiments become attack troops. By March 1918 there was no further doubt that the 26th Reserve Division was going to be used as an attack division. The pace of the activity grew faster almost on a daily basis as all missing items of equipment were replaced. The companies had the average battle strength of 100 men each, while this was considered a major increase; it was only 40 percent of what a company could field in 1914 and 1915. The horses were replenished, new wagons, teams and pack animals were received, the *Minenwerfer* became altered for flat trajectory fire and ammunition carts were completely filled.

The work on the practice field of attacking behind the advancing wave of fire, working forward in the crater field, developing the positions captured, the attack on machine gun nests and numerous other items became repeated until the men were proficient. By the middle of March the battalions were considered to be in excellent condition in regard to training, equipment and horse material. The soldiers were considered fresh, healthy and in a good mood; now the final advance could start.

In the second week of March the time for the breakthrough battle was close at hand; soon the regiments would be transported closer to the front. All unnecessary baggage became packed up and sent home or sent down to Lokeren, where the division had furnished a special warehouse. Until now, the transport, battalions and companies had accumulated numerous cows, chickens and dogs. The entire menagerie had to become left behind and the animals were assembled in Waasmünster.

Between 13-15 March 1918 RIR 121 began the journey to the new front. Despite all attempts to maintain secrecy about the upcoming offensive, it was felt that the Allies knew that Germany was preparing for a great blow; all of the massive preparations simply could not be completely concealed. However, the Allies did not know where and when it was to be executed. This key information had to be kept secret by all means possible.

Immense masses of German troops became unloaded far behind the front and little by little they moved forward toward the battlefield. All movement was made in night marches along the routes to the front. No traffic was permitted on the roads during the day. When the men were resting, all vehicles were placed under covers which were erected to prevent aerial observation; no one was allowed to be delayed unnecessarily on the roads during daylight hours.

The men said a hearty goodbye to the population of Hammes and the other billets, and on 13 March 1918 climbed on to the train in Dentermonde, to travel via Zottegem, Oudenaarde and Leuze to Barry-Maulde east of Tournai and then marched to Caurain–Ramecroix in Belgium, where quarters were received. This was where the men received their last vaccination against typhus. The battalions of RIR 121 had been unloaded on the railway line Leuze-Tournai and marched to the housing place Wiers and Callenelle on the Belgian-French border. The regimental staff was located in Château Arrondeau.

On 16 March 1918 a General Staff Officer arrived at St. Amand theatre and, behind locked doors, presented a lecture to the divisional commanders, staff and regimental officers assembled there. The officers found out that the attack would occur between Arras and La Fére; and that the offensive was set to take place on 21 March 1918. The 26th Reserve Division would belong to the newly formed 17th Army that was commanded by General Otto *von* Below; his Chief of the General Staff was *Generalleutnant* Krafft *von* Dellmensingen. These were well-known names with good reputations earned in the brilliantly led offensive in the autumn of 1917 in Italy. The 26th Reserve Division was designated as a reserve division that would help to block off the northern most end of the attack zone to the north and to possibly extend the zone if the opportunity arose.

The next few days passed agonizingly slowly as the troops waited for the assembly orders which did not arrive until 17 March 1918. The men of the 26th Reserve Division held a church service before departing and 'took care of their bill with heaven.' Now they were ready for the final battle, which, many hoped would lead to final victory.

Just before midnight on 17 March 1918 RIR 119 was ready to march. At exactly 11.00 p.m. the regiment marched off under cover of the late night darkness. The men marched as silently as possible, taking great pains to prevent any noise coming from their equipment as they marched. No signs of fire were allowed so there were no pipes, cigars or cigarettes that might give away the column to enemy observers. The march routes and march times were precisely regulated and had to be observed punctually. Inevitably there were long delays at railway crossings until the troop and supply trains were all past. Still, the regiment went quickly forward without incident or disruption along the prescribed route.

On 17 March 1918, with the onset of darkness, RIR 121 was assembled by Wiers, and moved via St. Amand-Douai and arrived in Tortequenne and Léclusse south of Douai at 3.00 a.m. on 20 March. The quarters provided to the regiment were in Millonfosse by St. Amand and Raches at Frais Marais. In the second night march the I/R121 was almost attacked by an enemy aircraft. The plane illuminated the terrain through a light ball with a parachute. Fortunately the battalions were protected by the high trees along the road so that they were not seen by the pilot.

It was as if the enemy suspected something was happening and wanted to know what was going on behind the German front. Enemy aircraft appeared overhead looking for any signs of activity; they lit up the terrain with flares on parachutes in order to be able to observe any movement on the roads. The hum of the propellers in the night quickened the heartbeats of many of the men, one was never sure if they would suddenly become the target of bombs.

If navigational lights were observed on the enemy aircraft flying over the road, the entire column stood quite still in order not to betray it to the enemy eyes. The march continued after lights out. By dawn the regiment reached its quarters in Brillon and Bousignies and the entire day was spent inside, out of sight, in order to conceal the movements from the ever present pilots. Everything needed by the men had been previously prepared, the housing was generally in mass quarters, but sufficient for the number of men in the regiments.

The second night march from 18 to 19 March 1918 was aided by the weather; the glow from the moon shone on the innumerable columns that hurried toward the battlefield on every road and allowed the men to see where they were going. Waziers was the second goal of the division. From there it went to Lecluse in the third night during torrential rains, after a small detour had been made. The diversion turned out to be a deception for the local inhabitants designed to imitate a troop concentration against Lens in case there any spies present.

The men had marched well during the advance toward the front. Still, many were unused to travelling so far by foot and even carrying the minimum amount of equipment needed, many had difficulties keeping up with the column. The officers, who were mounted in most cases, lent a hand and carried the packs of many of the men in order to lighten their load. This was much appreciated by the foot sore men.

Until this time, the Other Ranks in the infantry regiments did not know when or where the attack was going to take place. Only now, on the morning of 20 March 1918 the men were told that the massive breakthrough battle would take place on 21 March 1918. At 11.00 p.m. the battalions moved into the *Eterpigny Riegel* and in parts the *Wotan Stellung* south of Etaing. These were open trenches without dugouts, and the men waited for the attack while they froze in their rain soaked clothing. On 20 and 21 March 1918 RIR 121 remained in Tortequenne and Lécluse.

The artillery and *Minenwerfer* of the division were already in position for some time. *Minenwerfer* Company 226 had been moved by train to Douai and then marched to Tortequenne in conjunction with the 236th Infantry Division and set up their

Minenwerfer, created mined dugouts and helped to supply the *Minenwerfer* positions with ample ammunition. The 6/13 *Pionier* Battalion assisted *Minenwerfer* Company 226 in setting up the positions and installing the cumbersome *Minenwerfer*. When the attack started, the 6th *Pionier* Company would remain with the *Minenwerfer* and acted as support. Once the work was completed, *Minenwerfer* Company 226 was designated as a mobile *Minenwerfer* Company in Group Hasdrubal and was equipped with four medium *Minenwerfer*, new style. They would accompany the attack and be available as needed in order to support the infantry.

The 26th Reserve Division was subordinate to the 17th Army, Group Hasdrubal, which would form the northern pivot of the battle. In true Swabian humor, which did not fail the men even in this serious hour, they distorted the foreign name of the Punic general to one they were more comfortable with, Hasentrubel, or 'hare-whirlwind'. The division was located in the third line of the attack, in front of it stood the 236th Infantry Division.[3]

The 4/13 *Pionier* Battalion continued to work on position construction by Chèrisy southeast of Arras in the days before the offensive. On 20 March 1918 the 4th Company was located in Etaing, 8 kilometers behind the front. At 4.30 a.m. on 21 March 1918 the company was in alarm readiness as the *pioniers* waited in the thick dense fog that followed a very dark night.

On the morning of 21 March 1918 the thick, dense fog still lay over the cold ground, reducing visibility to a few meters at best. The men waited anxiously for dawn and what the German drum fire should inflict on the unsuspecting enemy lying opposite. At 5.40 a.m. the enemy positions were to be gassed and bombarded by the German artillery and *Minenwerfer* and at that exact time over 6,000 guns opened fire. However the impression of the bombardment on some veterans in the 26th Reserve Division was far from what they had expected. Whoever remembered the days of the first Somme Battle and the Flanders Battle and was up at dawn to swatch the bombardment became severely disappointed. However, what these men did not realize at the time is that the very element aiding in the attack, the dense fog, was also muffling the sounds of the bombardment so even the drum fire could barely be heard, yet the artillery was only a few kilometers in front of the division:

> At exactly 4 o'clock a blow sounds behind us. The large guns in the copse over there have fired and now? Silence! However no, a distant, weak rolling sound. Several kilometers from the attack field. Was it postponed? Because of the fog? Impossible. It is not allowed to be postponed. Is the wind, the fog, the terrain responsible for our disappointment?
>
> The morning passes in the tensest expectation of the first news and under the exchange of speculations. The day decides our large and also our small fate in the next days which is determined by these hours. About midday one heard altogether no more artillery fire. And the English artillery? Have they already advanced up by the enemy? Were they placed out of action through gas?[4]

It was also a somewhat different, pleasant experience for the men to be far away from the horror of the drum fire, almost as if they were disinterested spectators. The British artillery fire was negligible, as if the guns had simply been overwhelmed. At 9.40 a.m. the two southern armies, the II and XVIII, advanced and quickly broke through the enemy positions in the attacks designated Michael I, Michael II and Michael III. The 17th Army did not move and instead covered the British trenches with heavy mine fire. Group Hasdrubal would follow the southern attacks in the subsequent Mars portion of the great offensive:

> News came from the regiment at 2.00 p.m. The situation is good; the 17th Army has crossed over the forward most English positions on the entire line, and pressed forward in part up to the enemy artillery, Noreuil (approximately four kilometers from the exit position) was taken. And now came one joyful report after the other that admittedly only partially grasped the events, always evoking enthusiasm and also a little envy. You gradually obtain quite the feeling that one is once more again in the field. It becomes known that the 236th Infantry Division, the position division in front of us, made a determined attack on the Mühlenberg at Chèrisy, later that they had already crossed over the first enemy trench by Chèrisy (8 kilometers southwest of Lecluse) and were advancing.
>
> Therefore the 26th Reserve Division must come after. At 3.30 p.m. One moves on the march to Lecluse (4 kilometers south of Bellonne), at which also the officers once again carry the formally packed knapsacks. This march of 4 kilometers was our performance on the first day of the great offensive! Sitting around in the sun and lazing about was quite nice by the way after the march last night.[5]

The southern portion of the attack came under the code name Michael. Rumors had circulated that the attack had been betrayed to the enemy several days previously by two deserters from Lorraine. Regardless if these rumors were true or not, the attack by the southern armies had been successful and had broken open the British line along a wide front and forced the enemy lying in front of the 17th Army to retreat. A message was picked up at midday that reported that the first onrush was successful and the attack was progressing as planned. Great joy prevailed among the men in the ranks over this news. It would soon be time for the regiments of the 26th Reserve Division to join the attack. At 2.00 p.m. RIR 119 moved via Dury on the Cambrai–Arras Road into the *Hochwald Stellung*; the 236th Infantry Division attacked at 2.15 p.m. and took the first three British trenches, however the division did not advance any further. Towards evening RIR 121 became moved into the old second position, the *Wotan Stellung* between Etaing and Dury.

RIR 119's companies spent the night in the dugouts of the *Hochwald Riegel* and waited to see what 22 March would bring. The battlefront remained quiet the entire morning of 22 March 1918. Then, the II/R119 was ordered to move forward into the chalk pit located southeast of Chèrisy, to serve as the rear support for the 236th Infantry Division, which had suffered heavy losses on the previous day. At 2.00 p.m. the other battalions of RIR 119 also received the orders to advance, and to organize for an attack in the trench west of Fontaine-lez-Croisilles. The men moved forward into the chalk pit by Chèrisy in columns in where for a short time the entire regiment was crowded closely together.

9/RFAR 26 by Vis en Artois, 21 March 1916. (Source: *Die 26. Reserve Division 1914-1918*)

At the same time, RIR 121 moved forward via Dury on the Hendecourt Road that was well known to the regiment. The men marched forward to the *Hochwald Stellung* between Vis-en-Artois and Hendecourt and after a short rest marched further up to the chalk pit at Chèrisy. RIR 121 was now close behind the front line, the former Germans position that was occupied by IR 180. The British position lying opposite had been evacuated by the enemy due to the pressure of the attack proceeding further south at Croisilles. The British sent only a few shrapnel shells across, which fell in the middle of a battalion bivouac, without causing much harm, only three men were wounded.

Considering how many of the men were densely packed together it was fortunate that the enemy had almost completely discontinued his bombardment and only fired a few gas shells at Fontaine. The Sensée ground became crossed by the men while wearing their gas masks that then climbed the hill and assembled inside a trench at the top. The I/R119 was on the right, the II/R119 was on the left and staggered behind on the right was the III/R119. The British, who initially had not been overly concerned by the advance of the regiment, began to cover the German positions with severe annihilation fire at 5.00 p.m.

Many parts of RIR 119, which now stood under the control of the 236th Infantry Division, received the orders for the attack which was to take place at 7.00 p.m., too late to become organized in the terrain that was crisscrossed with a confusion of trenches. The confusion was compounded as there were no leaders present who were familiar with the terrain.

No one knew what areas were occupied by German troops and which were occupied by the British. There were no connections between the different battalions of RIR 119

Captured British trench by Chèrisy, 22 March 1918. (Author's collection)

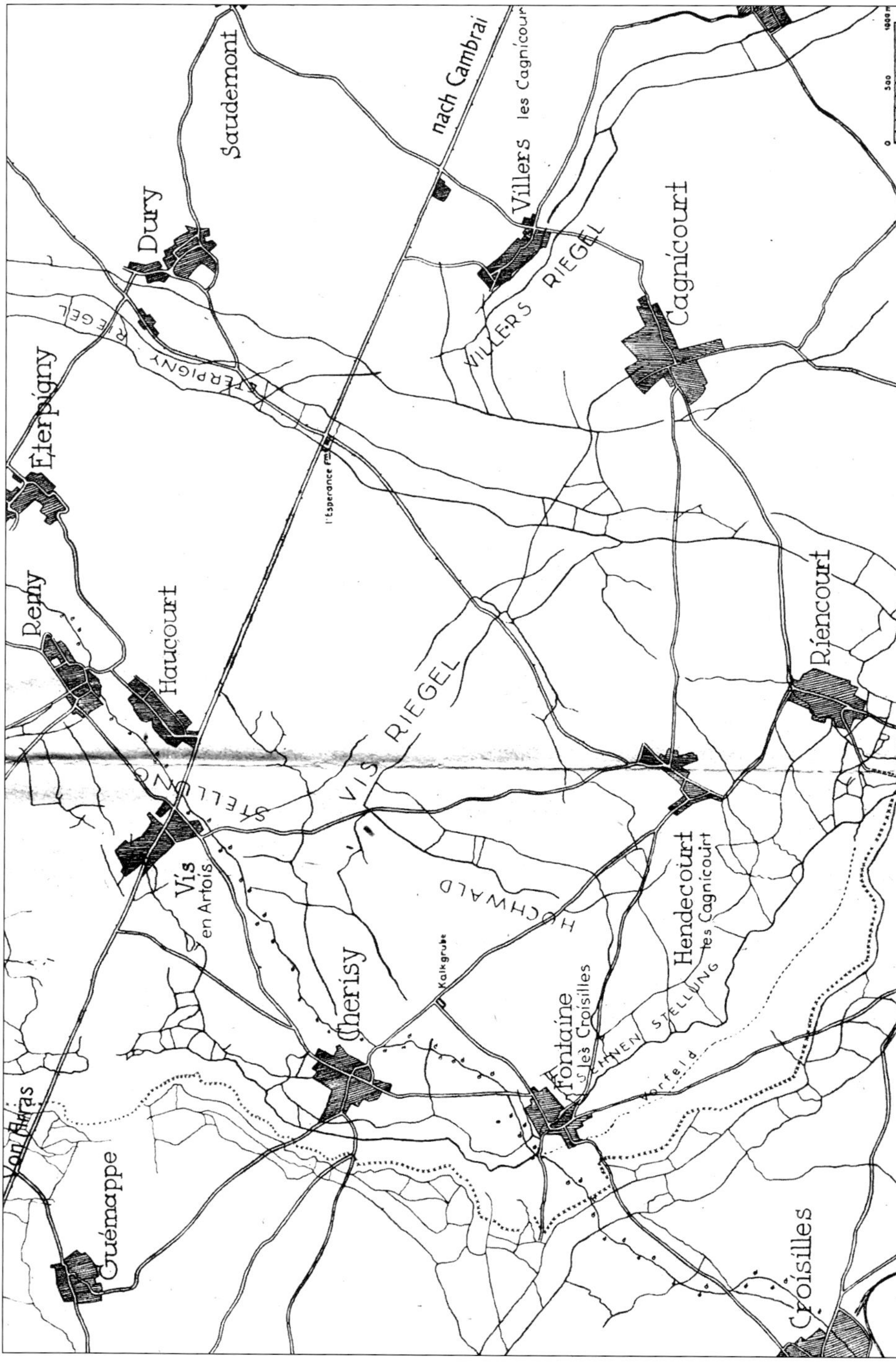
Saudemont
nach Cambrai
Villers
les Cagnicourt
Dury
Cagnicourt
VILLERS RIEGEL
ETERPIGNY RIEGEL
Eterpigny
L'Esperance Fm
Remy
Haucourt
Riencourt
VIS RIEGEL
STELLUNG
Vis
en Artois
HOCHWALD
Hendecourt
les Cagnicourt
Kalkgrube
Cherisy
Fontaine
les Croisilles
Vorfeld
von Arras
Guémappe
Croisilles

and with any other nearby troops, only the village of Hèninel had been given as a reference point. The officers of the regiment were opposed to risking a night attack on an entirely unfamiliar and unexplored position, however the order was unalterable. The organization for the attack would be difficult and would certainly take place under heavy losses in the enemy's annihilation fire. It was clear to everyone involved that there was a high probability of failure.

Regardless of this state of affairs, the I and II/R119 attacked shortly after 7.00 p.m. and parts of the 236th Infantry Division which held the trench it had captured the day before, were also carried along during the attack. As expected, the infantry did not advance very far. The enemy had strongly wired his new positions; his obstacles were not destroyed by artillery and mine fire as had been done on 21 March 1918, the enemy trench was filled with machine guns and his artillery fire was extremely fierce. The companies from RIR 119 still foolhardily threw themselves at the enemy despite these apparently insurmountable obstacles.

The attack started out with several jumps forward as groups of men attempted to cross the open ground in safety. These were immediately followed by an ominous hail of bullets and within moments many of the men lay shot down on the ground. Still, others did manage to reach the enemy position and rolled up several hundred meters of trench in hand grenade fighting and close combat. All connections between the attacking units were lost; it became a series of small battles with everyone fighting alone in the dark night. The 7th and 8/R119 were without any connections about 300 meters in front of the *Braunen Graben*.

Meantime, the 5/R119 worked forward and came up on the left of the 7/R119. Runners which sent back to battalion staff did not return. The three companies then advanced together on the *Braunen Graben*, suffering some losses while crossing the enemy entanglements; however the British apparently escaped to the rear in the face of this determined attack by the small number of men and they had abandoned the trench.

During this attack, *Leutnant der Reserve* Eugen Rettenmaier with 15 men of the 5/R119 also managed to snatch the strongpoint known as *Mühlenwarte* from the enemy. In the darkness the troops prepared their new position in order to be ready to repulse any British counter thrust. Towards dawn, the enemy machine gun fire continued to grow weaker and finally it ceased completely. When the sun appeared above the horizon the men began to realize that the enemy had withdrawn during the night and the positions facing the men of RIR 119 were empty and thick clouds of drifting smoke poured out of the old *Siegfried Stellung*. Under these circumstances the I/R119 moved forward and arrived on the hill north of Hèninel about 8.00 a.m. The II/R119 remained in the captured position and did not move forward until much later:

> We became awakened in the morning dawn through several shells which fell in the village, one struck in the quarters of the regimental staff, which after the morning toilet had been accelerated had escaped on the highway.[6]

At approximately 2.30 p.m. the battalions of IR 180 no longer marched in a closed formation, but dispersed by platoons, in double rows in spacing of 100-150 meters via

Dury and Esperance farm on the Arras-Cambrai Road into the *Hochwald Stellung* north of Hendecourt. This was two kilometers distant from the battlefield between Hendecourt and Bullecourt where the regiment had fought the previous summer. At the exit of Lecluse the regimental commander allowed the entire regiment to move past him. He had a serious look in his eyes and many of the men wondered if he was thinking of how many of the joyful men, who passed by, walked on their last road.

This was such a scene that the regiment had never seen before in the entire war; 'like at a festival' remarked one man from Stuttgart. This is where the comparison ended apparently, as the regiment was surrounded on both sides of the road by swarms of troops. Bivouacs, columns, cannons, troops, horses and automobiles were everywhere. German pilots flew overhead in numbers never seen before, only rarely allowing a British plane to slip through the tight net and drop bombs among the numerous targets. It was felt that the enemy airmen were surprised that so many worthwhile targets were spread across the countryside that could be seen from above far and wide, were not being taken under fire.

IR 180 provided artillery support upon arriving at the *Hochwald Stellung* which before 21 March 1918 had received a great deal of enemy fire but since then has received almost none, despite the position being covered with numerous guns. The artillerymen also told the arriving infantry that 'when the batteries moved into position there, they found everything prepared for them up to the smallest detail. Guns and ammunition stood prepared, ranges were made according to the Artillery Plan (*Messplan*).' 'We no longer had to shoot in before the 21st.'[7]

At 11.45 p.m. orders arrived at IR 180: 'The regiment will place itself by Fontaine, ready for the attack on Hénin.' Fontaine was two kilometers, Hénin approximately 7 kilometers west of the *Hochwald Stellung*. The company leaders, which were now being called to their battalion headquarters each night, heard the attack orders with skeptical faces.

Immediately following the reading of the orders, numerous questions arose. How would they find the specific storm exit position with so little information? Only according to the compass and chance? Would this questionable business become the regiment's first attack? It would be unbelievable luck, if it all came out right. However the regimental adjutant smiled mischievously during the reading of the orders and then said: 'Such an attack order is however truly no joke.' 'No, but it has already been cancelled. Hénin had already been taken.'

Early on 23 March 1918 patrols sent forward from RIR 121 found the enemy emplacements were empty, abandoned by the former garrison. Armed with this knowledge, the division began its advance on a broad front at 11.00 a.m. RIR 121 marched in double rows in a southwesterly direction over innumerable trenches and obstacles to the *Mühlenberg* and from there in the direction of Hèninel. This position system had been built as part of the *Siegfried Stellung*, which had been captured by the British during the Arras offensive in April 1917 and became further developed by them and now became occupied by the Germans once again.

During the descent into the Cojeul valley RIR 121 came under artillery and machine gun fire which resulted in only a few losses. The regiment then remained

Nachrichten Abteilung, IR 180 during the advance. (Source: *Die 26. Reserve Division 1914-1918*)

Troops from the 26th Reserve Division in the assault exit position, 22 March 1918. (Source: *Die 26. Reserve Division 1914-1918*)

all night in the British position that had apparently been evacuated very suddenly by the British, because he had left numerous pieces of equipment scattered about everywhere. The men found luxuries they had not seen for some years; warm coats, blankets, fur and leather vests, boots, and very soon almost everyone had plundered something useful.

The hills west of Hèninel were still strongly occupied by enemy troops. Powerful artillery and machine gun fire was directed against the companies of RIR 121 once the terrain was illuminated by the rising sun so that no further advance was presently possible. A warehouse was discovered in Hèninel filled with British beer which fell into the hands of the I/R119. Once this unexpected windfall had been discovered, the commander of the I/R119 immediately confiscated the beer for his troops and it was carefully administered to each man.

Everywhere the men searched there was an abundance of food, much of which the German soldiers had not seen for some time. The tinned food was especially valued, because the rations issued to the men of the 26th Reserve Division had become quite small and the soldiers joked that the entire attack was crudely described by the expression of the 'steamed cabbage offensive'. Shortly after 8.00 a.m. the III/R119 developed for an advance against Hèninel and three skirmish lines moved forth in front of the hillside; ascended the slope as if the men were unencumbered with weapons and packs, similar to a training practice. The men moved down the southern slope of the Cojeul brook and moved through Hèninel at 10.30 a.m., where they were allowed a short rest at the northern edge of the village.

The German advance did not remain undetected and the enemy now placed wild fire about Cojeul brook. Following the rest period, the III/R119 proceeded up the northern hillside in an attack against a strongly wired enemy trench, in which the brave defenders withstood the assault, unshakeable and undiscouraged. Once again the III Battalion suffered heavy losses and the attack came to a complete halt directly in front of the British obstacles, where the 10th and 11/R119 dug in. The 9th and 12/R119 became moved forward as reinforcements for the left wing. The regimental escort battery finally arrived at 3.00 p.m. and opened fire against the British trench. However, because the battery had approached too close to the northern hillside whose slope descended toward Cojeul brook, they could not engage close targets and over shot the enemy's front trench.

Nevertheless, at 3.40 p.m., the British strongpoint called *Tommyauge* became stormed and in methodical trench fighting, the enemy trenches were rolled up using hand grenades. To the men of RIR 119 it was an unparalleled heroic fight. The attack had disintegrated into small groups and these clashed with the seemingly numberless machine guns packed into the trench pieces of the *Tommyauge* and finally expelled the British in close combat.

Leutnant der Reserve Lachenmann was killed at the head of his platoon during the attack. His platoon was detained by wire obstacles through which he wanted to clear a path. He jumped up into the wire entanglements and instantly fell, shot in the head. Despite his death, the enemy strongpoint was taken. The men were able to cross hill and the valley between Neuville-Vitasse and Wancourt could now be overlooked. At 10.00 p.m. there were signs that the enemy appeared to be moving forward in a counter

Christliches Andenken im Gebete
an unsern lieben Sohn und Bruder
den ehrengeachteten Herrn
Josef Zehetmaier
Bauerssohn in Kummer,
Pfarrei Unterneukirchen
Sergeant im Würtemb. Res. Inf.-Rgt.
Nr. 119, 3. Komp.,
Inhaber des Eisernen Kreuzes und des
Würtemb. Verdienstordens,
welcher am 23. März 1918 durch einen
Brustschuß schwer verwundet und am
27. März früh 1/2 7 Uhr im 32. Lebens-
jahre im Kriegslazarett Nr. 194 den
Heldentod fürs Vaterland gestorben ist.

Die Pflicht rief mich zum Krieg hinaus,
Mit Gott ging ich vom Elternhaus,
Ich dachte euer fort und fort,
Wenn ich auch weilt am fremden Ort,
Und freute mich auf's Wiedersehen,
Wenn Krieg und Sturm zu Ende gehen.
Doch anders hats der Herr gewollt
Und hat von hier mich abgeholt.
Nun ruh' in fremder Erd' ich aus
Und bin bei Gott im Vaterhaus.
Weiß nichts von Krieg und Erdenleid
Und bin von jeder Sorg befreit;
Drum, meine Lieben, denkt stets daran:
„Was Gott tut, das ist wohlgetan."

Druck von Gebr. Geiselberger, Altötting

Death notice for Sergeant Josef Zehetmaier, RIR 119. (Source: Author's collection)

thrust; barrage fire was called up which apparently shattered this attempt; it became quiet again after midnight. During this fighting the II/R119 remained in reserve east of Hèninel.

By IR 180 the men were content to be in their holes in the pleasant morning, which promised the start of beautiful weather and offered a scene of peace time maneuvers. Infantrymen and artillerymen stood around in the open, chatting and laughing. They discussed the completely unaccustomed feebleness of the British artillery and the lack of British planes in the skies with the feeling of absolute superiority.

Suddenly, at 10.00 a.m., orders arrived to march-off to Chèrisy and by midday IR 180 moved into that village, which was badly shot up. However there are more wonderful items abandoned in the British position that are salvaged by the men. It was now very common to see men wearing British leather jackets; watching Swabians munching on British tinned food in both cheeks was no longer a rarity. At 7.30 p.m. IR 180 moved into the mill ravine west of Chèrisy and to the readiness position in the *Rosskopf Stellung*, north and south of the Chèrisy–Hèninel Road and there spends the greatest part of a cool night in the open trench or in craters.

Cojeul brook (Source: *Die 26. Reserve Division 1914-1918*)

On 24 March 1918 the troops of the entire corps were made ready for a concentrated attack. All three regiments of the 26th Reserve Division would be taking part in the assault. Following a period of artillery preparation RIR 121 would storm St. Martin. IR 180 was tasked with storming Hénin and the positions west of the village, while RIR 119 demonstrated against the line *Tommyauge–Löwenstern*. It would be the first time the division would be fully involved in the Mars portion of the offensive.

At 12.30 a.m. IR 180 received the attack orders from Brigade; at 1.00 a.m. the orders were distributed to the three battalions for their parts in the attack which was to take place at the eastern edge of Hénin. The only thing that was still unknown was the time set for the infantry assault. At the time the orders were being distributed, division headquarters had tentatively set the time for the attack for 9.00 a.m. The exact time would become given out to the various commands later in the morning once it had been confirmed.

At 3.00 a.m. the company leaders were ordered to their battalion headquarters. Now there was no doubt what this signified and within a very short time the following familiar attack orders were given to all of the officers present:

1. The attack goes forward on the entire front. Bapaume and Péronne have fallen, 38,000 prisoners.
2. III Bavarian Army Corps is in the attack upon Thilloy by Arras.
3. 236th Infantry Division and 26th Reserve Division stand ready for the attack on 24 March, the 26th Reserve Division upon Hénin, Karnickelberg (directly west of Hénin) and Mercatel (west-northwest of it). At 9.00 a.m. IR 180 was to proceed east of Hénin, then through Hénin in the *Taubenmulde* (south of

Karnickelberg) and then turn to the north, to support RIR 121 with its attack upon St. Martin (north of Hénin).

4. Beginning of the artillery preparation 9.00 a.m. Duration 1 hour. Regimental orders: Readiness position on the eastern edge of Hénin on both sides of the Hénin–Croisilles Road on the right the III Battalion, on the left the I, the II behind the right wing, front north-northwest.

Attack plan: The III would attack from the eastern edge of Hénin through the village in a northerly direction, making a stand on the northern edge. The I Battalion follows the attack of the III with the front to the west with the right wing on the *Karnickelhöhe*, with the left wing in the *Taubenmulde*, frontage about 500 meters. The II Battalion immediately follows the I Battalion behind the left wing, etc.[8]

Hénin, the goal of IR 180, was formerly a village of about 500 inhabitants. Now it was a ruin, out of which a few individual badly damaged houses could be seen. The village was nestled on the flat, valley of the Cojeul brook, a tributary of the Sensée stream. The Cojeul turns shortly before the village from an east-west direction to the north and divided it into two similarly large halves. In the middle of the village there was a bridge for wheeled traffic leading over it. South of this bridge the brook was 5-6 meters wide, north of it 4-5 meters wide and 1 1/2 meters deep. In addition to the bridge there were a few tree trunks and narrow bridges made of boards that had been laid across the stream spaced 30-50 meters apart.

The village ascended on both sides the hollow that formed the valley, on gentle slopes, slightly higher on the western side. The village could be completely seen from both sides of the valley rim. From the southeast, two sunken roads lead into the village, the northernmost road from Croisilles, the southernmost from St. Leger. With their entry into the village they left the road embankment, approximately 80 meters from the edge of the village where they were connected to the main road that lead crosswise through the village and over the above mentioned bridge. On the northwestern side there was another sunken road that ascended the slope of the valley.

The orders were clear, the exit position were clearly described, easy to find, only the time available to prepare for the attack was admittedly somewhat short. The company officers quickly returned to their commands and all companies immediately became alarmed.

The III/180 marched to its assigned position in the light early morning fog, completely unnoticed by the enemy. By daybreak, when the fog started to dissipate, the battalion gradually appeared in rows over the hill east of Hénin and about 5.00 a.m. it had reached good cover in the sunken Hénin–Croisilles Road. From there the companies safely moved into the readiness positions on the eastern edge of the village, with the 12/180 on the right, the 11/180 on the left in the front line. In the second line the 10/180 was on the right, the 9/180 was on the left, the 3MG/180 was at the exit leading to Croisilles, along with the battalion staff.

The I/180 marched out of the *Taubenmulde* along the *Mühlen Schlucht* and Croisilles–Hénin road and arrived at its readiness position at 5.45 a.m. located on

German field gun battery firing by Croisilles. (Source: *Die 26. Reserve Division 1914-1918*)

the Croisilles–Hénin Road. The battalion was distributed as follows: The 1/180 at the eastern edge of Hénin on the right of the sunken road, the 4/180 on the left, the 2/180 behind the 1st Company, the 3/180 behind the 4th Company. The Machine Gun Company and *Minenwerfer* were positioned behind the 4/180. The II/180 did not finish its support position in the sunken St. Martin–Croisilles until 7.30 a.m.

The I and III/180 took up their readiness positions quickly and quietly, barely disturbed through the fire from a single enemy machine gun on the left flank. On the other hand the readiness position of the II/180 had been discovered by enemy pilots and ground observers. While the battalion would not be involved in the attack, its role was not any easier. The men were squeezed into the sunken road where they were exposed to the enemy aircraft bombs and artillery fire, which continued to increase more and more until 10.00 a.m. and then continued in the same strength for the rest of the day.

The readiness positions of the other two battalions had been fully achieved by 6.30 a.m. The men of the III/180 found good protection against enemy observation behind the remnants of walls, bushes and shell holes. It was less favorable with the I Battalion located in its sunken road; however the men of the I/180 had also found a few British barracks nearby which were amply supplied with luxuries of all kinds, from food to equipment. The men made use of the items they discovered to help give them strength for the approaching struggle.

The numerous items discovered by the men of the I/180 did not allow any illusions that even if the British population had suffered any shortages through U-Boat warfare, it was obviously not allowed to be felt by the field army. The 'Tommies' were equipped with excellent materials, high rubber boots, vests that could be worn over tunics, sleeveless leather jerkins and ample provisioning with excellent food in the form of tinned meats, tea, chocolate and other delicacies. The men also discovered that there appeared to be little lacking in the type and abundance of trench construction materials, apart from wood. They did note that the British dugouts were by far not as solidly and safely built as the ones produced by the German troops.

Like all soldiers, once they were in a position to physically observe the enemy positions and equipment they were certainly going to make comparisons to what they were used to. Several questions arose in the minds of the German troops in regard to the trench materials and in particular the dugouts which were not as sturdy as those constructed by the Germans: 'Did our artillery allow them to be constructed in this manner? And of course, when looking at the dugouts, the consensus was also that they were not as homely furnished like the German ones.

When nearby cemeteries were discovered, the men of IR 180 felt that apparently the respectful honoring of the dead had decidedly less meaning for the very practical British than for the sentimental Germans. Perhaps this was only a comment in regard to the level of effort used to provide markers for the dead; no other explanation was provided for this particular comment.

In the construction of trenches, the men of IR 180 noted that while the Germans laboriously worked on covering their trench walls with woven fascine brushwood, the British soldiers used closely meshed fixed wire netting already furnished for this purpose making it far easier to create a solid trench.

According to the stocks of ammunition that were found in the British positions it also seemed there was little shortage of this crucial item as stockpiles were discovered everywhere. The thoughts of what the German soldiers had created under much severe conditions, was painful to many of men. Despite all of the harsh realizations that the stories of how effective U-Boat warfare had been had been false, the mood among the men was still joyful. After years of being on the defense, it was time to finally get at the enemy.

The entire village and the attack terrain could be overlooked from the position of the III/180. It was quickly noted that looking at the opposite hillside through binoculars showed an enemy position had been developed there. It was protected by prominently high wire obstacles, and the enemy troops were quietly awaiting an attack. Of course, the German guns would open gaps in the wire obstacles through which the attackers would be able to get into the opposing trench.

Patrols were sent into the village in order to establish the exact location of the German front line. It was expected that the 236th Infantry Division would still be in front of the 26th Reserve Division and it was considered to be odd that there had been no sign of this division during the march to the readiness position. The patrols sent to Hénin expelled a few British troops from the village and then returned with the report that there was absolutely no sign of a German front line. The patrols also confirmed that the enemy located beyond the village had filled up his trenches and were prepared in a well-constructed position that dominated the entire valley and the crossings over the Cojeul stream. None of this was particularly good news to the officers and men of the III/180.

Signal station on Croisilles hill. (Source: *Die 26. Reserve Division 1914-1918*)

At 9.00 a.m. the German artillery was scheduled to open fire. According to brigade orders, the effective fire of the artillery would be fully employed. When it became 10.00 a.m., and still no artillery fire the men simply waited. The troops soon became restless as they all knew perfectly well how much the success of the assault depended upon effective artillery preparation. Several messages were sent from the battalions to the regiment and from there to the division that without ample artillery preparation the attack would be impossible and would most likely be unsuccessful.

The biggest question in the minds of the troops was: 'Where was the artillery fire?' The opinion that the enemy was weakened because of German advance further on the left was considered irrelevant after the reports of the strongly occupied British position had been received. About 9.45 a.m. some shrapnel shells burst high above the British trench and a few light caliber high explosive shells impacted in the meadows far in front of the enemy trench. They did not even touch the British wire obstacles. It was a pitiful bombardment from the few batteries that had been able to come forward across the crater field Machine gun fire, especially from the left flank, spread across the open ground the men were soon to cross. The troops became increasingly annoyed and it did not bode well for the first assault waves. However, the problem was not that there were too few batteries; the problem was that the ammunition had run out. The infantry knew they would be unable to make any headway in the face of determined enemy resistance and the British machine gun nests could not be made harmless without direct artillery fire.

There was some initial hesitation about what should be done under these circumstances. 'To attack? Not to attack? Finally, to attack!' Regardless of the situation, the orders to begin the assault would have to be carried out. At 10.00 a.m. the regiments advanced with the II and III/R121 in the first line of the attack, the I/R121 followed in the second line. The front line managed to take the ruined houses of St. Martin-Sur-Cojeul, and threw back enemy sentries which had been positioned far out in front of the British lines. The men of RIR 121 continued to advance and worked forward across the Cojeul valley and up the hillside on the opposite side of the valley. The III/R119, which had established a connection with RIR 121 during the advance decided to make a risky, almost foolhardy left swing with an open right flank, joined RIR 121 in the advance to the northern slope of the Cojeul valley.

At the northern slope of the valley RIR 119 and RIR 121 ran into an entirely undamaged wire obstacle with a strongly occupied trench located behind it. The attacking troops could go no further in the face of determined British infantry fire and the sudden employment of British artillery fire as shells burst across the open fields. The I/R121 lying in the churchyard of St. Martin particularly suffered from this heavy fire. The two regiments were held firm, not being able to go forward, or back, and were suffering losses with each passing minute. They would remain in the open, pinned down by enemy fire until darkness fell. As night began to fall the forward most line was improved when the companies were able to dig in and the I/R121 was able to move into partially constructed British dugouts and battery positions. Only small parts of the 9th and 10/R119 with the 3MG/R119, which were in positions barely 20 meters distant from the enemy, could be safely extracted:

> At exactly 10.00 a.m. on the entire eastern edge: '1st wave out!' a few seconds later: '2nd wave out!' and now the process played out, on which the regiment could think back eternally with pride and grief. Many company leaders have not completely warded off that quiet concern: How would my position warriors behave in this unaccustomed task after three years of position warfare? It was unnecessary to worry. The waves raised up as if one man, hurled forward, the young platoon leaders advanced recklessly and dashing, the company leader with his staff initially with the 3rd wave, gradually working forward to the head of their company, the battalion leader, *Hauptmann von* Raben (III Battalion) and *Hauptmann* Schneider (I Battalion) moving forward impetuously amid their battalions. The enemy had scarcely noticed the movement, when it rattled, it banged, it whistled, it rushed from all sides. A hellish noise! 'How many dozens of machine guns have they over there?' Our own machine guns that were organized on a rise in the rear also fired, the path raised roughly above the head. 'They are all of our own machine guns!' shouted the company leader of the 12th Company; however he could no longer be convincing, as the first men fell. Our exquisitely firing machine guns succeeded in holding down this or that enemy machine gun. However the enemy is superior in numbers. The place is shrouded in dust. Bullets and stones flew about the head and hit, pattering upon the road and wall remnants. Now the enemy also placed barrage fire. Thank God his main effect lies upon the eastern part of the village, therefore with the storming we have already run under it. From shell hole to bush, from bush to wall remnants man by man scurries forward. He puffs for a few seconds in meager cover. Then with a jerk of will, he hurls forward again, falling.

> The man next to him on the same road, falls, but no one remains behind. Here takes place silent co-operation, there one falls with a glaring yelp falling over backwards, then hurrying over to the fixed picture of severely wounded man dying. A small young *Unteroffizier* of the 11th Coy – who had taken a couple of prisoners in Flanders and received the Iron Cross I Class for it; in the division he was ordered to a safe post, but not wanting to stay at home, he wanted to come back to the company, and he shouted: 'Everyone to me! We will soon get the chaps!' ran a few steps, and fell. The wave has also dissolved into individual Groups that attached to spirited leaders and went at them. Many bold men fell, cheering word, many heroic deeds became performed. However who could mention all of the names? One quickly worked through the village down to the Cojeul ground. There, balanced on tree trunks and swaying narrow bridges, one goes over the quite wide brook. I believe only one has fallen in. It was however useful that one has also practiced this art on the obstacle course. However it is a rewarding target for the enemy, how the brook must be crossed, man by man. The enemy fire hits terribly amongst the men, who in the urge of battle forget the warning of their company leaders, and wanted to force the crossing over the large bridge. A pile of dead men lies nearby the position.[9]

The III/180 reached the northwestern edge through the ascending part of the village. The 12/180, with the company leader at the head, did not halt the advance, but stormed along the British position which ran approximately 100 meters in front of the village edge, reaching the wire obstacles:

> Admittedly any advance from there was out of the question. No corridor, not the smallest gap was recognizable in the 10 meter deep, 2 meter high obstacles! Therefore they crawled back individually! One looks for and creates cover by carefully digging in under the strongest enemy machine gun fire in the willow bushes lying in front of the village edge and in individual small holes. The bold crew of Other Ranks of a light machine gun finds some protection behind a pyramid of stones in the vicinity of an enemy position and continued to fire stalwartly on them. At the edge of the village one remained in continuous frenzied machine gun fire and the artillery fire increased more and more.[10]

The I/180 pressed forth from its exit position in the Hénin–Croisilles Road, roughly in front of the village, immediately behind the last wave of the III/180, but in a more westerly direction. The 1/180 reached the middle of the village, the 2/180 advanced on the left of it. The two company leaders, *Oberleutnant* Widmer (1st Company), *Leutnant* Scheurlen (2nd Company), and the company leader of the 1st Machine Gun Company, *Leutnant der Reserve* Sannwald, became wounded a short time later.

Few men of the companies managed to cross over the stream in the enemy fire. *Leutnant* Menzinger, 2/180 and *Fähnrich* Hertkorn advanced with one Group over the dangerous brook crossing and found strong wire obstacles in the village until in the proximity of the southwestern village edge. They found this occupied by an enemy machine guns protected from behind by a sandbag barricade. In bold hand grenade attacks the machine gun crews became quickly expelled. The British troops then moved back a short distance into a small trench piece just to the west of the village edge.

There was no possibility of following the retreating enemy troops, as the men from the 2/180 came under fire from a machine gun on the left flank. The men slowly worked forward to the eastern edge of the village and from their position they observed a machine gun installed in a nearby trench with about 50 British soldiers.

> 'Come on now! Let's get that!' shouted the young leader in boisterous enthusiasm, he rose up, and fell dead in the arms of the *Fähnrich*. Cheeky and jubilant about the death of the leader, the British climbed up on the trench edge.[11]

The 3/180 had advanced with its right wing on the southern edge of the village until it had reached the stream. *Leutnant der Reserve* Kupferschmid with his company staff had looked hard for a crossing by the eastern edge of the village and to cross over the stream. Besides his servant, who had been wounded on the road there and had been bandaged by *Leutnant* Kupferschmid, no one else from the company staff returned alive. The 3/180 had received furious machine gun fire from the front, from the left and from the right over the top of the village.

Just an hour earlier, *Leutnant der Reserve* Kupferschmid had asked his men: 'What are you thinking?' Now, just one hour later he was dead. A bullet from the left flank struck a man of his company in the head while in the sunken road, he falls over silently. Kupferschmid looked at his men, some of which had shocked faces about the sudden death of a friend and remarked: 'Don't avert your eyes from that! Has it not always been in war that there are projectiles!' It was not too long before Kupferschmid was also a victim of the intense enemy fire.

The leader of a machine gun platoon, *Leutnant der Reserve* Kietschke, who had only just come to the regiment, looked for a position for his machine guns amid the infantry waves and 50 meters in front of them. As he hurried forward he saw that one of his machine guns had a jam and tells them in passing: 'Chaps shoot! You are letting the whole side down!' He then took cover in a shell hole, where he received a shot through the shoulder.

During this attack, the regimental staff of IR 180 was positioned upon the hill east of Hénin. On 23 March 1918 the staff had still inhabited a half mined dugout in front of Hèninel that the staff of IR 458 had evacuated, however grudgingly: 'O woe,' the adjutant remarked, 'now the Württembergers come, and with that there are no good cherries to eat. They simply threw us out!'

The view of the attack terrain from where the battle headquarters had moved at approximately 9.00 a.m. on 24 March 1918 was good, or rather would have been good if they had been allowed to use it undisturbed. The British artillery fire had already been shelling the area around the headquarters when the regimental signalers began to send messages to the various parts of IR 180. This activity was instantly spotted and the British fire increased in intensity, forcing the headquarters staff to change location several times. In addition to the constant artillery fire, machine gun fire from the opposite hill whistled around the ears of the headquarters staff. Many officers, who were otherwise accustomed to stand erect, had to learn the recruit's art of crawling on their stomach again.

The storm had not lasted very long; the companies of IR 180 lay scattered around the eastern edge of the village at individual positions the men had managed to reach. The troops were pinned down and any movement attracted enemy fire. The frenzied whistling of machine gun bullets zipped past over the holes and rocks where they had taken cover and they were forced to use extreme caution when trying to dig in, which was considerably difficult. Wherever the enemy recognized even the smallest movement or target, he showered it with fire. In addition, the enemy artillery fire on the village increased more and more in the course of the day with medium and heavy caliber shells.

The situation reminded many of the men of the worst days in Flanders, and this was the first day of the great offensive for the regiment. The impression of the failure of the attack, through no one's fault, combined with the heavy losses, paralyzed many of the men, especially the newer recruits. While they had performed well up to this point, many of the men had lost their enthusiasm and courage in the face of the harsh reality of war:

> Why has one forgotten the old lessons that we had frequently given the enemy in Flanders and on the Somme enough to his detriment? How often we have sent them home with bloody heads from our powerfully pounded position with the few preserved machine guns! And now we run up against a well-developed, entirely untouched position, covered with machine guns! At the moment of the attack the soldier does not ask such questions from himself. There is no why or where. However afterward, if what was to happen, had happened, if he buried the dead comrades in the shell hole, carried away the wounded, when the company assembled and was missing so many, so many![12]

With the onset of darkness the formations were re-organized and partitioned for the defense in depth. The 9/180 took over the position at the village edge position that had been reached by the 11th and 12/180, while the 12/180 became withdrawn to the eastern edge of Hénin, the 10th and 11/180, the *Minenwerfer* platoon and machine gun platoon with the battalion staff moved into a battery position east of Hénin. The I/180 occupied positions with the 1/180 at the western edge of the village, west of the brook, the 4/180 at the eastern edge, the 3rd and 2/180 with the battalion staff in the St Martin–Croisilles Road.

During the march through Hénin gas masks had to be worn when the enemy fired gas shells, however the gas was considered to be an advantage by the troops. The gas with the well-known sweetish smell was already known to simply cause tears, not death and the gas clouds helped to mask the German movements. Until this point, every attempt had been made to recover the numerous wounded men lying about the area. Unfortunately not all of the wounded could be brought back until the evening of the following day despite every effort to do so.

Dead horses and the body of a British soldier who had been wounded and died after being dragged into a nearby shell crater to have his wounds dressed, March 1918. (Source: Author's collection)

24 March 1918 was a difficult day for everyone involved in the attack, not just the infantryman. *Minenwerfer* Company 226 moved forward along the Hèninel–St. Martin Road to a fork in the road where it branched off toward Neuville and once there, ended up in heavy artillery and machine gun fire. Since any further advance during the day would only be possible with heavy losses, the company received orders to return to the exit of Hèninel.

Without really taking part in any of the fighting, *Minenwerfer* Company 226 had suffered considerable losses. The 'battle' on the *Cojeulbach* and Karnickel Hill on 24 March cost the company five men killed: *Pioniers* Ehnler, Schweizer, Aigner, Brandhoff and Saur. Three *pioniers* were severely wounded. five horses were killed, four severely wounded, two field wagons and four ammunition carts were destroyed by enemy fire which caused 45 medium mines, each weighing 135.5 lbs., together with fuzes to fly into the air and become scattered across the terrain.

The 4/*Pionier* Battalion 13 was ordered to create bridges over the *Cojeulbach* near Karnickel Hill by Mercatel to allow the infantry to cross the small waterway. However, the infantry met heavy resistance at the northern slope of this hill in the *Bachtales* (brook valley) and only a few men were able to cross over the brook; the attack stalled.

The 6/*Pionier* Battalion 13 was busy lugging up heavy loads of ammunition to the infantry during the attack on the British position on Karnickel Hill east of Mercatel as well as improving the roads so that vehicles and artillery batteries could move forward once the area was taken.

The British fire was extremely heavy and accurate during the day. During the fighting *Gefreiter Pionier* Biggel became severely wounded while carrying up ammunition.

Krankenträger Pionier Grüner went over to him to bandage his wound and then carry him out of the fire. They did not get far before Grüner was also severely wounded; Biggel later died while being transported to the rear.

Miraculously, the losses in RIR 119 were low on 24 March 1918, even though the attack had failed miserably because of insufficient artillery preparation. The companies then nested in the sunken road leading from Hèninel to St. Martin with every expectation that the attack would continue the next day following the same plan of attack as on the 24th. Then, orders arrived in the night that the 26th Reserve Division would only continue the attack again if the deployment of the artillery was completed and sufficient ammunition was available.

Towards evening on 24 March 1918, shortly after the II/180 had been reorganized 400 meters east of the sunken road, the enemy artillery fire increased to drum fire on the sunken road and the terrain to the east; at times the fire reached levels that were more reminiscent of fire raids that preceded trench raids. The day was unusual in that the companies of the support battalion had suffered heavier losses than those of the attacking battalions. No one was spared from the heavy fire; the II/180 leader, Major Keerl, became wounded on the heel by several shell splinters, while the leader of the 5/180, *Leutnant der Reserve* Häussler, was struck by several shell splinters on the hand.

25 March 1918 was a quiet day; the weather was cold and windy, but thankfully dry. Everyone in the division was squeezed tightly into earthen holes and the few existing dugouts. The battalions of RIR 119 were in part brigade, in part Corps reserve and had been assembled in the rearward position that was filled with equipment and material abandoned by the enemy. Eager collectors could still be seen at work everywhere, salvaging the considerable amount of spoils, especially locating the food stores that were often buried in shell craters by the retreating British.

Further forward, RIR 121 spent the next few days in the positions the regiment had reached at the end of 24 March 1918. The only annoying part was the random enemy artillery fire that rained down on the terrain. The men from IR 180 spent 25 and 26 March 1918 lying in the holes dug out of the ground and froze in the bone chilling cold, also bothered by the scattered enemy artillery fire. A few British dugouts were found in the support position, which however were considered poor domiciles, apparently as a result of the British lack of sense for tidiness and comfort of their residential areas.

The 26th Reserve Division's task for this day was to observe the enemy, especially because of an attack being executed on 26 March 1918 by the 6th Bavarian Infantry Division on the villages lying to the southwest of Hénin; Boyelles and Boiry–Becquerelle. As part of the overall plan, the 26th Reserve Division would push to the west and then turn off to the south, connecting to the Bavarian attack. This task became executed by the forward most companies and with patrols at the left flank of the division. The men of the 26th Reserve Division watched the attack by the Bavarians and observed as they took Boyelles and apparently also Boiry. However they could advance no further and waited for the attack of the 26th Reserve Division, just how the 26th Reserve Division had waited for the Bavarian attack on 24 March 1918. These actions raised some serious questions among the men of the 26th Reserve Division; why did the divisions always attack individually? The enemy in front of the Württemberg division did not break off as expected and instead afforded stiff resistance.

In the meantime, sufficient artillery and ammunition had arrived in the sector, so that on 28 March 1918 the attack by the entire 17th Army could continue once again following the artillery preparation. On 28 March 1918, the 26th Reserve Division had to take *Karnickel H*öhe east of Mercatel. At 10.15 p.m. on 27 March 1918 IR 180 received orders for an attack on the following day. The goal of the attack for the regiment was *Karnickel Höhe* that was positioned in a flat arc southwest, west and northwest around the village of Hénin. The hill gently ascended and reached its highest point about 800 meters southeast of Mercatel. At 3.30 a.m. a message arrived at the regimental headquarters that the support position of the battalions was finished: The II/180 moved to the right in the front line at the northwest edge of Hénin, the I/180, in connection with the II/180, at the western and southwestern edges with the left wing on the Cojeul brook, the III/180 in reserve in the two sunken roads near on the village edge.

At exactly 3.00 a.m. the fire preparation began and the men listened to the numerous shell impacts with great satisfaction, knowing that each shell could make the attack that much easier. The artillery fire worked from the rear to the front and the enemy artillery became bombarded first for one hour.

It was later determined that this fire had been very effective when the enemy barrage fire during the attack was weak and disorganized. From 4.00 until 4.30 a.m. there was a fire pause, to allow the barrels to cool down, and when new targets were obtained. At 4.30 a.m. the fire was directed on the rear enemy infantry positions and then it was moved forward up to the front line enemy trench, where it remained for one hour. At 7.15 a.m. the artillery fire increased with a huge crescendo to drum-fire:

> With grim ease the old soldier listens to the throbbing impacts through the small valley, the whistling, howling, roaring, rolling, deep impacts. He knows that the thousand arms that hit the enemy trench there with a clenched fist are his best helpers.[13]

It is at times such as this when the observations made by the men who were present for the attack surpass the basic description of troop movements and general details of the fighting. These observations bring a true sense of humanity to the story:

> The young nineteen year old recruit had never heard such as that. He spontaneously ducks and on a weeping reddish baby-face is the anxious question: 'I should storm into this hellish storm afterward?' However the terrible kettledrum whirl of the drum-fire has seized everyone like the pounding of the drummers to the storm of a departing force. Is it admittedly no small demand on the nerves, jammed five hours long in the narrow holes or tunnels, this thunder storm – and the inevitable? Short shots from our own artillery – that had to be indulged and always, only always having to wait, wait on the 'Out!' For victory – until death.
>
> Serious thought disturbs the soul. However they do not become spoken. Did it hit him? Did it hit me? Who has been marked for death? Is it the bearded old

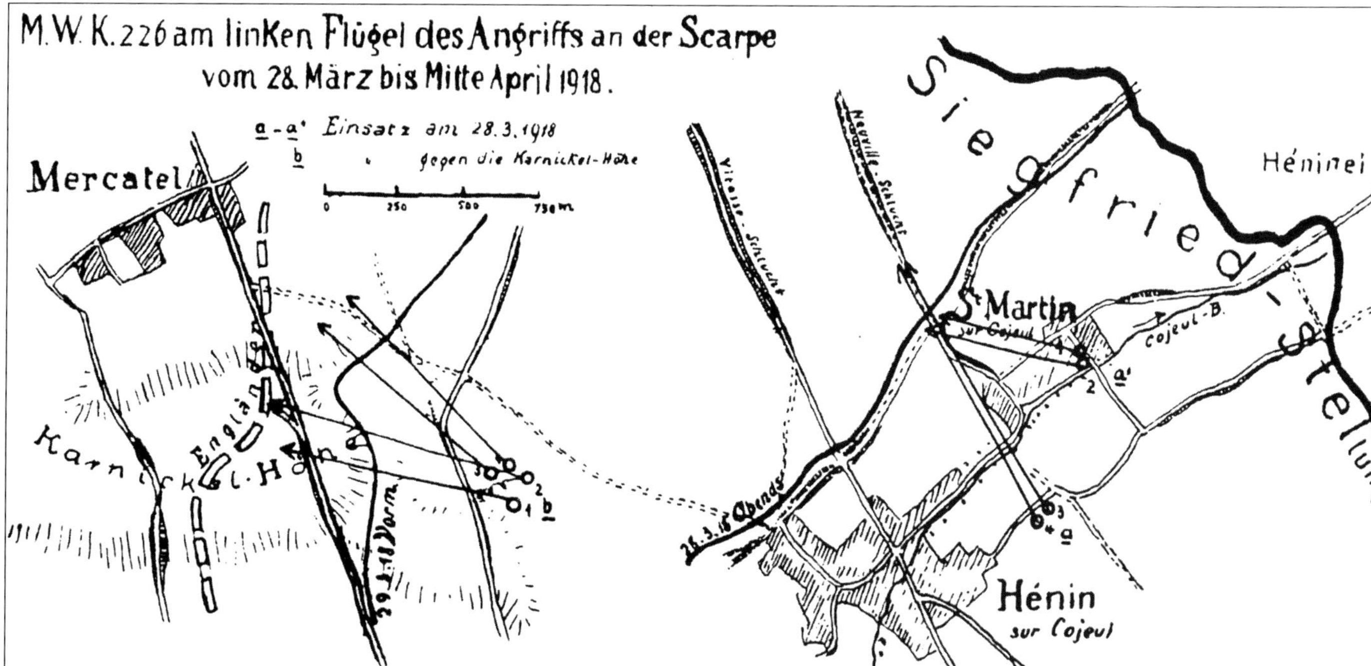

Minenwerfer Coy 226 firing locations.

one there, who stares so rigidly before himself brooding there, is it the boy, whose eyes are looking around so restless and inquiring? Maybe after an hour I will be so wan and quiet and still like that..... So, should this barren land become my resting place? A sharp ache; like a cut in the heart. Those at home, what will they say when they hear about it?

Maybe I could come home with a *Heimschuss*. [Blighty wound] Then I would go to Germany in the clean white bed! However each bullet doesn't hit! Today it must be, the day to obtain the Iron Cross I Class. Today is the opportunity, to stand out. If I succeeded in springing as the first into the trench! And to extract a couple of the tawny chaps! It will be good and I will take a few more hand grenade with me! Strangely, how the thoughts jump then again off to the most distant things and for a long last time, out of that forgotten experiences move from the soul with sudden conspicuous clarity! So go the restless thought that help one across on his path over the terrible tension, then however the other – there is a different man! Sleeping tranquilly and deep in his hole.[14]

The I and II/R119 followed the attack with a spacing of one kilometer; the III/R119 remained in St. Martin as the corps reserve. The Bavarians, which attacked south of the 26th Reserve Division, however, soon came to a stop and the II/R119 received flanking fire from the direction of Boiry–Becquerelle and was not able to advance any further as a result. Only the 8/R119 was able to extend the left wing of IR 180 and become involved in the fighting. The 7/R119 reinforced the 8th Company and together, both companies were essential to the success of the day.

While this account may sound matter of fact, it provides a clue to what was actually happening along the front as opposed to the accepted versions that have existed so many decades. It is true that all the infantry received specialized training in the new tactics used on the German offensives, exploiting the enemy weak points, penetrating the line wherever possible and ignoring the flanks until the enemy resistance is broken and the lines could move forward.

These tactics were used and did work, but only with the troops that had the most training, contained the fittest men and ample fire support. When it came to the basic infantry divisions, most of which had been previously designated as trench divisions, much of the fighting was done in the old style, where open flanks were considered dangerous and would often slow or completely stop a portion of an attack. The men of the 26th Reserve Division as well as many of the other divisions in the 17th Army were still trying to maintain cohesive battle lines:

At 7.30 a.m. the fire jumps back forward 400 meters, and now the village edge becomes alive. Out of holes and sunken roads, behind wall remnants and pastures bushes men push forth, without haste, quietly and surely first of all in clear recognizable waves. The enemy scarcely recognized the movement, because it rattled and whistled from all sides. Opening upon opening tear in the waves that soon loom up in small detachments, soon in rows flying asunder. Finally only man by man can proceed. However wonderful, how one after the other rushes forward,

> from hole to hole, from cover to cover! The platoon leader had a few men in his proximity still in hand. All others must make it by themselves. Now it shows the good soldier. He has found a protective hole. The bullets rush with venomous whistles roughly over the crater edge.[15]

RIR 121 was organized for the attack and the men waited for the signal to advance. After the preparation fire had ended, the men from three to four divisions rose up and advanced toward the enemy. After a short fire fight the British trenches opposite RIR 121 were stormed and about 150 enemy soldiers were captured by the regiment. RIR 121 went further until it reached the Hénin-sur-Cojeul-Neuville-Vitasse road; there the attack came to a stop. The British artillery was weak, it was either changing positions or the preliminary bombardment had been effective in silencing the batteries; it had barely fired at all against the attacking forces. Instead the attackers received strong indirect machine gun fire coming from a great distance, without there being any way to locate and silence the enemy machine gunners.

One British nest on the hill on the right wing of RIR 121 was particularly responsible for causing many losses in the regiment. The garrison of this nest fought back with extraordinary bravely and endurance, until they were shot out of the position by the regimental escort battery firing at close range. Towards evening the fire died down, and the enemy made off. Due to the high number of losses RIR 121 reorganized the regimental formations; the II and III/R121 became combined into a single battalion under the leadership of *Oberleutnant* Stark and remained in the position reached at the end of the fighting:

> Inside [his hole] he is secure. Most of his comrades are still behind him. He could remain lying down. No leader's punishing gaze finds him. And however- he stands up! Of course! He knows his goal and duty. The three are crowded together in the crater that barely offers any cover for one. 'I am going forward,' said one, he takes three steps, silently collapses. The next follows, falls down wounded. Should he lie in the enemy fire in his pain and bleed to death? Truly! Also, the third climbs out and drags the comrade back with effort and necessity in order to bandage him. Then he must leave him to his fate and continue his hard road. There an officer shakes the hands of the faithful lads that have not left his side and who now lay before him, with his last thanks and parting. 'You are a good soldier!' Then further, only further! One doesn't see so well what happened around him. Platoons, companies, battalions are mixed up. Now and then one looks unsuspected again into a well-known face, gasps a well-known voice in the shell-hole: 'Now however I have to take a breather for a while!' There waves the company leader. He jumped out of the lane into the enemy obstacles. 'Au! my older men are already there in the front, I must go behind three!' And now one slips after the other through the alley behind the leader here! The British however are still not smart and aware enough; otherwise he would have concentrated his fire directly on this point. Like lightning, how the picture changes through the swiftly rotating kaleidoscope. One hardly becomes to conscious thought. The impressions are like dreams. Also afterward all around cannot quite tell, what he saw and experienced.[16]

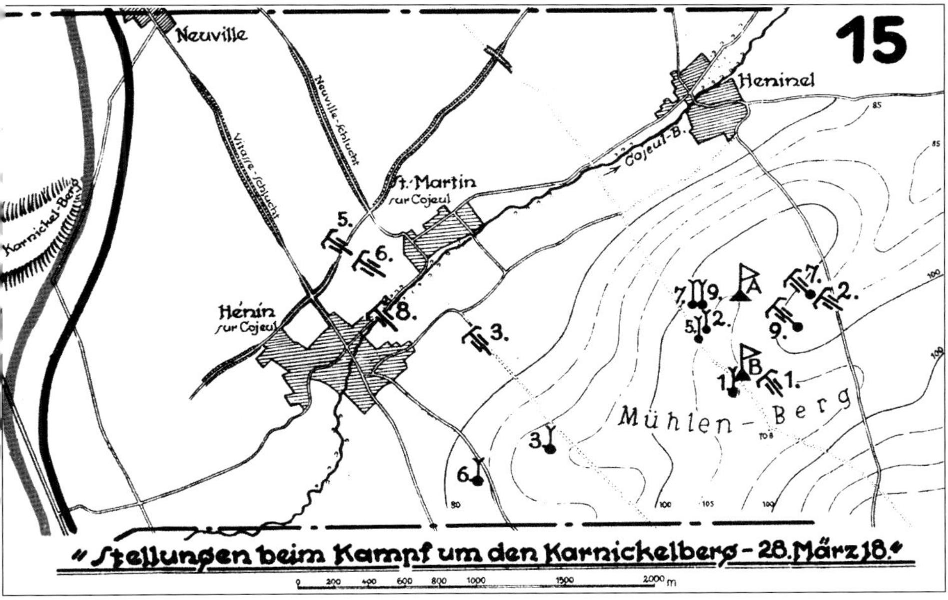

RFAR 26 positions 28 March 1918.

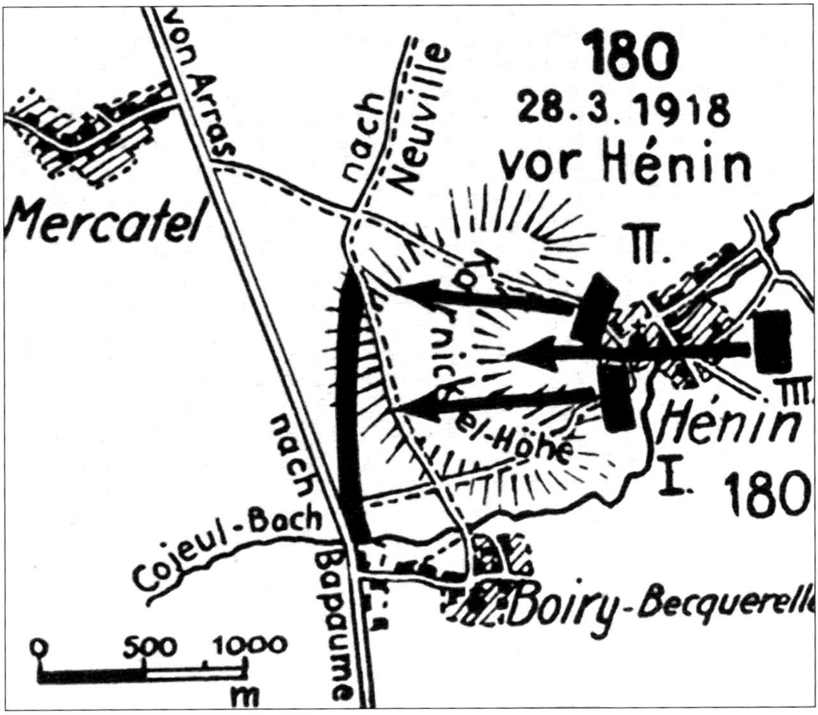

IR 180 in front of Hénin.

The view of the fighting is very narrow, generally just what was exactly in front of a particular soldier. There was little opportunity to gaze across the entire field of battle as machine gun bullets spread across the terrain from both sides making any attempt almost suicidal. The men took quick glimpses of the ground in front of their position, trying to see how far they were from the enemy, was there any cover?

Little could be seen of the opponents other than a couple heads looking above the edge of the enemy trench, a few flat steel helmets moving in the trench, a small group of brown shapes escaping to the rear. Further over there were two or three enemy soldiers with their hands raised high who would be quickly directed to the rear as prisoners. Once the enemy trench was reached, there were just a few crumpled shapes of enemy dead lying in the bottom and an occasional wounded man, looking helpless and in need of medical care.

There were a few cheerful sights, such as how towards evening a slightly wounded, small German officer trotted to the rear across the battlefield in the rear of very tall British soldier. Generally, undisturbed observation of the enemy was still impossible. At most positions machine gun fire swept across the terrain so strongly that wherever a head was raised it would be hit. Any movements must be made in swift, short jumps, or by crawling. Many of the knapsacks that the men wore while crawling forward into the shallow trench were completely perforated.

In certain instances during the attack no shots could be fired from some companies due to the terrain as well as the positioning of other friendly units. The main task for the infantry in such a battle is preferably to come up to the enemy position quickly and with the fewest casualties. The job of the machine guns and *Minenwerfer* and the escort batteries is to hold down the enemy fire. Rolling up the enemy trench, while demanding personal bravery, was however the easier part of the attack, especially as the men were no longer exposed to the heavy enemy fire, but instead deals with and comes to grips with the enemy.

The attack terrain facing the men of the 26th Reserve Division was covered with a bewildering number of smaller trench pieces, some apparently half dug out by the enemy in haste as a result of the German advance. Most of these trenches were running in a north-south direction on the slopes and on the hill. Then there were enemy machine gun nests and strongpoints that provided support for yielding groups of enemy soldiers.

The framework of the defensive system consisted of two larger intersecting trenches. One was not dug out especially deep; however it was furnished with wire obstacles. It cut through the terrain approximately 800 meters west of Hénin, 500 meters north of the sunken Hénin–Boiry Road in a south-north direction. The other, which was an old German trench, ran past the western edge of Hénin in a west-southwest direction.

On 28 March 1918, the II/180 had the task to take the highest point of *Karnickel Höhe*, about two kilometers west of Hénin, 800 meters southeast of Mercatel. The battalion was to advance from its support position at the northwest edge of Hénin. A connection with RIR 121 on the left up to the Hénin–Neuville Vitasse Road should have been established when the battalion relieved RIR 121 on the evening of 27 March 1918. The relief did not take place until about 5.30 a.m. on 28 March 1918 and because of the delay in completing the relief and the unfamiliarity with the position an unoccupied gap was allowed to form between the Hénin–Neuville Vitasse Road and the right flank of the II/180.

Immediately at the start of the assault the companies of the II/180 received severe machine gun and mine fire from half right out of a trench section that was not being attacked because of the gap. The 6/180 therefore changed direction, now moving to the northwest and across to the enemy trench and rolled it up. From there, the 6/180 swiftly moved forward from the northern slope and the hollow leading in the direction of Mercatel that had been evacuated by the enemy and soon reached the hill north of the hollow, from which the men could see the village lying just in front of them. The 8/180 had become attached to this attack in a similar manner. The route taken by the two companies crossed over numerous small trenches that in part were quickly captured, and in part soon full of British dead.

The 7th and 5/180 worked forward to the parts of the enemy position situated close to the village edge in hard, difficult fighting and from there advanced against a small trench piece, lying approximately 50 meters behind the first position, out of which several enemy machine guns fired. The difficult advance could not continue until the machine gun nests had been eliminated. The two companies advanced on trench sector A2, a large part in trench sector B1, then along the trench A2 against the Boiry–Neuville Road. About 2.00 p.m. the II/180 had reached *Karnickel Höhe* on the line of this road. At 3.00 p.m. *Hauptmann der Reserve* Vogler arrived at this point with his battalion staff.

The British were still strongly entrenches directly west of this position. A couple of well-placed shots from escort Battery Hahn, 2/RFAR 26, forced the British to withdraw. *Hauptmann der Reserve* Vogler wanted to risk one more advance with the assembled remnants of the different companies against the Arras–Bapaume Road. The 7/180 slowly moved forward approximately 500 meters until the company ran into undamaged obstacles on the road and strong British reserves that combined with the especially heavy rain that had started made any further advance impossible. During this time orders had arrived that the battalion was to stop and hold its ground.

The I/180 advanced at 7.30 a.m. from its readiness position in the Hénin-St. Leger sunken road behind the rolling barrage fire and attacked in a southwest direction, going across the Cojeul brook and after an uneventful crossing reached the first enemy opposition line on the Hénin–Boiry Road.

The terrain passed through by the battalion gently climbed toward the enemy positions and provided almost no cover. The companies advanced along the road, until they received strong machine gun fire out of the western and northern directions. The I/180 now found itself along the steep embankment of the road attacking against the strongly occupied trench A1 that ran perpendicular to the road. It was not until the trench was flanked by machine gun fire from several of the regimental machine guns from the northeast, did the men succeed in penetrating into the position at the place where the obstacles were slightly damaged and then, rolled up the trench.

The trench garrison appears to have received packages and letter mail shortly before the attack. The latest news from England did not interest the men at all; on the other hand the state of British nutrition was instantly recognized, especially with the discovery of a fresh apple flan among the packages. The main enemy opposition line was now in

British prisoners taken during the March fighting, (Source: *Die 26. Reserve Division 1914-1918*)

Trench B that proceeded from Trench A1 in an east-west direction, in which the British escaped the places in Trench A that they had occupied and had strongly equipped with machine guns. Then the attack seemed to hesitate.

Meanwhile, the III/180 was already proceeding on the same hill as the I/180, soon after the I/180 had started its attack. The III/180 in part penetrated into Trench A1; in part it went forward along both sides of Trench A1 to Trench B. Because of the artillery fire lying on Trench B and the pressure from the German attack from the south, the British moved further back to the west to Trench A2 and in Trench B2, in part also into a shallow Trench C.

Soon white cloths tied on the tips of bayonets appeared hesitantly out of Trench A2. After the artillery, mine and machine gun fire had been called off the *Krankenträger* ventured forward and found approximately 20 British soldiers with a wounded officer that a few men carried to the rear. The enemy, trapped between the attack from the south and the east by the II/180 could no longer have escaped. In a friendly and trustful manner they asked: 'Hénin?' and happily moved toward the village after the captors had confirmed that this was where they should go.

The British who had withdrawn to Trench B2 became in part driven back, in part killed by quite a few spirited men including *Unteroffizier* Bader, 11/180, *Vizefeldwebel* Rueff, 11/180, *Vizefeldwebel* Beck, 12/180, *Schütze* Lenz, 1MG/180. These men worked forward from traverse to traverse, throwing one hand grenade after the other, protected through rifle fire, while several comrades from the I/180 hastily carried hand grenades forward. The attack then came to a standstill due to a British machine gun set up on the edge of the trench on the left and whose crew was putting up a tough fight by spreading constant fire over the trench.

At first, the attackers attempted to silence the gun from a distance, using egg hand grenades. While these were well placed, they had no apparent effect on the gun or the crew. It was decided that something a bit stronger was needed and *Unteroffizier* Bader jumped forward, pulled the fuzes on three *Stielhandgranaten* at same time and quickly tossed all three into the area of the machine gun. A groan was heard, 'they are hit!' Bader continued to advance toward the enemy machine gun position through the smoke left behind by the hand grenades and found four severely wounded British soldiers lying on the ground. 'However, the machine gun? The rogues have taken the gun with them!'

The Germans continued the pursuit of the enemy remnants and discovered that the two men who had carried off the machine gun had left it standing in the trench; apparently the gun had become too heavy to carry and there was the danger the men could become captured. It had not taken Bader long before he was able to operate the foreign weapon. After tinkering about for a few minutes and studying the British machine gun he soon had it firing. Bader brought the machine gun into position in a shell hole, from which he fought against other enemy machine gun nests up to dusk, using up 5,000 British cartridges.

Meantime, the young, just promoted *Leutnant der Landwehr* Bächtle, 12/180 was advancing in Trench C at the head of a group of men he had quickly brought together, had not heard the warning shout from *Unteroffizier* Himmel, 12/180, who accompanied him, in the exciting urge to advance: '*Herr Leutnant*, there is a machine gun!' and he sank down, drilled through from several shots.

The escort battery with IR 180 had performed exquisitely on this day. It consisted of two field guns moving up closely behind the attacking troops, and the guns had performed miracles at times. Having this level of firepower close at hand and working in unison with the infantry was perhaps the most effective part of the new tactics. The battery leader, who was actually in the front ranks with RIR 119, immediately called back with his telephone after being contacted: 'Children! quickly! Where are the British? I have my guns with me and I will open fire!' the British defenders were having a very difficult time withstanding the effect of the well-aimed rapid fire from several 7.7cm field guns at close range.

The light 7.6cm *Minenwerfer* and *Granatwerfer* were also able to provide good assistance to the infantry on this day. Mixed in with the infantry, as well as in front of the infantry at times, was the platoon of *Leutnant der Reserve* Schlegel who proceeded along the Hénin–Boiry Road. Schlegel and his men were able to take enemy machine gun posts under accurate fire from the advanced firing positions and quickly eliminate them, much to the appreciation of the infantry.

Then, at 3.30 p.m. IR 180 received orders: the battalions would remain in their present positions for the time being, and would hold them. The formations become reorganized, connections were established between the units and patrols were sent out for reconnaissance.

During this time there was a great deal of confusion along the front. Men were moving from one position to another searching for their companies. Individual soldiers and small groups wandered through the terrain and officers hastened through the trenches to collect their men and as far as possible take them with them, leading them back to the company assigned position. At first only a small number of men could be located. A few who were still missing would eventually return, but many others were dead, but so many of the old proven company comrades who had been in the regiment since 1914 were among the killed and wounded on this day:

> The company leaders mourned the loss of so many good men, especially those who had been faithful soldiers, who carried on the tradition of the company, the irreplaceable teachers and leaders of the younger men, who, how they always have shown, so desperately needed the leadership of the war-tested men and who so gratefully accepted it. They were critical if the newer men were to cope in the trenches and crater fields, practical exploitation of the circumstances, the correct assessment of danger, precaution without nervousness, the feeling that not every shell hits and that the courageous were no more endangered than the coward. They taught the new recruits to trust their instincts, believe in their own superiority over the British, everything that the young boys learned first through the examples of the older men.[17]

28 March 1918 had been a very active day and the men could be proud of what they had achieved. Essentially the goal was reached; the successful storming of *Karnickel Höhe* was mentioned in the daily army report of 29 March 1918. The commanding general spoke of his special acknowledgement of IR 180 in the evening. There was still a consideration if the greatly thinned ranks of tired men could still successfully storm Mercatel in the late afternoon, fortunately no one would ever know if it would have been possible:

> At 7.15 p.m. brigade orders go out: On orders from the Group the brigade would still reach the Boiry-Becquerelle-Arras railway cut today ... if Mercatel was still occupied by the enemy, move heavy artillery in activity against it!
>
> 7.25 p.m. the regiment replied with light signals: Attack cannot occur today, because strong English positions with undamaged obstacles lie opposite the regiment. Following 8.00 p.m. a message from Brigade: Above all hold![18]

With the advance on hold, the new line began to take form. In the course of the following day the new outpost zone became established up to the large Arras–Bapaume Road, and in part placed forward of the regimental position.

The men had every reason to be happy about the success of this day; however there was no victory rejoicing among the ranks. The fatigue and strain of the fighting combined with an increasingly stronger rain that the men were exposed to, and the certainty of further heavy losses and the death of so many good comrades created a somber mood among the ranks. The rain and the cold and dampness made sitting in the earth holes almost unbearable. The men tried to create some meager protection against the inclement weather and constructed makeshift roofs made with tent cloth and pieces of corrugated iron found scattered around. Finally, the II/R119 relieved the exhausted III/180, while the I and III/R119 remained in reserve.

The 26th Reserve Division assault was discontinued because the connecting divisions had not advanced sufficiently far enough. Instead of the hoped for breakthrough, the enemy had only become pressed back a short distance. There was still some hope that if the attacks further to the south were successful it would have an impact on the situation facing the 26th Reserve Division, so the men waited, and waited. They would wait in vain as the war of movement that had barely started came to an end on this front, the '*Papierkrieg*' returned once again, all the more powerful, how one battalion adjutant grimly committed in his diary.

RIR 121 had suffered heavily on 24 and 28 March 1918, especially through machine gun fire. It had lost 37 officers and 1,000 men on both of these days of fighting. Amongst the losses were two battalion commanders, *Hauptmann* Irle who was killed and Major Benzinger who was wounded, and almost every company leader. Deprived of its best leaders and almost the half of its Other Ranks, the regiment was no longer capable of being involved in combat in the front line and was pulled back and became designated as the division reserve.

In the two attacks IR 180 had lost 20 officers and 800 men killed and wounded. The battle strength of the companies now ranged between 15 and 45 men each. The lack of officers was very serious, individual companies had no more officers at all, others only a few. The men's weapons were in bad condition. The largest part of the light machine guns lacked crews despite all of the previous efforts to train every man in the operation of this important weapon. In such conditions, there was little more the division could do.

Following this fighting, the men of the 26th Reserve Division discovered a large tunnel in the vicinity, a lengthy underground corridor that ran under the position and a noteworthy discovery was made by a few of the men. In the event of an evacuation the British had prepared to burn the tunnel by placing small piles of flammable materials against the wooden tunnel walls in containers the size of a field-mail-box and with the appearance of white stones. When the fire reached these containers they caught fire and burned in the manner of solidified alcohol, with red flames, which could not be extinguished even if earth was thrown up on it. However, taking advantage of the situation, the troops cooked their coffee on them.

During the progress of the attack on 28 March 1918 the staff of IR 180 followed in the Hénin– Boiry Road and nested in an earthen hole in the embankment of the road. In the evening they went back to Hénin and spent an unpleasant day and two still worse nights there. Following the attack the enemy placed continuous strong artillery fire from medium caliber guns on Hénin.

The staff had to be satisfied finding a recently started mined dugout with eight steps. There the regimental commander and his adjutant sat crowded closely together along with the Other Ranks on the steps, not in an orderly fashion according to rank, but all mixed together. The dugout was apparently filled with freezing water and was without sufficient illumination and the officers issued commands under these difficult circumstances.

The air inside the dugout corridor was stuffy and there was no circulation. Many of the men became drowsy in this situation, a luxury the officers did not have. Nearby lay 22 men of the Under staff in a small, corrugated iron hut, completely exhausted from the efforts of the day. The runners, signalers, wireless operators, Telephonists had all performed very well. The largest part of them had also participated in the attack, the runners had made many difficult journeys; they created their posts in the artillery fire, laid down wires and mended wires, usually with British wire that had been laboriously collected previously.

In the end, the events of the previous days had strained the limits of flesh and blood and the men had given all they could. As the men rested inside the rickety hut a dud shell tore a hole in the corner of their feeble roof, one man simply turned over on to his other side and continued to sleep. A few days later the staff moved into a quieter situation, especially when they found a comfortable habitation in one of the *Kalkgrube*, one of the numerous chalk caves in northern France, in which there was an artificial sun, an electrical spotlight, which provided some light.

The attack of the IX Reserve Corps and the XVIII Army Corps became temporarily suspended. The 26th Reserve Division was directed to prepare defenses, however without being conspicuous about it in order to deceive the enemy. The outpost zone was extended and there was lively patrol activity, all giving the appearance that the attack was finished.

The brief moment in time when the men of the 26th Reserve Division were involved in the war of movement was over. Now, it was like old times, brigade orders from the evening of 28 March 1918 said 'Above all hold!' The 'time being' mentioned in the orders would become a very long period of time. The division was once again involved in position warfare of the worst type.

The terrain occupied by the men was not too destroyed; the earth thrown up from the fox holes was good enough against being seen by the enemy, but useless against enemy artillery fire. Towards evening of 28 March 1918 it started to rain and the cold, wet conditions almost made life in the earthen holes unbearable. The men created meager protection, providing a roof made of tent cloth and salvaged corrugated iron which barely offered any protection against the rain, let alone against shells of any caliber. The reserve battalion was accommodated in shell proof mined dugouts as this portion of the defenses often received lively artillery fire, more so than in the forward positions as these positions could be easily seen in aerial photographs.

The monotonous routine of trench duty came into play once more with seemingly endless hours of sentry duty day and night that strained both bodies and spirits. Then, when rest was possible, it meant occupying a cramped, damp hole in the ground that quickly soaked the men through to the skin. The proximity of the enemy, who suffered much in the same way as the men of the 26th Reserve Division, required the utmost diligence by the expanded sentry duty. Constant observation of the enemy positions and the occasional strong artillery bombardment did not leave much opportunity for rest let alone sleep. When a man came off sentry duty, he was generally wet and muddy. In two hours, he was back on sentry duty in the same condition. There was no real prospect for the men becoming clean or dry. It was no different than when the division was in Flanders.

On top of the physical discomforts the men had to withstand, their morale also began to fail. The German offensives had taken precedent over all other needs of the army and this meant that the mail service was disrupted for some time as the transport wagons and horses had all been requisitioned for other duties. The field-mail which brought solace and joy to the men had simply stopped. It would be several weeks before the mail service would even approach normal levels once more.

While little could be done in regard to restoring the mail service, the lack of rest or sleep was offset somewhat by an increase in the size of rations. The mood of the men was apparently no better than the quantity and quality of the food being distributed. In the first days there were still plentiful supplies of English canned foods that had been found or dug up. Many of the younger soldiers longed for additional food to supplement the small rations they received as they always seemed to be hungry.

The large stockpile of captured food was being distributed freely to the men, which did help raise morale for the moment. Still, the question was made, could a piece of bacon really replace the positive impact of a letter from home?

When the captured supplies began to run out, no one despised horse flesh anymore and the horses that had been wounded in the vicinity of the men rarely made it to a Veterinary Military Hospital. Also, many of the Line of Communication dogs ended their existence in cooking pots thanks to nimble and resourceful *Korporalschaft*.

While the men pondered the fate that caused them to be positioned in such an inhospitable location, they did receive good news from the other parts of the front about great victories, particularly from the north. However, Arras, the huge fortress which was so close by, had not fallen and the enemy defenses only improved in strength from week to week. Still, despite the current circumstances, the men of IR 180 felt that one day Arras would fall and they would be counted among the troops that had conquered the city. Then, when the 17th Army gave their columns and batteries to the 6th Army in the north and to the 2nd Army in the south everyone knew it was no longer a war of movement.

Whilst the attack spirit of the men of the 26th Reserve Division was still intact, the physical strength of the regiments had dropped very low. The ranks of the regiments were thinned out and the front lines could barely be held with the small number of men still available whose bodies and souls were just about worn out. In the words of one regiment, 'the bow has been stretched to its limits.'

While the 26th Reserve Division occupied this sector the regiments were moved about from one location of the division front to another until finally, they were assigned to positions at the eastern edge of *Karnickel Höhe*, south of Neuville-Vitasse and west of Hénin.

When looking back at the brief period of open warfare, the losses suffered by the three regiments had been quite heavy. The losses consisted mainly of the older, more experienced veterans from the Vosges and the Somme. There were some subtle observations about the attitude and actions of the newer soldiers who apparently were reluctant to leave the strong defenses, or ignore the enemy artillery fire and advance along with their officers at critical moments of the attack, thereby exposing the older, more experienced men to suffer the highest losses. An example of the number of men lost can be seen in the ranks of the 11/R119 which participated in the assault with RIR 121 at the end of March. Of the 90 men in the company who started off in the attack only 30 men returned. On 30 March 1918 RIR 121, as the division reserve, was transferred into the old position on the *Mühlenberg*. Once there, the regiment received fresh replacements and could be divided into three battalions once again.

Enemy artillery activity was very low, sometimes quiet but it was always sensed to be close by. It was ten times the volume of the German fire and they often fired with gas shells. The carrying parties bringing up food and supplies had a difficult time walking through the fire zones.

There was a great deal of activity behind the front. Roads and field railways were built, heavy guns were brought into position, ammunition and construction materials were brought to the front. The two *pionier* companies, the 4th and 6/*Pionier* Battalion 13, were kept very busy over the next month with the 6/*Pionier* Battalion 13 restoring the Chérisy–Heninel Road with the assistance of the 4/*Pionier* Battalion 13, which also worked on the construction of a field railway. Once finished, the light gauge railway was able to carry large quantities of supplies to the front. Much of the work performed by the *pioniers* was aided by the seemingly endless supply of enemy construction materials that had been left behind by the retreating British. This sudden windfall made construction far easier than if the pioniers had to obtain fresh supplies from further in the rear.

The men in *Minenwerfer* Coy 226 spent the last days of March installing its weapons at the foot of the eastern slope of *Karnickel Höhe* from where it was able to place harassment fire on the enemy positions on the northern and southern slopes of this hill. At the beginning of April the company with then occupied with the construction of new *Minenwerfer* positions and with the creation of mined dugouts.

All of the work performed by the *pioniers* and *Minenwerfer* Coy suffered with the start of the rainy weather. After a few rainy days the terrain was so muddy that the field kitchens and the supply wagons with teams of six heavy horses remained stuck in the mud, including the horses. Only the tracked vehicles were able to move through the thick mud. These motor vehicles could easily drive through the bogs with their endless tracks, heavily loaded with supplies and equipment and even with a heavy gun being pulled behind it. The horses had almost all become broken down and exhausted from the heavy work they were subjected to, combined with their small ration of oats they now received. These unfortunate creatures all too often became shot and in part ended up in the cook kettles and frying pans.

In addition to the detrimental effects of the weather, the enemy artillery activity began to increase during April until it became a near constant danger. The artillery fire also included gas shells and there were many losses from gas poisoning in this month. The enemy artillery fire was quickly becoming an annoyance and forced *Minenwerfer* Coy 226 *Wurfminen* Column and the regimental transport to alter their bivouac location to Hatcourt on 9 April 1918 to avoid the enemy fire. However, the enemy long range guns were even able to reach as far back as Hatcourt so on 23 April 1918 the *Wurfminen* Column moved even further back until the entire company was in Dury.

As far as the eye could see there were no intact houses anymore and the First Line Transport bivouacked among the ruins of Chèrisy. However, the faithful drivers and

An Überlandwagen (A7V chassis) bringing up artillery ammunition. (Source: *Die 26. Reserve Division 1914-1918*)

horse keepers had soon collected so much building material that they were able to manufacture some modest cottages. The transport men rarely found stables when changing quarters, and in most cases they had to build them first. Then, when the stables were finally ready, they invariably were moved once again to a different place where the work started all over again. While fighting continued on other sectors of the front, the small remnants of the 26th Reserve Division spent an uneventful month holding a small portion of the line as a trench division once more. This was the life led by the men at the end of March and throughout April 1918.

In the night from 13/14 April 1918 RIR 121 moved to the position by Neuville-Vitasse and relieved IR 91. The position consisted of a few small trench-pieces and a few dugouts and had considerable shortcomings, making it difficult to hold in the event of a serious attack.

The men of RIR 121 soon found that they were facing Canadian troops once again, 'their elite troops next to the Scottish.' Soon it was time to determine the exact identity of the opposing forces and as such offensive patrols and raids began to occur with greater frequency. One patrol under *Unteroffizier* Schneider from the I/R121 succeeded in capturing a Canadian sergeant from out of the opposing trench following a period of fierce resistance.

Toward the end of April the weather improved, and subsequently the battle activity increased on both sides, with renewed artillery fire and trench raids. An extremely bold patrol was held on 28 April 1918 by *Vizefeldwebel* Herdtle, 1/R119, along with

Unteroffizier Lenz, *Gefreiten* Frick, *Musketieren* Köhn, Dietz, Walz 1/R119, Moser, 3/R119, Maier, Russ and Renkenberger, 4/R119. The patrol exited the German positions south of Neuville-Vitasse in broad daylight and the men crawled and climbed through German and British obstacles for two hours until they had arrived at the enemy position.

In a flash, Herdtle and his eight men sprang into the British trench while Maier and Russ remained behind as security. The raiding party fanned out and began to search the enemy trench and any dugouts they found. Walz and Köhn were the first to come across three British soldiers, who had been sleeping the 'sleep of the righteous' inside a dugout. Herdtle immediately rushed forward to help his comrades. The sleeping soldiers were rather abruptly awakened, were detained and then quickly taken back with the three raiders.

Frick and Moser also came upon two sleeping enemy soldiers in another dugout that were also very comfortable and had even taken off their boots. The two men were also grabbed and taken away. However, the two men were putting up a struggle with their captors despite being forcefully seized and were able to create a little confusion. Then, the Swabian password '*Sau*' was given which indicated an immediate withdrawal from the enemy trenches whereupon the raiding party had to give up any thought of taking the two enemy soldiers with them and allowed them to go free. The three other prisoners were taken back and were later found to belong to the 2nd Canadian Division and they were a 20 year old bookbinder, a 40 year old mason and a 44 year old butcher.

The men of the 26th Reserve Division were also subjected to enemy raids including one that occurred on 29 April 1918 in which a number of men from RIR 121 were captured. The raiders had come from the 2nd Canadian Division and had successfully captured nine men from the II/R121.

The raid was executed by the 19th and 21st battalions, 4th Canadian Brigade on the early morning of 29 April 1918. The following report was filed following the interrogation of the rather talkative prisoners:

> 2nd Canadian Division
> G.I. 204
> April 29th 1918
>
> Preliminary examination of 9 prisoners of 7th and 8th Coys and 2nd M.G.C. 121st R.I.R., 26th R.D. captured in N.19.a & o. on 29-4-18
>
> METHOD OF CAPTURE. Prisoners were in enemy outpost line during our raid and were taken prisoner.
>
> ORDER OF BATTLE. This is given from N. to S.: 121 R.I.R. – 119 R.I.R. – 180 I.R. The 21st Bavarian R.I.R. is stated to be on the right of 26th Res. Div. The N.C.O. of 7th Coy who seems very reliable is quite positive that on the 16th instant the 2nd Bn., 121 R.I.R. relieved in the sector in front of NEUVILLE VITASSE a Bn. Of the 452nd I.R. He stated that the 451 I.R. was North and believed that on relief the 452 I.R. went into line also North. This Prussian Division on their right was relieved on the 27th/28th by the 16th Bav. Div.

DISPOSITIONS. The Regimental Sector extending from N.13.c. 80.95 to N.19. c7.4 approx. is held by the II Bn, all four coys being in the line, the order N. to S. being 5, 6, 7, 8. I Bn. Is in support in the NEUVILLE VITASSE Switch system, one company from N.14.c.4.5 to N.14.c.8.0, and three companies S. of road from N.20.a.5.6 to N.20.d.6.7. there are sufficient dugouts in this system to hold all of the battalion.

The III Bn. Is in reserve in the *WOTAN STELLUNG* North and West of CHERISY.

COMPANY DISPOSITIONS. The 7th Company is in the outpost line from M.24.d.92.93 to N.19.a.7.6. It holds the following posts, by night, each of 3 or 4 men:

Post N.19a.6.7.		
Post & dugout (1 platoon)	N.19.a.45.50	Post N.19.a.16.28
Heavy M.G. Post	N.19a.37.44	L.M.G. Post N.19.a.10.21
Post	N.19.a.34.38	L.M.G. Post M.24.b.95.10
L.M.G. Post	N.19.a.30.35	L.M.G. Post M.24.d.92.93
Barrier & Post	N.19.a.22.28	
Post & dugout (1 platoon)	N.19.a.25.28	
Platoon shelter	N.19.o.36.91	

The two remaining platoons are in cellars at N.19.b.05.50 approx.

RELIEFS. During the last tour only three days were done in the line, but this time the period has been increased to four days. Prisoners say it is done in the hope of deceiving us as to days of relief, as lately many casualties have occurred from our harassing fire during reliefs.

ROUTES TO TRENCHES. The route from the WOTAN STELLUNG to the front line is as follows: Follow railway track N. of CHERISY to HENINEL, to H.28.d.0.7. along trench to road at M.27.b.3.7. then along road to N.21.a.1.0., track to N.20.b.3.0 and along trench through N.20.a.65.55, N.20a.20.45, or N.20.a.50.00, N.19b.3.2 to front line.

M.G's & T.M's. The 7th and 8th Companies have 4 to 6 L.M.G's each and in addition a heavy M.G. from 2nd M.G.K. is attached to each company. There are about 6 L.T.M's ("fish tails") in position close together at about N.19.a.2.0. There are also 5 M.T.M's spaced at intervals along N. side of road from N.19.a.80.25 to N.14.b.05.40. Casualties are caused at times by our M.G. harassing fire, but it seems that this is too high to be effective. T.M. ammunition is brought up in horse drawn vehicles as far as the neighborhood of the church, at night, generally unloading there between midnight and 4 a.m.

HEADQUARTERS. The church in NEUVILLE VITASSE is no longer a company headquarters which has moved across the road to N.19.b.05.50. The 6th and 7th Company H.Q. are both here. H.Q. of the Battalion in the line is in trench at N.20.a.5.4.

Headquarters of Support Bn. Is on road at N.21.c.8.4. H.Q., 121 R.I.R. in dugouts just off road between N.22.a.1.8 and cross roads at N.22.a.65.30.

TRANSPORT. The transport lines are about 400 to 500 yards S. of FONTAINE. 6 horses were killed there a few days ago by a direct hit. Losses are steady among the regimental transport through our night harassing fire.

RATION PARTIES Ration and field kitchens come to the West edge of HENINEL where they are met by ration parties from the Support Battalion at about 8.45 to 9 p.m. Ration parties come down road from N.20b.63.75 to cross roads at N.27.b.3.7 then follow old trench to road at N.28.c.9.6 and along road to HENINEL.

COMPANY STRENGTH. Is given as 60.

LOSSES. The whole Division is said to have suffered 60 percent casualties in the attacks on 24th and 28th March near ST. MARTIN. The 7th Company had 20 killed and 45 wounded out of 120 and casualties in other companies were equally severe. Since then losses have been normal till last when severe casualties are believed to have been inflicted on the 7th and 8th Companies. The II Bn. Commander and his Headquarters Staff were killed by a direct hit on the 28th March and the other two Battalion Commanders were wounded.

DRAFTS. A draft of 14 men received a week ago from the Recruit Depot at ECLOO is the only reinforcements they have had lately. All the men of this draft are 19 years old, and their morale[e] under shell fire is distinctly poor. They came out from the Ersatz Bn. Of the 121 R.I.R. from Germany about 3 weeks ago.

DEFENSES. There is no wire to speak of in front of the Outpost Line not in front of the Support position is the NEUVILLE VITASSE Switch.

PATROLS. These go out every night but appear to be mostly defensive patrols and have for their object principally the location of our posts, as these were not known at all accurately.

MOVEMENT OF 121 R.I.R. This regiment has been so severely handled on the 28.3.18 that it did not go into line again till the 16.4.18 being refitted and made up to strength during this period in the WOTAN STELLUNG. The Divisional sector was therefore held during this fortnight by the remaining two regiments.

INTENTIONS. N.C.O. of the 7th Company is certain that no attack is intended on this front. He states that there are no troops in reserve and that Divisions in the line are not considered fit for offensive action. An attack on the ARRAS front is not considered likely for the same reasons. During the first week of April when in the WOTAN STELLUNG this N.C.O. states that roughly 15 to 20 batteries of heavy guns were taken out of this part of the line and was told that these were destined for the Northern battle front. No troop movements have been seen or heard of.

AIRCRAFT. When in the Support Line the II Battalion was fired on by our aeroplanes with M.G.s and three or four casualties caused.

GENERAL. In case of an attack the orders were for companies to hold outpost line at all costs. The Support Bn. In the NEUVILLE VITASSE Switch was to carry out immediate counter attacks if the Outpost Line was driven back.

Prisoners state that they are told that if taken prisoner they will be very badly treated by the British. N.C.O. admits that British prisoners are treated very badly on the whole by the Germans, especially by the Prussians.

Prisoners had no idea that we would raid last night. Food conditions in Germany are said to be very bad and even worse in Austria where there is a certain amount of famine. Great dissent prevails among the working classes in BERLIN and the other large towns and there would have been strikes of a serious nature before this were it not for the official threat that all strikers would at once be drafted into the Army and sent to the front.

COMMANDERS	26th R.D.	– Lieut. General v. FRITSCH
	121 R.I.R.	– Oberst.Leut. v.
	II Bn.	– Ober.Leutnant STARK
	7th Coy.	– Lt. ELWANGER

HARASSING FIRE. Prisoners state that reliefs are changed periodically on account of our harassing fire. One platoon had 3 killed when coming into the trenches on the 27th. The platoon had great difficulty getting in and had to lie in shell holes on several occasions on account of our artillery and M.G. fire. Steady casualties have been caused by our harassing fire at night. Trench from N.31. central to N.26.b.1.5 has been evacuated on account of artillery fire, but prisoners state that it is occupied from N.31.central south by troops of the 180 I.R.

OBSERVATION. There are two O.P's in NEUVILLE VITASSE, one in old house at N.19b.10.48 and another in the ruins of the church at N.19.b.05.55. These are manned by Battalion observers and artillery F.O.O's. The T.M., O.P. is at M.34.b.95.10.

Battalion observers make sketches of the surrounding country and note all movement. F.O.O's and T.M. observers have orders to engage all movement in range. Attached map shows approx. field of view from these O.P's. Prisoners state observers reported a Headquarters at M.18.b.3.1 as runners could be seen frequently coming and going from this point. Prisoners state that there is no mining organization in their battalion and movement was left to for the artillery to engage. Prisoners stated that they had located 3 of our T.M's in M.34 by their flash. Locations given fairly accurate.[19]

At the beginning of May the enemy became restless. Large patrols attempted to break into the regiment neighboring RIR 119. On 3 May 1918 the III/180 was the designated as the Battle Battalion in the forward line. The 11/180 was in position with the main opposition line on the Arras–Bapaume Road, with the protection sentries of the outposts 100-150 meters further forward. The left wing of the company was on the Cojeul, the 12/180 connected on the right. The 11/180 had started work on new wire entanglements at 2 a.m. on this day and in order to protect the men while they were working, sentries were pushed forward even further, and by the 12/180 stood double sentry posts in spacing of 20-40 meters:

> The night is suspiciously quiet; I might just lie in the open air," said one experienced, old *Unteroffizier* to his sentry about the habits of the adversary. He had hardly spoken, when at 3.30 a.m. drum fire fell as with a sudden blow. A drum-fire – the most insipid invention of the brutal material war and will for annihilation, the fight that concerns the mind, the iron against the men's spirit – is already a huge test of nerves for the defenders in a well-developed position. Hovering and shaken, he sits worrying in his dark dugout if in the next moment one would not fall, coming in and bury him under its ceiling. However fully upon an open field, at most under a thin corrugated iron-roof, to allow this deafening and sense-bewildering thunderstorm to go over and not run away in abrupt fright necessitates the harnessing of all superhuman will-power. Only the most utmost refinement of will and morale strength gets the upper hand over the instinct of self-preservation. The organized, educated man frequently holds on better than the robust farmer's son.
>
> There is now the lonesome sentry in the middle in there, in the noise and smoke of hell, blinded by the lightning of the shrapnel and shells, the hand on the rifle stock, lurking at that moment, because the stream of sulphur that spits out yellow figures. 'They stand completely alone there.' Now they show what the man is worth. Never was he so dependent on himself, how on a nightly raid on a thin sentry line. It is good that the old *Unteroffizier* does not lose his head and eagerly shoots up his light ball. Altogether an old *Unteroffizier*! One such is priceless for his company, 'a tower in the battle.' For one moment with the start of the drum-fire the general excitement also takes hold of him. However once he has the enemy before his eyes, the old fighting spirit comes over him and the old confidence is master once again. However he often has sufficient experience in that a couple of well-placed hand grenades also do miracles to the superior enemy opposite.
>
> And this time the enemy is superior! A clearly sensed shift of the enemy artillery fire to the rear, and already immediately following the roll of fire rushed the flat

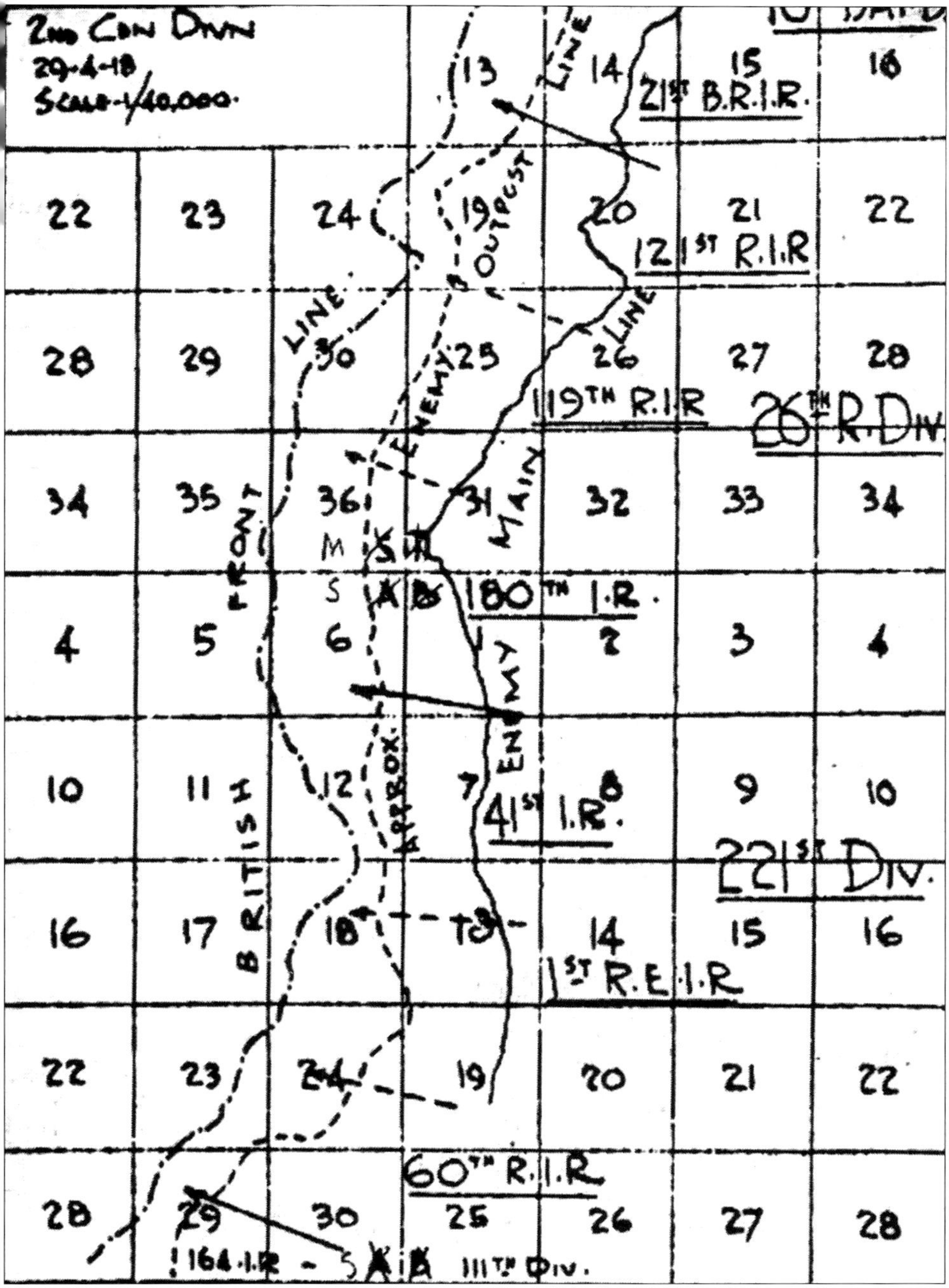

German trench occupation 29 April 1918.

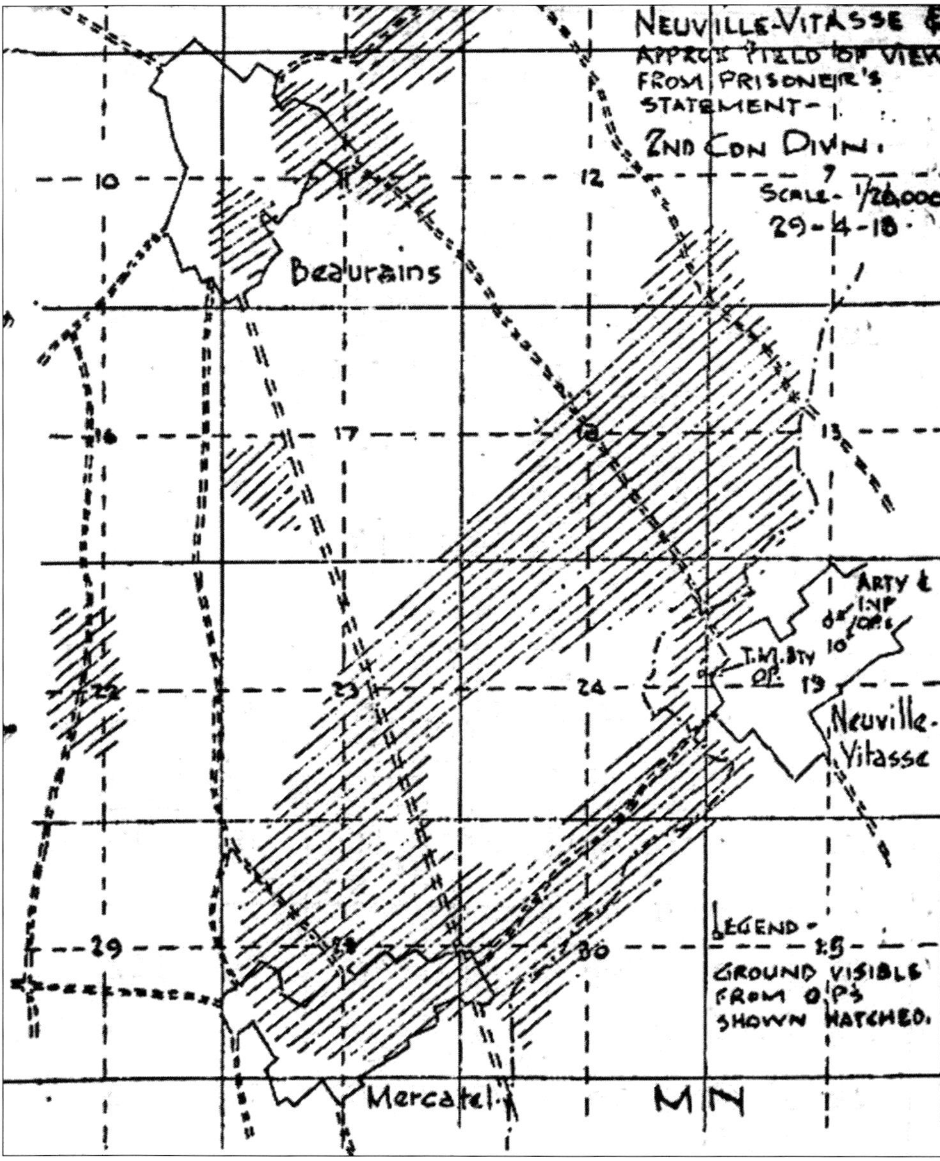

Approximate field of view of the Germans at Neuville-Vitasse.

steel helmets and the yellow face. With uncanny speed the dirty yellow flood rolled forth. They approached here in two waves in the spacing of about 20 meters, a heap of 200 to 250 men with white armbands. They fired in the swift advance. Where they met an enemy, they let out a devilish roar. It was no sincere cheer! But an ugly, guttural, Urrah!' The first hand grenades strike. The machine gun of *Unteroffizier* Frey (12th Coy) soon rattled. A couple of adversaries screamed, fell. The neighbors hesitated; the stream splits itself on the sentries like on the stone bridge pillars and flooded in coming through the unfortunately far too wide gaps of our sentry line. The *Schütze* swiftly throws his machine gun around. The most beautiful opportunity for destructive flanking fire! The gun fails! Now there are no more options. Back to the main opposition line! It is difficult working through the swarm of advancing Englishmen to strike through to the company leader tunnels that were by the crossing of the Arras–Bapaume Road with Trench B leading here from Hénin. The fewest sentries succeed in becoming detached from the bitter close combat with the enemy. A stout small Group under its young, courageous leader, *Gefreiter* Wizemann (12th Coy), fought stubbornly for every step of ground in a sap. The over powerful English mob shot down from both trench edges and stung that brave small heap of young heroes in that trench. A few were already wounded and however fight further, until they succumbed to the superior strength. The leader, wounded through a bayonet thrust and an unwounded young soldier are the only two survivors, who are able to provide news of this heroic fighting of our young men.

Leutnant der Reserve Griesinger.[20]

The left wing platoon of the 12/180 had been attacked as had the 11/180 on the left. The advancing enemy troops had also became split from the opposition of the sentries. The enemy advanced quickly and swiftly penetrated the main opposition line in two rows, each about 50 men. One half of the enemy assault came down on the Cojeul brook, where they were detained for a short time by the machine gun of *Unteroffizier* Knapp, however, the gun had to be abandoned because of a jam. The other half attacked further to the right, coming in across the outpost zone.

The sentries in the outpost zone who had assembled by the company leader, *Gefreiter* Queck, attacked the enemy line pressing from the south and west in a desperate hand grenade battle; however they then moved back, because they were already threatened from the rear, and reported what had occurred to the 8/180. *Leutnant der Reserve* Krauss, the leader of the 11/180, had gone along the road with his battle orderly in order to view the work of his people shortly before the beginning of the drum-fire. They were only gone three minutes, when they became surprised by the enemy artillery fire. A shell splinter hit Krauss in the back of the head in the *Strassen Graben*, where he had apparently sought protection. His orderly had also become severely wounded not far from him in a shell hole.

The replacement company leader of 12/180, *Leutnant der Reserve* Baur, wanted to throw his staff against the swiftly approaching Canadian infantry. He climbed on the edge of the trench (B) leading past his tunnel and immediately fell back into the trench with shattered legs. *Unteroffizier* Frey, who meanwhile had succeeded in striking back through up to the trench with a few men, held the British from this portion of the trench with hand grenades. The enemy then flooded along further on the left and right of the trench piece, while Frey bandaged his moaning *Leutnant*. Close behind the main opposition line the enemy bumped into two heavy machine guns. The one was met without a crew and was captured; the Other Ranks of the second gun struggled to withdraw 50-100 meters through enemy hand grenades, from where they continued to fire.

The men of IR 180 had received some welcome support in the form of heavy fire from *Minenwerfer* Coy 226 which placed barrage fire against the enemy trenches and into no man's land during the attack on 3 May 1918; just as it had done on 29 April 1918 when the 3/180 had been attacked by the enemy as a feint for the main raid against RIR 121.

The Canadians then made a sudden about turn after a green light ball had been fired off. 'They were insolent pigs; that demonstrated more than courage,' remarked one *Unteroffizier* afterward, who recognized the blustery bravery with all the superior strength of the adversary. However, what occurred next rendered no honor to the enemy. They fired into all shelters and shell holes in which wounded Germans were suspected as they withdrew. *Vizefeldwebel* Ruoff, who was lying quietly in the foreground with a shattered hand and also shot through the thighs, received a grazing shot across head and chest from passing British soldiers. Only by playing dead was Ruoff able to escape with his life.

Leutnant der Reserve Krauss's orderly observed how two Canadian soldiers, who had made the remark to him *Kaput*! and had gone past, turned back again and apparently came upon the corpse of *Leutnant der Reserve* Krauss. Krauss was later found without his Iron Cross I Class, his revolver and shoulder straps.

The two Group survivors, from which this testimony came, only managed to escape with their lives by lying motionless and unnoticed amongst a small heap dead man. The leader of the Group managed to find a safe hiding place inside a dugout after he had received a bayonet wound in the chest. Then the shelter then became loaded with combustible materials and set on fire by the Canadians and continued to burn out for a long time, but the Group leader managed to survive.

Meanwhile, *Vizefeldwebel* Stiehr, 8/180, came forward with some men he had gathered together from the 11/180 and the 3MG/180. He arranged the sentry line as well as he could with the existing men again and retained command over the 11/180, which only had three Group leaders; both *Fähnrich* Berroth and *Vizefeldwebel* Kahles were missing. On the next morning, *Leutnant der Reserve* Kramer came out during broad daylight and took over the leadership of the terribly frayed 11/180.

Some days later the survivors of the 11 and 12/180 stood solemnly by a long row of graves and gave their fallen comrades a last salute. The men rested in the soldier's graveyard of Estrées at the northern slope of the village that looked across to the towers of Douai. It was considered to be a beautiful resting place that had far too many of the regimental dead buried there. The troops that had stoutly held on 3 May 1918 could be proud of the praise which came from higher commands. The commanding general spoke of his 'full appreciation of his trusted troops' in the Corps daily orders.

Period drawing of Granatwerfer being used during an attack (*Illustrierte Geschichte des Weltkrieges 1914/18*)

At this stage of the war the regiments of the 26th Reserve Division were mere skeletons of their former selves. So few men manned the trenches that the division could be more accurately described as a battalion; the survivors desperately needed to rest and to refill the ranks if the division was ever to be considered a combat unit again. Regardless of the situation facing the division, it would remain in the front lines until the middle of May.

However, the Canadians had not finished with the 26th Reserve Division. On the night of 6 May 1918 the light machine gun of the 9/R119 helped to expel an enemy detachment that was attempting to sneak up to the sentries of IR 180 in the thick fog. The close range machine gun fire devastated the opposing ranks and the raiding party failed to enter the German position.

Aside from the occasional patrol or skirmish with enemy raiding parties, little occurred of note in the 26th Reserve Division in the next week or so; then, on 14 and 15 May 1918 the division was ordered to be relieved from the front line and was being sent to another location for a period of rest. On 14 May 1918, RIR 119 was relieved by RIR 28 of the 185th Infantry Division. IR 180 was also relieved by IR 161 and from 15 May 1918 the regiment was located in rest quarters in Arleux, nine kilometers south of Douai and in Palleul, one kilometer south of Arleux. The billets provided to the men in both locations were good.

While in the rear the 26th Reserve Division became the *Eingreifdivision* of the II Bavarian Army Corps, though how effective the division would be was questionable given its weak strength and exhausted troops. The companies in RIR 121, which on 21 March 1918 were 100 men strong, fresh and lively, impeccably equipped and clothed, when marching out through Dury, now came back with 25-30 men if they were fortunate, and were a picture of wretchedness with torn and dirty uniforms and worn out boots.

Up until the period of relief the two *pionier* companies in the division had been actively engaged in road and railway construction and other infrastructure work that was required to maintain the position. Both companies had suffered losses since the beginning of the year, but remarkably few considering all of the events that had taken place. The 6/*Pionier* Battalion 13 had lost four *pioniers* killed, *Gefreiter* Völlnagel, *Pioniers* Geldner, Schädler, Kugele and 19 *pioniers* wounded through mid-May, most of which occurred from a direct hit by an artillery shell on 10 May 1918 when the company was performing road work.

The first days spent in the rear were naturally used for rest, setting up the quarters, bathing, delousing, and the restoration of weapons and cleaning and repairing uniforms and other equipment, then however training started again; in particular, making the newly arrived replacements familiar with the various duties and to integrate them into the companies. During the morning there was infantryman training of the companies, in the afternoon the training in the specialty weapons took precedence. There were daily battalion courses on the light machine gun, light *Minenwerfer*, in communication methods and on use of the rifle grenade, furthermore stretcher bearer courses became held in all of the battalions.

With splendid spring weather, congenial billets and light duty, RIR 121 had the opportunity to recover once again. Other than the occasional enemy plane the men were not bothered by the adversary; as such the division was never used as an *Eingreifdivision* while in the rear.

RIR 121 also began construction of a monument to the fallen of the regiment in the cemetery in Estrées. In addition to the numerous Other Ranks of the regiment buried there, were the following officers: *Hauptmann* Irle, *Leutnants* Alt, Auerbacher, Bergold, Beutler, Boser, Buck, Bühler, Buschle, Friz, Hermann, Maier, Mayer, Maisch, Matthäs, Ruoff, Seeger, Schöller, Schweizer, Vollmer, Wiedemann, Wolf and *Offizier Stellvertreter* Sturm.

Each battalion in IR 180 also held a sports festival, during which beer was distributed much to the enjoyment of the Other Ranks. There were also numerous valuable prizes being given out for active in racing heats. Despite the heavy weeks and months of fighting the old humor of the men was still intact or possibly it was the effect of so much beer after a long period of moderation.

The *Zahlmeister* were quite proud of the prizes they were able to obtain, which were only possible through the savings earned from a well-managed market business. For a short time, the men were able to forget all of the dangers and strains of the past months, which they gratefully acknowledged were behind them for the moment. The festivities were made even more enjoyable when the regimental band played during the games as well as leading the men back to the quarters to accompanying marching music.

Decorated graves of men from IR 180 killed in the fighting in early May. (Source: Author's collection)

Notes

1. The Kempinski was and still is a well-known restaurant and hotel in the heart of Berlin.
2. G. Holtz, *Das Württembergische Reserve-Infanterie-Regiment Nr. 121 im Weltkrieg 1914-1918,* p. 69.
3. The 236th Infantry Division was formed at the end of December 1916 and consisted of Infantry Regiments 457, 458 and 459. The division was rated as third class by Allied intelligence and consisted mainly of men from the Class of 1918 (40 percent) and returning wounded.
4. Vischer, op. cit., p. 118.
5. Ibid.
6. Ibid.
7. Vischer, op. cit., p. 119.
8. Vischer, op. cit., p. 120.
9. Vischer, op. cit., pp. 122-123.
10. Vischer, op. cit., p. 123.
11. Ibid.
12. Vischer, op. cit., p. 124.
13. Vischer, op. cit., p. 125.
14. Vischer, op. cit., pp. 125-126.
15. Vischer, op. cit., p. 126.
16. Vischer, op. cit., pp. 126-127.
17. Vischer, op. cit., p. 129.
18. Ibid.
19. Canadian Intelligence Reports
20. Vischer, op. cit., pp. 131-132.

4

28th Reserve Division

January–March 1918

While the men of the 26th Reserve Division were destined to take part in the first major offensive of 1918, the sister division, the 28th Reserve Division, faced another type of future. After a subdued celebration of Christmas and the New Year, it had become 1918. The 28th Reserve Division was still located in Sedan where the men were training in offensive warfare and were helping to train other divisions for what was to come.

On 3 January 1918 His Royal Highness *Grossherzog* von Baden personally greeted all of the men of the 28th Reserve Division together for the first time on the parade ground set up on the Floin –St. Menges Road by Cachy, whereby a large number of awards were distributed to the regiments. The regimental commander of RIR 111 made a vow to His Royal Highness that the regiment would do its duty in the future with the same devotion as in the past. The regimental band of RIR 109 received particular praise, when His Royal Highness called out to the band after the parade march: 'The band has played marvelously despite the cold, bravo, bravo!'

The time spent by Sedan was quickly coming to a close. Along with the festive occasion of the royal visit came the news that orders had been issued for the 28th Reserve Division to relieve the 33rd Infantry Division in the Tahure sector. An advance party of 19 officers and 63 men were sent forward by rail on 3 January 1918 to St. Morel in order to become familiar with the new sector.

The beginning of the last year of the war found the 28th Reserve Division involved in position warfare in the Champagne by Ripont, west of the trenches previously occupied by the division. On 3, 4 and 5 January 1918 the battalions of RIR 111 embarked in Doucy and were transported by way of Charleville-Vouziers to the well-known places of Monthois and St Morel. They found makeshift accommodations in the *Sydow Lager* located in a ravine, 1,500 meters south of Marvaux.

In the nights of 4/5 and 5/6 January 1918 the II/R111 took over as the battle battalions and the III/R111 became the readiness battalion. The regimental sector was located at the left wing of the division sector. It was at this point where the German front

In addition to a brass band, RIR 110 also formed a small orchestra. (*Reserve-Infanterie-Regiment Nr. 110 im Weltkrieg 1914-1918*)

projected in an angle to the south between the Butte de Tahure and the Butte de Mesnil, both well-known names from army reports. The first days of January passed under mutual bombardments, gassing, as well as lively aerial activity, without resulting in any particular losses for the regiment.

The rest and training time for RIR 109 in the vicinity of Sedan also finally came to an end. Somewhat recovered from the exertions of the past months, RIR 109 was now trained for the attacks that were expected to take place in 1918. The regiment left its rest quarters and was loaded on to trains in Sedan, and was transported to the Tahure Sector.

In the nights of 4/5 and 5/6 January 1918 the I and II/R109 relieved the position battalion of RIR 135 in Sector G, northeast of Tahure. The III/R109 received rest quarters in barracks in the *Jonas Lager*. The new position could be described as quiet; however the shortage of dugouts and with the weather constantly shifting from frost to thaws and steady rain it was physically quite disagreeable. At this time the companies were equipped with a fourth light machine gun in order to increase their fighting strength, which also had the effect of further reducing the number of riflemen found in each company.

On 8 January 1918 the battalions of RIR 110 would board trains during very cold weather and driving snow in the railway station Carignan and traveled to St. Morel from where the men marched to their new quarters in Sugny and in the *Teschner Lager*. It had not been difficult to guess that that the regiment was going to the Champagne based upon the route taken by the transport trains. On the evening of 9 December 1918

Teschner Lager. (*Reserve-Infanterie-Regiment Nr. 110 im Weltkrieg 1914-1918*)

the I and II/R110 relieved the I and II/98. The regimental staff went into the position while the II/R110 was the rest battalion. The relief went smoothly and without losses.

The men of RIR 110 knew the sector from the Aisne to the *Kanonenberg* humpback quite well from the fall of 1917. They had first been sent there following the fighting on 1 July 1916. RIR 109 was located on the furthest right, in Sector G with the Butte de Tahure as the dominating point. RIR 111 was on the furthest left, occupied Sector D south of Ripont Mill. The dangerous point here was the *Wetterecke*, where the Champagne front bends to the north at a right angle. The middle regimental strip, Sector B, was taken over by RIR 110. The *Dormoise Mulde* was on the left flank, blocking this valley against the enemy was the main task of the regiment. The ruins of Tahure were before the front, dominated by Klitzing Hill. RIR 110 had taken over a sector that had seen heavy fighting in 1915 and that had often been mentioned in army reports.

The French designated the area as the 'Champagne *pouilleuse*' which was characteristic of the new battle terrain: 'lousy'. A large number of hills, ridges and humpbacks, between which ran ravines and hollows, gave the landscape its character. By day the miles of wide, shining white chalk piled up from the fire trenches could easily be seen. The farmers among the men of RIR 110 felt that the crop yield from this poor ground must be very small. Even the few wooded areas did not seem to want to grow; there were only small stands of stunted pine trees.

The local villages had all become completely destroyed in the fighting from 1915, and in their place stood barrack camps located on the steep slopes, which served as rest quarters. Roads were rare and the men would normally go into the positions using footpaths, crossing over hills and through ravines. Construction materials could become brought up from the regimental *pionier* park south of Maure on field tramway rails

Battalion dugout of the I/R110 on the Butte de Tahure. (*Reserve-Infanterie-Regiment Nr. 110 im Weltkrieg 1914-1918*)

using different ravines until they were behind the *Sprung Stellung*, and then were hauled over the hills by horses and dogs from Maure.

The work on the new position was impeded through stormy weather mixed with rain and snow, which caused all of the facilities to become covered in mud. The protection and patrol service placed considerable demands on the leaders and men employed in these duties as the French who were opposite were also active. On 11 January 1918 a sudden fire raid took place at midday, during which an enemy assault detachment penetrated the left wing of the outpost position of the 7/R111. The French soldiers threw hand grenades and incendiaries into abandoned dugouts and were eventually expelled through machine gun fire, so that when the picket went out to investigate the trench it was found to be empty. The French continued to hold numerous but unsuccessful raids to obtain prisoners.

On 13 January 1918 orders were issued by Brigade headquarters for a new distribution of the front line forces. Following several delays, the partitioning of the position took place. The lessons learned from the Battle of Cambrai and the unclear terrain which was suitable for surprise attacks, formed the basis for greater partitioning of the position. The new battle zone of RIR 111 ran south of Dormoise from the western slope of *Dumrath Höhe* via the *Altrock Stellung* to the east then curved around until to the *Prinz Karl Graben*, approximately one kilometer west of the Butte Dumois. The foreground was well protected with outpost positions, which were reinforced with light machine guns. The approximately 1,500 meter long right wing of the sector faced west and had the *Pionier Schlucht* and the lower *Goutte Schlucht* along its front.

The subsequent part of the front, about 1,200 meters long that turned to the south, also sloped from the *Altrock Stellung* down to the *Kuchen Schlucht*. On the other side of

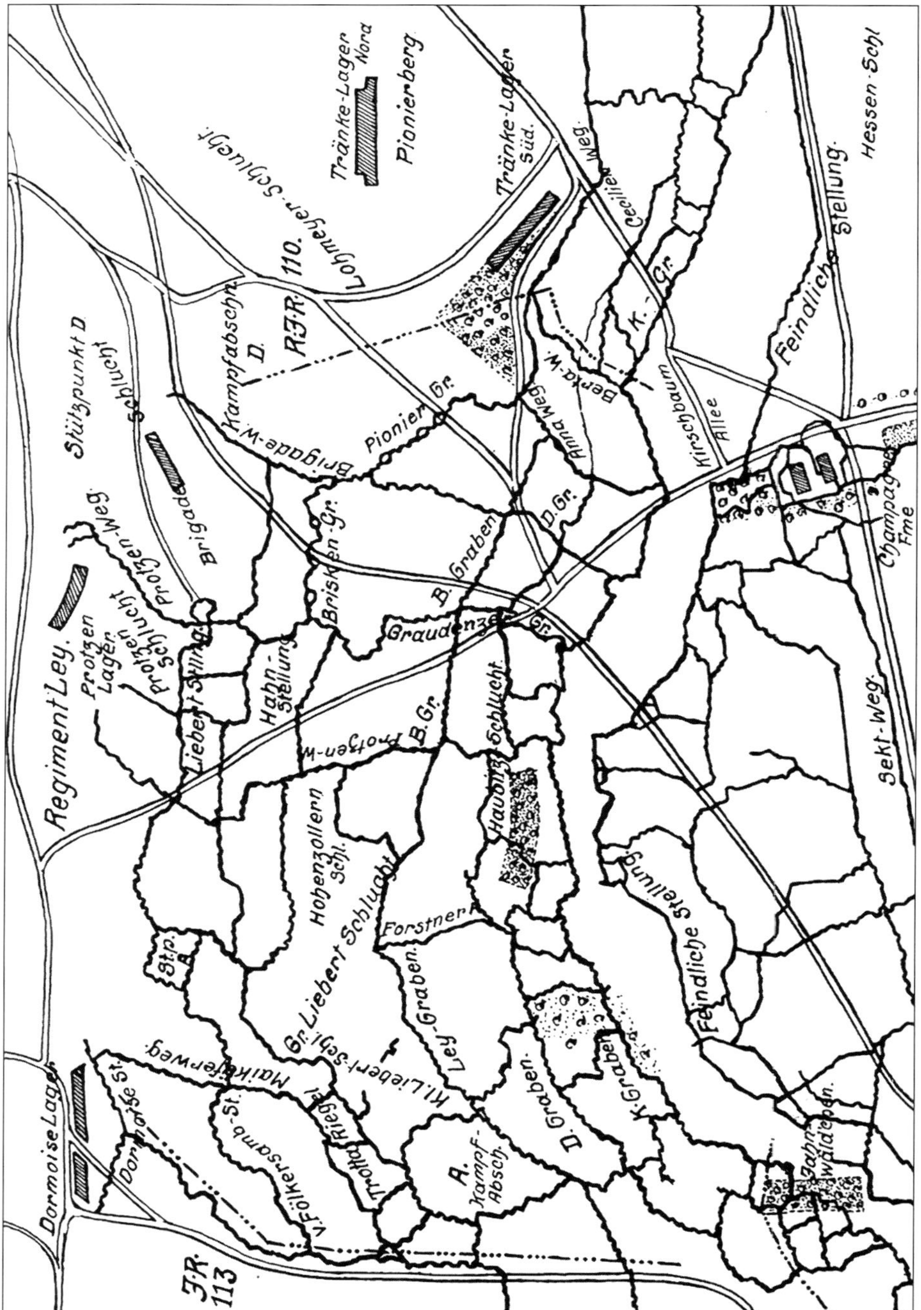

Sector held by RIR 111.

the line, the French were firmly situated at the *Wetterecke*. Between the opposing lines, which were some 30 to 40 meters apart, was a tangle of collapsing trenches, wire obstacles and craters, in which an active patrol war was played out. Two readiness companies stood under the possession of the KTK. in the main opposition line called the *Sprung Stellung*, or the HWL, both of which came from the readiness battalion.

The readiness companies were located with three other companies in the *Dormoise Stellung* by Ripont Mill and at the *Riegel Fleck* south of *Isbert Höhe*. The machine gun companies were located with their battalion sectors in specific zones that were provided with machine gun emplacements near the front lines; likewise the *Minenwerfer* Company that was provided with individual emplacements. It was very evident that the sector had already been hotly fought over. The ground was churned up from the numerous shell impacts, and the trenches were more or less destroyed; of the former wooded pieces only bald stumps rose on the hills. The dugouts did not offer sufficient shell proof cover for the entire garrison, so that the creation of new mined dugouts was necessary. Position kitchens were also planned for each company in order to provide warm food to the men in the front lines.

I/R110 took over as the battle battalion with three companies in the forward line and one company as reserve on the *Grönerberg* in the entire width of the regimental sector. Every method of communication was to be used and had to be tested to ensure that it worked properly. Special attention was also to be paid to furnishing runner and barrage fire chains in the event that all other means of communication failed.

In spite of its appearance the new sector appeared almost peaceful at first. The few light shells, the modest machine gun fire were not even noticed by the old front soldiers, even the level of enemy patrols and larger operations were not excessive. The only real issue with the sector was the weather, which was unpleasant and overcast, and which soon brought storms and rain. There was some excitement on 19 January 1918 as a result of an aerial battle. Following a thrilling battle between a French and German fighter the French aircraft fell burning to the ground and crashed into the company sector of the 4/R110. It was later learned that the enemy pilot had already shot down four German planes, as reported by his commander; but now he had met his fate. Enemy aerial activity had become increasingly lively since 22 January 1918, as did the opposing artillery and mine fire, which for the most part fell more and more on the right company sector of RIR 110. It soon became suspected that the French were planning a major operation.

While these events were taking place at the front, another event was taking place in the rear that would affect the men of RIR 109. On 23 January 1918 the highly admired and especially valued regimental commander, *Oberst von* Baumbach left the regiment. He had assumed command of RIR 109 at the beginning of the war, and shared three and a half years of fighting, hardship and deprivation with his men. There was no battle in which he did not personally participate, no position that he did not repeatedly visit until he knew it in the smallest detail.

He had the ability to recall the names of every man in the regiment even if they had met only once or if he had spoken to them; considered to be a sign of great concern for the welfare of everyone under his command. He was a leader, who led by example and was able to instill the spirit of opposition and fighting in his men, and he was held in high esteem by the rank and file. *Oberst von* Baumbach departed from the regiment with the following words:

> Through the highest Cabinet order I am appointed as the commander of the 12th Infantry Brigade. With it ends the time, in which I was filled with the proud feeling of standing at the head of one of the most beautiful regimens, a regiment, which I once led in the first victorious fighting. An affectionate thank you to the unnumbered men, whose task was made easier through the conscientiousness and bravery, and faithful memory of all fallen heroes! With everyone who belonged to the regiment, Officers as well as men, I always felt companionably connected with you and I gladly remember the pleasant, unforgettable times.
>
> Might the regiment stride further on the path of fame and honor! To everyone who belongs to the regiment, a warm farewell!
>
> Von Baumbach.[1]

His successor, Major *Freiherr* Göler *von* Ravensburg who arrived on 25 January 1918, had moved into the field with the regiment in 1914 as the leader of the 1/R109.

The reserve battalion of RIR 111 remained in the barracks of the *Sydow Lager*, where the men were actively training for the attack battle. The men stood on parade on 27 January for the celebration of the birthday of Kaiser Wilhelm, not realizing that it would be for the very last time. After ten days rest in the camp, where the peaceful countryside was disturbed through sporadic long-range enemy artillery fire, it was ten days in the readiness position and then ten days in the battle trench.

The rest quarters, the *Teschner Lager*, had apparently been a disappointment to the men of the II/R110. The barracks were in the poorest condition possible when the men arrived. Benches and tables barely existed; the boards of the beds and floors were missing, most likely forcibly pulled out and used as firewood. The 'reduced budget' of fuel was admittedly being addressed with a wood cutting squad located far behind in the Wood of Savigny, from where the freshly cut wood was laboriously brought forward. It was necessary to use half of the rest period to bring the camp into good condition, and gradually the accommodations improved, much to the relief of the men. In the remaining time the rest battalion focused on target shooting and practiced the new attack methods over and over again. Before leaving the rest area when the battalions were rotated the regimental commander would review each of the companies as they prepared to leave.

On the afternoon of 28 January 1918 any doubts about the meaning of the recent French activity were gone. The French suddenly attacked RIR 109 in Sector G2 after powerful artillery preparation fire. The French succeeded in penetrating into the first line east of the *Hermann Weg* using flamethrowers. However, he became thrown back through a counterattack by the 1/R109. One flamethrower, hundreds of hand grenades and other captured material fell into the hands of the regiment. The enemy had also simultaneously attacked RIR 110 and RIR 111; however he was also repulsed by these regiments while also leaving behind prisoners:

I already laid a few days in position with the 8th Company in the right company sector. Our forward most trench ran very close along the enemy trench and was only separated from this still through a strong, wide wire obstacle. At many places old, buried trenches led through the wire obstacles directly to the enemy. Our forward most trench was only occupied with sentries and with patrols. The machine guns of the company were set up at raised points. Cold winter weather with frequent fog, and from time to time sunshine about midday prevailed then. There were often fire raids, particularly upon the connection routes. During clear weather the pilots were high, which apparently directed the fire. At midday on 27 January, between 12 and 1.00 p.m. the enemy began to cover the right wing of my company sector and the left of the neighboring company (RIR 109) with mine fire. One of the first mines exploded in the vicinity of the sentry post. *Musketier* Wegmann fell, *Musketier* Stöhr, his comrade, moved back in accordance with orders.

I rushed with both of my battle runners through our trench from sentry to sentry, in order to see to the right and in all instances for orders to arrive. We even heard the further firing of a mine, and now still found time, to save ourselves in a dugout entrance and then earth and stones flew down with a crash into the dugout. The dugout entrance was buried. Fortunately there was a second unburied exit there. The undiminished intense fire allowed one to suspect that the enemy attack was imminent. The waiting and the uncertainty was the worst. Again we remained expecting the attack, but also by the onset of dusk it had not taken place. The company sector had collapsed, a few dugouts were buried. In the evening our artillery covered the enemy position with disturbance fire on my report. Again I went through the position, distributed the necessary repair work and spoke with the platoon and half platoon leaders who were to take incisive action for the counterattack. 'If only they should come, we will show them the light home, *Herr Leutnant*' was the reply of one of the platoon leaders. In the night the usual disturbance fire upon the trench; in the morning was fog: they did not come.

Then, shortly before 2.00 o'clock, powerful drum fire fell upon us like a blow upon the entire company sector. It was immediately clear to us that the French would now attack. Therefore I continued to fire off the barrage fire signal. *Musketier* Paul Schneider, the signal thrower, waited in the strongest drum fire with the greatest courage. The machine gun in the third line fired away over us against the French waves advancing upon us from out the hill. They vanished in the trench, moved back hastily and left behind hand grenades, fog bombs, Sulphur bombs, bundled explosive charges and objects of equipment in large quantities. The *Stosstrupps* of the company went forth independently, and would soon report that the patrol line was free from the enemy. Meanwhile, on the suggestion of *Unteroffizier* Rank a patrol under the command of *Musketier* Kempf with *Gefreiten* Kruse, the *Musketiers* Betz, Letzeisen, Stöhr and Beuter were sent by the platoon leader of the right platoon in the *Dresdner Weg*. There they suddenly bumped into a French patrol behind a traverse in the strength of one sergeant and four men. Close combat broke out, during which *Musketier* Kemp was wounded. *Gefreiter* Kruse took over the leadership. The French sergeant was wounded by a hand grenade splinter and surrendered; the remaining French threw smoke bombs and vanished outside the trench in the direction of the enemy position. A *Stosstrupp* under the command of *Unteroffizier* Rank captured two flamethrowers and got a French sergeant out of a dugout in the forward most trench, who had escaped from the artillery fire there.

The interrogation of the two prisoners would confirm the French *Régiment d'Infanterie* 18 (36th Infantry Division). Five assault groups in the strength of 88 men were to advance after a short artillery preparation until in our 2nd line and then roll this up. They found our trench empty, turned back and ran into our barrage fire. The patrol had losses from the machine guns. There one man fell; the sergeant came back into our trench and with it became captured.

Leutnant der Reserve Heuss, Company commander 8/R110.[2]

The enemy attack on 28 January 1918 was directed against RIR 109 on the right and against IR 235 on the left. As a result of the attack, the position of RIR 111 became threatened on both flanks, while the regimental sector lay under strong enemy fire and became covered with a smoke screen. The I/R111 had effectively prevented the enemy from breaking into the regimental position from out of the *Sprung Stellung* against the Butte de Mesnil with the fire from two heavy and two light machine guns. Elevated battle readiness had been ordered and the III/R111 moved out of the *Sydow Lager* by the afternoon and sent to the readiness position in the ravines west of Gratreuil, where the companies spent a quite cold night in modest housing.

The Army Report from 29 January 1918 did mention the recent fighting in a short statement: 'Our position between the road leading from Somme-Py and Ripont to the southeast lay under powerful fire in the early afternoon. Under its protection French infantry, with flamethrowers in a strong reconnaissance thrust against the front at several places. They were thrown back with heavy losses, in part in front of our obstacles, in part in close combat. Some prisoner remained in our hands. Several flamethrowers were captured.' Commendations and awards came from every level of command, up to Army Group Crown Prince. The regimental order from 29 January 1918 from RIR 110 closed with the sentence: 'The day was a proud page in the history of the II Battalion.'

On the same day another beloved and brave officer, *Hauptmann von* Wolff, left RIR 109. He had been assigned to the General Staff of the 220th Infantry Division. His command, the III/R109, greatly admired him, and he left the regiment with the awareness that he would always live in the hearts of all who belonged to his 'Grenadier Battalion.' The command of the III/R109 was taken over by *Hauptmann* Schulemann.

The French were apparently not yet finished with their local attacks. Soon after midnight on 31 January 1918 the enemy made two raids against the front of RIR 111 upon the *Prinz Karl Graben* at the left wing. They were repulsed by a picket outpost of the 3/R111 located in the *Sattel Graben*.

At the beginning of February, RIR 109 was under strength, both in the number of officers and men. In the first days of the month *Leutnants* Theissen, Croon, Motzkus, Krückner and 37 men arrived at the regiment as replacements. While not the numbers

RIR 111 officer in the Champagne. (Source: Author's collection)

that were required to bring RIR 109 back to full strength, any increase of the regimental strength was welcome.

On 3 February 1918 the companies of the I/R110 were already packing, because the relief was to take place on the same evening. Then, at 11.30 a.m., rumors spread through the camp like a wild fire; 'The commander-in-chief, His Imperial Highness the Crown Prince, was to visit the regiment'. His visit came as a complete surprise and after he visited the replacement regimental commander, Major Jena, he met with the men of the I/R110. While the Crown Prince reviewed the I/R110 on the grounds of the *Teschner Schlucht* he also made a special presentation to a number of men in the battalion. He had personally distributed three Iron Cross I Class and fifteen Iron Cross II Class medals to those Other Ranks that were present.

Then, all of the men who belonged to the battalion who were at the presentation were informally grouped on request of the Crown Prince. His Imperial Highness greeted the regiment and spoke of his appreciation for the fine work it had performed on 28 January 1918. After the awards were distributed the commander-in-chief spoke to the men. When he was finished, three loud hurrahs roared over the camp. The Crown Prince had talked with the Other Ranks in the most amiable manner, distributed cigarettes and allowed himself to be photographed amidst the men. It was reported there was loud laughing, pleased and thrilled faces wherever one looked. After staying 1 ½ hours His Imperial Highness drove off to visit other parts of the division.

At the beginning of February the patrols sent out by RIR 111 noticed increased activity and traffic inside the French trenches, especially at the *Wetterecke*; they also reported the presence of gas cylinders in the wire obstacles. Closer reconnaissance of the suspicious canisters and the enemy infantry were impossible because of the exceptional attentiveness of the French sentries. There was a corresponding increase in artillery and mine fire falling on the German positions; another enemy operation appeared to be imminent.

Starting from 10 February 1918 the French artillery activity became stronger once again. The French fired on the *Paderborn Weg*, *Hasenhügel* and *Geyer Weg*, the *Infanterie Schlucht* and the *Grönerberg* with medium and heavy caliber shells on a daily basis. He also held the *Infanterie Schlucht* and the *Höllen Tal* under fire with gas shells, particularly during the night and in the early morning hours, also on a daily basis.

13 February 1918 started off as a rainy, misty day. Strong French artillery fire began to fall on Sector D at 10 a.m. At 1.15 p.m. the artillery fire suddenly increased to drum fire, which at approximately 5.00 p.m. shifted over on the *Sprung Stellung* in Sector D, with the rear terrain lying under gas shells. At 11.30 a.m. the III/R110 ordered elevated battle-readiness for the 12/R110 as the connection company and at 3.30 p.m. the order was also sent to the other companies of the battalion. In the course of the afternoon the fire increased to the highest strength, and at 5.15 p.m. two French battalions attacked in several dense waves from the *Pionier Schlucht*, the *Kuchen Schlucht* and the *Prinz Karl Graben* against the middle sector of the 8/R111 and to the right against the left wing of the 5/R111. The pickets in front of the 5/R111 quickly became overrun, and French infantry penetrated Sector D by the *Wetterecke* in the width of two company sectors and advanced until they had reached the fourth line. French blocking fire blanketed the *Haupt Riegel Grönerberg* and *Hasen Riegel* in the sector of RIR 110 and all hollows lay under gas fire. As a portent of things to come, a report in the New York Herald dated 15 February 1918 mentioned that for the first time on French soil American batteries were participating in the artillery preparation during this attack.

The defensive measures by RIR 111 were being directed by the KTK, *Hauptmann* Glöckner. The German batteries and close combat methods attempted to hold down the enemy through disturbance fire. Once the French penetration of the German line became known, the 12/R110 immediately blocked off all trenches leading toward Sector D. It then took an officers patrol between two and three hours to re-establish the connection with the connection company of RIR 111, and the connection with the KTK The strong disturbance fire upon the positions of RIR 110 and the rearward connections continued on the following day. The II/R110 (the Rest Battalion) became moved forward to the hill where the Regimental command post was located. The companies of the Readiness Battalion, the I/R110, become accommodated in the *Infanterie Schlucht*, in the *Haupt Riegel* and in the *Dormoise Stellung* on the northern shore of the Dormoise for the protection of the left flank of the regiment. The II/R110 also provided work groups for the neighboring RIR 111.

The French troops had penetrated the third line, the main opposition line, and overpowered the garrison in the shattered battlefield. The 7/R111 which was behind in the *Sattel Graben* and at the *Fürstenberg Weg* under *Leutnant* Stauss prevented any further advance, primarily with the use of their light machine guns. However the trenches lay under such heavy fire that the *Stosstrupps* placed for the counter thrust were not able to advance. Machine gun nest Detlef of the 2MG/R111 in the *Fürstenberg Weg* under *Unteroffizier* Safferling deserves particular mention in the defense of this position. The machine gun was heavily bombarded and the gun-leader became wounded and the machine gun was damaged through shell splinters. Despite this, the gun continued to fire and had visible success against the enemy troop in the direction of the *Wetterecke.*

At the *Altrock Sap* the pickets of the 8/R111 under *Leutnant* Jöckle, stood on the parapet while firing at the enemy, until the light machine gun broke down, and they had to yield to the superior enemy strength. In the fierce close combat *Leutnant* Jöckle became wounded and the French reached the main opposition line. The leader of the 8/R111, *Leutnant* Beck, immediately began a counter thrust with his reserves and threw back sections of the enemy, which had pressed forth from the *Altrock Sap* against the *Sehne Graben.* The fighting at the 8/R111 became outstandingly supported through the machine gun nests *Diethelm* in the *Koppel Schloss* at the *Sattel Graben* and *Bonifazius* in the western *Sprung Stellung*, which despite the heaviest fire against the *Kuchen* and *Pionier Schlucht* had a noticeable effect on the French assault troops. One gun Captain, *Unteroffizier* Schwer, and five men of his crew were wounded in the fighting.

Two light *Minenwerfer* located in the *Sprung Stellung* and light machine guns of the 6/R111 located in the *Teschner Graben* joined in the fighting. The 6th Company, which was lying under strong artillery fire, did not become directly attacked. The company leader, *Leutnant* Gretz, then ordered *Vizefeldwebel* Reiser to block off the trench leading toward the enemy with barricades. Patrols were sent out to establish the connection with the 8/R111 and to determine the exact situation on the company flank.

The battalion command post at the Markgraf hill close behind the *Sprung Stellung* was especially covered with strong fire, so that every connection forward and to the rear had been broken. Runners could no longer make it through the curtain of fire and of those sent out earlier, none had returned. A patrol that was sent out under *Leutnant* Behrens on orders from the regiment in order to clarify the situation at the front was unsuccessful, because all of the participants were soon wounded.

In the course of the night *Hauptmann* Glökner did eventually succeed in obtaining a picture of the events taking place in the battle front after great effort, which he sent to *Leutnant* Kirsten, 7/R111, in a message. The report indicated that the enemy had become fixed in the main opposition line from the *Altrock Sap* up to the left regimental border and was sending out patrols against the *Sehne Graben. Leutnant* Beck, along with the remnants of the 8th Company, occupied the crater terrain in the area of the *Altrock Schlucht*, which were reinforced through Groups from the 6th and 10/R111. A barricade was erected near the *Altrock* Sap to prevent any further French advance.

Beck's small contingent had established a tenuous connection with the 6/R111 on the left in the *Wald Graben*; there was no connection to any friendly troops on the right. The 7/R111, whose position had become the front line, secured the eastern *Sprung Stellung* and the *Fürstenberg Weg.* Behind the 6th and 8/R111 lay the 10/R111 under *Leutnant* Freudenberger in the western *Sprung Stellung*, who was supposed to advance with a *Stosstrupp* through the trench of IR 65 to the *Sehne Graben* and in doing so establish the connection with the 8/R111. Subsequently on the right the 9th and 11/R111 were moved forward in the night as the rear support out of the gassed Dormoise valley and from Isbert hill that was lying under heavy French fire.

The 9/R111 under *Leutnant* Stoffler took on the protection of the *Wald Graben, Sattel Graben* and *Fürstenberg Weg* with sentry outposts. Everything now hinged on a quick and successful counterattack in order to throw the enemy back before he could become established. However, the strength required for the security personnel for the destroyed *Sprung Stellung* was too weak to undertake an immediate counterattack. The higher commands also realized that additional men were required and issued orders to postpone the attack for the time being.

The night was then used by reconnaissance troops under *Leutnants* Frey and Wiedhorn, who were to advance and establish connections with the neighboring units. While the reconnaissance was taking place, the troops had to be reorganized and become reformed as the commands had become mixed together during the fighting. The 12/R111 under *Leutnant* Höfler moved into the *Dormoise Stellung*. The I/R111 left the Sydow Camp and finally reached the ravine west of Gratreuil after a march impeded by rain and muddy ground, where the companies were made ready for the upcoming counterattack. This was followed by the fire of the German batteries, which became directed on the new enemy lines.

At 3.00 p.m. on 13 February 1918 the French had also bombarded the positions of RIR 109, in part with gas shells. RIR 109 became ordered to elevated battle readiness as a result of this attack and the I/R109, which had barely moved into rest quarters, was immediately moved forward and held in readiness. However, there was no enemy attack in the sector of RIR 109. On the night of 13 February 1918 the troops in Sector D succeeded in pressing the enemy back into the third line.

The decision to retake the lost trench piece was made by the KTK and by the regiment, which had its battle headquarters in Ripont Mill. On 14 February 1918 the necessary reconnaissance operation would be carried out, and if possible, to also roll up the trench pieces occupied by the enemy.

The positioning of the men required for the attack proved to be difficult, because the access routes to the front were entirely leveled and were still lying under strong fire. The reconnaissance had also determined that the adversary had been reinforced and was very alert. Everything appeared to indicate that another enemy advance was expected, so the rear lying parts of RIR 111 were moved closer to the front. The 12/R111 came into the vicinity of the *Sprung Stellung* and in its place two companies from the I/R111, which had previously moved up to Isbert Hill, became moved forward even further by Groups into the *Dormoise Stellung*. The 1MG/R111 occupied the machine gun nests in the terrain south of Knobelsdorf Hill. On the night of 14/15 February 1918 strong disturbance fire continued to blanket the terrain, and a large number of the patrols sent out on reconnaissance became involved in local fire fights with French patrols.

The 9/R111 occupied the battle line from the *Wald Graben* until the *Fürstenberg Weg*. The 7/R111 was in the 2nd line in the eastern part of the *Sprung Stellung*. The remnants of the 8/R111 became taken back with the existing parts of the 5/R111 to Ripont Mill. The 12/R111, which was struck by a direct hit from a shell while on the way, moved into the *Sprung Stellung* between the 10th and 11/R111. The I/R111 had moved the 2nd and 3/R111 forward to Ripont Mill, while the 1/R111 remained in the *Dormoise Stellung* and the 4/R111 remained on Isbert Hill. During the day the *Sprung Stellung* was bombarded under pilot direction, and the fire increased towards evening to such an extent that a new French attack appeared to be imminent. Listening patrols remained on alert but the enemy infantry behaved quietly during the following day.

The 28th Reserve Division immediately conducted the necessary counter-measures in order to recapture the lost terrain. With the loss of men, the garrison of the regimental sectors had been reorganized in order to maintain the defense in depth and support was being provided by the artillery. *Schlepptrupps* were formed in order to bring up the necessary replacements for the shortages of ammunition needed for the counterattack. A *Schlepptrupp* in the strength of 110 men was formed from troops in RIR 109 under the command of *Leutnants* Frisch and Eyssen and placed in possession of RIR 111.

News of the recent setback was quickly sent home by at least one officer in RIR 111, Oberleutnant Erwin Boy, RIR 111. In addition to discussing such mundane issues as a hoped for furlough, Boy apparently also let slip that there was a large offensive in the works. Who knows what might have happened if such a letter had fallen into the wrong hands?

> Oberleutnant Boy RIR111 Reg. Bar
> 14.2.18
>
> Dear Parents!
> Our hitherto tolerably calm position has recently become quite lively. Days of artillery fire yesterday followed strong French attacks, losing our front trenches. We are now very busy with preparations for the counterattack. I'm still doing very well. Since today the furloughs are closed and it will probably remain during the next months. So I am with the question of when I should drive off, and unfortunately have to let you travel alone to Hamburg. After happily surviving the offensive, the great peace furlough will probably come soon. Of the offensive, my regiment will not be there at first, because we are not sufficiently well-formed and are now tied here. For the newspaper that always arrives on time with Papa's greeting best thanks.
> Heartfelt Greetings Erwin.[3]

On 17 February 1918 the artillery began to fire upon the enemy positions, at times under aerial observation, in the direction of Klitzing Hill. On the morning of 18 February 1918 parts of RIR 111 and RIR 236 stood ready for the counterattack. However the preparations for the attack had not remained concealed from the enemy; who at 6.00 a.m. placed active artillery fire in a very wide area and took the German battery positions behind the steep slope by Habicht Hill and on the *Türkenberg* under fire with heavy and medium caliber shells. Despite the French fire, at 6.25 a.m. the German guns began the preparation fire for the attack that was being supported through the heavy and light machine guns of the regiments firing upon the enemy position on the ridge west of Tahure. The counterattack then took place which successfully recaptured the lost trench parts and captured 125 prisoners. The 3MG/R110 was given the task to support the counterattack by firing across on to Klitzing Hill.

However the newly recaptured position was soon lost again in the enemy fire and counterthrust. This new French assault was then pressed back by *Stosstrupps* from RIR 111 during which 28 Frenchmen suddenly appeared in front of the 12/R110 and were taken prisoner. At 4.00 p.m. a second German attack was undertaken, which however was smothered in the French artillery fire. Afterward, while the enemy infantry behaved very quietly, there was strong disturbance fire from the French artillery that lasted a time further.

On 18 February 1918 RIR 111 was ordered to counterattack and recapture the trenches lost on 13 February 1918 in connection with the left neighbor, IR 236. The *Stosstrupps* taking part in the counterattack were put into position in the night using every possible precaution to avoid making any sounds that might give them away to the French; sandbags were wound around the men's boots to muffle any noise. The men of RIR 111 went into action with firm confidence of a successful attack. The *Sturmabteilung* at the right wing, existing out of the 2nd and 4/R111, the *Stosstrupp* of a *Sturmkompagnie* and one half the 4/*Pionier* 16, broke forth out of the area of the *Wald Graben* under *Hauptmann* Wöhrle. The *Sturmabteilung* of *Hauptmann* Coester, III/R111, consisting of the 11th and 12/R111, two *Stosstrupps* of the *Sturmkompagnie* and also one half the 4/*Pionier* 16 assembled at the *Fürstenberg Weg* went forward to the *Sprung Stellung*. Lying behind the assault groups, the 6th, 10th, 9th, 7/R111 under *Hauptmann* Glöckner, acted as the security garrison, while the rest of the 5th and 8/R111 performed service as dispatch runners. The 1st and 3/R111 stood by Ripont Mill As the regimental reserve, which carried up ammunition and construction materials to the *Sturmabteilungen* in the night under great effort.

6.30 a.m. was the time set for the start of the assault. Four minutes before this time the combined fire of the artillery and *Minenwerfer* would fall with a blow upon the enemy batteries, which became gassed, and on the trenches, and from these to spring forward as a roll of fire. The French were lying in wait for just this moment as the enemy batteries immediately placed barrage fire on the German positions:

> Immediately at the commencement of our own fire *Leutnant* Geng, the leader of the 2/R111, jumped up upon the cover with the shout 'forward' and so brought his company still without losses through the barrage fire. The *Stosstrupps* of *Leutnant* Wolf, *Offizier Stellvertreter* Mutter and *Vizefeldwebel* Joos stormed along the 1b line. The trench, which was closed through a barrier of tree boughs, soon had to be left. They went further over the open field. At the *Altrock* Sap, where they found a trap door, there was stronger resistance to overpower. The first prisoners would be extracted out of the dugouts. *Offizier Stellvertreter* Mutter tells the following about his experience here: 'Because of the darkness and the powder-vapor as well as the leaping up and running in the zig-zag formed trench I did not know in the moment in which direction I should allow the French to be taken away. After some to and fro I was relieved when an old, small Frenchman, in that cried to me: '*Allemand* there' and with the hand indicated the direction. The prisoner hereupon marched at a fast speed in the implied direction.'[4]

The *Sturmtrupps* divided and then rolled up the *Riegel Graben* fighting and ran towards the *65er Graben*; with it they captured a further 133 Frenchmen. However the opposition strengthened, and a powerful French counter thrust broke forth. The losses began o increase; *Leutnant* Geng was fatally wounded and became carried to the rear on he back of *Vizefeldwebel* Heid. Ammunition and hand grenades became scarce. The platoon of the 4/R111 that was following as support, was shattered from the barrage fire. Finally the attackers could no longer hold the position and gradually fell back into the main opposition line. The defenses were barely organized when the adversary attacked once again. What hand grenades were still available were thrown against the advancing enemy assault troops. Two light machine guns in the 1b line opened fire into the French line and the concentrated fire dispersed the enemy troops.

However, despite the extra firepower there could be no thought of holding the position without additional infantry support. After the troops had struggled with the French for 1 ¼ hours, they moved back into the exit position in an orderly fashion, while the machine guns held the enemy in check. *Leutnant* Wolf attempted to roll up the *Altrock* Sap to the east with part of his platoon one more time; however he ended up in close combat with a superior enemy force and became cut off after courageous resistance.

The men from his platoon last saw him with *Hornist* Lebrecht, both men were firing while standing on top of the cover. One platoon of the 4/R111 under *Leutnant* Schuh had already attempted to penetrate into the *Altrock* sap previously. Three separate times the troops under cries of 'Hurrah' went against the sap in the flanking enemy machine gun fire over open terrain, and forced the enemy to retreat; however, every time they became forced back in the enemy counter thrust by superior numbers with hand grenades and machine gun fire. It was later determined that the enemy garrison of the sap consisted of a full company. Considering the disparity in numbers, the *pioniers*, supported by further parts of the 4/R111, did not succeed in breaking the opposition.

After the assault the remnants of the 2/R111 were assembled in the *Teschner Graben*, the 4th Company under *Leutnant* Dunkel occupied and held the *Wald Graben,* while patrols remained in contact with the enemy. At 11.00 a.m. the 3/R111 under *Leutnant* Büchner arrived in the *Teschner Graben*, which had already come under enemy fire during the march up to the front that had been directed by French pilots. The situation was too unclear for the newly arrived company to undertake an immediate counter attack; moreover enemy artillery covered the sector with scattered fire.

The results were similar by the *Sturmabteilung* of the III/R111. The *Stosstrupps* and the forward most parts of the 11th and 12/R111 fought from the *Fürstenberg Weg* until to the *Riegel Graben* and through the *ABC Graben*. Prisoners were extracted out of the dugouts, and the light machine guns were placed in position in order to bring fire against the escaping French. Captured French machine guns had been made unserviceable using hand grenades. The fighting took time, and so the fire wave of supporting artillery fire had meanwhile moved further away. Once the artillery fire had moved forward, flanking enemy machine guns became very disagreeable as these were no longer under bombardment and were free to fire into the German flank.

French counter thrusts were taking place, and during the time the position was being rolled up severe close combat flared up at different points, which caused strong losses on both sides. Among the losses was *Leutnant* Höfler, the leader of the 12/R111 and both of his platoon leaders, *Leutnant* Schuldenzucker and *Vizefeldwebel* Sälzler, who were wounded. The support of the 11/R111 was unable to come through the barrage fire and

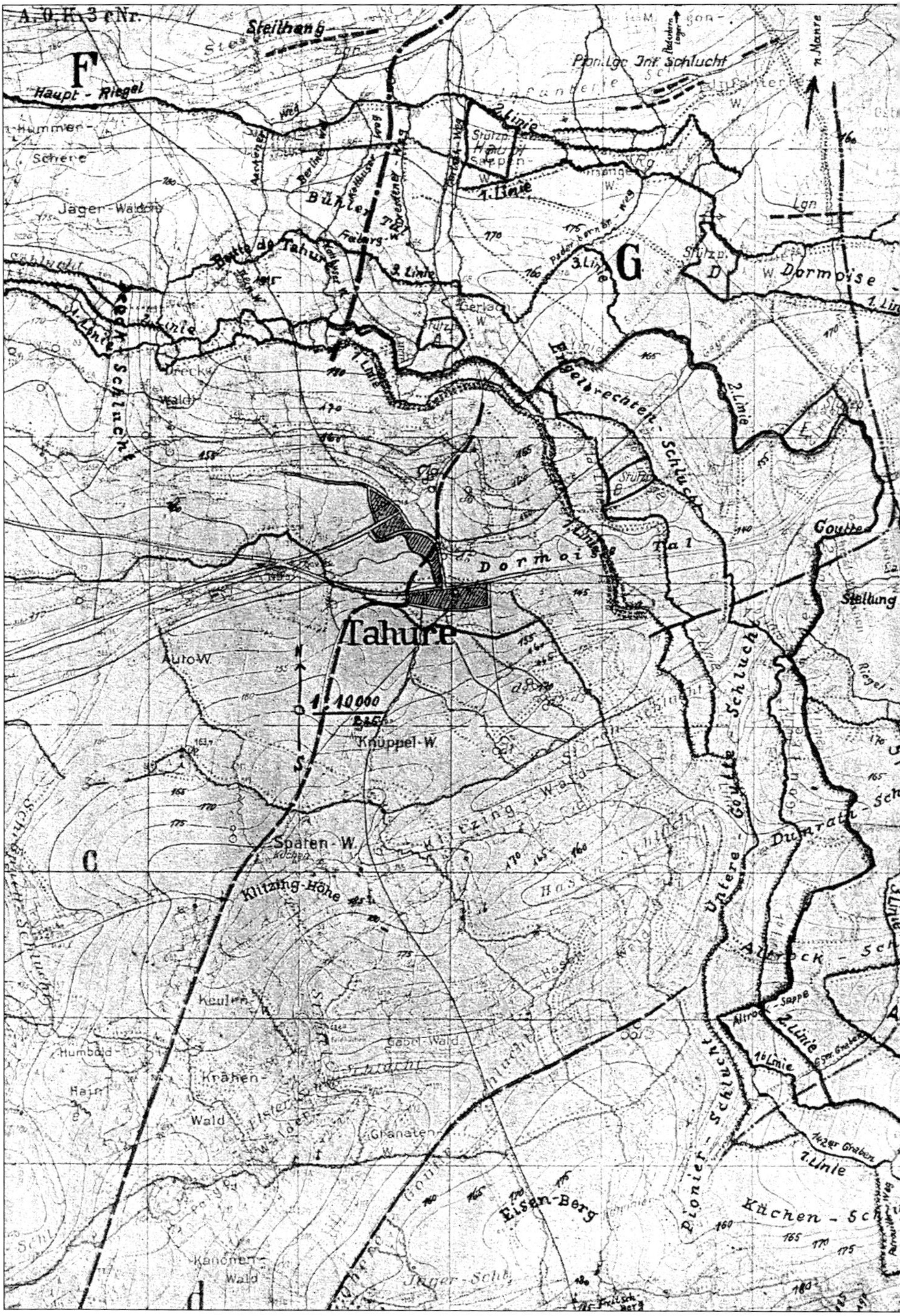

Tahure Sector occupied by the 28th Reserve Division.

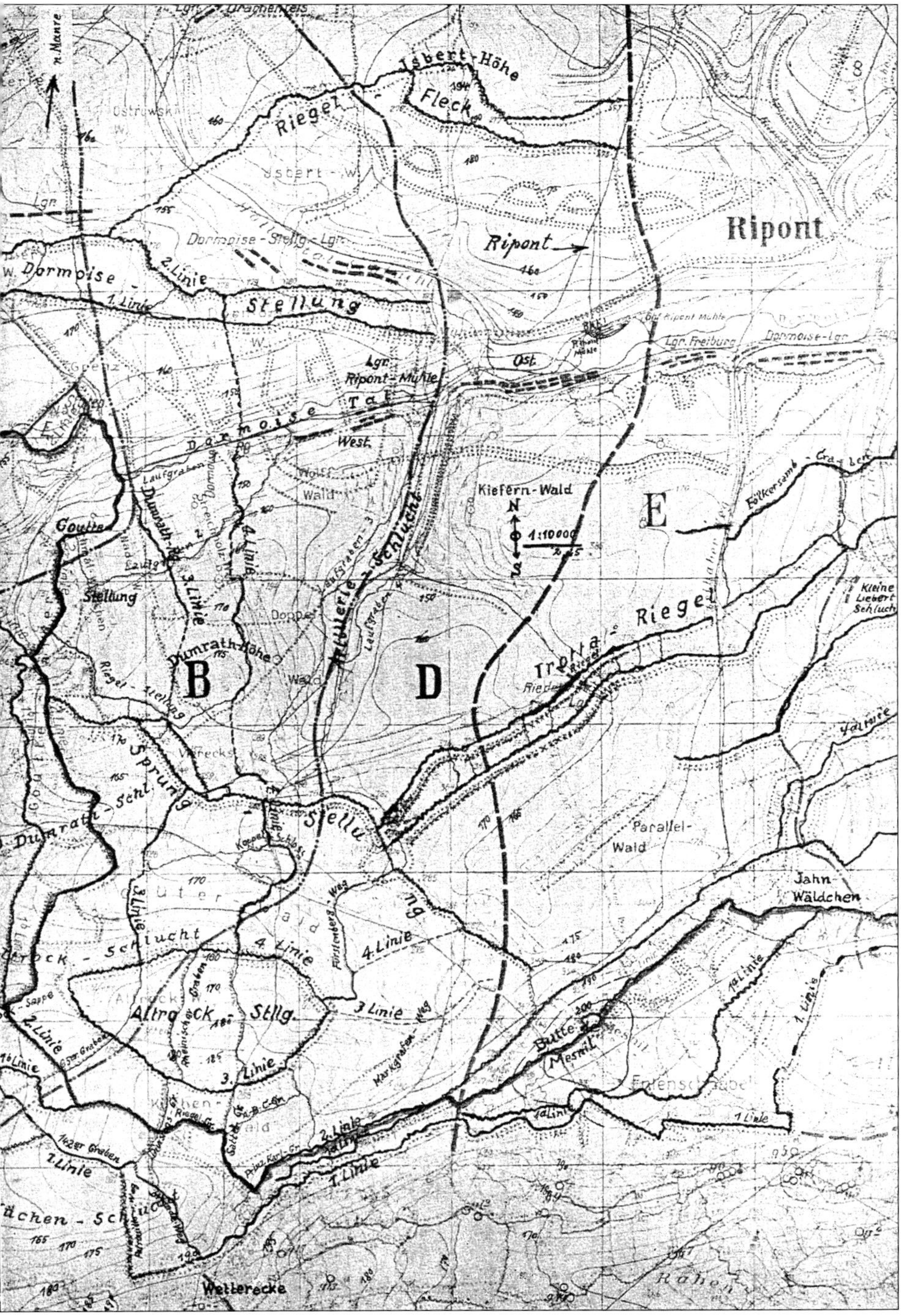
Isbert-Höhe
Fleck
Riegel
Ripont
Ripont
Dormoise-Stellg.-Lgr.
Dormoise-
2. Linie
1. Linie
Stellung
Lgr. Freiburg
Dormoise-Lgr.
Ost
Lgr.
Ripont-Mühle
Dormoise
Tal
West
Laufgraben
Kiefern-Wald
N
1:10000
E
Artillerie-Schlucht
Goutte
Stellung
Dumrath-Höhe
B
D
Riegel
Parallel-
Wald
Jahn-
Wäldchen
Sprung
Dumrath-Schl.
Stellu
4. Linie
4. Linie
3. Linie
3. Linie
Altrock Stllg.
Butte
Mesnil
1 Linie
2. Linie
1. Linie
Wetterecke

the company leader, *Leutnant* Rosenfeld, had been buried just after the beginning of the bombardment. Without this support, the *Stosstrupps*, whose hand grenades had run out, and light machine guns had been placed out of action, could no longer retain the upper hand over the enemy.

The remnants were forced to yield and retire back to the former main opposition line against which the French rushed at uselessly; losing a large number of men killed and wounded as well as additional prisoners. *Leutnant* Wiedorn assembled the dispersed parts of the 11/R111 and was going to attempt to advance from out of the *Sprung Stellung* through the enemy fire block to provide much needed support. While Wiedorn was still making his preparations, the enemy artillery fire increased, and shortly following, about 8.30 a.m., the French advanced in dense waves against the remnants of the 11th and 12/R111 as well as the *Sturmabteilungen* that were still firmly in the 3rd Line. The small group fought back desperately; and while only one man was reported as missing, most of the other men were wounded through revolver shots and hand grenade splinters.

The odds were too great and the combined units were unable to hold the position alone; there was nothing left to do but to give up the recaptured crater terrain again. Individual spirited men held back the French long enough so that all of the wounded were saved. *Krankenträger* Martin and Helms especially stood out for their care of their comrades. Meanwhile, the 1/R111 arrived by the III/R111 as rear support. The company sent out a patrol under *Leutnant* Schwarz and *Unteroffizier* Zeller, who with the troops of *Leutnant* Eckstein, 11/R111, established a connection in front in the 3rd Line. This operation resulted restoring the situation as it had been before the attack. The remains of the 11/R111, *pioniers* and *Minenwerfer* Other Ranks manned the positions in front of and in the eastern *Sprung Stellung*.

Brigade ordered that the attack would be attempted again after renewed artillery preparation at 3.30 p.m. On the right, the I/R111 positioned two *Stosstrupps* of the 3/R111 under *Offizier Stellvertreter* Wurth in the *Wald Graben*, on the left the I/R111 was ordered to advance from the *Fürstenberg Weg* against the 3rd Line. There was little time available for the essential reconnaissance of the attack field. The assembly of the *Sturmtrupps* in the full brightness of day in the destroyed and badly damaged trenches was observed by numerous French pilots; any chance of surprise had been lost. As a result heavy French fire was already placed upon the entire sector shortly after 3.00 p.m., which prevented every attempt by the 3/R111 to advance at the ordered time. It was not until later when *Offizier Stellvertreter* Wurth was able to proceed against the *Altrock Sap* and make the determination that it was still occupied by the enemy.

At 3.30 p.m. the 1/R111 under *Leutnants* Winterer and Schwarz swarmed into the wood on the right and on the left of the *Fürstenberg Weg* and already had suffered heavy losses through two direct hits. Meanwhile, the 3rd Line was densely occupied by the enemy and equipped with numerous machine guns. When the skirmish line left the wood, it received the strongest fire; also a pilot joined in the fighting with his machine guns. It was simply not possible to storm through the 300 meters of open ground; only one *Stosstrupp* managed to come forward in the shell holes of the *Fürstenberg Weg*, without however being able to penetrate into the enemy position. *Leutnant* Winterer quickly decided that the operation was hopeless and called off the attack. He then allowed his men to recover the numerous wounded and dead lying all around.

The night of 18/19 February 1918, during which the enemy artillery fire continued unabated and the machine guns sprayed fire over the positions, the time was used to rearrange the battle-tired German troops. On the right the I/R111 occupied the sector north of the *Wald Graben* with the 1st Company, while the 3rd and 4/R111 were assigned to the defenses. One company from RIR 110 lay behind in the western *Sprung Stellung*. The remnants of the 2/R111, which were assigned to the remains of the 12/ R111 under *Leutnant* Frey occupied the line up to the left regimental border. One company from RIR 110 moved into the eastern *Sprung Stellung*. The 6th and 7/R111 became the security personnel in the *Dormoise Stellung*; the 5th and 8/R111 provided hauling duty from Ripont Mill. Fortunately 19 February proceeded quietly, apart from some fire raids. By evening the relief began through RIR 110, and RIR 111 took over the right neighboring sector opposite Tahure that RIR 110 had previously occupied.

Following the fighting, the II/R110 relieved all parts of RIR 111 forward of the *Sprung Stellung* On the night of 19/20 February 1918 and occupied the new forward line from communication trench 3, *Waldgraben*, *Koppel Schloss* until *Fürstenberg Weg* and *Markgraf Höhe*. the III/R110 was relieved by the III/R111 and was placed in Sector D, Ripont Mill on 20 February 1918 as the readiness battalion. On the night of 20/21 February 1918 the I/R110 took over the *Sprung Stellung* in Sector D from the III/R111. On the evening of 21 February 1918 the III/R110 was relieved by the III/R105 and the I/R110 was relieved by the II/143. The two battalions of RIR 110 then marched to the *Teschner Lager* and the *Brandenburg Lager* while the II/R110 remained in the position.

The enemy still sat opposite in the *Wetterecke* which the regiment left to the succeeding one. When examining the reasons why the trench sections were lost on 13 February 1918, and that were not recaptured on 18 February 1918, a number of problems were exposed. At the beginning of February RIR 111 was more concerned about small enterprises and had not taken note of the indications that a large enemy attack was imminent. When this was discussed it was determined that there were insufficient reserves behind the battle front that were needed if the lost positions were to be retaken in an immediate counterattack.

The strength of RIR 111 alone was not sufficient in order to guarantee any success in the counterattacks. On 18 February 1918 the enemy had recognized the preparations being made for the attack and became reinforced accordingly. The preparation fire of the artillery and *Minenwerfer* was not adequate in preparing the enemy position to be stormed and to hold down the French batteries at the same time. On the day of the attack the enemy had superior strength by men and materials and was able to keep the upper hand. The regiment, leaders as well as the men, on both days of fighting, had fully performed their duty and fought in the position entrusted to them, as long as their strength lasted: The losses in RIR 111 amounted to: three officers, 33 men killed; three officers, 140 men wounded; two officers, 154 men missing.

The official tally of prisoners and booty brought in by RIR 111 was one officer and 63 men from two French regiments and one machine gun. The actual number of prisoners captured was higher, but as many of them went back through the sector of RIR 110 and were reported by this regiment.

The sector slowly returned to a period of calm in the days following the heavy fighting. While the infantry remained quiet the artillery remained active on both sides of the line. On 23 February 1918 a hauling party from RIR 109 that was carrying mines from Ripont Mill into the position, ended up in an enemy fire raid with gas shells, from which *Leutnant* Schuhmann and 30 *Unteroffiziere* and Other Ranks had to be transferred to the hospital because of gas sickness.

As a result of the recent enemy success by the *Wetterecke* the men of the 28th Reserve Division were placed on alert in order to avoid similar attacks and there was increased observation of the adversary. Patrols were sent into the foreground every night, which found the enemy to be very vigilant; even the smallest sound resulted in a salvo of hand grenades and numerous light balls being fired off, especially in the *Dreck Schlucht*.

The new position between the Butte de Tahure and Dumrath hill, taken over by RIR 111 in the days from 20 to 23 February 1918, strongly resembled the neighboring sector that had just been abandoned. The battle line became occupied with three companies of the III/R111. In order to provide relief for RIR 110, which was being prepared for an attack that would recapture the trenches lost on 13 February 1918, the 6th and 8/R111became placed at the western slope of Dumrath Hill from 27 February 1918, therefore in part of the former regimental sector. The Readiness battalion lay on the *Groenerberg* as well as at the *Infanterie Schlucht* situated north of it and at the *Drachenfels*.

The reserve battalion of RIR 111 was unable to rest while in the rear because of the possibility of further French attacks. The battalion remained in elevated battle readiness and was transferred to a position north of the Breitfirst (*Paderborn Lager, Uehsinger Lager, Russischen Schlucht, Tartaren Schlucht*). By 27 February 1918 two companies were also moved forward into the *Infanterie Schlucht*.

On 20 February 1918 RIR 110 had received the task to recapture and hold the trench recently taken by the enemy in cooperation with the neighboring IR 234. The area that was to be recaptured was 1,200 meters wide and from 500-800 meters deep, a sizeable area under any circumstances. The deployment and subsequent relief of the regiment gave the men who were to execute the attack the opportunity to rest. In addition, the troops would receive training on a practice work that was a copy of the target area. When the proposition had been approved, the *Sturmtruppen* were chosen from the I and III/R110 and on 21 February 1918 they were moved back out of the front line. The 1st and 4/*Pionier* Battalion 16, two squads from the *Sturmbataillon* with four *Flammenwerfer* and two artillery escort officers were assigned to the regiment for the operation.

The size of the attack demanded very thorough preparations. The II/R110, which was still in the front line position had to conduct the necessary reconnaissance which included:

1. Course of the forward most enemy sentry line.
2. Placement of the enemy barrage fire.
3. Reconnaissance of the Storm exit positions.
4. Reconnaissance of the approach routes to the lineup-places.

Further tasks performed by the II Battalion were:

1. Marking out of the readiness and storm exit positions with fluorescent paint signs.
2. Placement of tracing tape from the readiness place to the storm exit position.
3. Training of leaders to lead the *Sturmtruppen* up to the readiness place.
4. 4. Installation of runner chains from the *Sturmtruppen* until to the regimental battle headquarters.[5]

These tasks became accomplished by the position battalion by utilizing numerous patrols. These patrols were all led by company officers and *Portepee Unteroffizieren*. *Leutnants der Reserve* Schmolling, Vogt, Erdmann, Platzer, Penner, Leiner and *Leutnant* Egon Schild, *Vizefeldwebel* Kruse, 7/R110, *Vizefeldwebel* Rank and *Unteroffizier* Stolle, 8/R110 all drew special attention by their actions, and all of the patrols brought back useful information for the preparation of the operation.

The *Sturmbataillon* was allowed a full day of rest while 260 labor soldiers created the practice works on 22 and 23 February 1918 at Liry Mountain that came very close to the actual proportions of the French trench system. The higher command held meetings where detailed instructions were provided as well as discussions with the leaders of the undertaking about the purpose, goal and course of the operation that accomplished clarity and familiarity with the individual tasks assigned to them. Special diligence was used regarding the equipment being used by the men as every sound; every possible noise had to become silenced.

Once the labor soldiers had finished with their work on the practice site, the training on the model began. At first the companies practiced individually, then the two battalions together, and finally all troops who would be involved at the start of the storm, so that on 27 February 1918 a rehearsal could take place. The dress rehearsal went off smoothly, to the great satisfaction of all involved.

The regimental supply officer, *Leutnant der Reserve* Köhler, had material and food depots placed at strategic positioned and organized the hauling service. Bandaging stations and wounded assembly places were established, the artillery, the *Minenwerfer* and machine guns were assigned their tasks and provided with adequate supplies of ammunition, finally every possible means of communication was installed and tested; the preparations were all complete.

The weather during the last days of February was poor; rain and snow storms. 28 February 1918 began as misty and overcast, it then rained almost the entire day without pause. At 4.00 p.m. on 28 February 1918, the order for conducting the operation came: H Day was 1 March 1918 and the assault would begin at 6.15 a.m. under the code name *Darauf und Durch*. The two battalions making the assault were transported to the front on motor vehicles; the III/R110 travelled at 8.30 p.m., the I/R110 at 10 p.m. The column of vehicles rattled through *Fliegerhang-Nord*, Vieux–Ardeuil–Gratreuil until the mud bridge by Ripont. The overall mood of the men was reported to be serious, but confident.

The fully occupied vehicles moved slowly through the misty, humid night. The column containing the III/R110 reached Ripont Mill without incident, and the men were unloaded from the vehicles and allowed to rest for an hour. The head of the column transporting the I/R110 had just passed the barracks of the *Fliegerhang* when the entire column suddenly came to an abrupt stop: it turned out that the first vehicle in the column was firmly stuck in the mud, forcing the following vehicles to jam on their brakes.

There was apparently a great deal of swearing as the lead vehicle was unloaded and the men attempted to push it out of the rut; but it was all in vain, the vehicle remained immovable. The feverish activity continued in the attempt to move the vehicle out of the mud and finally, after an hour of strenuous labor the vehicle was finally free and could continue the journey. Time was running out if the men were to be in position for the attack; one more incident such as this and the I/R110 would not be in position in time to attack as scheduled. Fortunately everything went smoothly from this point on and the battalion arrived in Ripont and the leader of the II/R110 lead his men into the position via Ripont Mill.

The men of the I/R110 moved slowly through the dark night; the unfamiliar terrain was difficult to traverse but finally, at 4a.m. every man was at his assigned place, just at the last moment before the start of the artillery fire. The 4th and 1/R110 immediately went forward along the white tape until to the storm exit position in the *Sehne Graben* up to the *Lenzing Weg*. The 2/R110 found shelter in the *Wald Graben*. The 3/R110 was the last to arrive at the battalion battle headquarters.

It had been a miserable journey to the assault positions; the trenches stood knee deep in water and muck, the men could barely go forward and all of the weapons and uniforms were covered with thick Champagne mud. Nevertheless, the III/R110 reached the readiness position area at the *Koppel Schloss* at 3.30 a.m.; now the men stood in the trench and waited.

It was still quiet along the front, here and there a single rifle shot, the rattle of a machine gun, a shell impact. The watch hands moved slowly and finally reached 4.12 a.m., when suddenly a loud roar erupted when the artillery preparation began with a sudden blow. Numerous batteries bombarded the enemy artillery batteries for two hours. The sky in the rear of the men was lit up as if by lightning strikes with bright flashes suddenly piercing the darkness, and the shells rustling overhead could be heard as they sped toward the French lines. The French were not slow to react to the sudden shelling and yellow light balls began to climb up, out of the French trenches along the entire sector.

The French artillery response was quick. Most of the enemy fire lay in and north of the *Altrock Schlucht*, on the Readiness position area. Losses began to occur in the 10th, 11th and 12/R110, while the 4th and 1/R110 lay safely forward of the barrage fire zone. The 3/R110 had the worst of it when the company was caught in the middle of the French fire during the advance to the storm exit position and became torn apart. At about 5.00 a.m. the barrage fire in the area of the III/R110 finally let up entirely so that the companies could reach their storm exit positions in the *Sehne* without further disturbance, in accordance with the plan. Shortly before 6.00 a.m. the companies of the

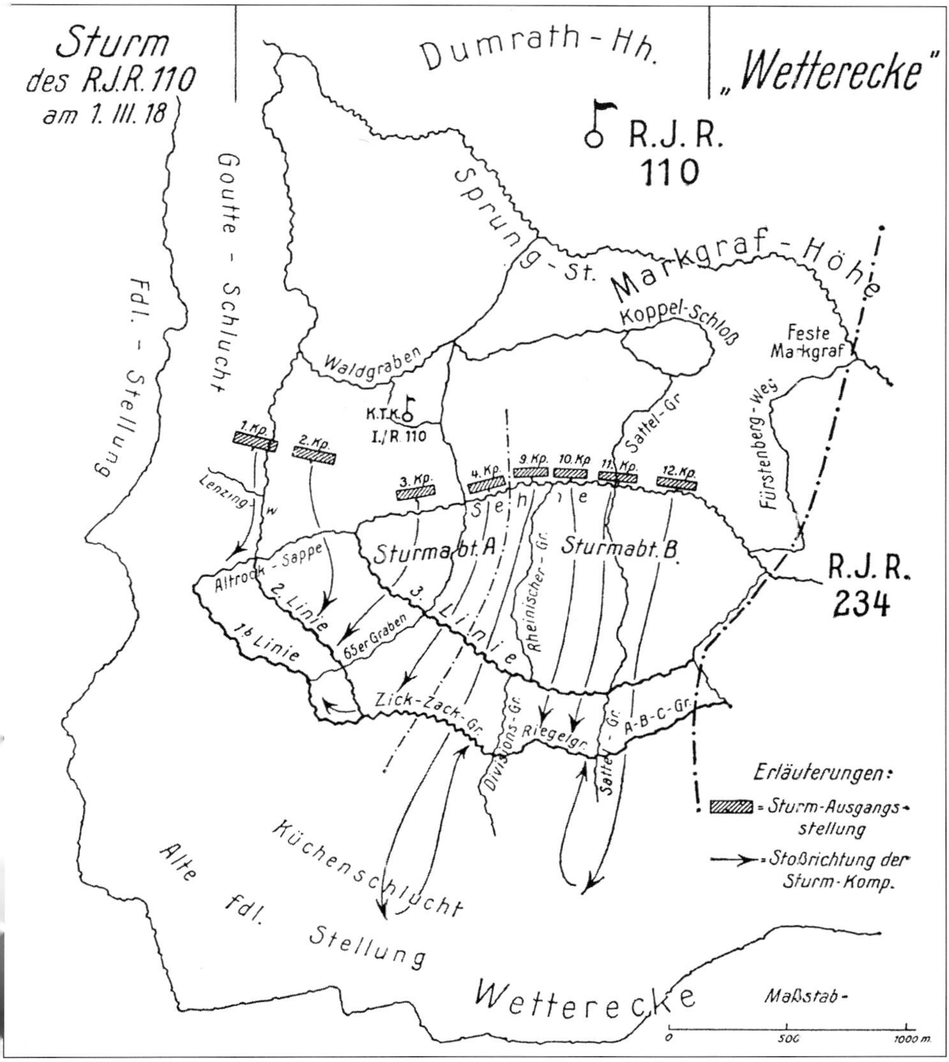

Darauf und Durch. The attack by RIR 110 on 1 March 1918.

I/R110 also reached their assigned places, however only weak remnants of the 3/R110 managed to come forward until the *Sehne.*

At the grey dawn of day, at 6.10 a.m., the *Minenwerfer* opened fire. The 5th *Minenwerfer* Company along with Light *Minenwerfer*, 12 medium *Minenwerfer* from the army reserve and 25 Light *Minenwerfer* from the 28th Reserve Division covered the enemy trenches with devastating destructive fire. The bursting, crashing and throbbing as the shells rained down on the enemy was described as appearing like fireworks. At 6.12 a.m. the German batteries opened fire on targets immediately in front of the

Sturmtrupps. Finally, machine gun fire targeted the enemy positions that were scheduled to be attacked in order to keep the enemy's heads down. It looked and felt like Hell according to the men of RIR 110. The assault leaders stared at their watches until the hands indicated: 6.15 a.m.: then *'Los! Raus!'* and the assault troops broke forth.

Sturmabteilung A: The I/R110 was under the command of replacement battalion leader *Hauptmann* Buch, from RIR 109. The attack by the 1/R110 under *Hauptmann* Tobye along with *Leutnants der Reserve* Bartling, Grapentin and *Vizefeldwebel* Höckele went forward as scheduled. Following behind the *Sturmtrupps* of the *Sturmbataillon* and the *Flammenwerfer* were the infantry companies, which penetrated into the *Lenzing Graben* and the *Zick Zack Graben* (Second line) and occupied these positions. The *Altrock Sap* was completely blocked off by a wire barricade; this barrier inside the trench quickly became blown up by the *pioniers*. At first, the French initially put up strong opposition, then suddenly they moved back rapidly. An enemy assault group of 25-30 men who advanced half left from the *Altrock Sap* became repulsed through hand grenades from the *pioniers* assigned to the assault group. A second enemy assault group from half right quickly moved back because of heavy German machine gun fire.

The captured trench quickly became occupied with infantry and machine gun posts were created according to plan and the connection to the 2/R110 was soon established. The enemy then covered the captured trench with strong shell fire until 9.30 a.m., from which numerous losses occurred. Among the losses was *Leutnant der Reserve* Bartling, who became severely wounded and eventually succumbed to his injuries at *Sanitäts Kompagnie* 5. *Vizefeldwebel* Höckele, who was only slightly wounded, became killed by a direct hit while being transported to the medical dugout in the rear.

The 2/R110 under *Leutnant der Reserve* Carstens had 15 men wounded and one light machine gun destroyed from enemy barrage fire. The *Stosstrupps* under the command of *Leutnant der Reserve* Breitenbach, *Offizier Stellvertreter* Schnörr, *Vizefeldwebels* Böhm and Holzinger, *Unteroffizier* Reich and *Gefreiten* Körbel penetrated into the enemy position and rolled the trench up from the right wing, during which one French machine gun was silenced through hand grenades. The French afforded fierce opposition between the *Altrock Sap* and the *65er Graben* however they gave up the position when their leader was killed. At 7.00 a.m. the 2/R110 had taken control of the *Zick Zack Graben* and the rearward lying trench from the *Altrock Sap* until to the *65er Graben*. The connection to the 1/R110 on the right was established, while there was still no connection to the 3/R110 on the left. While mopping up the captured trench *Unteroffizier* Reich and *Gefreiter* Reiser brought up 19 prisoners out of the dugouts; altogether the 2/R110 brought back 35 prisoners. The enemy troops that had attempted to withdraw to the main French line suffered heavy losses through machine gun fire.

The 3/R110 under *Leutnant der Reserve* Recklies and *Offizier Stellvertreter* Weinowski with about 13 men advanced along the *65er Graben* until the *Zick Zack Graben*. When both leaders became wounded, Sergeant Weber took over the command until the trench officer of the battalion, *Leutnant der Reserve* Jawandt, who had brought forward 20 stragglers, took over the company and established a connection to the 2/R110 on the right.

The 4/R110 under the command of *Leutnant der Reserve* Eggert began the assault as scheduled. Shortly after taking a few steps the company leader was severely wounded and during the transport to the rear was killed through a direct hit which also killed both *Krankenträger* who were carrying him:

> I stood next to the company leader. The time grew closer. A hellish noise of shells, mines and machine guns, as I have never experienced before at the front. *Leutnant der Reserve* Eggert stood there quietly, his watch in his hand. Sudden cries: 'The neighboring battalion is already advancing!' He does not let himself become influenced and waits for the set starting time. Finally his command: 'Fourth Company *raus*!' We hurled forth. However already after a few meters there was a terrifying impact in the still undeveloped company. We had thrown ourselves down, until the din of splinters ceased. Then we followed in a nonstop sprint behind the fire roll. Our preparation fire must have been terrifying for the enemy garrison; because the shapes that I saw crawl out of the dugouts like moles, almost looked pathetic. With high raised hands and distressed faces they stood before us and asked to be taken away. I have not seen anything further of *Leutnant der Reserve* Eggert. He was a very excellent leader of a company.
>
> *Leutnant der Reserve* Beuthe took over the leadership of the company and stormed forth with the left wing on the *Divisions Graben* until to the *Zick Zack Graben*. Individual people hurried out past the goal; however they were forced to turn around by their own artillery fire. Out of a dugout in the *65er Graben Gefreiter* Graf and *Musketier* Rüdes, two intrepid patrol participants, bring out 25 prisoners, amongst them a Captain, and captured important papers that at the last moment the French tried to hide in the crevices between the dugout frames. An enemy counterattack would be repulsed through hand grenades and machine gun fire. The connection to *Sturmabteilung* B (III/R110) was established. Between the 4th and 3rd Coy a gap originated in which a platoon of the 8th Coy was shoved into it.
>
> *Leutnant der Reserve* Ewald, 4/R110.[6]

Sturmabteilung B: The III/R110 was under the command of *Rittmeister Freiherr von* Bissing. During the time just before the scheduled assault the enemy barrage fire becomes so severe to the west of the *Sattel Graben that* heavy losses were feared. The company leaders of the 9th, 10th and 11/R110, *Leutnants der Reserve* Happel, Krichau and Schneevoigt attempted to evade the heavy fire and moved the companies out of the *Sehne Graben* toward the front, closer to the German fire. The 12/R110 under *Leutnant der Reserve* Wilser remained in the *Sehne Graben*. At the appointed time, the entire battalion moved forward as if on the practice ground and in a few minutes the *Stosstrupps* had reached the *Zick Zack Graben*.

With assistance from the *Flammenwerfer*, the assault companies cleared the dugouts and occupied the trench. Numerous prisoners were taken and sent back to the rear along with several machine guns and rapid loading rifles. During the storm, the *Stosstrupps* of the 9th and 12/R110 recklessly advanced beyond the goals set for the attack. The 9/R110 reached the *Kuchen Schlucht* and ran head on into an enemy counterattack. Under the prudent leadership of *Leutnant der Reserve* Happel the French attack was stopped and eventually thrown back. *Hornist* Stähle and *Gefreiter* Schröter prominently stood out in this fighting. The *Stosstrupps* of the 12/R110 penetrated up to the *Wetterecke*, then returned to the first trench, when they found more French troops.

An enemy counterattack from the direction of the *65er Graben* in company strength was repulsed by parts of the 9th, 10th, 11th and 4/R110, from which one captain and 28 men were disarmed and captured. 2 machine guns and 30 rapid loading rifles were also taken.

Musketier Bartler, 9/R110 drew particular attention to himself for his actions during the attack. He stood upright with a captured rapid loading rifle (*Chau-Chat*) without any cover and took a French machine gun under fire. *Leutnant der Reserve* Macholz, *Gefreiter* Reinig, *Krankenträger* Hinze and *Gefreiter* Schroeter cleared one enemy dugout and captured one captain, one sergeant and 24 French soldiers. The connection with the neighboring troops of RIR 234 existed from the start up to the conclusion of the attack.

The attack was entirely successful, all goals were obtained, and only one trench was still to be taken on the right wing. At 3.00 a.m. two *Stosstrupps* from the 2/R110 under the command of *Unteroffizier* Reich and *Gefreiten* Körbel and one *Stosstrupp* from the 8/R110 under the command of *Vizefeldwebel* Rank rolled up the first trench. At first the enemy afforded strong opposition, but then quickly moved back. The enemy artillery was comparatively quiet following the attack as the artillerymen did not where friend and foe were located. The *Stosstrupps* took advantage of this lull and organized a defense in depth and realigned the different formations.

As part of the defensive plan the 6/R110 became placed in possession of the III/R110 and put in between the I and III/R110. At 12.00 noon the 8/R110 filled up the gap between the 4th and 3/R110 and participated in the defense of the sector. The 7/R110 placed 12 runners between the regimental battle headquarters and the III/R110 and a hauling party under the command of *Vizefeldwebel* Pohl in a strength of three *Unteroffiziere* and 30 men, who despite enemy fire, immediately brought forward materials and ammunition after the successful attack and carried the wounded to the rear.

At 12.30 p.m. the rest of the 7/R110 was put in by the 12/R110 on the left wing. At 7.25 a.m. the 5/R110 was placed in possession of the III/R110 as support, however the 5/R110 ended up in heavy enemy fire and became dispersed. Part of the company managed to reach the 9/R110 and reinforced the forward line. The rest remained in the *Sehne Graben* as the security garrison in possession of the III/R110.

Saturday 2 March 1918 was quiet; the expected French counterattack never took place. However, in the evening hours, quite strong fire of varying lengths of time fell on the rearward trenches and approach routes. On the night of 2/3 March 1918 the three battalions of RIR 110 that were in the forward line, were relieved by two battalions of RIR 109; the relief went smoothly.

In the subsequent review of the attack, the results were seen as a stunning success. Not only was the entire former German position recaptured and firmly in German hands, but three French counterattacks were completely repulsed and more than two hundred prisoners were taken along with their weapons. The final tally was three officers, 201 men taken prisoner, along with several dozen machine guns and rapid loading rifles. All command posts sent their congratulations to RIR 110 and spoke of their appreciation

Funeral preparations for the men killed in RIR 110 during the raid *Darauf und Durch*. (Source: Author's collection)

Funeral preparations for the men killed in RIR 110 during the raid *Darauf und Durch*. (Source: Author's collection)

of the raid. The Crown Prince personally telephoned and gave his congratulations to the division for the successful operation as well.

When *Leutnant der Reserve* Carstens, the leader of the 2/R110, became ordered to the commanding general and questioned about the raid:

> Were you also there when the trench was taken? No, Your Excellency! Not I! However I heard … Not I, but my people! Ah, so! However, you were there? Aye, Your Excellency! However it was no big thing. It had to succeed if everyone did his duty.[7]

News of the successful battle also made its way quickly back to Germany in letters from the front:

> Hauptmann Boy RIR111 Staff
> 3.3.18
>
> Dear Parents!
> From the newspaper you will have learned that here yesterday was again great battle Day, which brought us 170 prisoners. How hot the wrestling was, you may realize from our artillery in a few hours over 120000 shells were fired. The fights are not finished yet, but my division will soon be in rest. I'm doing very well. I look exquisite and feel fresh despite all this. We will probably not join the big offensive because we are already exhausted …
> Best regards your Erwin.[8]

This was seen as an example of the modesty of the leaders and the spirit that instilled a sense of duty and loyalty among the men. The raid had succeeded because everyone had done his duty, which was not easy to do at times. However, the successful raid did not come cheaply: two officers (*Leutnant der Reserve* Eggert and *Leutnant der Reserve* Bartling) and 37 men were killed, six officers, 245 men were wounded and four men were missing. This was the true cost of the operation of 1 March 1918.

On the evening of 2 March the I/R110 took over the readiness position in Sector 5, the right division sector. The 2/R110 was accommodated in the *Haupt Riegel*, 1st and 3/R110 in the barracks at the *Steilhang* and the 4/R110 in the *Türkenwald,* where the Readiness-Troop-Commander (BTK) was positioned. The III/R110 received accommodations in the *Paderborn Lager*, however it returned to the *Teschner Lager* on 6 March as the rest battalion. On the night of 3/4 March 1918 the II/R110 relieved the II/R109 on the Butte de Tahure, with the 5th and 8/R110 in the front line, the 6th and 7/R110 in the *Haupt Riegel*. Connections were established on the right to RIR 239, and on the left to RIR 111.

On 4 March 1918 the 28th Reserve Division occupied Sectors G, B, D, from right to left with RIR 110 and RIR 111 and RIR 109. The enemy was still behaving quietly since their unexpected defeat of 1 March 1918. Then strong drum fire was placed on the German trenches, probably as preparation for a renewed counterattack, which appeared

Grave of Gefreiter *der Reserve* Heinrich Bischoff 4/R110, killed on 1 March 1918. (Source: Author's collection)

to have been planned for 6.50 p.m. on 5 March 1918. Barrage fire was immediately called for, supported through *Minenwerfer* and machine gun fire and the enemy attack was apparently nipped in the bud.

The new position occupied by RIR 110 was the badly shot up and churned up chalk dome of the *Butte de Tahure*. The shallow *Bühler Tal* separated it from the *Signalberg* and the northern hillside fell in several steep embankments, which and offered excellent possibilities for dugout construction. The KTK and two readiness companies and all possible depots were accommodated in this hillside. The so-called *Dreck Schlucht* [Muck ravine] ran along the western flank of the Butte toward the enemy position. The rearward connections led from the precipice through the *Brigade Schlucht*, past feeble looking pine copses up to the Challerange-Somme-Py railway line, where the regimental battle headquarters was located.

The men needed days of rest and relaxation after the exhausting days of battle. The position was very quiet; there was no conspicuous activity by the enemy. On bright days the French artillery fired a few shots on the forward line and the left wing and on the rearward connections, without causing any damage. The weather was mostly good, so that the companies soon recovered from the recent exertions. Replacements came from Germany and were distributed to the battalions, reliefs were held regularly and without disturbance from the enemy.

Because of the recent fighting the trenches, dugouts and obstacles taken over by RIR 109 were in extraordinarily bad condition. Sector D clearly demonstrated the power of the heavy fighting that had taken place for its possession. The dugouts had all been destroyed; where the trench walls were not damaged through shelling, they had suffered from the bad weather. The trenches were only knee deep, filled with water and mud and furthermore easily seen by the enemy. Then came the prolonged bad weather and quite frequent hostile fire raids that seriously hindered the immediate restoration work needed so badly. The fighting troops and especially the hauling troops and food carriers suffered terribly under the poor conditions. No one who had not personally experienced life in the trenches or the long hikes carrying heavy loads of supplies through the pitch black night, in mud and knee deep water under enemy fire could understand the misery the men were experiencing.

Then, if the situation could not get any worse, a divisional order was discovered on a French corpse:

> Captured orders of the 11th French Division.
> Private! Nr. 3341/1
>
> The divisional commander has been informed that a type of tacit traffic between our troops in the first line and the enemy opposite appears to prevail respecting the recovery of wounded after fighting. So reported the 69th Infantry Regiment on 15 February when a detachment of seven Germans, who, under the protection of a Red Cross flag moved out of the Wood of Le Fays toward Beaumont. Nothing has been reported about a salvo on this important target. This procedure must cease! The division commander enacts the specific rule that any German, when and where he is at the recovery of wounded – is to be immediately taken under fire. It is no longer needed to be reminded that with the successful fighting manner of the enemy opposite, this signifies compassionate weakness. The sector commandant is made personally responsible for any violation against this rule.
>
> Voiullemont, Commander of the division.[9]

The already dangerous work of the medical personnel had just become virtually impossible in respect to recovering the wounded lying in the open. This was seen as a typical example that the French no longer recoiled before the most spiteful methods for the annihilation of the German soldiers. In contrast, the men of the 28th Reserve Division had learned to recognize the British as humane opponents during the Battle of the Somme.

With the recent actions, the 28th Reserve Division was once more understrength. The flow of replacements continued throughout this period of time as the regiments slowly recovered from the loss of so many good men. On 6 March 1918 12 *Unteroffiziere* and 168 men arrived as replacements for RIR 109, with that the regiment had the ration strength of 105 officers, 2.680 *Unteroffiziere* and Other Ranks and 208 horses. On 28 March 1918 an additional 16 *Unteroffiziere* and 49 replacements arrived.

Life at the front returned to normal very quickly after the events of 1 March 1918. On 16 March 1918 the patrol Operation *Willkommen* took place against the enemy trenches in the *Dreck Schlucht* under the command of *Hauptman von* Zeddelmann, I/ R110. The purpose of the operation was to capture French prisoners in order to establish the identification of the opposing enemy units, a seemingly endless task, but necessary if accurate intelligence information was to be provided to the high command on enemy troop movements across the entire western front. Of late, this activity was seen as being quite important by the OHL and every attempt was made to take enemy prisoners or at least to identify the opposing enemy units.

The leadership of the patrol was given to *Leutnant der Reserve* Leiner, 2/R110. The *Stosstrupp* leaders were *Vizefeldwebel* Reich, 2/R110, *Vizefeldwebel* Ewald, 4/R110 and *Unteroffizier* Pfeifer, 1/R110. The raiding party consisted of three *Unteroffiziere* and 50 men from the I/R110 and nine *pioniers* from the 4/*Pionier* Battalion 16. In addition to the artillery support, eight medium and 10 light *Minenwerfer* would provide additional preparation and blocking fire. The regimental heavy machine guns were to provide support by firing on fixed points in the enemy lines with elevated fire.

All preparations for the operation had been thoroughly completed. At 4.00 a.m. the three *Stosstrupps* left the trench at the slope of the Butte to the *Dreck Schlucht*, they worked through the ravine until they had reached the French wire obstacles and waited there for the preparation fire to start, which opened with full strength at 4.50 a.m. At exactly 5.00 a.m. *Trupp* Reich penetrated into the enemy trench, searched the position thoroughly in accordance with its instructions. The enemy trench was found to be unoccupied and *Trupp* Reich returned to the exit position at 5.30 a.m. with all men accounted for.

The advance of *Trupp* Ewald was difficult; it found the wire obstacles in front of the enemy trench undamaged. With help from the *pioniers*, lanes were blown up in the wire while the men were taken under enemy machine gun fire. Once the lanes were created, *Vizefeldwebel* Ewald, *Gefreiter* Starck and *Reservist* Grüber (4/R110) were the first men to jump into the French trench. Ewald found the trench section searched by him also empty and returned in accordance with orders.

Leutnant der Reserve Leiner had better luck; he entered the French trench and found the route leading to the right blocked through a fallen door. He pressed through this obstacle into the trench and his men were able to extract nine French soldiers out of four dugouts. Sergeant Striebig, 3/R110, *Musketier* Bitz, 4/R110 and the *Pioniers* Weissgerber and Wegerich, 4/*Pionier* Battalion 16, performed the main work, stoutly supported by *Musketiers* Runkel, Winter and Witter, 3/R110. A bundled explosive charge had to become thrown down into one dugout, because no one came forth when ordered. During the search for more prisoners Sergeant Striebig ran up against a Frenchman, who was prepared to shoot at him. Striebig was faster and shot the man down with his pistol. An enemy sergeant who was also hurrying to the site of the raiding party reluctantly surrendered when faced with being shot down by Striebig. At 5.45 a.m. *Leutnant der Reserve* Leiner returned to the exit position with ten prisoners and without any losses in his detachment.

The prisoners were from *Régiment d'Infanterie* 24 and had only come into the position on the previous evening, after one month of rest behind the lines. With this information, it was established that the French 36th Infantry Division had been relieved by the 6th Infantry Division, which was very valuable information for Army Headquarters. All command positions spoke of their thanks to the participants and their appreciation; *Leutnant der Reserve* Leiner and Sergeant Striebig received the Iron Cross I Class. There were also awards, promotions and monetary rewards to the Other Ranks of the raiding party.

There was no further large fighting action in the Tahure position and life had become quite bearable for the men. Then, on 18 March 1918, 12.00 noon, the 28th Reserve Division separated out of the association of Group Dormoise and would become subordinate to the newly formed Group Perthes (XVI Army Corps), commanded by *Generalleutnant* Wild *von* Hohenborn. The commanding general of Group Dormoise said goodbye to the 28th Reserve Division through the following daily order:

> On 18 March of this month the 28th Reserve Division separates out of Group Dormoise. It is with reluctance that I separate from the brave division. Inserted for weeks at numerously fought over positions, the division had honorably fulfilled its duty under difficult circumstances. In difficult work they improved their position, they had in the upbeat spirit of the undertaking forced the enemy to constantly hold their breath, advanced its line and obtained clarity about the enemy for the upper leadership and in proven fighting spirit, on 1 March, suffered heavy losses in the glorious fighting, tearing the momentarily acquired success out of their hands and safely holding on to it. A further page of honor in the history of the division and its proven troops. With appreciative thanks I wish the 28th Reserve Division further success, soldiers luck and an honorable home coming after the coming war time after imposing an honorable end to the fighting.
>
> The Commanding General: *Freiherr von* Watter *Generalleutnant*.[10]

No time was wasted in making the switch to the new Group. On orders from Group Perthes, a mine explosion was planned for 19 March 1918. The mine would be detonated between 10.00 and 11.00 p.m. in the enemy's wire entanglements, accompanied by two patrols from RIR 109. The raid was successful and all of the participants of both patrols came back unharmed in their own trench along with fresh intelligence information.

Further patrols from RIR 109 also obtained important information about the enemy sentries, advanced defensive works and weakly occupied points of the enemy position. *Leutnants* Beil, Hartwig, Seufert, Motzkus, Frässle and *Unteroffiziere* A. Ratzel, Riexinger, Lacher, Zieger, Burghardt, Rainer and numerous Other Ranks were particularly prominent in this work.

Gefreiten Starck and *Reservist* Grüber, 4/ R110, were not very happy with the failure of their raid on 16 March 1918 and could not leave it alone. On 19 March 1918, three days after the relief of the I/R110, they went to the battle trench without orders, reported to the trench officer about penetrating into the enemy trench again, on their own; the officer apparently approved the request. After approximately two hours the sentries inside the trench could hear hand grenade fighting taking place in front of the position; the two man patrol did not return. The French Army report from this time stated: 'A few prisoners were taken at the Butte de Tahure.' In the spring of 1918, Starck was returned home from captivity as being unfit for duty. He was able to provide the first news of that fateful night. He was with Grüber in the trench fighting, surrounded from all sides and had been severely injured with a shot to the knee, a shot in the shoulder and a bayonet thrust. Grüber was also wounded but nothing ever became known about his fate. It was suspected that he had been killed on the night of the raid and buried nearby.

All intelligence gathering had been in support of the great breakthrough battle of the German Army that was about to begin. In preparation for this major event, heightened battle readiness was ordered throughout the 28th Reserve Division at 8.00 p.m. on 20 March 1918. The III/R109 was moved out of the *Jonas Lager* to Ripont Mill and the *Dormoise Stellung*, so that the entire regiment was employed in the front lines. At 3.00 a.m. on 21 March 1918 the German batteries covered the entire Tahure Sector with powerful destructive fire, especially on the enemy artillery positions. In addition, the enemy camps and billets and wire obstacles were bombarded with gas shells. The bombardment was joined by all of the heavy, medium and light *Minenwerfer* so that in the Tahure Sector, as on the entire western front, the enemy might be deceived about the real attack location through powerful artillery fire and numerous patrols. It was not until late on the same day when the men of the division first learned that the great offensive had begun. The men wondered, 'would they succeed in forcing the breakthrough?' 'Every soldier believed it would succeed.'

At 2.40 p.m. on 21 March 1918, *Stosstrupps* from RIR 109 broke forth out of the front line in the execution of the Operation *Sauhatz* against the French position. *Stosstrupps* 1 and 1a under the command of *Leutnant* Beil and *Vizefeldwebel* A. Ratzel, both from the 7/R109, crossed over the trench of IR 158. They immediately received machine gun fire from the direction of the *Hasenwald*, so that only the first men made it through the position. Simultaneously placed enemy barrage fire not only hindered the patrol from pressing forward, but also from being able to go back. It was not until about 4.15 p.m. when the participants succeeded in making their way back individually to the German lines.

Stosstrupps 2 and 2a under the command of *Vizefeldwebel* Armbruster, 8/R109 and *Unteroffizier* Waibel, 5/R109 went forth to the western hillside of the *Pionier Schlucht*. They too ended up in strong enemy machine gun and artillery fire and could not come back until the barrage fire had died down.

Gefreiter Imholz, 7/R109, the leader of a light machine gun located in the second line, recognized the danger his comrades were in, and fought back against the enemy machine guns along with *Grenadiers* Heptig and Weid, 7/R109, as long as they could despite the enemy barrage fire, until a direct hit killed Imholz and wounded both grenadiers. Also, *Vizefeldwebel* Dansig, *Unteroffizier* Weidkamp, *Schützen* Gehrs, W. Schmidt and Wieber, all from the 2MG/R109, fired as long as possible, until they were all wounded through artillery fire. It was felt that the brave determination of these men and the fire of the *Minenwerfer* platoon were mainly responsible that the patrols were able to come back to their own trenches with comparatively few losses.

It was later determined that a mine explosion in the enemy obstacles on the day before the operation and the attacks that followed in Sectors G and B shortly before Operation *Sauhatz* had contributed to the increased alertness of the adversary and to the failure of the raid.

By RIR 110 the beginning of spring started with a gas bombardment of the enemy artillery from 3.00 to 5.00 a.m., followed by ten hours of artillery fire upon the enemy positions. In the early afternoon the patrol Operation *Willkommen* was to be repeated by the III/R110. At 12.39 p.m. two *Stosstrupp* broke forth against the French trenches.

Each *Stosstrupp* consisted of 20 men under the command of *Leutnant der Reserve* Macholz and *Vizefeldwebel* Deckert. The *Stosstrupps* reached the French position and found ample evidence of the devastating effect of the German bombardment. The trench was badly damaged, many of the dugouts had been pressed in, or the garrison had already evacuated the position. The patrol could only bring back objects of equipment and weapons, through which however the presence of *Régiment d'Infanterie* 24 was confirmed.

The men of RIR 111 were advised that the reasons given for these operations was to prevent the enemy from sending reserves to the portion of the front threatened by the offensive, much the same as the attack on Gommécourt on 1 July 1916. For this purpose RIR 111 had been ordered to hold a *Stosstrupp* operation codenamed *Frühlingsanfang* [The start of Spring]. Under the guidance of *Leutnant* Winterer, the enemy position became reproduced at a training works where the *Stosstrupp*, which were formed from volunteers from every battalion, would practice the attack.

At 12.10 p.m. on 21 March 1918, the preparation fire began. At first the enemy replied only weakly. At 1.05 p.m. the *Stosstrupps* advanced from their readiness positions. *Stosstrupp* I under *Vizefeldwebel* Küpper initially received machine gun fire while leaving the trench, which was immediately silenced by supporting German machine gun fire. They moved forward quickly up to the first enemy trench. However the wide and strong wire obstacles were completely undamaged and it was only after great effort that the men succeeded in crossing the obstacles and penetrate into the trench. The French dugouts, which in part were placed inside a sunken road, were strongly constructed; however they had suffered badly through the mine fire. While part of the garrison fled out of the dugouts or gave themselves up as prisoners, fierce opposition was afforded at others, which became overcome with hand grenades.

Stosstrupp II under *Leutnant* Rüttenauer succeeded in advancing until at the northern edge of Tahure and took numerous prisoners. The *Stosstrupps* were already on the return route to their own positions, when the French barrage fire began and they were able to reach their own position without losses and with their loot – 36 prisoners and 2 *Musketen*. The patrol undertaking had shown 'that the dashing attack spirit was still in bloom in the regiment,' how the division commander, *Generalleutnant von* Held, said in the division orders. The men of RIR 111 felt great satisfaction for this compliment, after the difficult days in February; 'they had shown the enemy that they were superior to him.'

After the beginning of the great offensive in March 1918 it became increasingly restless in the sector of the 28th Reserve Division. The artillery of both sides became more active, which according to the men of RIR 109 betrayed the apparent nervousness of the adversary. The positions and approach routes often lay under the strongest bombardment day and night. The installation of a blocking trench between the Butte and the *Jäger Copse* became necessary by RIR 110. The increased enemy fire did result in a number of losses including *Oberleutnant der Reserve* Hänlein, the proven company leader of the 9/R110, who was severely wounded during entrenching work during a fire raid On the night of 4/5 April 1918.

Patrol activity in no man's land increased on both sides in the final days of March and heightened battle readiness became repeatedly ordered, which also apparently increased the enemy's anxiety. *Leutnants* Dürr, Wolf, Frisch, *Offizier Stellvertreter* Wiegand and *Vizefeldwebels* Hauger, Alies, Wetzel, Rapp, Heller, Pfahler, Lange, A. Ratzel and the *Unteroffiziere* Burkhardt, Braun, Waibel and Neese, furthermore many good Other Ranks especially stood out in RIR 109 for their actions while on patrol. The bravery of *Leutnant* Beil, *Offizier Stellvertreter* Frank and *Vizefeldwebel* Pfahler were also rewarded with the bestowal of the Iron Cross I Class.

By the end of the month the French were wary of the German patrols. At 12.30 a.m. on 31 March 1918 a patrol of the II/R110 under the command of *Leutnant* Egon Schmid, advanced into the French trenches after a short fire preparation. The garrison had quickly moved back to avoid the attack. Situations such as this were becoming the norm and few enemy soldiers were taken prisoner let alone found inside the French lines.

Then, the tables began to turn at the beginning of April when the enemy made numerous attempts to penetrate into the German positions, in order to obtain information about the German distribution of strength. The battalions of RIR 109 were instructed to elevate all patrol activity in order to make it impossible for the French to obtain any useful information at all. During one of these patrols On the night of 14/15 April 1918, *Leutnant* Eder become so severely injured through a hand grenade explosion that he died 10 days later in the field hospital.

On 16 April 1918 the French began to fire on the German position by RIR 109 with such force that the highest alarm readiness was ordered. On the next day, just after 12.00 midnight, the enemy fire was directed upon the main opposition line between *Dumrath Schlucht* and *Altrock Schlucht*, and despite barrage fire being immediately ordered, one enemy patrol succeeded in penetrating into the forward line, exactly where part of the 3/R109 was occupied with entrenching work. The men quickly moved back on the main opposition line in accordance with orders at the beginning of the enemy drum fire, nevertheless a direct hit struck between the work groups, from which one man was wounded and one man was buried. Two *Krankenträger* ended up being taken prisoner by the enemy patrol while they were performing their duty in bandaging the wounded *Grenadier* Wolfsberg; who later died from his injuries.

The French also raided the trenches of RIR 110 on this day. An enemy raiding party appeared in front of the left company sector of the 11/R110. During the ensuing fight, the officer on duty, *Offizier Stellvertreter* Bilger was severely wounded in the thigh through a revolver shot. The trench patrol under *Unteroffizier* Muck and *Reservist* Reinhard finally expelled the enemy with hand grenades.

Later in the evening of 16 April 1918 the *Prinz Karl Weg*, *Sattel*, A-B-C *Riegel* and the division trenches came under the heaviest enemy blocking fire once again. A new French advance followed the bombardment against Sector D2 by RIR 109, which was refused through machine gun and infantry fire.

As the days passed the enemy attacks did not appear to be letting up at all. At 5.20 a.m. on 18 April 1918, a powerful mine explosion suddenly took place at the left wing of Sector D4. Simultaneously 40 Frenchmen pressed into a German sap held by RIR 109. Three sentries who were in the sap were taken prisoner after brave resistance, or how it was presumed from the numerous blood trails found. A fourth sentry succeeded in alarming the *Stosstrupp,* who immediately went forward in a counterattack and together

Christliches Andenken
im Gebete

an den tugendsamen Jüngling

Georg Fußeder

von Benk, Gefreiter b. Res.-Feld-Artillerie-Regt. Nr. 28

welcher am 7. April 1918 infolge eines Granatschusses in einem Alter von 32 Jahren den Heldentod fürs Vaterland starb.

Dein Grab im fernen Feindeslande
Ist uns wohl eine schwere Pein,
Doch nimm dies Wort zum Unterpfande
Dein Grab soll nicht verlassen sein,
Allabend wenn die Glocken summen,
Zieht liebend unser Geist dorthin,
Und streuet betend Andachtsblumen,
Aufs Heldengrab mit frommen Sinn.

Kambli'sche Buchdruckerei G. m. b. H., Pfarrkirchen.

Memorial card to Gefreiter Georg Fusseder, RFAR 28. (Author's collection)

RIR 110 Decker's Circus. (*Reserve-Infanterie-Regiment Nr. 110 im Weltkrieg 1914-1918*)

with the *Stosstrupp* of *Leutnant* Beil and *Vizefeldwebel* Alisat expelled the enemy. Two French prisoners remained in the hands of RIR 109. The Battalion *Lux*, *Vizefeldwebel* Frisch, 7/R109, had been unable to contact battalion headquarters despite using every means available to him. He decided to act and directly contacted the supporting artillery batteries and personally ordered barrage fire, so that the enemy suffered heavy losses while withdrawing.

The men of RIR 109 were not complacent about the increase in enemy activity. In the morning hours of 20 April 1918 a patrol advanced from the German lines under the command of *Leutnant* Hell until it had gone past the third enemy trench. There it came to close fighting with an enemy patrol that ended with losses on both sides. *Unteroffizier* Neese was killed by a hand grenade, and one other man was wounded. When the French received reinforcements, Hell's patrol was forced to move back, leaving the dead and wounded behind. However, *Leutnant* Hell immediately went forth again with the reserve *Stosstrupp* and he succeeded in recovering Neese's body and the wounded man.

The recent conduct of the enemy prompted the 28th Reserve Division to report the following to Group Perthes: 'The enemy appears to have changed his behavior. Through daily patrols he looked to determine our current strength distribution. His disturbance fire in the rearward terrain was used constantly. Presumably thereby he wanted to determine the presence of stronger forces and prevent us from moving away fighting strength divisions.'

Many times it was through the alertness of the sentries on duty that the enemy plans were foiled. In one such instance a great disaster was avoided when at 4.30 a.m. on 21 April 1918 *Unteroffizier* Mussler, *Gefreiter* Pipenpott and *Musketier* Firnges, 5/R110, discovered an enemy patrol in the strength of about 40 men in the wire entanglements. The three men immediately threw hand grenades among the enemy soldiers and alarmed the *Stosstrupp*. The *Stosstrupp*, under command of *Leutnant* Egon Schmid, went forward over the German patrol trench into the wire entanglements.

Hand grenades were thrown back and forth everywhere and flashes of light flickered in the darkness flickered from the explosions. *Leutnant* Schmid personally captured one prisoner who belonged to *Régiment d'Infanterie* 24 and his men brought in a second, severely wounded Frenchman. During the fighting, *Musketier* Firnges was fatally wounded and died a short time after. The behavior of the men was praised and *Leutnant* Schmid was recognized with the Iron Cross I Class. The presence of the III Battalion *Régiment d'Infanterie* 24 in the opposing trenches was confirmed through a patrol by *Unteroffiziere* Stolle, 8/R110, along with 19 volunteers several days later.

RIR 109 suffered a particularly poignant loss from French shellfire on 26 April 1918. *Feldhilfsarzt* Ganter had become buried in the medical dugout through a direct hit. Rescue teams immediately began the work of opening the collapsed dugout entrance but were too late; Ganter was dead when they arrived. He was considered an extremely conscientious doctor and a philanthropist, and through his modest nature and his helpfulness he had earned the love and esteem of everyone he came into contact with.

Enemy activity continued into the end of April without let up. On the night of 27/28 April 1918 the French sent three assault detachments, each about 20 men, against different points of the forward trench by RIR 110. The first detachment ran into the Group of *Unteroffizier* Stolle, 8/R110, which was protecting the 7/R110 while the men were entrenching. It quickly turned into a hand grenade battle, when a French flamethrower suddenly appeared and a stream of liquid fire sprayed across the terrain. *Vizefeldwebel* Kruse and *Musketier* Krause, 7/R110, rushed back to help. The flamethrower was eventually dealt with, but *Unteroffizier* Stolle and *Musketier* Krause were wounded.

When a second French assault detachment arrived at the scene of the fighting the men of the 7th and 8/R110 were forced to move back. *Musketiers* Grieshaber and Billing of the 5/R110 repulsed a further enemy advance against the sector of the 5/R110 with hand grenades. The third enemy assault detachment did not succeed, in penetrating the German trench, because of the resolute behavior of *Musketiers* Seitz, Müller, Hecht, Wosniska and *Unteroffizier* Schneider.

Whilst the front line was under attack daily, the rest battalion of RIR 110 was expediting the machine gun and target practice training of all officers and other ranks. The new attack procedures and fighting against machine gun nests was eagerly practiced. Larger practices exercises in battalion strength, in collaboration with other weapons were also held.

During RIR 109's occupation of the Tahure sector, the *Jonas Lager* became a rest camp for the regiment in the rear. Barracks next to barracks stood in the shallow, curved hollow that was formed in the shape of a hook, some of which also moved up on the slopes of the hollow. The battalion relieved from the front had barely arrived in the *Jonas Lager* and had become somewhat cleaner and recovered from the exertion of front line duty, when the men were required to perform fatigues and training.

Much of the training revolved around the large-scale offensives that had taken place along the western front. The men were provided with the latest techniques used for the break through battle, taking of machine gun nests and battle firing and training in large formation and with close support artillery. Several inspections from higher leadership soon made it evident that the regiment would soon be leaving the Tahure-*Wetterecke* Sector.

Activity in the rear areas pointed to the imminent relief. Rumors began to spread that the 28th Reserve Division would soon be assigned to play a part in a major attack. The men also used this time to forget about the war, even if only for a short while. While the II/R110 lay in the *Teschner Lager* in the Readiness position, spring weather had arrived and began to change the landscape. At this time, a very strange rumor spread through the Other Ranks; *Leutnant der Reserve* Deckert was apparently up to something.

The rumors were true; Decker was organizing a circus to provide amusement for the troops. Approximately 100 chosen men became coached daily in the evening free time and trained for their particular roles. By the afternoon of the Assumption of the Virgin Mary the men located in the rear had all assembled for the festivities. The regimental band, the officer corps of the II/R110, and all of the men arrived at the position punctually and lined up together in the arena on the open hill in full expectation of the event. The regimental commander Major *von* Schmelling had barely arrived when the band began to play and the door of the mighty circus tent opened up. All of Decker's artists passed out of the tent while the circus director rode a lively white horse that belonged to the battalion leader. Decker rode a personified donkey as his replacement.

RIR 110 Decker's Circus. (*Reserve-Infanterie-Regiment Nr. 110 im Weltkrieg 1914-1918*)

The circus was a great success and everyone thoroughly enjoyed himself. There was much laughter and merriment among the troops present and many were able to forget their current circumstances and recall fond memories of home. Meanwhile further north the large attack battle flared up of which the supreme leadership hoped would finally decide the war. The news about the intense fighting had become eagerly sought after, and the regiments waited for the command that would call them to join this battle. Until that time came, the men had to remain content to stand guard in the Champagne. There was little to report in the final days of April and early may other than the change of leadership of the division. On 29 April 1918 *Generalleutnant von* Altrock was ordered to be the commander of the 28th Reserve Division.

Toward the middle of May, rumors spread of an imminent relief once again; this time it appeared to be true. Everything pointed to the division being moves as equipment was being packed, the company, battalion and regimental offices were being prepared to move. The relief became a fact when the 228th Infantry Division took over Sector A. On 12 May 1918 the rest battalion, II/R110, marched from the *Teschner Lager* to Vandy, north of Vouziers. In the evening hours the III/R110 was relieved in the readiness area by the II/R207 and subsequently marched to Terron. In the nights of 13 and 14 May 1918 the position battalions of RIR 109 were relieved through IR 35.

In the days from 13 to 15 May 1918 RIR 111 was relieved through IR 48 and was sent to the Army camps St. Martin, St. Marie and Sugny. On the evening of 13 May 1918 the I/R207 took over the battle sector of RIR 110, so that the I/R110 could move into billets in Brizy. On the next day the regimental staff turned over the command and was accommodated in Brizy and when the 1MG/R110 arrived in the evening, all parts of the regiment were moved out of the position. On 18 May 1918 the 28th Reserve Division ended its attachment to 3rd Army.

With the relief, the position time in a front sector which was never mentioned in the army reports, was over. While the sector received little notice in the official reports, the experiences and the men who had become casualties were remembered by their comrades. RIR 109 had suffered 38 killed, 151 wounded and eight prisoners during the time it was in position.

The 3rd Army commander issued the following statement regarding the 28th Reserve Division:

On 18 May 1918 the 28th Reserve Division separates from the 3rd Army. After long employment on both sides of the Aisne, at the beginning of this year the division defended the important Tahure Sector. An attempt in this time by the enemy to become firmly established on the severely notorious *Wetterecke* occurred, had failed. On 1 March the division had completely recaptured the trench pieces that had temporarily fallen in the hands of the French and repulsed further attacks by the enemy.

I speak of my appreciation to the brave Badener for standing firm during their affiliation to this Army and my thanks and wishes for them that they achieve the same successes in the great battle front, as they did in the tough fighting at the Sector 'Tahure.'

The commander-in-chief, von Einem.[11]

Notes

1. Frisch, op. cit., p. 242.
2. Greiner & Vulpius, op. cit., pp. 224-225.
3. Feldpost letter Hauptmann Erwin Boy, RIR 11, courtesy of Felix Fregin
4. Bachelin, op. cit., p. 192.
5. Greiner & Vulpius, op. cit., p. 231.
6. Greiner & Vulpius, op. cit., pp. 235-236.
7. Greiner & Vulpius, op. cit., pp. 237-238.
8. Feldpost letter Hauptmann Erwin Boy, RIR 11, courtesy of Felix Fregin
9. Greiner & Vulpius, op. cit., pp. 237-238.
10. Frisch, op. cit., pp. 246-247.
11. Frisch, op. cit., pp. 247-248.

5

28th Reserve Division on the Offensive

May–June 1918
Chemin des Dames

Trench warfare, which had begun at the end of 1914, now appeared to be at an end. The troops of the 28th Reserve Division looked forward to the coming events with firm confidence. All leaders and men in RIR 111 were firmly determined that the regiment would have the same great successes they had already experienced. Most of the men of 1914 were no longer found in the ranks of those who formed for the attack in 1918. The new men could not replace the experienced fighter, however the spirit of the troops promised that the regiment would accomplish the tasks that it was given.

Following the lengthy Aisne deployment, the regiments of the 28th Reserve Division were going to participate in one of the major offensives planned for the Western Front. The months of training the men had undergone in open warfare, clearing machine gun nests, close cooperation with escort batteries and the specialized offensive training provided by *Sturmbataillon* Rohr were finally going to be put to use.

From 17 to 22 May 1918 the men of the 28th Reserve Division were in their new quarters north of Vouziers. The days were spent making final preparations for transporting the regiments to a new front where the division would take part in the great breakthrough battle on the Chemin des Dames. Everything being taken with the regiments was packed according to a schedule, all officer's mess, orderly rooms, documents and other items not required for the upcoming attack were sent to the division Field Recruit Depot. All extra vehicles were turned in and the companies practiced attack procedures on a daily basis. The exercises being held were focused on the capture of machine gun nests. Under the watchful eyes of the *Pionier* Commander the men also practiced the rapid construction of bridges and the crossing of the Aisne Canal between Vrizy and Vandy. Finally, there was a larger regimental training event north of Vandy on 21 May 1918.

In the days between 23 and 25 May 1918 the 28th Reserve Division was loaded onto transport trains and was conveyed into the areas around Cuirieux, Goudelancourt, Bucy and Puissieux where the division would be brought together for the upcoming attack. The final movements to the assembly area were completed in night marches according to a rigid schedule, used to prevent the enemy from learning the location of the attack. No unnecessary movements were allowed during daylight hours in order to remain hidden from the ever present enemy observation aircraft.

This would be only the second time in the war when the 28th Reserve Division would be on the offensive. The 28th Reserve Division would take part in the battle in the area between Soissons and Reims where it would cross the Chemin des Dames and advance toward the Marne. The division was part of the 7th Army under the Supreme Command of His *Excellenz Generaloberst von* Böhn. The 28th Reserve Division was assigned to the XXV Reserve Corps, Gruppe Winckler along with the 197th Infantry Division, 10th Reserve Infantry Division, 1st Guard Infantry Division and 33rd Infantry Division. The 28th Reserve Division was first assigned as the reserve by the OHL and took up position in the area of Bruyres –Athis.

Two spring offensives had already taken place. Each attack had resulted in numerous prisoners and guns being taken, as well as piles of valuable war materials. Wide areas of Northern France had been captured including the desolate wasteland of the Somme, the result of Operation Alberich in early 1917. However, neither 'Great Battle' had been successful in breaking through by Amiens and by doing so separate the French Army from the British. The attack undertaken in April on the Lys did not succeed in taking Calais and Hazebrouck and failed to break the logistical spine of the British Army.

The goal of the high command remained the same as it was at the start of the year, to breakthrough to the sea. Some of the areas being looked at for the next phase of the offensives were considered too strong since the cessation of the attacks in April. Before any further major attack could be contemplated the enemy forces needed to be weakened or there was no hope of any success. The goal, to force the Entente to discuss peace had still not been reached.

Time was passing quickly and with each passing day the enemy had time to recover from the previous blows it suffered in the long pauses between battles. Then there was the issue involving the arrival of American troops. While still untested in battle, the large numbers of men filled up the ranks of the enemy reserves. As these troops were still inexperienced they did not come into consideration in the planning and organization of the anticipated decisive battles for the time being. Still, inexperienced or not, the Americans would be able to replace battle proven French divisions in quiet sectors of the front.

The OHL therefore considered the possibility of holding a new thrust as a distraction, where large numbers of enemy troops would be required to meet the new threat as well as forcing troops to be withdrawn from Flanders. If successful, this would allow the offensive on the Lys from April to be resumed.

The OHL came to the conclusion that an attack directed against key enemy positions, ones that the French and British could ill afford to lose would provide the best chance to accomplish its goals. The selection for the attacks in late May fell to the

Aisne front between Soissons and Reims, at whose center was the Chemin des Dames ridge. The OHL came to the conclusion that only further large blows in swift succession would decisively change the overall situation. Therefore, on 17 April 1918 General Ludendorff advised the Army Group Crown Prince to make preparations for an attack on the Chemin des Dames.

This location had been considered almost impregnable for some time by the French High Command, especially by Foch. It was felt that the natural defenses of the region, enhanced through artificial fortifications, were ample protection against any enemy attack. As such, Foch had withdrawn the strong divisions located there and in their place inserted jaded, worn out troops, amongst them five British divisions which had been badly mauled in the earlier German offensives.

All of the details of the immense attack were distributed to the divisions on 22 May 1918. The main thrust would be executed by the 7th Army in the sector between Mortier Wood, west of Anizy le Château and Sapigneul on the Aisne. This would be joined by the 1st Army between Sapigneul and the Brimont north of Reims. A few days after the main attack the right wing of the 7th Army and the 18th Army would capture the terrain south of Noyon in the direction of Compiégne. The German attack front would have a width of 120 kilometers when all parts of the plan were put into action.

The final preparations had begun; absolute secrecy and speed was required if the attack was to have a chance. All departments had to follow the strict orders from the 7th Army. Supervision of the immense effort was assigned to special observation flights and observation balloons who would report every violation of the orders. The men were marched only at night, the horses were allowed to go to the pastures only during relief, even the tires and wheels of the batteries and columns became provided with special attachments made out of wood covered in wool so nothing would clatter as the guns and wagons moved toward the front.

The efforts required to ensure the attack started at the designated time were almost impossible to complete. Every Group required about 200 artillery batteries of all calibers to be inserted into their positions between 14 and 26 May 1918 and provided with sufficient ammunition, without the supervisory pilots being able to determine their position through wheel tracks. There was something new with the artillery preparation fire which had never been attempted until now. For the first time the artillery would open fire at the start of the attack without one shot being fired beforehand to register the guns. Because of the limited time to prepare for the offensive and the difficult terrain, total surprise was necessary if the attack was expected to have any success.

Starting from 21 May 1918 the assault divisions arrived in their designated positions. On 24 May 1918 the *Sturmtruppen* were inserted into the assembly areas, which were no further than 5-6 kilometers behind the battle front and the readiness positions.

The main thrust of the German attack would come from the 7th Army and would also involve the 1st Army on the left wing and the 18th Army on the right wing. The attack would be delivered out of the line Anizy-le Château until northwest of Berry au bac in the direction of Soissons-Fismes-Reims. Strong opposition was expected in the area by Soissons and every precaution was being taken in order to overcome the anticipated enemy resistance.

Apart from the powerful defensive system of the enemy there were also exceptional terrain difficulties to overcome: the wide, swampy and churned up Ailette depression, the steep slopes of the ridges with the barriers and crater fields, the raging Aisne with few bridges which were dominated from the heights on the southern shore and in the end the Vesle. The German thrust must reach a depth of 20 kilometers if there was any prospect for success.

The mountainous terrain lying behind the attack front with its steep hillsides and forested ravines created a natural veil for the assembly of the extensive preparations required for the attack. The same conditions found on the enemy side of the line were formidable defenses and gave a false sense of security to the French who were holding this portion of the line.

In reality, whilst formidable, the Allied defenses were not in good condition. The sectors the divisions were holding were too wide for effective coverage. The trenches and wire entanglements were in poor condition and there was limited visibility of the German lines. Of the five British divisions placed on this part of the front, Major-General Campbell of the British 21st Division doubted that his division could hold the sector assigned to it for more than 24 hours if attacked.

General Duchêne, commander of the French Sixth Army, had decided to ignore the edict sent out by General Petain that the front line should be lightly held and the battle zone further to the rear would be held in strength as the main line of opposition. Instead, Duchêne was convinced that a fully manned front line was the best option for stopping any enemy attack and as such he filled up the front line trenches until they were overcrowded with men and left the main battle zone almost defenseless.

Despite all of the precautions being taken by the Germans, small pieces of the upcoming attack had been slowly leaking out to Allied Intelligence. In the weeks before the attack the sub-section of American Army Intelligence called 'Order of Battle' had been piecing together all of the different clues about the attack. In mid-May the 'Order of Battle' section provided a well-argued warning about an impending German attack along the Chemin des Dames.

Unfortunately, at this time, there was a great deal of friction between the American and French commands and the warning was 'scornfully disregarded' by the French command. Intelligence reports that followed which supported the warning provided by American Army Intelligence were simply ignored by General Duchêne until a fateful event on the night of 26 May 1918 following the capture of several German prisoners. The interrogation of the prisoners provided clear evidence that the Germans were going to attack the Chemin des Dames in the next day or two. Even Duchêne could not ignore all of the warnings forever and following the statements made by the prisoners he ordered even more men into the French front line. While believing he was providing a solid defense against the German attack, he was in fact providing more targets for the planned German artillery preparation fire developed by *Oberst* Bruchmüller.[1]

According to the attack orders, the 28th Reserve Division was under the command of the XXV Reserve Corps (Group Winkler) in the 7th Army. It had orders to take the heights of the Chemin des Dames between Malval farm and Bovelle farm and deliver the attack across the Aisne and Vesle until at the heights between Mont de Soisson farm and Bruys. The attack was divided into the following segments:

1. Taking of the height of the Chemin des Dames.
2. Taking of the ridge between Chemin des Dames and the Aisne.
3. Forcing of the Aisne crossing and firmly placed on the heights south of the Aisne.
4. Taking of the heights between the Aisne and Vesle and the Vesle crossings.
5. Taking of the heights south of the Vesle.

After obtaining all of these attack goals the infantry should dig in.[2]

The men of the 28th Reserve Division faced the approaching attack with firm confidence. The leaders and men were determined that the regiments would succeed as they had done in the past.

The men of the 28th Reserve Division marched to their assigned positions on 26 May 1918. They passed battery upon battery, vehicle upon vehicle, tethered balloons, infantry, labor troops, columns of every type, medical detachments, bridging trains, and more, all preparing for the attack set to begin at 1 a.m. on 27 May 1918. Surely with such forces at hand the attack could not fail, much the same feeling as the men of the British army felt on the eve of 1 July 1916.

In the afternoon of 26 May 1918 there was a discussion held in division headquarters, whereby the regimental commanders and adjutants of the division were given the final attack orders: 'The 7th Army would attack the Chemin des Dames on the fourth day, firmly in the possession of the heights of Ailette and the Aisne and thrust forth over the Vesle until on the heights between Soissons–Bruys–Erugny–Reims.'

Placed in the First Line: On the right the 1st Guard Infantry Division; in the middle the 33rd Infantry Division; on the left the 10th Reserve Division. The 197th Infantry Division, the position division up to this time, would follow in three attack groups. On the morning of the attack the 28th Reserve Division was designated as the reserve of Gruppe Winckler and located in the area of Bruyeres-Athies. In accordance with these orders the division marched at 10.00 p.m. from its camp and took up positions several kilometers behind the front line.

The German prisoners recently captured had provided the French with accurate information regarding the impending attack. However, *Oberst* Bruchmüller had successfully positioned 3,719 guns of every caliber as well as numerous *Minenwerfer* along the attack front. At precisely 1.00 a.m. the guns and *Minenwerfer* opened fire without warning, firing a combination of high explosive shells, gas shells and shrapnel. Every part of the front was covered with fire. The front line trenches disappeared in an immense series of explosions as heavy mortars fired on the masses of defenders. Artillery emplacements, crossroads, headquarters, depots and any other targets of value were all being struck at the same moment.

At 3.55 a.m. all of the guns concentrated their fire onto the front line trenches for a total of five minutes. At 3.40 a.m. the first *Sturmtrupps* advanced toward the enemy lines, some 20 minutes before first light. The preparation fire had been so intense that it was often difficult for the *Sturmtrupps* to recognize where the enemy front line trench had once stood. Nothing was left of the defenses or wire entanglements to indicate that a trench had once stood there a few hours earlier.

The volume of fire was described by some of the men as if a hurricane was raging. A tremendous crashing, roaring, hissing and bursting filled the air. It was a level of fire that even the oldest front fighters had never experienced before. Some of the men thought back to the days on the Somme and Verdun, where they described their existence as being in Hell. Today it is the opponents turn to experience such destructive fire and this thought alone helped to raise the morale of the men.

The men of the 28th Reserve Division waited anxiously for any news about the fighting while they were behind the lines, ready to advance; the division had been ready to move since 4.30 a.m. The men knew the attack was making good progress when the sound of the artillery fire grew weaker and weaker. This could only mean that the guns were advancing behind the infantry as they moved deeper into the enemy positions. Some of the first reports arrived at the headquarters of RIR 111 at 9 a.m.: 'Corps Winkler was in the fighting at the Vesle. However the regiment would remain in its accommodations, but it should be ready, so that an hour after the arrival of marching orders it can move off.'

At 1.15 p.m., more news reports from brigade: 'The attack moves forward well. The Aisne was crossed on all parts of the front. The artillery already moved forward across the Aisne. The advance of the division over the Ailette must be considered.' Later the division reported: 'The attack troops had reached the heights north of the Vesle.'

The orders for the advance by the 28th Reserve Division did not arrive until 2.55 a.m. on 28 May 1918. 'Division moves forward into Ailette valley. At 4.30 a.m. the battalions should be prepared to start at the entrance of Bruyeres, ready to march further to Chamouille.' RIR 109 marched at 4.00 a.m. via Bruyeres to Monthenault and from there continued to march through the Aisne valley to Bourgat 10.20 a.m. The midday meal had barely been distributed to the troops when orders arrived to continue the march to Courcelles. RIR 109 arrived there at 12.00 midnight and received billets on the Courcelles–Bazoches Road.

In accordance with orders RIR 110 moved out of Chamouille and at 7.30 a.m. was allowed a short rest period. The regiment was now in the positions where friend and foe lay opposite one another on the previous morning. There were traces of the heavy fighting everywhere one looked. Mountains of projectile baskets were piled near former battery positions, obstacles were torn apart and trenches were smashed. As yet only a few bodies still lay on the battlefield, covered with a tent tarpaulin provided by their comrades. The *pioniers* had already made the roads passable and thrown bridges across the Ailette. Large groups of prisoners were filing past as they were directed toward the rear. Judging from the loud noise coming from the front, the battle still raged further in front. At 10.30 a.m. RIR 110 marched until the men reached the heights of the Chemin des Dames, and now descended via Vendresse to the eastern slope of Hill 175, known as the 'Coffin cover', where the regiment arrived at 2.30 p.m.

The men of RIR 110 discovered that I/155 had captured a French General and four of his staff, 35 machine guns and 340 men on Hill 175. The spoils included four 15cm long barrel guns that were still loaded with their shells, all indicating just how startling the assault by the *Sturmtruppen* had been. At 5.30 p.m. RIR 110 received orders: The 28th Reserve Division would remain in the advance until Courcelles; RIR 110 would

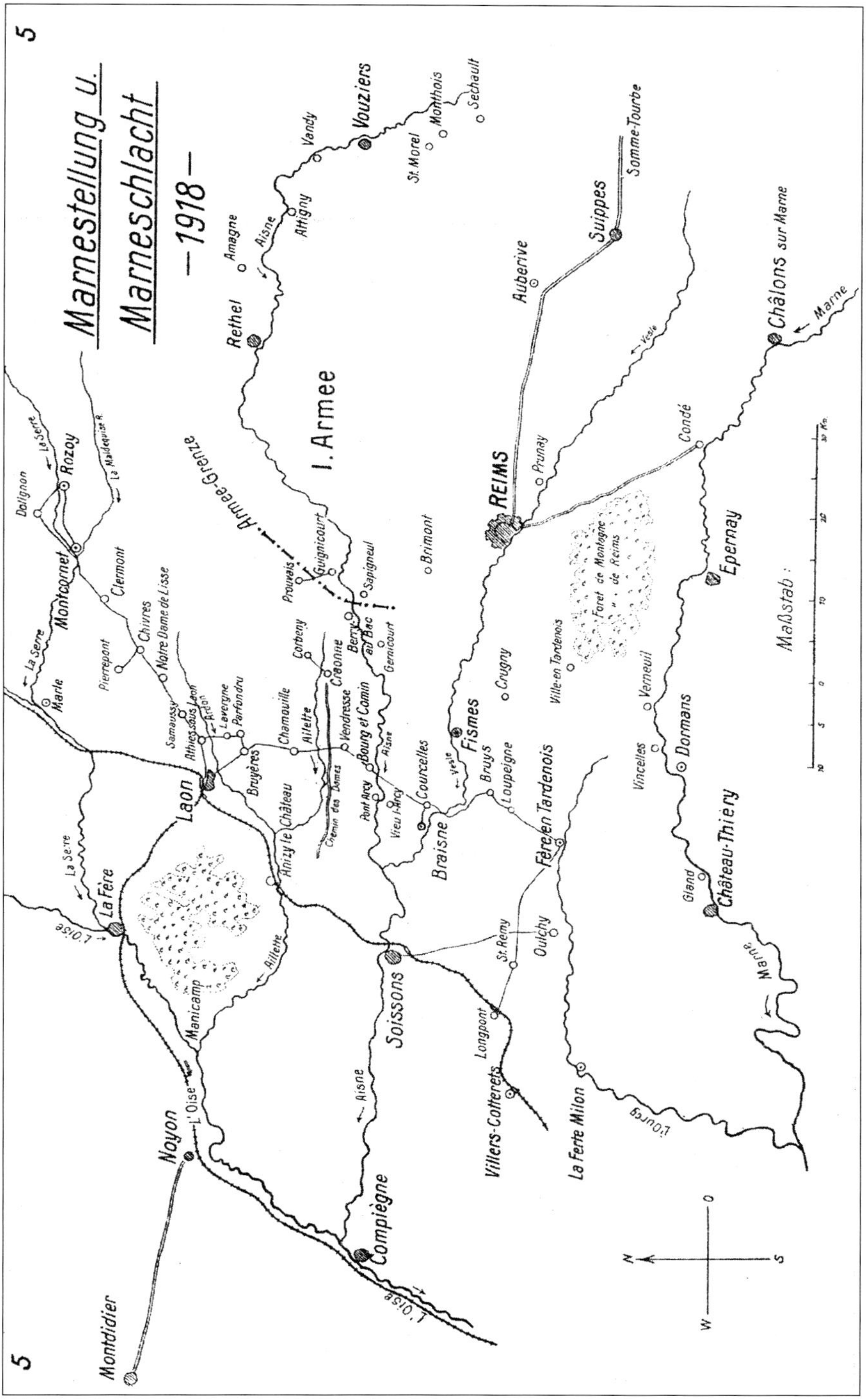

The Marne Position.

march behind RIR 111 via Bourg et Comin to Courcelles in the following order II, III, I Battalion.' The battalions moved on as the regimental commander had ridden in advance of the column along with the mounted orderlies.

It was discovered that Bourg et Comin on the Aisne and the Aisne canal, had been captured without much opposition, and the large bridge located there was still undamaged. The passage over the river and canal by Point-Arcy was considered to be difficult because the steep towering hills on the southern shore of the Aisne by Vieil-Arcy could effectively block any attempt to cross the waterways. Yet even here, the enemy resistance had been swept aside and the German troops streamed across the river and canal without much effort.

As the columns marched past, the men could see the numerous French machine gun nests, now silent. More bodies were scattered about these positions, all wearing the familiar Field Grey uniforms. Apparently the French had been able to provide some effective resistance as the German troops forced their way across the river.

The 28th Reserve Division continued to march on the hot dusty roads and eventually reached Courcelles, completely exhausted, between 10.30 p.m. and 12.00 midnight and the men were provided with billets for the night. There was no real concern if the supply columns could keep pace with the infantry. The men were provided with ample food taken from the numerous, well-stocked enemy supply depots captured in and around Braisne.

On the early morning of 28 May 1918 RIR 111 moved into the wood north of the Ailette, at about 10.00 a.m. the march would continue to Bourg on the Aisne in the following order III, I, II Battalion. After a brief rest in Bourg, the regiment moved forward in the afternoon until it had reached Courcelles on the Vesle. There the regiment would bivouac in Courcelles Château. During this time the regiments of the 28th Reserve Division had marched without being troubled through enemy artillery fire or by enemy aircraft. The greatest enemy was the unaccustomed exertion of marching with full packs and the heat which placed considerable demands on the troops. By the end of the day the regiments recorded that only a few men had fallen out on the march and that by far foot ailments were being reported above anything else.

29 May 1918 would be a day of rest for the troops of the 28th Reserve Division. While many of the men rested their sore feet, others were sent out to gather all possible food supplies. Livestock were slaughtered and stewed or fried, all types of wine had been found in the vicinity of the division so no one went lacking. Even freshly picked asparagus was offered as part of the meal. It was a sight that had not been seen in the division since the early part of the war of movement in August 1914. Once the feast had been consumed the regiments made ready to march forward but no such order arrived and the men were allowed to rest.

The rest time was of short duration; at approximately 9.00 a.m. on 30 May 1918 the 28th Reserve Division received orders, to advance on the right wing of *Gruppe* Winkler which meanwhile had reached the line: Hartennes – Hill 206 – Grand Rozoy. RIR 109 was joined by the 1st *Ersatz Pionier* Battalion 16, *Minenwerfer* Company 228 and RFAR 29 and designated as March Group B. The regiments started to move at 10.20 a.m. and reached Cuiry – Housse at 3.30 p.m. where RIR 109 received billets. Many

Men from RIR 111 in the trenches. (Author's collection)

of the men had very good memories of seeing this name on the wine bottles contained in the château cellars and of the carp found in the château pond. There were a few especially eager 'fishermen' in RIR 109 who were determined to have a fish dinner. After several of these 'fishermen' had taken mud baths, the carp were finally caught and consumed with great delight.

RIR 110 marched in the morning and moved closer to the right wing of Gruppe Winkler with the division. R111 marched at 10.30 a.m. and went along the Vesle to Violaine, where the battalions bivouacked in the surrounding forests. RIR 110 marched in the summer heat until Namteuil was reached between 2.30 and 3.30 p.m. and the I and II Battalions received billets in the village while the III Battalion was accommodated in former French barracks just west of the village. The men were greeted with roses and carnations blooming in the village gardens which sent out a beautiful fragrance while the murderous battle still raged in the front:

> Advance! The highest mood! The regiment hurried forward under light blue skies, shrouded in dust. A few kilometers in front us the Guard fought, we were following in the second line, and did not allow us to become drawn into the fight. The long chain of our tethered balloons showed us approximately where the battle front ran. In the evening we believe we are coming closer to them, but on the following morning they stand in great distance to the south. The Chemin des Dames already lay far behind us, the Aisne and Vesle had been crossed over. Long rows of prisoners, white and black Frenchmen, from England and Italy fascinate us as they pass;

discarded pieces of equipment, shot up vehicles. Dead and horse cadavers mark the route that the yielding enemy has taken. We were almost without hope to still be able to catch him; we carry on further in the burdensome heat. As such the companies reached the small, completely abandoned Namteuil worn out and tired on 30 May about 3.00 p.m.

Leutnant der Reserve Fritz Schmitt, RIR 110.[3]

Once in Namteuil the thunderous sound of the artillery was now quite close and the line of observation balloons was nearby. The opinion among the troops that they might become involved in the fighting on the next day had grown considerably. Still, looking at the men, it would be difficult to picture them involved in a life and death struggle with the enemy. An almost playful mood had taken over the Other Ranks and even the most serious men had played all sorts of pranks. Looking around the village one could see a man swaggering around in a bridesmaid dress while wearing a top hat. Another presented himself as a coquette with a dainty night cap and other props and with the general cheerfulness all of the previous and forthcoming fatigues appeared to have been forgotten.

All of the clever men had quickly obtained mattresses and bed-pillows so that in the event there was a shortage of straw in the bivouac they would have a soft place to sleep. A few of the men who considered the future worried that once the bivouac was destroyed, the men might have to return to the hard floors of the now empty houses. Even the officers enjoyed this brief respite from the realities of the fighting that was surely to take place shortly:

Together with *Leutnants der Reserve* Gerstner and Heuss I looked upon the Château Muret et Crouttes in the evening, which was lying in the vicinity, a beautifully situated, stately property that likewise had been quickly evacuated. The view from the tower offered a wide, extensive full view. The glow of fire lit up the horizon and loud cannon thunder reverberated across from the battle line. Before we left the Château, we found out that all three of us had grown up in the *Kurpfälzischen* city of Heidelberg, a similar impulse followed, and the song '*Heidelberg, du Jugend and bronnen*' was sung. The echo from this song throbbed in the nightly silence and filled the old walls of the Château corridors with youth and gaiety. A few hours later we stood with our companies in the battle in front of St. Remy.

Leutnant der Reserve Fritz Schmitt, RIR 110.[4]

Up until this time the 28th Reserve Division acted solely as the Corps Reserve and had not taken part in the fighting. This situation was about to change when fresh troops were needed in the battle lines due to the loss of men from wounds and fatigue from three days of heavy fighting. In the night from 30 to 31 May 1918 the 197th Infantry Division relieved the 10th Reserve Division and at the same time the 28th Reserve Division was assigned to the front line where it was sure to see action.

Once the necessary orders had been issued, the regiments of the 28th Reserve Division began the long march to the front lines. At 5.00 a.m. RIR 109 took the lead as

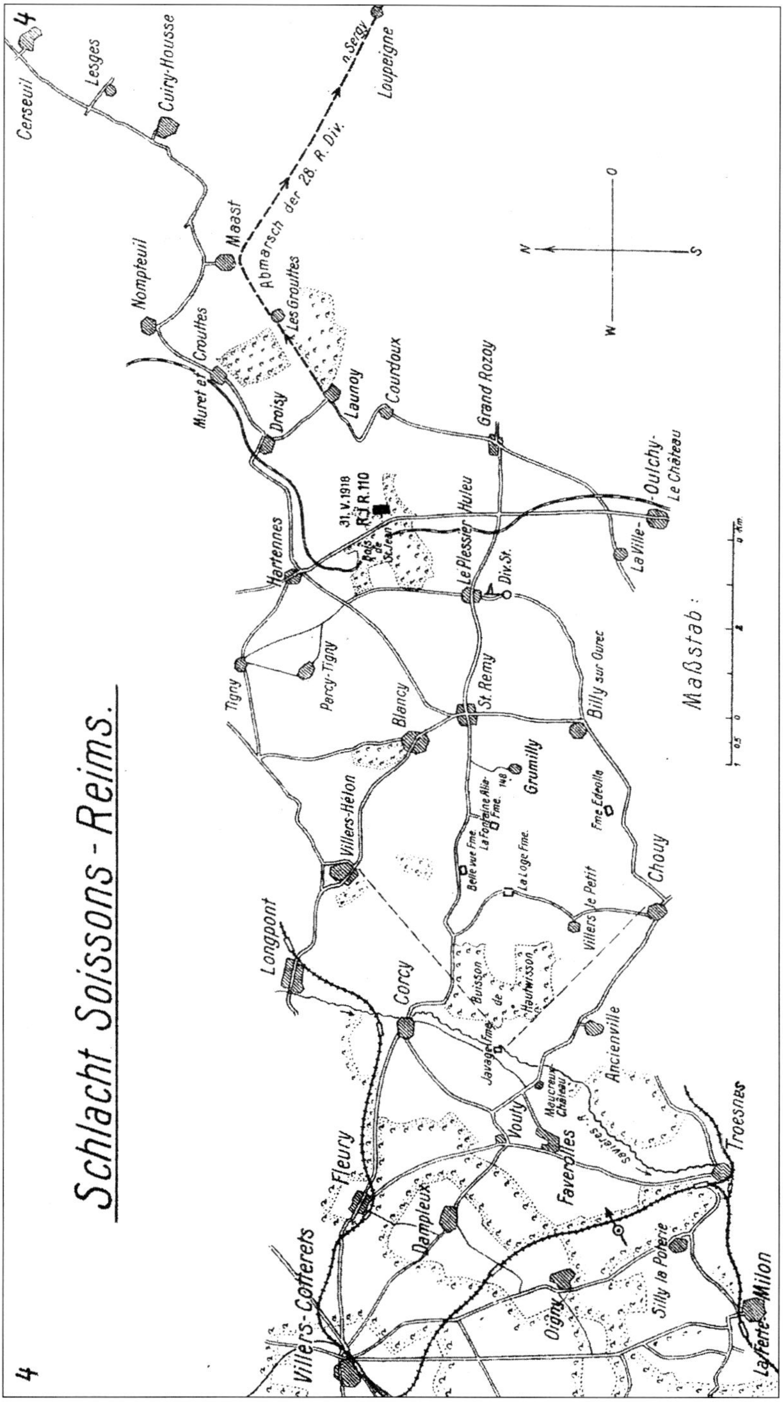

Fighting between Soissons and Reims.

the battalions marched off. Over the next few hours the remaining regiments also took to the roads and moved toward the front. All three regiments moved in the direction toward the villages of Le Plessier-Huleu. The route was under French artillery fire for most of the way and when dawn approached, the inevitable enemy aircraft appeared overhead in large numbers. Due to the threat of artillery fire and attacks from enemy aircraft the columns advanced with large intervals between the units, normally one kilometer between each battalion.

As the men approached the front lines the sounds of heavy fighting continued to almost grow stronger with every step the men took. As the columns approached the area behind the front the enemy activity increased substantially. Other units were already involved in fire fights against the French troops by Tigny and enemy machine gun bullets soon whistled past the men as they marched along the roads. Finally, after reaching the Bois de St. Jean the columns were stopped for a much needed rest and the men took cover in the dense forest.

At 12.37 p.m. division orders arrived which provided some insight into what the men were about to experience:

> There was fighting in the Line Parcy-Tigny Hill west of St. Remy. RIR 110 and the I/RFAR 29 under Major von Schmeling would move forward to St. Remy and until further orders they would be subordinate to the Guard Infantry Division.[5]

In accordance with the new orders, at 1.00 p.m. RIR 110 moved closer to the front line, leaving the field kitchens behind under cover in the Bois de St. Jean. The regiment advanced toward St. Remy with the I Battalion as the vanguard, followed by the II Battalion, III/RFAR 29 and the III Battalion in the rear. At 2.45 p.m. the column was halted in front of Plessier-Huleu and the men were ordered to take up positions at the eastern exit of the village. Every attempt was made to provide as much cover as possible against enemy aircraft. As such, every house and garden was occupied by horses and men and all unnecessary movement was forbidden.

While the men rested the regimental commander and his orderlies rode over the division headquarters of the 1st Guard Division which had stopped nearby, at the southern exit of Plessier-Huleu. At 2.50 p.m. Major *von* Schmeling received new verbal orders as the situation had already changed from a few hours earlier. The 28th Reserve Division was now ordered to protect the right flank of the 1st Guard Division. In fact, RIR 110 was needed immediately to fill a gap that had formed between the Guard Division and the neighboring 37th Infantry Division. At 2.50 p.m. Major *von* Schmeling received verbal orders:

1. The I Battalion would occupy the Fontaine-Alix farm and the wooded piece by the farm as the vanguard. If possible, without considerable fighting, also occupy La Loge farm.
2. The II Battalion would take position in the ground north of Grumilly.
3. The III Battalion would take position in the ground south of St. Remy.[6]

Captured French artillery. (Source: Author's collection)

Whilst the regimental commander and his staff were receiving the new orders an enemy squadron of bombers flew over the positions of RIR 110 and evidently observed the troop concentrations in the village. Within moments bombs began to explode in the positions held by the III/R110 and in just a few minutes approximately 70 men from the 11th and 12/R110 had been killed or wounded.

Furnished with the new orders, the regimental commander rode out with his staff and mounted orderlies on a reconnaissance around St. Remy and the other locations provided to the regiment. By 3.45 p.m. the regimental staff had firmly established that the Fontaine Alix farm was occupied by French troops and that one company from IR 150 (37th Infantry Division) was involved in a fire fight with the French defenders in the farm.

With an exact knowledge of the overall situation facing his regiment, Major *von* Schmeling issued orders that the I/R110, located at the southern exit of St. Remy, should occupy the wooded piece on Hill 148 west of Grumilly. The battalion immediately formed for the advance with the 2nd and 3/R110 in the front line and the 1st and 4/R110 in the second line. During the movement by the I/R110 a connection was established on the right flank with IR 150. There was no connection with any German units possible on the left flank as the battalion moved forward.

The II/R110 arrived at the southern exit of St. Remy at 4.00 p.m. was given verbal orders by the regimental staff. The battalion would take up a position west of the St. Remy–Billy Road with the 5th and 7/R110 located in the hollow by Grumilly and the rest of the battalion in a wooded piece east of the village.

Just then, an orderly officer from IR 150 galloped up and reported to the regimental staff that directly west of St. Remy strong enemy forces had pressed back parts of the I/150 on Blanzy. The orderly officer urgently asked for support. Major *von* Schmeling rode back with the officer and observed how the skirmish line from the I/150 was withdrawing from Blanzy in an easterly direction, closely followed by advancing French troops.

> Our regimental commander just arrived out of the church square in St. Remy, and with full clarity he sprang from his horse and shouted to us: The Frenchmen sit in front of us upon the hill; the battalion would immediately develop to the right and begin the counterattack!
>
> *Unteroffizier* Ehling, III/R110.[7]

Suddenly everyone was in motion as officers issued orders to their assembled men. The III/R110 ordered the 11th and 12th Companies to attack the enemy between Blanzy and the St. Remy– Corcy Road, take Blanzy and the hill southwest of the villages. The 11th company would be on the right, the 12/R110 on the left. The 9/R110 would follow behind the 12/R110; the 10/R110 would be in reserve behind the right wing of the battalion. The 3rd Machine Gun Company would support the attack by firing into the French lines above the advancing companies.

The companies of the III/R110 were rapidly organized and within a short time were advancing toward the French lines. The attack was supported by the batteries of the III/RFAR 29 which opened rapid fire against the French positions, in some instances using open sights. The well placed fire of the batteries provided some protection to the men advancing across the open terrain.

The French had already set up a number of machine gun nests in the gardens and hedges around Blanzy in order to defend the village and the guns quickly opened fire into the advancing lines from RIR 110. The German infantry in the front line as well as light machine guns and a platoon of heavy machine guns opened fire; the din of so many guns firing made it almost impossible for the men to hear one another.

The concentrated fire from the machine guns, infantry and artillery were beginning to have an effect on the French skirmish line and soon individuals, then small groups began to withdraw toward the village. The 11/R110 under *Leutnant der Reserve* Ziegler quickly observed the enemy movement and followed closely on their heels, giving them no time to form a new defensive line.

Ziegler's men assaulted machine gun nest after machine gun nest in the manner they had been taught over the last few months. The new tactics were successful as each nest fell into German hands. Within a short time Blanzy was stormed and the connection with the I/150 was established in the village. At approximately 5.00 p.m. Blanzy was firmly in German hands. The men of the 11th Company continued their assault upon Hill 180 west of the village, accompanied by two platoons of the 3rd Machine Gun Company. The attack was successful; the enemy garrison that survived the attack was either forced back or taken prisoner and the 3rd Machine Gun Company quickly set up their guns in defensive positions.

During the attack a number of men from the 11/R110 were singled out for their actions in the attack: *Leutnant der Reserve* Heim, *Offizier Stellvertreter* Ronde, *Unteroffizier* Splittdorf, *Gefreiters* Waschle and Jost, *Reservist* Reinhardt, *Musketiers* Bienecke, Löhr and Langenese.

During the initial attack the 12/R110 had already run into several enemy machine gun nests 500 meters west of St. Remy. These were surrounded on all sides as had been practiced for so many weeks and were eliminated one by one. The gun crews that had survived the assault were taken prisoner and sent to the rear.

In one case, a lone German soldier assaulted a French machine gun nest, *Unteroffizier* Demmler. Demmler successfully stormed the nest and took most of the garrison prisoner, two French officers were killed and several French soldiers had been wounded in the attack. As each machine gun nest fell, other French defenders began to fall back. Sergeant Lampert and *Unteroffizier* Demmler pursued the retreating enemy with their groups. *Leutnant der Reserve* Happel, 12/R110, then took up positions in a small group of trees where he organized defensive machine gun nests. During this assault a number of men from the 12/R110 were recognized for their individual actions: *Vizefeldwebel* Sachs, *Gefreiter* Kaiser, *Gefreiter* Hellinger, *Unteroffizier* Gerstel and *Gefreiter* Sauterer.

Losses were inevitable during the successful advance by RIR 110. During the attack the 9/R110 extended its front to the left on its own. The platoon of *Leutnant der Reserve* Macholz captured an enemy machine gun nest, which was occupied by at least 100 enemy troops. During the assault, Sergeants Hahn and Geiger, two men who had belonged to the battalion since the beginning of the war, were both killed. Losses such as this were irreplaceable.

During the brief assault, the 10/R110, which had been echeloned on the right of the battalion, then became ordered to shift behind the middle. When the company received strong machine gun fire from the left flank from the St. Remy–Corcy Road, *Leutnant der Reserve* Schweigert ordered the first platoon to take position south of the road and the second and third platoons north of the road. *Leutnant der Reserve* Holzinger ordered his light machine guns to provide concentrated fire against the enemy positions.

While the men were being deployed, *Leutnant der Reserve* Hemberger suddenly saw one of the enemy machine gun nests in the wood opposite his position. He shot down one Frenchman and four others surrendered. While the second and third platoons were engaging the enemy the first platoon pressed forward until it had reached the sunken road which led from the St. Remy-Corcy road to the La Fontaine-Alix Farm. In a short time the enemy ceased all firing and in the subsequent advance one officer and 43 men were sent back as prisoners.

Unteroffizier Mack, *Unteroffizier* Skibb, *Gefreiter* Schade, *Musketier* Leyk, Heimbächer, Engels, Böhme and Müller were all singled out for their actions of this day. The III/R110 had successfully restored the situation, helped to throw the enemy out of Blanzy and advanced with the I/150.

While successful, the actions of RIR 110 had thrown off the planned attack of the 28th Reserve Division. Just as the III/R110 had become involved with the attack on Blanzy with the I/R150 the 28th Reserve Division headquarters in Le Plessier-Huleu received attack orders at 4.00 p.m. In this attack, the boundaries of the division were designated as follows: on the right of the division the St. Remy–Villers Hèlon-Longpoint Road; on the left: the Chouy-Javage Farm. RIR 111 would attack on the right RIR 110 on the left.

The first goal of the attack was the heights of the Savières stream. RIR 109 would take the advance with the 3/RFAR 29 and one platoon of the 4/*Pionier* Battalion 10 and continue on to Billy sur Ourcq, in order to take up reserve positions behind the attacking regiments. When RIR 109 reached the designated position the attack orders were changed as RIR 110 had been called away to assist IR 150 by Blanzy.

Then, at 4.30 p.m., a new division order arrived. It came at the time when the I/R110 was advancing against La Fontaine-Alix farm and the III/R110 was assisting the I/150 by Blanzy. Under these circumstances, the new order was already out of date and was no longer feasible. The replacement regimental adjutant of RIR 110, *Leutnant der Reserve* Greiner, went as fast as possible to Plessier-Huleu and verbally reported the situation to the division headquarters.

After learning of the new situation the division issued another attack order, which arrived at the regimental headquarters of RIR 110 at 5.40 p.m. According to the orders RIR 110 remained in the right sector, RIR 109 remained in the advance via Billy sur Ourcq and d'Edrolles farm and would take over the left wing of the attack. RIR 111 which was already in the advance upon St. Remy, marched from there to Billy sur Ourcq. However, before the order could be distributed to the battalion and company leaders, RIR 110 received the following changes in a new division order at 6.30 p.m.

> As the right border of the division probably shifted in the line St. Remy, Bellevue farm, southern edge of Dampleux, the regiment will not go forward via the La Fontaine-Alix farm and stop the attack north of this new border against Blanzy and vicinity.[8]

With each subsequent order, the regimental staff would have to make new arrangements with the different battalions who in turn would have to inform the individual companies. Even with the receipt of new orders, it always took time to get everyone positioned and to determine exactly what was expected of each platoon in the regiment.

While the changes were taking place, smaller actions continued across the front line. At 5.00 p.m. *Leutnant der Reserve* Schneider from the 2/R110 with *Unteroffizier* Körbel, *Gefreiter* Rosenthal and other people of the company stormed La Fontaine-Alix farm, and took 22 men prisoner. At 6.40 p.m. the II/R110 shot down a low flying French aircraft and the Platoon of *Leutnant der Reserve* Deckert from the 6/R110 took the wounded pilot, an officer, prisoner.

Then, at 7.55 p.m. a new attack order from the division arrived at the regiments. In RIR 110 the new attack orders were finally sent down to the battalions at 8.25 p.m.:

1. The new attack direction goes directly to the west. The right border: RIR 110 (the same division border) from St. Remy via Bellevue farm to the southern edge of Dampleux. The left regimental border: from Villers le Petit, northern edge of Ancienville, southern edge of Faverolles, southern edge of Oigny.
2. The start of the attack: 9.00 p.m.
3. Goal of the attack for today: the Savières stream west of the Buisson de Hautvisson.

4. The attack: on the right the I, on the left the II Battalion La Fontaine farm. La Loge farm falls in the strip of the I Battalion.
   The described wood Buisson de Hautvisson is to be attacked by both battalions at the projecting end and rolled up.
5. …
6. …
7. III Battalion follows the attack in the second line.
8. …
9. …
10. III Battalion received orders, to abandon its former strip, and be placed at the ready in the wood piece on the St. Remy-Corcy Road. The 10th Coy would establish the connection between the I Battalion and the I/150 here. Part of RIR 109 would deploy with it.[9]

With RIR 110 occupied the position intended for RIR 111 and was heavily engaged with the enemy, RIR 109 took over the position specified for RIR 110 and developed for the advance via Billy sur Ourcq on the d'Etrole farm between La Fontaine Alice, Chouy farm. RIR 111 would now be the division reserve. Finally, at 8.45 p.m. RIR 109 stood ready on the right of the division line with the III/R109 and two field guns on the right, the II/R109 and one field gun on the left; the I/R109 with one platoon from the 4/*Pionier* Battalion 16 in the second line. During the time needed to rearrange the regiments, severe losses occurred on the march through enemy artillery fire.

By the time everyone was in place dusk had fallen. Then, at 8.57 p.m., a third attack order with further changes of the order of battle for the division had arrived. The right border of the division was now: St Remy de Bellevue-Dampleux Farm; left border: Chouy–Noroy–Troësnes–Silly-la Poterie. The line separating the regiments would be the Villers le Petit–Faverolles–Oigny Road. On the right would be RIR 110, on the left RIR 109 with RIR 111 in the second line. The attack would begin at 9.00 p.m. and would still be delivered up to the Savières brook. Once again, the delay needed to regroup into the new attack positions allowed the French artillery to inflict a number of losses to all three regiments.

It was not until 9.30 p.m. until the battalions could finally advance with the onset of darkness. The III/R109 on the right wing immediately received strong artillery fire coming from Hill 188 and severe machine gun fire out of la Loge farm lying one kilometer to the southeast. The 12/R109 worked toward the farm under the leadership of *Leutnant* Jenne, who was killed during the advance. *Feldwebel der Reserve* Lehmann immediately took over the command of the 12th Company and continued the attack against the farm, supported by four machine guns from the 3rd Machine Gun Company as well as additional support from the 11/R109 under *Leutnant* Straub.

The farm was finally taken after heavy fighting, 34 prisoners and four machine guns were captured. The III/R109 continued to advance in total darkness in the line la Loge farm until it was east of Buisson de Hautvison where the men entrenched under the protection of an advanced skirmish line. The III/R109 could not advance any further because of severe flanking fire coming from the right. Apparently RIR 110 had not advanced as far as RIR 109 and had remained approximately 800 meters to the rear; the situation was somewhat tenuous.

Due to the brevity of time, the formation of the battalions of RIR 110 did not take place until 9.00 p.m. and the regiment was finally assembled by 10.30 p.m. During this time full darkness had fallen and simultaneously there was strong artillery fire directed upon the II/R110, so the new deployment of the regiment had proven to be impossible. The connection to RIR 109 had not been established as expected resulting in the large gap between the two regiments.

The situation facing the division had become even more critical when the II/R109 had already started its attack before the latest changes in orders had made it to the battalion. Part of the battalion was already involved in fire fights against French machine gun nests south of Chouy when the newest order finally arrived about the current order of battle.

The II/R109 west of Chouy immediately made alterations to its attack and the formations were rearranged once more. However, the 8/R109 which had advanced in a southwest direction in the darkness could not be informed of the third attack order. The company moved forward in the night, without any connection with the rest of the battalion, until it was in the vicinity of Noroy. Parts of the 5th and 6/R109 had also been unable to establish any connection again with the battalion, along with two light *Minenwerfer* and the escort field gun. They had guided on the advance of the III/R109 on the left wing in the direction of Château Maucreux in the dark night.

The regimental staff and I/R109 followed the attack of the II and III/R109 and the staff was in Villers le Petit by 12 midnight. Finally, towards 3.30 a.m. the II/R110 was ordered to entrench in front of la Loge farm, with the I/R110 already positioned 200 meters west of La Fontaine-Alix farm. It would take some time to determine just where each regiment, battalion and company in the division were located, which needed to be done as quickly as possible before any further offensive action could be taken.

In the early morning darkness of 1 June 1918 the II/R109 continued the advance and except for the time the battalion was on the hill northeast of Noroy it was constantly under enemy artillery fire. Once at the hill the II Battalion attacked the French positions at 3.00 a.m. The II/R109 had no connection to any friendly troops on the right wing despite several patrols being sent out to establish a connection with the III/R109. One of these patrols under *Leutnant der Reserve* Beil, 7/R109, received strong machine gun fire from the area around Ancienville, during which the leader and a several of his men were wounded. Through the stalwart conduct of Sergeant Hörrle, 7/R109, with the remaining Other Ranks in the patrol, all of the wounded were brought to safety.

The missing III/R109 had strayed too far to the right in the previous evening and was eventually found to be in the sector assigned to the II/R110. Fortunately for the men of the II/R110 the III/R109 had already captured La Loge farm and the II/R110 no longer had to complete this task. In an attempt to straighten out the confusion in the regimental ranks, brigade orders arrived at RIR 110 directing the III/R109 to return to its regiment and leave the battle zone of the II/R110.

The II/R109 did eventually establish a connection on the left wing with the 1st Guard Infantry Division, which provided some security for the battalion. Once back with the

Staff of II/R110. (*Reserve-Infanterie-Regiment Nr. 110 im Weltkrieg 1914-1918*)

regiment, the III/R109 took up a position in the right regimental sector and with its front directly to the west the battalion attacked west of Villers le Petit. A platoon from the 4/*Pionier* Battalion 16 which had taken over the protection of the division lines west and northwest of Villers le Petit in the night; was now assigned as the reserve behind the II/R109.

At 5.30 a.m. the II/R109 had reached Noroy. After a short pause in the fighting the battalion resumed the advance at 8.00 a.m. and penetrated further into the French lines in a westerly direction and reached the heights of the Buisson de Cresnes toward midday despite powerful infantry and machine gun fire. The fighting continued in this area until 1.00 p.m. when the attack on the western edge of the wood hesitated. Until now the fighting had been against small groups of enemy infantry and machine gun nests. Now, when enemy artillery fire fell along the battalion front and enemy aircraft joined in the fighting, attacking any movement the pilots observed with machine gun fire, the II/R109 began to suffer heavy losses.

Attempts were made to obtain supporting artillery fire by the II/R109 as well as the regimental staff but despite all efforts the German artillery support was missing. The swift advance by the II/R109 up to this point had been successful, mainly as a result of the veiled waves of the 5th and 7/R109 under the command of *Offizier Stellvertreter* Wiegand, *Vizefeldwebel* Frisch as well as the Group leaders: *Unteroffizier* Bödigheimer (killed), *Gefreiter* Wieland (killed), *Gefreiter* Nutz and the invaluable support from two machine guns of the 2nd Machine Gun Company. The losses in the battalion were high, particularly to the leaders. *Leutnants* Dressler, Armbruster, Kindevater, Schulz, Allies and several *Offizier Stellvertreter* and platoon leaders were placed out of action through wounds.

The III/R019, now back with the regiment, took position as the right battalion in the advance and after taking time to reform the ranks, would begin the attack at 6.00 a.m. During the time the battalion required to reform and take up position the activity was observed by low flying enemy pilots and within a short time heavy French artillery fire from the hills southwest of Corcy fell on the assembled battalion and powerful machine gun fire coming out of Lionval farm cut through the ranks.

Fortunately, the III/R109 was able to quickly advance by swinging very wide and the battalion literally ran out from under the enemy barrage fire. Once on the move, the men of the III/R109 attacked in an unstoppable advance against the towering hills of Faverolles. Ancienville became taken in this advance whereby 36 enemy prisoners fell into the hands of the 10/R109. The French continued to provide a solid defense and the Savières ground became closed off by strong artillery fire. The French tenaciously defended Maucreux Château through powerful machine gun fire.

Parts of the 10th, 3rd and 12/R109, under the command of *Leutnants der Reserve* Weigele II, Mayer and Schretzmann, captured the large, solidly built château at 8 a.m. together with the parts of the 5th and 6/R109 which had not been able to establish a connection to their battalion on the previous evening. Shortly before RIR 109 advanced into the château the enemy occupying it had waved white cloths and caused the attack to hesitate in the face of what appeared to be surrender by the enemy troops. Instead, the time was used by the enemy to escape into the nearby wood and in part using automobiles to drive in the direction of Faverolles.

A French field howitzer detachment which had not completely left its position yet, stopped and fired a few shot against the attacking Germans, then the guns were packed up and rapidly driven toward safety. When the men from RIR 109 entered the château they found that everything had already been plundered and the interior of the stately home looked terrible. Apparently the French had destroyed everything; there were no food stocks or wine to be found inside the building.

The III/R109 keenly pressed after the retreating French. The 3/R109, which was subordinate to the III/R109, reached the crossroads northwest of Maucreux shortly after 8.00 a.m. and took a number of prisoners there. They fired at the enemy automobiles that were departing the château, loaded with infantry and artillerymen on the Corcy–Vouty Road for as long as they were in view and then carried the attack further under their leader *Leutnant* Hell, supported by a platoon of light *Minenwerfer* under *Feldwebel Leutnant* Schäfer, *Leutnant* Hell's group circumvented Faverolles which forced the enemy to evacuate the village but were soon stopped when French resistance proved too strong.

The III/R109 along with the 3/R109 were unable to continue the advance without artillery support. The French were able to reform and mounted several strong counterattacks with artillery support and eventually were able to press back the 3/R109 and recapture Faverolles. The main body of the III/R109 that was about 400 meters east of Faverolles then received extremely severe enemy machine gun fire coming from the church tower and out of the houses of this village, which the light *Minenwerfer* were unable to silence. Only one gun from the escort battery was in position and was also unable to effectively silence the enemy machine guns. The heavy infantry fire was accompanied by well positioned, powerful enemy artillery fire which was being directed by low flying French observation aircraft which could see every movement made by the companies lying in the open terrain. With the increasing enemy pressure the attack by the III/R109 hesitated and then came to a full stop and the losses suffered by the men continued to grow rapidly.

With the III/R109 in an exposed position and under heavy fire there was an urgent need to establish a connection with the neighboring troops before the battalion could be isolated and possibly cut off. Patrols were sent out from each flank, looking for the nearest friendly troops. The patrols sent off to the right managed to make contact with the neighboring RIR 110 which was still slightly to the rear of the III/R109, but there still existed a gap between the two units which could not be occupied without more troops. The solution was found by positioning several machine guns to cover the open ground and prevent any possible enemy advance into that area. The patrols sent off to the left did not succeed in establishing a connection to the 1st Guard Infantry Division. As a result of this, a gap formed between the II and III/R109 approximately one kilometer wide.

Once the stray battalion from RIR 109 had been sent back to its regiment, the men of RIR 110 prepared for the renewal of the attack from 31 May 1918. The division order written at 4.20 a.m. which arrived at regimental headquarters at 5.25 a.m. changed nothing in the disposition of the regiment. The goal of the attack for 1 June was the Villers Cotterêts–la Ferté Milon Road. At daybreak the battalions moved forward with two companies each in the first line, and two companies in the second line.

The attack of the II/R110 on the left wing made good progress. Enemy machine gun nests scattered about by Villers le Petit were taken by the 8/R110, one after the other. Platoon Halbrock took five prisoners during this time. A machine gun Group of the 5/R110 under *Unteroffizier* Blömecke captured a machine gun by Ancienville during which six Frenchmen surrendered with their hands raised high. The 8/R110 and one platoon each from the 6th and 7/R110 circumvented Buisson de Hautvisson to the south.

The waves of men from the remaining companies advanced through the wood and reached the slope which led to the Savières brook. Two enemy machine gun nests located in the Savières ground slowed the advance until they were both placed out of action by the platoon of *Vizefeldwebel* Rüdiger, 8/R110, together with a machine gun from RIR 109. With the nests cleared, the men were able to cross the brook. Once on the opposite bank several enemy machine guns opened fire from out of the Maucreux Château which the men of the III/R109 had not yet taken.

Platoon Hock of the Machine Gun Company successfully fought against the enemy machine guns from a position at the northern edge of Ancienville. A battery ascending the Javage Farm–Faverolle Road on the right of the château also became shot up in the shortest period of time and frantically galloped away in the fire from the machine guns. Platoon Lorenz of the 2nd Machine Gun Company successfully fought against enemy machine guns positioned on the hill north of the Savières brook.

Under the protection of this fire the companies were able to reach the safety provided by the walls of Château Maucreux at the time the residence was being captured by III/

R109. The men from RIR 110 could also watch as the French, apparently a headquarters staff, drove away in an automobile. The men were eager to pursue and all parts of the battalion surged forward upon the hill at the eastern edge of Faverolle. Once there, strong French machine gun fire forced the men to halt. Meanwhile, the II/R110 staff is also entered the château at approximately 8.00 a.m. and immediately set up a command post:

> The attack ordered for the evening of 31 May was postponed at the last minute and moved forward to the next morning, because in the darkness and in the enemy artillery fire it was not possible, to reach the readiness position. The III Battalion spent the night east of the La Loge farm. The companies camped in the small groups of trees that were scattered around or in the grain fields and also dug in partially there. The night proceeded comparatively quiet. The enemy artillery and enemy machine guns only scattered fire down on the terrain. However it was nevertheless an unpleasant night that brought no relaxation to the troops.
>
> When the morning of 1 June dawned and the last preparations were completed, our battalion moved to the advance. My machine guns were distributed with the infantry companies and to be sure two platoons (*Leutnant* Lorenz and *Offizier Stellvertreter* Hock) were with the front companies, one platoon (*Vizefeldwebel* Willenweber) was with the companies in the second line. I remained with my battle orderlies by the rear platoon in the vicinity of the battalion staff.
>
> The attack moved forward well in the delightful summer morning and it was pressed forward most energetically. The enemy infantry afforded only individual opposition, on the other hand the enemy machine gun nests afforded more opposition, which were distributed across the entire terrain with great skill and that had to become fought down individually. Our heavy machine guns afforded good work here and supported the advancing companies with the best results.
>
> About 5 a.m. we came upon a small farm south of Buisson de Hautvison, in whose immediate vicinity a large herd of beef and sheep was accommodated in an enclosure. It was apparently the livestock depot of a larger troop association, which could no longer become transported away with the rapid withdrawal of the French troops and was now inconsiderately destroyed by them. The shells fell down continuously on the animals which were frantically running about and caused a horrible blood bath among them. I had to watch this horrible drama for a long time during the advance, until a wave in the terrain masked my view. When we then strode through the southern edge of the grove, we came into the strongest artillery fire. The wood pieces were showered with shells and shrapnel and the otherwise so splendid high wood became throbbing throughout from the terrible noises of the crashing and bursting projectiles. I ran forward with my orderlies and a gun crew as quickly as possible in this hail of shells, each moment in danger of becoming torn apart. And nevertheless we came through safely, and afterward it appeared like a miracle that we had come out of this fire with no losses. Then, when we moved out of the wood somewhat later, the valley ground of the Savières stream lay in front of us, and on the rise of the other side we saw

the white sandstone Château Maucreux brightly lit up, which according to the map lay in the battle strip of the battalion and the area was already well-known to us. Now, after observations, we could see how a few vehicles left the château in a hurried journey. It was, as we later found out, the staff of a high command post that had been accommodated in the château and that was surprised by our rapid advance, and which still in the last minute could be brought to safety. We immediately opened fire upon the vehicles traveling away, however we could no longer prevent their escape. Still later we found in the château the complete baggage of the staff and amongst them therefore an entire crate full of French war crosses (*Croix de Guerre*), with which we were mutually decorated with. The valley ground still lay under strong infantry and machine gun fire from the château, and it lasted a long time, until our machine guns (Platoons Lorenz and Hock) had silenced the fire. Beneath the château lay a small mill with a few out buildings, in the vicinity of where we crossed over the brook. As I came over there with my people, it offered me a humorous picture. An immense pig had been killed through machine gun fire, and now our good *Schützen* fully regretted the circumstances of the animal in that they could not participate in the battle party. They would have surely all been grateful guests, and likewise we would have certainly gladly participated with them. However, we must continue to answer the call of duty.

In a swift tempo we went up the rise and after a few minutes we had arrived at the château. It was about 8 o'clock, when I walked through the château yard and there I met with the company leaders of the 7th and 8th Companies (*Leutnant der Reserve* Schmitt and *Leutnant der Landwehr* Heuss). The château was, how we later determined, the property of *Marquis* de Lubersca and made an imposing impression with its numerous battlements and spires. Also the interior was exceptionally luxurious. We barely dared to go inside in our soiled and dusty clothes, and I still remember how full of wonder we were when walking the splendid halls and when the troops carefully ascended, still completely dazed from the splendor that surrounded us. None of us had suspected in this minute that this magnificent château should become involved in our fate. And however it was so! Our attack came to a halt in front of its walls and in its park and its cellars we spent 8 more terrible days. And when we then became relieved and left it, the French transformed it into a desolate wreck.[10]

One platoon of the 7th Coy with the company leader, *Leutnant der Reserve* Fritz Schmitt, swung north of the château in the direction of Vouty. They remained lying 200 meters in front of the village. The village and the Corcy Road were strongly occupied. Skirmishers went forward against the Savières stream being forced to return in our fire. Enemy cavalry that galloped on Javage farm about 11 o'clock were taken under fire and dispersed.

During this the right wing of the II Battalion – 5th Company and one platoon each from the 6th and 7th Coy – went via La Loge farm through the Hautvison wood. Nine French would become taken prisoner in this advance. However, by the Javage farm and the mill situated in its vicinity the French afforded tough

> opposition. Two machine gun Groups of the 7th Coy (*Unteroffizier* Bender and *Unteroffizier* Lorenz) went forth against the mill, they stormed with people from the 6th Company under Sergeant Marburger and took 22 prisoners. With fire support from out of the mill the 6th Company under *Leutnant der Reserve* Deckert went forth against the farm; the 7th Company under *Leutnant der Reserve* Fritz Schmitt, encompassing the left. Five prisoners remained in our hands, the fleeing French ended up in our machine gun fire. At 8.45 a.m. the farm is in our possession. The companies came up to 300 meters east of the Vouty–Corcy Road; however because of severe machine gun fire and shrapnel fire on the hillside closely west of Javage Farm they withdrew. At 10.00 a.m. the hill west of the Savières steam was in our possession.
> *Leutnant der Reserve* Gerstner, 2 Machine Gun Company/R110.[11]

> The advance on the right wing by the I/R110 under *Hauptmann* Zeddelmann was very difficult. Bellevue farm became stormed by the 3/R110 under *Leutnant der Reserve* Senger and the garrison found inside the farm was taken prisoner. Because the right neighboring division did not advance as far the right wing of the battalion suffered under heavy machine gun fire coming from the right flank. The heavy fire becomes frustratingly noticeable especially during the passage through Buisson de Hautvison in the direction of Louatre and Violaine. About midday the Savières ground laid under powerful artillery fire, so that the I/R110 could not cross over the stream until between 11.00 a.m. and 12.00 noon by Javage farm and occupy the hill west of the stream. On the left the connection to the II/R110 was established, on the right to the I/150, which had now also advanced up to St. Pauls farm south of Corcy. During the afternoon strong artillery fire lay upon our position. *Leutnant der Reserve* Beuthe, 4th Company was slightly wounded. *Leutnant der Reserve* Grapentin was buried.
> *Leutnant der Reserve* Fritz Schmitt, RIR 110.[12]

While the infantry companies continued to press forward against increasingly strong French resistance, the regimental staff of RIR 110 was constantly shifting position in order to keep pace:

> At 7 a.m. the regimental staff is at the Fontaine Alix farm, at 9 a.m. the battle headquarters would be moved by the La Loge farm and at 11.30 a.m. to the edge of Buisson de Hautvisson. It had become very hot. The magnificent beech wood provided cool shade. 'I might remain here!' I remarked jokingly to the regimental commander Major *von* Schmeling. We will remain there! At midday the regiment reported to brigade: Faverolles and the tip of the wood nose north of Vouty were occupied by enemy machine gun nests. The enemy heavy artillery, according to statements from prisoners, stood in the ground of Oigny-Troësnes. As long as the right neighboring division was not in the possession of the hill between Longpont and the Buisson de Hautvisson, the regiment cannot deliver the attack further, because its right battalion would otherwise become fired at here from the rear. I

Hauptmann Rösch, MG *Offizier* on the Staff of RIR 110 in Buisson de Hautvisson. (*Reserve-Infanterie-Regiment Nr. 110 im Weltkrieg 1914-1918*)

ask after messages about the situation by the right neighboring division and about the bombardment of the reported heavy enemy artillery.

Leutnant der Reserve Fritz Schmitt.[13]

While both regiments, RIR 109 and RIR 110 were heavily engaged in battle with the opposing French forces, the men of RIR 111 were being held in reserve. It was not until 12.00 noon until the regiment moved forward toward the fighting and by 1.00 p.m. it had reached the vicinity of Villers le Petit. The regiment was halted and the battalions were positioned to protect the edge of the wood. While in the position an officer patrol established a connection with RIR 110.

Little changed along the front held by the 28th Reserve Division as both sides were exhausted from the heavy fighting of the last few days while each side maintained a steady rate of machine gun fire designed to prevent the other from considering a new advance. Towards 2.00 p.m. powerful artillery and machine gun fire was placed against the right wing of the II/R110. The 6/R110 under *Leutnant der Reserve* Stumpf took the dense waves of Frenchmen advancing out of the high fields of grain under fire and easily repelled the attack.

Later in the afternoon, with the unfavorable situation of the gap still existing between the III/R109 and RIR 110, a new division order arrived at 3.15 p.m., directing RIR 109 to continue the attack, and, after reaching the Fleury-Faverolles–Troësnes Road the new goal assigned to the regiment was to reach the Dampleux–Oigny–Silly-la Piterie Road. The attack would commence at 4.00 p.m. One battalion from RIR 111 would protect the right flank of the division by Javage farm against threats from the north, the 1/*Ersatz Pionier* Battalion 16 and *Minenwerfer* Company 228 located by Noroy would protect the left flank against any surprises from the south.

The time from the receipt of the division order until the time fixed for the attack however was not enough to provide all of the battalions, companies, batteries, *Minenwerfer* etc. with the attack orders. While some neighboring regiments attacked, others did not. There was absolutely no artillery support for the attack and the enemy artillery fire increased minute by minute under the guidance of observation aircraft. Then, reports arrived that enemy tanks were observed moving west of Troësnes, which could not be fought effectively with the lack of support from artillery and *Minenwerfer*. The attack was an utter failure and only resulted in increasing the number of casualties suffered by the infantry.

During this latest attempt to continue the offensive the villages in the rear and approach roads were attacked over and over again by squadrons of enemy bombers. These aircraft came upon a *pionier* company that was on the march in Oulchy le Château and within moments the column was turned into a scene of carnage. The entire company and all horses lay scattered around, wounded or killed. Part of the regimental band from RIR 109 were also struck by the bombs and Musician *Landsturmmann* Dirr and *Grenadier* Kautz were both wounded, the former eventually succumbed to his wounds.

The III/R111 moved forward at 4.00 p.m. according to orders from the division by way of Javage farm and press on to the heights north of Vouty with the instructions to protect the right flank of the division to the north. Corcy and Vouty, as well as the road between both villages at this time, were still in enemy hands. The German front line proceeded from St. Paul farm to the heights northeast of Vouty and from there to southwest of Javage farm in the Buisson de Cresnes Faverolles. The III/R111 had already received strong artillery fire during the march to the Savières ground and had also been attacked several times by enemy aircraft squadrons dropping bombs. The advance could only be carried out with great difficulty and had to be accomplished in jumps by small detachments. The Savières ground lay under the heaviest enemy bombardments, so that only individuals in large intervals could cross over it. The strong enemy bombardment of the Savières valley continued into the night of 1/2 June 1918.

At 4.00 p.m. on 1 June new division orders arrived by RIR 110:

> 1. …
> 2. The division places the new attack goal: after reaching the Fleury–Faverolles–Troësnes road to then attack and reach the Dampleux–Oigny–Silly la Poterie Road. The Fleury–Faverolles–Troësnes Road will become crossed over at 5 p.m. in the attack to the west, etc.[14]

At 4.15 p.m. the following orders went out to the battalions for the continuation of the attack.

1. The attack continues until to the road Fleury–Vouty–Faverolles–Troësnes.
2. The I Battalion would occupy Vouty, II Battalion would occupy Faverolles, the III Battalion moved forward as the reserve to Javage farm, to bring its light machine guns and heavy machine guns into position.
3. The howitzer *Abteilung* will fire from 8-8.05 p.m. on Vouty and Faverolles and then transfer its fire upon wood lying behind them.
4. The battalions already worked closer to the villages during this bombardment, so that at 8.05 p.m. the attack can begin.
5. …
6. The III/R111 was placed on the right next to the I/ R110 for the protection of the right flank of the division.[15]

The I/R110 started the attack punctually, with the 3rd and 4/R110 in the first line, the 1st and 2/R110 in the second line, with six heavy machine guns that were in raised positions. The light machine guns were not in position on time because of the loss of a driver and a horse due to shell fire, delaying the arrival of the cart carrying the weapons and ammunition until a replacement horse could be obtained.

The front line approached close to the Corcy–Vouty Road. During the advance *Leutnant der Reserve* Carstens, the company leader of the 2/R110 who had been with the regiment since August 1914 was killed, along with another company officer, *Leutnant der Reserve* Breitenbach. Any further advances at this point became impossible because of the accurate enemy barrage fire that appeared with every attempt by the infantry to advance. Strong enemy machine gun fire also came out of Vouty and the wood north of the village. The connection to the right was lost because of the slow advance by the neighboring regiment. By the onset of darkness, the companies returned to the exit position where they dug in and had failed to make any progress at all.

The *Minenwerfer* platoon of the II/R110 under Leu*tnant der Reserve* Nowsky successfully bombarded a machine gun post in the church tower of Faverolles during the preparation fire. The II/R110 promptly began the attack with the 8th, 7th and 5/R110 in the front line; and the skirmishers were able to reach the Vouty–Faverolles Road and the eastern edge of Faverolles. Then, strong machine gun fire coming from the houses and fruit gardens of Faverolles and Vouty, which the I/R110 was unable to take, and well placed enemy barrage fire also detained the advance of the II/R110, which was forced to dig in 200 meters east of the Vouty–Faverolles road; the attack had failed:

> Our attack continued firmly in front of the villages of Vouty and Faverolles behind the backdrop of the mighty forest of Villers Cotterêts where there was an advance by a far superior French force, under which even cavalry was used north of the village of Vouty in an attempt at a surprise and to create air there, which was refused outright. That evening at 7 p.m. a renewed general attack was ordered on our side. The formations had become extremely mingled in the course of the 16 hour battle action. I stood with part of my company in the area of Javage Farm; one platoon under *Leutnant der Reserve* Penner supported the 6th Company. Our punctually employed preparation fire of the artillery was short and modest to

anyone who listened; all the fiercer raged the French barrage fire that will be run through in a desperate advance. And we are already grabbed from the holes of the numerous scattered and skillfully positioned enemy machine gun nests. The first enemy machine gun could be captured and prisoners were taken in bitter close combat. The losses increased. The confusion struggled around and could be seen with every look across, but the watchword was still 'Onward.'

With a few people of my company I saw more open terrain and now ran, with what strength I still had, at a clover field lying a few hundred meters forward, toward the enemy and moved into a row of trees on the Vouty–Corcy Road, which was designated as our first attack goal. In the middle of the sprint the strongest machine gun fire pattered against us from all sides. Gasping, we threw ourselves down in the green field; above us the bullets chirped angrily. Every attempt to get up was the signal for the enemy to cover us with fire. We saw ourselves firmly fixed and without cover and had the horrible feeling of sitting in a trap. The well camouflaged enemy could not be seen. There, as we still received fire from sharply right and on the left, no doubt existed that our small group was too far pressed forward and had no more connection. To crawl to the rear in the ascending terrain, was hopeless. Now also our machine gun fire started in abundance from the rear that luckily spread away high above us. So no choice remained but to stay put until the onset of darkness which enabled us to go back. The following 2 hours would probably remain in everyone's living memory, of those that survived it. Even the smallest movement on our side demanded target practice by the enemy with machine guns and shrapnel. A few steps next to me laid *Unteroffizier* Martin Bender, one of my best and trusted under-leaders, awarded with the Iron Cross I Class, a brave and prudent soldier and a more splendid portly comrade anywhere.

I always had to admonish him to take better cover and always looked for the small Martin Bender to come up on the knee, then to disappear again as fast as lightning when the fire started again. The sun slowly sank behind the western edge of the wood. Not much longer and we would be delivered. I looked across inspecting the line at the skirmishers lying scattered in large spacing and saw how Bender was propped up again; my shout 'lie down' came together with the sharp crack of the sheaf of bullets and the crying out from them hitting. Softly groaning Bender lay on the ground. We crawled toward him from two sides. The blood gushed out of his shoulder and stained his uniform and the clover. The wound was bandaged in a makeshift manner with my own and bandage packets thrown to me, and I had the best hopes that he would come through. However, his wound was unfortunately a very severe type. A few weeks later the good and unforgotten comrade died in a military hospital in Germany and found his last rest in the cemetery in his home town of Eschelbach. With the beginning of darkness I brought my people back safely again to the western edge of the Savières ground. Our own insufficient artillery preparation had, in spite of the most considerable bravery, made it impossible for the attacking troops to reach the stretched attack goal, the Vouty–Corcy Road and further to the Wood of Villers-Cotterets.

Leutnant der Reserve Fritz Schmitt, RIR 110.[16]

Between 7.00 and 8.00 p.m. on 1 June the III/R109 made repeated attempts to continue the attack that had been ordered; however the battalion was taken under enemy annihilation fire by artillery and machine guns so that the battalion became disorganized and remained lying in the exit position while suffering heavy losses. The III/R110, as the reserve battalion, moved forward to the western edge of Buisson de Hautvison and was placed at the ready about 7.00 p.m., to follow as the reserve. During the night it continued to receive strong artillery fire from light and medium caliber guns as the battalion dug in at the eastern edge of Buisson de Hautvison during the early morning hours.

At 8.20 p.m. a new division order arrived whereby the attack would be renewed at 5.00 a.m. on 2 June 1918. There would be one half hour of artillery preparation prior to the assault. Fortunately the night remained comparatively quiet so that the battalion formations could at least become moderately organized. Despite this, it had been impossible to close the gap between the II and III/R109 during the hours of darkness.

It was well-known that the adversary was affording tough opposition by Vierzy and Chaudun as well as south of these villages with strong forces. The situation at Villers-Hélon and Lôuatre was still unclear. What was known was that in the woods of Villers Cotterêts stood two to three enemy cavalry divisions with vehicles.

Despite the obstacles, the men of the 28th Reserve Division strived to comply with the orders they had been given. The men of the III/R111 did not manage to cross the Savières ground until 9.00 p.m., when the companies of the III Battalion reached the readiness position location on the eastern slope of the hill northeast of Vouty. Security detachments immediately became pushed forward to the west, and one of these detachments under *Vizefeldwebel* Wessing joined an attack by the I/R110, which lay in front of the III/R111, on an open area. Wessing and his men succeeded in digging out an enemy machine gun nest and taking the crew prisoner in the intermediate field.

About 10.00 p.m. the enemy made a counterattack upon the entire line in front of the II/R110, supported through an artillery bombardment that fell with a sudden blow. The platoons of *Leutnant der Reserve* Edelmann, 8/R110 and *Leutnant der Reserve* Penner, 5/R110 immediately opened fire at the advancing French troops and repulsed the attack with support from the *Minenwerfer* platoon.

Major von Schmeling, RIR 110, assessed the situation on the evening of 1 June 1918 as follows:

> The enemy had powerfully reinforced his artillery from hour to hour and engaged with fire. His infantry was in a favorable, exquisitely protected position, had good observation and ample ammunition.
>
> The regiment did not have to deal anymore with individual machine gun nests and a withdrawing enemy, but with an enemy in a fully developed defense that was provided with strong, deeply partitioned artillery (light and medium calibers).[17]

At 12.45 a.m. on 2 June 1918 RIR 110 received the division order from issued at 9.20 p.m. on 1 June 1918:

1. …
2. The 56th Reserve Infantry Brigade would still take the Fleury–Faverolles-Troësnes Road in its possession this evening under all circumstances.
3. The attack will continue on 2 June. Attack goal: Dampleux, Oigny–Silly la Poterie Road.[18]

At 12.45 a.m. the brigade ordered the artillery preparations to begin at 4.00 a.m. with the duration of 30 minutes. The infantry attack would then begin at 5.00 a.m. The general bombardment of the Savières valley continued in the night to 2 June 1918.

At 2.00 a.m. the headquarters of RIR 110 transmitted the new orders to the battalions for the continuation of the attack. The regimental commander of RIR 110, Major *von* Schmeling then went to see the brigade commander in Villers le Petit, where Schmeling made his superior aware that the artillery available for the proposed attack was insufficient and that there was no available ammunition for both the attack and the defense for the counterattacks that would surely follow. In Schmeling's opinion there was no hope of any success in the attack and holding the area expected to be gained. Many of the guns supposedly assigned to support the upcoming attack had not even arrived in position.

The 1st Guard Infantry Division, which connected on the left of RIR 109, had also reported repulsing a tank attack at Marizy St. Geneviève. Considering all of these factors, many of the commanders of the 28th Reserve Division had great doubts that the proposed attack stood any chance of success without a large increase in artillery support.

I/R110 did not receive the attack order until 4.25 a.m. because of delays transmitting the message through the strong artillery fire, which lay like a steel curtain on the Savières ground. Due to the lack of time and the heavy enemy fire it was impossible for the I/R110 to reach its starting point in order to be ready for zero-hour.

German artillery preparations began simultaneously with the preparation of a major French attack. Towards morning the enemy fire increased to the level of drum fire, and French reinforcements were observed moving into positions and apparently preparing for a counterattack. Then, at 5.00 a.m. strong enemy attacks took place, in part accompanied by tanks, along the entire division front.

The French troops had managed to penetrate the weak chain of sentry outposts of RIR 110 unobserved under the protection of a field of high corn and once through the field, advanced against the companies of the III/R111. The 9th, 10th and 11/R111 supported by machine guns, brought the French attack to a halt and then went against the enemy in a vigorous counterattack with fixed bayonets. The companies of the III/R111 threw the French back to his exit position and continued to pursue the enemy beyond it. When the counter thrust came to a stop the men of RIR 111 had captured 34 men from *Régiment d'Infanterie* 167.

However, this victory was purchased at a high cost. *Leutnant* Albrecht was killed at the head of the 11/R111. The leaders of the 9th and 10/R111, *Leutnants* Rasche and Frey, were both wounded as were *Leutnants* Dengel and Ruhle among numerous Other Ranks. The troops had no connections on the right and on the left, so that the danger of becoming isolated and captured became very real. The companies were therefore forced o come back to the eastern slope of the hill northeast of Vouty. Still, despite the sensi-ive losses, the French attack had been repulsed.

The continued fierce enemy fire raids demonstrated that the French had not given up the intent to attack once again. In addition to enemy infantry, French tanks were observed opposite the sector of the 9th and 12/R111. A deserter, who came into the German lines by RIR 111 in the afternoon, also confirmed that the French were determined to continue to attack.

A new enemy advance began that moved across the hill south of Corcy by the I/R110 until it reached the battle headquarters of the I Battalion which was located in the vicinity of a sunken road northwest of Javage Farm. The battalion leader, *Hauptmann von* Zeddelmann, led a counter thrust with all available forces he had at hand and was able to throw the enemy back into its exit position at the wood edge north of Vouty. About 30 French soldiers were taken prisoner during the counter thrust and by the neighboring RIR 111.

The attack by the II/R110 on 1 June became repeated; however the German artillery preparation was inadequate and did not have the desired effect. All of the enemy machine gun nests were intact and fired at the advancing troops from RIR 110. French barrage fire lay in front of the German line and the resulting losses were heavy, the mood of the men was depressed. The II/R110 was forced to withdraw into the exit position and strong enemy artillery fire lay upon the position of RIR 110 during the entire day.

The commanders had been correct in their assumptions. The attack on the morning of 2 June 1918 was unsuccessful, because there was almost no artillery preparation fire and minimal artillery support when the attack occurred. The fighting did not last long before the troops were recalled and resumed the positions being held the previous night. The only result of this feeble attempt was to increase the number of casualties in the division.

Then, about 7.30 a.m., strong machine gun fire became audible behind the right wing of the II/R109. A report arrived simultaneously indicating that the enemy had broken through the wood of Cresnes with strong forces, through the menacing gap that existed between the II and III/R109, which threatened the regiment in the rear. Within a very short time an enemy detachment had already passed through the wood and had reached the battle headquarters of the regimental staff on the Noroy Road.

The regimental staff immediately recognized the threat and quickly ordered two *Stosstrupps* and the machine gun reserve to attack the advancing enemy detachment as well as sending a messenger to the neighboring RIR 111 asking for additional support. Following a brief fire fight with the *Stosstrupps,* one enemy officer, three sergeants and five men were captured and the enemy detachment retreated. Additional support was provided by the employment of the 8th, 1st and 2/R109 as well as parts of the 2nd Machine Gun Company that were lying in the second line. They attacked in a 'dashing manner' and succeeded in completely repulsing the enemy that had threatened to break through the regimental line and threw them back with heavy losses.

The actions of *Vizefeldwebel* Försching, 1st Machine Gun Company, who, with the Gun Captain and *Schützen* Küstner, Würz and *Gefreiter* Kast decisively interfered in the fighting with machine gun fire and were recognized with the Iron Cross I Class.

The support of the battalion from RIR 111 that was approaching RIR 109 was no longer needed. According to statements from the prisoners the enemy had positioned two battalions for a planned break through from Troësnes to Ancienville.

Simultaneously with the attack upon the III/R111 the enemy had been fighting with RIR 109 which had been inserted at the left wing of the division in the Bois de Cresnes and east of Troësnes and in part had been thrown back upon Noroy. The I/R111 had received the order, to move to Noroy, and take up a connection with the parts of RIR 109 that were withdrawing and to further occupy the old position by Troësnes. The II/R111 had also become placed ready for a counterattack following the report of the enemy advance against RIR 109; however the battalion was not needed in the fighting.

Just before 8.00 a.m. on 2 June 1918 the I/R111 marched off and reached Noroy, without becoming shelled by the enemy. Once there the battalion received the assignment from the commander of RIR 109, to attack in a northwesterly direction and to clear the Bois de Cresnes from the enemy. The 1st and 3/R111, which was already progressing well in the attack upon Troësnes, were turned off in a northwesterly direction. Meanwhile parts of the 2nd Guard Infantry Division went forward upon Troësnes from the south, so that the attack by the I/R111 was no longer needed.

On orders from brigade the companies of the I/R111 assembled in the southeastern part of the Bois de Cresnes and pushed forth security detachments to the edge of the wood. One of these sentry groups under *Vizefeldwebel* Mutter succeeded in destroying an enemy machine gun nest and with it freed several men from RIR 109 that were already in French captivity. During this movement the 4/R111 and the 1st Machine Gun Company formed the fire protection for the battalion. However they were discovered by enemy aircraft, which directed strong fire on the positions. The day of fighting had caused numerous losses to the battalion. From the 1st Company *Leutnant* Schwarz was killed, and with him 48 men were either killed or wounded. At 2.30 p.m. the companies were individually withdrawn via Ancienville and Lioval farm to the Buisson de Hautvison.

Once order had been restored the regimental staff retained control over the I/R111 from the battle headquarters in Buisson de Cresnes. An enemy bomber squadron had observed the movements of the men from RIR 111 and dropped a large number of bombs on the tempting target, which caused heavy losses to the I/R111 as well as the regimental staff of RIR 109. A second attempt by the enemy to thrust through the gap between the II and III/R109 failed in strong defensive fire.

Towards midday the regimental staff of RIR 109 transferred the battle headquarters to the village of Noroy. Just before 2 p.m. division orders arrived in Noroy that the 28th Reserve Division was to shift to the north in the width of about one regiment and the 2nd Guard Infantry Division would be inserted between the 1st Guard Infantry Division and the 28th Reserve Division.

The 3rd Guard Regiment received the task to capture the Hill of Troësnes, from where the enemy could observe all of the German movements since 1 June 1918, and from where they made attacks against the German line. Despite attempting several assaults, the 3rd Guard Regiment was unable to capture the hill due to extremely fierce enemy resistance. Following these unsuccessful attacks RIR 109 was assembled by Ancienville on the night of 2 June 1918 as the division reserve.

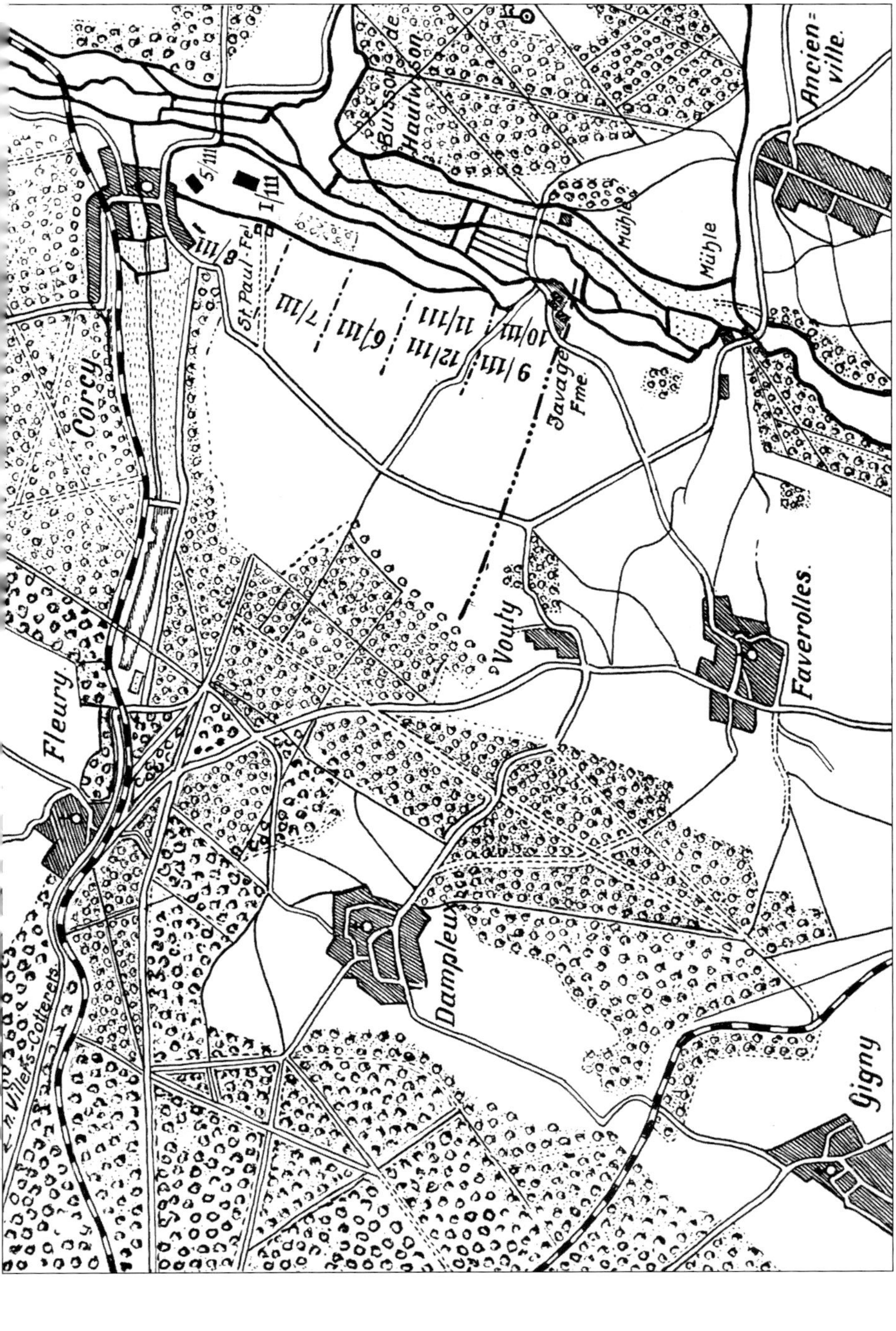

Position of RIR 111 near Faverolles.

While this was taking place, the enemy had placed strong forces in the wood northeast of Villers Cotterêts, giving the impression that the French and British were preparing to change from defense to the attack. The OHL determined that in order to prevent this from occurring, Corps Winkler should take possession of the massive wooded area of Villers Cotterêts and expel the enemy from it.

In the course of 2 June 1918 a new distribution of the battle front was ordered from which RIR 111 was assigned the northerly skirmish line of the division. The northern border of this strip lay along the railway embankment north of Corcy. The southern border which also connected to RIR 110 moved from the Javage farm via the southern edge of Dampleux along to the southern edge of Villers Cotterêts. The southern half of this strip was already occupied by the III/R111.

In the night to 3 June 1918 the II/R111 was supposed to relieve one battalion of IR 150 in the northern sector. While the II Battalion prepared for the relief, the order went out for the continuation of the attack on the following day. The 28th Reserve Division was given the job to take Villers Cotterêts, and the first attack goal assigned to the regiment were the heights north and south of Dampleux. According to orders, the attack would begin at 5.30 a.m. after 15 minutes of artillery preparation fire.

In the night to 3 June 1918 the battalions of RIR 111 were arranged in the following manner for the attack. In the northern battle strip the II/R111 was in the forward line with the 8/R111 on the right wing, the 7/R111 in the middle and the 6/R111 on the left wing. The 5/R111 was the reserve and was positioned behind the right wing. One platoon of the 2MG/R111 was distributed to each of the three forward companies and in addition the *Minenwerfer* platoon was placed with the 6/R111.

The III/R111 was partitioned in the left sector so that the 9/R111 on the right and the 12/R111 on the left should attack in the forward line in two waves. The 10th and 11/R111 would follow behind as the third wave. The battalion reserve was one platoon of the 11th Company and two heavy machine guns. The remainder of the machine gun company was distributed with the second and third waves. The I/R111 formed the regimental reserve at the eastern slope of the hill south of Corcy behind the right wing of the attack. The escort battery was placed ready at the western slope of the Savières valley and would hopefully soon reach the hill west of Corcy if the attack progressed.

On the morning of 2 June 1918 two *Sturmtrupps* from *Sturmbataillon* 7 had arrived at RIR 110 in the strength of two officers and 60 men that were to take part in the upcoming attack with the regiment, in addition one officer and 24 men of the 4/*Pionier* Battalion 16 also joined RIR 110.

RIR 110 had become newly partitioned following orders from division and brigade. The III/R110 took over the northern half of the regimental battle strip and receives the task to take Vouty by storm, and then advance through the wood south of Dampleux until it was in the ground of Oigny. The I/R110 assembled at the regimental battle headquarters and became the reserve battalion. The II/R110 took over the southern half of the regimental battle strip.

The task was to capture Faverolles, then to thrust through the wood until to the ground of Oigny. Both *Sturmbataillon* would then join the attack and take the hill south of Dampleux and penetrate forward through the large wood. The *Sturmtrupps* of the

Sturmbataillon become allotted to the III/R110. Another division order arrived at 5.00 p.m. describing the further attack goal of the division as Villers Cotterêts. *Minenwerfer* Company 228 would provide support for RIR 110.

At 6.00 p.m. the regiment sent its requirements for artillery fire preparation and support for the rolling barrage fire to brigade headquarters. As the men rested and waited for the moment of the new attack, they watched the blood red sun sink down behind the wood of Villers Cotterêts. The men spent an eerie night from 2 to 3 June 1918, in the wood of Hautvison. The forest appeared to glow in the crashing and bursting of countless enemy shells. The night was filled with screams and swearing, moans and wailing as the shells found victims among the troops massed for the attack.

At 12.30 a.m. a further reminder arrived about the joint attack by the divisions for 3 June 1918 for the entire Group Winkler that had already been set for 5.30 a.m. The brigade orders also reminded the men that the goal ordered in the attack for the 28th Reserve Division had the greatest importance for the OHL, Villers Cotterêts, which must be reached under all circumstances.

The positioning of the light and heavy machine guns and the escort battery took place under the command of *Rittmeister Frhr. Von* Bissing for an operation that was scheduled to take place on the evening of 2 June 1918 at the exit position of the III/R110. The operation took place as scheduled and it resulted in a number of casualties including *Feldwebel Leutnant* Biedermann who was fatally wounded. Once the raiding party returned, the regimental commander and *Rittmeister Frhr. von* Bissing paid a visit to the brigade commander to discuss the raid and what the men had reported upon returning to the German lines. The brigade commander was advised that based upon the results of the raid and from observations made during the recent days that any attack against the enemy positions by Villers Cotterêts had little chance of success.

In their point of view, the attack against an extremely strong enemy position, equipped with ample artillery with apparently unrestricted ammunition supplies which the weak German artillery force, provided with little ammunition was doomed to fail. However, following the discussion and the strong opinions of the two regimental officers, there was no change in the attack order.

During the entire night strong artillery fire lay in Buisson de Hautvison and in the valley ground of the Savières stream. Shifting the infantry which were going in position with the light and heavy machine guns and the escort battery appeared almost impossible. Still, it needed to be finished if the attack was to take place as ordered and the men and equipment were moved without regard for casualties.

At 12.00 midnight the III/R110 crossed over the Savières stream and to the men it was the route through Hell. The artillery fire falling about the men increased to hurricane strength, completely dispersing the battalion. The battalion commander was wounded and the leadership of the III/R110 was then taken on by the replacement *Hauptmann der Landwehr* Rösch. Due to the heavy enemy fire only a small part of the troops were able to reach the other side of the river bank. Despite all efforts, the III/R110 did not reach its assigned place in time for the attack.

The main attack had been ordered to begin at 5.30 a.m. on 3 June. In the context of the overall-attack the 28th Reserve Division had been given the task to take Villers

Cotterêts. The infantry attack would be prepared with 15 minutes of artillery fire which was considered adequate for the task ahead. There was also another consideration, the low stocks of artillery ammunition at hand. In reality, the 15 minute bombardment was all that could be spared if the guns were to have any reserves of shells in the event of an enemy counterattack.

The men of RIR 109 were ready at 5.30 a.m. in the Savières Ground between Javage farm and St. Paul farm. The regimental battle headquarters was located at the mill at the western edge of Buisson de Hautvison. While RIR 109 was ready, the I/R110 had not yet reached its readiness position by daybreak. Instead, the battalion assembled at Javage farm and the III/R110 followed behind as the reserve.

At 5.30 a.m. the companies from RIR 111 stormed forth in the attack with 'determined enthusiasm'. However the men had barely left the position when devastating machine gun fire was directed against them, coming from emplacements by the embankment and from the copse north of Corvy. Simultaneously, shells began to burst among the attack waves and clouds appeared above the troops from shrapnel fire. Nonetheless RIR 111 continued to attack despite the heavy losses being suffered by the regiment. The regiment advanced against the wood north of Vouty and the forward enemy position on the Corcy–Vouty Road were overrun in the initial attack.

The surviving French flooded back to the wood north of Vouty where they were taken under fire from the heavy machine guns, which was so effective that only a few succeeded in reaching cover. 'Forward' was shouted as the watchword, and the wood lying in front of RIR 111 was successfully taken. Under the exemplary cooperation of the *Schützen* with the machine guns and *Minenwerfern* it was possible to fight down a large part of the enemy machine gun nests, part of which were in the intermediate terrain, part at the edge of the wood and hidden inside the wood.

The first waves of the III/R111 as well as the right wing of the II/R111 reached the wood in the first fifteen minutes of the attack before transforming into a stubborn struggle with the enemy machine gun nests. This occurred over and over, and losses increased to a point where the attack began to hesitate. The fighting at the right wing by parts of the I/R111, where the attacks were also joined by the 6th and 7/R111, was particularly bitter. Along with many brave men the leader of the 7/R111, *Leutnant* Harrer, who had personally lead his Group forward against a machine gun nest, was killed. *Leutnant* Kirsten, the leader of the 5/R111, who was close to the 7/R111 with two platoons, was also killed by enemy fire. *Leutnant* Büchner, the leader of the 3/R111, and *Leutnant* Schuh from the 4/R111 which were in support were killed.

Enemy flanking fire directed against the left wing of the III/R111 caused particularly heavy losses. The left wing of the battalion was open; no connection existed to the neighboring RIR 110, because the neighboring battalion of RIR 110 had been blown apart in the readiness position. Along with many other comrades *Leutnants* Höfler, Marx, Stelz and Weimer become wounded and placed out of action.

When Zero hour arrived, the II/R110 stood ready. However, there was no sign of the III/R110. The regimental commander took it upon himself to order the I/R110 that was in the reserve readiness position by Javage farm to move forward into the gap in the first line. The I/R110 moved into position at the ordered time. The companies of the I/R110

2nd Machine Gun Coy, RIR 111, April 1918. (Source: Author's collection)

had already attacked here twice in vain, but despite this, the 2/R110 under *Leutnant der Reserve* Schneider, and the 1/R110 under *Offizier Stellvertreter* Ober advanced with their men with 'particular pluck' in the morning fog and reached the wood edge north of Vouty and the eastern edge of the village.

The II/R110 had also started its attack and *Leutnant der Reserve* Lorenz and *Offizier Stellvertreter* Hock from the 2nd Machine Gun Company reached Faverolles in the forward most infantry wave. The machine guns of the 2nd Machine Gun Company fought effectively against the enemy machine guns firing out of the village while the 7/R110 occupied a wood piece in front of Faverolles. Then, the fog vanished and all of the intact enemy machine gun nests and batteries directed a horrible crossfire from close vicinity of the German line in front of Faverolles–Vouty.

The fire had become so intense that the survivors were later forced to withdraw behind the Vouty –Faverolles Road and later in the evening back into the storm exit position. The losses in the regiment were heavy, particularly in the 8/R110. *Offizier Stellvertreter* Trapp, 4/R110, who had been in the company since the beginning of the war, was missing and likely killed; *Vizefeldwebel* Otter, 3/R110, was also killed and *Offizier Stellvertreter* Becker, 3/R110, was severely wounded.

RIR 109 would act as the reserve for the initial attack and was ordered to follow behind the first attack waves:

> We had reached the enemy in exhausting marching and immediately became transitioned to the attack at those places. The superior strength of the enemy artillery, especially however the bombardment through the enemy flyers with their

> ill-fated string of bombs however, made it impossible for us, to urge the enemy further back, and also that we replaced a *Maikäfer* regiment at this position that had not succeeded in this. The relief however signifies no rest for us, but a new attack order that began with the words 'It is of great importance for the *Oberste Heeresleitung*, that still today the wood of Villers Cotterêts becomes occupied…' So therefore the I Battalion waited in the morning dawn for the start of the attack. In front of us was one battalion from R111. The preparations and so-called drum fire by our artillery began. Our ears accustomed to completely different opening concert found this quiet and timid music as completely insufficient, and in that action the shortage of ammunition and guns has caused the continuation of this so brilliantly started operation to hesitate, and the infantry had suffered the most amongst them.
>
> *Leutnant der Reserve* Affolter,1MG/R109.[19]

What had quickly become evident was that the attack of the 28th Reserve Division had unluckily collided with a large-scale French attack, which broke forth with support from five tanks. The tanks were the big surprise of the day. They were new, small and extremely maneuverable vehicles, probably the small Renault FT17 with a two man crew. In the face of such force RIR 111 became pressed back by the superior enemy strength until it was in the wood east of St. Paul farm. It was there that the I/R109 became embroiled in the French attack. The 4/R109 stood out in particular, along with 1st *Minenwerfer* Platoon from *Minenwerfer* Company 228 as well as the 5/R111, in that they advanced against five enemy tanks and placed several of them out of action and forced the other tanks to withdraw. Once this had been accomplished, the 3/R109 tried to deliver the attack at the right wing again, during which its leader, *Leutnant der Reserve* Hell, was killed at the head of his company. Sergeant Jacob Schäfer took on the leadership of the 3/R109 when he heard the shout that the last company officer, *Leutnant* Mayer, had also become wounded.

Even if the enemy plan had been disrupted through the attack by the 28th Reserve Division, the French succeeded in bringing forward part of their attack troops at 6.30 a.m. out of the projecting wood piece northeast of Vouty where the five tanks were observed in movement. The III/R109 claimed a notable share in the defense against the French tanks when parts of the battalion were attacked by three of the enemy tanks from the flank during the march to St. Paul farm.

The tanks had penetrated the very thin forward line of the 28th Reserve Division and then turned against the III/R111 located at the right wing. The battalion reserve with the battalion staff immediately occupied the Corcy–Vouty Road and attempted to stop them with infantry and machine gun fire. Dense masses of French infantry followed behind the tanks and the German defensive fire resulted in heavy enemy losses. However, the weakened troops of RIR 111, who attempted to cling to the positions in the terrain, could not stop the enemy advance. The men of RIR 111 were forced to yield step by step until they were back at their exit position. The enemy pressed afterward as far as the Corcy–Vouty Road. There was no opportunity for the men of RIR 111 to counter attack and it was enough that the thinned ranks could hold their ground at all.

Meanwhile three of the tanks had quickly advanced against the II/R111 on the right wing, and two of them succeeded in penetrating the weak skirmish line. They traveled south past St. Paul farm and in doing so they showered the skirmish line from the side and from the rear with machine gun fire. The tanks turned off to the north east of St. Paul farm and fought against the parts of the 2nd, 3rd, 4th, 5th and 8/R111 which were placed in the wood piece north of the farm. These companies were soon inundated in a hail of bullets seemingly coming from all sides.

While the circumstances looked bleak, the men from RIR 111 succeeded in placing the tanks out of action. The first was fought down through the machine gun fire of Platoon Crzybowski of the 2nd Machine Gun Company and through the fire of a flat trajectory 7.6cm light *Minenwerfer* under *Offizier Stellvertreter* Haas. The other tank remained at the eastern slope of the hill south of Corcy where it had become hung up in the trees. The tank stuck in the trees was stormed by parts of the 1/R111 and people of the battalion staff; the crew ended up in captivity:

> The specified time, which we should follow after the battalion from R111 had passed, without the enemy fire having weakened and that somehow always became stronger since the beginning of the attack. Nevertheless *Hauptmann* Herrmann decided to proceed. However, when we swarmed out from the hill we had reached in light waves, we ended up in severe enemy fire that inflicted heavy losses on us. The situation was critical in the highest degree, when suddenly enemy tanks appeared out of the edge of the wood of Villers Cotterêts that slowly and surely inexorably came toward us. There was probably many a good Grenadier whose heart pounded, and I confess, that we were stunned. *Hauptmann* Herrmann demonstrated he was worthy of admiration here; he prevented the men hurrying back in the further withdrawal and calmed the bewildered and hesitant men through quiet commands. And then see how one had quickly become accustomed to the traveling monsters and began to fire at them from all sides. One soon moved back into the wood, a different one had to stop on the open field and the brave 109er stormed at it, tore the leader out, a very young officer, who had been injured through a shot on the eye, who quite coldly asked 'Is there a doctor here?' The other tank remained behind us, standing on the slope. This or the other we wanted to bring behind the front on the next day, because we heard that a large reward was offered for this. Unfortunately however, the tank was badly damaged, and the spark plugs were removed, so that bringing it back was impossible.
>
> The sight that offered itself to us was unforgettable to me, when we reached the farm in further slow progress since the start of our attack. There, lying man next to man was an entire skirmish line of R111er as if ready to attack, but stretched out there through a burst of machine gun fire. It also appeared to be crazy, to proceed against a wood edge in the open field almost without trees and shrubs, which was densely occupied by the enemy. From out of the farm one could observe, for example, how the enemy machine guns in trees dominated the entire terrain, and this knowledge convinced us to begin the retreat to the hillside, behind that we had so expected a successful attack in the morning. We moved ourselves back

> slowly. Active artillery fires was directed closely to the straw stacks, where the staff was, and enemy pilots fired upon us with machine guns from low heights of only 20 until 30 meters. It was a costly day in losses of dead and wounded; it has also proven however that our men's view of the tanks, which how one knew, compelled excellent troops into wild flight, conserved their serenity and unflinching and successfully picked up the fight against them. If the French had been only half so courageous and immediately followed their tanks, probably not one of us would come back.
>
> *Leutnant der Reserve* Affolter, 1MG/R109.[20]

The battle with the enemy machine gun nests continued. Elements of the 5th and 7/R111 with the cooperation of the 1st Machine Gun Company took on the two most dangerous nests, and finally the French garrison began to wave white cloths in a signal that they wanted to surrender. As *Leutnant* Brenker, the leader of the 1st Machine Gun Company approached them and asked them in French if they would come over to him, at this moment he was shot down by the skirmish line of the French counter attack that had just started. The devastating fire accompanying the attack also quickly forced all parts of the regiment to be taken back out of the wooded piece east of the Corcy–Vouty Road.

According to the regimental account, the attacking spirit of the regiment was not broken. At Corcy the staff of the II/R111 assembled the parts of the I and II/R111 found there and lead them in a counterattack against French skirmishers, who apparently believed they were still advancing under the protection of the tanks. The French were thrown back under heavy losses back over the Corcy–Vouty Road. However, enemy machine gun fire instantly opened up from the wood north of Vouty to engage the attackers.

At the same time, other parts of the I and II/R111 were assembled by *Leutnant* Beck, 8/R111, in the wood piece north of Javage farm and he led them forward with support from RIR 109 against the machine gun nests once again. However, flanking machine gun fire from the embankment by Corcy effectively stopped Beck and his men. The attackers had suffered heavy losses once again, including *Leutnant* Beck, a proven company leader in many battles, who was killed in the enemy fire. About 8.00 a.m. the fighting finally ended and despite all of the effort made by the 28th Reserve Division there was little to show in comparison to the losses suffered, in spite of great bravery. The losses of RIR 111 alone were seven officers, 73 *Unteroffiziere* and Other Ranks killed, 236 *Unteroffiziere* and Other Ranks wounded.

Many of the reasons given for the failure of the attack had already been discussed before the first man had left the exit position when the attack started. The opinions of the regimental commander and *Rittmeister Frhr. Von* Bissing had unfortunately turned out to be correct. One reason given for the failure was the inability for the attack taking the enemy by surprise. It became known later that the French had the intention to bring the German advance to a halt in the extensive wooded terrain east of Villers Cotterêts and at the same time to launch an integrated counterattack.

The far numerically superior enemy infantry supported by tanks and an especially large force of artillery were in place and ready for the German attack. It was also clearly evident that the German forces did not have the strength needed in order to overcome

Château Maucreux. (*Reserve-Infanterie-Regiment Nr. 110 im Weltkrieg 1914-1918*)

such superior numbers, especially when the German artillery was also very inferior in numbers, caliber and furnished with insufficient stocks of ammunition.

The failure was not only due to numbers, there was also the issue that the connecting troops on the right and on the left of RIR 111 had not advanced at the same time, leaving the flanks of the regiment wide open. Still, RIR 111 had complied with the instructions of the leadership, and had carried out the attack and in doing so apparently splintered the large French counterattack and as such prevented the enemy from capturing any substantial amount of terrain.

Once back in the original German lines, the battalions became reorganized while under intense fire and were partitioned side by side for the defense of a continued enemy attack. The attack on the left wing of the division also failed to gain any ground, so that on the night of 3/4 June the attack was suspended on higher orders when it was realized that the available strength was barely enough for the defense of the terrain, which afforded hardly any cover, let alone another attack. Like RIR 111, the men of RIR 109 dug in as deep as possible in positions dictated according to the needs of the defensive battle. The regimental staff of RIR 109 moved its battle headquarters to the northern corner of Buisson de Hautvison.

With such heavy losses suffered by the 28th Reserve Division, every man was needed at the front if the line was to be held. The II/R109 becomes inserted into the line between the II and I/R110 as support and the II/R109 dug in. It was urgent that an effective defensive position become created even if only just to help preserve the lives of the remaining men. For the rest of 3 June 1918 and through the night to the early morning hours of the next day strong artillery fire lay upon the positions of the regiments, which had increased in the evening hours and towards morning of 4 June 1918 had reached its fullest intensity.

The division order that arrived at the different regiments at 11 p.m. included the following details:

1. The divisions, with their present day morning attack, smashed a French counterattack… RIR 110 has behaved magnificently in the varied fighting about the villages of Faverolles and Vouty and despite the strongest enemy artillery counter effect completely held its position.
2. For the time being the attack is not continued tomorrow.
3. The division will hold the front of its captured position in its entire extent and dig in there.[21]

The attack battle had to come to a stop; the defensive battle began. The transition from the offensive to strictly defensive fighting was sudden and unexpected to the men of the 28th Reserve Division. In the past, when the regiments were involved in position warfare, there were always strong defensive positions already created where the men could find shelter from enemy fire and where they could rely upon artillery support, barbed wire obstacles, etc.

Now, sitting in the positions where the men were ordered to halt, there was little cover and most of the men were exposed to enemy artillery and machine gun fire. *Leutnant der Reserve* Armbruster, adjutant of the III/R109 had become so severely wounded on the evening of 3 June 1918 that he died shortly afterward in the field hospital. *Leutnant der Reserve* Heuberger took over the office of the adjutant of the III Battalion in his place.

Orders issued at 2.00 a.m. 4 June 1918 regulated the partitioning of the regiments for the defensive battle. The current line would be extended into a defense in depth. The light machine guns formed the framework of the position, the heavy machine guns and *Minenwerfer* were deployed east of the Savières stream; each weapon was to create its own protection. The idea of a continuous defensive line was abandoned, depots of food and ammunition supplies became created and footbridges were thrown across the Savières stream in the event of a withdrawal. Listening posts and patrols now took over the protection of the different companies.

Throughout 4 June 1918 the positions held by the division were pounded by French artillery fire. The constant shell fire in the mornings quickly turned into extremely strong barrage fire which gave every indication of an imminent enemy attack, however none followed. To some it appeared as if the enemy was anticipating further German attacks and was taking every precaution to prevent this from happening.

Losses were inevitable as the men attempted to create some sort of makeshift shelter by digging into the ground as best they could. No one was spared from this fire regardless of rank. The commander of the I Battalion, *Hauptmann* Herrmann, became so severely wounded by shell fire that he soon succumbed to his injuries. The shortage of officers in RIR 109 meant that battalions were now being commanded by company officers. In this instance, *Oberleutnant* Müller took over the command of the I/R109.

The unusually high losses of company officers meant that replacement officers needed to be assigned to command many of the hardest hit companies. *Leutnants* Hürdle, Gras, Schade, Deuss and Sachse took over the command of the leaders of the 1st, 3rd, 5th, 9th and 12th Coy for the leaders that had been placed out of action due to death or wounds.

In addition to the ever present artillery fire, the enemy aircraft were a constant threat day and night. Throughout the day bomber squadrons appeared over the positions in large numbers and strings of bombs seemed to constantly fall on infantry and artillery positions and the wood of Hautvison. The enemy aircraft hit the troops lying out in the open quite hard at first. While the bombs being dropped did not have enough force to penetrate into the ground they did have a dangerous splinter effect which proved deadly to anyone caught in the open. Soon the soldiers looked for additional protection from the constant bombing and found that if the fox-holes were covered with a layer of thick tree trunks it gave the occupants adequate protection against these weapons. Over the next few days the men worked eagerly to provide these shelters for everyone and when finished the losses from aircraft bombs no longer occurred. Still, these temporary shelters gave no such protection against even the lightest artillery shells if they suffered a direct hit.

In the night to 5 June 1918 the troops received hot food once again from the field kitchens, the first time since the beginning of the fighting. Over the next few days the men remained in their improvised defenses, waiting to see what would happen next. On 6 June 1918 the III/R110 relieved the II/R109 in the forward line: the I/R110 was inserted on the right, the II/R110 on the left, the III/R110 in the middle. In the afternoon of 9 June 1918 Major von Schmeling, commander of RIR 110 assembled the battalion leaders and adjutants in Maucreux Château in order to discuss the next phase of the Aisne Offensive. The discussion held by the officers of RIR 110 was no longer found in one of the luxurious rooms or resplendent halls of the château that was present only a short time earlier. The days of constant bombardments had badly damaged the once beautiful home. Since the division had reached the château it was being utilized as a command position, accommodation for the reserves and dressing stations, all of which were eventually transferred into the large, spacious shell proof cellars. Even the route to the château was permanently under enemy artillery fire.

The assembled officers learned that there was a possibility that the attack would continue and the advance would allow the 28th Reserve Division to reach Villers Cotterêts. There was an attack pending between Montdidier and Noyon which should destabilize the enemy's front before the sector of the 28th Reserve Division. Once this was accomplished, RIR 110 would also attack again. The goal of the attack remained the same as on 3 June, Villers Cotterêts which must be reached under all circumstances.

By 3.00 p.m. on 9 June 1918, RIR 110 was ready to begin the attack once more. The men sat in their positions awaiting the order to begin their advance. Hours pass and no orders arrive. Finally, the regiment learned that the enemy front between Montdidier and Noyon had not broken; in the contrary the strength of the enemy fire was reinforced. Whether the men were sorry to hear that the offensive was over or not will never be known. Shortly following the failed attacks the regiment learned that it was to be relieved; the advance party of IR 37, 10th Reserve Division had arrived. The full relief by elements of IR 37 followed in the night from 9 to 10 June 1918. RIR 110 once again crossed the Savières brook, marched through the menacing Buisson de Hautvison, and finally to Droizy, Launoy and Courdons, where billets were provided to the men.

RIR 109 remained in position until 10 June and did not become relieved until the night to 11 June 1918, also by element of the 10th Reserve Division. RIR 111 became relieved in the night from 9 to 10 June 1918 when the battalions were relieved by IR 155 and marched to Hartennes in the darkness, where they received a bivouac in a wooded are. On the morning of 11 June RIR 111 continued to Cierges, where the I R111 received billets. The other battalions bivouacked in small woods between Cierges and Ronchéres.

Everyone in the division had been looking forward to a period or rest and relaxation following the hard fighting of the past few days. This was not to be the case however. Already on 13 June the 28th Reserve Division was inserted on the Marne once again. The regiments took over positions at the northern bank of the Marne between Treloup and Vincelles where the division relieved the 50th Infantry Division.

In looking back at the recent battle, the 28th Reserve Division had only attacked for four days but in that short period of time the division had suffered heavy losses, many of which were irreplaceable veterans who had been with the division since the start of the war. The actual number of losses suffered by the division might never be known. Some of the records so painstakingly kept since August 1914 were destroyed through enemy fire or lost in the confusion of the final months of the war.

What is known is that in the period of time between 31 May and 6 June the II/R109 lost 34 men killed, 6 officers, 3 *Offizier Stellvertreter,* 167 Other Ranks wounded and 23 Other Ranks missing. The regiment reported that the losses of both other battalions were similar but that it was no longer possible to accurately determine them when the history of the regiment was written.

RIR 110 total losses to 10 June 1918 amounted to 641 Other Ranks of which 107 Other Ranks were killed, 479 Other Ranks were wounded and 55 were missing while RIR 111 reported similar losses. Given the level of fighting and the heavy casualties suffered by all three regiments, the losses to the 28th Reserve Division amounted to approximately 2,000 officers and men. This was a crippling blow to any division in the German Army at this time.

While the division had failed to reach its goal in the end, the men looked back at the fighting and declared it a victory. They viewed their sacrifices as proof that their division had performed its duty to the fullest.

Notes

1. Georg Bruchmüller (1863-1948) entered the army in 1885 and commenced his military career in the *Fussartillerie.* He remained in the artillery for the remainder of his career. During his time on the Eastern Front Bruchmüller developed and perfected his techniques involving sudden, accurate artillery preparation fire instead of the accepted prolonged artillery preparation period.

   A. His plan called for assigning specific fire missions to each battery on a specific timetable. Ranging of guns on their targets was done using details on the individual gun characteristics, weather, etc. The first stage of fire was directed at headquarters locations, command posts, telephone centers, enemy batteries and infantry positions. The use of high explosives was mixed with various types of gas. The second stage involved increasing the number of batteries involved in bombarding the enemy artillery and the third stage had specific high value targets assigned to batteries according to their range. These targets included close range infantry positions as well as long range targets that were targeted by heavy guns. For his work, he received the nickname *Durchbruchmüller*.

2. Frisch, op. cit., p. 254.
3. Greiner & Vulpius, op. cit., p. 251.
4. Ibid.
5. Ibid.
6. Greiner & Vulpius, op. cit., p. 252.
7. Greiner & Vulpius, op. cit., p. 253.
8. Greiner & Vulpius, op. cit., p. 254.
9. Ibid.
10. Greiner & Vulpius, op. cit., pp. 255-257.
11. Greiner & Vulpius, op. cit., p. 257.
12. Greiner & Vulpius, op. cit., pp. 258-259.
13. Greiner & Vulpius, op. cit., p. 259.
14. Greiner & Vulpius, op. cit., pp. 259-260.
15. Greiner & Vulpius, op. cit., p. 260.
16. Greiner & Vulpius, op. cit., pp. 257-258.
17. Greiner & Vulpius, op. cit., p. 261.
18. Ibid.
19. Frisch, op. cit., p. 262.
20. Frisch, op. cit., pp. 262-263.
21. Frisch, op. cit., p. 263.

6

26th Reserve Division

May–September 1918

The rest period that followed the fighting in May seemed to fly by according to many men in the 26th Reserve Division. Suddenly it was June and orders had been received that the division was going back into the front line. It was a place quite familiar to the men as the new sector being taken over was just north of the old Serre position, opposite Hébuterne, in the sector northwest of Puisieux. The 26th Reserve Division was once again in *Oberamt* Bapaume.

On 6 June 1918 , RIR 119 boarded trains in Arleux and was transported to Vélu and quartered in the destroyed village of Frémicourt. Far in front lay the terrible cratered fields of the Somme battle. The impression of returning to this well-known spot was seen quite differently by each regiment. RIR 121 described the scene where spring had covered over most of the visible death and destruction and covered the shell craters and ruins with a layer of fresh, pleasant greenery that beautified the barren area. Men repeatedly asked about one village or another and the answer was always: 'men, you stand in the middle of it here!' The villages were simply gone, the piles of rubble were overgrown with stinging nettles; it would be impossible for a stranger to suspect that years earlier hundreds lived in this barren wasteland.

It appeared quite different to the men of IR 180; the terrain had taken on a hideous appearance because no houses existed any longer, just ruins, weeds, well-built British barracks lay scattered everywhere in the terrain, made out of half-round corrugated iron-sheets, surrounded by low walls for protection against the explosions of aerial bombs, badly damaged enemy tanks and at the front a disgusting smell of putrefaction from the numerous horse cadavers, of which no one seemed to have thought of burying.

On 4, 5 and 6 June 1918 the battalions of RIR 121 were loaded in Arleux and transported to Vélu. RIR 121 lay for a few days at Frémicourt, Lebucquire, Achiet le Grand and Boursies where aircraft bombs disturbed the men's rest, and unfortunately caused considerable casualties from bomb fragments. The regiment was now in the area where it served between November 1914 and November 1916. However the terrain was no longer recognized by the men. The battle of the Somme, the withdrawal to the *Siegfried Stellung* vith the destruction of all military significant buildings and facilities on Operation Alberich, the subsequent Battle of Cambrai in November-December 1917 and now the great offensive battles in France had completely erased the old familiar landscape.

However, if there was one constant, it was the never ending amount of hard labor that was needed to maintain the position and improve the defenses. The front line fortunately did not consist solely of a crater position, but actually had a rudimentary trench system running through it and the Battle as well as the Readiness battalions for the most part could be fully accommodated in incomplete mined dugout entrances that had been previously created.

On 8 June 1918 IR 180 took over the position and placed the II/180 as the Battle Battalion, with the Readiness Battalion by Puisieux and Rest Battalion in the cellars of Bapaume in the vicinity the *Place de Faidherbe.* However already on 10 June the rest battalion had to be transferred out of Bapaume because of the frequent enemy bombardments with heavy caliber shells and the daily attacks by enemy bomber squadrons. The men were moved into a camp about one kilometer west of Bapaume on the Bapaume–Arras road. The regimental staff moved its battle headquarters about 600 meters northeast of Beauregard Farm and 200 meters east of the Miraumont–Puisieux Road, both areas well-known to the veterans of the early Somme fighting.

Most of the houses in Bapaume had been destroyed or damaged. Even the impressive city hall had been blown up as a result of Operation Alberich. Ironically, only the corners with the typical French café signs were still intact after the buildings had been demolished. At least the city streets had been cleared of debris so that troops and supply vehicles could travel on them. RIR 119 used empty British barrack camps to house the rest battalion, in which the troops who had come from the east were still not familiar with the level of fighting in the west, undressed before going to sleep. This was something the men familiar with the fighting on the western front had long ago ceased to do. The eastern front men uttered 'Rapid fire' when the Swabians moved into the well-built barracks as a result of the perceived intensity demonstrated by the men of the 26th Reserve Division.

Biefvillers was nothing more than a giant park, Irles had disappeared from the earth, the stone church had disappeared and all that could be recognized was the old road leading to Grévillers. Miraumont Château, where the divisional staff were previously billeted, was still somewhat intact; the entire village, however, was completely destroyed. It was not any different at Pys. Because of the wholesale destruction the carrying troops rested in small holes inside of a sand quarry near the Miraumont railway station when they were not travelling to and from the front lines. Due to the close proximity of the front line the provisions could be brought forward by carrying troops and still arrive in a warm condition to the battle battalions.

On the night of 6/7 June 1918 RIR 119 relieved IR 152 east of Hébuterne. The enemy occupied the slope in front of the village and could see deep into the German rear. The line held by RIR 119 projected far forward of the rest of the line because the 26th Reserve Division had advanced to this point while the flanking divisions had not come as far forward. The bulge in the line was called the 'Swabian belly' by the men as a form of soldier humor. At this point of the front line only a single trench ran through the position where the men had to remain quiet for days at a time in order to prevent from being seen. There was no thought of working on the exposed trench and as such four fifths of the men lay in rabbit holes, one fifth were in old mined dugouts.

At first the enemy was quiet, only firing mines during the day and random machine gun fire across the terrain at night in order to impede carrying parties. The situation became worse when rain started to fall and the numberless craters dotting the landscape quickly filled with water and formed a sea of churned up earth and mud.

Carrying troops were required to move across this terrible ground in enemy fire for hours at a time and when they finally made it back to their fox holes they were able to get only a few hours of rest before the next journey. The infantry were restricted to observing the enemy positions and rarely opened fire. The numerous old, crumbling trenches that crisscrossed the foreground greatly impeded patrol activity on both sides.

Enemy artillery fire increased in strength at the end of June, an indication that the adversary was becoming increasingly active and attacks could be expected. The newest danger came from the enemy gas batteries, the very dangerous Livens Projectors, which could throw a large number of gas mines into the German positions all at once. This form of attack often surprised many men who did not have their gas masks close at hand and the number of troops reporting gas sick increased accordingly.

On 10/11 June 1918 RIR 121 was placed in the forward line by Serre that was approximately the same position held before the fighting in June 1915; south of Hébuterne until La Signy Farm inclusive. This portion of the front was a crater position, without dugouts. Only the Readiness battalion had a few completed dugouts, in part constructed by the regiment in an earlier period of the war, otherwise the old defenses and facilities of the regiment from 1916 had been almost erased from the face of the earth.

The mass grave from July 1916, the large kitchen dugout by the *Fünf Weiden*, *Feste Soden* with its dugouts were all gone; Serre was completely overgrown with stinging nettles. RIR 121 found the area also filled with dead horse and special orders issued for their removal took several weeks to complete.

In the weeks that followed there was constant low level battle activity; continuous artillery fire, particularly at night, strong fire raids accompanied by enemy patrol advances, hand grenade fighting, mine fire, systematic bombardments of individual dugouts with gas shells, and mutual bombardments of the approach routes. Enemy planes were a constant presence, firing with machine guns and dropping bombs from low altitude on the German positions. The Reserve battalion in Grévillers was often targeted by enemy aircraft and on 11 June 1918 the I/R121 alone had one man killed and 22 men wounded from an aircraft bomb. The British pilots dominated the sky in every direction and few German aircraft were ever seen by the men.

At 2.00 a.m. on 16 June 1918 the enemy artillery fire powerfully increased on the forward line by IR 180 and the rearward trenches of both left company sectors, the 9th and 12/180, which was accompanied by strong mine fire. The artillery fire had barely been transferred to the rear at 2.15 a.m., when two enemy detachments in the strength of 50-60 men each approached the sector of the 9/180. As the enemy raiding parties reached the forward most sap, the sentry inside of it threw hand grenades at the dark shapes and a nearby machine gun opened fire.

Quarters of the I/R121 in Grévillers following an enemy bombing raid. (Author's collection)

The British attack failed due to the quick response by the alert sentries and the effective infantry and hand grenade fire of the trench garrison. Afterward a severely wounded British First Lieutenant from the 1st Manchester Regiment was found and brought in as a prisoner. The British made a second attempt in the following night at 2.15 a.m. against the northern sap of the 11/180; however it too was spotted by the alert sentries and expelled through machine gun fire and hand grenades.

On the night of19/20 June 1918 the battalions in IR 180 exchanged positions, the I/180 became the Battle battalion and in the next night the 1/180 had to a repulse another enemy attack. At 12.30 a.m. strong artillery fire of light, medium and heavy caliber guns suddenly fell on the forward line as well as the rearward positions and communication trenches of both northerly company sectors. The barrage fire from the German guns that was called up with light balls started quickly, however it was a thin defensive barrage due to the lack of guns and the extensive width of the sector.

The artillery was soon joined by the rapid barrage fire of the light 7.6cm *Minenwerfer*. Shortly after the beginning of the British drum-fire two enemy detachments of about 40-50 men each advanced against the sap at the right wing of the 1/180, with one detachment attacking the sap head, the other the base of the sap. The main body of attackers was refused through infantry and machine gun fire, the other part, which had successfully penetrated into the trench, were immediately thrown out in a counterattack with help from the 2/180. A series of further enemy raids occurred in the following night along the front of the 26th Reserve Division. At midnight on 20/21 June 1918 heavy artillery and mine fire fell across the several regimental sectors. At 12.30 a.m. the enemy infantry advanced at several points, all of which were successfully driven back by infantry fire and barrage fire from the light *Minenwerfer* of *Minenwerfer* Coy 226 which lost one man killed and several men wounded during the attack.

RIR 119 had expected an attack on 20 June 1918 however the enemy did not approach the regimental sector on this day. British planes did drop bombs in the battle zone and rest camps of RIR 119 but without causing any real damage. Large enemy patrols continued to raid the lines held by RIR 119 on a regular basis in the following days with some success in taking prisoners and causing losses, something the regiment could ill afford. While there had been no major attack yet, everything pointed to one being imminent.

Following the latest enemy attempts to breach the German lines there were daily bombardments of the opposing positions by the light 7.6cm *Minenwerfer*. The *Minenwerfer* crew alternated the bombardments with the work needed to replenish their ammunition stocks and restoring the position to good order following the damage caused by enemy fire. One noted success occurred on 28 June 1918 when an area taken under fire by *Minenwerfer* Coy 226 by La Signy Farm struck and blew up a large enemy gas mine depot. The crew of *Minenwerfer* position 'Ulm' who had fired the lucky shot had to wear their gas masks for the next 30 minutes as clouds of gas filled the air.

The *Minenwerfer* platoon of *Leutnant der Reserve* Schlegel had great success in destroying enemy machine gun nests, and which would have been even more effective if the ammunition being used did not turn out to have so many duds. It was a sign of the troubles German industry was having in supplying good quality material to the troops at this stage of the war.

What came next was very unwelcome to the badly understrength 26th Reserve Division; an influenza epidemic. At the end of June influenza spread through the division and neighboring divisions causing numerous men to report sick. On 30 June the 6/*Pionier* Battalion 13 reported all officers and 22 percent of the ration strength of the company were ill with influenza. This not only disrupted all work being performed at the end of June, it continued into July with more men falling sick while others were still recovering from the effects of the illness.

The increase in the number of men reporting sick in early July corresponded with an increased battle activity of the enemy, particularly mine fire with gas and high explosive ammunition as well as numerous patrol advances. The British and Canadians were not allowing the men of the 26th Reserve Division any time to catch their breath. The enemy used every weapon in his arsenal to harass the Germans from the forward most sentries to the rest areas far in the rear day after day in order to unnerve the German troops. Enemy aircraft dropped leaflets covered with enticing ideas or provocative pictures and articles directed against the German leadership that were designed to encourage men to desert.

The British were not the only ones actively raiding at this time. The men of the 26th Reserve Division, while tired and far less in numbers than their opponents, still managed to hold numerous patrols and raids against the opposing lines. At 12.30 p.m. on 1 July 1918, *Leutnant* Zirn, company leader of the 6/180, along with a few men made a bold patrol against an enemy sentry post. Zirn had explored the route to the enemy post several days earlier and had worked out all of the details of his raid. He divided his men into two *Stosstrupps* and two detachments of protection troops and crawled forward at the head of his men at 11.15 a.m. on a bright, sunny day. Zirn and his men left the German trench and crawled toward a barricade, where he knew an enemy sentry stood guard. At 12.30 p.m. both *Stosstrupps* were located five meters in front of the enemy sentry, without having become discovered.

Zirn then gave the signal for his men to proceed and the *Stosstrupps* rushed fell against the sentry post, with *Leutnant* Zirn at the head, followed by *Unteroffizier* Lang and *Kriegsfreiwilliger* Kilgus and all three men jumped into the deep, narrow sentry hole. However, they did not simply find a lone sentry in the sap; they found seven enemy soldiers inside the post which was a slit trench that was so deep and narrow that the men following, *Gefreiter* Helber and *Musketier* Alber, were forced to remain outside the trench.

The enemy sentry, although surprised by the sudden appearance of three German soldiers, immediately prepared to defend his post while his comrades reportedly wanted to give up. The sentry, described as a 'powerful, broad-shouldered Englishman,' fought back against Zirn and his companions. On seeing this, the rest of the enemy soldiers also joined in and offered resistance against the invaders. Three of the enemy soldiers were shot down through well-aimed head shots with a pistol. *Leutnant* Zirn, along with *Unteroffizier* Lang and *Kriegsfreiwilliger* Kilgus then became embroiled in a brawl using their hands and feet and attempted to bodily lift the large sentry out of the steep and deep trench, which failed.

When more of the enemy garrison approached the sap they became shot down through numerous well-aimed pistol shots by the raiding party. The sentry, who still desperately fought back against being captured, succeeded in becoming free, however he was then shot in the chest and head by *Leutnant* Zirn and *Kriegsfreiwilliger* Kilgus and fell to the floor of the trench. Zirn and his men now had to beat a hasty retreat back to the German lines, which they managed to reach without suffering any losses. While the raid did not succeed in capturing any prisoners, it did demonstrate that while the 26th Reserve Division was understrength, the men still had the pluck to attempt a raid in broad daylight.

The entire front line was restless throughout the month of July that included one failed enemy attack by Albert on 13 July 1918. On the next day the normal routine was interrupted when five British aircraft chased one German plane over the lines by Hébuterne as the men on the ground could only watch the uneven contest taking place over their heads. Then, just before midnight on the same day, patrols from both sides were active in the foreground until a downpour forced them all to withdraw.

The battalions of IR 180 rotated in the night from 14/15 July 1918 and the II/180 became the Battle battalion. RIR 119 connected on the left of IR 180 while the neighboring division connected on the right. At 4.30 a.m. on 15 July 1918 the enemy opened heavy drum fire from numerous guns of every caliber on the entire German forward line, then, at 4.45 a.m., an enemy raid took place. The enemy attacked the boundary between the 6th and 7/180 with about four detachments of about 50 men each. Simultaneously followed an attack in battalion strength, about 4-5 companies strong, against the left wing of the 8/180, the 5/180 and against the left neighboring regiment.

The enemy overran the forward line by the 7/180 and advanced until they were in the vicinity of the company leader dugout. The enemy also succeeded in breaking-in at the left wing of the 8/180 and in the area of the 5/180. The attacks took place along a portion of the line held by IR 180 that projected far out into no man's land by Hébuterne where the *Minenwerfer* position called 'Altona' was located. The initial enemy attack was not recognized immediately by the *Minenwerfer* crew so 'Altona' was only able to fire three shots once the enemy skirmish line was spotted, then the British appeared immediately in front of the position.

The gun crew defended the position with carbines and hand grenades during which *Unteroffizier* Hag and *Pionier* Engelhardt were killed while *Pionier* Müller was reported missing. 'Altona 1' was not able to fire anymore, as it became buried by the enemy fire. 'Altona 2' fell into enemy hands and the gun was lost.

Counterattacks were organized immediately but because of the low strength of the companies and the high losses already suffered during the bombardment and the infantry attack they were only partially executed. The KTK then ordered the readiness companies, the 2nd and 1/180, to counterattack, which did not succeed in throwing back the enemy to his exit position, because the British had already created a defensive position in the captured trench piece and erected barricades. A second enemy attack on the outpost zone by IR 180 in the evening of the same day enlarged the initial enemy success.

The raiding parties had also succeeded in penetrating the line by RIR 119. The portion of the line held by RIR 119 experienced the same level of enemy drum fire on the morning of 15 July 1918 at 4.55 a.m., followed by an infantry attack soon after, at 5 a.m. The British had sneaked into an old trench in front of the German lines and organized for the attack. Three strong skirmish lines suddenly advanced out of the old trench; overran the front line and reached the *Habichtsweg*.

The remnants of the 1st and 2/R119 soon brought the attack to a stop. The II/R119, the Readiness battalion, was in front of the artillery positions and filled the gaps in the line. The III/R119 was in Biéfvillers became alarmed and the 9th and 12/R119 were moved forward in the event the companies were needed.

A counterattack was planned at 4.00 a.m. on 16 July 1918 that should throw the enemy back. The German artillery batteries began a bombardment of the enemy positions in preparation for this attack, while the 7th and 8/R119 with the remnants of the 1st and 2/R119 advanced into the *Habichtsweg*. The leader of the *Stosstrupp* which was to take the first trench was the replacement company leader of the 7/R119, *Leutnant der Reserve* Bunk.

The first enemy troops were encountered in the *Habichtsweg* and were taken with hand grenades and bayonets by the *Stosstrupp* under Bunk and further to the right by another *Stosstrupp* from the 7/R119. Contact to the left was made in the sunken road which was recaptured in part and blocked off. Then *Leutnant* Bunk thrust forward into the old first trench leading to the sunken road at the regimental border on the right and had almost reached it, but enemy resistance prevented him from going any further.

Just as some of the British troops were seen going to the rear a strong enemy fire raid suddenly struck the terrain just recaptured by *Leutnant der Reserve* Bunk and his men and caused large losses to the 7/R119, and at the same time the British attacked once again. *Leutnant* Bunk held out in his position with the few men remaining with him until the last hand grenade had been used and then moved back fighting to the 3/R119.

The counterattack by the 8/R119 was under the command of *Offizier Stellvertreter* Fessler, who had taken over the company in place of the severely wounded *Leutnant* Wörner. When Fessler's company had been forced out of the *Habichtsweg* by the sudden enemy counterattack he held his position with one *Unteroffizier* and two Other Ranks, one of which he later sent back as a runner. This small group held off the enemy until 4 p.m. and prevented the adversary from taking full advantage of his attack and made it possible to create a main opposition line in the rear; however, the position of the 1/R119 was lost.

The trenches of the 3/R119 were prevented from being rolled up by *Leutnant* Frank, 3/R119 with his two orderlies and six men from the 7/R119. Despite the strong resistance, the left wing of RIR 119 had to be curved back during the course of the fighting and the entire outpost zone was lost. Further advances by the enemy were attempted, all failed in the opposition of the weak garrison. To give the reader some idea of just how devastating the losses had been in RIR 119, following the fighting the 2/R119 numbered five men, the 1st, 7th and 8/R119 had six men each. The 3rd and 4/R119 contained 20 men each while the 5th, 6th, 9th and 12/R119 had 25 men each.

The regimental combat strength of RIR 119 was less than 300 men, a far cry of what a regiment should contain normally. Since the other regiments were of similar size the division was extremely weak, containing slightly more men than what a single company would consist of in 1914. The weak strength of the 26th Reserve Division was not the exception, it was the rule and as such when looking at the history from this period of the war the reader should take into account that while regiments and divisions are mentioned, the size is more like companies and battalions in actual strength.

The incredibly small number of men were holding a front 2,200 meters in length against an attack by an enemy brigade, which was found to consist of the best enemy attack troops; New Zealanders. The New Zealand troops had a reputation among the German infantry as being first rate fighting men with a terrible hatred of the Germans and they were well known for taking few prisoners. Perhaps this impression allowed the few remaining men of the 26th Reserve Division to put up a strong defense, far greater than the small number of men would be expected to provide?

The superior enemy strength did not allow for the recovery of the lost outpost zone however it did allow the men of the 26th Reserve Division to stop the enemy advance. Recovering the lost outpost zone again was not possible, and would only be feasible with the insertion of stronger forces and thorough artillery preparation. It was eventually decided to create a new defensive position with the current front line that was held that should prevent adversary from making any further headway.

Once the fighting died down the artillery held fire raids the rest of the day. Enemy pilots dropped bombs on the battlefield and toward evening German infantry flights appeared overhead, something quite unexpected and very appreciated by the hard-pressed infantry on the ground. The companies holding the front line fired light balls at the ground in order to provide the friendly infantry flights with an idea of where the front lines stood. Even when darkness fell, numerous enemy pilots flew above the position the entire night resulting in a state of constant alarm readiness.

German pilot and observer in their Hannover CLII. These aircraft could provide valuable support to the infantrymen by use of machine gun fire, dropping small bombs, flares and harassing enemy infantry. (Author's collection)

The increased activity along the front by the 26th Reserve Division continued until the morning of 17 July 1918 when it began to rain steadily and it became quieter on both sides of the line. From the random pattern of enemy artillery fire it was assumed that the opponent still did not have a clear idea about the exact location of the German line and was firing in the dark. In the night to 20 July 1918 the main opposition line was moved back, the remnants of the I/R119 were relieved and the outpost zone was only occupied by sentries; this change was apparently not noticed by enemy observers.

Then, shortly after 8.30 p.m. on 21 July 1918 the enemy attacked without any fire preparation with a large force. After a period of powerful hand grenade fighting the outposts of the 6th, 8th, 9th and 12/R119 were forced to withdraw to the main opposition line; only the 5/R119 was able to hold out. There were plans to recover the lost outpost zone and the terrain was covered by heavy annihilation fire from the German batteries on 21 July 1918 from 5.00 to 10.00 p.m. When the offensive patrols of the different companies moved forward, the enemy let loose powerful retaliation fire, however, sentry positions were set up at various locations in the outpost zone despite the heavy fire.

From 22-23 July 1918 the badly frayed RIR 119 was finally relieved by IR 440 and the 26th Reserve Division became an *Eingreifdivision* once more. RIR 121 remained in the position until 22 July 1918 when it was relieved by IR 418 that followed in the nights from 22, 23 and 24 July 1918. On the next day the regiment received rest quarters near Bapaume, in Bus Le Mesnil. *Minenwerfer* Coy 226 was relieved by *Minenwerfer* Coy 401 on 24 July 1918 and moved to the rear but soon came under long range artillery fire.

Zur frommen Erinnerung im Gebete
an

Georg Knaus

von Köfingen

Unteroffizier beim Res.-Inf.-Regt. 121, 8. Komp.
Inhaber des Eis Kreuzes II. Kl. und der
Silbernen Verdienstmedaille

geboren den 23. Januar 1895
gestorben den 19. Juli 1918
den Heldentod fürs Vaterland.

G e b e t.

Vater der Barmherzigkeit und Gott alles Trostes, erbarme Dich Deines treuen Dieners G e o r g, der im Kampfe gefallen ist. Fern von der Heimat liegt er begraben, doch Du, o Vater, sei ihm nahe durch Deine Liebe. Vergib ihm die Vergehungen, laß ihm alle zeitlichen Sündenstrafen nach, lohne seinen Tod, den er fürs Vaterland erduldet hat mit dem ewigen Leben, schmücke ihn mit dem Siegeskranz des treuen Soldaten und gib uns allen die Freude des Wiedersehens im Himmel durch Jesum Christum unsern Herrn.

Bopfinger und Neresheimer Tagblatt.
Agentur M. Ledl, Neresheim.

Death notice for Unteroffizier Georg Knaus, RIR 121. (Felix Fregin)

While in the rear the company helped prepare anti-tank mines, construct foot bridges over the Sensée stream and started construction of a concrete dugout for the division staff.

The fighting that had taken place by Hébuterne was just a small part of the events taking place along the entire front and received only brief mention in the German Daily Report: '15 July 1918. Southeast of Hébuterne a strong enemy attack was repulsed. And on 16 July: Enemy attack southeast of Hébuterne was unsuccessful.'

RIR 119 was now housed in captured British camps, trying to recover from the strain of the last weeks. The rest time was regularly interrupted by enemy aircraft dropping bombs on the camps, something the men had become used to. The weather soon turned hot and rain started to fall while there was a further appearance of the Grippe [influenza] from which everyone in the area suffered from. Whether it was a sense of honor, or not, the men of RIR 119 refused to report sick, only going to hospital if they had a high fever and they were ordered to go by the doctor.

The men of the 26th Reserve Division desperately required rest and refitting following the months of fighting behind them. However, the tense military situation facing the German Army in the west did not allow the luxury of rest for any division involved in the fighting. Once in the rest quarters training was resumed as normal. Now, everything was being directed toward providing an effective defense with only a few men. Much of the effort centered upon the light machine guns as the core of each infantry group. This allowed for the most firepower from the smallest number of troops.

The news that the division was being relieved and moved further to the rear by Douai at the beginning of August was greeted with great joy by the men of the 26th Reserve Division. The regiments of the division were soon marching to the new rest quarters, a goal that always made the journey that much easier and resulted in fewer complaints about sore feet and sore backs than usual. The billets in Douai were very good, however night after night more aerial attacks took place so that many of the men felt that they could never elude the long reach of the enemy.

The next fourteen days were spent in trying to increase the combat effectiveness of the 26th Reserve Division. There were still pitifully too few men in the division and of these, many were recent recruits with little training behind them. The only solution to this problem was to ensure that each man was capable of utilizing all of the weapons available to the infantry, especially those that provided the most firepower. Still, even with such training, the men lacked the necessary combat experience that would make them effective soldiers in the type of fighting taking place in 1918. There was daily live fire practice on the machine guns, pistols, rifles, and *Minenwerfer* as well as in hand grenade tactics. In the free time following the training the men were able to visit the city of Douai with its beautiful buildings, parks, swimming pool, cinemas, etc. that offered all sorts of variety and enjoyment and where they could relax, even if for only a short time.

The quarters provided to the men were generally comfortable and for the most part consisted of individual quarters in local homes. The 26th Reserve Division was still designated as an *Eingreifdivision* and as such the regiments must be alarm ready at all times, which moderately impaired the training of the companies. Even in the higher state of alert, all of the exercises were held and in particular, the training on specialty weapons progressed rapidly.

The regiments had barely settled in at the rest area when the alarm cry was sounded on 8 August 1918. It quickly became known that the enemy had made a massive infantry attack accompanied by 300-400 tanks that had been brought up to the front in silence and had then smashed through the German lines.

A corps order arrived at 3.00 p.m. and the battalions of RIR 119 were quickly assembled and loaded on to motor lorries and moved to Chuignes where it became the corps reserve with the front facing Proyart. While the men marched to the new position they could hear the sounds of artillery fire coming from almost every direction, never a good sign. While on the roads enemy aircraft frequently bombed the column, causing numerous delays in the advance. When the regiment arrived at its assigned location the men were provided with shelter in poorly constructed British dugouts.

Leutnant der Reserve Wörner, RFAR 26 (*Das Württembergisches Reserve-Feldartillerie-Regiment Nr.26 im Weltkrieg 1914-1918)*

RIR 119 was then joined by RIR 122 and IR 478, which formed a provisional brigade. The men were quickly exposed to the first signs of tank panic as soldiers streamed past their new position in terror, shouting 'everything is lost!' The men of RIR 119 had never faced tanks before and were unfamiliar with the dread they had caused among the front line troops, it would not be long before they experienced this first hand.

Part of RIR 119 was being used for artillery protection, while other parts were used as pickets in order to protect the main German line. The situation was very unclear at the front and the exact location of friend and foe was unknown. A patrol led *Leutnant der Reserve* Herdtle went forward in the night and was able to establish that the British occupied the nearby village of Proyart.

The 107th Infantry Division counterattacked during the night and the provisional brigade which included RIR 119 was to follow behind and act as reserves. However, the attack failed when the 107th Division ended up running into a British attack and was forced to retreat.

While the remainder of the 26th Reserve Division was enjoying the rest quarters, the men of RIR 119 faced renewed enemy attacks on 9 August 1918, including some with the dreaded tank. The German divisions were completely on the defensive following the massive Allied attack of the previous day. RIR 119 was now shifted into a readiness position and when new orders arrived, the regiment moved to the eastern edge of Bray-sur-Somme:

> In the course of the afternoon of 9 August I received an order from my new division. I was to become placed in readiness in possession of the brigade west of Etinehem. Before the orders could be promptly sent to the commands, the drum

> fire of the Englishmen came, so that I could not reach the command place and therefore went to the brigade that was southwest of Bray. The I Battalion marched there in the evening, crossing the severely bombarded Bray by leaps. The brigade even wanted to depart to the east, when I arrived there with my battalion, which reached the new provisional location without losses as if through a miracle, and could report.
>
> *Hauptmann der Reserve* Rueff, Commanding I/R119.[1]

The men could watch the fighting from their positions which consisted mainly of small holes where the men could find some shelter. They could feel the bombardment that seemingly fell on every square foot of ground as the shock waves rippled through the chalk soil. If they looked toward the sky, they found it filled with numerous enemy aircraft and not a single German plane could be seen.

Darkness had fallen on the battlefield where RIR 119 was positioned and the black night only made matters worse when it came to the fear of enemy tanks. Whenever a sentry thought he observed a dark shape moving in the foreground it was always considered to be a 'black monster', an enemy tank. Panic began to take over the men as the alarm cry was sounded over and over in the night for the imaginary tank attack. The men all recalled the cries of 'all is lost!' by retreating troops as the Württembergers advanced to the position. However, aside from individual cases of panic, for the most part the men of RIR 119 remained calm. While sitting in their small, cramped wet holes, the men were thinking more about their comrades in RIR 121 and IR 180 who were resting behind the front. These thoughts filled many of them with secret envy and resentment.

The overall situation facing the German army was dire. There were far too many situations requiring immediate reinforcements while too few men were available for this purpose. On the following day RIR 119 was split up with the I/R119 being attached to the 42nd Infantry Division and the II/R119 to the 27th Infantry Division. On the night of 9/10 August 1918 the III/R119 with the regimental staff was also assigned to the 27th Infantry Division.

Brigade ordered the I/R119 to support IR 138; however the battalion went to the location where this regiment was supposed to be but could not find it in the dark night. The I/R119 would now have to act independently:

> Until now we had only met Swabians. The situation there was completely unclear, the 3rd and 4/R119 received orders, to begin to clarify the situation in front with light skirmish lines on a broad front. Although it was night and the entire terrain was completely unfamiliar, the two platoons and the patrols sent out accomplished their tasks in the shortest time, so that by 2 a.m. the situation before our front in the largest part was assessed. Also, the regimental staff we were to support from the Prussian brigade, was located at 2 a.m.
>
> *Hauptmann der Reserve* Rueff, Commanding I/R119.[2]

On 9 August 1918 the II/R119 had been attached to Grenadier Regiment 123 and had taken a position with the III/123 east of Bray. At this time Bray lay under the fire of heavy mortars and long range enemy batteries. The steep sided Somme valley with its grey stone made quite an impression on the men of the II/R119, even in these uncertain times. In the evening the II Battalion moved forward 1,700 meters west of Bray. Two companies dug in as artillery protection, the 8/R119 on the right and the 7/R119 on the left of the Bray-Corbie road. The battalion worked forward under heavy fire and the companies took up positions 300 meters in front of the artillery position.

What the men in the II/R119 did not know was that in the night all of the troops lying in front of the battalion had moved to the rear; the artillery had been limbered up and driven back, leaving the II/R119 alone upon the open fields in the forward most position.

On the evening of 9/10 August 1918 the British attacked Bray-sur-Somme at the fall of darkness. The enemy troops advanced from the west and had captured considerable ground. Troops from IR 120, IR 137, IR 265, IR 478, IR 479 and *pioniers* were still positioned west of Etinehem, however, the total number of men in all of these 'regiments' amounted to less than 1,000 men.

At 2.00 a.m. the 3/R119 reported it had to swivel back on the former connection they had on the right, because the British had broken through on the right wing of the company. Also, they had lost contact with the 4/R119 that was dug in at the second line. Bicycle patrols under *Leutnant der Reserve* Pfau and *Unteroffizier* Elsässer immediately sped off, which received British machine gun fire from the right and the rear. They bravely continued to pedal on in order to clarify the situation but everywhere they went, there were no German troops:

> There were powerful attacks again which advanced by the way of the place where the battalion was to move as the brigade reserve readiness position. It now received orders, to occupy Etinehem and there to serve as the rear support for the troops in front of us, and to establish where our own troops were through patrols. The companies moved from their positions and took up a connection to the right and the left. The enemy did not attempt anything, instead they only scattered the village with uninterrupted machine gun fire. When the morning dawned, the first big surprise came: The so-called rear support position was shoved far forward in front of our own line, there in the morning dawn all what lay in front of the battalion out above Bray had moved back. During the entire day, the British wanted to march into Etinehem with two large patrols from the Bois Gressaire. However the 1st and 3rd Companies denied it to him with a few belts of machine gun ammunition. He was badly offended by it and placed the heaviest artillery fire on the irritating village situated on the Somme from 12-6 p.m. However the position of the battalion had been so skillfully chosen under avoidance of the village that in a miraculous way no losses occurred. It became evening; the brave food carriers provided the battalion with warm food. The entire day we probably saw Englishmen marching forward toward Etinehem from the heights lying opposite us; however the sharp morning greeting of the 1st and 3rd Companies forced them to remain at a respectful distance. They sensed that a different breeze blew here. So it became night.
>
> *Hauptmann der Reserve* Rueff, I/R119.[3]

The patrols of the I/R119 continued further on and they found that five kilometers north of the I/R119 the German line had stood firm and unshaken in the night attacks. What had happened to the other troops which the I/R119 was to support but were missing without a trace? It was later discovered that they had marched off according to orders they received from Brigade headquarters. The four companies of the I/R119, in the firm hands of the leaders, *Leutnants* Klipphahn, Bönsel, Gammertsfelder and Malblanc were as prepared as they could be for the expected enemy attack.

The morning of 10 August 1918 was generally quiet but in the afternoon there was heavy drum fire north of the regimental sector and enemy troops were visible opposite the neighboring 54th Reserve Division. However, the regimental sector of RIR 119 was not attacked. It became very lively during the night. Numerous enemy planes swooped down low over the battlefield and the whine of their engines and propellers along with the uninterrupted fire from the enemy guns hid the approach of a new threat. Enemy drum fire began towards 3.00 a.m., and after a short time two tanks appeared on the Bray-Corbie road. Tanks also appeared further south where the regimental companies had orders to withdraw if they were strongly attacked north of Bray:

> The dark monsters slowly rolled on the road, vomiting firing from the front and the sides. Bands of light broke out of the loopholes and observation slits from the interior electric lighting and offered the machine guns good targets. The wagons were taken under fire with steel core bullets from two heavy and a few light machine guns of the II Battalion. Bright flashes came from the splash of the bullets on the armor that was strong enough to keep them out.
>
> The tank crew apparently did not like the spooky throb on the steel walls which appeared horrifying and they put out the lights in order to impede the targets. When the wagons came even closer and did not become detained, a small part of the 7/R119 was seized by the tank panic and went to the rear. Only one brave platoon held firm, together with the 8th Company under its intrepid leader, *Leutnant der Reserve* Siegle, who held his men together through his cold blooded calmness. They crawled into their fox holes as the monsters arrived here and let them drive past. Then they stood up, carefully at first, then boldly man by man and looked curiously at the tank from behind. 'It was the purest theater.' The men said later. The British infantry should have followed 1,000 yards behind the tanks. However when they noticed that the Swabians did not run away and still fired, the attack hesitated before RIR 119. The two tanks travelled in to Bray, one until the eastern edge of the city, and when they found no opposition or anyone who noticed their rolling advance, they turned and travelled back. The III/R119 had not become attacked. However the left wing of the II/R119 hung in the air. The Grenadiers must yield to the attack. So I would curve back the line of the II Battalion until at the western exit of Bray. However that scary night of Bray will not soon become forgotten, although it was not lacking in a cheerful episode. So when a dashing *Hauptmann* of the neighboring regiment, who wanted to collect the remnants of his troops about him, stalwartly shouted about in the darkness: 'Grenadiers to me!' Finally two stout field grey swarmed about him and when

he asked them their names, one said: 'I am a 119er and belong to the Seventh Company.'

Hauptmann der Reserve Rueff, I/R119.[4]

By 5.00 p.m. it was firmly determined that the battalion was completely exposed and that there were no other German troops within five kilometers of its position. Fortunately, it was also determined that there were no more enemy troops nearby as well. The British had apparently not discovered the size of the German force during the fighting in the previous night and had moved farther back:

> Behind me the swampy Somme. A serious decision stands before me, either to pointlessly gamble with my battalion of about 150 men like Leonidas with his flock or to still use the early fog to cross over the river on narrow path some 30 centimeters wide. Because simultaneously powerful drum fire was employed south of the Somme and the English light balls hailed advances being made, the order to change shores became given. The march off occurred in exemplary calmness and order. The complete battalion was placed in possession of the senior regiment west of Cappy at 7.00 a.m. Two light *Minenwerfer* that we could not carry over the wobbly bridge were blown up. Two cannons from the platoon of our forward moved battery must be left behind, however they later became recovered. First of all the battalion occupied the bridge head by Cappy. There, since one could not know what surprise could come from the south, the bridge heads of Laneuville and Froissy became occupied to the north as well as to the south on orders from Brigade.
>
> *Hauptmann der Reserve* Rueff, I/R119.[5]

The firm stand at Etinehem by the I/R119 made it possible for IR 137 to assemble the remnants of the regiment and, after becoming rested, become led back over the Somme. IR 137 could now take over its old position which the enemy had not succeeded in capturing.

In the early morning hours of 10 August 1918 the III/R119 was placed north of Tailles Wood and the battalion pushed the 10/R119 into the front line. As there were no accurate maps following the great chaos of the defeat of 8 August 1918, two companies moved forward in the fog and ended up in the fire of German artillery batteries and suffered losses. The battalion adjutant, *Leutnant der Reserve* Kull then pulled them back. The British saw this movement and followed. However, while the companies were still withdrawing they opened fire on the British who were breaking forth from Tailles Wood at a range of 600 meters and effectively stopped the enemy advance.

On the afternoon of 11 August 1918 the 2nd and 4/R119 were be placed in possession of the troops advancing over the river. The two companies extended the right wing of IR 137 along with two heavy machine guns and boldly moved forward. In the course of 12 August 1918 Bray become occupied by the Germans again and a connection was established to the II/R119, which together with the III/R119 had stood firm in the enemy night attack.

The situation was still far from being under control. Hundreds of men who had become separated from their regiments, either by accident or design, wandered behind the front south of the Somme. These men spread dozens of rumors from the situation facing the army and brought forth uncertainty and excitement among the troops who had remained with their officers:

> There a further bold patrol was made to Chuignalles by *Leutnant der Reserve* Herdtle with *Unteroffizier* Elsässer and *Musketier* Gurr who also found Swabians from IR 478 on the southern edge of the village. They saw strong enemy skirmish lines moving to the attack and brought the report back, whereupon the highest readiness level was ordered. IR 478 repulsed the attack. The fighting did not proceed so fortunately in the sector of RIR 119. How it had been anticipated, the English sat waiting on the dominating positions only waiting for the opportunity about which parts were to go further over the Somme.
>
> *Hauptmann der Reserve* Rueff, I/R119.[6]

On 12 August 1918 the position of the III/R119 was taken over by units from the 54th Reserve Division. All four companies had still been in the front line and there were regular rotations of the men. Enemy attacks were expected at any time and there were rumors of tanks being in front which proved to be false. However, early on 13 August 1918 the British attacked the hill west of Laneuville just after 2.00 a.m. after a short period of artillery preparation fire:

> Already the sentries put in by the 2nd Company on the right wing were seized from the rear and given up for lost. However light and heavy machine guns open fire; the English hesitated, the 4th and the largest part of the 2nd Coy can use the moment to evade and move back to the battalion again on the same weak bridge as on the morning of the 11th. The remnants of the Prussian regiments must leave more hair.
>
> *Hauptmann der Reserve* Rueff, I/R119.[7]

Now, barely 50 men still remained and formed the outpost troops of the division in the I/R119. The average battle strength of a company was 26 men; the 2/R119 only having 17 men still standing. The connection was established with Grenadier Regiment 123 west of Bray. Numerous patrols fanned out along the front and bravely and boldly moved forward in order to detain the enemy if possible and firmly locate the new front line. The patrols of *Vizefeldwebel* König, 4/R119, *Unteroffizier* Jeuchner, 3/R119, Sergeants Krauss and Schietinger, 1/R119 and Gehring especially stood out:

> 13 August also remained quiet. During the night the Somme ground was blocked off by heavy machine gun fire. The protection of the bridgeheads at Fraissy was accomplished through pickets and patrols. My brave men were marvelous and by their hands the connection to the right and to the left were preserved with patrols and the enemy was prevented from any opportunity of crossing the Somme

through machine gun fire, so that so far for the last 2 days there was an orderly situation there. The security was soon so pronounced that on the morning of 14 August the brigade general personally came to thank me and my brave battalion.

Hauptmann der Reserve Rueff, I/R119.[8]

I/R119 was relieved on the morning of 15 August and on 15/16 August it was returned to the regiment where it remained in the railway hollow between Bray and Curlu until 20 August 1918. In the course of 16 August 1918 the enemy worked closer to the German positions in front of the II/R119. The position of the regiment was then moved along the Méaulte-Etinehem road.

Only small remnants of the regiments from the 27th Infantry Division still remained, who, immediately before the English attack on 8 August 1918 had made a successful and bloody assault on Malancourt and then took part in the defense of the British attack and had suffered terrible losses. The largest part of the men had no leaders and were scattered across the battlefield. *Oberstleutnant* Schäfer, commanding RIR 119 and his staff took command over the scattered men on a front sector three to four kilometers wide north of the Somme in which the men of the II and III/R119 stood shoulder to shoulder in thin lines in defense of any further enemy attacks. Part of IR 27 from the 243rd Infantry Division, along with men from the 54th Reserve Division fighting further to the north formed part of his fighting reserve.

There were enemy gas attacks On the night of 15/16 August 1918 and the men were forced to wear their gas masks up to five hours; the gas reportedly smelled like sour apples. At this time the OHL desired to know the identity of the enemy troops opposite the division and had planned to make a series of raids in the early morning hours of 18 August 1918.

Meanwhile, about 10.30 p.m. on 15 August 1918 *Leutnant der Reserve* Rettenmaier, leader of the 5/R119, heard the sustained fire of a machine gun on the right wing of the company. Along with his orderly, *Gefreiter* Hetzel, he left his shell hole and moved toward the firing gun. In the glow of a light ball he saw the British lying about 200 meters in front of the position. He was immediately determined to take advantage of the situation. Rettenmaier was determined to go on the offensive; he first of all cocked his pistol, left orders for his *Stosstrupp* to follow him immediately and asked for anyone nearby who would voluntarily accompany him. Hetzel and a Machine Gun *Schützen* decided to accompany Rettenmaier. While the British machine gun prevented them from rushing out, Rettenmaier and his companions were still able to work forward. Then, once the *Stosstrupp* under *Vizefeldwebel* Schwung arrived, Rettenmaier gave the order to attack.

In the next moment he had the first British soldier by the collar. In the darkness of the night the *Stosstrupp* looked for other adversaries, however they only caught two living enemy soldiers and found two more that had been killed. Furthermore, one Lewis Gun was captured and numerous pieces of equipment were brought back. The quick resolve by Rettenmaier had spared the II/R119 from an enemy operation and had provided the OHL with the prisoners they desired. The next few days passed under artillery fire of varying strength, until the regiment was relieved on 20/21 August 1918. The remnants of RIR 119 assembled in Curlu and were sent back to Douai.

Part of the success experienced by RIR 119 could be traced to the fact that most of the regiment was apparently unaffected by tank panic with the exception of a small group from the 7/R119. In the chaotic situation following 8 August, the regiment, no matter how small it had become, formed a strong battle line in the position of the 54th Reserve Division, and which alone had withstood the powerful enemy attacks.

Whilst RIR 119 was heavily engaged in the fighting, the pleasant days of rest for the men of IR 180 had come to an abrupt end on 19 August 1918. The regiment was transferred and moved toward the front lines as a detachment of the *Eingreifdivision* of the I Bavarian Army Corps on the embankment by Quiéry la Mott, 6 kilometers west of Douai. At 4.30 a.m. on 20 August 1918 the battalions moved into their billeting areas on the railway embankment. Two battalions from RIR 121 also arrived there on the following day.

The first piece of business was the manufacturing of shelters for protection against the weather and enemy bombardments. This work was started immediately after the men arrived and they received assistance from a *pionier* company that was placed under the control of regiment for this purpose. The materials required for the work came from the *pionier* park in Quiéry la Motte.

All of the hard work performed by the men was apparently in vain when at 2.00 a.m. On the night of 23/24 August 1918 IR 180 marched away in a southerly direction and in the course of the morning the battalions reached the *Hochwald Stellung* south of the Arras-Cambrai Road, where the men were distributed in the position, mostly in open trenches. As the left neighboring division had moved back, IR 180 was moved into the position once held by IR 101 and as the *Eingreif* regiment occupied a position south and southwest of Fontaine. The front line of the battalions was in the *Siegfried Stellung* southwest of Fontaine.

According to the news arriving from the front, British attacks were expected by Arras at any moment. As the division was now an *Eingreifdivision*, it must send forth individual reconnaissance troops to the front on a daily basis in order to explore the terrain for areas to use as possible counterattacks. On 21 August 1918 parts of RIR 121 were moved closer to the front in order to be quickly in position if needed.

RIR 121 remained in the area between the western edge of the Douai-Brayelle Farm and the railway by Quiéry-La Motte until the morning of the 24th. Reconnaissance patrols were sent out toward Oppy and the area around it in order to establish the opposing lines as best they could. In the night from 23/24 August 1918 the battalions of RIR 121 moved forward to Boiry-Notre Dame.

The last part of the division, RIR 119, would soon rejoin the division but not until the men had been given some time to rest. While marching back to rest area on 22 August 1918 the men and horses of RIR 119 were so worn out that the regimental leaders stopped the column and placed the men and horses in temporary quarters, the march was continued on the next morning. The regiment was then informed that the 26th Reserve Division was an *Eingreifdivision* once again.

The regimental transport suffered a great deal at this time. The horses were in poor condition from overuse and limited rations in comparison to the immense effort required of them. Also, there was little protection in the ravaged Somme terrain thanks to the efficiency of Operation Alberich and they were subjected to enemy aircraft bombs, long range artillery fire and often had to be moved further back to the rear to find a safe location. RIR 119 reached the rest area where the men hoped they could spend some time relaxing following the effort of the last weeks. Then, on 23 August 1918, fresh drum fire fell and the regiment was alarmed while in rest quarters.

Suddenly, on the 24th, there was a massive enemy attack that penetrated deep into the German lines. The 26th Reserve Division was now designated as the *Eingreifdivision* for the II Bavarian Reserve Corps. RIR 119 was then positioned east of Vis-en-Artois, RIR 121 in Boiry-Notre-Dame and IR 180 in the *Hochwald Riegel* north of the Chérisy–Hendecourt Road. The men marched to the positions in clear weather and there were numerous enemy aircraft in the skies. The men could easily hear the bombs being dropped all around them.

Every man was needed to repel this latest enemy attack, and shortly after the British assault had begun, the 6/*Pionier* Battalion 13 was sent back to the front by Boiry Notre Dame. Part of the company then acted as artillery protection and part became involved in the infantry fighting.

In the night from 25/26 August 1918 RIR 121 was moved further forward. An attack was expected south of Arras and the regiment had to be prepared to meet the enemy in the area of Vis-en-Artois. This area was well-known to the older veterans of RIR 121, particularly the III/R121. Part of the regiment was placed in the *Hochwald Stellung*, part on Vis hill.

Drum fire began to fall on both sides of the National Road at 4.00 a.m. on 26 August 1918. The fire fell on and in the area of Croisilles to the north until north of Monchy le Preux, the heaviest fire on the latter location. One half hour later the enemy infantry attacked with numerous tanks, forcing the German line back. The men could see the enemy troop concentrations from their raised positions and the progress of the fighting. The morale was raised when the troops saw a burning tank on the National Road and another one that *Leutnant* Dambacher, 3/RFAR 26 had destroyed with his guns. The 35th Infantry Division attempted a counterattack which initially gained some ground, but the enemy forces were too great and the division failed to reach its goals.

Despite heavy fire, IR 180 completed the position change without incident and the regiment was held ready if it was needed to become used for a counterattack. At 9.30 p.m. the III/180 was ordered to support IR 126 and received orders from this regiment to establish a connection with the parts of IR 126 lying in front of it and to fill an existing gap between the right wing of IR 87 and the left wing of IR 126.

The regiment succeeded in completing the assigned tasks despite the dark night in unfamiliar terrain including when the patrol of the 11/180 under *Vizefeldwebel* and *Offizier Aspirant* Sprenger, with Sergeant Greiner and eight men were forced to wear gas masks. The patrol was eventually forced to return because German gas had blown back on their position. Aside from this incident the night proceeded quietly and nothing exceptional occurred until the following morning.

Then on 27 August 1918, in union with the remnants IR 126 and IR 172 the old main opposition line of IR 126 was recaptured. The III/180 attacked at 3.30 a.m. on the 27th from its position in the *Siegfried Stellung* with two companies advancing from the *Mühlen Graben*, one behind the other in the forward most line (12th and 9/180) and two companies in the second line (10th and 11/180). The British sentries were pressed back in hand grenade fighting while toughly defended opposition nests were successfully taken. Finally the enemy opposition stiffened making any advance beyond 250 meters west of the Héninel–Croisilles Road impossible. Except for a small section, the main opposition line of IR 126 had been regained and the task was essentially fulfilled.

On 27 August 1918, new artillery fire raids by the British artillery began at 5.00 a.m., apparently as a continuation of the enemy attack. The British now appeared in front of the main opposition line of the 35th and 39th Infantry Divisions. In order to determine the exact location of friend and foe, the 2nd and 4/R119 sent patrols into the foreground to clarify the situation and to firmly establish the location of the III/476 that was supposedly by Boiry and southeast of the village. The danger in the north and south grew from hour to hour. It seemed that the enemy attacked everywhere with immense confidence in victory.

At 10.00 a.m. RIR 119 received orders to send the I/R119 east of Vis-en-Artois and the II/R119 west of Remy where they were to be ready to prevent the British from crossing the Cojeul stream. Before the battle battalions could reach these spots, the enemy had already attacked at 10.30 a.m. and had overrun Chèrisy. The 39th Infantry Division, already under great pressure, was forced to yield to the rear.

During this time, the II/R119 occupied the hill west of Remy between the Cojeul and Sensée streams on the Boiry-Notre-Dame and Vis-en-Artois Road. The I/R119 placed the 1/R119 on the right next to the 2/R119 and closed the gap between the II/R119 and the I/R119. The 3/R119 extended the left wing of the 4/R119 lying in front of Vis and sent a group of light machine guns to the artillery platoon of the 3/RFAR 26 south of Vis.

The new dispositions were barely completed when the enemy attacked again at 11.50 a.m. south of the National Road. The 39th Infantry Division fought against repeated attacks and was eventually smashed and forced to yield to the rear even further, leaving the crossing of the Sensée stream to the British.

With the withdrawal of the 39th Infantry Division the I and II/R119 were still under the impression they were *Eingreif* Battalions. They suddenly saw an enemy flushed with victory in the forward most line opposite them. However, while they still held a front facing west, the British had pressed on and attacked 4th and 2/R119 from the rear and in the flank. The Württemberg field artillerymen of RFAR 26 attempted to repulse the enemy attack by firing at close range over open sites into the advancing mass of British infantry without success. The 4th and 2/R119, each barely with a battle strength numbering 40 men, under *Leutnants der Reserve* Klipphan and Gölkel, were attacked from three sides with overpowering force and moved back in the direction of Remy-Haucourt while being closely pursued by the enemy.

The II/R119 also moved to a new location by withdrawing to the rear. The British continued to drive forward from of the eastern edge of Vis just as the companies of the I and II/R119 moved in double time and managed to make it back to the rear. However, the danger was far from over. Every man in RIR 119 and RIR 121 by Vis-en-Artois and to the south was placed in the line to form a block against the quickly advancing enemy

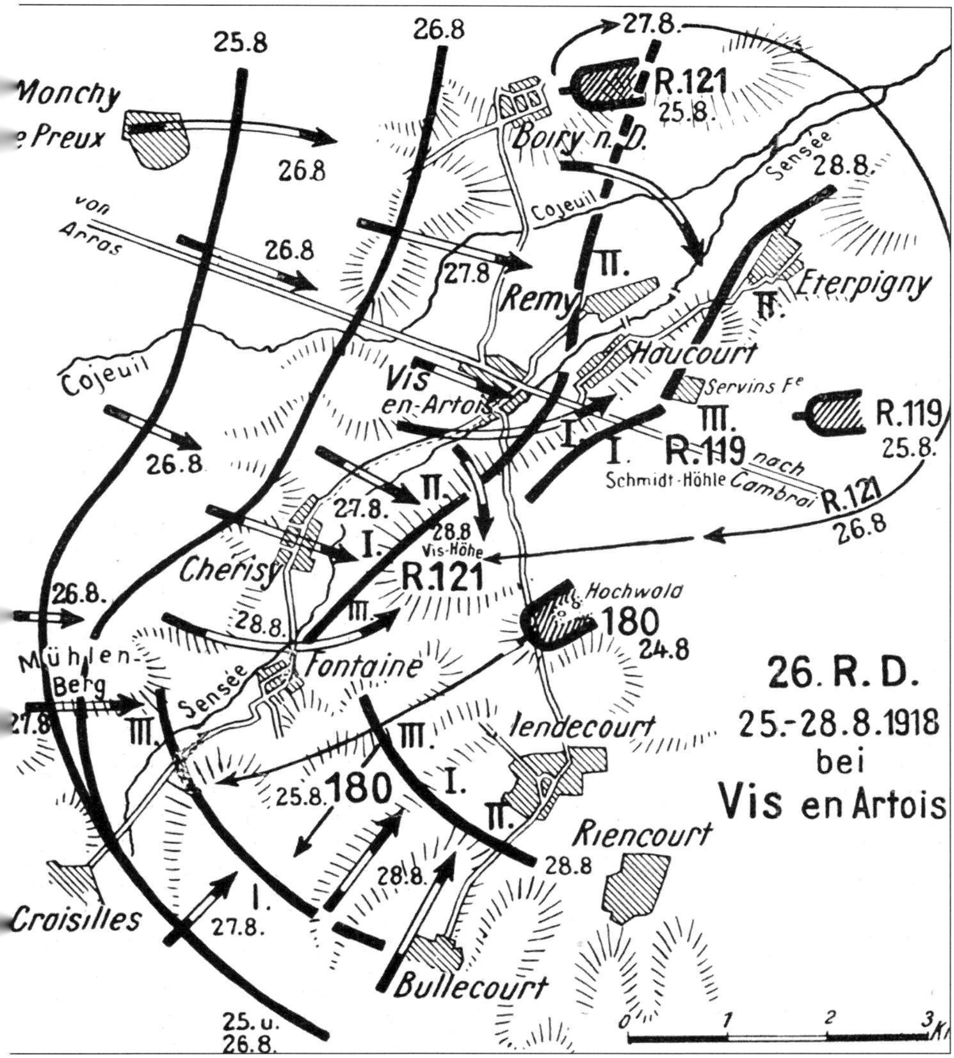

26th Reserve Division by Vis en Artois 25-28 August 1918.

troops. Despite this effort, enemy artillery fire and heavy machine gun fire threw the two regiments even further back in the village ruins. The heavy fighting continued there as the 2nd Guard Reserve Division, 4th *Ersatz* Division, 16th Infantry Division formed behind the 26th Reserve Division and prevented the front from breaking.

IR 180 was positioned behind the 39th Infantry Division when the division was forced from its position and the men were streaming to the rear. The troops of IR 180 gathered up as many of the stragglers as possible and received the advancing enemy troops with heavy fire and brought the British attack to a stop. With the collapse of the

39th Infantry Division, IR 180 had become the forward most line and was fully occupied with defending the position against further attacks. The II/180 was the farthest on the right of Schmidt hill, the I/180 was on Vis hill and III/180 was the farthest left by the *Hochwald*.

At 8.00 a.m. the III/180 came under attack once again; proceeded by powerful drum fire. The battalion received the British soldiers with effective infantry and machine gun fire, causing the enemy skirmish line heavy losses. However, for every enemy soldier disabled, additional reinforcements continued to arrive on the field so that in a short time the flank and rear of the defenders were seriously threatened. Now the men of the III/180 fought step by step as they moved back, having to become economical with the ammunition that gradually became scarce, especially for the machine guns. The fighting by the III/180 was being supported through the effective fire of *Leutnant der Reserve* Schlegel with his platoon of *Minenwerfer*, until he also finally ran out of ammunition and Schlegel became fatally wounded, struck by an infantry projectile.

The *Minenwerfer* officer, *Leutnant der Reserve* Schlegel, had only a few 7.6cm *Minenwerfer* with limited ammunition at hand. He was a very competent *Minenwerfer* officer who had successfully interfered in previous situations, both in the defense of a position as well as in the attack. Using his expertise, Schlegel provided the range for his weapons and waited for the advancing enemy troops to move into position:

> Now the enemy thrusts in the most favorable shot area. Therefore fire! The mine hisses across and struck in the middle of the enemy waves. It is good. Under the few following shots the ranks of the enemy split apart and generally look for possible cover behind a concrete chunk and surroundings. Out of there the unshaken defenders looked to work on a machine gun. However a direct hit thwarts the attempt and also forces the adversary to quickly escape. And now there is a rich harvest for the few *Minenwerfer*. The masses flooding to the rear offers the most welcome, most grateful target.[9]

It was at this moment as Schlegel was searching for new targets, standing up in his position, he was struck in the neck by a bullet and was fatally wounded. He reportedly died while being attended by his *Sanitäts* Sergeant.

The staff of the III/180 had observed the British attack since the start of the drum fire from the battalion battle headquarters. During the fighting the battalion leader, *Hauptmann der Reserve* Vogler, became wounded by a shrapnel ball in the abdomen and on the right thumb. As the British assault waves came closer the battalion orderlies and a light machine gun from the 9/180 participated in the defense. At the same time the wounded *Hauptmann* Vogler took up a rifle and began to fire on the approaching British.

The British troops were quickly approaching the battalion headquarters, forcing the staff to withdraw through the trench, fighting from traverse to traverse. Eventually, the battalion staff came to the road leading from Fontaine to the west, which lay under powerful enemy machine gun fire. The staff made their way across the bullet swept road and continued their retreat but without *Hauptmann* Vogler. He was with the group one minute and gone the next. No one knew what had happened to him.

Southwest of Fontaine in the Sensée Ground the remnants of the III/180 met up with the companies of the I/180, as well as the platoon of *Vizefeldwebel* Haas of the 3MG/180. Together, the two battalions succeeded in preventing the British from crossing over the hill from the Mühlenberg down to the Sensée Ground and brought the enemy attack to a stop. *Unteroffizier* Knapp of the 11/180, was reported to have performed outstandingly during the defense against the enemy attack after he was provided with new ammunition and cooling liquid for his light machine gun.

Leutnant Merker took over the III/180 as the replacement battalion commander after Vogler had gone missing. On orders from the regiment he assembled the carrying troops of the battalion as well as every straggler he could locate at the regimental battle headquarters in the road south of Hendecourt.

At 1.30 p.m. the II/180 that had been with the 41st Reserve Infantry Brigade on the right wing of the 21st Reserve Division between Hendecourt and Fontaine become moved to protect the right flank of the division and now all parts of the regiment were together on the right wing of the 21st Reserve Division.

Losses for IR 180 on 27 August 1918 were small in numbers but very damaging to the overall strength of the regiment. *Leutnant der Reserve* Schlegel. 11 Other Ranks killed; *Leutnants der Reserve* Ziegler, Klenk and 54 Other Ranks wounded; *Hauptmann der Reserve* Vogler, *Leutnants der Reserve* Beck, Gustav and 36 Other Ranks were missing.

While the infantry was heavily engaged with the enemy, the *pioniers* attached to the division were no less busy. The 1st Platoon of the 6/*Pionier* Battalion 13 was located in the forward line by Hendecourt where they carried mines to the front as well as supplies of ammunition and hand grenades. During the initial enemy drum fire, *Pioniers* Reule and Friedrich Maier were carrying hand grenades up to the front lines. They not only had to survive the numerous enemy shells falling all around them, they were also subjected to numerous air attacks. The British planes were flying so low to the ground they were being hit from splinters from their own bombs as they exploded.

Reule and Maier had barely returned from the front when they saw approximately fifteen British soldiers penetrating into the position. Both *pioniers* engaged the enemy with hand grenades and within a short time forced the small group to surrender. The far outnumbered *pioniers* were faced with a dilemma, what to do with the prisoners. They quickly decided to deliver their captives to the neighboring 6/180 and then hurried once again, alone through the position where they were able to save the severely wounded *Unteroffizier* Rank. Later, the *pioniers* went back with the infantry on orders from an infantry officer. The losses in the 1st Platoon on this day of fighting was Sergeant Huber and *Pionier* Kurz killed, three *Unteroffiziere*, four *Pioniers* wounded. The 2nd Platoon of the 6/*Pionier* Battalion 13 was kept busy escorting the *Stossbatterie* and had also suffered some losses, while the 3rd Platoon constructed new gun positions.

The night of 27/28 August 1918 proceeded relatively quiet, as was the early morning hours of the 28th. Then, towards dawn of the 28th new enemy attacks began with the same strength as the previous day in the area controlled by RIR 119. An anti-tank gun from the 9/FAR 30 was moved forward to Servins Farm as protection against the seemingly numberless enemy tanks that were accompanying the attack in this area.

Württemberg Pioniers fighting in the open. (*Lehrer im Krieg*)

After 11.00 a.m. strong enemy skirmish lines were observed advancing out of Chèrisy toward Vis. Dense masses of enemy infantry could also be observed advancing from Monchy on Boiry-Notre-Dame. Annihilation fire was called up which held the enemy in place for a short time and caused a number of losses.

At 11.00 a.m. powerful artillery fire suddenly began to fall on the sector held by RIR 121 that quickly increased to the strongest annihilation fire. The bombardment was followed by attack after attack by enemy infantry in dense waves, supported by numerous tanks, however they were all refused. The British were successful in penetrating the outpost line only at individual places. The nests of enemy soldiers were individually counterattacked by *Stosstrupps* using hand grenades and by evening they had all been eliminated with the occupants killed, captured or forced to withdraw.

During the early morning hours I and II/180 were occupied with shifting units in order to secure the connections between the different battalions and the neighboring troops. At 11.00 a.m. drum fire fell on the entire front from the Arras–Cambrai Road as far as Bullecourt, 'in an intensity hardly seen in the Somme days according to IR 180's post-war history. After 15 minutes of heavy fire the British attack began in individual swarms, similar to *Stosstrupp* tactics, along the entire line, especially in the direction of the *Kalkgrube*–Hendecourt Road and on the western part of the *Kabel Graben*. The Fontaine–Bullecourt Road and the terrain on the right and left of it was attacked with vastly superior forces.

The I and II/180 immediately opened rifle and machine gun fire across the entire regimental sector. Over and over the two battalions succeeded in bringing the enemy attack to a stop through their fire. Eventually both battalions had to give up their positions when they were strongly encompassed by enemy troops that had broken through the German line by the neighboring division. The men from IR 180 fought on until almost every hand grenade had been thrown and the machine guns were in part destroyed and in part almost completely out of ammunition. Finally, the survivors from the I and II/180 were forced back and occupied rearward positions where they formed a new defensive line.

Whilst the attacks against the 26th Reserve Division had been brought to a stop, mostly with rifle and machine gun fire, with little gain by the enemy troops, the attacks further north by the neighboring divisions were more successful. The British had broken through the defensive fire and poured through a gap in the line and then attacked the companies of RIR 119 from the flank and the rear.

Leutnant der Reserve Dick, RFAR 26 (*Das Württembergisches Reserve-Feldartillerie-Regiment Nr.26 im Weltkrieg 1914-1918)*

The 6/R119 was almost destroyed in this breakthrough and the few survivors were forced to change fronts and moved back across the Sensée. The British quickly pressed into the vacated positions of the 6/R119 and then advanced against the 5/R119 which had already reinforced its right wing and was able to hold firm under the increased pressure. The lynch pin of the defense by the 5/R119 was the light machine gun under *Unteroffizier* Gottlob Bauer, who caused the enemy heavy losses.

Bauer eventually ran out of ammunition while two other machine guns in the company had been placed out of action from enemy artillery fire. The ammunition was collected from the two damaged guns and carried up to Bauer who then continued to fire. Suddenly, a heavy shell exploded nearby and shell splinters wounded Bauer who poured fire into the enemy ranks while blood dripped from both of his hands. Bauer continued to fire despite his wounds and the British attack soon stopped.

The respite was short lived as a British officer aggressively drove his men forward once more, only to hesitate in the point blank fire of the MG 08/15. The enemy quickly recovered and they courageously stormed the position of the 5/R119 again. The right wing defenders of the 5/R119 inflicted terrible losses on them and finally forced the surviving enemy troops to seek cover.

While the fighting was going on by the 5/R119 the enemy reached the northern edge of Remy that had already been completely evacuated by the 6/R119 and continued the attack against the 5th Company from the north with even more force than before. Whoever could carry a rifle was pushed to the right wing of the company by the company commander, *Leutnant der Reserve* Rettenmaier, and opened a desperate rapid fire at the approaching enemy skirmish line.

When the machine guns had completely run out of ammunition and the infantry were down to a few rounds apiece, *Leutnant* Rettenmaier gave the order to retreat to Servins

Farm. Only the dead remained behind, amongst them *Leutnant der Reserve* Wörne who was killed by shell splinters from an artillery projectile. Most of the wounded ha already been carried to the rear during the fighting. The I/R119 covered the withdrawa of the company through effective flanking fire and prevented the enemy from pressin after the retreating men.

However, the 8/R119 under *Leutnant der Reserve* Seal that was positioned in th second line was attacked on the right rear by the British advancing from the north an did not yield the position to the superior enemy force. Then, at 4.30 p.m., the III/36 arrived southwest of Eterpigny and in conjunction with the 8/R119 brought the enem attack to a stop. Towards 1 p.m. the I/R119 had become attacked twice and both time had knocked back the attackers under heavy losses.

In order to avoid a breakthrough one platoon of the 11/R119 became inserted betwee the II and I/R119. Toward 5.00 p.m. the situation stabilized and a line running throug from Eterpigny via the Servins Farm to the south up to RIR 121 was created. The pris oners brought in that evening provided the exact identity of the 'British' troops tha had attacked the division. According to enemy prisoners the attackers had suffered th heaviest losses and that Scottish regiments had attacked RIR 119, with the 1st and 2n Canadian Divisions involved in the attacks against RIR 121 and IR 180. The two latte divisions apparently had to be relieved by the 3rd and 4th Canadian Divisions becaus of the heavy losses they had suffered.

Prisoners captured during the night by the men of RIR 121 confirmed that the 2n Canadian Division had become so badly shot up on 28 August 1918 that it had t become relieved by the 3rd Canadian Division. That was very gratifying news for th men of the regiment and the performance of the 26th Reserve Division was recognize in the following army report:

> The main thrust of the English attack met Württemberg regiments on both sides of the Arras–Cambrai Road. The enemy stormed seven times in vain. Deep echelons of tanks on and alongside the road followed here over and over with new infantry. They remained lying in the fire of our machine guns and in the guns driven forward in the forward most line. Where the enemy had penetrated into the position, our counterthrust threw him back again entirely.[10]

By IR 180, the fighting in the area to the west and south of Hendecourt came to a hal at 7.00 p.m., and the enemy voluntarily evacuated the terrain north of the *Neckarweges*. Support had arrived in the line Raperie-Bullecourt where parts of the 58th Infantry Division were assembled in order to be ready to interfere in the defense if needed. During the heavy fighting in the morning the regimental staff transferred its battle headquarters from Hendecourt to the sand pit on the Hendecourt–Cagnicourt Road.

In the evening a regimental staff officer was sent to the 51st Reserve Infantry Brigade to give a verbal report about the situation of the regiment and with the plea that the order placing IR 180 under the 41st Reserve Infantry Brigade be rescinded and the entire regiment be made subordinate to the 51st Reserve Infantry Brigade once again, where it would have an opportunity to reform behind the front. Later in the evening IR

80 did become extracted from the front on orders from the 26th Reserve Division and assembled in Saudemont without any enemy interference.

When the losses were tallied at the end of the day it was discovered that IR 180 had lost: *Leutnant* Trost and 18 Other Ranks killed; *Oberleutnant* Widmer, *Leutnants* Gmelin, Albrecht, *Leutnants der Reserve* Schöll, Härle, Ottmar, Herlikofer (remained with the troops), Flaig, Pietzker, Baier, Sonnewald (remained with the troops) and 9 Other Ranks wounded; *Leutnants der Reserve* Glück and Spielmann and 76 Other Ranks missing. While seemingly a small number of losses following such heavy fighting the reader should keep in mind that these losses probably represented 65-70 percent of the entire regiment as it existed at that time.

The losses suffered by the 26th Reserve Division were no different than those of numerous other divisions in the German Army at this stage of the war. Replacements were almost non-existent and the divisions would have to make do with the men at hand. Shortly after this period of fighting, orders were issued by the division to disband the fourth company of each battalion and to divide these men among the remaining three companies. Each battalion would now only consist of three companies and one machine gun company. Even with the new three company battalion formation the only thing that was saving the units from becoming completely eliminated was the large increase in the number of automatic weapons issued to the infantry companies.

The morning of 29 August 1918 began quietly, and it was assumed that the large loss inflicted upon the enemy was the reason for this. However, it is quite likely that if several enemy divisions were being replaced there would be a period of time when fighting activity would be quite low. It did not become more active along the front until about 10.30 a.m. when the artillery from both sides commenced to fire and *pioniers* blew up the bridges over the Sensée stream. The greatest danger facing the 26th Reserve Division came from the north, where the enemy had created a large hole in the German front alongside the position of RIR 119.

Toward midday the men from RIR 119 could clearly see movement everywhere in the enemy lines. A field artillery battery drove up north of Vis-en-Artois, columns of infantry marched on the National Road and everything pointed toward a new attack. Towards 5.00 p.m. a large enemy patrol moved forward through Remy against the Sensée brook, however it was repulsed with heavy losses. During this fighting, the platoon of light machine guns under *Leutnant der Reserve* Wachtler stood out in particular.

The situation in front of RIR 121 was very similar on 29 August 1918; it was generally quiet. However, the men sitting in their small holes could clearly see as gun after gun were brought forward, infantry columns moved forward and tank behind tank slowly driving forward on the opposite slope, some 2,000 meters distant. Every man knew all too well what the next day would bring and made every preparation possible in order to be ready.

The enemy artillery continued to fire upon the German positions throughout the day; on all advance roads and hollows in which they suspected were being used as assembly areas. The German guns also covered the Sensée ground with annihilation fire, in areas where British readiness positions were reported to exist. Other than the few enemy patrols and constant artillery fire, there were no new major enemy attacks. In the evening a new sector was created for the division into which the II/R119 was partiall extracted from the front line and was moved to the right, the III/R119 inserted th 11th and 12/R119 between the I and II/R119 and the size of the sector was materiall reduced, in keeping with the small number of men still available.

The new positions had barely been occupied when fresh orders arrived. The divisio commander, 'who was far behind the front with a blue pencil happily organized th maps lying on the table, barely suspecting, what pain and effort his light lines cause the battle troops. Each front soldier had a justifiable aversion to traveling around a night and in fog in unknown terrain, churned up from the fire.' Despite this resent ment, the men were moved once again.

Ammunition supplies were of great concern to the small handful of men holdin the front lines. In the previous fighting, positions had to be abandoned and an effec tive defense was almost impossible as units began to run out of ammunition and han grenades. Fortunately, the Russian carts from the regimental transports brought u ammunition and other close combat supplies in the frenzied enemy searching fire so tha ample supplies were at hand for the anticipated enemy attack that would surely follow.

A relief planned for RIR 119 for the morning of 30 August 1918 by IR 360 ha to be postponed, because the enemy attacked along the entire front as the men ha expected the previous day. At 5.00 a.m. drum fire began to fall that was quickly replie through weaker German barrage fire. In the early morning there were several strong British patrols that successfully crossed over the Sensée stream and a line of skirmisher advanced against the position of the 11/R119. However *Leutnant der Reserve* Gra 'greased them off bloodily with his stout flock.' Repeated enemy attempts, to brea forth in dense waves between Remy and Haucourt all failed in the fire of the infantr and machine guns. The platoon of *Leutnant der Reserve* Offermann particularly stoo out in this period of fighting.

The situation by RIR 121 was unclear as no reports had come from this portion o the line so additional men were sent forward to bolster the defenses with the 1/R11 being placed next to the 3/R119 on the National Road. It was then discovered that th neighboring II/R121 had held its position for the largest part. However, the succes came with a heavy price in dead and wounded, including the battalion commander *Hauptmann der Reserve* Kühnlen. Kühnlen had marched out at the start of the war wit RIR 119 and for two years he commanded the 7/R119. During his time in the regi ment he had been wounded several times when he became exposed to enemy fire whil commanding his men.

To the south of the division position were the Viser hills with the corrugated iron barracks and stables that were visibly in the hands of the enemy. Machine guns spread fire in the hollow in front of the Viser hills from out of a cave, the so-called '*Schmidthöhle*'. The enemy attacked repeatedly the entire morning, accompanied by strong artillery fire. Each attack was met with well-aimed defensive fire by the battle troops and the enemy infantry were driven back each time. The attackers stood out clearly in the open terrain and the men of the 26th Reserve Division noted that some units advanced with packs, some without packs as they moved through the village, before assembling on the western and northwestern edge of Vis-en-Artois. Just after 11.00 a.m. there was a pause

In the fighting and as countless British aircraft flew above the sector, the 9th and 10/R119 received orders to move further forward.

At 12.30 p.m. a German heavy howitzer battery fired upon the sunken road southwest of Servins Farm, which was occupied by the 3/R119 as well as the terrain surrounding the farm. The company signaled this to the rear and the short shots stopped falling on its position a short time later. Then, just after 2.00 p.m. more short shots fell on the company and while this was taking place the enemy renewed his attempts to cross over the Sensée stream between Remy and Haucourt.

Initially, machine gun fire prevented the enemy from crossing the stream in any great strength. However, more and more enemy troops flooded into Remy and while additional defensive artillery fire was requested it became increasingly weaker despite the urgent requests. Now, even with every machine gun in service there was no way to prevent the British from completely occupying Remy.

At 3.00 p.m. *Vizefeldwebel* Dittus, 4/R119, led a patrol back to Haucourt and found that the village was still free from the enemy. However the heavy British fire increased in strength slowly until 4.00 p.m. when the fire suddenly fell with full force on the sector of RIR 121. At the same time the rear terrain was obscured by enemy gas shells. Then, shortly before 5.00 p.m. the enemy fire died down, but at exactly 5.00 p.m. it fell on the regimental sector in a massive blow from guns of every caliber. Dense swarms of British infantry advanced on both sides of the national road, out of the Sensée ground and out of Remy and quickly took hold of the positions of RIR 119.

Barrage fire was called for; infantry, machine guns and *Minenwerfer* threw everything they could against the enemy and the attack soon faltered and then hesitated. An anti-tank gun was positioned near Servins Farm, ready to fire at any approaching tank. The enemy reformed and attacked once more, this time he was able to penetrate along the National Road. The 10/R119 received orders to counterattack but at that moment German heavy field howitzer fire fell on the 10th and 11/R119 and the KTK of the I/R119. The headquarters dugout entrance was destroyed; *Unteroffizier* Karl, the leader of the Telephone Troops, who had mended the destroyed telephone wires in the enemy fire numerous times, became killed along with two infantrymen. The 11/R119 suffered heavy losses and was forced to avoid the friendly fire.

During the confusion caused by the friendly German artillery fire the British succeeded in advancing from the hill. *Vizefeldwebel* Neth fired into the flank of the enemy skirmish lines with his heavy machine gun and mowed them down in rows. In front of the 4/R119 another machine gun was forced to change position further back where *Vizefeldwebel* Dittus took over and moved into a position in the sunken road.

The situation was quickly becoming dangerous as position after position was captured by the enemy troops. Part of the 6/R121 came up and was attached to the 1st and 3/R119 and still the three companies only numbered approximately 50-60 men. The III/R119 staff saw that the close combat field gun on the hill was in danger of being captured and ordered 10th and 11/R119 and some *pioniers* to recapture the position and secure the gun. The German artillery continued to fire on the positions of RIR 119 and light balls were used to signal the German guns that they fired too short; the reply was only fiercer fire and the losses continued to increase.

Disgust, anger and rage gripped the infantry; panic threatened to spread through the thin ranks as the farm continued to be targeted by the heaviest German fire. The friendly fire had finally proven to be too much to withstand and the I/R119 was ordered to retreat to the eastern edge of the farmstead. The few remaining men withdrew from the dangerous positions while trying to avoid the heavy shells falling all about as well as the advancing enemy infantry.

The artillerymen on the gun crew of the anti-tank field gun from the 9/FAR 3… tried to help out in the withdrawal by rapidly firing 36 rounds at the advancing enemy. The close range fire caused numerous losses and confusion in the enemy ranks but it was too little, too late. The German artillery fire falling on the farm grew in strength and suddenly spread toward the rear. The fire also forced the defenders to abandon the eastern edge of Servins Farm along with the anti-tank gun.

The Prussian artillerymen were able to remove the breach blocks of their cannon. *Leutnant der Reserve* Grau and *Leutnant der Reserve* Bayer, who had made one last attempt to retake the farm with parts of their two companies, were both killed in the attempt and the last opportunity to recapture the position failed. The entire zone to the east of the farm was still under German fire and within a short time, also under British annihilation fire making any assembly of men impossible. The order to retreat on the *Eterpigny Riegel* was verbally issued, where at 8.00 p.m. a total of 97 men along with one heavy and two light machine guns gathered around their leader, *Hauptmann der Reserve* Eugen Rueff, in well-ordered formations. This small group was not the remnants of any one company or battalion. As far as Rueff knew, it was the entire regiment; the few survivors of RIR 119.

But what had happened to the rest of the regiment? What disaster had befallen the others? While Rueff had assembled a small handful of survivors from RIR 119 the fighting still continued at the front. The new front line following the loss of Servins Farm stood on both sides of the Arras–Cambrai Road. It was a precarious position, not from the pressure of the enemy attack, but still under the rain of friendly German shells in the form of annihilation fire from the German batteries. The III/R119 stood in this fire with the two remaining companies, the 9th and 12/R119, as well as the companies of the subordinate III/362 in the line from the eastern edge of Haucourt to the area at the southern edge of Eterpigny. This small force then connected to the II/R119 at the eastern edge of Eterpigny, where the fighting against the enemy climbing up out of the Sensée ground was intense.

After a short time this front was also lost, as were the withdrawing parts of the I/R119 and RIR 121. If the British succeeded in occupying the ridge northeast of Servins Farm, they could take the entire terrain under devastating machine gun fire; preventing any chance for the few remaining men from making it back to safety.

The retreating men of the I/R119 advised the parts of the 12th and 9/R119 they ran into that their flank was threatened. The leader of the III/R119, *Hauptmann der Reserve* Rupp, had already recognized this threat. Through his encouragement of the Other Ranks flooding to the rear, along with active support from the leaders of the 9/R119, *Leutnant der Reserve* Schäfer and the 3MG/R119, *Leutnant der Reserve* Irion, as well as the energetic involvement of the company leaders of the III/362 he succeeded in bringing the wavering line to a stand once again; the situation appeared saved.

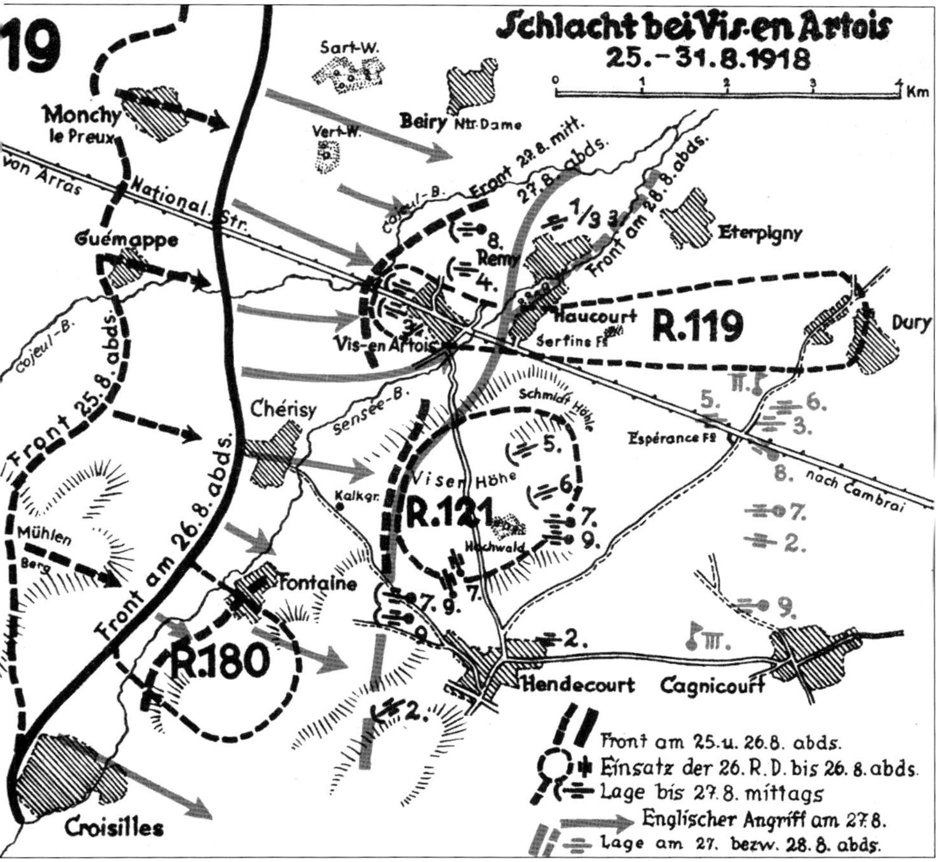

Battle by Vis-en Artois, 25 - 21 August 1918.

Rupp sent a sketch of the new front line back to the regimental headquarters by messenger dog, which alone could still safely run through the roaring storm of British annihilation fire that was falling between the new forward line and the regimental battle headquarters. Then, heavy German shells began to impact the area, at first individually, which quickly turned into a dense hail, smothering the new, barely stable line. Every attempt through light balls, waving helmets, white cloths, even messages transmitted through messenger dogs to inform the German batteries proved to be useless; the heavy fire continued and brought new losses among the few remaining defenders.

It was a heavy decision and the difficult responsibility of the leader to firmly hold the infantry companies in the line that was lying under both German and enemy artillery fire. However, if a disaster was to be avoided, it had to be done. Also, individuals who had enough of the intense fire and began to move further to the rear on their own were collected at the battle headquarters and placed in a newly formed line. The last machine gun existing in reserve by the leader was used to fill in the gaps made by the rapidl disappearing infantrymen.

Parts of the I/R119, which had not received the order to retreat became assemble by the adjutant of the I/R119, *Leutnant der Reserve* Pfau, and the leader of the 1/R11 *Leutnant* Klipphan, and organized into a reserve. The Communication Officer of th II/R119, *Leutnant der Reserve* Stengel, made every attempt to establish a connectio with RIR 121 through the hail of German and British artillery fire, however, he becam fatally wounded by a shell splinter while moving through the open ground. With hi loss the connection between the III and II/R119 was broken.

However the II/R119 had held its position east of Eterpigny; and repeated attempt by the British to break forth out of the ruins of Eterpigny had been prevented in the fir of the 5th and 8/R119. Finally, when evening fell and the artillery fire from both side slowly died down, the decimated companies of both battalions and the III/362 reorgan ized as best they could with the few men still left and waited for the urgently require relief that was reportedly pending. In what was considered almost a miracle troops from IR 62 did arrive at the front and the few survivors from RIR 119 and IR 362 hande over the positions in an orderly manner. It was soon learned that IR 62 was relieving th entire regiment in the night from 30/31 August 1918.

There was a subsequent investigation held by the division commander about th cause of the friendly artillery fire that had been directed against the regiments. I was found to be the fire from artillery batteries of a newly placed division, which ha inadequate orientation about the position of the front line. The division in questio had mistaken the men of 26th Reserve Division for advancing British troops an the anti-tank gun deployed at Servins Farm for an enemy battery. The fire continue despite all of the sketches and reports from the battalion leaders and the regimenta headquarters that had continuously advised the higher leadership about the course of the battle line that was being held by friendly regiments. Later, as these events became known, some of the regiment's survivors withdrew. At 6.30 a.m. on 30 August 1918 strong drum-fire began to fall on the positions of RIR 121, which was followed shortly by an enemy attack involving strong forces. The heavy fog that covered the terrain was reinforced with artificial fog from the British shells, which reduced visibility to only a few meters. Despite the dense fog the attack against the regimental position was repulsed and following the successful defense, the I and II/ R121 believed that the attack was over.

However, during the attack the enemy had been able to penetrate the regimental position at several places. The staff of the I/R121 advanced against these enemy nests with hand grenades and was engaged in the clearing the position by the 4/R121 and it was here that the battalion commander, *Hauptmann der Reserve* Kühnlen, was killed. When the entire position was in the possession of the regiment, British and Canadians troops suddenly appeared in large numbers at the left flank and in the rear of the regiment. It was quickly apparent that the enemy had broken through the German lines by the left neighboring regiment and rolled up the position of RIR 121 from the south.

This had proven to be a disaster for RIR 121, there was nothing that could be done to save the understrength regiment. The III/R121 had become overrun, as did the I/

R121. Only the II/R121 at the right wing was still able to hold out. During the heavy fighting and confusion following the enemy attacks from the flank and rear the I and II/R121 were entirely worn down, and only a few men from the two battalions, about 50 men, escaped. All other men who had survived the attack had ended up as prisoners of war, including both battalion staff. On 31 August 1918 the remnants of RIR 121 were assembled in Palleul where the pitiful remnants of RIR 119 were also found.

To say that the division was exhausted would be an understatement. The 26th Reserve Division had to become extracted from the front lines and marched off to the north, where it became sent to an area south of Lille where the division became the army reserve for the Sixth Army on 2 September 1918. It was a division only on paper as the combat strength of the regiments consisted of only a few hundred men who were at the end of their strength.

Much of the journey to Ennevelin, Seclin and Thumieres was by foot, which only weakened the division even further. Along the route the men were provided with quarters that were in the homes of local civilians or in large factory rooms that had been equipped as living quarters, all of which were generally good. The next day was devoted to rest as well as replacing missing weapons, ammunition and other pieces of equipment that had been lost in the recent fighting.

A daily order of the II Bavarian Reserve Corps dated 2 September 1918 gave the Swabians of the 26th Reserve Division the highest praise:

> To the leaders and troops of the 26th Reserve Division I want to particularly speak of my fullest praise for their outstanding performances. The division had provided a brilliant example that was decided by the spirit of the troops and not the numbers. The division defended its sector unshaken and tenaciously, until they reached the hand of its comrades again in the counter thrust. The positions could not become held if the 26th Reserve Division had not stood at this place. It was a joy to me to have the division that I grudgingly saw separate at the beginning of June, back under my command in this great battle, Krafft von Dellmensingen.[11]

General von Soden, the former division commander, also observed:

> It is with the highest admiration that I have read the news about the fighting by the glorious 26th Reserve Division southeast of Arras. How for two years on the Somme, so therefore here had the Swabian division formed the rock of ore amid the surf of the battle and so this formed the backbone. What spirit that is placed in troops, to be able to afford that it has also brilliantly demonstrated here again. The division had prevented the total rupture of the German Arras front and saved Cambrai in these heavy days.[12]

With regard to IR 180 the stay by Seclin only lasted a few days when the regiment was ordered to change quarters as it was being moved forward as reserves and at 6.00 a.m. on 6 September 1918, it received its new quarters. The quarters were west of Seclin in the area east of La Bassée, in Hantay, Grand-Moisnil and Don. When IR 180 arrived in the new sector each battalion received a *Nachrichten* platoon and a *Minenwerfer* platoon equipped with two throwers.

The accommodations provided to the regiment were bad for the most part; either in barracks or in mass quarters. The companies were initially occupied in being filled up with men combed from the rear echelon of the division and trying to make their quarters moderately inhabitable.

Small drill exercises were held near the quarters as often as they could without being seen by enemy observation aircraft, which seemed to be overhead almost every daylight hour. Since drilling in the open proved to be quite difficult, the Instructional Officer held talks with the different battalions inside the quarters.

As there was apparently no hope for any substantial numbers of replacements coming from home to fill up the thin ranks of the division, it was here that orders were issued that one company in each battalion would become broken up and the Other Ranks would be distributed into the three remaining companies. Starting from 5 September the regiments consisted of nine weak companies.

On the night of 13/14 September 1918, IR 180 was relieved by IR 175 and in the morning the battalions marched to their new quarters in Carvin-Epinoy, southwest of Seclin, where the entire regiment was accommodated. The village was quite shot up; completely empty of civilians and the houses were badly damaged, many were without roofs or windows. There was much work needed to make the quarters even moderately habitable.

Situated in the middle of the village, the railway station received sporadic enemy artillery fire at night and sometimes also bombs that were dropped by enemy aircraft making the stay in the village somewhat less than pleasant. The troops were quite happy when the regiment was transferred once again on 19 September into two areas between Carvin and Seclin.

During the stay by Lille there was a momentous event by Moncheaux when the division was reviewed by His *Excellenz Generalfeldmarschall von* Hindenburg. At 9.00 a.m. on 20 September 1918 the regiments stood on the Phalempin Road for observation by von Hindenburg, who handed out awards including three Iron Cross I Class and ten Iron Cross II Class to men who belonged to IR 180. It was a great delight to the men of the regiment that the victor of Tannenberg and Field Army Chief of the General Staff personally wanted to hand out the decorations during his inspection of the front and shook the hands of the men in a comradely manner. It was an exciting day for the men of the division. The troops were able to see the man who was directing the fate of Germany face to face for the first time and on whom they placed their trust despite all of the recent disasters.

On 21 September 1918 IR 180 became transported from Phalempin by railway to Bouchain, and then moved between Cambrai and Valenciennes where the regiment received quarters in Marquette, Mastaing and Paillencourt. At 8.00 a.m. on the 21st RIR 119 was alarmed when the regiment received a telephone call from headquarters. The men frantically began to prepare for a sudden move and in four hours the men of RIR 119 were ready to be loaded on transports. The regiment marched to Ostricourt in the middle of the night, where the battalions were loaded aboard trains and transported to Lourches. Only a few of the original veterans still numbered in the regiment, mostly in the baggage and transport sections, who remembered how almost on the exact day four years earlier the regiment marched out from Lourches to begin the campaign against the French in the first invasion of the Somme.

The 26th Reserve Division was now *Eingreifdivision* for XVII Reserve Corps. Starting from 23 September 1918 the training duty became established once again that however soon suffered from numerous interruptions as the regiments were shifted behind the right wing of the 2nd Army by Cuddy, southeast of Cambrai on 25 and 26 September 1918 where the men were quartered in Bethencourt. Later, the division was transported to Jwuy and Thun-Léveque by motor lorries on 27 September 1918 in accordance with the 26th Reserve Division being designated as the reserve of the High Command on 26 September 1918.

RIR 119 was apparently given the impossible task of preventing the untimely fall of Cambrai to the enemy. Shortly after reaching Lourches the regiment was pushed forward in the evening to the areas around Bantigny, Sancourt and Abancourt which were reached on 23 September 1918. RIR 119 was designated as the *Eingreif* Regiment of the XVIII Reserve Corps. The British had made major attacks north and south of Cambrai, pressing back the German line, but because of heavy losses had not resumed the attack, and the next day had been quiet. RIR 119 was shifted once again to Bévillers and Beauvois.

On 27 September 1918 sixteen Canadian divisions assaulted the German lines between Arras and Péronne and the 1st Canadian Division successfully smashed deep into the German defensive zone. The Canadians drove back the remnants of the shattered German divisions facing them and by the afternoon the 1st Canadian Division had reached the line Oisy le Berger – Haynecourt and seriously threatened the city of Cambrai. Towards evening orders went out to the 26th Reserve Division to move north into the gap that had opened north of Cambrai and to make preparations at Jwuy-Thun to prevent any further advances by the enemy. In the night from 27/28 September 1918 IR 180 was the first regiment to move and traveled in motor lorries via Carnières–Rieux– Jwuy to the crossroad southwest of Jwuy by Thun, where it arrived at .200 a.m.

The men from RIR 119 could hear heavy drum fire out of the area of Moeuvres. The battalions were alarmed, and the I/R119 moved to Beauvois where the men were loaded aboard motor lorries and transported to Haucourt-Lesdains and to Vaucelles, where the I/R119 moved into a readiness position located in a small wood southeast of Le Pav. The massive enemy attack was stopped on both sides of Marquion, between Moeuvres and Graincourt, Ribécourt and Villers-Guislain. However at Inchy two Canadian divisions advanced on Bourlon, Then the 3rd British Division advanced from Flesquieres by Havrincourt, widening the area of the break through and forced the defenders to bend back the line.

The 26th Reserve Division was subordinate to the XVII Army Corps; and with its arrival, IR 180 received orders from the 51st Reserve Infantry Brigade located in Thun-Léveque, to assemble in the area around Eswars to oppose the enemy in the line Abencheul–western edge of Sancourt– western edge of Sailly–western edge of Petit Fontaine. The assembly of the regiment and the I/RFAR 26 was completed at 6.00 a.m. with the I/180 inside the village and behind it, the II/180 at the northeast exit, the

III/180 at the southern exit of Eswars. The regimental battle headquarters was at the exit to Thun-Léveque. At 7.50 a.m. the II/180 was moved forward to the sunken road west of Ramillies and it was assigned to support one platoon of the attack battery because the enemy was supposed to have penetrated at St. Olle.

IR 180 was now made subordinate to the 1st Guard Reserve Division and when the message came at 10 a.m. that the enemy had broken through north of Tilloy and at Blecourt, the battalions were alarmed and became arranged as follows: two battalions on the hill east of Tilloy (II/180 on the right, I/180 on the left, the separation line was the rail line Sancourt–Ramillies), the III/180 was behind by Ramillies. These preparations were completed at 1.30 p.m., the regimental battle headquarters was at the western exit of Ramillies. When the message of an enemy breakthrough at Tilloy and Blecourt had proven to be incorrect, the I and II/180 were moved forward until they were west of Tilloy; the I/180 on the left connecting with the 1st Guard Reserve Regiment, the II/180 on the right of it with the instructions to establish a connection to RIR 121.

The constant movement of troops was becoming a problem as the roads were overcrowded with columns of all types including evacuating civilians fleeing from the intense fighting as they walked to the rear with their modest belongings, looking 'sad and heartsick' according to the men of the 26th Reserve Division. Long range enemy fire seemed to fall along every route behind the front and threatened Jwuy, where a large ammunition depot was located. The battalions from RIR 119 marched from Thun-St. Martin to Eswars, and from there to Ramillies, where RIR 119 was placed at the ready as corps reserve; the I/R119 to the southwest, the II/R119 to the east and the III/R119 to the north of the village.

After the loss of the canal position by Marquion the front was taken back to the line Arleux-Aubigny-west of Cambrai. The enemy had already attacked the railway line Aubencheuill-Sancourt on 28 September 1918. The 207th Infantry Division that formed the rear support for the 26th Reserve Division, supposedly still held positions at Sancourt and Sailly. RIR 121 lay in the north on the embankment Sancourt–Tilloy, IR 180 was in the area of Tilloy. However the situation facing the 26th Reserve Division turned out to be far more threatening than the reports indicated. Of the battle divisions, which should lie in front of the 26th Reserve Division, almost nothing still existed of them.

On the evening of 28 September 1918 the British pressed into Tilloy; however they became thrown out again by IR 180. Ramillies lay under enemy fire through the night as patrols of the 2nd and 3/R119 advanced toward Tilloy, where they found parts of IR 180, and the regimental staff that was in Morenchies. The patrols also found disorganized relics of the shattered 207th Infantry Division. On the morning of the 29th the British attacked again and patrols from the 2/R119 reported observing German troops flooding to the rear in the direction of Sailly, Tilloy and Sancourt. RIR 121 effectively stopped the British thrust on the Sancourt–Tilloy railway; while Neuville and St. Remy were still held by IR 180; however a break in the line threatened Tilloy.

The escort battery, 1/RFAR26 constructed earthworks in the area east of Tilloy. Towards midday on 28 September 1918 the enemy attacked on the line Sancourt-Sailly and ended up in the effective fire of the batteries of the regiment that had gone into position in the area Cuvillers-Eswars-Ramillies. The enemy won ground regardless of the heavy losses. Towards evening the II/RFAR 26 received orders to go into position as an independent Flanking position Group at the southern exit of Cambrai at Faubourg de Paris.

That evening, on orders from 1st Guard Reserve Brigade, the II/180 moved west of Tilloy, the I/180 was located at the western edge of Neuville, a fortified village, and the III/180 was in the gravel pit 400 meters northeast of the church of St. Olle. The regimental battle headquarters became transferred to the former battle headquarters of the 1st Guard Reserve Regiment by the canal bridge. Losses had been light in IR 180 on the 28th: one officer wounded. one *Unteroffiziere* and one Other Rank killed, nine Other Ranks wounded.

An old acquaintance of the 26th Reserve Division was located close by, RIR 99, which had been part of the 26th Reserve Division until early 1917. Towards midday on 28 September 1918 the men of RIR 99 had marched to Lewarde and Roucourt and they were exhausted by the time they reached their destinations. After a brief rest orders came for the regiment to immediately march to Cantin in order to prevent the enemy from the crossing the canal. Then, later in the afternoon, RIR 99 marched to Villers au Tertre, in order to be in position between these villages and Fressain for a counter thrust. About 3.00 p.m. the lead elements of the regiment arrived and the troops immediately began to dig in and create shelters.

However, after a few hours, orders arrived that the 220th Infantry Division was to become an *Eingreifdivision* with the XVIII Army Corps, and the regiment immediately moved to Wasnes au Bac with an escort battery. The battalions were quickly fed before they marched off in heavy rain and strong head winds and reached their goal shortly before midnight. The regimental commander who had ridden in advance received orders for the regiment to march even further. However the troops were so exhausted the final leg of their journey became postponed to the morning of 30 September 1918. This experience was not an isolated matter as many of the divisions were shifting troops across the front to bolster weak points in the line and as a consequence, the men who were already tired from lack of sleep and malnourished from inadequate rations became almost comatose and could barely move.

The official report concerning the events of the following day, 29 September 1918, was short and to the point:

> Two enemy attacks occurred on 29 September at 4.50 p.m. and 6.20 p.m. directed against the entire front of the 26th Reserve Division from Sancourt until Ste. Olle which broke down before our lines. A small break in west of Tilloy immediately became restored again in a counter thrust through reserves of the II/180.[13]

It was too matter of fact and did not truly represent the events of this day when looking at the actions by the different units within the division. The events that occurred on this day, the events that led to the successful defense against two enemy attacks was more complicated than the 'official' version.

At 1.30 a.m. on 29 September 1918, the III/180 had reached the support area in the gravel pit north of St. Olle. The I/180 was forced to deploy north and northwest of

Neuville because the area west of the village was continuously under extremely heavy artillery fire and offered no protection against the shelling whatsoever. The II/180 had already moved into the deployment area west of Tilloy that had been assigned to the battalion and established a connection with the RIR 121 by 8.30 p.m. on the 28th.

At 8.00 a.m. the most severe enemy drum fire fell along the front with a blow and soon after parts of Infantry Regiments 98, 209, 213 and small remnants of the 7th Cavalry *Schützen* Division were observed falling back on Tilloy and Cambrai. The retreating troops were closely followed by the enemy advancing in strong, dense waves. The I/180 quickly moved toward the front line and immediately took the enemy assault waves under very effective rifle and machine gun fire and succeeded in breaking up the enemy attack in the concentrated fire of the battalion. While the battalion had successfully stopped the initial attack, repeated attacks followed quickly with fresh forces close to the Cambrai–Aubencheul Road.

The I/180 now found itself in a precarious position. After moving closer to the front lines following the British attack, all connections to other German units on the left were missing and could not be established despite numerous attempts by patrols from the I/180. This was probably attributed to that the enemy was gradually able to firmly place individual machine guns directly opposite and to the south of the battalion, forcing the battalion to curve back the weak left wing. The rest of the battalion position held its position unchanged despite continuous heavy artillery bombardments.

At 10.00 a.m. the German batteries placed heavy fire from medium caliber guns on Tilloy and the terrain southwest of the village that forced the I/180 to temporarily evacuate the position. Once the friendly fire had been stopped following repeated attempts to notify the artillery that the village had been occupied by German troops, the village was reoccupied.

At 11.00 a.m. IR 180 notified Brigade about the situation by telephone and asked for reinforcements in regard to the weak occupation of the sector, and especially about the necessity of a rear support in area east of Tilloy. As a result of this request at 1 p.m. the III/R119 with one platoon from the 3/RFAR 26 moved to the eastern edge of Tilloy and into earthworks one kilometer to the east of the village, in order to prevent a breakthrough out from that village. The I/R119 was positioned on the railway embankment southeast of Tilloy and the crossing of the Schelde canal. RIR 225 lay on the opposite side of the canal within shouting distance, and the II/R119 was placed east of Morenchies.

In the morning hours the III/180 had also repulsed the enemy infantry attacks with its two forward companies, the 10th and 11/180 following the enemy's drum fire. The casualties among the British troops had been considerable yet there always appeared to be fresh reserves. Following the last British attack the III/180, under the command of *Hauptmann von* Raben, was ordered to counterattack. The battalion was effectively supported by the machine guns of RIR 31, and had been able to throw the British back over the hill southwest of St. Olle.

Once behind the hill the British quickly set up a new defensive position despite heavy losses. The advance by the II/180 continued and *Stosstrupps* from the 10th and 11/180, under the company leaders *Leutnants der Reserve* Ziegler and Schmid, broke into the new enemy line and drove the tenacious enemy back upon Fontaine Notre Dame in severe hand grenade fighting. The thrust by the two companies continued until the British had been pressed back across the *Hagen Stellung* which the III Battalion then occupied.

With it the mission of the III/180 had been accomplished. It was noted by battalion headquarters that the attack occurred without any support from the 2nd Guard Reserve Regiment and as such the right flank of the III/180 was completely open. The new position occupied by the III/180 was successfully held against numerous powerful advances by the British that were directed against the front and right flank of the battalion over the next few hours.

The British managed to recapture St. Olle by 12.00 noon; then the British advanced on Petit Fontaine and simultaneously pressed back RIR 31 south of the Bapaume–Cambrai Road. Under these circumstances the III/180 decided to evacuate the *Hagen Stellung*, and occupied Petit Fontaine with the front to the north. Immediately following these moves, and in accordance with orders the troops of the 1st Guard Reserve Division and the regiment connecting to the south went back to the eastern bank of the canal and the III/180 received the assignment to occupy the eastern bank of the canal from St. Olle Bridge–Cambrai to the south.

In the course of the afternoon the enemy discontinued the attacks by Tilloy and following the extraction of the remnants of IR 209, IR 213, IR 98, the II/180 had to occupy the gap that had formed between the I/180 and RIR 121 and consequently was also inserted into the front line.

By 3.30 p.m. the regimental battle headquarters of IR 180 was by the canal bridge west of Morenchies, where a telephone and wireless radio connection existed to Brigade and through lamp signals to the II/180. At 3.30 p.m. the I/180 also reported that all of the troops up to Neuville and to the south had withdrawn to the canal.

In the course of the afternoon parts of the 207th Infantry Division came back from the front line and brought news that the enemy attacks had essentially failed. However the situation was completely unclear and there was a strong possibility that the enemy was in Neuville-St. Remy, the suburbs of Cambrai. With this possibility, the I/R119 was located in the first line instead of being positioned in the second line. When this situation became evident, the battalion looked for a close connection to the I/180 which was located in Tilloy.

The front lines stabilized in the afternoon and little occurred for the rest of the day except for occasional skirmishes, patrols and the ever present artillery fire. It had been a warm day, accompanied by local rain showers that made the ground wet and soaked the men's uniforms. At 9.30 in the evening the remnants of the 9th and 11/180 which had returned to the regiment in the course of the afternoon became placed in possession of the II/180, the 10/180 was sent to the I/180. An emergency bridge west of the destroyed railway bridge suddenly flew into the air with a thunderous roar in the evening when *pioniers* set off explosive charges. The men dug in as best they could; there would be little time to rest as toward evening the artillery from both sides continued to fire with considerable intensity and rumbled the entire night. The losses in IR 180 on 29 September: one Officer killed, *Leutnant der Reserve* Meyer; four officers wounded. 12 *Unteroffiziere* and Other Ranks killed, 82 Other Ranks wounded, one Other Ranks missing.

Throughout the day the German batteries greeted the advancing enemy companies and British artillery fire continued to fall upon the position and rear terrain. The artillery fire had begun at dawn with heavy drum fire, followed by major attacks. The Canadians had stormed against the railway embankment by Tilloy-Sancourt with fixed bayonets and had rapidly pursued the remnants of the troops that stood in front of the 26th Reserve Division. The situation had demanded the fiercest resistance from all weapons, especially the artillery batteries.

According to the 26th RFAR 'the Canadians had advanced upon the railway embankment Tilloy-Sancourt upon the 26th Reserve Division – here the route was only over corpses.' The 1/RFAR 26 stood at Cuvillers, the 2/RFAR 26 west of Ramillies on the dominating hills that afforded unobstructed views into the low areas between Abancourt and Tilloy. The batteries fired into the masses of the attacking enemy with direct fire, accompanied by the 10.5cm light field howitzers that were situated in positions north of Eswars from the III/RFAR 26.

One platoon of 3/RFAR 26 moved to Tilloy with the III/R119 and fought back against the enemy who had broken-in to the German lines and the enemy onrush became broken, then the attack hesitated. All during this time heavy British fire continuously fell on the German batteries which for the most part were firing from very exposed positions. By the end of the enemy attacks the position had held. Where ever the enemy had penetrated the German lines, they were thrown back again in counterattacks.

The guns of RFAR 26 had provided invaluable assistance to the infantry regiments of the division in the heavy fighting of 29 September 1918:

> Report by the *Abteilung* Staff about 29th September: In the night from 28/29 September 1918 the group (II *Abteilung*) received the order, to move into position with the 4th, 5th and 6th Batteries RFAR 26 and 2nd Battery *Fuss* Artillery Battalion 59 in Faubourg de Paris by Cambrai as a Flanking Position Group.
>
> After traveling through the city of Cambrai that was lying under active fire with losses, the positions were explored at daybreak and taken up. Because of cautiousness in the morning an observation of the ordered targets first of all was impossible.
>
> Thick, apparently artificial fog on this day allowed us to expect an attack expected from the direction Noyelles–Bourlon wood on Faubourg de Paris with certainty. The group determined, independently in this case, to interfere in the fighting that developed here.
>
> The batteries were in possession of ammunition out of limbers and wagon lines, the 6th Battery furthermore had 300 more rounds out of the column.
>
> To establish a telephone connection to the rear was impossible despite all efforts and trying to place and maintains a direct line in consideration of the approximately 10 kilometer straight distance across heavily bombarded terrain could not be even considered.
>
> Between 8 and 9 in the morning very strong artillery fire began. From 9 o'clock on our own infantry flooded back inexorably, first individuals, then in groups up to 20 men with wounded. Parts of the Marine Infantry Regiment still held the hills of Pronville until Hill 85 with a few machine guns.

In the meantime the view had become better. Officer patrols and volunteer patrols from the Other Ranks of the staff clarified it in the front. A Sergeant of the 5th Battery fell during this. The entire roadway from Faubourg de Paris lay continuously under the strongest fire, one house after the other was knocked down.

After the danger from the left flank had become threatening, the batteries of the group directed their fire upon the enemy, who was working forward on Hill 85 lying in front, after he had already crossed over the canal a long time before. The position artillery apparently had orders to retreat, everywhere saw batteries leaving. Behind the position of the Group railway crossings had already been blown up and later the guns.

In this moment the Group gave the batteries orders: one platoon from each FK Battery [field gun battery] was to go with all ammunition on the western edge of Paris in the hedges into open positions, in order to fight against the advancing enemy. Such a favorable position was one a position battery had just previously abandoned. The 2/59 was to fire off their ammunition from out of their position. The second platoon of each battery each moved to a reception position in the area Niergnies–Awoingt. One platoon was sufficient in consideration of the situation of the ammunition in the front.

The batteries made the position change in the heaviest fire. The 5th Battery, when the leader of the Group personally wanted to deliver the orders, was already underway to the front with one platoon on the personal initiative of the battery leader. The 6th Battery followed swiftly, only the 4th Battery no longer came into action, because the platoon chosen for the open position was delayed through 2 direct hits in its horse teams and ammunition wagon.

All available ammunition came to the front. Ammunition lying around from other batteries became collected. The 6th Battery finally used ammunition from the FK 96 for their FK 16 after the projectiles were separated from its cartridges; as they had used much of their ammunition out of the first position when it had fought against an artillery *Abteilung* of 3 batteries driving up and had shattered them. Soon worthwhile targets became available. The adversary was just about to climb down from Hill 85. As long as there was still ammunition in their possession, they became prevented by the batteries. Over and over he withdrew behind the hill. A counterattack by IR 84 on the left wing was supported.

Individual infantrymen who remained with their machine guns still lay between the batteries. The mass of our own infantry had gone back to the north and northeast. Ammunition had become very scarce about 1 o'clock in the afternoon; replacements from the suburbs could no longer be counted on, because a quick connection to the rear didn't exist. Therefore the group gave the order at 1 o'clock that the platoons, after the ammunition was fired off, would withdraw to the positions of the rearward platoons.

The 2/59 fired off a further 175 shots out of the reception position that their column had brought here. In the night from 29/30 came orders, the Group shall again go back into the division association.

Losses for the day: 3 men dead, 8 horses dead. 14 men wounded, 6 horses wounded.

Signed: Martin *Hauptmann der Landwehr* and *Stellvertreter Abteilung* leader.[14]

The II/RFAR 26 became deservedly acknowledged by the division commander with the following letter:

> The *Abteilung* did not turn out to be Flanking Position Troops, but an extremely useful part in the fighting in the major combat and did this through its own, brilliant personal activity.
>
> The large success that *Hauptmann* Martin achieved and has personally experienced, has been a fair reward for his exemplary behavior; and I want to extend my fullest acknowledgment and my sincere thanks to him and his brave *Abteilung*.
>
> Signed *von* Fritsch.[15]

The thunder of artillery continued uninterrupted throughout the night along the entire front. At 3.00 a.m. drum fire suddenly fell on Tilloy and the Canal position. Under the protection of artificial fog enemy infantry advanced to the attack, breaking through at Tilloy and became firmly established on the railway embankment. However, when the veil of fog lifted, the British suffered heavy losses from infantry fire, supported by the batteries of the I/RFAR 26 firing from open positions. The accurate fire from the field guns either destroyed the nearby tanks or forced them to withdraw. The 2/RFAR 26 also succeeded in firing upon enemy batteries while they were driving up to the front and caused them heavy losses.

The II/RFAR 26 arrived at the threatened sector and provided effective blocking fire along with the III/RFAR 26. However the British recognized the danger posed by the guns of RFAR 26 and directed numerous guns for counter-battery fire against the German batteries with considerable intensity. The losses were heavy, especially by the I/RFAR 26. At the 1/RFAR 26 *Leutnant der Reserve* Holtzhausen became fatally wounded. A direct hit destroyed the 4th gun and killed the entire crew. The disabled battery then had to be extracted or become completely destroyed. At the 2nd Battery *Leutnant der Reserve* Weizsäcker fell with his men. In a short time, no more than two men were still operating each gun. The 3rd Battery also suffered considerably, losing *Leutnant der Reserve* Dambacher, who had provided an exceptional performance at Vis en Artois.

Tilloy changed possession four times on this day. However, in the end, the 26th Reserve Division held the position, although with significant losses. The enemy plan to take Cambrai had failed thanks to the stubborn defense of the German troops and the supporting batteries.

Opposite page: clockwise from top left:
Leutnant der Reserve Buck RFAR 26 (*Das Württembergisches Reserve-Feldartillerie-Regiment Nr.26 im Weltkrieg 1914-1918)*
Leutnant der Reserve Holtzhausen RFAR 26 (*Das Württembergisches Reserve-Feldartillerie-Regiment Nr. 26 im Weltkrieg 1914-1918)*
Leutnant der Reserve Dambacher RFAR 26 (*Das Württembergisches Reserve-Feldartillerie-Regiment Nr.26 im Weltkrieg 1914-1918)*
Leutnant der Reserve Weizsäcker RFAR 26 (*Das Württembergisches Reserve-Feldartillerie-Regiment Nr. 26 im Weltkrieg 1914-1918)*

Leutn. d. R. Buck
gef. bei Eswars 30. 9. 1918

Leutn. d. R. Holtzhausen
30. 9. 1918 schw. verw. b. Ramillies
gestorben 17. 10. 1918

Leutn. d. R. Dambacher
gef. bei Bouchavesnes 30. 9. 1918

Leutn. d. R. Weizsäcker
gefallen bei Cuvillers 30. 9. 1918

During the entire night of 29/30 September 1918 strong enemy disturbance fire fell upon the entire sector. All approach routes and the rear terrain until far behind the front line became bombarded with heavy caliber guns.

Because RIR 121 had suffered heavy losses, particularly through artillery fire, when it was positioned on the railway embankment, one battalion from IR 451 had to become inserted into its position during the night. This movement suddenly became stopped by orders from Corps headquarters and IR 451 now became subordinate to the 22nd Infantry Division. The shortage of men was becoming critical and there were no longer enough reserves to meet all of the needs of the front line troops.

The night of 30 September 1918 proceeded quietly in general and without any particular incidents. There were only individual enemy patrols that approached the position and these were repulsed. As expected, the British continued the attack at daybreak on the following day, a blustery day. The strongest drum fire fell and smoke screens covered the observation posts along with bomb attacks on the command posts and division headquarters in Bouchain northeast of Cambrai, the main infantry attack took place with 16 fresh divisions, accompanied by numerous tanks was directed against the greatly weakened and very thin lines of RIR 121.

At 5.00 a.m. drum fire began to fall upon Tilloy and the terrain north of it. Runners from the regimental observers that had been inserted in the area of Ramillies, who had settled in during this day and the following days had proven to be splendid. The observers reported at 5.50 a.m. about the transfer of the enemy fire to the rear on the terrain east of Tilloy and the withdrawal of the individual German skirmishers on the hill northeast of Tilloy. These reports were soon confirmed in detailed written and verbal reports which followed and which had been delivered to the battalion through officers.

The 1st and 3/R119 were positioned on the railway embankment in connection with the 1MG/R119 and successfully fought off all attacks. With this effective defense, the II/180 on the flank was able to hold the northern edge of Tilloy and the sunken road to Blécourt.

The enemy attacked with strong forces immediately following his drum fire, which fell in the greatest strength on the embankment position and the hill at the northern exit of Tilloy, as well as on Tilloy and the Tilloy–Blécourt Road, on the position of the II/180 and RIR 121.

At 5.30 a.m. two tanks crossed over the railway line northwest of Tilloy and one turned off to the south and very effectively bombarded the garrison of the railway embankment from the flank and the rear. It became fired at very lively by machine guns and after approximately 3/4 of an hour went back over the railway line. The other came in the area of a *Minenwerfer* platoon:

> The *Minenwerfer* platoon that *Leutnant der Reserve* Gallmann commanded was installed on the northern edge of Tilloy. The assignment of the platoon was to support the II Battalion with the defense of that place. This task was accomplished in an exemplary manner by the young officer.
>
> It is fair to say that thanks to the untiring activity and prudence of its leader, the platoon was supplied with enough ammunition so that it could look toward

the attack by the enemy that was surely expected with confidence. Today the *Minenwerfer* once again proved what invaluable help well aimed mine fire afforded to the hard pressed infantry. And maybe one also finally receives for once the hotly longed for target, a tank, in front of the tube.

In dark dawn the drum fire fell as with a blow. The place, the surrounding terrain and especially severely at the northern exit of the village, even the position, where Platoon Gallmann lay, was showered with fire. It was now critical to maintain calm amid this hellish noise. All eyes were directed on the leader. With imperturbable calmness he observed, looked for and finds his targets, gave his orders clearly and specific. The certainty and calmness of the leader was shared by the entire platoon, who mechanically, without hesitation, how on the practice field, implements his hold. The first target was the enemy support position. It was already effective before the actual attack, to cause disorder in the masses of the enemy and so to demolish the enemy attack strength.

Gradually it became lighter and one could notice how from out of the forward positioned railway embankment our own Other Ranks were going back. What is going on! Why the hasty flight by the infantry? The mystery solved itself, when on the hill of the railway line two tanks appeared, from that the one in front of the embankment moved in the direction of the thrower position. And now this precious game opposite the leader and his stout platoon caused a burning desire to hunt. Mine upon mine thumped out of the barrel in flat fire. Already the second shot hits home, however it doesn't slow down the movement of the monster. The third hit only appears to have forced him to rest. A piece springs off and smokes for a long time. The tank struggles arduously back up to the embankment, but its strength is no longer enough to overcome this, it remains lying there. The rejoicing is great by the leader and Other Ranks. However there is no rest. The rest of the ammunition becomes fired off on the advancing British. However, the last mine is barely out of the tube, when the leader grasps the carbine, and out of a *Minenwerfer* he becomes an infantryman, who with his men in of course of fulfilling their duty want to participate in the fighting with the infantry until the arrival of fresh ammunition. A short personal report to the KTK about his situation and intent with the request about supplies of infantry ammunition! Then he stormed with a few men from his platoon right through the frenzied machine gun fire against the enemy. He came upon a superior mass of British on the village street. Out of a close proximity he was stretched down by an enemy bullet.

Always in the middle with the will to help, where he always operated and moved about everywhere, he died as a hero with a joyful, courageous heart. Unfortunately all efforts by his companions to recover the body of the adored, admired leader were useless. A hail of machine gun bullets made access impossible.

Leutnant der Reserve Schlegel IR 180.[16]

Despite the desperate resistance, the enemy succeeded in breaking through a gap between the II and I/R121 at 6.45 a.m. and advanced to the south in the direction of Cambrai. The II/180 located at Tilloy then became compelled to curve back its right

7.7cm anti-tank gun, RFAR 26, by Vis en Artois, August 1918. (*Die 26. Reserve Division 1914-1918*)

wing on the northwestern edge of the village. In order to close the emerging gap in the line, one battalion from IR 190 (220th Reserve Division) was sent from Bantigny and became placed in the possession of the two regiments of the 26th Reserve Division. This action had a ripple effect on the line and when the II/180 was forced to curve the line back and the enemy was able to penetrate the middle of the village the 1/R119 became threatened on the right flank.

After the first attacks had failed, the British attempted new advances over and over again, now under the protection of tanks. RIR 121 also experienced attacks by British tanks and despite the fear of these strange weapons, managed to successfully drive them off but not before losing a number of men. Three tanks were brought to a stop through machine gun fire from the II/R121, one tank was dealt with a direct hit from a light *Minenwerfer* of the I/R121, one other was destroyed the by officers and Other Ranks of the escort battery, the 2/RFAR 26 who steadfastly stayed by the guns despite the strongest bombardment falling around the guns causing heavy losses.

Bitter fighting raged throughout the entire day on the open terrain that was free of any real cover. Only a few sunken roads cut through the flat fields between Blécourt and Tilloy. The valiant companies of RIR 121 and IR 180, where the enemy had broken through multiple times and then attacked the flanks and rear by tanks, fought back to the very last. They were also skillfully supported from batteries standing far out in front alongside them, often firing over open sites with direct fire.

Whilst II/R121 succeeded in refusing all attacks from a position inside a sunken road leading from Blécourt to the southwest, the I/R121 that consisted of approximately 60 men combined from the existing companies now became pressed back on the sunken Blécourt–Tilloy Road by the enemy's superior strength. Nevertheless the British suffered the heaviest losses in the infantry and artillery fire of this small group.

Of the numerous British tanks, nine alone were dealt with by the infantry and several others were destroyed by the artillery. The British now sat on the railway embankment and regrouped.

When the I/R121 and II/180 withdrew from the embankment, the men did not stop again to offer any opposition until they were at the western edge of Tilloy. Now the right wing of the I/180 had to establish a connection to the western edge of the village because of this withdrawal. There was some good news to report when at 11.00 a.m. the I/190 arrived north of Tilloy and occupied the Tilloy–Blécourt Road.

The British then renewed their attack and successfully advanced deeper into the German lines and the situation began to change for the worse. Already at 11.00 a.m. a lamp signal message from the II/180 stated that the enemy had penetrated into Tilloy. The Brigade positioned the III/119 for a counter thrust and both the I and II/180 received orders from the regiment to hold Tilloy under all circumstances if it was retaken in the counter thrust.

At 11.00 a.m. the battalion staff of the III/180 which had already rejoined the regiment in the evening of 29 September 1918. Now four heavy machine guns of the III/180 became available and after replenishing their ammunition the gun crews marched to the I/180 and by 2.00 p.m. were made subordinate to the battalion.

Meantime, the enemy had spread out more and more in Tilloy and had already begun to install machine guns inside houses. The arrival by the 11/R119 at 11.45 a.m., together with parts of the II/180 which still lay in the park at the northwestern edge of Tilloy, were designated for clearing of this wooded piece and the village. However, they were simply too weak to advance any further into the village. The 11/R119 became assigned to occupy the recaptured park and the northern corner of the village. It was clear that more reinforcements were needed but further parts of the III/R119 did not come forward despite numerous requests from the KTK of the II/180. The 11/R119 did manage to close the gap between RIR 119 and IR 180 and brought help to the II/180. The started a counter thrust on the park and entered the village about midday with part of the II/180 and cleared it from the invading Canadians in bitter close fighting. The men of RIR 119 had discovered that they were opposing Canadian troops supposedly through statements from an 'inebriated prisoner'.

The I/180 finally had to evacuate the embankment southwest of this village under the pressure of the enemy from Tilloy and now occupied the road at the eastern edge of Tilloy as well as the earthworks east of the village. The *Minenwerfer* of the battalion that could no longer be brought back, were blown up.

Bitter house to house fighting surged in Tilloy until half of the village was occupied by the British, the other half by the Germans. In order to be able to bombard the enemy with artillery, the German line withdrew away from the eastern edge. The men of IR 180 and RIR 119 had been fortunate on this day. Much of the British artillery fire fell on the British troops and completely avoided the German positions. It appears both sides were having problems trying to determine where friend and foe were located.

However, the reserves that were to support the advance did not appear, there were simply no more reserves that could be spared without weakening another portion of the German line. The troops that were in the village had been surrounded on three sides, they suffered heavy losses in the course of the afternoon through concentrated English infantry fire and toward evening were forced to evacuate the village in the face of superior enemy forces which were advancing toward the village once more.

Once the German forces had withdrawn from the village the artillery was notified and heavy German annihilation fire was placed on Tilloy and the Canadian troops occupying the ruins. The entire line in front of and north of the village had been moved back and the 11/R119 was reinforced by the 9th and 10/R119. The III and I/R119 reorganized the occupation of the sector closely together and the companies of the II/R119 were pulled out of Ramillies and moved closer to Morenchies. Elements of IR 180 still successfully occupied the northern edge of Tilloy and the eastern edge of the village when the front line stabilized but they were isolated and the connection to friendly forces was tenuous at best. Manpower losses of 26th Reserve Division were heavy, especially in the number of officers. By the morning the II/R121 only had one company officer besides the battalion staff.

At 1.10 p.m. Corps Headquarters received the following question from the 26th Reserve Division: 'The division, in the current situation, is to retake the embankment and Tilloy with the local reserves. Should the counter thrust begin?' Corps headquarters at least realized that the divisions under its control were overtired and extremely weak. In order to save the divisions from the prospect of further large losses in the planned operations, Corps headquarters ordered that the line currently occupied was to be held with the insertion of one battalion each from RIR 119 and RIR 99, which had been moved to Ramillies as reinforcements. In the course of the afternoon several more English attacks became refused.

The fighting on 30 September 1918 could be viewed as a complete success for the 26th Reserve Division over a far superior enemy. According to captured maps the British had intended to thrust over the canal at Escaudoeuvres and take Cambrai from the rear. In spite of the unrelenting employment of masses of infantry with numerous tanks the English breakthrough attempt failed.

While failing to capture Cambrai, the British continued to hold the German positions under strong disturbance fire during the night. It was obvious that regardless of the success on 30 September 1918, the next day would not prove to be any easier.

The formations of the XVII Army Corps had become badly mixed together with the employment of battalions from many different regiments. In order to create a clear command situation, the following four regimental sectors became designated: RIR 121 would hold the front excluding Blécourt until half way to Tilloy, then subsequently RIR 190 until the northern edge of Tilloy. IR 180 would follow next until by the southern edge of Tilloy. RIR 119 would then hold the line up to the canal.

After the failure of the attacks utilizing tanks early in the attack, the strength of the enemy infantry thrust was also apparently weakened. The reports and statements from prisoners indicated that they had suffered heavy losses but still always appeared to have fresh troops at hand. The men of RIR 121 were of the opinion that the attackers were at the end of their strength and could easily have been refused, if all troops stood firm like the Württemberg units. The daily report from the OHL on 1 October only seemed to support this opinion:

> On the afternoon a newly inserted Canadian division succeeded in pushing forward, passing north of Cambrai upon Ramillies. Under the leadership of *Generalleutnant von* Fritsch the especially proven *Württembergische* 26th Reserve Division threw the enemy back again by way of Tilloy in the fighting between Arras and Cambrai.[17]

The British had been successful in achieving important gains north of Cambrai, while south of the city all of their efforts had failed. It was expected that on the following days his attempts to outflank the city would be renewed with all possible strength. The regiments of the 26th Reserve Division prepared as best they could for more major fighting. RIR 119 discovered that it was wedged in the angle between the railway embankment and the Schelde canal. To the north it appeared that only the badly damaged RIR 121 and IR 180 had managed to hold firm and as such RIR 119 saw its connections and its retreat route to Ramillies threatened.

IR 180 losses on 30 September amounted to: two officers dead (*Leutnants der Reserve* Niggel and Gallmann); nine officers wounded. 13 *Unteroffiziere* and Other Ranks dead; 94 wounded and 27 missing.

Notes

1. Gerster, op. cit., p. 113.
2. Ibid.
3. Gerster, op. cit., pp. 113-114.
4. Gerster, op. cit., p. 116.
5. Gerster, op. cit., p. 114.
6. Gerster, op. cit., p. 115.
7. Ibid.
8. Ibid.
9. Vischer, op. cit., pp. 139-140.
10. Holtz, op. cit., p. 75.
11. Stühmke, op. cit., p. 72.
12. Ibid.
13. Vischer, op. cit., p. 144.
14. Klaus, Major a.D., Justizrat Max, *Das Württembergische Reserve-Feldartillerie Regiment Nr. 26 im Weltkrieg 1914-1918,* pp. 110-112.
15. Klaus, op. cit., p. 113.
16. Vischer, op. cit., pp. 145-146.
17. Stühmke, op. cit., p. 82.

7

28th Reserve Division

June–September 1918

Following the period of fierce fighting near Villers Cotterêts, the 28th Reserve Division desperately required rest and recuperation. However, nothing had changed, the troops simply could not be spared and it was once again deployed to another part of the front. In the days that followed, the division would relieve the 50th Infantry Division in the Verneuil–Marne sector.

At 6.00 a.m. on 11 June 1918, RIR 110 assembled at Les Crouttes and marched to Sergy, a distance of 25 kilometers, where the regimental staff, II and III/R110 were provided with poor accommodations. The I/R110 marched further until Chamery and received billets there. Shortly after moving into quarters the advance party sent out to inspect the new position returned. The relief took place on the night from 12-13 June 1918; the companies marched with fifteen minute spacing to Origny. The villages passed on the way to the new sector lay under the fire from light and medium artillery and the regiment lost two killed and six wounded as a result.

The I/R110 relieved the II/53 on the right of the new sector; the III/R110 relieved the I/39 on the left, the Readiness battalion, III/158, was relieved by the II/R110. The connection was established on the right to RIR 109, on the left to RIR 116. The regimental machine gun companies moved into the position 24 hours later. On the night to 11 June RIR 109 marched via Arcy-St. Restitute to Cuiry Housse and Ledges and in the early morning hours of 11 June 1918 via Fère-en-Tardenois-Villers sur Fère to Courmont.

On 12 June 1918 the advance detachment of RIR 109 was transported into the portion of the Verneuil Sector on the Marne where the regiment would be positioned. It was to become the middle regimental sector of the division. On the night to 14 June 1918 the II and III/R109 moved up to the front and relieved the two position battalions of *Füsilier* Regiment 39. The III Battalion received the reserve position in the Bois Meunière, the regimental staff and battle headquarters were in the la Grange au Bois Farm east of Ronchéres. RIR 111 would be on the right of the regiment. RIR 110 would be on the left. The orderly room of the battalions and companies as well as the regimental band lay in Courmont.

RIR 111 took over a position on the right wing of the division, which was positioned on the northern bank of the Marne between Treloup and Vincelles. The regiments of the 28th Reserve Division now belonged to Group Kathen, XXIII Reserve Corps:

> When the morning fog disappeared on 13 June, the river lay before our eyes, whose name had become fateful for Germany. The Marne valley moved in deep notches from the east to the west in considerable meandering. The hills upon both banks rose over the valley floor about 170 up to 200 meters. The steep hillsides held vineyards; the hills were covered with wide deciduous forests. On both sides deep notched side valleys led to the Marne. We are at the place, where the German front turns off sharply to the northeast from the Marne. There, where the Sômoigne brook entered into the Marne from the north, it moves by the mountain slope up to the houses of Verneuil; opposite lies the village of Try, a few kilometers upstream Troissy; 1 1/2 kilometers downward on this side of Vincelles and opposite on the southern shore in French possession was the city of Dormans with the towering church spires and the large, now however quiet railway station.[1]

On 15 June 1918 the sector lay under the heaviest artillery fire of the largest calibers as well as the Wood of Gèvres. The battalion battle headquarters in the right sector was destroyed by a direct hit and the commander of the II/R109, *Hauptmann* Isermann, as well as the Civilian Doctor Dr. Rüst and *Leutnant* Bielefeld were wounded. *Oberleutnant* Möller took over the leadership of the II Battalion, *Leutnant* Gnacke assumed the duties of the Machine Gun Officer with the staff and *Leutnant* Grüttner took command of the 2MG/R109.

On the same day the sector held by the regiments was shifted to the right, so that the village of Courcelles would be occupied by the 28th Reserve Division. The four companies of the Battle battalion from RIR 111 were inserted into the forward line and became secured by the river through pickets, sentries and patrols. The Readiness battalion was accommodated in the woods south of La Chapelle-Hurtay and the Reserve battalion was in the Meunieres wood east of Ronchéres.

Losses sustained by RIR 109 in the offensive in late May and early June, needed to be made up as soon as possible. The first replacements arrived on 16 June in the strength of three *Vizefeldwebel*, 11 *Unteroffizieren* and 112 men. While not enough to restore the regiment to full strength, the new men helped to fill out the thin ranks of the companies.

The enemy artillery never seemed to let up, almost as if they had unlimited supplies of shells. Vincelles, Verneuil and the sunken road in the regimental sector were the targets of very active enemy bombardments day and night. No one was spared from these bombardments and rank offered no protection. On 27 June 1918 the regimental commander of RIR 109, Major *Frhr.* Göler *von* Ravensburg was killed by a direct hit in Champvoisy.

At 9.00 p.m. Major *Frhr.* Göler *von* Ravensburg, accompanied by *Leutnant der Reserve* Platt from the regimental staff, were looking to pick out for quarters for the staff of a Bavarian regiment that was proceeding to the village of Champvoisy. At

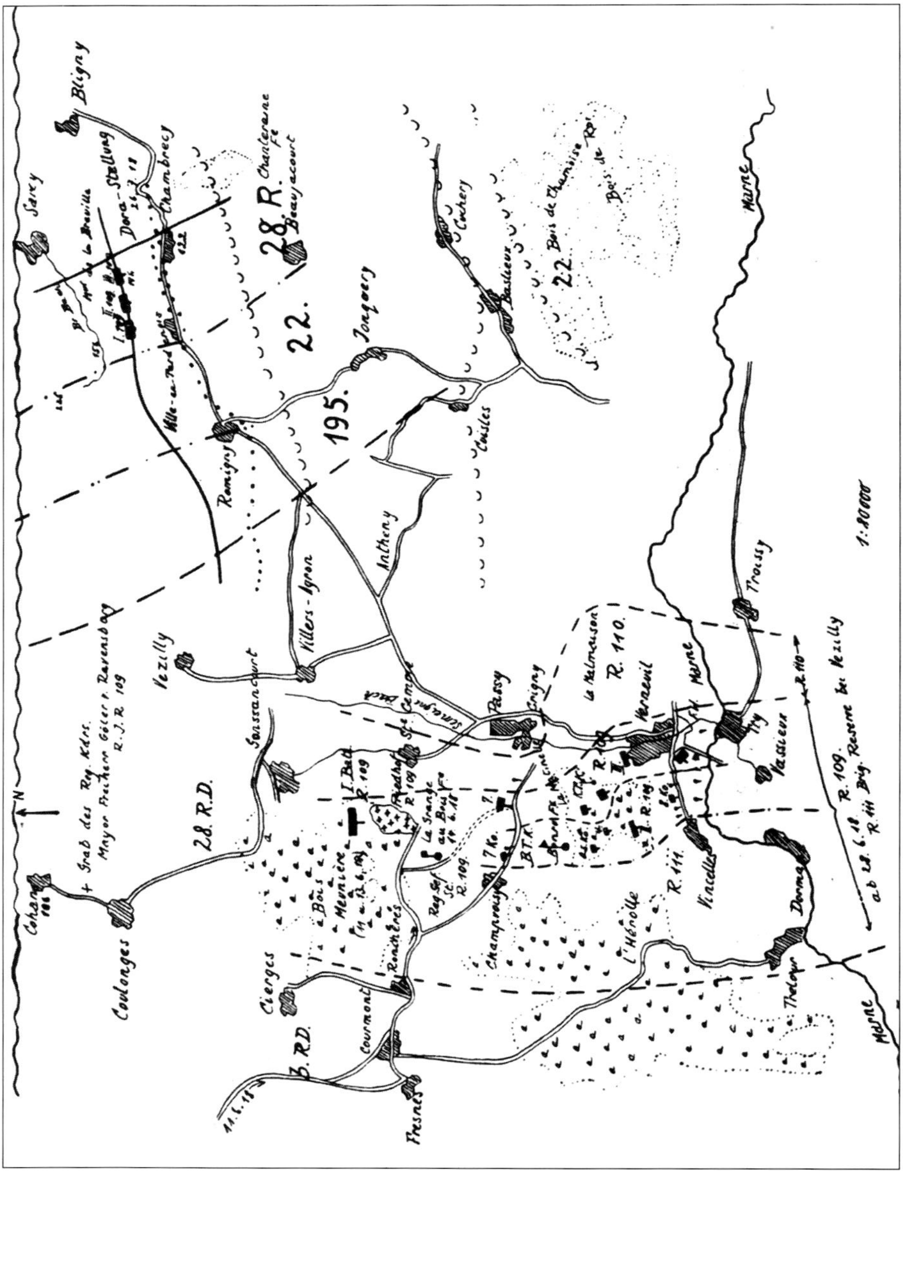

Advance by 28th Reserve Division

·.30 p.m. the enemy covered the village with several medium caliber shells. The first shell fell 30 meters in front of Major *von* Göler and shell splinters injured him on the left side of his face so severely that he fell over and lost consciousness. *Leutnant* Platt, who was wounded on both hands, called for Medical personnel to assist them. Major von Göler was treated by *Regimentsarzt* Dr. Mitter who immediately had him transported to *Sanitäts* Company 514 at Morfontaine Farm. Major von Göler never regained consciousness and he died during the transport at 12.25 a.m. on 28 June 1918, shortly before arriving at the Morfontaine Farm.

At 11.00 a.m. on 30 June 1918 there was a funeral in the church of Coulonges for Major von Göler. It was attended by the commander of the division, the brigade and the other regiments belonging to the 28th Reserve Division. The 1/R109, which Major *Frhr. von* Göler led into the field at the start the war, was made the honor company. While the regimental band played, the twelve *Feldwebel* of the regiment carried his body in a solemn procession to the cemetery of Coulonges.

On the night from 18 to 19 June 1918 there was a new partitioning in the division sector, when the battle line became divided into two battalion sectors, with the border of RIR 111 east of Treloup. The regiment remained in this position until the end of June. The front was relatively quiet, with the exception of reciprocal bombardments. The greatest demands placed on the men were sentry and patrol duty so the troops were able to slowly recover their strength with the favorable weather. In the new partitioning RIR 109 took over the left sector of RIR 110 by Vincelles.

RIR 109 occupied Verneuil and the regimental border was the eastern edge of the village, where nearby the 1/R110 was placed in cellars by Bunot Farm. The other companies of the I/R110 were positioned in gravel pits and in a copse southwest of La Malmaison Farm on the rear hillside of the ridge that ran from Verneuil to the Bois de Navarre. At night the companies push forth pickets, double sentry posts and patrols against the Marne and in the vineyard terrain. The III/R110 is in the northern edge of the Bois de Navarre, called Bois Pareuil, whose southeast corner and the hill of Bois de Trotte were both occupied by the adversary. The left regimental border went from the eastern edge of Passy via Pareuil right through the Bois de Navarre. The II/R110, as the Readiness battalion, was accommodated by the Malmaison Farm, by Grigny and the Gourdonnerie Farm, where the regimental staff also lay. Because of strong bombardments, which resulted in losses, the regimental *Unter Stab* became transferred on 14 June 1918 first to Goussaucourt and then on the 17th to Coulonges.

The defenses occupied by the 28th Reserve Division were not developed positions. The forward line was located approximately where the earlier attacks in the area had halted. Continuous trenches did not exist and with the wide expansion of each regimental sector and the weak strength of the companies there was no possibility of trenches being created. The companies and staff lay in earthen holes, poorly protected against rain and shell splinters. The outpost zone was occupied by advance pickets, double sentry posts and patrols. By day no one dared to be seen and the immense summer countryside appeared empty of people.

The position was generally quiet except at night when a machine gun rattled here and there, or a sentry shot sounded. However the villages and approach routes, particularly in the evening and night hours, lay under strong shelling that greatly impeded bringing up materials, ammunition and food. Lively pilot activity prevailed, Verneuil, which had been quickly evacuated during the earlier fighting had already been stripped of anything that could be useful to the men. The previous regiments occupying the area had thoroughly cleared the village of all cows, pigs and chickens. Hunting rabbits now took place at dusk in order to supplement the meagre rations. Despite augmenting the rations with rabbits and other small game, food was becoming scarce and monotonous. However, one item was still found in abundance, Marne wine. Wine literally flowed in streams from the cellars of every house in the area. The company leaders were very happy when finally the last drops were gone.

Replacements continued to fill up the ranks of the regiment; on 27 June six *Unteroffiziere* and 64 men arrived at RIR 109. Major *von* Becker from RIR 111 took over the regiment on 15 July 1918, while *Rittmeister* Auer *von* Herrenkirchen from Grenadier Regiment *zu Pferd* 3 arrived on 28 June 1918 and took over the II/R109. On 30 June 1918 orders were sent to Major *Frhr. von* Rotberh, Knight of the *Pour le mérite*, former commander of the *Garde* Reserve *Schützen* Battalion, from the AOK to take command of the regiment, replacing the interim commander Major von Becker.

The companies in RIR 110 received replacements of *Unteroffizieren* and Other Ranks. However the number of new men did not come close to bringing the regiment back to full strength. The company leaders also had worried faces when they examined the new men and their papers. Many of them were not fit for front line service and should never have been sent to the regiment. Because of poor rations, stress, overwork and feverish intestinal illnesses a large number of men reported sick from the regiments. Simply said the majority of the men were just not in good health.

Under these circumstances, the army was not as strong as it was only a few weeks earlier, and even at that time, it was in poor condition. The German offensive on 27 May 1918 in the area between Ailette brook and the Aisne had ended on 14 June 1918. The crucial question for the High Command now was if the attacks would continue or should the army transition to the defense?

The 7th Army, which the 28th Reserve Division belonged to, was in an extraordinarily unfavorable situation after the end of the offensive. The position between the Aisne, west of Soissons and Reims, up to the Marne formed a wide bulging arc, almost a triangular projection, a 'sack,' with the top in Château-Thierry and the corner pillars Villers Cotterêts and Reims which was encompassed almost on three sides by the enemy. The position being held by the 7th Army was untenable; the adversaries by Reims and the Wood of Villers Cotterêts were in positions where determined attacks from the west and east could completely cut off the German troops inside the bulge, resulting in a disaster the German Army would not be able to recover from.

For the supply of the troops in the Marne salient there was only the railroad Laon-Soissons available, and this lay so far behind the front, that its capability through long range fire could be greatly reduced. On the other hand the situation for an attack by the French on both flanks was extraordinarily favorable.

Whilst the higher commands debated what to do next, the routine in the rank and file was unchanged. The main task facing the 28th Reserve Division was the exploration f the enemy disposition through raids and patrols. Position construction had made nly small progress, in part due to the small number of men available, in part due to the weak condition of many of the soldiers. Fortunately it was beautiful summer weather, a easonably quiet position and a place where the men could recover somewhat from the train of the recent fighting. Then, rumors began to circulate of something big that was oing to take place and that new preparations were being made, but for what, no one new exactly.

Within a short time the regiments of the division began to be shifted around the ront as part of larger troop movements, possibly something to do with all of the recent umors. On the night of 24/25 June 1918 the II/R110 relieved the I/R110 in the right ector. On 27 June 1918 the battle sector was newly divided: the Battle battalion now used three companies in the forward line and one company in reserve. The left battalion ook on the sector of the III/83 with two companies on Trotte hill. From the Readiness attalion, the I/R110, the 4th Company was transferred to Grigny as the security arrison and the 3/R110 was transferred to Belle Idée Farm. Then, on the night of 30 une/1 July 1918 the I/R110 relieved the III/R110 in the left sector: the 2nd, 3rd, and 4/ R110 occupied the position, while the battalion staff and 1/R110 were in Pareuil.

On 29 June 1918 the 6th Bavarian Infantry Division had become inserted between he 10th *Landwehr* Division and the 28th Reserve Division of Group Kathen, and when on 5 July 1918 RIR 111 occupied the largest part of the former sector of RIR 109, RIR 110 moved to a position southwest of Bois de Navarre by RIR 109 and was distributed as follows:

Battle Battalion I/R110 had four companies in the forward line between Bois de Navarre inclusive until the western edge of Trotte hill; the command post was in Pareuil. The Readiness Battalion, II/R110, had one company in Pareuil, three companies at and near La Belle Idée Farm. The Rest Battalion, III/R110, bivouacked in the wood of Vezilly in tents.

Between 28 and 30 June 1918 RIR 111 was relieved by troops of the 6th Bavarian Reserve Division and the regiment received billets in Arcy le Ponsart, in Bois de Vezilly and in Bois d'Aiguisy. The rest time was used to thoroughly clean the uniforms as well as repairing the weapons and pieces of equipment. It was however too short, to be able to give the troops any real relaxation after the recent fighting. Already on the night of 4/5 July 1918 the I and III/R111 were moved forward to the Marne defenses again, with the III/R111 as the Battle battalion with one company at Vincelles, and three companies on a hill north of the village; the I/R111 was the Readiness Battalion at and south of the Champvoisy-Passy-Griny road.

The situation facing the 7th Army only allowed for two possibilities for the OHL: to either abandon the projecting arc by the Marne and by doing so take back the German line to its former position, or continue the offensive with the goal of taking Reims and penetrate the wood of Villers Cotterêts. There were other considerations that needed to be addressed in addition to the situation facing the 7th Army. The German allies: Austria-Hungary, Bulgaria and Turkey were obviously at the end of their strength. It would not be long until the decision of the war would fall solely on the actions of the German army.

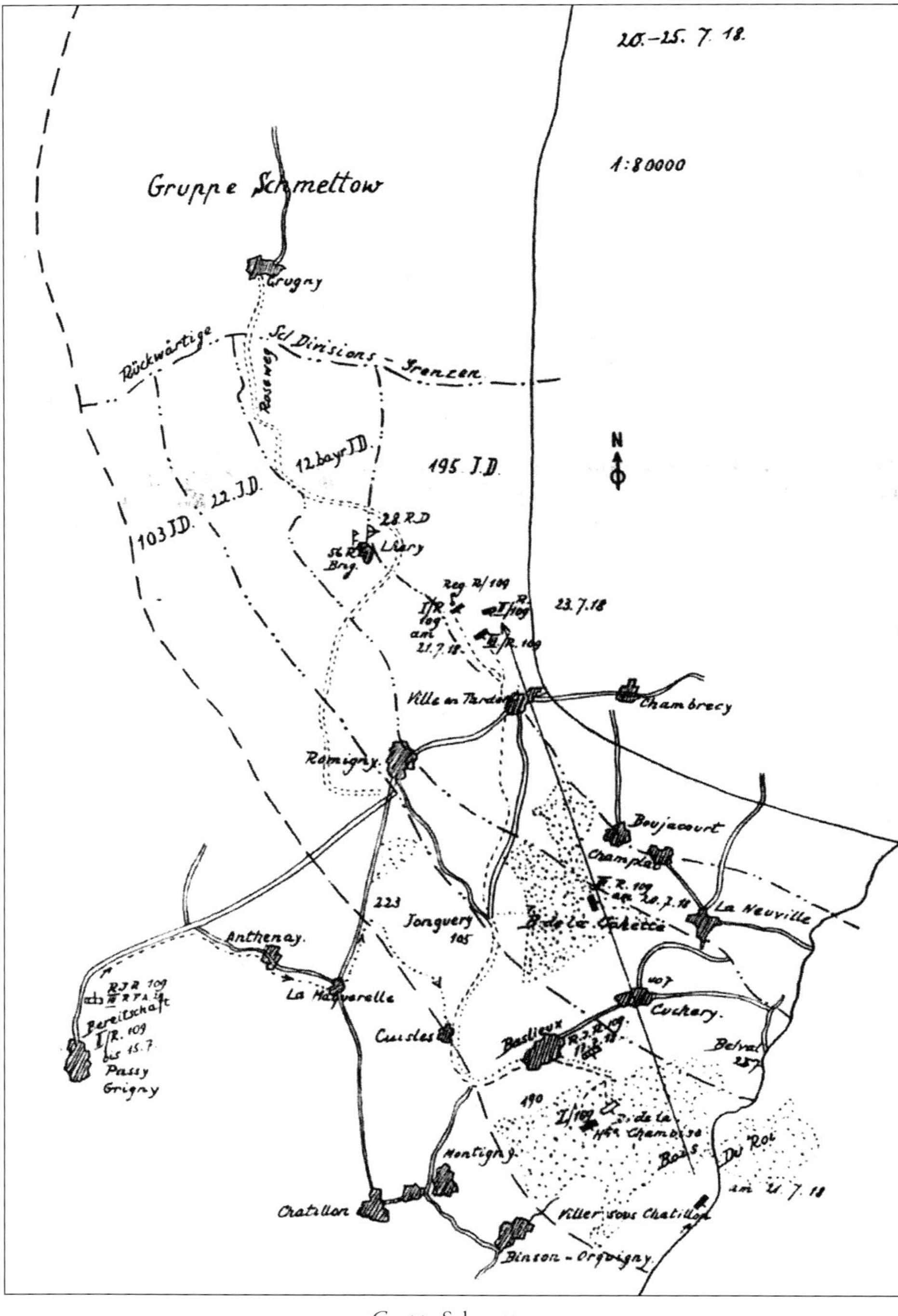

Gruppe Schmettow.

The consideration of all of these issues as well as with respect to the morale and spirit of the troops with the masses of American divisions arriving in France, and the deteriorating conditions at home, led the OHL to the decision that the offensive ordered on 1 June would continue. *Heeresgruppe* German Crown Prince was to be employed and on 21 July 1918 the three involved armies were assigned their final task: The 7th Army would conduct the thrust on both sides of the Marne on Epernay. The 1st Army should break through the front between Prunay, southeast of Reims and Aubérle and between Cond, and Châlons – Somme – Tourb. The area around Reims would not be attacked. The Reims position would fall with the push on Epernay and Châlons.

These attack orders signified a difficult Marne crossing for the right thrust wing – the 7th Army from the strength of this obstacle in the enemy fire who dominated all crossings from excellent positions on the high hills of the southern shore. However the left wing of the 7th Army would also encounter great difficulties with the advance through the steep wooded terrain by Reims – Fôret de la Montagne de Reims – with its deep incised river valleys, hills and extended wooded areas. The 1st and 3rd armies would have to overcome the cratered desert of the Somme battlefield in order to advance.

Four Groups were formed in the 7th Army: Groups Kathen and Wichura would cross over the Marne between Gland and Vincelles and thrust southward. Group Conta brought its right wing between Vincelles and Verneuil on the southern shore of the Marne, its left wing however remained on the northern bank. This group would thrust up the Marne; its goal on the first day was Epernay. The fourth group, Group Schmettow would attack the Reims mountainous terrain; then turn to the southeast.

General Foch had also not given up his plans for a large offensive against the eastern flank of the German position – Aisne-Ourcq – and was determined, to conduct the defense of the German attack and his own offensive as interrelated operations. On 13 July 1918 General Pétain fixed the beginning of the Allied offensive for the 18th.

Meanwhile, the OHL was completely unaware of enemy offensive plan and the preparations being taken on the Allied side even by the evening of 14 July 1918. As such, on the night from 14 to 15 July 1918 Y Day was designated as 15 July 1918 and X hour was 1.10 a.m. While the fighting was expected to be difficult, there was a firm belief in the success of the attack and that by the evening the *Sturmtruppen* would be in Epernay.

The original day intended for the attack by the OHL had been 10 July 1918. However the enormous preparations required for the offensive, which was designated *Marneschutz Angriff*, could not be finished in time to meet this deadline and as such the beginning of the offensive had been postponed to 15 July 1918.

The preparations included moving 1,700 batteries into place and provided with sufficient ammunition for the task they were assigned. The *pioniers* had to make preparations to carry all necessary equipment and materials across the Marne, the attack divisions in the first line had to be conducted into the readiness position areas and made familiar with their attack zones. All of this activity and many other preparations all had to be completed during the short nights that occurred at this time of year in order to avoid the preparations from being discovered by enemy observation aircraft.

The preparation work required for such an attack placed a great deal of strain on the nerves of the staff and the troops and great activity by everyone involved. The secrecy

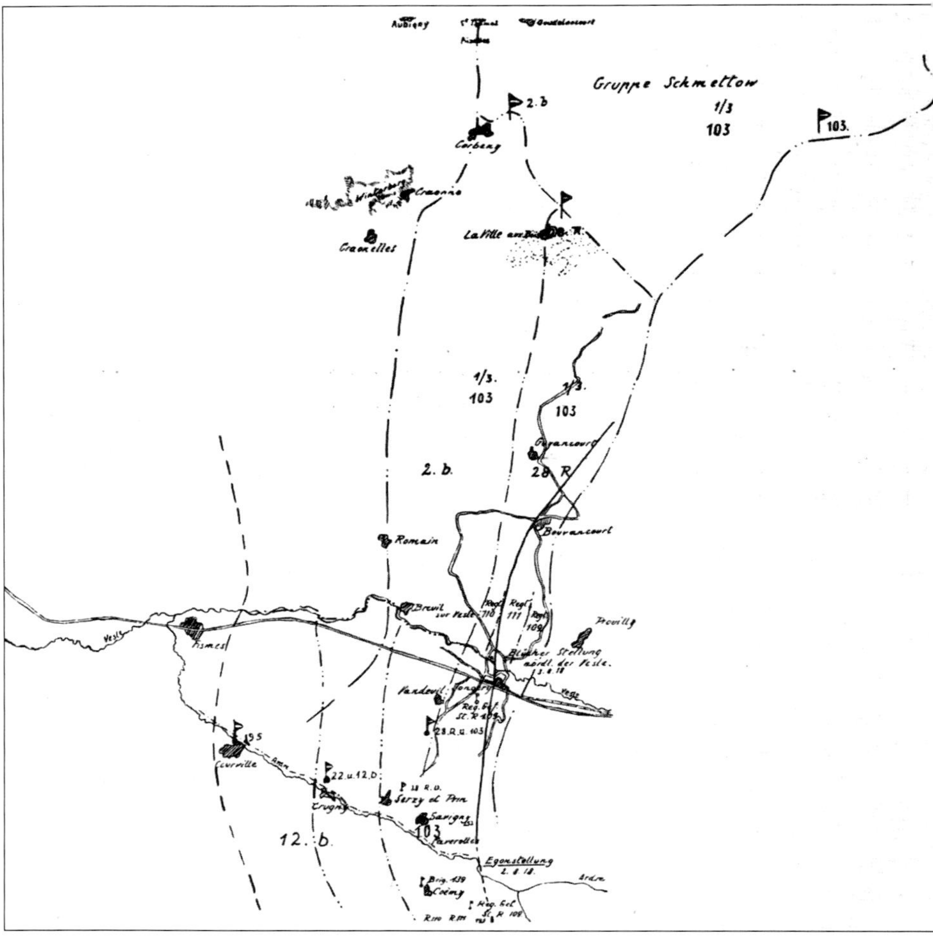

Gruppe Schmettow.

over the attack goals was of particular importance if the offensive had any hope of succeeding. In this instance, the frenzied activity of moving artillery batteries and troops was easily observed by enemy observation aircraft and any thought of surprising the enemy was gone, so that the offensive was almost doomed to failure before it had even started.

During the attack preparations by the 7th Army, RIR 109 lay in its position in front of Verneuil. Verneuil came under extremely severe bombardments by gas shells between 10 and 12 July 1918 which resulted in the 2nd and 3/R109 losing about 90 men to gas poisoning. The enemy also exhibited heightened levels of activity in these days; indicating that an Allied attack might take place, however the expected attack did not occur. Instead, on the night of 14/15 July 1918 the enemy blew up the remnants of the bridge on the Verneuil-Dormans road that lead over the Marne.

On 11 July 1918 the II/R110 took over the battle sector, the III/R110 moved to the readiness area and the I/R110 marched in the Vezilly Wood. Little had changed in the forward line since the insertion on the Marne, but what was noticeable was the increased activity in the rear areas. There was ground reconnaissance, surveying of battery positions, bringing up ammunition and then camouflaging the growing number of stock piles, mounting of *Minenwerfern*, carrying detachments to transport the mines and a myriad of other activities, all apparently preparations for a large attack.

It also seemed odd that the French barely fired on the forward positions at all, but the rear terrain, the approach routes, billeting areas and wooded areas all lay under strong artillery fire. At night the uninterrupted rattle of columns could be heard moving back and forth in the rear. Enemy aerial activity was also exceptionally lively, each night low-flying enemy aircraft appeared overhead, which illuminated the approach routes with parachute flares and then sprayed machine gun fire on them as well as dropping bombs. All of the increased enemy activity resulted in stockpiles of ammunition suddenly exploding and burning throughout the rear area.

Throughout preparations for the attack the 28th Reserve Division was a position division. Since 12 July 1918 it belonged to Group Conta and was to follow the attack divisions as the third wave as the Army reserve. While it was extremely important that the enemy did not recognize the preparations for the attack or the actual date it would begin, it became known later that Generals Foch and Pétain were clearly aware of this information as early as 12 July 1918 through statements from prisoners and from superb ground and aerial observation. The postponement of the German offensive from 10 to 15 July 1918 allowed the Allies even more time to complete their defensive measures in time to meet the opening assault; there would be no surprise when the first German soldiers advanced across no man's land.

The main defensive measure taken by the French commander-in-chief had, who had correctly assessed the direction of the German attack, was the ordered evacuation of the largest part of the first French position at the front. The positions remained occupied only by weak sentries for the deception of German observers. With this move, the German attack would fall upon an empty position and the main fighting would not take place until the second position was reached and this would be occupied by an unshaken enemy.

A large number of machine gun nests, pickets, *Unteroffizier* and double sentry posts from RIR 109 that had been pushed forward up to the riverside secured the foreground between Verneuil and the Marne. Further replacements arrived at the regiment at the last minute in the strength of three *Unteroffizieren* and 63 men; in addition the 1st Machine Gun Company of a Bavarian Machine Gun Battalion was assigned to the regiment as added firepower.

RIR 110 received orders on 12 July 1918 as part of the attack of the 7th Army that the position battalion should undertake the clearing of the Bois de Navarre through heavy and light *Minenwerfer* in preparation for the attack, and then after passing through the forest, to occupy its eastern edge.

After the attack was carried out the I/R110, which lay in rest in the Bois de Vezilly, would move forward with the entire regiment until reaching the La Belle Idée Farm.

The Readiness battalion, III/R110, lying at the La Belle Idée Farm had to occupy readiness position in the Brandouille valley, northwest of Trotte hill. The time set fo the advance would be provided by the regimental headquarters.

The position battalion, the II/R110 under *Hauptmann de Landwehr* Rösch, ha inserted the 8th, 5th and 6/R110 in the forward line. The 7/R110 lay in reserve at th left wing. They would provide protection after the beginning of the attack against th Bois de Trotte from its position, then, moving behind the middle of the battalion advance to the Bois de Navarre. On 13 July 1918 the advance detachment of IR 3 (113th Infantry Division) arrived, and on the night two battalions of IR 36 were accom modated by Gaudonnerie Farm.

On the night of 14/15 July 1918 all batteries and *Minenwerfer* were finally read to fire, the last attack battalions marched to their exit positions, the *pioniers* campe by their pontoons. The watch hands slowly moved toward 'X' time, and at 1.10 a.m precisely to the second the German batteries opened fire on the enemy positions i order to clear a path for the infantry attack. In the early morning of the 15th the 133r Infantry Division attacked as planned, going past RIR 109 in a southeast direction with the goal of the day: reaching the line Cuis-Weg, Cuis-Chouilly.

On 15 July 1918 the following order was distributed: 'Under the orders of the Germa Crown Prince the 7th, 3rd and 1st Armies will attack the enemy on the Marne in a easterly direction. His Majesty the Kaiser will arrive at the battlefield tonight. All of hi good wishes accompany the troops, to which he calls out: 'With God for the Kaiser an the Reich':

> On 15 July silence prevailed at the II Battalion in the forward line, but Pareuil and all approach routes lay under powerful fire. At 1.10 a.m. – X time; the hurricane breaks loose, our preparation fire began. It appears to us that the throbbing does not seem as strong this time as it was on 27 May. Or did we deceive ourselves? The enemy artillery was not silent!! Powerful disturbance fire lay in the vicinity of the wood of Vezelly. By the II Battalion the bombardment since 3.30 a.m. had become weaker, however from 4.50 a.m. on it increased again. However, that is not according to plan! La Belle Idée Farm and the regimental battle headquarters also lie under unchanged strong fire during the entire night.
>
> 4.50 a.m.! Now quickly out of the holes! Forward! It is still pitch black in the dense forest foliage. It is difficult to advance in the undergrowth. Now the French machine guns rattled. Our companies lie before wire obstacles, which were skillfully positioned between the trees. Our *Minenwerfer* had not taken hold of the scattered and flanking placed machine gun nests. In his narrow, but deep trenches sits an unshaken enemy. Losses occurred. Particularly the 6th Company that lay outside the wood and must overcome open terrain up to the wood edge, only advanced step by step. 7.50 a.m. *Leutnant der Reserve* Teeg (5/R110) reported that he lay in the second French trench. On the right of him one platoon from the 3/36 and the 8th Company came forward. *Leutnant der Reserve* Jörger from the 2nd MG Company requested support at 7.00 a.m. The 7th Company was put in, likewise the 12th Company, which rolled up the Bois de Navarre from the

> northeastern end. At 9.05 a.m. *Leutnant der Reserve* Gerstner (2nd MG Company) reported: IR 66 (113th Division) had crossed over the Marne and was advancing upon Troissy with all transport. The I/36 had connection to the II/R110. It stood with two companies in the vineyards west of the Bois de Navarre, however it did not come further forward, because the Rebgelände was covered with machine gun nests. One other battalion (IR 36) attacked the Rebgelände from the south. Our own troops came forward between Bois de Trotte and Bois de Navarre. It was the III/37 and the Württemberg Mountain Regiment of the 10th Reserve Division.[2]

At 9.30 a.m. the II/R110 reported that the Bois de Navarre was in the hands of the battalion and with it the attack goal had been reached. In accordance with orders the three *Sturm* Companies were used in depth, one became eliminated as battalion reserve.

The III/R110 moved at 9.10 a.m. on orders of the regiment to the readiness position in the Brandouille valley. The escort battery, 2/RFAR 29, remained in the vicinity of the Belle Idée Farm and during 14 and 15 July RIR 110 remained in its place.

The capture of the Bois de Navarre produced 150 prisoners, three *Minenwerfer*, three heavy machine guns, ten rapid loading rifles and a great deal of ammunition. *Leutnant der Reserve* Jörger with his machine gun platoon alone took 30 prisoners. Our losses amounted to: *Leutnant der Reserve* Fischer severely wounded, *Leutnant der Reserve* Heuss slightly wounded, eight men killed and 25 men wounded.

The I/R110 advanced according to orders at 7.30 a.m. with the regiment in the Wood of Vezilly and reached La Belle Idée Farm via Villers-Agron at 9.10 a.m. When the battalion arrived at its goal there were some disturbing concerns. Where were the large numbers of prisoners? Why did the enemy artillery still fire? What do these squadrons of enemy aircraft signify? 'Gloomy thoughts passed through our minds! Has the thrust not succeeded?' What was the situation at the front?

The Marne had been crossed by the attack divisions of the 7th Army and the *pioniers* had performed admirably in in their efforts to restore the bridges over the river that had been blown up, while all the time under strong enemy fire. The crossings were made; however the troops soon realized that the enemy had not been surprised by the attack. In terrain extraordinarily difficult for the attacker, extraordinarily favorable for the defenders there was hard fighting at every village and at every piece of wood. On the evening of the 15th the assault troops lay in and in front of the second French position. Epernay, the desired goal, was not obtained. However Group Schmettow on the left wing of the 7th Army had managed to break into the second French position.

As early as the evening of 15 July 1918 the attacks by the 1st and 3rd Armies must already be looked upon as failures and as such cutting off of the Reims salient appeared to be very unlikely. The only thing that could change the situation was if the attack by the 7th Army succeeded in capturing the hills southwest of Reims, then the evacuation of the Reims salient could still become accomplished.

The fighting on the southern bank of the Marne had made no progress. The enemy had positioned his reserves for defense and while some portions of the line were able to be captured they could only be held under heavy fighting. The circumstances north of the Marne were more favorable. The attack by Group Schmettow remained in flux, in

Courton Wood the 22nd Infantry Division had managed to break through the secon French position. If these successes could be expanded, the advance against the hi southwest of Reims on the left wing of the 7th Army could succeed.

At 7.30 a.m. RIR 109 received orders with the other regiments of the 28th Reserv Division to be placed at the ready as the army reserve in the area of Vincelles-Bois d Navarre-St. Gemme. In order to create a permanent position on the southern Marn bank, the continuation of the attack by the 7th Army was ordered for 16 July 1918 Under these circumstances the 28th Reserve Division as the army reserve was move behind the right wing of Group Schmettow.

At approximately 3.00 a.m. RIR 110 marched in the following order: I/R110 with th 2/RFAR 29; II/R110 with *Minenwerfer* Company 228; III/R110 on the Passy-Grigny Romigny road to the wooded piece south of Romigny and took up positions unde cover against aerial observation. RIR 109 marched at 4.00 p.m. via Passy-Grigny t Anthenay, where it arrived at 7.00 p.m. At 10.30 p.m. the regiment continued furthe via Violaine to Cuisles, where the regiment was placed in support of the 195th Infantr Division.

The attacks continued in the mountainous terrain on 17 July 1918, and while th fighting raged in front of the division, the 28th Reserve Division was still not put int the fighting. On 17 July 1918 Group Schmettow took Hill 263 west of Fleury, whicl dominated the Marne valley for quite a distance.

Army Oberkommando 7 had wanted to put in its last reserves, the 28th Reserv Division, to help with the attacks on the left wing. Army Group German Crown Princ did not agree with the intended participation of the division and the troops did not tak part in the attacks. Even if the division had been deployed in the fighting it would no have made any difference in the final results.

The goal of the day for the left wing of the 7th Army would not be reached; the attacl strength of the troops had become completely used up in the heavy fighting of the las days. In recognition of the serious situation it now faced, the 7th Army arranged fo the transition to the defense for the entire front that evening. At midnight the OHI acknowledged the need for the systematic withdrawal of the troops on the southerr Marne shore; the Marne Battle had ended.

Only the II/R110 had participated with the attack on the Bois de Navarre. The mer knew nothing definite about the overall situation, but it was suspected that the Germar divisions had been unsuccessful in spite of every effort made by the troops. Would the Marne decide the fate of Germany for the second time? On the afternoon of 17 July 1918 General Pétain ordered the start of the battle to recapture the lost terrain along the entire to begin on the morning of the 18th.

While these major events were taking place, the men of the 28th Reserve Division were still waiting to see what happened next. Orders arrived at 4.00 p.m. for RIR 109 to be placed in readiness behind *Jäger* Regiment 8 in the Bois du Roi, and, together with the *Jägers*, to clear the enemy from the wood and push through until it was at the southeastern edge of the wood.

RIR 109 proceeded to the assigned location through heavy rain from sudden cloudbursts and heavy artillery fire, from which 12 men were killed and 36 men were wounded. The regiment reached the readiness position by 9.00 p.m. on 17 July 1918. RIR 109 remained at the readiness position until 4.00 a.m. on the 18th in the streaming rain; then new orders arrived that the attack would not take place and the regiment marched back to Baslieux where it was transported on vehicles to Cuisles. Parts of the 2/R109 which had not received the marching orders, became surprised by an enemy attack, which the men repulsed with the help from two light machine guns and one group from a Machine Gun Marksmen Detachment.

Once in Cuisles, the battalions distributed food to the men, when at 12.30 p.m. the regiment was suddenly alarmed. The II and III/R109 were placed in possession of the 101st Infantry Brigade in the wood of Rodemat with the orders that the battalions would only be employed in the most extreme emergency. The I/R109 stood as the brigade reserve in Chamoise Wood and there suffered heavy losses through powerful enemy artillery fire. The 4/R109 succeeded in capturing a five man strong French patrol while occupying the woods. The I/R109 returned to the regiment again in the evening and was inserted between the II and III/R109, in order to work on the creation of a main opposition line.

On the early morning of 18 July 1918 the 28th Reserve Division moved in an easterly direction to the readiness position behind the right wing of Group Schmettow. The battalions of RIR 111 with the escort battery and a *pionier* company marched to Aougny, where they took up defensive positions in wooded pieces and the route in a southern direction to the front was explored by patrols. On the afternoon the wooded pieces northeast of Olizy-et-Violaine also became occupied. About 3.00 p.m. a strong enemy counterattack took place against the German front, and the I and III/R111 marched in a southerly direction to Cuisles and later on the night became moved forward via Baslieux-Cuchery to la Neuville. The II/R111 was placed in possession of 22nd Infantry Division and moved via Jonqury-Champlat to Cohedon and with it the battalion was eliminated from the regimental association.

Generally, it was an exhausting day for the troops. It became worse when at 6.00 p.m. a thunderstorm with torrential rain began, which lasted until the night and completely soaked everything. On this day the 10/R111, which already suffered greatly during the bombardment of Vincelles with gas shells, leaving it with a fighting strength of four *Unteroffizieren* and 22 men, become disbanded and the men were distributed to the other companies.

At 4.30 a.m. on 18 July 1918, the 56th Reserve Infantry Brigade telephoned: 'Situation in area west of Pourcy, unclear. Breakthrough attempt by the adversary possible. RIR 110 must expect the possibility to become swiftly inserted in the direction of Cuchery-La Charmoise or La Neuville-Pourcy.' The regiment was ready to depart at 5.00 a.m. and at 5.40 a.m. the marching orders arrive: RIR 110 with escort battery and the III/RFA 29, which moves under the command of the regiment, to march immediately to the southern corner of the wood of Cohette as the army reserve and position itself there at the ready, protected against aerial observation.

The forward movement went very slowly, because the road was congested by thick columns of traffic and strong artillery fire was falling in the direction of Bois du Roi. At 11.00 a.m. the batteries reached their readiness position places in Cohette Wood.

The escort battery and III/RFA 29 stopped in the wood on the right and on the left c the Jonquery–Champlat Road. RIR 110 was in the attack terrain. Traces of the bitte fighting could be seen everywhere: French trenches, machine gun nests, exceptionall skillful positions, wire entanglements and the dead.

The enemy had attacked the 195th Infantry Division, the 12th Bavarian Infantr Division and the 22nd Infantry Division with fresh troops at 10 a.m. following severa hours of preparation fire. While the French had not been able to make any headway i the attack, the 7th Army placed the 28th Reserve Division in the possession of Grou Schmettow as a precaution. At 3.45 p.m. RIR 110 become subordinate to the 12t Bavarian Infantry Division and received orders, to immediately travel with the escor battery to Orcourt and once there be placed in readiness in the possession of the divisio and to establish a connection with Bavarian IR 26.

The companies of the regiment immediately moved along the advance routes in th wood pieces south and west of Orcourt. At 6.00 p.m. the regiment was assembled in th new position and the support battery, 2/RFAR 29, had established a surveillance position at the southern edge of the Bois de la Cohette. At 8.00 p.m. the regiment receive the following mission from the 12th Bavarian Infantry Division:

> 1. One battalion of the regiment would be subordinate to Bavarian IR 26. 2. RIR 110 had to locate and occupy a main opposition line in the wood, 500 meters west of Belval, with the front to the east. Because of these orders the I/R110 becomes subordinate to Bavarian Infantry Regiment 26. The II and III Battalions moved to Belval wood and occupied it. At the eastern edge of the wood lay machine gun nests with fields of fire in the direction of Belval and Grand Pr. The regimental staff was accommodated in Cuchery. The II and III/R110 were therefore the security garrison of the main opposition line. In the *Vorfeld* lying on the right in the wood at La Fortelle and west of Grand Pr. Was Bavarian IR 26, on the left of it Bavarian IR 28.[3]
>
> Bavarian IR 26 and 27, which had been seen by the enemy at la Poterne out of the valley of La Charmoise, stormed the steep valley sides under the severe enemy fire, and advanced until the regiments were close in front of Grand Pr. and La Fortelle. The two Bavarian regiments had been fighting for several days and were becoming exhausted. Despite repeated attempts, the regiments were unable to make any headway against the determined enemy resistance, while at the same time the French could also not attack due to the presence of the Bavarians. This situation could change at any moment as the ranks of the two Bavarian regiments had grown dangerously thin due to the number of losses suffered in the past days.
>
> On 18 July the French did attempt an attack; but he had been repulsed. On the evening of the 18th the I/R110 was placed in possession of Bavarian IR 26 and received orders, to take over the support position of the regiment. What the I Battalion found when it arrived in the position was that the Orcourt-Grand Pr. road climbed steeply up the hillside. On the hill between La Fortelle, Grange de Grand Pr, and the small wood north of it, the II/B26 was lying on the right and the I/B26, on the left were involved in a battle with the French. The I/R110, as the

> support battalion, occupied the *Franzosen Graben* with the 1/R110 under *Leutnant der Reserve* Fauler; behind it, lying at the eastern edge of Belval wood, was the 3/R110 under *Leutnant der Reserve* Senger and the 4/R110 under *Leutnant der Reserve* Meuret. The battalion staff was in a gap that was covered with a very thick wood. The 2/R110 under *Leutnant der Reserve* Leist was slightly pushed forward in a small wood at the left wing. The different companies had all occupied their respective positions by 12 midnight where they came under lively disturbance fire on the night and on 19 July, particularly on the sector of the 4/R110 and the battalion staff, which fortunately does not cause any losses. The task given to the I/R110 was to throw any attacking enemy force back in a counter thrust.
>
> *Hauptmann von* Zeddelmann, RIR 110.[4]

The II/R111, attached to 22nd Infantry Division, now moved forward on the hill between Nappes and the Bois d'Eclisse on the night of 18/19 1918 July and was placed under the commander of IR 39. The 7/R111 occupied the left wing of the wood edge west of Nappes on the Cohedon-Chaumuzy road. The three other companies remained about 300 meters behind as the reserve and provided protected to the north. The 6/R111 was employed at wiring of Nappes and les Haies.

On the night of 18/19 July 1918 the I and III/R111 were placed ready at the western edge of the Bois de Courton, east of Neuville, where they found some cover against the bombardment in old Italian shelters. In the course of the morning of the 19th the regiment received an order to develop a blocking position at the western edge of the Bois de Courton, and to find cover against the expected artillery bombardment, the work continued until the morning of 20 July 1918 . On this day strong artillery fire began at 7.00 a.m. which gradually increased to drum fire. The I/R111 on the right and the III/R111 on the left were made ready for battle, and occupied the existing *Riegel Stellung* that existed out of a line of fox holes.

However, before the companies had reached the position they were already embroiled in the fighting. In front of them, northwest of Paradis, the French and British had successfully broken through the German lines, and when the 12/R111 as the lead company reached the area approximately 500 meters north of Paradis, they ran straight into the attacking British forces. The *Schützen* and machine guns immediately joined the fighting as quickly as the guns could be set up. There was no connection to other troops on the right and the left, and the British threatened to outflank the 12/R111 on both sides, so the company withdrew until it could reach the 11/R111 with its right wing, which had just arrived. Both companies, despite their low rifle strength, had brought the enemy attack to a halt. The 9/R111 came up and took over the protection of the left wing. The I/R111 was also successful in throwing back the adversaries, who had crossed over the battle line with weak forces.

RIR 111 felt that this success provided reputable proof that despite the weakened strength and despite the ongoing artillery fire it was still a fighting unit on which the leadership could rely. It was also mentioned that watching the troops that had been manning the forward line flooding back was not an encouraging sight for the men of RIR 111. The regiment simply wanted to have it acknowledged that the enemy attack was stopped at this position by the two understrength battalions; the I and III/R111 There were numerous reports about the exemplary behavior of the troops in RIR 111 especially that of a patrol of *Vizefeldwebel* Allgeyer from the I/R111 and *Leutnant* Weiss who, bleeding from two wounds did not go to the bandaging station until he gave a detailed report to the battalion commander about the confusing situation.

The success of this day had not been achieved without loss. There were so few veteran left among the men that any loss was significant. One especially grievous loss for the regiment was when *Leutnant* Winterer was killed while at the head of his 1st Company. He had proved to be a superb leader since the year 1917. Among the fallen was *Oberleutnant* Lantelme, who had been with the regiment since November 1914 and who had afforded valuable services to the regiment in many positions, namely as construction officer. He was killed together with a few men of the Construction Company.

At 1.00 a.m. on 19 July the II/R109 was placed in possession of *Jäger* Regiment 6 a the reserve for the defense of an enemy attack that was expected to originate from the Ferme des Savarts. The II/R109 marched via the Champ brook and became positioned in the wood east of the farm. While the anticipated attack never occurred, the enemy machine guns and artillery were very active.

In the afternoon the German artillery fired on the position of the II/R109 resulting in the loss of two men killed and seven men wounded. The II/R109 could only avoid this friendly fire by withdrawing to the northeast and once there, the men dug a new defensive line and wired the southern edge of the Bois du Roi. Later, three French prisoners were brought through the position by the III/R109.

During the night of 18/19 July companies of RIR 110 suffered under a fierce bombardment of Belval Wood and on the 19th their adversaries bombarded the wood, villages and roads with heavy fire raids. Because of a new organization of the battle strength of the 12th Bavarian Infantry Division, the II and III/R110 moved as reserves to the 23rd Bavarian Infantry Brigade into the so-called old French positions east of Cuchery and by Menicourt up to the Belval river. Unfortunately these positions do not actually exist except as lines on a map, so that the men were without any cover; while the III/R110 had artillery positions in front and behind it. The night was very restless. Despite all of these problems, it was still more agreeable than being further south at the Marne, where on the night of 19/20th July 1918 the *Sturmtrupps* were taken back to the northern shore.

On the night from 19/20 July 1918 the I/R110 began to work on the construction of the main opposition line according to orders from the Bavarian IR 26. The 2/R110 became transferred to a sunken road in a wood piece north of the Orcourt-Grand Pr. road as rear support for the II/B26.

On 20 July 1918 strong artillery fire fell upon the artillery positions starting at 6.30 a.m., then it became transferred onto the sector of the 1st, 3rd and 4/R110 and the battalion staff. At 9.30 a.m. the enemy fire reached its greatest strength: medium and light shells, shrapnel with new, odd fuzes and gas shells were all mixed together. Barrage fire signals rise up into the air by the front line as the French infantry attack. The machine guns from the I/R110 were employed in the defense; the 1/R110 placed two light machine gun groups ready for the counter thrust against the so-called *Erlenbusch*. Finally the message arrived: 'the attack was bloodily refused'. Two prisoners were brought back from the fighting: 'Senegalese, repugnant chaps. One is severely wounded; about his neck he wears a string of cowry shells.'

By 5.00 p.m. the I/R110 was under strong fire again, which continued until 7.30 p.m., when it finally died down, only to become revived again during the night. The day had cost the battalion: 13 men killed, *Leutnant der Reserve* Senger and 42 men wounded, 27 men gas sick. The *Franzosen Graben* became occupied by the 1st and 3/R110, while the two light machine gun groups of the 1/R110 returned into the company sector. The 2/R110 then sent two light machine gun groups to Bavarian IR 26. They become placed in the front line. The I/R110 then received two heavy machine guns from the 1MG/R110 as replacements.

At midday on 20 July 1918 the I/R111 becomes moved back to Cohedon. While this movement occurred the left flank of the III/R111 was without any connection with the neighboring troops. The 2nd and 4/R111 as well as the machine gun company became stopped and made subordinate to the III/R111, with the instructions to close the gap. The 1st and 3/R111 meanwhile moved to a reception position with the machine gun platoon on the hill north of Cohedon and came under the 103rd Infantry Division as the division reserve. In the early dawn hours of 21 July 1918 the remaining five companies of the regiment located in the Bois de Courton become relieved through a battalion of IR 83 and moved to a readiness position at the western edge of the wood. In the course of the afternoon the 2nd and 4/R111 with the 1st Machine Gun Company re-established a connection to the I/R111 at Cohedon. In the late afternoon the III/R111 moved into a bivouac in the wood piece east of Lhéry. During all of these movements the First Line transport in the rear was not immune from the enemy actions as it became attacked by enemy pilots and had suffered losses from bombs and machine gun fire.

At 8.30 a.m. on 20 July 1918 the enemy began to bombard the front and rearward positions of the 12th Bavarian Infantry Division with guns of all calibers, destroying all connections between the different units as well as causing large losses. The baggage section of the train of RIR 110 was covered with aircraft bombs, whereby one *Vizefeldwebel* and three Other Ranks of the Baggage Section were wounded, one man was killed and two horses became injured. At 11.20 a.m. the situation became clarified: the adversary had attacked and had been refused everywhere.

During the enemy drum fire on the morning of 20 July 1918 the 7/R111 occupied the northern edge of the Bois de Courton, the 6/R111 was subsequently on the right, and the 8/R111 filled the gap between the II/R111 and the I/71. At 10.00 a.m. the enemy broke forth by Marfaux-Espilly, however they flooded back again in the barrage fire of the German batteries. At 3.00 p.m. the II/R111 advanced in a counter thrust, where the 8/R111 moved to the wood edge of les Haies until in the heights of the lane leading from Paradis to Espilly. There the company met with the remnants of the I/116 and found out that the main opposition line had been taken by the enemy. During this time the 5th, 6th and 7/R111 advanced almost without losses until in the copse north of Espilly. The 6th Company then developed and advanced in waves against Hill 234, one kilometer east of Espilly. Lively machine gun fire struck into the advancing ranks, and the men were only able to overcome the open field by moving slowly forward in short rushes. The 8/R111 received orders, to take the northern edge of the Bois de Courton and to go through the wood and roll up Hill 234. The 7/R111 became inserted on the right next to the 8th Company.

Because there was no artillery support, the 2nd Machine Gun Company was ordered to suppress the enemy machine gun nests on Hill 234. At about 7.30 p.m. the enemy fire was noticeably lighter and the companies took advantage of this by advancing once more, and the first wave came on to Hill 234 almost unfired upon. At 8.10 p.m. the hill was in the possession of the battalion. The enemy on Hill 234 had been completely taken by surprise and after a short fire fight took flight to the rear. Soon after the taking possession of the hill the companies received machine gun fire from the right coming out of the Bois de Courton and from the left out of the direction of Marfaux.

Companies of IR 32, which were to advance on the right of the II/R111 were not successful in advancing into the Bois de Courton, and also all connections on the left of the battalion were missing. Without this support the ground that had been gained could not be held and the II/R111 received the order to move back to the exit position in the line of the Paradis-Marfaux lane. After a severe fire raid the British reoccupied the hill on the night.

On 20 July 1918 the I/R109 was ordered to work on the construction of masking screens along the Cuisles–Baslieux-Coucherty and Olizy–Violaaine roads. This order could not be implemented; because uncommonly strong enemy artillery fire was placed upon the length and breadth of the position in the morning. Then at 9.15 a.m. the I and II/R109 were alarmed and were given orders at 10.00 a.m. to become placed in readiness on the right and on the left of a glade in the Bois de la Cohette, the II/R109 remained with *Jäger* Regiment 6.

At 11.30 a.m. the III/R109 was sent at the quick march via Baslieux to Jonquery where it occupied the eastern edge of the Bois de le Cohette and it stood under the command of the 41st Infantry Brigade as the reserve of the OHL. The enemy had attacked the left neighboring division, where he was repulsed. The stay by the III/R109 in the Bois de la Cohette brought heavy losses, because the entire wood lay continuously under searching fire by the enemy artillery.

On the afternoon the RIR 109 returned to the 28th Reserve Division. The regimental staff and the I/R109 moved via Baslieux-Cuisles-Jonquery–Ville-en-Tardenois to the stone bridge two kilometers southeast of Lhéry. The III/R109 received the same march goal in the wood of Cohette. While marching back *Leutnants* Gushurst, Losch and Kaucher and nine men were wounded by enemy fire. The III/R109 was covered in bombs dropped from enemy bomber squadrons twice on the march, however without suffering losses.

Because of the unusually high losses amongst the officers *Leutnant* Rapp took over the 9/R109 for *Leutnant* Gushurst, *Leutnant* Hartwig took over the 12/R109 for *Leutnant* Losch, *Feldwebel Leutnant* Hagge took over the Communications platoon of the III/R109 for *Leutnant* Kaucher; *Leutnant* Grüttner took over the 1/R109 for the sick *Leutnant* Duss, *Leutnant* Aha took over the 7/R109 for the sick *Leutnant* Seufert and *Leutnant* Werver Hoffmann took over the 1MG/R109. Through orders from AOK dated 15 July 1918, *Rittmeister* Auer von Herrenkirchen was promoted to Major, *Vizefeldwebels* Hoppe, Annen and *Offizier Stellvertreter* Kaucher were promoted to *Leutnants*.

On the evening of 20 July 1918 the II and III/R110, without the 6/R110, and the 2nd and 3MG/R110 moved into the wood between Bois de la Cohette and Champlat as the division reserve. The machine gun companies became inserted for the defense of the intermediate field between the main opposition line and the artillery protection position. The new position was a horrible place according to the men: 'It is terrible in this wood! The dark, sparse trench pieces, earth holes, no dugouts! And also the continuous strong disturbance fire that was doubly unpleasant in the wood.' The enemy also attempted an attack on the 21st by the left neighboring division, however still without any success.

On 21 July 1918 the 10/R110 relieved the men from *Pionier* Battalion 26 in the wood northeast of La Neuville. The remaining companies of the II and III/R110 worked on the extension of the artillery protection position at the southern edge of the Bois de la Cohette under the guidance of the *pionier* commanders. The work proceeded slowly, because Cohette wood lay constantly under enemy disturbance fire.

On the night of 21/22 July 1918 the 12th Bavarian Infantry Division placed Bavarian IR 27 on the left of the division sector, and shifted the I/R110 as well. The 3/R110 became transferred into the wood piece forward of the 2/R110. Following the extension of the main opposition line, the company occupied the position from the Orcourt Grand Pr, road until la Fortelle. The 4/R110 moved into the wood south of the road by La Fortelle and there relieved a *Jäger* Company. The 2nd, 3rd and 4/R110 and battalion staff was the support for Bavarian IR 26. The 6/R110 under *Leutnant der Reserve* Deckert, which until this point was the regimental reserve, moved into the *Franzosen Graben* in place of the 3/R110. The 1st and 6/R110 became subordinate to Bavarian IR 27 as the support companies. Four machine guns of the 1MG/R110 were put in into the Intermediate field according to orders from Bavarian IR 26:

> No infantry attacks take place up to 25 July inclusive. Nevertheless, it is not agreeable in the positions. In fact, what concerned us was if Orcourt, Cuchery and the artillery position lay under heavy fire! However then the enemy particularly bombarded the wood at La Fortelle on the Orcourt-Grand Pr, road and the *Franzosen Graben* in a frightful manner. It becomes especially active, if something was going on at the right or on the left, then the Frog also becomes nervous by us.
> *Hauptmann von* Zeddelmann, I/R110.[5]

On 22 July 1918 the companies became accommodated in the old position of Bavarian IR 27 and 28 in the wood south of the Jonquery-Champlat road on orders of the division, but it was not any more pleasant there. The task given to RIR 110 was an Intervention unit, but all other possible uses became discussed with the leadership.

On the morning of 22 July 1918 a strong enemy attack came from the direction of Marfaux-southern tip of Reimser wood, and the commander of RIR 111 received the order, to march forward with the III/R111 to Cohedon, to take command over the I/R111 located there and become placed in readiness as the connecting regiment between the 7th and 1st Armies. On the night of 23/24 July 1918 the 2nd and 3MG/R111 were replaced in the intermediate zone by the *Gebirgs* Machine Gun *Gruppe* 6 and returned to their respective battalions. The 10/R111 also returned to the III/R111 on the 24th.

The II/R111 was supposed to return to the regiment again on the night of 22 July 1918; however it could not move off because the relief still had not arrived. It was not until the evening of the 22nd when two battalions from IR 32 moved up, and the II/R111 received a readiness position in the *Hecken Schlucht* east of Nappes. The area however was so narrow that the 5th and 6th Companies with the *Minenwerfer* platoon and parts of the machine gun company moved in the copse north of Espilly.

The 5th and 6/R111 suffered losses on the morning of 23 July 1918 through German barrage fire, which was replying to the drum fire of the adversary. Under the protection of the artillery fire enemy skirmishers advanced behind tanks, which could be successfully stopped by *Minenwerfer* fire and machine guns using *K-Munition*. Meanwhile the adversaries successfully pressed forward in the Ardre ground until Marfaux and in the copse southeast of it. A counterattack that had already been ordered had to be cancelled as the two companies, the 7th and 8/R111 consisted of only 60 rifles.

By daybreak of the 23rd the III/R111 stood at the southeastern edge of the Bois d'Eclisse, north of Cohedon and the I/R111 stood at the wood edge north of the village. The battalions were not required to participate in the defense, because the battle line refused the enemy attack. The entire sector lay under heavy fire, and the situation was uncertain. *Leutnant* Gorgel of the III/R111 explored the forward line and came to the conclusion that Marfaux had probably fallen into enemy hands, otherwise the attacks, executed with support of tanks, had all been refused. The companies were often forced to change their locations because of the violent fire raids, and found meager protection in old earthen holes in the wood.

On 24 July 1918 the I/R111 became moved forward at the wood edge east of Cohedon and there established a connection with the parts of IR 32 standing by Nappes. The battalion remained in these positions until to the night of the 26th. On the night to 24 July 1918 the II/R111 protected the left flank of IR 32 in a position that stretched north of Espilly via Nappes until at the northeast corner of the Bois de Courton. The battalion remained here until the night of 26/27 July 1918.

While the enemy artillery covered the positions with frequent fire raids, the infantry only attempted partial attacks by the afternoon of the 24th in the Bois de Courton. On this day the 2MG/R111 shot down an enemy aircraft. The II/R111 then received orders on 25 July 1918 to march off to a rearward position. Then, on the 25th, at 11.00 p.m., the following message from the 12th Bavarian Division: 'On 22 July the 28th Reserve Division became the *Eingreifdivision* behind the left wing of Corps Schmettow in the area of Lhéry–Ville en Tardenois–Les Malades Farm.'

17 July 1918 had been the last day of the German offensive on both sides of Reims; any further attacks planned by the 7th and 1st Armies against the Reims salient were no longer possible because of the start of the large French offensive on 18 July 1918. The Marne in 1918, as in the autumn of 1914, was a fateful river for the Germans.

In addition to the constant Allied attacks, the enemy fire barriers also prevented any further German attacks. The enemy could concentrate his forces quickly using the extensive rail system behind the front while the Germans were forced to move large bodies of troops by foot. Squadrons of enemy aircraft spread death and destruction with bombs and machine gun fire in the German lines and the rear supply depots day and night, which did not allow for any rest. Every enemy attack began with waves of tanks, which bewildered the German infantry and provided encouragement and relief to the enemy forces. The German troops could no longer withstand the ever increasing enemy's strength, materials, weapons, etc. which appeared to double in size from day to day. On the German side, the problems with supplying adequate ammunition, food, etc. to the men was increasingly difficult. The supplies must be managed with trucks or horse drawn wagons on bad, almost impassable roads.

The earlier intent by the OHL, to thrust forward in the terrain west of Reims, had failed, and it must be recognized that with the strong enemy resistance a successful breakthrough was no longer to be expected. On the other hand the German opposition with the weakened and tired troops in undeveloped positions and in the unfavorable terrain against enemy attacks; was chaotic. The leadership therefore had been forced to take back the attack divisions into prepared rearward positions. Considering all of these circumstances, the OHL finally made the decision to withdraw from the Marne front and go back to the Vesle Line.

The losses among the regiments of the 28th Reserve Division had been high. As an example, the total losses in RIR 109 from 16 to 23 July 1918 were one *Offizier Stellvertreter* and 16 men killed, three officers, one *Offizier Stellvertreter* and 99 men wounded, of which five of these men were also missing. While seemingly small, these losses actually represented a large percentage of the existing regimental battle strength. Many of the companies consisted of some 25-30 men or less.

At 11.00 p.m. on 25 July 1918 the following orders were issued to RIR 110 from the 12th Bavarian Division:

> Tonight the III/R110 would shift via Ville-en-Tardenois West in the hollow 400 meters south of Aulnay Farm, where it will receive further orders from the 28th Reserve Division. In the remaining the task for the other parts of the regimental staff and II/R110 remain unchanged.[6]

The III Battalion immediately moved off and late on 25 July 1918 the majority of the three regiments of the 28th Reserve Division were reunited once again and were engaged with the extension of a new position by Ville-en-Tardenois and Chambrecy. Group Schmettow held the *Dora Stellung* at this time, occupying it from the right to the left with the 196th Infantry Division, 22nd Infantry Division and 28th Reserve Division.

RIR 111 was assigned to the middle sector of the division east of Ville-en-Tardenois. Two battalions occupied the battle line, with one company from each battalion positioned in the foreground at the small railway line running from Sarcy to Ville-en-Tardenois. The main opposition line on the hill south of the Breuille stream was occupied by two companies from each battalion with the fourth company of each battalion serving as the rear support in the grounds of Breuille stream. The Readiness battalion lay south and north of Aulnay Farm. On 26 July 1918 the III/R109 was in the line, on the left was the I/470 and on the right the II/R111.

The men from RIR 110 that were working in Cohette Wood were gradually becoming accustomed to this 'accursed wood'. However since 7.00 a.m. on 26 July 1918 the entire wood, particularly the artillery positions, came under extremely active artillery fire. The question on everyone's mind: Will the enemy attack?

At 9.45 a.m. orders arrived from the 12th Bavarian Infantry Division: 'The II/R110 was to immediately occupy the artillery protection position. The enemy has penetrated between the right and middle regiments. Connection with BIR 27 is to be established.' However a message soon arrives that the attack by the adversary, which involved infantry and tanks had been refused outright. The position regiments were still holding the line. On orders of the 22nd Bavarian Infantry Brigade, two companies, the 5th and 7/R110 become placed in possession of Bavarian IR 27.

On 26 July 1918 the enemy fire increased more and more on the I/R110 since 4.45 a.m. This was no longer the usual disturbance fire, this time it clearly indicated that an attack was about to take place. Dense smoke mixed with gas filled the hollows and valleys. At dawn barrage fire signals rose up from the ground at the front, however, the German guns did not open fire. The situation was confusing in the heavy fire and the limited visibility. It was possible that the batteries in the rear had failed to see the barrage signals due to the smoke and gas but there was also the sound of firing on the plateau on the left flank of the I/R110.

Suddenly, the company leader of the 6/R110 arrived at the battalion headquarters completely out of breath. He reported: 'The enemy had overrun the front line of the Bavarians with 6 tanks and strong infantry. He now sits in the *Franzosen Graben*.'

No one knew exactly what was happening at the front. Orders were issued only to be countermanded a short time later; there was confusion everywhere. The 2/R110 had been ordered to occupy the main opposition line during the fire preparation. When the 2nd Company arrived at the front the II/B26 advised that all was in order and independently waved them off to the left. Then the 3/R110 and two machine guns of the 1MG/R110 under *Leutnant der Reserve* Brand were placed in position for a counter thrust on the *Franzosen Graben* from the Orcourt-Grand Pr, road. Yet before the *Minenwerfer* could open fire, the 2nd and 3/R110 and a few men of the 6/R110 advanced on their own toward the enemy with shouts of hurrah.

The *Franzosen Graben* had been occupied by about 267 Frenchmen, who had been just carried to the front from Châlons on vehicles after a long period of rest. Following the fighting two of them become taken prisoner. *Leutnants der Reserve* Leist and Deckert also advanced against the position from the right, in order to free the *Kampf-Truppen-Kommandeur* of the I/B27 from the hands of the French as he had surrendered during the initial enemy attack. Now the French were invited to surrender and the situation had been restored, the enemy attack had failed.

The counterattack resulted in a number of losses for the I/R110: *Leutnant der Reserve* Brand, 1MG/R110, became severely wounded and died a few days later in the military hospital. *Leutnant der Reserve* Gallier and *Offizier Stellvertreter* Weber were wounded; *Offizier Stellvertreter* Ober was missing, four Other Ranks were killed, 20 were wounded and 27 were missing.

On the afternoon of 26 July 1918 the two battalions of RIR 110 that were still attached to the 12th Bavarian Division were given orders to retreat at 11.00 p.m. and the 1st, 3rd, 4th and 1MG/R110 marched off. At 11.15 p.m. the battalion staff and 2/

R110 marched out of the position. The battalions of Bavarian Infantry Regiment 26 evacuated the position after midnight; however each battalion left behind one light machine gun group in the position under the command of an officer until 2.00 a.m., which would deceive the adversary by firing light balls and with small arms fire. The men of RIR 110 were confused as they had not contemplated a retreat after they had recently refused French advances so brilliantly.

At 2.00 a.m. the security patrols also moved back to the rearguard positions in the line Cuisles-Champlat, and then at 3.00 a.m. went back further into the main opposition line. The outpost line was to be occupied by powerful fighting pickets and machine gun nests, which would pay special attention to the river valley between Chambrecy and Sercy. The battalion battle headquarters of RIR 109 was located in the hollow de la Breuille, while the regimental battle headquarters was on the slope of the hill north of Malades Farm. The brigade headquarters was in Coémy, the division battle headquarters was on the Sercy et Prin–Vandeuil Road.

The men were engaged in creating a strong position within the available time and manpower limitations. Wire obstacles were installed, rudimentary trenches were created, the extension of available shelters, exposed fields of fire, the installation of sentry and observation posts, machine gun nests, *Minenwerfer* and *Granatwerfer* positions. Everything possible was being done in order to make the *Dora Stellung* as defensible as possible.

The former positions became evacuated without being disturbed by the enemy, who had apparently been completely deceived by the retreat. However, not everyone in RIR 110 had been informed of the withdrawal. On the morning of 27 July 1918 two men from the I/R110, who had transported French prisoners back during the night, were returning to the former position again in the morning and it was fortunate that the French had still not advanced into the abandoned German defenses. Once the men realized they were completely alone, they quickly packed up their equipment and safely returned to the battalion.

While disengagement from the enemy had been relatively simple, the retreat to the new position was extremely disquieting. The companies of the I/R110 marched individually to Jonquery, where the battalion was assembled. When the battalion staff of the I/R110, as the last part of the regiment to pass Cuchery, a doctor standing in front of the medical dugout advised them that there was a severely wounded regimental comrade still lying in the cellar. There was no thought of leaving the man behind so the staff carried him back on a stretcher.

With every man on the staff being heavily loaded with equipment, it made it difficult to transport the wounded man. The staff, including officers, alternated carrying the stretcher and so they finally reached Jonquery in the streaming rain and soft ground through the thick wood. Upon reaching the village the wounded man could be transported on a wagon taken from one of the regimental columns.

The II/R110, which now included the 6/R110 that had returned, along with the *Gebirgs* Machine Gun Group 6 had taken up a reception position at the southern edge of Cohette wood under the command of Major von Schmeling, which covered the withdrawal until 3.00 a.m. before rejoining the regiment. The I and III/R110 had marched via Jonquery through Ville-en-Tardenois that was lying under enemy artillery fire. The II/R110 received a position beside the III/R110 in the Breuille hollow, 400 meters south of Aulnay Farm. when the I/R110 arrived in Aulnay Wood northwest of Aulnay Farm the rain was streaming down and in these miserable conditions the men set up a bivouac.

The I/R110 had moved back under the control of the regiment again and under the orders of the 28th Reserve Division which was fortunate as the regiment had been reduced in strength considerably in the past two weeks. The losses of the regiment from 14 until 27 July 1918 was 436 men killed, wounded and missing including 96 men sick in hospital.

The III/R110 was positioned on the right with the 12th Company in the western most part of Ville-en-Tardenois, with the 9th and 11th Companies at the reverse slope of the hill 800 meters north of the village, the battalion staff and the 10th Company as the readiness company in the Breuille valley. The II/R110 was inserted on the left of the III/R110; from which the 9th Company established a connection to the 2/83. The I/R110 moved forward from Aulnay wood into the Breuille ground as the Readiness battalion on the night from 27 to 28 July 1918. The regimental staff lay in the Malade Farm east of Lhéry.

The men of the 28th Reserve Division had barely become acquainted with the new position when by daybreak on the 28th powerful enemy artillery fire started to fall across the division sector, particularly on the village of Bligny. Observation and bomber squadrons appeared above the division sector and at 11.30 a.m. the enemy attacked the position of RIR 109 with approximately one company; however the attack became suffocated in artillery and *Minenwerfer* fire. Afterward, in the afternoon, the rear terrain became covered with severe artillery fire and the enemy attacked the positions of RIR 109 again towards evening with approximately one battalion. However, the enemy suffered such considerable losses through machine gun, artillery and *Minenwerfer* fire that the attack soon hesitated and the outpost position remained in German hands.

Following the disastrous enemy attacks, patrols from the 9/R109 pressed forward until they were by the southern edge of Chambrecy and there captured a man of the 7th Gordon Highlanders and a captain of the British 153rd Infantry Brigade. The enemy on the following day renewed attacks against the left sector only to be repulsed there as well.

The enemy did not make any attempts to follow the withdrawal and cross the Romigny –Ville-en-Tardenois Road by RIR 110 until early on the 29th. When the enemy did advance, they ended up in flanking machine gun fire from the 12/R110 and 3MG/R110, so that he was not able to advance any further. The opponents did not succeed in attempts to advance on 30 and 31 July 1918 for the same reasons.

At 10.00 p.m. on 31 July 1918 the I/R110 was transferred to the steep hillside in the vicinity of Malade Farm. With this move, the further withdrawal into the *Egon Stellung* on the Ardre stream had begun. The II/R110 took on the forward line of the entire regimental sector on 31 July as the KTK. Furthermore, four machine guns each from the 2nd and 3MG/R110 were employed in the forward line under *Leutnant der Reserve* Schwerberger. The III/R110 became the Readiness battalion in the Breuille valley.

Very little took place on 1 August 1918 other than reconnaissance patrols by the company leaders of the outpost position by Château Prin and Serzy in the morning. Then, at 10.00 p.m., the I/R110 withdrew via Coemy in the Ardre valley and once there occupied the outpost position: the 4/R110 protected the sector from the Château Prin-Brouillet Road until Coemy exclusive and the 3/R110 from Coemy until the Ardre stream. On the right there was a connection to the 8/R116, on the left to the 11/R111. The 2/R110 was distributed in the area between the railroad from Serzy-Savigny and the Serzy-Savigny Road. The outpost commander and the 1/R110 were at the eastern exit of Serzy-et Prin.

The 1MG/R110 was positioned in nests between the Ardre and the main opposition line, which ran from the southern edge of Serzy on the slope to the Savigny-Jonchery Road. The regimental staff of RIR 110 moved into the copse south of Vandeuil. All of the dispositions of the units were finished by 12 midnight.

The III/R110 protected the retreat in rearguard positions at Malade Farm until 3.00 a.m. By 3.30 a.m. the II/R110 was located in the outpost line. This only left *Leutnant der Reserve* Holzinger with the 12/R110 and a few men from the 5/R110 in the forward position. For two hours they deceived the enemy through light balls and small arms fire and then followed the battalion without being molested by the enemy. The II and III/R110 and the rearguard under *Leutnant der Reserve* Holzinger reached their assembly points in the hollow one kilometer north of Serzy at approximately 5.00 a.m. The retreat into the *Egon Stellung* was successful and without the loss of men or equipment. Then, on the night, artillery fire lay on Château Prin, in the wood pieces nearby and upon the Savigny–Serzy Road.

At 11.00 a.m. on 2 August 1918 the bridge across the Ardre stream was blown up by the 1/*Pionier* Battalion 16. Towards midday the enemy was observed advancing upon Coemy from the hill by Malade Farm and soon infantry and cavalry patrols pushed forward until they were in the Ardre valley and began to make contact with the outpost guards. On the evening of the 2nd enemy sentries lay close in front of the division outpost line. The German artillery fired proficiently, unfortunately too short at times, which resulted in a number of losses. The sector of the 28th Reserve Division was now occupied with RIR 109 on the left, RIR 111 in the center and RIR 110 on the right.

From the very start the *Egon Stellung* was only supposed to be an intermediate position. Already on the night from 2 to 3 August 1918 the withdrawal into the *Blücher Stellung* behind the Vesle took place. More space was needed between the opposing lines in order to prepare the defenses and in order to gain the necessary distance from the French and British forces, the Vesle was crossed over in the following night by way of Jonchery and the *Blücher Stellung* was occupied in the Bois de Goulot.

It was critical to hold the *Blücher Stellung* at all cost. Orders were issued that where the enemy pressed after and crossed the Vesle he was to be instantaneously thrown back across the river again. After the withdrawal into the *Blücher Stellung* was accomplished, the bridges over the Vesle were blown up by *pioniers* and the terrain between the Vesle and the main opposition line was covered with wire obstacles. There were almost no doubts that there would be crucial fighting in this new position.

On the evening of 2 August 1918, with the onset of darkness, the III/R110 marched via Vandeuil and took over the sector of the regiment north of the Vesle as the battle battalion from the railroad junction south of Montigny until le Goulet Château exclusive. As of 1.00 a.m. it received a readiness position east of Montigny.

At 1.00 a.m. the I/R110 took the outpost units out of the main opposition line and moved north of the Ardre. They succeeded in this completely unnoticed by the enemy and without losses. The battalion staff and the 1st Machine Gun Company occupied the main opposition line while *pioniers* blew up the cellars of Serzy, an exceptionally gruesome sight, as the villages of the Ardre valley went up in flames that could be seen far and wide. At 3.00 a.m. the battalion staff, 1st, 2nd and 1MG/R110 marched out of the main opposition line. The route taken: Vandeuil, Jonchery, Montigny, slope of the hill north l'Orme Farm where the I/R110 moved into the reserve position.

At 3.15 a.m. the 3rd and 4/R110 also moved out of the main opposition line, however the two companies remained on the southern bank of the Vesle on the Fismes–Reims Road where they had to repulse attacks from several strong enemy patrols. Two Officer patrols along with Other Ranks of the I/R110 under the command of officers of the II/R110 formed the rear guard. The two companies remained upon the southern Vesle bank until 6.00 p.m.; then they crossed over, because the neighboring connection troops were also going back on bridges over the Vesle, and then marched into the reserve position. Once everyone was across, the bridges and footbridges were blown up leaving the Vesle as a barrier between the Germans and the enemy. The retreat into the *Blücher Stellung* was successful.

The British cautiously followed the withdrawal at some points and rapidly at others. Already at 6.45 a.m. on 3 August 1918 an enemy cavalry patrol was sighted south of Jonchery and was fired at. At 8.15 a.m. enemy infantry advanced in a skirmish line, about two companies strong, out of the wood west of Branscourt and was brought to a stop through machine gun fire. At 11.00 a.m. an enemy cavalry detachment and smaller infantry detachments appeared again south of Vandeuil. By midday more enemy cavalry patrols and infantry skirmish lines suddenly appeared in the foreground and were taken under fire from which the 9/R109 succeeded in taking two prisoners from *Régiment d'Infanterie* 46.

On 3 August 1918 only two companies of the III/R111 still remained behind on the southern shore of the Vesle as the rearguard. One battalion of RIR 111 was in the *Blücher Stellung* as the Battle battalion, which was inserted at the small railway line leading past le Goulot Château. The Readiness battalion was close behind. The withdrawal action had lasted from 18 July to 3 August 1918, and was called a 'brilliant performance which involved leaders and troops' by General Ludendorff.

What did the men think about the withdrawal from position to position? No direct enemy pressure had been applied to the left wing of the 7th Army to force such a massive withdrawal and the men had been growing anxious about the reasons. After much discussion and conjecture it was finally decided that events taking place on other sectors of the front must be the direct cause of the evacuation of the Marne salient.

The formations of 7th Army, including the 28th Reserve Division, were admittedly tired and worn out from the events of the previous two months. Since 25 May 1918 the men did not have quarters that had a roof over them as protection against the weather. The requirements placed on the men in the attacks as well as in the defense placed great strain on their nerves and there were heavy losses, which were not fully replaced. Food was scarce, monotonous and supplies had been irregular. Despite all of these setbacks, the OHL still believed that after a period of rest, renewed attacks would give the German Government the freedom of bargaining a peace with the Allied countries.

RIR 110 manpower losses from 14 July to 3 August amounted to 57 *Unteroffiziere* and Other Ranks dead; 12 officers, 316 *Unteroffiziere* and Other Ranks wounded, one officer, 81 *Unteroffiziere* and Other Ranks missing; in total 461 men. While not the same numbers of losses experienced by the regiment on the Somme, the numbers were telling in that when compared to the overall regimental strength, they were in fact a higher percentage of the regiment than those suffered on the Somme in July and in October 1916.

The common themes found in the accounts listed above were of relatively small numbers of losses being seen as having a major impact on the effectiveness of the regiments of the 26th and 28th Reserve Divisions. We need to take a closer look at the overall situation that existed at that time in order to see the larger picture instead of just bits and pieces of the problem.

The constant concerns over the number of troops at the front, the number of troops needed on a monthly basis to make up normal losses and to expand the size of the army that had been plaguing the German High Command had finally come to a head.

The army was considered to be extremely exhausted after four years of war. The defensive fighting in 1917 and the 1918 German offensives had used all resources at its disposal. The rear guard actions that followed simply continued to sap the strength from the army. In looking at all of the details of the German positions, the losses the army had suffered, the food shortages at home and at the front and the constant pressure applied by the Allied armies, adequate numbers of men and critical supplies no longer existed.

The trench divisions had been left far too long in their defensive positions without relief and the men in these divisions were considered listless and unfit to cope with enemy attacks in the summer of 1918. Most of the divisions designated as attack divisions had suffered heavy losses in the different offensives and had lost most of their effectiveness.

German Army losses could no longer be replaced as before, even with taking steps such as reducing the number of regiments in each division or the 'accepted' strength of infantry battalions. Because of the critical shortages of men, 10 complete divisions were disbanded in August 1918 and the men were used to replace losses in other units.

Examination of Crown Prince Rupprecht's Army Group documents reveal calculations of troop strength were based on battalion 'field strength'. This included combat troops as well as the men being utilized for other duties, the sick and missing, stragglers and men on leave. Using such methods, the total number of men drawing rations was not an effective method of determining the fighting strength of the battalions.

Before the March 1918 offensive the official battalion strength was shown as 850 *Unteroffiziere* and men. This was in line with the actual battalion strength at the end of 1917 where the average field strength of a battalion was approximately 900 men. After deducting the sick, men on leave, seconded, etc. the average fighting strength of the battalions on the western front was about 640 men. Other than the Class of 1899 the only other men available as replacements were men discharged from hospital and those transferred from the eastern front. This situation required 'making the most economical use of the available manpower' by the Supreme Command.

The new face of warfare: Air raid damage to street in Stuttgart. (Author's collection)

At the beginning of 1918 the first recruits from the Class of 1899 were sent to the front. 26,350 men were sent in January and February with the goal of sending them to the front in March 1918 after completing their training. Despite all efforts, there were insufficient replacements for all of the divisions that desperately needed them so the bulk of available men were sent to the divisions participating in the attacks.

In April 1918 several cavalry divisions were disbanded and the men were distributed among other divisions. In May two infantry divisions were disbanded and also distributed among other divisions. Even with these drastic actions the gap between the number of replacements needed and those supplied continued to expand and the army could not completely replace the men lost in April and May from the offensive at Armentieres and even the attack divisions could not be brought up to full strength.

The average field strength of a battalion at the end of February 1918 had been 807 men, by the end of May it had been reduced to 692 men. Almost all replacements in the following months were sent to the divisions involved in the Hagen operation. Trench divisions received no replacements for the most part and grew weaker and more exhausted holding their positions. Crown Prince Rupprecht's Army Group suffered heavy losses in May, June and July. At the end of July the Supreme Command was compelled to reduce the official field strength of battalions on the western front from 850 men down to 700 men.

It was quickly determined that even this reduction could not be met and further attempts were made to locate additional replacements. Approximately 60,000 men were withdrawn from the Quartermaster-General service, the Chief of the Field Railways, the Chief of the Motor Transport and the Air Force. Services on the Line of

Communications were limited, *Landsturm* Battalion strength was reduced even further and convalescent sections were decreased.

Re-examination commissions combed Germany and the lines of communication for all men, who until then were considered unfit for front line service and designated in the following categories:

> 'Gv.' *Garnisonsverwendungsfähig* = Suitable for garrison employment.
> 'G.V.E.' *Garnisonsverwendungsfähig im Etappen gebiet* = Fit for duty on the Line of Communications.
> 'G.V.F.' *Garnisonsverwendungsfähig im Felde* = Fit for duty with regimental transport, etc.
> 'G.V.H.' *Garnisonsverwendungsfähig in der Heimat* = Fit for garrison duty in Germany.
> 'K.f.b.Z.' *Kriegsverwendungsfähig für besondere Zwecke* = Fit for active service in certain capacities.

Following cursory examination, many of the men formerly considered unfit for front line duty were designated as 'KV' *Kriegsverwendungsfähig* = Fit for Active Service.

Other divisions were disbanded during the following months which still did not meet the ever increasing demand for men. In addition, with the transfer of so many men that had been working behind the front there were critical delays in providing everything from food to ammunition to the front line troops. Also, the inferior quality of men (physically) and the inexperience (lack of training) at the front and in the recruit depots created even more difficulties for the army command.

The drain on available manpower strength continued to grow despite all of the measures just mentioned. In August 1918 the average field strength of the battalions in the army group was between 660 and 665 men. In reality, the actual combat strength of the battalions was far less, especially with the trench divisions. What was hidden among the 'official' numbers were still the men in hospital, on the sick list, on leave, and seconded. For three months the 'field strength' also included the names of the missing men, whose numbers increased daily during the summer months. As a result, the actual fighting strength of the divisions that had been at the front for a long time was considerably lower than the reported field strength. This was the situation facing the German Army as the men of the 28th Reserve Division took up positions behind the Vesle.

The natural obstacle in front of the troops in the *Blücher Stellung* was the Vesle. It was not very wide and it had marshy banks, which were covered with dense shrubbery. Approximately 200 meters distance from the river the terrain ascended gradually at first, then steeper. A strip of woods ran through the entire regimental sector of RIR 110, on average 500 meters wide, called the Bois de Goulet, which had glades and forest paths.

A single road led to Voisin Farm from Goulet Château on the left wing of RIR 110 in RIR 111's sector. The hillside then moved up the road from Goulet Château to the village of Montigny. North of this road and in the wood the French had placed massive ammunition depots. Railroad and Field railway tracks led to these storage places. The companies of RIR 110 now found shelter in the mined tunnels and huts formerly used by the French Ammunition workers. It was not the safest place to be considering the ever present danger of explosions if the nearby ammunition depots were set off, but they were better than nothing.

Battle Battalion III/R110 was directly east of Montigny; however it soon appeared advantageous to move three companies of this battalion to the northern edge of the wood on the hill by the KTK and move the fourth company of the Battle battalion into the ridge line. The reader must still remember that while companies, battalions and regiments are being discussed, the actual numbers of men involved are ridiculously small by early war standards.

The *Bereitschaft-Trupp-Kommandeur* (BTK) lay in a cellar at the eastern exit of Montigny, close to his four companies. The Rest battalion, I/R110 was accommodated at the northern slope of the hill north of L'Orme Farm however, later it was placed on the slope 700 meters south of the regimental battle headquarters in Voisin Farm.

In the early morning hours of 4 August 1918 the position of RIR 110 lay under heavy artillery fire, following which enemy detachments in the strength between 200 to 250 men advanced from the slope south of Jonchery. Additional enemy detachments were observed in the afternoon at the northern exit of Jonchery, which were taken under machine gun fire. It was evident that the enemy had already moved up to the Vesle.

On the night of 4/5 August 1918 an enemy patrol of about 20 men crossed the Vesle by the mill of Jonchery and attacked a picket detachment of the 5/R109 on the northern riverbank. The picket fired at the enemy with a light machine gun however, they were forced to move back into the main opposition line with the loss of one man dead and one man wounded. In the early morning of 5 August 1918 the enemy troops by the mill of Jonchery were thrown back across the Vesle by *Stosstrupps* of the 5th, 6th and 7/R109, leaving behind three dead.

In the early morning hours of the 5th individual enemy assault groups pressed forward over the Vesle and the railway embankment once again until they had reached the main opposition line inside the woods. Machine gun fire and the prompt deployment of well-placed barrage fire prevented the adversaries from making any further advances. Within a short time, a counterattack by the 10/R110 under *Leutnant der Reserve* Happel, the 11/R110 under *Leutnant der Reserve* Reich, the 12/R110 under *Leutnant der Reserve* Holzinger, in first line and the 6th and 8/R110 in the second line threw the enemy back across the Vesle.

A French machine gun was firmly established on astride the Jonchery–Montigny Road, one kilometer south of these villages. *Leutnant der Reserve* Holzinger ordered this machine gun nest to be taken under fire by *Vizefeldwebel* Lewineck, 3MG/R110, which forced the French to withdraw along with their light machine gun. *Leutnant der Reserve* Deckert, 6/R110 simultaneously attacked another enemy the nest from the north. Two additional groups stormed another machine gun nest where the French officer and two men were killed, 24 men were taken prisoner and two rapid loading guns were taken.

While this fighting had been taking place by RIR 109 and RIR 110, additional smaller enemy units had evaded sideways into the Wood of Goulot, therefore in the sector of RIR 111. In the face of this new threat, a counter thrust became scheduled for 10.30 a.m. on 5 August 1918, which managed to drive the French back over the

Vesle along with their machine guns. Given the ease in which the enemy had crossed the Vesle, the forward line now became occupied by all four companies of the Battle battalion, one placed next to another in a continuous line.

Following these attempts to negotiate the Vesle the enemy infantry stopped their reconnaissance advances by RIR 109. The opposing artillery became increasingly active so that in the time from 7 to 20 August 1918 RIR 109 suffered losses of eight men dead, two officers and 59 men wounded. On 17 August 1918 twenty nine replacements arrived from the *Ersatz* Battalion, far too few to make up the recent losses let alone those suffered in the previous months.

On 6 August 1918 the French attempted once more to gain a foothold upon the northern bank of the Vesle opposite RIR 110. At approximately 4.30 a.m. the French attacked with strong forces from *Régiments d'Infanterie* 46 and 89 from the French 10th Infantry Division. The sentries and patrols from RIR 110 moved back into the main opposition line in accordance with orders. Without encountering strong opposition, the enemy troops advanced until they were close in front of the main opposition line where they became held in place by machine gun, *Minenwerfer* and artillery barrage fire.

During this attack, there was a huge explosion in the German lines by RIR 110 when a stack of hand grenades had been hit and exploded all at once. Fortunately there were no losses among the men of RIR 110, but there was considerable confusion in the French ranks. The III/R110 took advantage of the situation and quickly formed a counterattack that was soon joined by the 7th and 8/R110. In the face of this counterattack the enemy moved back across the Vesle and left one officer, 67 men and several rapid loading guns in German hands. On the evening of 6 August 1918 the II/R110 relieved the III/R110 in the battle sector. The patrols sent out by the battalion encountered scattered enemy detachments in the foreground, they were quickly expelled, leaving behind two prisoners and a rapid loading gun.

Then, between 1.00 and 3.00 a.m. on 8 August 1918 more French patrols attempted to cross over the Vesle, they were quickly spotted and machine gun fire prevented them from making it across. After this last attempt, the French began to bombard the sector held by RIR 110 with artillery fire. All key points in the rear terrain were covered with powerful disturbance fire and strong fire raids. Among the men killed or wounded in the heavy fire was *Leutnant der Reserve* Schweigert who was severely wounded. During the bombardment of Bouvancourt on the night of 14/15 August 1918 *Leutnant der Reserve* Köhler, the Supply Officer of the regiment, was killed.

Finally, on the night from 19 to 20 August 1918 the battle battalion of RIR 110 became relieved by IR 357 from the 199th Infantry Division. The relief proceeded without incident and was completed at 2.00 a.m. The companies marched separately to the Bois de Gernicourt, where the battalion was assembled by the Baggage section of the train. The II/R110 in the reserve position was relieved by the 1st and 2/357, finally the I/R110 in the readiness position was relieved on the night from 21 to 22 August 1918 by the III/357.

On the night to 21 August 1918 the Battle and Readiness battalions of RIR 109 were relieved by IR 114. The division was being shifted to another portion of the front and the men had to be in the area of La Malmaison and Lor on 21 August 1918 and ready to be loaded on trains. In accordance with orders all troops were allowed to rest until the division was scheduled to be transported on 23 August 1918.

The manpower shortage was reaching a critical point and this meant that changes were needed in the makeup of the German army units almost on a weekly basis. By the middle of August 1918 the Supreme Command decided that if the average field strength of the battalions was less than 650 men then the divisions would divide their battalions into three companies instead of the normal four. During the rest time, the RIR 109 received top secret orders which required the battalions to be formed using only three companies. The 4th, 8th and 12/R109 would be disbanded and the men distributed among the remaining companies. The *Feldwebels*, each one now listed as a clerk on the regimental establishment would be placed with the Baggage section of the train and in the 3rd, 7th and 11/R109.

During this time, the sector held by RIR 111 had been very quiet with very little battle activity in the regimental sector. Still, the previous days of fighting, the withdrawal and the long position time had placed considerable demands on the mental and physical strength of the troops. The health of the men had visibly deteriorated and there were losses from the bombardment of the position. On the last day in the current position, on 20 August 1918 the regiment lost 20 men from a gas bombardment.

Finally, on the night to 21 August 1918 RIR 111 became relieved and marched to the Plesnoy Wood *Lager* southeast of la Malmaison. Then, on the 23rd IR 109 was transported in four troop trains from the railway station Roberchamps and traveled via Asfeld, Rethel, Mohon, and Sedan to Marancourt and arrived there on the 24th.

After the relief of RIR 110 had taken place the battalions marched via Gernicourt-Berry-au-Bac. The men found that they were in the battle zone of the Nivelle offensive from 1917 and beyond the large Laon-Reims Road they could see the ruins of Craonne and behind it the Winterberg. The first destroyed French tanks still lay now as then in front of the regiment's old position and French prisoners were occupied repairing the roads. The regiment eventually marched to Plesnoy Farm, where the regiment was accommodated. The men were allowed to rest and have a good sleep up until 24 August 1918, during which time they were given no duties that would interrupt their relaxation.

The numerous reports by Group Headquarters and the General Headquarters about tank defense, infantry attacks, counterattacks etc. allowed the men to suspect that there had been a serious crisis at another position of the front. They later learned that 8 August, which had been a quiet day in the sector of the 28th Reserve Division, was to become known as the 'Black Day of the German Army.'

The British and French had advanced deep into the German position by the 2nd Army. It was considered to be the first crucial defeat of the German army in the field. Six days later there was the ominous Crown Council in Spa, at which there was the prospect of peace negotiations. The men of the 28th Reserve Division had not suspected anything of this as news of these events had not reached the men.

Manpower shortages continued to plague the 28th Reserve Division and on 23 August 1918 the battalions of RIR 110 also become formed from three companies, the fourth company of each battalion was disbanded and the Other Ranks divided among the remaining three. RIR 111 suffered the same fate as the other regiments of

The new face of warfare: Air raid damage to street in Stuttgart. (Author's collection)

the division at the same time when the 4th, 8th and 12/R111 were disbanded and the men were distributed to the other companies of the battalions. Replacement had been arriving from home but only very sparsely and could barely fill the gaps in the ranks of the companies, in which the absence of battle proven soldiers was made very noticeable.

On 24 and 25 August 1918 the battalions were loaded at the railway station Roberchamp Farm and transported via Sedan-Longuyon to Landres, in order to receive rest quarters. While in these billets the troops, as far as it was possible, were not begrudged the desperately necessary relaxation. The regiment remained in these quarters until 11 September 1918. During this time training was eagerly promoted, during which special attention was placed in tactics used to fight against enemy tanks.

While the men in RIR 109 had hoped for time to relax and recuperate, the quarters in Domremy were considered to be fair, while the same in Eton were considered very poor because the village consisted of only ruined houses. The housing in a forest camp was just moderate, especially because the large mass quarters, in which entire companies were packed together with poor illumination and piles of equipment lying about, one next to the other.

In order to improve the housing, part of the rest time had to be used to work on the quarters, something the men were not unfamiliar with. Also, immediately after arriving in the rest quarters the entire regiment was to be newly equipped. The clothing had been available in crates for a long time; however there was never enough time to distribute it to the men so that the regiment gradually took on a very ragged appearance. After a few days of complete rest, the normal duties and fatigues associated with periods of rest began once again.

This was the first time in a very long time that the men of RIR 110 were accommodated in proper houses. They were able to wash, undress, become deloused; many even had good luck and could sleep in real beds. Regardless of where they were staying, the men were allowed to sleep undisturbed.

During this time, the companies gradually become melded together with the new replacements. There were sports and gymnastic games on a daily basis, there were lessons about tank defense and taking machine gun nests. There was the important gas room used to test gas masks, target practice and finally battle practices were held in small and larger associations. The regimental *Nachrichten* Company became disbanded and was replaced by a regimental and three battalion communication platoons. The regiments gradually became combat ready for deployment again.

The idyllic time was coming to an end as events on the front demanded the participation of every available unit. On 4 September 1918 the regimental and battalion leaders of RIR 109 were transported into the sector of Division Damloup, because of an enemy attack and the possibility of using the 28th Reserve Division as a sector reserve to assist in the defense had been considered. Fortunately, the front stabilized and the division was not required.

The needs for replacements continued to grow at a frightening rate and in addition to the steps already being taken to provide new men, veteran units in the army continued to be disbanded and the men and equipment released were being used to fill up the gaps in the infantry battalions. During this rest period two officers, 65 *Unteroffiziere* and Other Ranks and 18 horses from the disbanded *Minenwerfer* Company 228 arrived at RIR 109 with their throwers to become the *Minenwerfer* Company of the regiment and were distributed in the III/R109.

Finally, on 12 September 1918 the rest period was over and the division came under orders to move to the front by Verdun once again. The orders specified that the division would be held ready to march at a moment's notice as the enemy had attacked by Army *Abteilung* C in front of Verdun. The 28th Reserve Division was ready to march by 10.00 a.m. but as usual, the men had to wait in line for the order to move forward. Finally, at 7.00 p.m., the order arrived and the regiments marched toward the Bois de Rouvres.

The division arrived at the Bois de Rouvres late in the evening and was supposed to be accommodated in a camp located in the wood. However, the camp was already overcrowded by the time the regiments arrived and they were forced to bivouac at the western edge of the forest. Once in position several regiments were placed at the ready on the right and on the left of the Eton–Rouvres Wood Road. An old acquaintance of the division also arrived at the Bois de Rouvres at this time, the men of RIR 40. It had been almost 30 months since RIR 40 had left the 28th Reserve Division and it now appeared that they were to be reunited once again.

The arrival of RIR 40 was one more indication that the shortage of replacements had apparently reached a critical point. The three regiments of the 28th Reserve Division; RIR 109, RIR 110 and RIR 111 were all far understrength despite receiving new replacements. Part of the problem was solved when on 19 September 1918 a large number of replacement troops arrived in the division from the recently disbanded regiment, RIR 40.[7]

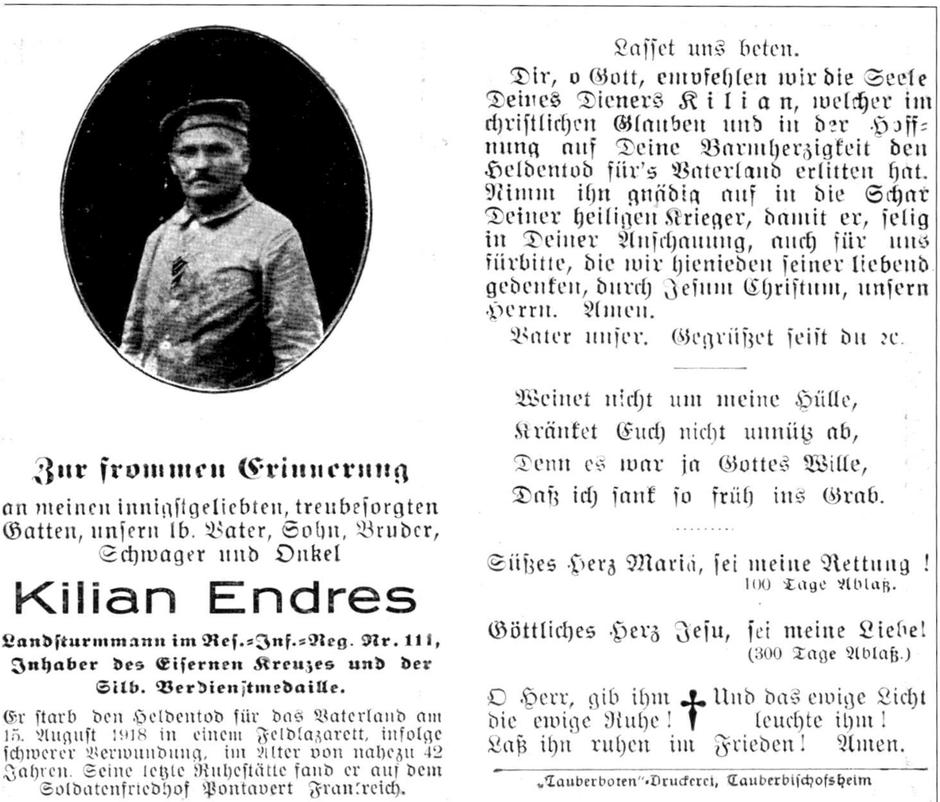

Zur frommen Erinnerung
an meinen innigstgeliebten, treubesorgten
Gatten, unsern lb. Vater, Sohn, Bruder,
Schwager und Onkel

Kilian Endres

**Landsturmmann im Res.-Inf.-Reg. Nr. 111,
Inhaber des Eisernen Kreuzes und der
Silb. Verdienstmedaille.**

Er starb den Heldentod für das Vaterland am 15. August 1918 in einem Feldlazarett, infolge schwerer Verwundung, im Alter von nahezu 42 Jahren. Seine letzte Ruhestätte fand er auf dem Soldatenfriedhof Pontavert Frankreich.

Lasset uns beten.

Dir, o Gott, emvfehlen wir die Seele Deines Dieners Kilian, welcher im christlichen Glauben und in der Hoffnung auf Deine Barmherzigkeit den Heldentod für's Vaterland erlitten hat. Nimm ihn gnädig auf in die Schar Deiner heiligen Krieger, damit er, selig in Deiner Anschauung, auch für uns fürbitte, die wir hienieden seiner liebend gedenken, durch Jesum Christum, unsern Herrn. Amen.

Vater unser. Gegrüßet seist du 2c.

Weinet nicht um meine Hülle,
Kränket Euch nicht unnütz ab,
Denn es war ja Gottes Wille,
Daß ich sank so früh ins Grab.

Süßes Herz Mariä, sei meine Rettung!
100 Tage Ablaß.

Göttliches Herz Jesu, sei meine Liebe!
(300 Tage Ablaß.)

O Herr, gib ihm die ewige Ruhe! Und das ewige Licht leuchte ihm!
Laß ihn ruhen im Frieden! Amen.

„Tauberboten"-Druckerei, Tauberbischofsheim

Memorial card for Landsturmmann Kilian Endres, RIR 111. (Author's collection)

However, the men who were returning to the 28th Reserve Division were not the same men who had left several years earlier. Most of the veteran soldiers of RIR 40 had been killed, wounded, fallen ill or captured in the fighting on the western and eastern fronts. The men who survived were for the most part untrained soldiers with little or no combat experience. Several months earlier, on the morning of 18 July 1918, RIR 40 had a combat strength of 35 officers and 902 *Unteroffiziere* and Other Ranks. The regiment was engaged in heavy fighting on this date defending the line against a French attack. By the evening of the same day the regimental combat strength was 23 officers and 264 *Unteroffiziere* and Other Ranks, barely the size of a single company by 1914 standards and a regiment in name only.

At the end of September orders were issued by the OHL that if the field strength of a battalion decreased to below 400 men the infantry regiments were to be divided into two battalions instead of the normal three. By the middle of September fifteen divisions had been reformed utilizing this new standard. By taking the surplus men from these divisions and all fit or reasonably fit men combed out from the rear areas, industry and garrison duty the average field strength of the battalions in Crown Prince Rupprecht's army reached 594 men at the end of September.

The Class of 1900 had been called up far earlier than normal, about 300,000 men, in June. These men would reach the recruit depots in the field by September and October 1918. Additional men arrived during this time from the eastern front. However, many of these men had been prisoners of the Russians and were infected with Bolshevism and of little actual value in the fighting in the west.

The men taken from well-paid jobs in German industry were less than eager to face the dangers of combat for far less money. Also, many of them were infected with anti-war sentiments and the lack of experience proved to be more of a drain on the system than a help with higher sick and desertion rates. Men who had been employed in various rear echelon areas were simply physically unfit to be in combat as it existed in 1918.

In the weeks and months that followed the disastrous day of fighting on 18 July 1918 RIR 40 had received drafts of replacements in an attempt to fill up the depleted ranks. Many of these 'men' were young boys, barely 19 years old. Others were returning wounded who had not yet fully healed from their injuries or were men who had been combed out of German industries and rear echelon units and had little interest in becoming involved in combat. Even with the arrival of replacements RIR 40 was considered unfit for major combat.

The decision had been made to eliminate RIR 40 and it was decided to take the remaining officers and men and distribute them to the three regiments of the 28th Reserve Division. RIR 40 received the division order at 6.00 p.m. on 10 September 1918:

> The regiment will separate out of the division and become moved to the 28th Reserve Division.
>
> It is with sincere regret that I take my parting of the trusted unit that had belonged since the formation of the division and had its full share in the glory. I thank RIR 40 in place of the absent division commander for the outstanding services that it has afforded the division. An honorable memory of the regiment by those who belong to it and in the history of the 115th Infantry Division is certain for all time.
>
> Our heartiest wishes for the future follow the departing comrades. I hope RIR 40 is privileged to also preserve its old reputation in the new association and in the accustomed excellent manner contribute to the success of our cause.
>
> Signed, *von* Hahnke.[8]

Throughout 11 to 13 September 1918 the individual battalions and the regimental staff were relieved and marched into the billeting area that had become available with the recent departure of IR 173. In the middle of the relief there was the possibility that an enemy counterattack would take place. Accordingly, the machine guns and the *Minenwerfer* crews of RIR 40 remained in the position one day further and in addition the relieved troops were retained in elevated battle readiness and assigned alarm places. Once the danger was over, the regiment traveled via Stenay, Montmédy, Longuyon to Nouillon, from where it marched to the Rouvres *Wald Lager*.

On 13 September 1918 the 28th Reserve Division was placed on alert and moved into the sector of the 8th *Landwehr* Division as support because statements made by prisoners indicated that an enemy attack would take place in the next day or two along the front line in the direction of Moranville-Blanzèe. RIR 109 occupied the *Ornes Riegel* about one kilometer southwest of Etain; RIR 110 was placed into the *Hagen Stellung*, one and a half kilometers west of Warcq, and RIR 111 was moved forward into the *Bois de Herméville*.

On the morning of the 13th the regimental staff of RIR 110, the I and III/R110 were accommodated in barracks, the II/R110 in the *Schwaben Lager*. The battalions were ready to march from 8.30 a.m. and at 10.30 a.m. the regiment, along with the 2/RFAR 29 as the escort battery, immediately advanced on the Rouvres-Etain Road. When the *Hagen Stellung* was reached, the I/R110 was positioned on the right, the II/R110 on the left and the III/R110 with the escort battery as the reserve were in concrete dugouts in Warcq. Etain lay under strong artillery fire and was avoided by the companies, and the impacts of the heavy shells reverberated horribly in the ruins of the village. At 6.00 p.m. the readiness position was occupied and the regimental staff lay at Hospital Farm west of Warcq.

On 13 September 1918 RIR 111 reached Buzy Gussain-Ville marching in small detachments because the route was under enemy observation at all times. By evening the battalions moved forward in a westerly direction in the wood of Herme-Ville because an enemy attack was expected on both sides of the Verdun–Etain Road. Once in position the regiment established a connection with LIR 109 lying in the battle line and on the night to the 14th became organized on both sides of the Herme–Ville-Braquis Road.

The Group reserve, to which the II and III/RFAR 29 belonged, was also assigned RIR 40 which still acted as an independent regiment and received the task on 14 September 1918 to intercept a possible enemy break-in by the 56th Reserve Infantry Brigade on the Orne and to counterattack if it was required. The approach routes to the *Volker Stellung* had to become explored in great haste.

On 14 September 1918 an enemy attack took place further south between Manheulles and Fresnes which then resulted in RIR 111 being placed at the ready with the I/R111 south of Braquis for a possible counterattack. It quickly became recognized that the regiment was not needed to intervene in the situation and the regiment received orders in the evening to be placed at the ready once again as the division reserve by Cussain-Ville.

The elevated alarm readiness concerned the fighting by St Mihiel where American troops employing tanks and gas drove a wedge into the *Schlauch Stellung*, making the position untenable thereby forcing a withdrawal as well as the loss of considerable quantities of material and men. The 'Yankees' stopped their advance on 14 September 1918 and dug in after sacrificing entire divisions in the fighting along the line Norroy–Rembercourt–Manheulles in front of the *Michel Stellung*. The main goal of the attack was apparently Metz along with Longuyon, an important railroad junction, which if lost would cut off the interior rail lines and needed to be prevented under all circumstances.

With the immediate concerns over the enemy attack ended, the planned relief of the 56th *Landwehr* Brigade in the sectors Hautecourt and Herméville could take place on the night to the 16th. RIR 109 occupied the right division sector on the National Road

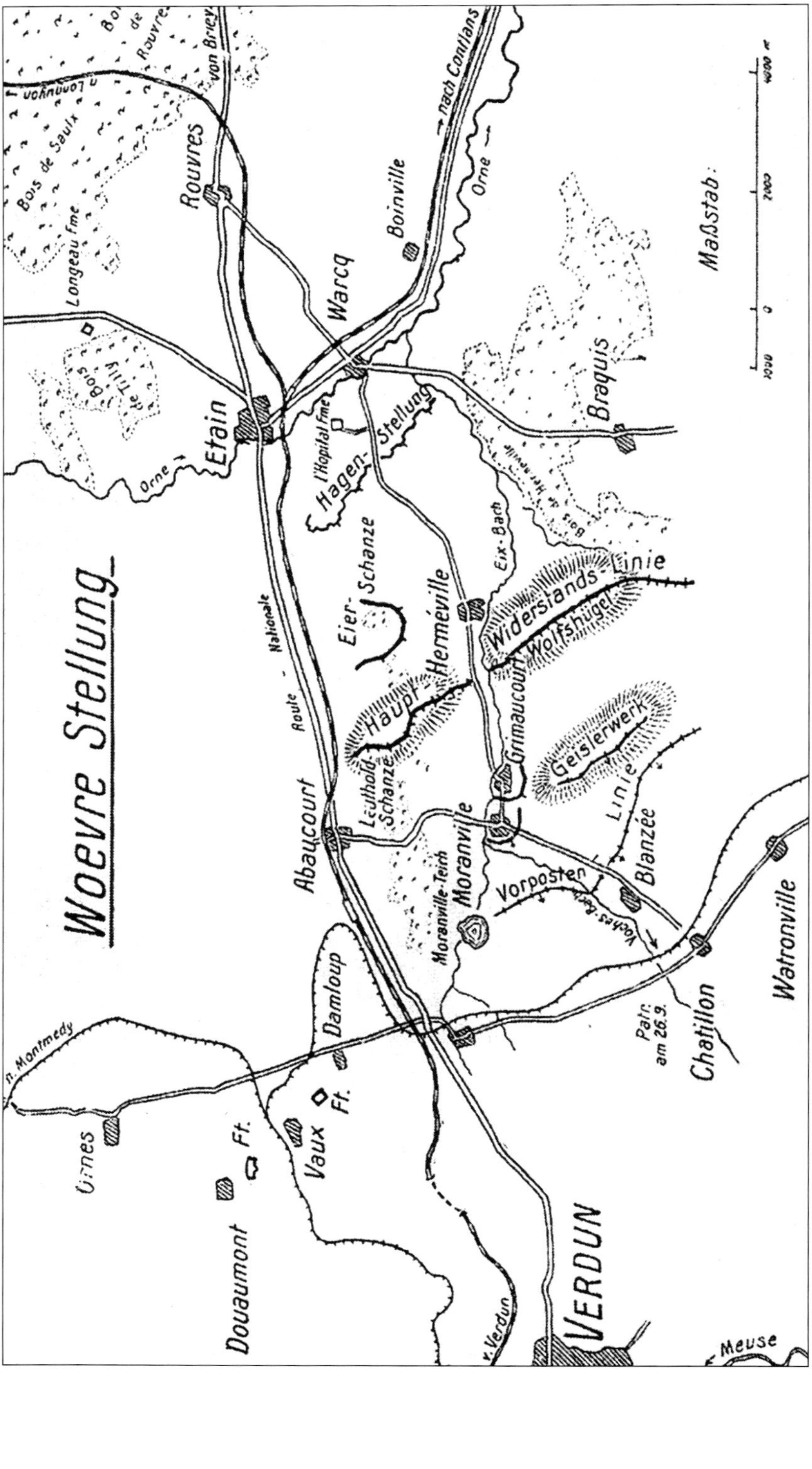

Woevre Stellung.

o Verdun with the III/R109 in the battle position, the II/R109 in the readiness position nd I/R109 in reserve in the *Ornes Riegel*.

The position *Ornes Riegel*-Etain had an outpost line several kilometers deep before the nemy line was reached. A large distance existed between the main opposition line and he outpost lines so it was necessary to provide reconnaissance sentries and patrols in the arge expanse in order to protect the regiment against a surprise breakthrough attempt.

On the night of 15 to 16 September 1918 RIR 110 took over the sector of *Landwehr* R 110. In the same night RIR 111 relieved *Landwehr* IR 109 from its position. The attle battalion, II/R111, occupied the main opposition line and the rest of the regi- nent remained in the French *Lager*. Two outpost companies of LIR 109 did not become elieved until the evening of the 17th.

The 16 of September 1918 was also the day when the *Hohenzollern Fusiliers* (Fusilier Regiment 40) arrived in the nearby Wettinger *Lager* in the Bois de Woupremont. This vas probably the only time during the war when so many related regiments were in such lose quarters as LIR 40 was also camped nearby. Everyone who wore the number 40 n his shoulder strap, Active, Reserve and *Landwehr* units, were enclosed together for a hort time in a small area.

Sixteenth September 1918 was also the day when RIR 40 ceased to exist as an inde- endent regiment. The amended division order from the 28th Reserve Division dated 15 September observed:

> This is an amended order. Originally the II/R40 was to join RIR 110 and the III/ R40 would join RIR 109: The battalions of RIR 40 were now divided as follows: I/R40 with 1st Machine Gun Company to the RIR 111, II/R40 with the 2nd Machine Gun Company to RIR 109, III/R40 with 3rd Machine Gun Company to RIR 110.[9]

This order required a rearrangement of the existing regiments in the 28th Reserve Division and as such one battalion each from RIR 109, 110 and 111 was ordered to be dissolved and the men reassigned to the remaining two battalions. One major aspect the order required that the men from RIR 40 would remain intact as a single unit in the regiment they were assigned to: 'All in the existing Hohenzollern infantry regiment would become united for maintaining the tradition and solidarity in a closed formation with the inserted battalions of RIR 40.'

Additional orders followed which provided exact details of the transfer of men: 'From the Regimental staff RIR 40, the following were dissolved and were transferred:

Leutnant der Landwehr Vohl as the regimental adjutant to RIR 111
Leutnant der Reserve Lamey, Albrecht to RIR 111 under the simultaneous commandeering to the staff of the 56th Reserve Infantry Brigade
Leutnant der Reserve Spengler to RIR 110, also to the staff of the 56th RIB
Leutnant der Reserve Czerny to RIR 109
Leutnant der Reserve Tutein to RIR 111

Hauptmann der Reserve Thomas was first the M.G.O. RIR 111, later to the possession of the brigade.
The Regimental band was assigned to RIR 109

Battalion leaders:
III/R109 *Hauptmann* Domizlaff with his former staff
III/R110 *Hauptmann* Beckmann. Adjutant: *Leutnant der Reserve* Stahl, Karl with III/R40 staff
II/R111 Major Derichs. Adjutant: *Leutnant der Reserve* Schurhammer with his former staff.[10]

On 16-17 September 1918 the men of RIR 40 received new equipment, including new shoulder straps that would represent the regiments they were joining. On the following day the old RIR 40 was reviewed by the new division commander His *Excellenz Generalleutnant von* Altrock. The men also said goodbye to their old commander *Generalmajor* Lamey.[11] The small number of troops still remaining in RIR 40 marched past in review, when finished General Lamey addressed his men. It was an emotional time for many of the troops as well as General Lamey who had commanded RIR 40 since 1914 and was genuinely moved as he said goodbye to his men. The usual viewing and presentations had to be finished quickly. Fortunately the enemy had grown very quiet at this time so along with normal battle readiness these 'domestic issues' could take place undisturbed.

On 19 September 1918 RIR 40 ceased to exist as a regiment in the Imperial German Army. While the men would remember their service in the old regiment, all indications of its existence were eliminated as the men changed the shoulder straps on their tunics to indicate their new regiments. The II/R40, 2MG/R40 and regimental band now became the III/R109. The former III/R 109 became disbanded and divided among the other two battalions. In addition, 16 officers and 186 *Unteroffiziere* and Other Ranks arrived as replacements for the regiment. Major Engelmann transferred to the regiment from RIR 40 and took over the leadership of the I/R109.

Despite reinforcements from II/R40, the battle strength of the companies was quite weak. Fortunately, other than the occasional enemy artillery bombardments and minor patrol activity on both sides, the position could be described as 'quiet'. This allowed the new men, replacements from home and the men from RIR 40 to be integrated into the regiment. During the patrol activity it was determined that inexperienced American units were opposite the regiment, possibly the reason the enemy was behaving so calmly.

On 18 September 1918 the III/R110 marched to the Rouvres *Lager* and later was transferred to the stone bridge southeast of Etain. There on 19 September it was disbanded. *Unteroffiziere* and Other Ranks became distributed to the I and II/R110. The former III/R40 and 3MG/R40 became the new III/R110 in the regimental association.

The sector occupied the 28th Reserve Division was on the wide Woevre plain near the Etain– Verdun Road. The ground was covered in small wooded areas, low rolling hills with wide and meadows lying in front of them. Several small brooks crossed the terrain nd in some areas formed marshes that would be difficult for infantry and especially anks to cross. Only a few areas were considered to be vulnerable, especially the strip of neadow lying between Fayelle and Chabotte woods. The sentries had been told to keep watchful eye out for any sudden enemy activity.

Only remnants remained of the villages of Moranville, Grimaucourt and Herméville. To he west the vista became limited by the Côte Lorraine. In the northwest, Forts Vaux and Douaumont lay noticeably close in front of the division, the scene of such intensive fighting in 916. The main opposition line in the regimental sector ran across the ridge *Leutholdschanze-Tonberg-Wolfshügel*, north and south of the Herméville–Grimaucourt Road.

I/R111 was the readiness battalion and located in the Bois de Herme-Ville, while the II/R111 was in reserve in the *Autrey Lager*. A patrol under *Leutnant* Schildenberger irmly established that Chabotte copse had been evacuated by the enemy and there vere no indications of an imminent enemy attack. The regiment believed that with ts current strength its defensive capabilities were very limited and in order to be able o hold the partly swampy forest terrain the troops needed immediate reinforcements. This need was fulfilled in part when on 20 September 1918 the I/R40 and 1MG/R40 became inserted into the regiment as the II/R111. The former II/R111 was divided among both other battalions, so that the average trench strength of the companies ncreased to 70 men each.

Due to the extremely low battle strength of the battalions the battle sector of RIR 111 was occupied by two battalions. Each battalion had one company in the outpost line, one company in the main opposition line and one company in reserve, a total of 210 men more or less. The sentries, many of whom had little combat experience or training were quite jumpy at their posts, especially during the early morning hours around dawn when the sentries could swear they saw enemy shock troops and tanks approaching the lines when none existed.

The company assigned to the outpost zone occupied the most tactically important strongpoints, while double sentry posts were established in between these positions. Constant patrols were moving through the outpost zone establishing connections with the various sentry posts. The outpost zone in the sector held by the 28th Reserve Division was four kilometers deep and should allow time for the main opposition line and reserve companies to respond to any enemy attack.

The main opposition line was well developed with numerous dugouts for the men. The troops enjoyed the luxury of electric lighting and the field railways that were used to bring up men and supplies. Open areas in the woods, paths used by the troops were all being protected by anti-tank guns, generally the 7.7cm M.96 field gun. The high velocity 7.7cm shell could easily penetrate the armour of an enemy tank if the crew could hold on to their nerve while firing over open sites. In order to be completely prepared against any sudden enemy tank attack additional measures were taken as the men sited numerous machine gun nests, the guns being equipped with *K-Munition* (armour piercing ammunition). Flat trajectory 7.6cm *Minenwerfer* were also placed in strategic locations in order to be able to engage enemy tanks. While not as powerful as the high velocity 7.7cm field gun the 7.6cm *Minenwerfer* shell had been shown to be effective in stopping an enemy tank.

Contact mine barriers were established at vulnerable points. Most mines at this tim were simple in design, generally employing a high explosive shell or charge and a crud detonating system that the weight of a tank would set off.

Even in quiet sectors, patrols and raiding partiers were sent out on a regular basis t identify the opposing troops, capture prisoners or equipment and to generally try an maintain the upper hand over the enemy. A series of raids was carried out on the nigh of 26/27 September 1918. One of these raids took place in the right hand portion of th sector held by RIR 111, northeast of Watrouville. The raiding party moved out unde the cover of darkness and made their way toward the French lines. Just as the raidin party was about to make their attack an alert French sentry sounded the alarm and th situation quickly became a fire fight, man against man. During the melee French reinforcements arrived that forced the raiding party to withdraw.

While no prisoners were taken, the raiding party claimed to have killed or wounde a number of French soldiers and did return to the German lines without suffering an losses. The men quickly realized that they would be expected to be vigilant and on th highest alert for the anticipated enemy response.

Another patrol under *Offizier Stellvertreter* Schäfer, RIR 111, succeeded to ente Souselages Farm inside the enemy lines on the night of 26/27 September. The patro became discovered by alert French sentries and quickly became embroiled in han to hand fighting. The enemy reportedly suffered losses but as reinforcements wer approaching the patrol had to withdraw, back into the German position that wa reached without losses. It is odd that two patrols could be engaged in close fighting wit the enemy yet neither lost a single man. Perhaps the cover of darkness was the reason perhaps the patrol reports were slightly embellished? It is most likely we will never know which possibility is correct.

The raiding parties sent out by RIR 110 were having different results. Several patrols were sent out from the I/R110 in the same night, one under the command of *Leutnant der Reserve* Harksen and the other under *Offizier Stellvertreter* Böhm. The plan was a coordinated attack against a French sentry post located by Blanzée. While Böhm's men worked their way toward the enemy post and occupied their attention, Harksen's men would attack from the opposite side.

Almost at once everything began to go wrong. Instead of surprising the French sentries the raiding parties were greeted with numerous hand grenades and machine gun fire. Despite the dangerous situation *Leutnant* Harksen, accompanied by his servant Schmidt and six men leaped over the embankment and attacked the sentry post. The sound of intense fighting could clearly be heard in the darkness but the volume of enemy fire was too great for Böhm and his men and he withdrew back to the German lines with one man severely wounded, *Musketier* Steinbrenner 2/R110. The fate of *Leutnant* Harksen was not known, he was formally reported as missing and probably killed.

The French had the same idea as the Germans on this night and while Harksen and Böhm were attacking the French sentry post about 50 enemy soldiers crept up toward the German picket line near Boches brook. After a short fight the French withdrew, empty handed. Only Sergeant Danner, 1/R110, had become wounded during the fighting.

Unteroffizier Ludwig, 2nd Machine Gun Coy, RIR 109, September 1918. (Author's collection)

Poster reminding the troops to use standard ammunition against the 'Tommy' and leave the tanks to the artillery. (New York Times Mid-Week War Pictorial Extra)

On 26 September 1918 the French troops also succeeded in capturing two strong points in the sector of the left neighboring regiment. A counterattack was planned an the I/R111 reinforced its left wing company in the event it was needed. The fire c the German batteries however was sufficient to convince the enemy to evacuate th captured terrain.

Regardless of the patrols and raids the position occupied by the 28th Reserve Divisio was by all definitions a quiet position. There was lively aerial activity during the day even bombs were dropped on the positions at times. Even though the artillery on bot sides was active day and night, the men still felt that the position was relatively calm.

The wide and deep outpost sector was something new to the field sentries and require long patrols. Special diligence was also paid to the preparations of tank defenses, th fight against machine gun nests and *Minenwerfer* and the installation of the mine barrier In late 1918 the issue of tank defense was taking a pre-eminent role in the training o German troops, something that was not even considered when the war started.

The effectiveness of enemy tanks was a major factor in the ultimate destruction of th German army and the ever increasing loss of prisoners in 1918. A representative of th Supreme Command made a statement to the *Reichstag* leaders on 2 October about th deployment of this weapon:

> The enemy employed them [tanks] in unexpectedly large numbers. Where they appeared unexpectedly and when in addition our lines had been plentifully treated with artificial fog, they were often more than the nerves of our men could stand. At these points they broke through our front lines, paved the way for the infantry, and appeared in the rear, producing local panics and completely upsetting the conduct of the fighting. If they were recognized beforehand, our anti-tank weapons and artillery dealt with them speedily. But the damage had already been done, and the large number of prisoners taken, which reduced our strength so considerably and caused a more rapid consumption of the reserves than we had been so far accustomed to, is to be explained only by the successes achieved by the tanks. We were not in a position to confront the enemy with the same number of German tanks. To manufacture them was beyond the strength of our industry, which was strained to its utmost capacity, or else other matters would have had to be neglected.[12]

Notes

1. Greiner & Vulpius, op. cit., pp. 266-267.
2. Greiner & Vulpius, op. cit., pp. 270-271.
3. Greiner & Vulpius, op. cit., p. 274.
4. Greiner & Vulpius, op. cit., p. 276.
5. Greiner & Vulpius, op. cit., p. 277.
6. Greiner & Vulpius, op. cit., p. 275.
7. RIR 40 had been part of the 28th Reserve Division at the start of the war and had remained with the division until April 1915 when German divisions were reduced from four to three regiments each. The surplus regiments were combined to form new divisions, thereby expanding the size of the German Army. RIR 40 became part of the 115th Infantry Division at the end of

Soldier setting the fuze of an artillery shell being used as a mine. (Author's collection)

Artillery shell being used as an anti-tank mine (*New York Times Mid-Week War Pictorial Extra*)

March 1915. In the time since RIR 40 had been with the 115th Infantry Division the regiment had been involved in numerous actions. The 115th Infantry Division was formed in April 1915 near Tournai. It later became involved in the fighting at Notre Dame de Lorette and Neuville St. Vaast, with casualties numbering 5,208 men according to the *Verlustlisten* reports. At the end of July 1915 the division was sent to the eastern front and operated near the Narew. It participated in the summer offensive including the fighting by Kovno and Lake Narotsch. In August 1916 the division was sent to Galicia, in the middle of December to Rumania. The 115th Infantry Division was relieved from the Eastern Front in February 1918 and in April it was transported to the Western Front in the area of Antwerp where the men were put through an intensive training course. In early June 1918 the division was sent to the Aisne where it suffered heavily in the Allied counterattack at Corcy in July 1918. Following the fighting on 18 July the division was relieved. RIR 40 had probably suffered the worst casualties and as a result the decision was made to disband the regiment and replace it with IR 173 that had been attached to the 223rd Infantry Division which had also been disbanded as a result of heavy losses in the fighting in March and August 1918. In 1917 Allied intelligence rated the 223rd Infantry Division as a good division. The 223rd Infantry Division was involved in the Mars offensive on 22 March 1918. It was later involved in the Oise Offensive and remained on that front until August 1918. French attacks on 18 August forced the division back and caused heavy losses. As a result of the heavy losses morale was low in the division and Allied intelligence ratings indicated that the authority of the officers was low and desertions were frequent. In September 1918 the entire division was dissolved and the various regiments were sent to the 52nd, 103rd and 115th Infantry Divisions. By the time the division was dissolved, Allied intelligence had rated it third class.

8. W. Gallion, *Das Reserve-Infanterie-Regiment 40 im Weltkrieg*, pp. 318-319.
9. Gallion, op. cit., p. 320.
10. Ibid.
11. General Herbert Lamey was born in Freiburg i.Br., 6th December 1858, a son of a Professor of Law at the University located there. In 1860 he came to Karlsruhe, as his father became a Minister. After the War of 1866 the family moved to Mannheim. While there he attended the Gymnasium. In 1879 he took the officers examination in Berlin and then became an *Advantageur* on 1st May 1879 with the 1st Baden *Leib* Grenadier Regiment. On 14th October 1880 he became promoted to *Leutnant* in the 2nd Baden Grenadier Regiment 110 and assigned to the III Battalion. He was married in 1887 to Miss Elisabeth Dilger, daughter of a former Baden artillery officer. Following the war he lived in Donaueschingen with his wife and daughter. He suffered a personal loss during the war when his only son, a *Leutnant* in Grenadier Regiment 110 fell in front of the enemy on 20th August 1914 in the battle by the Saar.
12. R. Lutz, *The Fall of the German Empire*, p. 461.

8

28th Reserve Division

Final Weeks of the War, Armistice and Demobilization

In the first few days of October RIR 109 received replacements in the strength of 105 *Unteroffiziere* and Other Ranks. With these replacements and others received at this time the average field strength of the battalions increased to 700 men; the Machine Gun Company and *Minenwerfer* Company to 150 men. RIR 110 and RIR 111 also received additional drafts of men and could fill up the depleted ranks of their companies. Whilst the numbers in the ranks had increased, the effectiveness of the new men was very doubtful as they were almost completely untrained and many were physically unfit and unable to stand the rigors of modern combat.

The much anticipated French response to retaliation raids launched in late September occurred on the night of 13 October 1918. The countryside was shrouded in mist and fog and this cast a dull grey appearance over the terrain. The wind rustled autumn leaves in woods and copses. While this sort of weather and general conditions called for increased alertness it is more than likely that the natural instincts of the men in the outpost zone was to stay as warm and dry as possible under the circumstances.

It was during the inclement weather that a French patrol succeeded in approaching the German lines to cut their way through the wire entanglements near Chabotte Copse without detection. The raiding party then came up in the rear of several German sentry positions and surprised the small garrisons. Within 10 minutes of the start of the raid it was over. One *Vizefeldwebel*, three *Unteroffiziere*, nine Other Ranks and one machine gun were missing, all taken back with the French raiding party.

As soon as it had become known that a raid was taking place the neighboring sentries formed together and moved off toward the sound of the fighting, joined by three Groups from the Outpost Company. They arrived too late; the raiding party and most of the German sentries were gone. The sentries had managed to put up a fight and four of them who avoided capture were wounded while several others had fled the area to avoid capture. The empty sentry positions were quickly reoccupied in the expectation of further French attacks.

Following this raid rumors began to circulate that the division would be leaving thi sector for a distant part of the front. This rumor gained some credibility when the me were ordered to take inventory of their equipment and the packs were to contain onl the minimum items required. On 14 October 1918 all furloughs were cancelled; every thing pointed toward an imminent move.

In the days that followed rumors continued to circulate yet there was no relief o orders to move the division. The normal trench routine continued with companie taking turns manning the outpost line, main opposition line and reserve positions Enemy activity remained low with the exception of patrols, regular artillery fire and a occasional bomb dropped from a passing enemy aircraft.

On 18 October 1918 *Leutnant der Reserve* Mattig along with nine men from the 10 R110 penetrated the enemy lines and captured a prisoner of the US 35th Division, American Army Corps. The was the first American prisoner captured by the division.

At last, at 9.00 p.m. on 20 October 1918 the official orders arrived that the divisior was to be relieved by the 5th Guard Division. RIR 109 was to be relieved by the *Königin Elisabeth Garde Grenadier* Regiment 3. The regiment would be embarked on transpor trains at Mancieulles bei Briey, Jarny and Briey and transported to Boussu. The quie times for the regiment on the Woevre plane had come to an end. Over the coming days the regiments would be relieved from their positions and marched to the point of embarkation.

The III/R110, being the Rest battalion, marched to Briey, where it arrived on at 11.30 p.m. on the 21st and received quarters. On 21 October 1918 the III/R111 as the Reserve battalion left its position and moved to the railway station Jarny. The I and II/R110 was replaced on the night of 22/23 October 1918 by two battalions of IR 20 and marched via Rouvres *Waldlager*, Mouaville, Jeandelize, Conlans to Jarny, where they were loaded aboard troop trains.

On the night of 21/22 October 1918 the position battalion from RIR 111 was relieved by two battalions from Bavarian IR 23. In the evening the battalion marched to the rear to the *Rouvres Lager* and at 4.00 a.m. the rest of the division marched in the direction of Conflans, where it would be transported on the afternoon of the 22nd.

There was much supposition about the destination of the division. Every officer and man had an opinion of where they might be sent next and numerous wagers were made as to what part of the front they would end up on. The trains travelled through Diedenhofen, Trier, through the Eifel where the dry autumnal weather gave many of the men a feeling of homesickness as the journey went across the German-Belgian border still further to Lüttich, Brussels and into northern Belgium. This was an ominous move in the minds of many aboard the troop trains. The men had all heard of the desperate fighting in the blood drenched fields of Flanders. This possibility elicited much cursing and swearing.

The division had indeed been scheduled to be inserted into the Flanders Sector. However, the OHL expected a large enemy attack in the area of Valenciennes, a key rail and supply center. New orders were issued diverting the 28th Reserve Division to the threatened sector. RIR 111 had been the first of the regiments to depart and had almost reached its original destination. The I and II/R111 which had already been transported

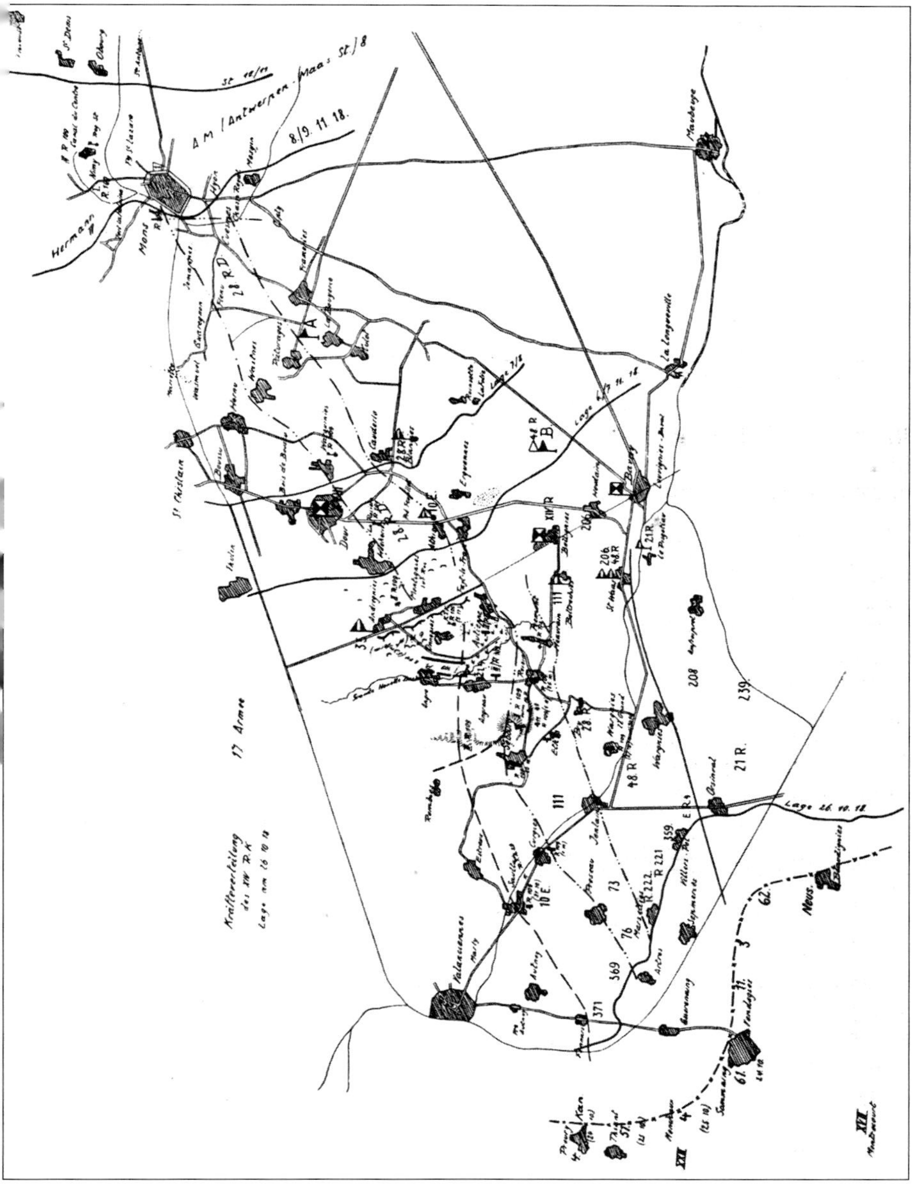

Situation as of 26 October 1918.

further north, had their trains diverted to St. Ghislain. The III/R111 which had already arrived in Gent was forced to march 25 kilometers to a different railway station where it became loaded onto a troop train and in the following night was also transported to Saint Ghislain. The III Battalion arrived there on the morning of 26 October 1918 and immediately after being unloaded the battalion was driven to Roisin using motor lorries.

When the transport trains of the regiments following behind changed direction into the area southwest of Mons, the men quickly learned that the division was being sent to the vicinity of Valenciennes opposite the northern French border where the 17th Army was fighting. The 17th Army was dealing with increased opposition from the Belgian Army and the British troops that supported it.

Over the previous month the 17th Army was involved in large-scale, tenacious enemy attacks. The German tactics of making spirited counterattacks during the forced withdrawal resulted in numerous losses to the Belgians and British and slowed their progress and limited their gains of territory. However, the enemy losses of men and equipment always appeared to be replaced quickly. Also, the lavish employment of tanks and artillery by the Allies had finally resulted in the loss of Cambrai and Valenciennes.

Perhaps the greatest blow to the German position was the loss of so many trained men whose numbers grew smaller on a daily basis. The new replacements that had been arriving in the past months did not have the same spirit or motivation as the older veterans and could not be counted on in the same manner. If not for the lavish use of machine guns by the German defenders the enemy gains probably would have been far greater. But even these weapons could not completely stop the powerful enemy attacks; it was only a matter of time before all German defenses would crumble.

The disintegration of the German Army continued to occur at a rapidly expanding pace. Twenty two more divisions were disbanded in October 1918 and the men released were sent to bolster other divisions along the front. The defensive fighting in October 1918 resulted in the average battalion field strength to be decreased to 545 men in the first days of the month; to 508 men by the middle of the month and 450 by the end of October. When non-combatants were removed from these numbers the actual fighting strength of a battalion would have been 250, 208 and 142 men respectively. On 22 October 1918 the first 18 year olds from the Class of 1900 were sent to the front. Even in situations where drafts of replacement troops were sent to units at the front, there were ominous signs of deeper troubles:

> The young men sent from their homes to replace casualties were infected and demoralized. The lack of discipline of these troops was already apparent during their journey to the West, and increased to insubordination and open mutiny. Such men could be of no advantage to the front. These were the men who, during the fighting, shouted to the steady, advancing troops that they were 'prolonging the war', and who called the artillery which held its ground 'strike breakers'.[1]

It would not be long before the 28th Reserve Division was thrown into the thick of the fighting. On the day the first troop trains arrived in 17th Army sector, the Allies attacked with numerous tanks and infantry. Within a short time the enemy had made gains in the German lines one kilometer deep at places. The newly arrived troops of the 28th Reserve Division were quickly loaded into motor lorries and were transported toward the front where they were needed the most. However, the front stabilized before the men could be placed into the line. With the situation under control the men were assigned housing in and around the village of Angreau, Flamengries, Roisin, and on the following day in Curgies, Wargnies le Grand and Jenlain. Within two days the entire division had been formed as the trains carrying the rest of RIR 110 arrived on 26 October 1918. The last campaign of the division had begun.

Upon arriving, the 28th Reserve Division was attached to its old unit, the XIV Reserve Corps that was now under the command of *Generalleutnant von* Morgen. In the afternoon of the 25th the division commander, *Generalleutnant von* Altrock, travelled to Corps Headquarters and requested that his division be placed under his command so that the 28th Reserve Division could act as a coordinated unit in the attack, defense or retreat.

However, *Oberkommando* 17 decided to retain full control over the employment of the three regiments. In part this was a result of the situation facing *Oberkommando* 17. The relatively fresh 28th Reserve Division had received enough replacements in the last few months to bring the division almost up to full strength, or what full strength was considered to be in late 1918. The situation at the 17th Army had been growing increasingly difficult as losses mounted and few replacements had arrived.

The 28th Reserve Division was so large at this time that the division's battle strength was as great as all of the other divisions in the 17th Army combined; such was the sorry state of the German forces in late 1918. Instead of using the division under a unified command it had been decided to make each regiment subordinate to different divisions at locations where they were needed the most. *Generalleutnant von* Altrock continued to argue against breaking up his division without success. From 27 October to 31 October 1918 the three regiments of the 28th Reserve Division were constantly being shifted back and forth along the front of the 17th Army as one sector after other critically needed reinforcements.

On 26 October 1918 RIR 109 assembled in Roissin, a village on the Belgian-French border east of Valenciennes, from out of which in the year 1914 the 28th Infantry Division began its advance to Lens at the start of the war. Orders arrived at 12.45 a.m. on 27 October 1918 placing each regiment with a different division. RIR 110 became transferred to Jenlain into the area of the 111th Infantry Division and reached the village by daybreak. RIR 111 received billets in Curgies in support of the 10th *Ersatz* Division while RIR 109 marched to Wargnies le Grand in support of the 48th Reserve Division. All three regiments acted as the army reserve and each morning at dawn the men were quickly assembled and the companies were made ready for a counterattack if required. Nothing of any great excitement occurred in the first few days other than the 2/R109 being able to rescue a British pilot whose plane had been shot down by a German fighter near Sébourg.

The billets provided to the men of RIR 110 in Jenlain in part were in cellars and in part in earthen holes located at the village edge. The village and its surroundings were constantly under strong artillery fire, especially at night. Then, something new appeared to be taking place when on the 29th the regiment was allotted a *Kampfwagen Abteilung*.

The *Abteilung* consisted of captured British Mark IV tanks that had iron crosses painted on their sides in order to prevent misidentification. Finally, because of the continuous bombardment of Jenlain the III/R110 became transferred to Wargnies le Grand on 29 October 1918. Up to 30 October 1918 RIR 110 had already lost 42 men from enemy artillery fire.

Corps orders from the 31st directed RIR 110 to march from Jenlain to Sébourg on the night of 31 October/1st November. Following arrival at 8.00 a.m., the battalion was duly informed that the departure had already been ordered. At this time, the enemy artillery fire became even stronger; allowing the men to suspect that an attack by the British was taking place on the front line. Under these circumstances the regimental commander of RIR 110 held back the I and II/R110 from marching off to Sébourg. At 8.05 a.m. the III/R110 was assembled in Sébourg and moved back to Jenlain, where it was made ready as regimental reserve in the hedges north of Notre Dame Farm.

On 31 October 1918 RIR 109 was transferred to Wargnies le Grand, where it too was assigned a *Kampfwagen Abteilung* consisting of five captured British tanks under the command of *Hauptmann* Regenborn. Furthermore the regiment received an escort battery, the 1/RFAR 29.

Early on the morning of All Saints Day, 1 November 1918, the Allies began a major attack against the German lines by Valenciennes that involved a large amount of artillery, seemingly numberless men and numerous tanks. At approximately 7.00 a.m. the enemy attacked the 111th Infantry Division (IR 76, IR 73 and IR 164) and subsequently the 48th Reserve Division (RIR 221, RIR 222 and RIR 223) south at Artres and Maresches in their positions east of the Rhonelle brook.

What came next would become the last attack made by the regiments of the 28th Reserve Division in the World War. At 8.30 a.m. the order issued by the 48th Reserve Division arrived at RIR 110 that the advance would begin at 9.20 a.m. The goal was to take possession of the hills from the Préseau-St. Hubert Farm up to the ground by Fond des Veaux.

RIR 110 developed between Préseau and Jenlain. The I and II/R110 dug in as best they could under the circumstances. The III/R110 advanced to the nearby Fort de Curgies, situated between Jenlain and Préseau, whilst under enemy fire.

I/R110 was deployed on the right for the counter thrust, the II Battalion on the left, with the direction of attack toward St. Hubert farm. The 2/RFAR 29 and five tanks from *Kampfwagen Abteilung* 12 were allotted to the battalion. The I/R110 under Major Höhne had the 1st and 2/R110 in the front line, with the 3/R110 as support along with the allotted machine guns and *Minenwerfer*. The II/R110 under *Hauptmann der Landwehr* Rösch had placed the 7th and 8/R110 in the first line with the 2nd Machine Gun Company, behind them the 6/R110. The combat strength of the companies included four light MG 08/15 machine guns each.

With the support from two captured tanks and a platoon from the escort battery the counterattack of the II/R110 was delivered in impeccable order. The battalion made contact with the British on the Préseau–St Hubert Farm–*Punkt* 104 Road and forced them to abandon their position. The British troops moved back to the hill between the Préseau-St. Hubert Farm–*Punkt* 104 Road and the Rhonelle brook where they took

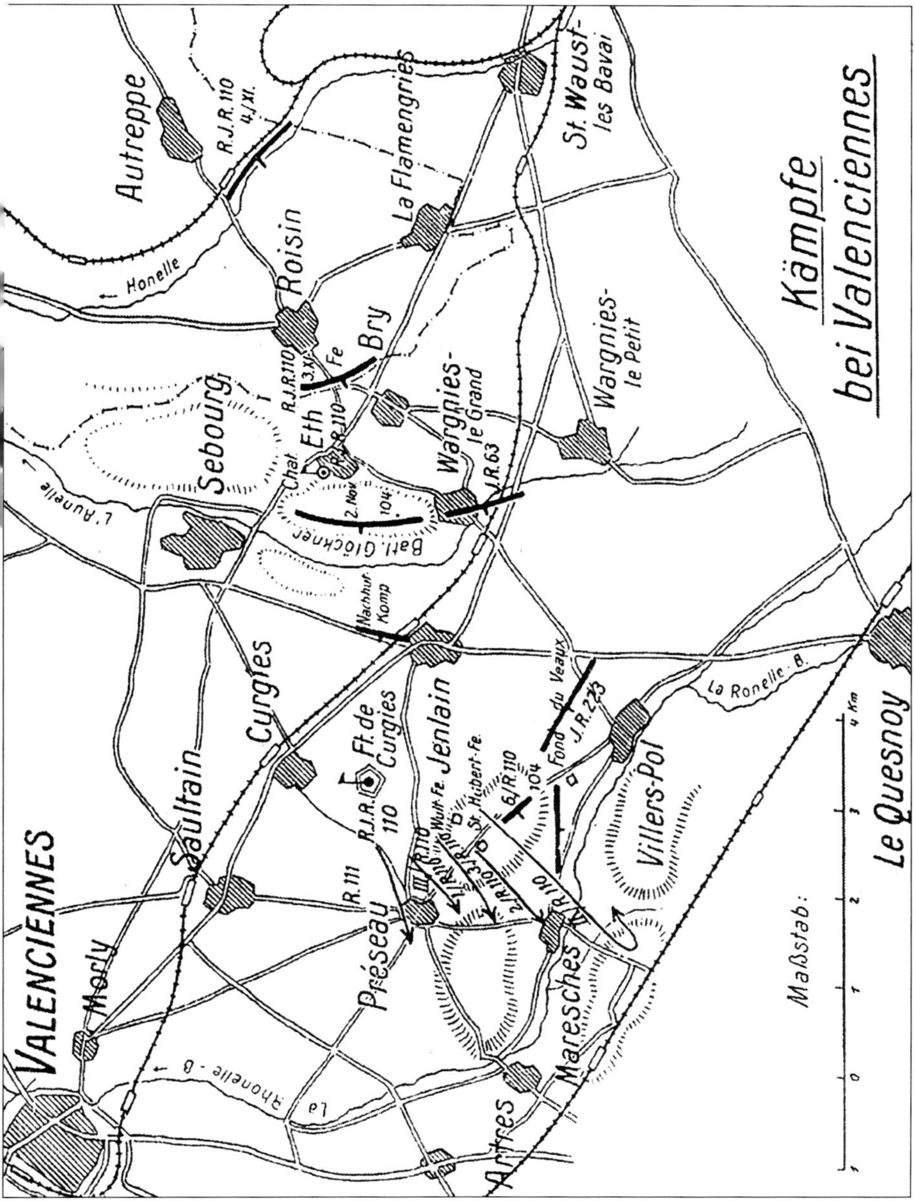

Battle by Valenciennes.

up new positions. The men of RIR 110 continued their attack and advanced against stiff opposition toward Maresches and the area south of the village across the brook and occupied much of it except for the hills south of the village that were still being defended by British troops.

Once the battalion reached Maresches it was unable to establish any connection on the right or the left. As a result the men withdrew a short distance to the northern bank of Rhonelle brook and occupied the attack goal: the position in the eastern part of Maresches and the area 400 to 500 meters east of it. There was still no connection on the left by the brook. The supporting 6/R110 lying on the hill behind Maresches did establish a connection on the left to RIR 223. The right flank was still threatened where the 7th and 8/R110 retained a connection to the platoon of *Leutnant der Landwehr* Sturm (2/R110) during the entire battle. However, at the right flank, in the western part of Maresches were British troops.

At the same time RIR 110 was engaged in the counterattack, RIR 111 had been made subordinate to the 214th Infantry Division. RIR 111 received the task, to counterattack from Curgies in the direction of Préseau and to throw the enemy out of that village. While RIR 110 would capture and hold the hill of Mareches, RIR 109 would move to the village of Saultain where it would remain in reserve in the event the regiment was needed.

On the front by RIR 111 the British had crossed over the Rhonelle-brook in the early morning hours after a short period of drum fire and had penetrated into Préseau. At 9.00 a.m. the II and III/R111 advanced in a counterattack in the direction of the church of Préseau. The two battalions were reinforced by *Kampfwagen Abteilung* 13 consisting of three captured British tanks.

Despite being on the receiving end of enemy tank attacks in the past, the men of RIR 111 had little trust in the new weapon as being reliable. Still, the presence of such weapons did raise the overall morale of the men. However, their mistrust turned out to be well placed in this instance when two of the tanks remained motionless at the exit position because of motor trouble, and apparently the third tank was never engaged in the fighting. According to the men of RIR 111 they had better support from their escort battery, the 3/FAR 29.

The infantry advanced in waves and initially did not meet any opposition worth mentioning. The eastern edge of Préseau was reached at 10.15 a.m. Apparently the British had not made any real preparations to defend the village and as the skirmish lines of RIR 111 approached they evacuated the village. During the search of the village a few British troops who had missed the order to withdraw were found in cellars – mostly very young British soldiers, who were taken prisoner.

At the eastern edge of Préseau *Leutnant* Conrath was fatally wounded by a shell splinter a few minutes after his return from a reconnaissance on horseback. Préseau was now in German hands again but the enemy still held the hills between Andres-Maresches in his possession. At 3.00 p.m. the brigade ordered the storming of this hill in connection with IR 363 and IR 64 fighting on the right of RIR 111. The attack gained ground at first. However, when IR 64 was pressed back at 5.30 p.m. by a British counterattack that advanced in dense columns, IR 363 and RIR 111 were forced to return to their exit positions. There was no strength left for a renewed advance on this day:

Shortly on the left side of the village as our battalion came to develop, two tanks took on the leadership; they strengthened the morale fighting courage. However o woe, after barely 100 meters the right hand one supposedly received a direct hit and the one on the left also hesitated shortly after and remained behind. Despite the artillery fire we started our unobstructed march in a quiet pace away, past the artillery position 'without ammunition', we strived toward the village of Préseau. It was probably in the midday time, when we reached a rise of ground, and the command to dig in became given. With the first thrust of the spade the artillery fire from the enemy began with all calibers. On the right of me lay the *Schütze* Leute, shortly after he became wounded, he left me the Light pistol and disappeared. Afterward, *Schütze* Sulger pressed himself into the slight depression. Also he caught it, when after a few minutes a shell ½ meter distant from my assault pack tore it apart in thousands of pieces. Helping him up and binding him, had been madness. On his requests I left that hole, in order to look for protection with the next gun. A terrible sight greeted me here. The gun of *Gefreiter* Steiert had received a direct hit, 2 *Schützen* were mixed together in a mass of pulp, 2 *Schützen* were wounded. *Gefreiter* Steiert as the *Gewehrführer* remained uninjured on this day. I hurled myself to the front and reached the deep trench of the infantry, fortunately for me a vacant trench, where therefore before a shell found its victims here. I endured the next half hour like that. The drum fire, which lasted 1 hour, let up and I looked for my starting point. A short report of the losses to the company leader *Leutnant* Reitinger followed. The gun on the far right was altogether no longer able to be found, the other was also eliminated with a direct hit; so I still remained with Gun Kretzer with 2 *Schützen*.

We began digging away, but not for long. Engine sounds forced us to take cover. However what helped it, 40-50 pilots barely 100 meters high threw a series of bombs. The most audacious came down except for 20 meters behind our line and fired into our thin ranks with machine guns. Fortunately as before, we were spared further losses. It was altogether inexplicable that one could still stand up in an open field during this bombardment with intact bones. So the evening broke that was followed by profound silence. It was unforgivable in this night to change the positions of individual guns, what would have a portentous effect on me on the next morning. Food was received at midnight; I received the mailbag. With a tent square over my head, I sorted the mail in the newly dug hole, somewhat deeper than that during the day. Gun wise, I knew the individual crews very well. About 2.30 o'clock I brought the company leader and his good runner Schuhmacher the mail with the words: 'In the event that something happens tomorrow morning.'

Platoon leader, *Vizefeldwebel* Geuter, 1MG/R111.[2]

In the early morning RIR 109 was still at Wargnies le Grand. At 9.00 a.m. the regiment advanced to Curgies. On the hill west of Sébourg the regiment came under enemy barrage fire. For approximately two kilometers the men had to run through the heavy fire in groups and platoons. Once out of danger orders called for it to move to Saultain through heavy fire again the entire way:

> The light barrage fire doesn't do much harm. The cheeky low flying pilots that continually attack us are annoying. A tank detachment goes forward with us.
> *Leutnant* Schurhammer.[3]

The attack against Préseau and the hill of Mareches began at 9.00 a.m. At first, the enemy afforded only little opposition to the counterattack so that already by 11.00 a.m. the eastern edge of the village was reached. The British then withdrew from Mareches Hill in the face of the advance by RIR 111. The attack was witnessed by a member of the *Radfahrer* Company of RIR 111:

> The regiment had moved to Curgies, as the reserve for the 214th Infantry Division. Nearly every night we were moved to a different position of this endangered sector. Up to the early morning of 1st November however, the enemy remained completely quiet. Suddenly strong drum fire began; simultaneously the British attacked in part with artificial fog with large superior strength and overran the forward lying division in the dark. The enemy first of all remained content with his success and stopped. RIR 111 together with RIR 110 received orders for the counterattack and recapture of the lost position. The battalions arranged themselves in the village for the attack, which was scheduled at 8 o'clock. The regimental staff was on the eastern edge of the village near the railway station, where the I Battalion also reported. The attack started to unwind as if on the parade ground. In front was the regimental commander with the adjutant and the orderly officer, on the left beside it we 3 cyclist, 20 steps behind the Battle orderlies and the Telephone Section in the march column, then with a spacing of 50 meters a platoon of infantry in skirmish line with wide spacing. Behind the skirmish line were the rest of the companies in company columns. The other three companies and machine guns followed with wide spacing also in company columns. When the regimental staff reached the Curgies–Fort Rocharbeau road, the first English shrapnel came that burst in a great height and caused no losses whatever. The old soldier types immediately became making jokes about the marksmanship of the British. Approximately 300 meters south of the named road the regimental staff received English infantry fire. We had a small rest stop and allowed the now developed companies to pass by us. The two other battalions had meanwhile begun the attack through the village. Also we were allotted tanks to participate in the fighting. On the evening of first November the position of the 214th Infantry Division, despite continuously strong counterattacks, was firmly in our hands.
> *Radfahrer* Wilhelm Klein, 5/RIR 111.[4]

However, the further advance by RIR 111 against the hill became disrupted through a strong mass counterattack by the British on IR 64 lying further to the right. In view of this new threat the officers in charge of the attack in RIR 111 felt they needed additional men before continuing. The men of RIR 111 moved back into the position at the western edge of Préseau and created a defensive position. RIR 110 provided support for this movement and established a connection with RIR 111 in Préseau.

The British, who at first had withdrawn in the face of the German counterattack soon recovered and were now pressing forward against the newly captured positions. Up until the onset of darkness Préseau and the hill between Préseau and Mareches were in German hands. However, in view of the powerful enemy artillery fire that had started up again there was no further question that in a few hours a British counterattack would throw out the Baden troops, if they did not become surrounded beforehand.

During the counterattack, the regimental headquarters of RIR 111 took up residence in the nearby Fort de Curgies, one of the outer defenses of Maubege:

> The regimental staff transferred its command post into the fort. It was not occupied by our troops; only one Group of infantry had been placed in both sentry rooms at the entrance gate. An observer from the field artillery, who had set up a stereo telescope in an unprotected observation post, fell through enemy artillery fire. In the afternoon the British also bombarded the entrance of the fort with heavy guns. During this bombardment I traveled to the division with a report. I positioned myself at the entrance and wanted to travel quickly out of the fort after the next succession. One of the next shots went into the loophole of the northern sentry room and wounded almost every occupant. The shot had torn out large pieces of the sandstone wall and thrown them through the entrance, so that I could no longer travel through it. I waited for the next two shots to hit, jumped after the impact, carrying my bike, away over the debris, swinging myself on the rampart ditch bridge on my bike and drove on. However, I only made it a few meters when the next series already came. One shot went into the entrance again; the other went on the left beside me under the pavement of the access road. The air pressure hurled me, including my bike, into the branches of a large tree standing beside the road, from where I landed together with the hail of splinters and paving stones on the grass. My bike fell on me, likewise a few of the paving stones and wood and iron splinters. Jumping up, taking the bike, I attempted to get up on the bike to see if it still worked and proceeded on to Curgies, this all happened quicker than writing it. How already like so often during the war I had come away again with my skin intact. I was not wounded; however, still before the village I could no longer step on my right foot. One of the paving stones had fallen on my ankle and caused me intense pain. Also otherwise I now sensed aches everywhere on my body. I became securely bandaged about my ankle in the medical dugout in Curgies that had already fully swollen. The investigation of the remaining body resulted in only many discolored areas that had resulted from the stones and large wood splinters. I then traveled even further and gave my report at the prescribed place. Because I could no longer walk, I went to the regimental quarters, where I remained up to 8th November. I could, to be sure, still not quite walk, but could bicycle moderately. With a quite firm bandage around the ankle I reported to the regimental staff again for duty. Meanwhile, it had not gone well for my regiment. The neighboring division was ordered to go back on the night of 1st to 2nd November.
>
> *Radfahrer* Wilhelm Klein, 5/RIR 111.[5]

The 1/R110 soon became forced out of Préseau through enemy artillery and machine gun fire. Only weak parts of the company under the leadership of *Leutnant der Reserve* Reich managed to reach the Préseau-Maresches road. There they met severe opposition and could not move any further. On their right RIR 111 had barely advanced via Préseau and immediately moved back again to the edge of the village. On the left *Leutnant der Reserve* Reich had no contact with the 2nd Company during the entire day, which together with the 7th and 8th Companies and Platoon Sturm had reached the attack goal and the remnants of these companies were positioned in the churchyard of Maresches. In taking this position the company leader, *Leutnant der Reserve Leist*, 20 prisoners were dispatched to Fort Curgies. The British, however, remained on the right flank in force. The heavy enemy machine gun fire prevented any connection being established with *Leutnant der Reserve* Reich across the open terrain during the day. in the course of the fighting two British field guns were silenced by the 2/R110, one withdrawing toward Artres, the horse team of the other were shot down, preventing the gum from being removed. Throughout the day numerous low flying British aircraft directed artillery fire upon the companies of the regiment. The moderate losses until now became considerably increased by the fire raids from guns up to 18cm in caliber.

At 11.45 a.m. orders arrived at RIR 110 from the 221st Infantry Brigade that the old front positions of the 111th Division should be taken again. The attack sector of the regiment was between 3-4 kilometers in width. The Préseau–Artres Road was designated as the regimental right flank.

At 12.20 p.m. the regiment issued a corresponding order to the companies, however in the current situation it was simply impossible to implement. The situation at the front line had continued to deteriorate hour by hour. About 2.00 p.m. *Leutnant der Landwehr* Sturm was ordered by *Leutnant the Reserve* Leist (2/R110), his platoon leader, to take some of his men and attempt to throw out the British that were still occupying the western part of Maresches. It was an impossible order as already the combined efforts of the I and II/R110 had not succeeded in this, because of the steam of British reinforcements at the steep slope on the Maresches–Artres Road.

In the fighting that took place during the afternoon hours the British superior strength forced the men of RIR 110 out of the village. The losses to RIR 110 were very high in the fighting. Among others *Leutnant der Reserve* Kleyer (7/R110), *Leutnant der Reserve* Jacky (8/R110), the *Vizefeldwebel* and *Offizier Aspirants* Genter and Brand were killed. Finally, because of the loss of so many dead and wounded it became impossible to hold the village. The remnants of the 7th and 8th Companies moved to the east in an arc, back to the position of the 6th Company.

The remains of the 2/R110 under *Leutnant der Reserve* Leist were not able to retreat from the village. They were surrounded in Maresches, because the British lying on the Préseau– Maresches Road had extended to the right and occupied the churchyard:

> We were in a house and expected to come through in the darkness. This plan would fail when I saw that the British artillery moved forward. Still however, I would not give up my freedom. An attack from our side could help us, which was

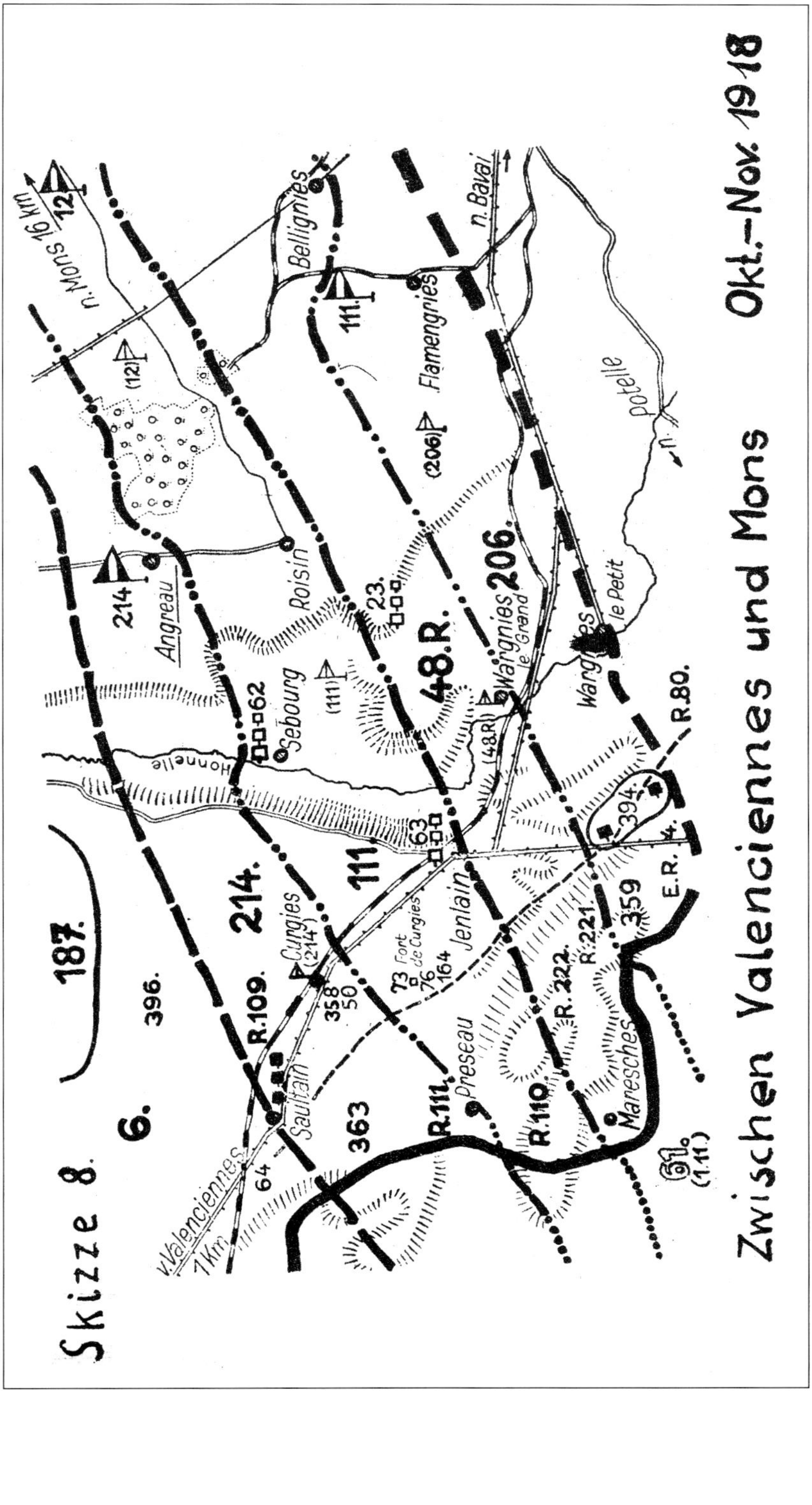

Between Valenciennes and Mons, October-November 1918.

our silent hope. The night was dreadful: gas, our own artillery fire, British, now and then even in the same house.

Leutnant der Reserve Leist, 2/R110.[6]

While RIR 110 and RIR 111 were engaged with the British, RIR 109 was still held back in reserve. Even without being directly involved in the fighting this regiment had suffered considerable losses through artillery bombardments on the village billets and on the march to reach the position. 1 November was also the day in which the regiments of the 28th Reserve Division fought together as a united division again.

Early morning on 1 November 1918 RIR 109 was placed in support at the north-western exit of Eth in alarm quarters. At 9.35 a.m. the orders came for the regiment and the escort battery to march to Curgies via Sébourg to the support position; the regiment and escort battery arrived in Sébourg about 2.00 p.m. The regimental staff was accommodated in the Château Curgies, also the headquarters of the 214th Reserve Division. The march to Curgies was carried out during clear weather under extraordinarily active aerial observation. The approach roads and village exits of Curgies lay under strong shrapnel fire as a result that caused numerous losses among the men.

Following a brief rest the regiment marched to Saultain at 3.00 p.m. to take over a battle sector. The battalions moved along the Valenciennes–Maubege Road. Throughoutthe march, enemy aircraft directed artillery fire on the columns, whereby more losses occurred. The escort battery followed to the western edge of Saultain, where the regimental staff also took up housing in the cellar of the château.

That evening the British probed the right of the regiment. However, they were driven back. On the night of 1/2 November 1918 officer patrols became sent out from the II/R109 in an attempt to clarify the situation. On the return route the patrol of *Vizefeldwebel* Ratzel, 7/R109, bumped into a British detachment, by which several soldiers from the 'York Regiment' were killed and a British machine gun was brought back as spoils.

The patrols had discovered that while there was a connection between RIR 110 and RIR 111 there was also a gap in the lines that could spell disaster for both regiments if the British took advantage of it. More troops were needed to fill this gap.

At 9.30 p.m. the headquarters of RIR 110 sent orders to the front, shortly afterward additional orders arrived from the 221st Infantry Brigade which basically provided the same details:

1. The regiment will defend itself tomorrow on the hills between Préseau and Maresches churchyard.
2. The III Battalion would be on the right, east of the Préseau–Maresches Road, with its front to the west. Connection on the right to RIR 111 at the western edge of Préseau.
3. I Battalion on the left, front to Maresches until the churchyard inclusive.
4. Both battalions were partitioned in depth. Rear boundary: Préseau-St. Hubert Farm Road.

5. II Battalion would become the support battalion and become placed north-east of the Préseau–St. Hubert Farm Road on the rear hillside in support. Provide flank protection! The hill line Préseau-St. Hubert farm indicates the middle of the main opposition zone.[7]

This order reached the I and II/R110 and both battalion leaders literally reported almost identical responses that any movement to the rear by the II/R110 was impossible, because the strength, which was needed to be inserted into the approximately one kilometer wide sector was simply not available. Both battalion leaders were asked to examine the question if taking the front back was possible. Both battalion commanders fully expected the continuation of the attacks by the British in the morning of 2 November 1918.

Upon receiving the information from the battalion commanders, the regimental commander of RIR 110 contacted the brigade commander of 221st Infantry Brigade by telephone. He reported his views about the threatened situation of the regiment, which was in a strong angle projecting to the west. He especially raised the issue that there was no secure connection on the left wing and also made the suggestion to move the position back to the line St. Hubert Farm–Préseau. The regimental commander emphasized once more that there was very great danger of his regiment being encircled from the south if an enemy attack came from this direction.

In the opinion of the regimental commander of RIR 110 the brigade commander was positioned far in the rear and did not understand the situation at the front. The brigade commander rejected the recommendation by his regimental commanders and promised that the left neighboring brigade would establish a secure connection with the right wing at the churchyard Maresches.

Of the tanks that had been assigned to support the attack, little had been accomplished. *Kampfwagen Abteilung* 12 and 13, each originally equipped with five tanks, could only field a total of five tanks in the fighting on 1 November, and these had shared the fate of the two regiments. Two tanks accompanied RIR 110 in the initial attack, both of which soon became disabled as a result of British artillery fire. Of the three tanks with RIR 111 two broke down at the start of the action and for some unknown reason the third tank in *Kampfwagen Abteilung* 13 appeared to lag behind the infantry advance and did not take part in the fighting. All tanks attached to the division that were capable of being moved were withdrawn at the end of 1 November 1918 and transported back to Germany.

To many it was evident that the war was rapidly coming to an end. Still, there were a few who still felt that by some miracle an honorable peace could still be obtained. Most of the officers who believed the latter did not really know how bad the situation at the front had become. They were cut off from the reality of the situation and continued to direct the movements of corps, divisions and regiments as if they were still at full strength and not the skeleton formations they had become.

While the regiment and brigade headquarters discussed the situation at the front, one officer personally went out along the front lines to determine the situation firsthand. At 11.00 p.m., 1 November 1918, the adjutant of the II/R110, *Leutnant der Reserve* Laasch, went down to the front line of the regiment where he organized the distribution of the companies and made the following findings: On the left there was a connection to the 9/R223 who also had two MG 08 heavy machine guns; the 6/R110 under *Leutnant der Reserve* Regel with four *Unteroffiziere* and 22 men occupied a sector 400 meters wide. On the St. Hubert Farm–Maresches Road was the 3/R110 under *Leutnant der Reserve* Halberstadt with about 25 rifles, on the right of them *Leutnant der Reserve* Reich with a few men of the 1/R110. There was still no sign of the III/R110.

Leutnant der Reserve Reich, I/R110, moved to the left by the 3/R110 in the darkness, filling in the gap in the regimental line, however, the open space to RIR 111 had become larger. The threatening danger of a break-in by the British between RIR 110 and RIR 111 became reported to the regiment.

The I and II/R110 continued their attempts to make contact with the battalion staff of III/R110 in the course of the night in the effort to have more troops sent forward to close the gap between RIR 110 and RIR 111. Despite all efforts, no connection could be established. Finally, a runner must have successfully reached the III/R110 and not until shortly before dawn did parts of the 10th and 11/R110 arrive and were quickly pushed into the gap between RIR 111 and the I/R110 along the Préseau–St. Hubert farm Road. With their arrival the front of the regiment was fully manned. However the occupation was very thin and completely insufficient for the defense against an attack. Battalion battle strength had fallen to approximately 100 men at this time.

On the right the regiment had made a connection with RIR 111 on the eastern edge of Préseau, on the left with the forward companies of RIR 223. The leader of the I/R110, Major Höhne, reported to headquarters at 11.00 p.m.:

> After drum fire between 9 and 10 p.m., the British attacked in the sectors of the 1st and 2nd Companies and the neighboring company from RIR 222. The attack was refused. One platoon was missing. The II Battalion did not become attacked. At 10 p.m. the enemy infantry behaved quietly, the artillery placed their fire raids further back.[8]

Sometime after 3.00 a.m. a battalion commander from IR 222 arrived by RIR 110 with the task, to take on the front line on the left of the St. Hubert Farm–Maresches Road, which was the sector of the II/R110. Altogether the battalion commander had only 25 men under his command. These few men became inserted in the sector of the 8/R110; the 8/R110 was then taken back in the vicinity of Wult Farm, as battalion reserve. Also, measures for the defense of the St. Hubertus farm were completed by the II/R110: five machine guns became positioned in the trenches and hedges, and finally the connection with the III/R110 that had meanwhile been inserted into the gap, was established.

Following the costly success on 1 November 1918, the 28th Reserve Division was no longer capable of an offensive action let alone able to adequately defend its sector with so few men. In the early morning of the 2nd the British continued their extensive attacks along the line. The British quickly thrust through the German positions on both sides of the village of Préseau.

The connection by the battalions with the regimental staff of RIR 110, which since 4.00 a.m. had moved its battle headquarters into Fort Curgies, could not be preserved through telephones. It could barely be maintained through runners and the orderly officers of the regiment. An orderly officer of the 221st Infantry Brigade, arrived by the battalion staff of the II/R110 on the night. He was specifically informed of the fact that the battalions of the regiment were almost non-existent and that those of the battalions of other regiments supposedly still in the sector were no better off. The command position should be made aware of this and therefore the orders being issued from higher commands were only 'juggling' battalions that did not exist.

It seems to be obvious to everyone at the front that according to the situation, everything possible had been done by the battalions of RIR 110. At 3.00 a.m. on 2 November 1918 enemy artillery fire fell with a powerful a blow upon the entire regimental sector, as well as on the right and on the left of it. The British probed along the entire line. In the sector of the I/R110 there were only a few individual machine gun nests that remained scattered around the front line in the hopes of keeping the British at bay for the time being. To make matters worse, at 5.00 a.m. Major Höhne, I/R110; was advised he has been made a regimental commander in another regiment in the front line. *Hauptmann der Landwehr* Rösch therefore took command of the I/R110. Höhne, one of the most trusted and competent leaders in RIR 110 would be missing when the British attack fell on the regiment.

At 6.00 a.m. enemy artillery fire fell on the regiment like a blow once more, with shells from heavy caliber guns impacting on St. Hubert farm. Still, no attack against the regiment followed. The obvious reason for the shelling of the farm; two guns from the escort battery were positioned on the left rear of the farm and could be observed from the British lines.

After one hour of heavy fire the orderly officer of the II Battalion, *Leutnant der Reserve* Roser, observed British troops near the guns. Shortly thereafter the British had also penetrated from the right flank and from the rear into St. Hubert farm, while the entire front line garrison of the regiment and the machine guns in front of the farm remained silent as they had no enemy in front of them. At the moment *Leutnant* Roser entered the cellar containing the battalion headquarters and reported his observations, the British tossed hand grenades into the only exit. A few men inside the cellar were wounded and any opposition was impossible. It became very evident that the British plan was to outflank the position of the regiment in a wide arc from the right and then the roll up the sector from the right flank and from the rear.

When the enemy attack began the only available reserves, two heavy machine guns and about 15 men located at Fort de Curgies with the regimental staff, became inserted at the right wing of the artillery protection position. *Leutnant* Blecher, the company leader of the 11th Coy RIR 110 had just fulfilled his task in forming a connection with R111, when the British started their counter-thrust:

> I now sat in a hole and manufactured a sketch with a message about the connections. While I was still so occupied, according to my watch at 6.15 o'clock in the morning the English drum fire struck with a blow. Our sunken road was under an extraordinarily strong bombardment. The shells burst on the road surface and mowed everything down. I immediately allowed all machine guns to make ready

> to fire and observed the front, but there was nothing to see of any infantry attack in front of us. Also no machine gun or rifle fire was audible by us. Therefore the English artillery fire was not transferred back further. Suddenly about 7.30 a.m. I was sure that on the right of us the British were already in the village of Préseau, partially thrust up the sunken road and were already involved in close fighting with the 10th Company. What happened now was all the work of an instant. How they suddenly appeared out of the ground, the Tommys seized us with their light machine guns. From all sides the British suddenly stormed here. Our gun had still barely sent out a few shots when we were bagged by a superior strength. I still see the *Unteroffizier* Rosendahl, how he wildly struck around with the gun, but in the next moment he has also overpowered.
>
> *Leutnant* Blecher, 11/R110.[9]

The British attack was devastating and the German lines quickly crumbled, either as a result of a direct attack or from being taken in the flank:

> About 6 o'clock on 2 November the companies reported the positions occupied in accordance with their orders. At 6.30 a.m. 2 runners with the battalion runner departed for the Regimental Headquarters in Jenlain, when shortly after 7.15 o'clock *Unteroffizier* Bachmann from the Telephonists of the battalion came running to the staff and shouted: The Tommys have broken through north of us and hurried forward with their light machine guns behind the German positions on a broad front. We could observe from the slope of the sunken road, how the Tommys were in position 200 meters behind us, when strong artillery fire began to fall upon the positions of our 3rd Company, upon the sunken road and upon the positions of the I Battalion of our regiment standing to the left of us. Under this artillery fire the British advanced against our regimental sector and went into position.
>
> The British that had penetrated in the north directed their machine gun fire on our position from the flank. In the meantime it had become daylight and the Tommys could continue rolling up our front to the south. The staff of our battalion could observe how troop upon troop of our companies were taken away as prisoners, going past to the north of Préseau. Also any movement by the 11th Company was no longer possible because they lay between two fires. About 11 o'clock a.m. large patrols of Tommys (Scottish) searched the area south of the village of Préseau and took the staff of the III Battalion prisoner, who had sought protection against the artillery fire in the opening of a cellar of a destroyed shed, hoping in the coming night to be able to strike through to the regiment in Jenlain.
>
> Officers and runners from the staff immediately became searched. Watches and insignia were removed as 'souvenirs' and the transport to the British Headquarters began. We had destroyed the telephone equipment before and torn up and buried the cryptography and orders. *Hauptmann* Beckmann, the leader of the battalion received wounds on the upper arm, in the chest and on the upper thigh from a Scotsman, who was blindly shooting about himself. After we had bandaged him

in a makeshift manner, the march went to the Scottish headquarters; we had to alternate carrying *Hauptmann* Beckmann, because he could no longer walk. From the Regimental staff of the Scottish we went to the Division Staff, there would the battalion leader and his adjutant be loaded into a personal automobile and in a journey with two English officers and two men as guards went approximately 1½ hours, speeding past by immense columns of American troop marching forward, into the Army headquarters. It had already become night. We became screened by an interpreter, who greeted us with the words: 'Oh, there they are, the men of the regimental staff!' One believed both of us to have been the captured regimental commander and adjutant, after our short explanation and our total apathy the interrogation was still courteous but swiftly ended. *Hauptmann* Beckmann was brought to the field hospital where I accompanied him. There we could still look after the severely wounded *Hauptmann* Wöhrle from RIR 111 (*Landrat*). Beckmann remained in the hospital and I became delivered to a prisoner collection point with an automobile and guarded by 2 men at 11 o'clock at night, where I met *Leutnant* Held, our *Ordonnanz Offizier* from the battalion, and about 80 officers and approximately 1,200 men from all regiments. That night the men in the collecting point were transported away by mounted Canadians and towards morning, safely delivered into a farmyard that had been fenced in with barbed wire. There the officers and Other Ranks were separated, and after two days we were brought to the railway station, loaded into livestock cars that became sealed and transported to Le Havre.

Leutnant Karl Ott, III/RIR 110.[10]

The situation facing the men of RIR 111 was not much different than what RIR 110 had experienced. On the night of 1/2 November 1918 the regiment was positioned as follows: The I/R111 was on the right wing on the road that ran from Préseau to Aulnoy–Valenciennes. The III/R111 occupied and held the western edge of Préseau. The II/R111 was in reserve and remained in the hollow between Préseau and Fort Curgies. The regimental staff was in Fort Curgies.

Numerous battalion and regimental staff, without troops, were slowly crowded together in Fort Curgies as it was considered to be the safest location in the vicinity. By observing the frenzied events taking place all around the fort it slowly became evident that the British had broken through north and south of Préseau and had surrounded RIR 111.

The attack on the morning of 2 November 1918 did not come as a surprise to the men defending Préseau. However, they had expected the British to directly attack the village and instead the main enemy thrust, including tanks, came north and south of the village. At 6.00 a.m. strong artillery fire was placed on the entire line that was soon followed by the British attack. When the British broke through the German defenses north and south of Préseau they were able to circumvent the I and III/R111 that had so far successfully defended the western edge of the village, and these battalions quickly became cut off. At 9.00 a.m. the II/R111 also became attacked from a northerly direction. The situation inside the village quickly became confused and chaotic as enemy fire came from all sides:

> It was a nasty race in the machine gun and artillery fire up the hillside. However it succeeded with few losses. Also our escort battery that stood in the hollow on the right raced back with us and showed up in our new line. The brave cannoneers fired off shot after shot. The Tommy attempted to pursue us further four times, but every time finished the attack in a wild flight. Unfortunately we could not push after them with our few men. The brave cannoneers received exalted praise above all, in that they remained in our line without any cover. The staff went back into the fort that already lodged a large number of orphaned staff. Also a large number of straggling troops from all possible regiments and a *pionier* company came together here, with that we could form one more quite fairly connected position in the end. At midnight the staff in a hero's cellar went back to Curgies.
>
> *Leutnant* Schurhammer, Adjutant II/R 111.[11]

Platoon leader, *Vizefeldwebel* Geuter, 1st Machine Gun Company, also provided a personal account of fighting on this day:

> About 6 a.m. my words were fulfilled. The rolling fire was immensely employed, and however the losses were comparatively low. After, the rolling fire began about 7 a.m. and had reached the artillery which before the attack was the 'artillery without ammunition'. I could now first orient myself on what my fields of fire were. On the left it was up the hill, on the right downward, so that on top of everything because of the irregularly dug in infantry I only had a limited field of fire to the front.
>
> 'A tank comes' shouted one man. 'The Tommy comes' cried the other, without however the bombardment picking up. I allowed them to approach here within 150 meters, and then fired into the attackers. The attack hesitated immediately. Now the Tommys jumped behind the supposed tank which the pulley of the well looked deceptively like the firing mechanism. When a dozen British went into cover behind this I opened point blank fire. The tank transformed itself into a cloud of bricks, and from on the left I then called to a *Vizefeldwebel*, who could no longer stand up from in front of there. With binoculars I observed the entire terrain again. At 250 meters a dense hedge ran in front of an extended orchard. Only dimly did I notice lively activity by the enemy behind it. Immediately I scattered the entire hedge with a new belt. Now it became quiet. The attack was repulsed. Unconsciously, a particular feeling of apprehension ran through me. No shot had fallen on the right or on the left; everyone stared with interest on our gun. I had fired slightly over 2 1/2 belts and had been absolutely certain against any further attacks, when upward from the hill, where my company leader was also, a command sounded that I understood as 'everyone to buckle up', because I had hoped for a counterattack by our side. However o woe, I undoubtedly saw a reserve company was coming from behind, however behind were the Tommys. Also the artillerists came charging up without weapons and from on the left he continually yelled: 'Everyone to unbuckle'.

On the hill stood an individual Scotsman who waved. The Scotsman greeted me, not far from him lay the severely wounded gun leader Steiert. Four of us took him in my blanket and carried him past the British waving around with an 08 pistol. In the village we heard for the first time in these 2 days our artillery firing, especially with gas. We must place our wounded comrade in an entrance to a home, because only two of us were equipped with gas masks and were concerned when the bombardment fell precisely on the village entrance.[12]

While this all of this occurred, one company was given the task of preparing a counter-attack in a northerly direction, when they also received infantry and machine gun fire coming from the south. The British had apparently also reached the eastern edge of the village. Inside Préseau it now came to bitter house to house fighting where only a few officers and men managed to find their way to the rear and safety:

The British attacked the western edge of Préseau after a short, but exceptionally severe artillery fire about 7.30 o'clock. The attack broke completely in our infantry and machine gun fire. The enemy was only successful in occupying a few houses at the northwest corner of the village; where he could be thrown out again in the hand grenade battle. A further attack didn't follow. We already thought the attack was refused on the entire front. I questioned the report of a *Gefreiter* that the enemy had penetrated into the village from the south and was in our rear. However, soon afterward I firmly determined that we were actually cut off from our reserves. The circle of the enemy closed always tighter around us. About 10.30 o'clock we consisted of 5 officers and about 30 men. *Hauptmann* Dierich, who expected a counter attack by our reserves, gave the order to hold the western edge. A short time after we also firmly determined our infantry was advancing one kilometer north of Préseau in a westerly direction. Our counter attack apparently gained ground. However, when we looked with our binoculars these were German prisoners, it came to us that we wanted to escape the same fate, and we had to attempt to reach the higher situated eastern edge of the village with our last strength. Already at the next cross street we determined that we were in a virtually hopeless situation. Beyond the street lay an English platoon spread out in a grass garden. I quickly allowed a machine gun to be put into position in a second story of a residence masked behind a curtain. The platoon became worn down from our sustained fire from our close distance. The road needed to obtain a connection to our reserves seemed open. However, made aware through our fire, the British had brought two machine guns into position on the street on the left of our house. He spread fire on the street that we had to cross. I suggested that we take advantage of a fire pause, simultaneously reaching the edge of the opposite street with the greatest speed. With three large wide jumps I was also over there. Nobody had followed me. Immediately following, *Hauptmann* Dierich became shot by an English Sergeant in close proximity with a revolver – so I became told after the war. The remainder were wounded and in captivity. I sneaked through gardens and houses, attempted to reach the eastern edge now. From out of the window of a house I had to watch, how comrades from the 9th Company, among them *Vizefeldwebel* Küppers, became led away as prisoners by the British a few meters from me.

About 12 o'clock I had the village behind me. I was in a grass garden surrounded by a hedge and now wanted to breathe a sigh of relief. There I saw, immediately on the right beside me, only concealed by the dense beech hedge, was an English skirmish line. Silently I crawled on the ground through the tangle of branches. I now had the open field in front of me. However 15 meters to the right lay the British in position. 40 meters quickly on. Up to the English position, I was hiding in a shell hole. Anxious minutes. Would the enemy follow? Again a jump. And again I was in a crater. About 1.15 o'clock I met the first Germans. Two artillerymen lay beside their gun. They were also glad, to see a Germans face and to learn about what I had seen in Préseau. A quarter of an hour later I left them again. At 4 o'clock I arrived as the only officer of the III/R111, who had escaped capture.

Leutnant der Reserve Frey, Adjutant III/R111.[13]

The only other officer to escape capture was *Oberarzt* Dr. Merker. Besides the two artillerymen who were found between Préseau and Curgies Frey encountered no other soldiers. The British had not followed and had apparently been content with the conquest of Préseau. Only remnants from the three battalions could be assembled in the artillery protection position. The guns of the 3/FAR 29 that had to be left behind in front of the infantry position, however, they could be recovered after nightfall. The situation had become untenable. On the afternoon the left sector in the artillery protection position from Fort Curgies until to the railway Curgies–Préseau became transferred to Major Derichs. The retreat via Curgies to the southern part of Sébourg began that night.

The men of the battalions from RIR 110 and RIR 111 defending the western edge of Préseau had become killed or wounded in the bitter fighting or prisoners. In total, five battalion staff were captured on 2 November 1918. Only Major Derichs II/R111, who had remained with part of the regiment as a rearguard in the artillery protection position was able to move back at night to Sébourg with his small group.

RIR 109 was the most fortunate of the three regiments of the division as it was in reserve and had avoided most of the initial fighting on the morning of the 2nd. When the attack occurred the II/R109 occupied the sunken road and fruit gardens east of the village of Saultain just north of Préseau.

When the enemy drum fire began at 6.30 a.m. upon the entire line, it was soon was followed by an attack. At first it was directed mainly against the troops connecting on the right of RIR 109. The British troops had quickly penetrated the German lines so that soon the right wing of the regiment was in contact with the enemy and was able to prevent them from advancing any further. More attacks occurred during the morning however they broke down in the defensive fire of the companies of RIR 109.

On the left of RIR 109 the British were also successful in gaining ground in the direction of Curgies. As a result of this a gap opened at the left wing of the regiment; which required the 9th and 10/R019 and all of the guns of the 3rd Machine Gun Company to close it again. During the afternoon the enemy attacks continued, supported by low flying aircraft, which flew despite the rainy weather. *Unteroffizier* Müller from the 1st Machine Gun Company succeeded in shooting down one of the aircraft, which was flying above Saultain, at 3.45 p.m.

In the late afternoon the British continued their attacks against the right wing of the regiment. The German troops on the right of the regiment could not hold out against the superior British numbers and began to withdraw. This left the right wing of RIR 109 open and vulnerable and as a result of this the right wing of the regiment was also taken back.

At least one man was of the opinion that the reason the two regiments from the 28th Reserve Division had suffered so greatly was due to the neighboring division being ordered to go back On the night of 1st to 2 November:

> This order had not reached RIR 110 and 111, so that on the morning of 2 November they were alone in the old position. In the early morning hours the British placed a major attack again, surrounded the two regiments and only a few succeeded in striking through to the rear. Approximately 200 men still came back from the regiment. Starting from 2nd November it went back a bit each night, so that by the Armistice we had reached Mons.
>
> *Radfahrer* Wilhelm Klein, 5/RIR 111.[14]

The situation at the end of 2 November 1918 was critical. The two other infantry regiments of the division, RIR 110 and RIR 111, had suffered such severe losses when they had been used at other divisions in the last days and that their fighting strength was used up. In the course of the afternoon of 2 November the regimental staff of RIR 110 was relocated in Eth, where they had become ordered by the 221st Infantry Brigade to gather the dispersed Other Ranks of the regiment. Out of these Other Ranks one battalion became formed consisting of about 150 men that were formed in three companies. Also, a newly composed machine gun company of six guns, a *Minenwerfer* platoon with three *Minenwerfer* and a signal platoon arrived as well. *Hauptmann* Glöckner was placed in command of the composite battalion.

By 3 November 1918 there was a fighting withdrawal and RIR 109 fought daily in the front line of the division during the retreat, while in other divisions the regiments could alternate positions. A single regiment, RIR 109 now became the infantry troops who performed all of the tasks of the 28th Reserve Division. Only two *pionier* companies were still in its possession.

The withdrawal fighting played out so that when the fighting stopped each day, usually at the onset of darkness, the division carefully broke off from enemy contact. When going back into the new position that in the meanwhile had been selected by the regimental staffs of RIR 110 and RIR 111, the British usually followed afterward in the early hours of the following day.

Perhaps the last to leave the battlefield near Curgies was *Leutnant* Maischhofer, RIR 111, who was with a patrol in the artillery protection position. When confronted by the superior enemy forces he and his men moved back on Sébourg, fighting the entire way. The rest of the battalion, reinforced through the stragglers who had been collected, finally occupied the outpost line on the western edge of Sébourg on 3 November with two Groups. The remainder of the regiment, in a strength of about 20 men, who at the time were without rifles, held the main opposition line on the hills immediately east of Sébourg. Fortunately, the enemy only came very slowly after.

3 November 1918 was spent trying to reform the different regiments and to create a unified defensive line against the inevitable British attacks that were expected at any time. One battalion from RIR 110 occupied the assigned sector on the hill west of Eth, the right wing in the ground that led from Eth to Sébourg, the left wing on the track to Jenlain On the night of 2/3 November.

The meager remnants, approximately 200 men, of RIR 110 and 100 men of RIR 111 were assembled on the 3rd. It was perhaps the most disastrous day for these regiments in the war considering that both regiments had gone into battle together with 4,200 men. The successful attack on All Saints Day – and the hopeless defense on All Souls festival – was the end of these formations.

At 1.00 a.m. on 3 November 1918 the order came that the position was to be evacuated at 3.00 a.m. So far, all of the emphasis of the regimental accounts concentrated on the combat troops and the fighting they had experienced. Very little was ever recorded of the support troops, the First Line Transport, the communication service and the medics and in particular the men who staffed the field kitchens and the difficulties they faced in such circumstances:

> On one morning I received the order, to come to the Orderly room of the regiment. There I was greeted by *Leutnant* Schurhammer and he gave me the following order: 'You will travel tonight with the onset of darkness with the field kitchen up to the village of Sébourg, in fact up to the church. (The road became shown to me on the map.)' There the food would be collected from the ration distribution area. There, as it is possible that nearby enemy patrols could detain them, we received 12 more men (slightly ill, etc.) for protection. Under the onset of darkness I collected the 12 men and gave each one a rifle ready to fire and moved with the field kitchen – the driver was Heilig, from Gerichstetten in the Bauland – out of the place where the transport was in quarters. We had hardly left the village when we also already received shrapnel fire. This did not have any effect on us, the shells followed closely in front of and behind the vehicle. We moved further quietly on our route, when suddenly a shell came so close behind our vehicle that it was as if a miracle that everyone remained uninjured. In the same moment however, I also saw no more of the escort men, they were gone without a trace.
>
> Nothing was different for my driver Heilig and I, as we were to execute our mission and as quickly as possible and reach the protective wood lying in front of us. Because of the blustery, rainy weather it was so dark that it was impossible to recognize the road without more openings. However, in order to reach the village of Sébourg, we were tied to that road. I then hurried, always 50-100 meters in advance, looked for the road and allowed Heilig to follow with the vehicle. So we reached the church of Sébourg after many obstacles. There the horses would be well covered and everything was made ready for the distribution of the food.

After we had waited approximately one hour, a soldier came with his collar turned up and called to us: 'Is this the field kitchen from RIR 111?' When we answered in the affirmative, he explained that on orders of *Leutnant* Maischhofer we had to drive to the position in the front, because it was also impossible, to send back even one man to fetch the food. I explained, I have orders to drive up to the church of Sébourg and there give out the food. On my further refusal to drive forward, the soldier suddenly explains: 'Then I order you to drive forward.' Under the use of an unceremonious expression I also leaned down, where I was introduced to the soldier as *Leutnant* so and so. After I had really convinced myself that I was dealing with an officer, I was also ready to execute this order, if he, as the relevant officer assumed the responsibility for the vehicle. This he affirmed. So we drove in a westerly direction to the village exit of Sébourg. Suddenly a soft voice called: 'Where do you intend to go?' Thereby the *Leutnant* and I went about 20-30 meters in front of the vehicle, we reached the caller first. To our astonishment we saw *pioniers* here that were occupied with mining work in order to blow up the road. The leader of the same professed to us that they were going to blow up the road in the next few minutes, so that we would have no more opportunity to drive back. Despite all persuasions the leader of the *pioniers* remained to blow up the road after we passed, because his man still have had no food and if an attack followed, the demolition would be too late because the enemy was no more than 100 meters distant. I professed I was ready to give the *pioniers* food and some bread, however the same were not ready to postpone the explosion, until I gave them a bottle of Schnapps to them, which was in the field kitchen as Iron Rations. Now to set off out across the village edge; still approximately 100-150 meters to where our comrades lay in their rifle pits. No one could leave their places upon orders from *Leutnant* Maischhofer, so we approached along the rifle pits and gave everyone food in his poorly dug out cover. Here the British were barely more than 100 meters distant. Allowing the desire to spare the health condition of our comrades, *Leutnant* Maischhofer had therefore ordered that no one was allowed to go back to get food.

After the food was given out, *Leutnant* Maischhofer considered it necessary that the man also receive coffee. Of course it was also the same for us in this sense of duty to provide for our comrades. We immediately drove back to the village and with further gifts and good words allowed the *pioniers* to be persuaded to wait still longer, until our comrades and therefore they had hot coffee. The village was entirely destroyed, it was hardly possible to find water anywhere in the pitch black night. Finally we also succeeded in this, and so in the morning, at approximately 3 o'clock, we could provide the sought after hot coffee to our comrades. The coffee had barely been distributed, when we received fire, presumably from the clinking of the cooking pots. We had still not completely reached the edge of the village with the field kitchen, when an attack also followed, and we were barely past over the mined place, when the explosion occurred. Through the impact of the shells and the explosion our horses were very restless, especially the horses being led, so that it took great effort for us to hold the horses. Thereby we barely noticed that the British had stormed into the village from both sides. Through a narrow angle

> we left the village and now drove over the open field with an unknown destination. We drove away further, until we could finally become moderately oriented at dawn and so about 8 o'clock in the morning reached the First Line Transport, which was already prepared to march. However, our comrades, who we had fed at night, also arrived here with us simultaneously, because they had to yield to the superior strength of the enemy. However, I and my driver, Heilig, had executed the orders we received and could notify the Adjutant, *Leutnant* Schurhammer that the vehicle had safely come back.
>
> Kitchen *Unteroffizier* Nästle, II/R111.[15]

The final retreat had begun. From this point until 11 November 1918 the 28th Reserve Division was constantly moving closer to Germany, closely followed by British troops. At 3.00 a.m. on 3 November 1918 the battle line was taken back until Sébourg, the new opposition line became occupied by the II/R109, while the bulk of the regiment, the I and III Battalions marched through Sébourg and lay in reserve by Angreau. The British swiftly followed, so that contact was regained shortly after.

III/R109 occupied an opposition line in front of the village. Two companies were positioned in a quickly formed trench in the front line, while somewhat further back the rest (Battalion Staff and 1st Company) were placed at the ready. The I/R109 was in reserve, lying in the village where it was later joined by the II/R109. On the afternoon the III/R109 and eight machine guns of the 3rd Machine Gun Company were inserted into the right division sector. The losses to RIR 109 on this day amounted to: *Leutnant der Landwehr* Aha, killed, four men wounded and 16 men missing.

The position chosen that night by RIR 110 was improved the next day when it was further strengthened by machine gun nests. A rearguard company was sent forward to the western edge of Jenlain and on the road to Sébourg. This sector, consisting of approximately 1,300 meters, was occupied with only six picket posts, altogether 60 men. Having reconnoitered the entire sector, the regimental commander sited five machine guns on the right in a staggered deployment. The danger of an enemy advance there appeared imminent. The commander of the neighboring regiment, IR 76, agreed to occupy the position with machine guns. The connection on the left to IR 63 was considered firm. The troops dug in as best they could. It did not take the British long to fully explore the new German defensive line. At midday approximately 50 enemy aircraft circled above the position and flew down to altitudes as low as 20 meters. No German aircraft were in view during this time.

At 6.30 a.m. on 3 November 1918 drum fire fell upon the neighboring sector. The sector of RIR 110 only received modest fire at this time. At 6.45 a.m. a telephone report arrived from the *Kampf-Truppen-Kommandeur* of the regiment in Eth that the enemy had been seen on the right, east of Sébourg and by the hills there. At 7.35 a.m. a message arrived from *Hauptmann* Glöckner: 'Even after reports arrived from the main opposition line the enemy advanced on the right of our sector with strong forces. Everything is placed in order in our main opposition line, however the occupation was weak.' At 7.45 a.m. the message arrived that enemy machine guns fired toward the exit of Eth leading to Sébourg from the north. The last reserves of the regiment received the task, to

† Jesus! † Maria! † Josef!

Zum frommen Andenken

an den am 14. Dezember 1878 geborenen und am 3. November 1918 gefallenen

Kaufmann Karl Aha

Leutnant d. L. und Kompagnieführer, Inhab. des Eis. Kreuz. 2. und 1. Kl., der hessischen Tapferkeitsmedaille u. des Ritterkreuzes 2. Kl. mit Schwertern des Ordens vom Zähringer Löwen.

Bei Kriegsbeginn wurde er am 4. Mobilmachungstage zum Ersatz.-Batl. des Res. Jnf. Regt. 83 in Kassel eingezogen, im Dez. 1914 aber als g. v. wieder entlassen. Am 14. Feb. 1915 durch das Bezirkskdo. Hersfeld wieder angefordert, kam er zum Landsturmbtl. Erfurt und von da zum Ausbildungsbtl. 11/13 nach Hersfeld. Hier wurde er für k. v. erklärt, und im Dezember 1915 zum Ersatzbtl. L. I. R. 83 nach Eschwege versetzt. Am 27. April 1916 rückte er zur Westfront ab in das Rekrutendepot Brieulles s. bar. Am 15. Juni 1916 wurde er dem L. I. R. 116 zugeteilt, bei dem er bis zu seiner im August 1917 erfolgten Beförderung zum Leutnant d. L., verblieb. In der Folgezeit kämpfte er bei dem bewährten und angesehenen Res. Inf. Regt. 109 der 28. R. I. D. und verdiente sich bei diesem durch hervorragende Tapferkeit und Pflichttreue das E. K. I., das ihm am 21. Sept. 1918 höchstpersönlich von seinem Kaiser in Briey überreicht wurde. Bei den Rückzugskämpfen im Herbst 1918 war ihm

Leutnant der Landwehr Aha, RIR 109 (Courtesy of Felix Fregin)

occupy and defend this exit. The regimental staff of RIR 110 now transferred its battle headquarters to the farm south of Roisin. The regimental adjutant, *Leutnant der Reserve* Reichwald, remained in Eth until 8.05 a.m. At this moment the enemy penetrated here into Eth from the park terrain.

It quickly became evident that the handful of men who now formed RIR 111 was far too weak to defend the sector assigned to the regiment, almost the same width that a full division once held. At 11.30 a.m. the II/R109 under *Hauptmann* Heffner became assigned to the regiment. On the afternoon of the 3rd the battle strength of the regiment was reinforced even further. Men who had been on leave, stragglers, men that had been relieved from their command, had increased the number of the fighters. Also four heavy machine guns from the 3rd Machine Gun Company were assigned to the outpost company.

Throughout the British advance on 3 November 1918 the main opposition line of the 28th Reserve Division was not attacked by infantry. Instead, mine throwers and machine guns had provided barrage fire. Nearby, the enemy penetrated into the meadow terrain (park terrain) between Sébourg and Eth and was prevented from thrusting forward against the château through two machine guns set up for flanking protection. Employing this protection, I/R110 withdrew as it was obvious that the current position was untenable. I/R110 fell back on the artillery protection position, where it was mixed in with the firmly placed parts of IR 76. In an agreement with IR 76 two sectors became formed: IR 76 on the right, RIR 110 on the left. The sector of RIR 110 reached from the farm on the Roisin–Eth Road up to the farm on the Roisin-Bry road.

In the afternoon the British advanced against the rearguard position of RIR 109 and pressed the companies back. RIR 109 left behind patrols by the brook and on the Wargnies le Grand–Sébourg Road as protection for the withdrawal of the main body of troops. The remaining parts of the rearguard companies assembled at the KTK in Château Eth:

> At 5 p.m. the British went forward over the old main opposition line of RIR 110 south of Eth in large numbers. IR 23 on the left came back out of Bry. This withdrawal closed off the remnants of the Other Ranks that were lying in the regimental sector. A new front was formed approximately half way on the road to Roisin. At 12 o'clock at night the remnants of the regiment moved on its return march from Roisin to the railway embankment south of Autreppe. The rear march had proceeded without impediment. The rest the regiment, two heavy machine guns and three *Minenwerfer* were distributed in the sector of IR 73.[16]

On the evening of the 3rd RIR 111 occupied the following locations: The high ridge west of Sébourg was occupied by an outpost Company in the strength of two officers and about 30 men with machine guns under the leadership of *Leutnant* Maischhofer. Directly east of Sébourg were the remaining forces of the regiment in the strength of four officers and 30 men in position in the main opposition line.

The overall situation was confusing and no one really knew where the opposing side was located at any given point. *Leutnant* Frey had been assigned to the outpost company of RIR 111 and his description of the events of the night of 3 November 1918 clearly emphasizes this confusion:

> On the afternoon of 3 November I was assigned to the outpost company. I received the command over 20 men and two heavy machine guns. About 5 o'clock in the evening we had brought the guns into position on a ridge. The company occupied a sector about 600 meters wide. On the left we had connection to the pickets of a north German regiment. Towards evening *Leutnant* Maischhofer and *Leutnant* Gottmann, the leader of the 3rd Machine Gun Coy RIR 111, became convinced that according to human discretion with the good field of fire of our guns barely had any prospect for success in an enemy frontal attack. The evening and the night proceeded quietly. In the dawn we expected an enemy advance. However nothing stirred after the infantry fire and the rattle of the machine guns concluded, when about 7.30 o'clock, 1 1/2 kilometers on the right of us, an infantry battle was taking place. Also south of us we heard the sounds of fighting. However, you could

not see anything because of the fog. At 8.30 o'clock I received the message that the pickets of the neighboring regiment on the left of us were missing without a trace. We did not receive any messages from the main opposition line. Also there was no food. When now even *Leutnant* Maischhofer and *Leutnant* Gottmann, who had promised me, they would come to me again before the early morning, had still not appeared at 8.45 a.m., I felt that something was not right in Sébourg. In the meantime we had also lost the connection on our right flank. So at 9 o'clock I gave the order for the return march to the main opposition line. Without enemy interference the guns moved off in intervals of 300 meters.

We assembled in front of the church in Sébourg. In close formation we marched through the village. The inhabitants cleaned their residences and prepared for the reception of the British. We came to the bridge, which led over the Aichelle stream. So were the *pioniers*, who, in accordance with orders, were to blow the bridge up into the air after the withdrawal of our company? The matter became still eerier to me, when I noticed that the streets lay filled with German knapsacks, rifles and other pieces of equipment. We had no idea that the village here had already become occupied by the British shortly after 8 o'clock, coming from the south. *Leutnants* Gottmann and Maischhofer, as I later found out, were already standing against an attack by the British with barely one Group. We on the other hand had not even observed sentries. As we turned off at the exit of the village at a crossroad, there came from the right in march step a closed company of British! We had almost bumped into each other's nose tips. The consternation on both sides was equally great. In a few seconds we as well as they had sprang back 20 meters. We had found cover in a garden. Also one of our machine guns already rattled. The British had also recovered from their surprise and pushed machine gun around the corner of the road. 5 minutes of machine gun fire. We had no losses. The British could not aim, if they did not want to expose themselves to our machine gun fire. What to do now? Was our main opposition line that lay 300 meters east of us, already forced by the British? At any event the road there was blocked by the English company. We attempted to strike through to the north. Instinctively I had chosen the correct route. By climbing over the walls and hedges the machine guns were found to be in the way. They were made unserviceable. We now crawled up the hillside to the main opposition line. We had barely raised our heads when we already also received fire. The main opposition line was therefore still in our possession. In front of us the Germans fired at us and behind us were the British. An unfortunate situation! How could we make ourselves noticeable to our comrades? All shouts were of no use. Soon suggestions were also made here. A steel helmet became placed on a bean pole and held up high. They had recognized us. We became joyfully greeted by our comrades again. They had already given up on us. I immediately gave orders, to shoot only if English steel helmets were observed without any doubts. Towards midday the entire company had returned again with the exception of 4 men. I could now still hold the main opposition line with the last reserves. A transfer to the rear from the front however could not be avoided.

Leutnant der Reserve Frey, Adjutant III/R111.[17]

At 6.30 a.m. on 4 November the British bombarded the main defensive line with numerou guns. The enemy quickly broke through the line and became firmly established. The I R109 was quickly moved to the support position south of Angreau whilst III/R109, unde *Hauptmann* Domizlaff, was placed on the left of the regimental line in order to provid reinforcements and to lengthen the front line that now curved back as a result of the Britisl penetration. The III/R109 quickly formed a defensive flank with the 11th Company, ir order not to become overrun. The 9th and 10/R109 were on the left in staggered formations

> The 11th Company then received orders from me to counterattack against the break-in place that connected with the next battalion. It succeeded in throwing the enemy back. With this the 11th Company captured a few machine guns and several British prisoners were taken. Further attacks were completely refused.
> *Hauptmann* Domizlaff.[18]

The 11th Company quickly recaptured the old line with a counter thrust. Five prisoners and three machine guns were brought back. *Gefreiter* Güntert, 7/R109, drew special attention to himself through his decisive behavior, in that he shot down three enemy soldiers and with this detained any further advances by the British. All further attacks of the enemy were repulsed completely. The losses in the regiment on this day were very heavy: 20 men killed, three officers and 46 men wounded, furthermore one officer and 72 men missing.

The withdrawal order arrived at 11 p.m. At midnight the detachment from the adversary took place. The march to the rear went through Angreau to a small copse south of Onnezies. During the withdrawal the rearguard came under the command of Major *von* Auer, commander of the II Battalion. The I/R109 occupied a new opposition line east of Honnelle brook between Angreau and Onnezies.

The III/R109 had ended up in the heaviest British artillery fire during the return march and had suffered considerable losses. When the rearguard withdrew on the hills directly west of Angreau because of the heavy drum fire at 6.00 a.m., the replacement commander of the II Battalion, *Hauptmann* Häffner, became wounded. During the march through Angreau the rearguard received fire from different houses. The regiment was certain that the fire was coming from Belgian civilians. The II/R109 became positioned behind the I Battalion at Onnezies as the reserve and the III was located in the wood piece south of Onnezies as support.

After fierce drum fire on the old position east of Sébourg the enemy followed in the morning hours of the 5 November 1918 until they had reached the hills west of Honnelle brook. In the afternoon strong disturbance fire was placed on and behind the entire regimental sector, however, no attacks followed. The regiment lost on this day: Wounded; two officers and 26 men and 17 men missing.

The loss of officers had already been high and as the RIR 109 withdrew even more had become sick or wounded. *Oberleutnant* Ochel took over the leadership of the III Battalion from *Hauptmann* Domizlaff, who had taken ill. *Oberleutnant* Siegert took over the II Battalion for the wounded *Hauptmann* Häffner. *Leutnants* Thom, and Langenhan took over the leadership of the 3rd and 2nd Companies respectively.

On 4 November 1918 the enemy had penetrated into the main opposition line at the left neighboring regiment. The Outpost Company of RIR 111 held its position. However, the connection to the rest of the regiment was lost, and at 9.30 a.m. when the Outpost Company came under extreme pressure, fighting against the enemy advancing from a southwestern direction, through the village, it withdrew to the main opposition line.

Tactics up to this point were the same. One company from each battalion remained as the rearguard company and approximately up to the commencement of the counter-thrust, usually employed about 6.00 a.m., masked the retreat movement. The relief that followed was carried out under enemy fire and usually with heavy losses, naturally at the quick march. At 6.30 a.m. on 5 November 1918 the British conducted their attack as usual and then transferred his fire onto the rear terrain in order to attempt to catch the majority of the defenders because he had figured out the German tactics.

On the evening of 5 November 1918 the III/R109 received orders, to relieve two *Pionier* companies in the right regimental sector. The 9/R109 became put in on the left, the 10/R109 on the right and the 11/R109 staggered behind the right at the southern edge of Angreau. The battalion battle headquarters with the 4/*Ersatz Pionier* Battalion 16 were the reserves in Onnezies. On the same day the remnants of RIR 110 assembled in Pâturages. The men were completely exhausted and had to be taken out of the front lines.

III/R109 was exposed to strong enemy fire again on the 6th. A British attack employed at 4.30 a.m. became refused by the 9th Company with support of a Machine Gun Company. On the other hand the enemy succeeded in a momentary break-in at the position of the 2nd Company. He had more success again at the neighboring regiments 64 and 73, where he became firmly placed in their positions. The 11/R109 immediately blocked off this threat and thereby prevented the sector from being rolled up. New enemy attacks proved quite threatening to the German position, becoming surrounded seemed inevitable. Then, the front was taken back even further on the road west of Montignies, delaying the moment when the 28th Reserve Division would have been completely destroyed.

On the night of 5 November 1918 RIR 111 moved behind the Grand Honnelle stream. Because RIR 111 had no more battle strength, it was assembled in Montignes sur Roc and was newly organized. On 5 November 1918 the regiment reported that it had a strength amounting to eight officers, eight *Unteroffiziere* and approximately 72 men. One company consisting of five officers and about 80 *Unteroffiziere* and men was formed which contained three platoons. Of these men, crews were available for the last four light and five heavy machine guns in the regiment. In addition, there was a *Minenwerfer* Company with four officers, seven *Unteroffiziere* and 43 men which possessed one light and two medium *Minenwerfer*.

The men of RIR 109 still formed the bulk of the defenses for the entire division though the strength of the regiment was dwindling rapidly. The unceasing disturbance fire On the night of 6 November 1918 increased at 6.30 a.m. to drum fire. At 7.30 the British attacked. The 9th Coy repulsed the attack supported by the right *Minenwerfer* Coy. On the other hand it the enemy succeeded in penetrating at the left *Minenwerfer* Coy. Through immediate counter thrusts by the 4/*Ersatz Pionier* Battalion 16 they succeeded in throwing the enemy back again. With the break-in the 2/R109 at the right wing of the left sector became encompassed on its flank and suffered considerable losses. Two heavy machine guns inserted behind the 2/R109 succeeded in holding the enemy back until the 6/R109 managed to escape from Onnezies by the railway embankment and reached the sunken road lying behind it.

At 8.30 a.m. the situation was restored once again and the line was firmly in German hands for the time being. At 9.30 a.m. the British attacked again out of the line Angre-Angreau and were able to penetrate the front of the regimental sectors held by IR 64 and IR 73. The 11/R109 standing behind the right wing of the regiment immediately blocked off the right wing and thereby prevented the regiment from being rolled up. Later, the 11/R109 threw the enemy back to Angre through an independent counter thrust. The 9th and 10/R109 had also repulsed fierce attacks, during which parts of both companies became isolated and were taken captive.

In the left sector the 1/R109 had to withdraw to the railway embankment when their left flank became threatened. The 2nd and 3/R109 also withdrew to the railway embankment trying to avoid the constant short fire from the German batteries. The 6/R109 moved forward as reinforcements and became subordinate to the I/R109 and was placed at the threatened left wing.

In order to prevent the regiment from being encircled the order was given to transfer the front to the road west of Audregnies-Montignies sur Roc at 11.00 a.m. During the detachment, which took place without disturbance by the enemy, the II/R109 without the 6/R109 moved into a reception position southeast of Onnezies. By 1.30 p.m. the regiment had occupied the new line with the III/R109 on the right, the I/R109 on the left and II/R109 as the reserve in Montignies.

A composite battalion, more the size of a platoon, was formed from RIR 111 in Montignies and became subordinate to the regiment to prevent the British from circumventing the left wing of RIR 109. The men from RIR 111 occupied the northeast corner of the wood of Autreppe. In the course of the afternoon the 6/R109 became pushed forward into the foreground until it was by the western edge of Onnezies for the protection of the regiment. When RIR 109 was ordered to withdraw to the western edge of Montignies, RIR 111 took up a support position behind the left wing of the regiment. The losses in RIR 109 on 6 November amounted to four men killed, one officer and 32 men wounded.

On the night of 7 November 1918 the front of the 17th Army was transferred into the line Thulin-Elouges-Wiheries-Athis-Fayt le Frane-Fontenoy-château-Hergies; the battle zone of the 28th Reserve Division consisted of the southern exit of Wiheries to the western exit of Athis. An outpost zone became created in front of the main opposition line with the deployment of machine guns. The withdrawal was carried out as scheduled, without becoming observed by the enemy.

The regimental staff and the remnants of RIR 111 moved to the sugar factory east of la Rosieres. From here the regiment blocked off the front to the north. Through officer patrols it was firmly established that Clouges had been in British hands since 9.00 a.m. on 7 November. The new front line now ran from the railway station at the southern edge of Clouges to the east up to the northwest corner of the wood piece southwest of Dour, then to the north bending in the direction of Thulien.

On 7 November 1918 RIR 110 marched via Quaregnon, Mons, Nimy to Maisieres, where it received billets in a château park east of the Nimy–Casteau Road. There it was greeted by the division commander and he spoke to the individual officers and Other Ranks and informed the men that the regiment could be proud of its performances until the last. Many of the men he spoke to came from the last detachment of replacements which came from Airship duty, Electrical, Mechanical and Transport troops and Line of Communication formations. These men had little interest in fighting to the last and had virtually no infantry training; many had never even fired a rifle. They were unable to withstand the fierce artillery fire and either became casualties, reported sick or in some cases simply disappeared to the rear. The only truly reliable soldiers in the regiment were the handful of veterans who stood firm until finally, they were killed by machine gun fire or fell into captivity through no fault of their own.

The enemy cautiously followed in the early morning hours of 7th November. At 5.00 p.m. patrols sent forward by RIR 109 prevented the enemy from any further advances on this day. Despite the almost complete absence of fighting, RIR 109 lost three men wounded, two officers and 16 men missing on the 7th.

The British were quiet the morning of 8 November 1918 in front of RIR 109. On the other hand, on the right a severe artillery battle raged, which at noon also encroached on the sector of the regiment. During this time the troops connecting on the right went back. The regiment immediately closed off the right wing by the 11/R109 to the north with the 1/*Ersatz Pionier* Battalion 16 and later placed the I/R109 at the right wing of the regiment. For the time being, the danger of a flanking breakthrough was eliminated.

In the late afternoon strong enemy forces attacked the entire division line. Aided by mine slag heaps and houses the enemy succeeded in repressing the outpost line, so that the outpost troops finally had to withdraw to the main opposition line. Then all attempts by the enemy to advance further became repulsed under heavy losses. The machine gun fire coming from the elevated slag heaps effectively contained the enemy at the southeast edge of Dour and inflicted heavy losses.

At 6.00 p.m. the withdrawal continued and the men moved back into the Antwerp-Maas *Stellung*. Then, in association with the army, the XIV Reserve Corps went back into the *Hermann IV*, also known as the *Mons Stellung*. While the new positions had been given unique names, this did not indicate that they were any real obstacle to the advancing Allied troops. In many instances, the positions were simply lines drawn on a map along a natural barrier such as a canal or a river.

The detachment by the II and III/R109 from the enemy took place without interference, as did their withdrawal. On the other hand, the I/R019 bumped into a strong British detachment in the darkness while marching back on the designated withdrawal route. Only by luck did the battalion escape capture. The lead company swarmed out from the column and forced the British back. At first the British troops had been mistaken for withdrawing German troops until both sides were literally on top of one another. If not for the sudden confusion and darkness, the entire battalion would have been overwhelmed.

Still, some men were lost, including *Leutnant* Bergner, the adjutant of the I/R109 who possessed the overall retreat orders, which fell into enemy hands. In addition to *Leutnant* Bergner, *Leutnant* Zieger was reported missing along with a small number of men.

On 8 and 9 November 1918 the division reached the vicinity of Mons. The morning of 9 November 1918 was quiet and nothing special occurred, a welcome relief to the weary men. The dense fog helped the situation as the British hesitantly probed forward with patrols and in the evening became firmly positioned in front of the division with approximately two companies.

A food warehouse located at the railway station of Mons had been plundered by Belgian civilians and by stragglers from the Line of Supply and Column Other Ranks. The warehouse was quickly cleared of intruders by one platoon of the 3/R109 who then guarded it with armed sentries. Up until the intervention by the 3/R109 food and other materials with a value of several hundred thousand Marks had already been plundered or destroyed. The town commander of Mons thanked the regiment for its unerring and swift intervention.

The long, exhausting march went through the mining area of Mons. The sky was lit up like lightning from the fires and explosions, because behind the Germans all bridges, crossroads and railway lines were being blown up by *pionier* detachments. Towards midnight the column reached Nimy east of Mons:

> The men were provided with luxurious quarters, because the owners of the homes did not dare to come out of the cellars because of the constant artillery fire. When we looked at each other in the white sheeted parade beds, we must laugh because we looked so funny, unshaven, gaunt, bleary eyed front swine. 9 November is quite quiet. Tommy only advances slowly, because the many mine explosions detain him and he still does not trust our retreat. A very damaged tank left behind that we had to leave standing by a village edge, held his brother, how a captured officer told me, for two days because they had feared to run into a trap and the tank without a crew was considered to be a poorly masked support position.
>
> *Leutnant der Reserve* Schurhammer, Adjutant, II/R111.[19]

Leutnant Gallion kept a brief diary of the ten days of defensive fighting at the end of the war:

> Alternating with the second youngest company leader I led the rearguard of the III/R109 as the youngest company leader. We crouched in wet holes a part of the night, feeling chilly and hungry. We sent our comparatively plentiful lead about the ears of the British and out of our light machine guns. So he might believe first of all that the Germans formations were still in full strength and expected his attack. When he then let loose his vastly extravagant steel on the following morning on our bodies, he still did not trust us any further. He moved after cautiously. We must certainly pay for our 'sitting across' with real losses. Henceforth we were cunning and more careful. Still we were pounded in the following days, tired, freezing and starving in the wet ground and counted the quarters of an hour of the sluggishly creeping night, however we smelled the approximate time of the early morning pounding and already had a noticeable spacing, when the Tommys inundated our rearguard position. His fire blows always became shorter, longer however

> on our road and also more dangerous. English cavalry patrols could snatch us up easily, those who remained behind on and on from the majority. It went along like that for miles long and almost without space and subsequently became jammed in industrial villages for hours so that we were very ill at ease with the possibility of a partisan ambush occurring. For the stumbling tired men, their decrepit bodies and great mental depression barely allowed them to move any further. The heavy weight of the light machine gun and the growling empty stomach didn't go with each other.
>
> *Leutnant* Gallion, III/R109.[20]

On 10 November 1918 the 28th Reserve Division marched to Sablain and on the same day reached the western edge of Mons.

> It was also here, where I met an old Bavarian *Jäger Hauptmann*, who was in his 60's, a large, tall figure with white hair, accompanied by his servant and a sheep-dog. The Old man had a carbine and a telescopic rifle hanging about him, his servant also a rifle and two haversacks with cartridges. He told me that his *Jäger* Battalion has dissolved, the men fallen or captured. Now he conducted the war on his own. He was continuously between the two lines, a terror for the Tommys. The patrol would regret coming in front of his rifle. He sorrowfully said: 'Maybe I will also be hit by a bullet once, what was I supposed to do without my battalion.'
>
> *Leutnant der Reserve* Schurhammer, Adjutant, II/R111.[21]

In accordance with orders the Mons position was held on 10 November 1918. The enemy moved forward that evening and was firmly established in the outpost zone and battle contact came in the first morning hours of the 10th with the left regimental sector, II/R109. At 10.00 a.m. the enemy destructive fire was placed on the railway station Mons; simultaneously the enemy attacked the left wing of the regiment with strong forces. However, he became repulsed with support from German batteries. Further attacks that followed in the afternoon also failed. RIR 109 lost five dead, 11 wounded and 15 missing this day.

At 8:20 a.m. on 10 November, Major *von* Schmeling assembled RIR 110 and announced that His Majesty the Kaiser had renounced the throne. After the recent fighting at Valenciennes, the regiment had reached the end of its strength in numbers and psychologically. The Other Ranks returning from the fighting were completely numb and dazed and also no longer fully conscious about the significant decision of the renunciation of the throne by the Kaiser. They only possessed one thought in their apathy: home, home, as soon as possible!

The end of the Great War came suddenly to 28th Reserve Division. One day there was still fighting and suddenly it was finished, the turmoil, suffering and death of the past 50 months was over. It was an odd feeling that in the blink of an eye all concerns about death and wounds were gone and many of the men were unsure how to handle the new feelings that came over them. A sense of relief and uncertainty came over the men regarding the immediate future. All that anyone could think about now was that

Hotel Brittanique in Spa, Belgium where the Kaiser abdicated. (Author's collection)

the war was over and they would be going home. The basic infantryman in the 28th Reserve Division was not overly concerned about the defeat, especially after what they had experienced in the last year of the war. Now the overwhelming concern was the thought of having survived the fighting and to finally return to a normal life if that was possible after what so many had experienced.

The withdrawal by the men of RIR 109 that had taken place the past days and weeks continued into the night of 10/11 November 1918. Then, at 11.00 a.m. on the morning of the 11th a report arrived that British cavalry had broken through the German line in the direction of the village of Noas and had already occupied that village. Immediate counter measures were quickly undertaken by the men of RIR 109 to face this new threat when the order arrived that all hostilities would end at 12.00 noon. Apparently the *Waffenstillstand* (Armistice) that had been rumored for some time had been concluded. The men of RIR 109 no longer had to face fighting a far superior enemy in what was looking more and more as a hopeless situation.

For RIR 110 the Armistice was announced to the men at 12.00 noon on 11 November 1918 by the company leaders. The hostilities were suspended immediately and for all intents and purposes the war was over. In retrospect, the author of the regimental history wrote: 'Whoever by us suspected then, what a cruel end that was! Nobody knew the murderous conditions of this armistice.' The author was correct as the rigid terms and conditions of the Armistice would not be known for some time, not until after the Peace Conference had finished.

In RIR 111 the small crowd of men that still remained of the regiment received a telephone call at 10.00 a.m. on 11 November 1918 that the hostilities would cease promptly at 12.00 o'clock. The following division order arrived shortly thereafter:

28th Reserve Division Division Headquarters, 11th November 1918

1a Nr. 8006 Division order.
Comrades! The cease fire has been concluded. The years long, terrible fighting has come to an end. The division will become marched homeward. However our situation is still serious. We are on a long road that stretches far from home, amid a population that hates us. The homeward journey goes through areas which in part are barren and little settled. Therefore leading the division home requires the good will of everyone, severe order and discipline; then it will succeed in leading everyone who belongs to the division back home without the loss of life or limb. Behind us lies the World War, which was imposed upon Germany by jealous foreign countries. We were finally overwhelmed but have not been vanquished. The 28th Reserve Division has performed admirably during the entire war in terrible fighting. We return home with polished shields and our honor intact. Germany and Baden can be proud of such warriors, who also survived in hopeless situations and have honorably fought to the death. In the emotion of the passion of our time one hardly has the time or the mood to appreciate the heroic deeds of the division. Not until the coming generation will read with proud amazement, how our warriors have afforded superhuman effort and have withstood stalwartly up to the last breathe. In reverence we remember the fallen heroes in what is called hope that this heroism in the coming generations to Germany's fame and world wealth and consequences will accomplish again. In Germany the transition is carried out of old relationships in the new nation state. We will have to be content with a difficult transition time before we can thrive in the new economic relationships. We must all play a part; because out of subjects we have become citizens. We have received new directives, so the duties of the subject became still greater and more significant. The new Federal Chancellor Ebert, who belongs to the Social Democratic party, published the following:

The new government has taken over the business of leadership, in order to preserve the German people from a civil war and famine and assert his justifiable demand on self-determination. They could only fulfill this task if all authorities and officials in cities and the land offer their helpful hand.

I know that it will become very hard, to work with the new men that have taken over the management of the empire, but I appeal to their love for our people. A failure of the administration in these serious hours consigns Germany to anarchy and the greatest misery. Help everyone only with serving the fatherland through undaunted further work, with everyone at his post, until the hour of the relief has come.

Berlin, 9th November 1918. *Reichs* Chancellor Ebert.[22]

The divisional commander to what had already been presented to the men:

> It is good we are obliged that everyone to stay put at his post, to play a part in the new work, to guide our severely tested people through the turbid transition time in the new situation. Everything hangs on our trusted cooperation, our own fate and the indulgences of our children and children's children. Faithfully and with self-sacrifice, we want to play a part in the work in that Germany rises once again and in the future it strides along the world -paths in its old strength.
>
> *Von* Altrock.[23]

While the news regarding the Armistice arrived at each regiment in a slightly different manner, it is clearly evident that the concepts of the army being 'stabbed in the back' and the idea that the Allies had failed to defeat the German Army in the field were being sown and were to take root within the next generation and set the stage for the next major upheaval to be experienced in the 20th Century, the Second World War 1939-1945.

Now, on 11 November 1918, the Armistice effectively ended fighting on the western front. In looking back at the events of the war the regiments of the 28th Reserve Division could see that following the short period of victory in the advances of 1914 the regiments of the division had heroically afforded opposition to the enemy armies for four years and in their perspective they had protected the homeland with their lives.

Despite the concept of remaining undefeated in the field or the subsequent 'stabbed in the back' theory, by November 1918 the troops, as far as they still existed, were at their last strength, they had nothing left to give and could not have continued fighting even if they had wanted to. Even if the Armistice had not come, the troops no longer wanted to fight. The end of hostilities was founded in the military situation at the front as much as in the political situation at home, the severity of which the men at the front knew nothing about. It was seen as being undeserved for an army that had given its all for honor and the fatherland until the very last.

It would probably be impossible to describe the emotions that passed through each individual at the moment the Armistice was announced. A war that the world had never experienced before was finally concluded even though the Armistice was technically only a temporary end to the hostilities. The men of the 28th Reserve Division slowly emerged from the hastily prepared earthen holes and shallow fire trenches in the wet November earth, very hesitantly at first. When nothing happened to the first few brave souls, more and more men stood up. It was almost like a miracle, to be able to stand up in the open by the front line without becoming instantly fired at by the enemy.

Within a short time small groups of men could be seen standing about everywhere, discussing the momentous event with emotional words and gestures. The extreme tension of the last few weeks slowly faded and became a feeling of joy with the notion that these men will see home again. All of their comrades who had fulfilled their duty to the fatherland with a hero's death would not be forgotten. They would live in the hearts and minds of their companions in arms.

The timetable for the withdrawal from occupied territory had to start immediately if it was to be accomplished on schedule. Thus Belgium had to be evacuated by by 22

November 1918. In order to accomplish this, the army had to march until it crossed the border. Rest for men and horses was not permitted until the frontier was crossed. Strict discipline was required to move the vast quantities of men and material. Order was called for by the High Command, otherwise the entire situation could collapse into chaos and confusion.

Field Marshal von Hindenburg was well aware of the need for strict discipline in the withdrawal and he issued a general statement to all of the German troops still in occupied territory:

> I stand as before at the head of the General Headquarters, to lead the troops in an orderly and steadfast manner home. I expect that all command authority, officers, *Unteroffiziere* and Other Ranks furthermore will also do their duty.
>
> Von Hindenburg.[24]

While the march was perceived differently by each man in the long columns, for most it was a relief that the war was finally over and that they had survived. For others, it was not the result they had expected when they had marched off to war with such high hopes of returning home in a joyous victory march. Victory or not, they were finally out of the great struggle in which so many of their comrades had died. 'Now it was the thought of home, parents, wives and children!'

For the men of 28th Reserve Division, who had survived to see this day, they found that they were in the streets of Belgian villages and cities that had suddenly become decorated with Belgian flags, which had seemingly appeared instantly on every structure they could see. To some German soldiers the populations appeared as if they were drunk with victory, filled of national pride and looked scornfully down on the German soldiers. How would the men react to such conditions? Would mob rule suddenly take over and result in even more misery for the people on both sides? It was considered to be a point of honor for the Baden soldiers that the honor of their regiments was upheld, and most were proud that it could be said: 'No crude lack of discipline occurred.'

The task facing the German command was going to be a difficult one, to bring all of the troops across the Rhine River in the shortest time, without rail any transport, crossing large rivers and high mountains on the long route home. That the task was successful could be considered the last masterful achievement of the General Headquarters Staff. Even at the end of the war, the officers whose entire military career was spent in handling the logistics of millions of men continued their duties until the last second.

For the return march the 28th Reserve Division was divided into four columns. Each infantry regiment formed one of the columns. Each column was assigned a large number of different formations; *Pioniers*, *Minenwerfer* detachments, light and heavy artillery, medical companies, military hospitals, Bakery, provision and ammunition columns and more. This is also where the first signs of unrest and revolutionary influence could be seen among the men who had been fighting at the front.

The column containing RIR 111 was assigned a Württemberg *Landsturm* Battalion, which was the only formation in the column that wore the red cockade. Further evidence of revolutionary ideas could be seen with the transport park column where individual small red flags could be found. All other troops used Baden and German flags for their field symbols, items that they had obtained in Belgium. Almost every infantry group had a Baden flag. The infantry units were distributed throughout the columns to protect all of the different formations, because there were still safety concerns while moving through the civilian population.

The 28th Reserve Division, which formed part of the 17th Army, consisted of four army corps, marching in parallel columns. The first part of the journey would follow the Löwen–Eghezee– Namur Road. On the road that led to the Maas two corps marched in advance, with two corps following. The 4th *Ersatz* Division marched in front of the 28th Reserve Division, behind it as the last in line was the 206th Infantry Division. The 28th Reserve Division was divided into four groups: March Group Three, where RIR 110 was located, was being led by the commander of RIR 110. The troops in this portion of the column consisted of RIR 110, I/RFAR 29, *Landwehr Fuss* Artillery 56 and 2/ *Feld Rekruit* Depot from the 107th Infantry Division. While in 1914 this would have consisted of a very large body of men and horses in a long column, at the end of 1918 the combined number of men and horses was barely a fraction of the early war number.

Within RIR 111 the three battalions were so understrength that each one became formed into a single company along with Machine Gun Company Gottmann. The four companies were subordinate to the regimental commander, *Hauptmann* Boy. The men were tired and only longed for home, but just what could they expect once they did arrive in their old towns and villages?

News about the real condition at home had only sparingly reached the troops at the front. Some of the circumstances awaiting the men were known from the changes the men on leave had witnessed firsthand. Also, the few replacements that had arrived by the regiment had much to say about all of the turmoil at home. Much of what they said appeared unnatural and foreign to the men who had become accustomed to the war at the front. However, until now, the fighting had not allowed much time to contemplate the information. For many, understanding the radical changes that had occurred would require them to see it in person before they could even attempt to understand any of it.

There were a few troublemakers in the companies that brought the contamination from home. However, it was particularly pointed out that the small crowd of stout men who at the end formed RIR 111, the troublemakers did not find any sympathetic ears. The troops remained loyal and firmly in the hands of their leaders, who had the added weight of responsibility in that they still entrusted the Other Ranks with weapons, equipment and ammunition as they lead them back home.

Problems on the long march home did not take long to become evident. While the front line combat units were well in hand and retained discipline, the Line of Communication units which were not combined into larger formations more often than not marched on their own and without much consideration of any central authority. As a result, in the first days of the withdrawal there were numerous halts and frequent delays caused by confusion and traffic jams on the small number of roads available to the men.

The unruly behavior was soon resolved when the Line of Communication formations became integrated into the larger groups. In addition to the difficulties caused by the Line of Communication units, others, in their eagerness to get home, did not use the specified march routes, utilized the wrong billets that were assigned to other units and did not move punctually in the morning as required under the extremely well ordered schedule.

Most of these problems were eventually corrected within a few days through the hard work of the headquarters staff of the regiments, divisions and corps, so that the marching during the beautiful, cold weather and frost proceeded smoothly and without many losses of men or horses.

The columns travelled an average of 22 kilometers each day, quite an achievement considering that the route lead through the high Venn and lasted a total of 21 days. It was an especially good performance if you consider that the men were tired and worn out, many had bad footwear; the food for men and horses was often insufficient and of poor quality and the quarters, even if not in poor condition, were usually very cramped.

The men viewed the journey home with different eyes. To some, the beautiful rural areas with numerous castles and villas were a sight to enjoy. They found the rolling hills with peaceful farms quite soothing after the horrors of more than four years of trench warfare. The cool, autumn weather was also a relief on the march. In the early mornings, fog often prevented the men from seeing much of the countryside but this soon passed as the day warmed up.

The historians in the regiments knew they were walking through areas rich in history. Gemappes, where the pursuit of the French Army occurred after the catastrophe of Waterloo, Ramillies, where the English were victorious over the Army of Louis XIV in 1706. Not far from the road the wide Maas depression extended over to Gembloux, which was the scene of a battle during Dutch War of Independence in 1578. Now, with the withdrawal of German troops into Germany they realized that a new chapter of history was being formed.

The route taken by RIR 111 through Belgium was went through many small towns as Germany came closer and closer. On 12 November 1918 the regiment reached Baulers. On the 13th Limal, on the 14th Roux Maroir and on 15 November 1918 Bonesse. Whilst there, the Soldiers Committees were chosen according to orders issued by headquarters, another sign of the altered relationship between officers and men that was never even dreamed of before the war began. On 16 November 1918 the men reached Vaux et Borset, on the 17th Horion. On 18 November 1918 the march brought the men to Lüttich, where the combined battalions of RIR 111 took over guarding the railway station and provisions office. The regimental staff and baggage were given billets in Ougreè.

The regiment was placed in readiness against what they perceived as a malicious mob, probably civilians who, after four years of near starvation, were frantic to obtain food and other scarce items. There was also a concern that the crowds contained Belgians who took strength in seeing their enemy being forced to withdraw in defeat and would try to take advantage of the situation. The regiment was determined to prevent any looting of the supplies that were desperately needed by the columns and set up machine guns and were being supported by tanks, which kept the civilians at bay as well as the large groups of army deserters.

On 18 November 1918 RIR 110 reached the Chotier *die* Maas and moved to Seraing, a suburb of Lüttich, across the large river. While passing through the industrial areas and the larger cities of Belgium the regiment also found the population hostile and all precautions were taken to provide security for the columns and supplies.

On 19 November 1918 the 28th Reserve Division marched from the Maas valley into the valley of the Vesdre, and now the route lead through the industrial city of Verviers where the local civilian population continued to be bolder and more threatening to the passing German soldiers. Fortunately, there were no incidents and the column continued to Limbourg and Gülpen, with the Öde River and the German border being close by. Early on the following morning the columns were in sight of the German homeland. In honor of this moment the vehicles and horses were decorated with black-white-red and yellow-red flags.

While the civilian population appeared to be increasingly hostile, not every contact with local civilians was unpleasant or stressful. The few *Radfahrer* still left with each regiment were used to maintain contact with the different parts of each column and between the different columns. It was very tiring work and it seemed to the *Radfahrer* that they were always in motion during the withdrawal:

> We *Radfahrer* had very exhausting duties on the return march. One was only rarely allowed to sleep and then only for a few hours. We had to travel in advance for all formations to secure the quarters, then back again to the troops and notify each formation of their billets, guide the marching column, now and then travel back by the column to make sure everything is still together, and if necessary to deliver the orders for the next day to the formations at night. Once it actually happened to us that the march column was torn asunder. At a crossroad an unaccompanied vehicle drove through a gap in our marching column. The leader of the next vehicle had fallen asleep, and the horses then followed after this foreign vehicle, all behind also followed. My scare was not small when during a control trip I only found half of the marching column. There we were already a few kilometers distant from the relevant crossing I naturally did not know when the vehicles had turned off. Nothing could be seen of our vehicles far and wide. However, after three hours I had found them again and brought them to the main troop on a byway. Namely, all formations must begin precisely at the ordered time on the ordered roads, because otherwise they could end up in danger of missing the march column. All streets and roads that led to Germany were so exactly distributed on the rear marching army that day and night each road was entirely covered for a particular specific marching column. At larger railroad junctions and canal ports one saw many German railroad trains and transportation boats with subsistence and fodder, ammunition, clothing, etc. that had simply been completely deserted by their transportation and accompanying personnel and becalmed and now fell victim to being plundered by the Belgian civilian population. Also, many powered vehicles of all types, which were left by their drivers and were now derelict in the road ditches. So, for example, on a canal bridge in Verviers stood a completely new automobile with an anti-aircraft gun and a heavy machine gun that was even still loaded. We took the machine gun with us. Naturally, the delivery of all of this valuable army property did not become charged against us. So many millions of the nation's fortune went lost there by unprincipled red comrades.

Niemand hat größere Liebe, denn die,
Daß er sein Leben läßt für seine Freunde.
Ev. Joh. 15. 13.

†

Zur
christlichen Erinnerung
im Gebete
an den Kaufmann
Wilhelm Blanknagel
Fernsprecher im 1. Nachrichtenzuge
des bad. Res.-Inf.Regt. 110,
Inhaber des Eisernen Kreuzes 2. Kl.
und anderer Auszeichnungen,
welcher am 30. Oktober 1918 infolge
schwerer Verwundung bei Mons in
Belgien nach Empfang aller hl Sterb-
sakramente auf dem Verbandplatz zu
Roisin sein Leben dem Vaterland opferte

Schlaf wohl, mein tapf'rer Sohn und Held
In fernem Land, auf fremdem Feld
In Gottes heil'gem Frieden
Entrückt dem Streit hinieden!
Auch uns wird kommen einst der Tag,
Da wir befreit von Erdenplag
Zum lieben Vater gehen,
Bei ihm uns wiedersehen.

[illegible]

Telephone operator in RIR 110, Died 30 October following a severe wound received by Mons. (Author's collection)

German troops retreating through Luxembourg. (Author's collection)

> That there are also good persons in Belgium, the following experience might demonstrate. *Radfahrer* Legutke and I came very late one evening during bad weather into Verviers. We made quarters there on a different day. It was too late to look for the Commandant's office, and so I went into the first house and asked about lodging for the night. In the first and second stories comrades were already in the quarters, but on the third story we found an old mother who lived alone with her approximately 40 year old son. We even received a hot night meal, without therefore having to ask. For it we gave the old mother a large can of preserved sausage that I had still found at a plundered railroad train. We naturally wanted to sleep on the ground, but both said we had not slept in a bed for a long time. On the next morning we still received a good coffee and after warm thanks went on our way again.
>
> *Radfahrer* Wilhelm Klein, 5/RIR 111.[25]

On the afternoon of 21 November 1918 the column crossed over the river by Eupen-Haas and into Germany. The columns continued and made an exhausting march into the high Venn. The columns had taken on a festive appearance when, along with the flag decorations, the men spontaneously broke into song with the old soldier's song '*In der Heimat, da gibt's ein Wiedersehen*'. The men were back in Germany; home!

However, not all was pleasant or friendly as the men crossed back into Germany. The new realities of revolution and unrest were present everywhere. During the withdrawal it was normal routine to send an officer into the next town or village where the men were to stop for the night and make arrangements for quarters to accommodate the men. When *Leutnant der Reserve* Schurhammer, II/R111 rode in advance of the column into the first German city his reception was less than friendly:

> I want to describe my reception on German soil in the entry into Eupen. I rode in advance, in order that I could inquire about quarters. At the city entrance stood a mob of 20-30 chaps with red armbands and red cockades on their caps and inversely draped rifles. Naturally, no greeting. I nevertheless rode over there and asked the lads for the Commandant's office. The reply: 'Here, we are in command; we are the soldier's council. Off with the shoulder boards, the medals, off!' Shouts like this and similar ones mixed up in the mob. My answer was not exactly very socially acceptable and already a couple of such chaps were hanging on me and wanted to tear me from the horse. That, however, did not go so easily, as these nice lads probably expected it to be. I raced my good animal into the middle of the mob that forced the noble lads to fly on the right and on the left side. And then I gave a persuasive speech with my heavy riding crop, a piece of spoil from Lüttich. It was a pleasure to see, how much understanding these men had for this language. In the meantime my bandsmen platoon had also come into view, and when they saw what was taking place here, they played one more small tune on my behalf that worked so well that as long as we were in Eupen, we saw and heard no more from the soldier's council.
>
> *Leutnant der Reserve* Schurhammer, Adjutant II/R111.[26]

German troops retreating through Luxembourg. (Author's collection)

By far, this was the worst incident of lack of order and discipline by revolutionary rowdies who played the part of the Soldier Council in Eupen. In the words of *Leutnant der Reserve* Schurhammer, 'it was a sad example that sufficed for many.'

On 22 November 1918 the troops were finally given a day to rest. The men spent this day with the poor, but friendly villagers in the Venn. The pleasant memory of a very friendly reception by the citizenry remained in the hearts of the men. In the melancholy sternness of the impoverished high moor scenery of the high Venn, the columns became lost in thought for a few days. The column then slowly marched across the high ridges of the *Vennkreuzes Rötgen* that was situated in a forested valley. The columns continued to Zweifel on ever changing steep ascending and descending roads. Due to the congestion of the roads to the Rhine by the large numbers of men another day of rest was provided that was greatly appreciated by the footsore men.

With the main roads crammed with men and wagons any further advance was considered questionable until the mess could be sorted out. Instead, the columns with the 28th Reserve Division marched forward along nearby secondary roads which were not really equipped for such traffic but it was better than sitting still for long periods of time. On 23 November 1918 the men passed through fir wood covered in sugary hoarfrost that gave the appearance of Christmas lights. In Winden the men remained in the modest and very hospitable farmhouses set in a backdrop of pristine nature. All during the march rain and sun alternated each day, still the weather was such that it did not impair the journey home.

The men of RIR 109 travelled through Eupen and on the 23rd marched toward Cologne. On 24 November 1918 the men stood at the western edge of a large brown coal-region with impressive open mine pit facilities stretched across the countryside. RIR 110 reached Rideggen on 24 November 1918 and climbed down to the Rhine plain. Quite soon the spires of the Cologne cathedral slowly appeared in front of the column, a welcome sight to many of the men.

At 2.30 p.m. on 25 November 1918 RIR 109 marched in identical step in group columns which visibly made a big impression on the civilian population, who provided the warmest welcome for the regiment. At the end of the route RIR 109 held the last massed parade marching past the regimental commander in review at the city *Heumarkt,* a large square that contained a large statue of King Friedrich Wilhelm III. The men remarked that the ceremony certainly did not give the appearance of a vanquished army.

The journey home had been accomplished within the time frame provided by the Allied forces. Much of the credit for the success of the long and exhausting march home was given to *Vizefeldwebel* Schandert, the leader of the regimental band who played marching music throughout the entire journey, day and night.

For the men formerly in RIR 40 the tension among the ranks increased as the city of Cologne grew closer and closer. The friendly reception by the local population thrilled the tired men. The troops found their entry into the city accompanied by music, flowers and shouts of welcome as the people provided an honorable homecoming to the unbeaten fighters.

The 'Red Mob' was very active in Cologne at this time but apparently the reputation of the Baden division must have convinced them 'to crawl away cowardly in their dark hideouts during our presence' as was described by one regimental historian. As such the men of the 28th Reserve Division were assured an undisturbed time in the pleasant *Rheinischen* capital with the charitable and enjoyable circle of citizens:

> Something should not be forgotten. On the return march shortly before the German border our regimental commander, Major Derichs, allowed the regiment to be called together in an old cloister yard. He climbed on a large barrel that was lying around there and said approximately the following: "Comrades, I just received the message that we had to turn over our weapons and ammunition to the soldier council in Cologne. Do you understand that?" A vigorous No resounded from all sides and cries were loud: "We march with our weapons back into home, just as we marched off. The soldier council in Cologne could take the weapons from us, if they also have the courage." The regimental commander replied hereupon: "That is only what I wanted to know, I thank you comrades." With the march through Cologne we marched for the last time past our division commander in the old military order. No soldier council was allowed to see that we had not turned in our weapons. It would also be received badly for him. The regiment returned home with its honor intact. We were proud about it.
>
> *Radfahrer* Wilhelm Klein, 5/RIR 111.[27]

On 27 November 1918, at 9.30 a.m., RIR 110 marched over the new hillside bridge across the Rhine. For the last time the division commander von Altrock allows his division to march past him. The march continued through the beautiful Sauerland with its mountains and valleys, villages and cities.

Men from RIR 109 on the journey home. (*Das Reserve-Infanterie-Regiment Nr. 109 im Weltkrieg 1914 bis 1918*)

RIR 111 also crossed over the Rhine by Cologne on this day between 12.00 and 1.00 p.m. on the hillside bridge. The march through the festively decorated and flag bedecked city took place in exquisite marching order and without any stopping. The baggage wagons were decorated with black-white-red and yellow-red-yellow flags. The inhabitants of Cologne greeted the troops heartily and distributed gifts to the men as they passed by. The brigade commander allowed the battalions to march past him at the *Heumarkt*, and everyone watching were extremely appreciative over the good composure of the RIR 111 servicemen:

> On 28 November we crossed over the German border by Eupen. Everything was festively covered with flags and covered in garlands. After a further days march through the Eifel we had the first rest day. Then it went further again via Düren, Cologne to Hüsten–Neheim. The entire division lay in quarters in the District Arnsberg. With completely few exceptions we quite kindly received everywhere up and well fed. We were especially grateful here to one butcher's widow I believe to be in a large village between Eupen and Cologne, who on one day cooked an entire cow. Every soldier that visited the house was invited for a meal.
> *Radfahrer* Wilhelm Klein, 5/RIR 111.[28]

Once across the Rhein, all of the men from that region who were in the different regiments were discharged home, the regiments then marched away on 29 November 1918.

On 2 December 1918 RIR 109 was one of the last formations across the Rhine. The regiment marched through the mountainous terrain somewhat hastily and finally reached its march-goal. The journey through the Westfalian ground took the men into the area of Arnsberg, Hachen, Hövel and Hüften *an* der Ruhr, a small industrial city. RIR 110 reached Niedereimer by Arnsberg in Westfalia on the 2nd and become accommodated in good quarters. In 21 days of marching the regiment had travelled 447.5 kilometers.

RIR 109 remained in Hüften *an der* Ruhr until 10 December and demobilized 70 *Unteroffiziere* and Other Ranks each day. On 5 December *Leutnant* and Regimental Adjutant Böhne left the military service after he had performed his responsibilities over two and a half years in an exemplary fashion. On 6 December 1918 *Leutnant* Kirchenbauer also left the regiment, who had served the regiment as the Supply, Judicial and Orderly Officer almost throughout the entire war.

On 6 December the Acting Commanding General sent a wire containing the Demobilization orders for the regimental staff, I and II/R109 including machine gun companies and the *Minenwerfer* Company which were embarked at 10 a.m. in Arnsberg. The III/R109 moved into the quarters of the I/R109 and awaited the final orders.

At 10.00 p.m. on 10 December 1918 RIR 110 began the rail transport from Arnsberg to Baden, and home. Arnsberg was the rail hub from which most of the men of the 28th Reserve Division were sent home for demobilization. The days spent waiting to be sent home were used by the regimental staff to process the necessary paperwork for men who were being released from service early for pressing needs. It was also used to make repairs to the uniforms and pieces of equipment, and the important business of getting rid of vermin. Frenzied activity prevailed in the orderly rooms and offices as they prepared for demobilization. With the prospect of being discharged from the army at hand, the mood of the troops was good. Also, the marching of the last days had not been very exhausting, and the billets were comfortably furnished.

At 3.00 a.m. on 11 December 1918 RIR 110 traveled from Arnsberg via Werdohl, Finntrop, Dillenburg, Wetzlar to Aschaffenburg where the regiment arrived at 2.00 p.m. on the 12th. On the same day the regiment continued further via Eberbach, Bretten, Mühlacker to Pforzheim and Wildbach. After a short rest the regimental staff and the I/R110 made the last march to Gernsbach and Hörden in the Murg valley. The II and III/R110 were transported by rail to Durlach and from there marched to Ettlingen. The three battalions were then demobilized in the middle of December in Gernsbach and Hörden and in Ettlingen, and the Other Ranks were discharged to return home.

The II/R109 with the Machine Gun Company was ready to be transported on 11 December 1918 in Arnsberg while the III/R109 (the former III/R40) moved again and arrived in Arnsberg where the men were billeted until the 16th.

At 1.30 p.m. on 13 December 1918 the I/R109 arrived in Durlach and marched via Ettlingen to Busenbach, where it received quarters. From 14 until the 18th the horses, vehicles, weapons, ammunition, clothing and pieces of equipment were handed over to the Demobilization *Abteilung* E 109 in Ettlingen. All officers and Other Ranks from the Classes of 1896 through 1899 became transferred to the *Leibgrenadier* Regiment; all other class years were discharged. Major Engelmann managed the handling of the I/R109.

III/R109 was be transported from Arnsberg and arrived in Bruchsal on 18 December where the men received quarters in the boy's school. There were a few delays in transporting all of the men and equipment. It was not always easy putting together transport trains because of material shortages. The management of this battalion took place under the leadership of *Oberleutnant* Siegert.

The II/R109 arrived in Durlach at 7.00 a.m. on 14 December and marched to Reichenbach, where it was disbanded under the guidance of the Battalion commander, Major Auer from Herrenkirchen. The men were all discharged before Christmas with the exception of the youngest Class year. Once discharged, the men made their way home to every corner of Baden.

Starting from 14 December 1918 RIR 111 became embarked for home by battalion. The regimental staff and the III/R111 arrived in Konstanz about midnight on the 17th, where they were received at the railway station and greeted by the city authorities and music played by the band of *Ersatz* Regiment 114.

On 15 December 1918 the I/R111 reached Donaueschingen at 8.00 a.m., while the II/R111 reached Stockach on the 16th at 10.00 a.m. Both battalions also received a joyous welcome from the city officials and the local populace of those places. Before the end of the year, the regiments of the 28th Reserve Division had all ceased to exist; the war was over.

Notes

1. R.H Lutz, *The Causes of the German Collapse in 1918*, p. 86.
2. Gallion, op. cit., pp. 326-327.
3. Gallion, op. cit., p. 326.
4. Geiger, op. cit., pp. 357-358.
5. Geiger, op. cit., pp. 358-359.
6. Greiner & Vulpius, op. cit., pp. 289-290.
7. Greiner & Vulpius, op. cit., p. 290.
8. Ibid.
9. Gallion, op. cit., p. 329.
10. Gallion, op. cit., p. 328.
11. Gallion, op. cit., p. 326.
12. Gallion, op. cit., pp. 327-328.
13. Gallion, op. cit., pp. 329-330.
14. Geyer, op. cit., p. 359.
15. Gallion, op. cit., pp. 330-331.
16. Greiner & Vulpius, op. cit., p. 293.
17. Geyer, op. cit., pp. 220-221.
18. Gallion, op. cit., p. 332.
19. Gallion, op. cit., pp. 332-333.
20. Gallion, op. cit., p. 333.
21. Gallion, op. cit., p. 332.
22. Frisch, op. cit., pp. 286-287.
23. Frisch, op. cit., p. 287.
24. Greiner & Vulpius, op. cit., p. 293.
25. Geyer, op. cit., pp. 359-360.
26. Gallion, op. cit., p. 335.
27. Geyer, op. cit., pp. 360-361.
28. Geyer, op. cit., p. 360.

9

26th Reserve Division

October-November 1918
Armistice and Journey Home

At 4.00 a.m. on 1 October 1918 the 51st Reserve Infantry Brigade reported that it had implemented the reorganization of the units that had been ordered. The gaps that existed in the line were closed through machine gun posts. The 26th Reserve Division was holding a considerable length of the front with the three under-strength regiments and the only reserves in possession of the division were two battalions from IR 190 located at Blécourt and Cuvillers, two battalions from RIR 99 and the II/R119 at Ramillies. One battalion from RIR 99, the I/R99, was inserted into the sector of IR 190. After three quarters of an hour of artillery preparation combined with gas fire that surpassed everything experienced by the division until now, the enemy attacked at 5.30 a.m. on the whole Army Corps front. Numerous tanks followed the dense waves of advancing infantry.

The initial enemy attack was repulsed along the division front; however the enemy broke through at the border between the 22nd Infantry Division and the 26th Reserve Division, overran the reserve battalions from IR 190 that were positioned at Blécourt and Cuvillers and began to thrust into the area of Eswars, into the artillery positions of the division. The 8/RFAR 26 fired at point blank range until the last shot, which came when the enemy penetrated into the gun positions after the machine guns of the battery had all been destroyed. Still, despite this disaster, the gunners succeeded in blowing up one gun before abandoning the battery.

Several other batteries were overrun by the enemy troops before the advance could be brought to a stop by the direct fire of other nearby batteries that were shooting using open sights. The attackers had advanced within a few meters of several batteries that after firing at the Canadian troops at point blank range were unable to fire the guns anymore and the artillerymen defended the gun positions with carbines and hand grenades.

Later on the same day many of the batteries were successfully recaptured in a counter-thrust. The heroic action of the 2/RFAR 26 that snatched away the lost guns from the enemy again, is described in the division order below:

> Division Headquarters, 3 October 1918. On the afternoon of 1 October *Vizewachtmeister* Wildermut, *Vizewachtmeister* Leitz and *Unteroffizier* Röck from the 2/RFAR 26 with drivers and gunners from the battery succeeded in salvaging two guns that had fallen into English hands in the morning at Cuvillers under the most difficult circumstances and heaviest enemy bombardment. I speak to all participants for their intrepid, energetic behavior, my special acknowledgment.
> Signed von Fritsch.[1]

At 5.00 a.m. on 1 October 1918 renewed drum fire broke across the sector held by RIR 119 that was followed by an enemy attack a short time later. According to captured document three British divisions advanced from Tilloy and the north towards the east; a fourth division was in support, and after the successful breakthrough would make a large right swing and grab the triangle at the railway embankment from the rear, force the crossing over the Schelde and storm Cambrai. The city at this time was being defended Guard and *Jäger* units. The plan was well contrived, but when the enemy encountered the men of the 26th Reserve Division the plan was thrown off track.

The enemy made every attempt to dislodge the men of RIR 119 from their positions, in vain. The regiment held tenaciously, inflicted heavy losses on the attackers through infantry and well directed machine gun fire and didn't yield a single foot of ground. The situation became so critical at one point even the battalion staff also took up rifles and joined in the fighting. However north of the regimental position the German defenses had been overrun and were inundated by swarms of enemy troops.

The 9/R119 and a platoon from the 3MG/R119 became caught up in the confusion and encircled. The men quickly became destroyed or taken prisoner, only a few managed to escape to the rear including the platoon of the 3MG/R119 that managed to avoid being captured. The enemy then was able to fire into the flank and rear of the 10th and 11/R119, both of which had successfully fought off all frontal attacks.

What the men saw now would have been considered unthinkable only months earlier; swarms of fleeing German soldiers, crying out in panic, pouring back northeast of Morenchies and abandoning the positions to the enemy. 'It was such a shocking sight, how manliness and the sense of duty had disappeared and shattered and how disastrous faintheartedness gripped them.'

While the neighboring troops fled from the battlefield the men of RIR 119, what few were still left, continued to hold on to the positions and 'looked with defiant eyes, staring in the face of threatening danger.' The situation had become extremely serious. The right flank of the regiment and the division hung in the air and a giant void opened north of Ramillies. RIR 119 was now in a very precarious position. The front the regiment held in the morning faced west, now it had to form lines facing north and in part facing northeast. The only salvation of the regiment was in the rear, one of the last intact bridges across the canal, which was also under heavy enemy fire.

While the heavy fighting was taking place the men of RIR 119 could see a British artillery battery travelling east of Tilloy. British patrols and larger detachments of infantry advanced from the hill north of Morenchies and moved to the south. Machine gun fire was directed against these targets and they were driven back over and over.

Unteroffizier Balb of the 2MG/R119 destroyed an officer's patrol east of the Châteat Park and captured maps, sketches and the plans of the entire enemy attack.

The 5th, 6th and 7/R119 became supports for the I and III/R119, with the 6/R11 in the northern corner of the park of Morenchies, and the 5th and 7/R119 on the roac to Ramillies with a front facing northward in order to prevent the position from being encompassed.

The British and Canadians had thrust forward via Abancourt, Bantigny, to Blécourt where units from IR 190 had been posted and continued forward to Ervillers and had surrounded the men of RIR 121 who held Blécourt. Neuville-St. Remy had already been lost the day before and in its houses and those of Tilloy enemy marksmen and machine guns had been posted that overlooked the entire terrain from their elevated positions and made any movement in the open impossible. Sheaves of bullets swarmed over the terrain without interruption. Enemy disturbance fire and short shots from the German guns depressed the spirits of the men even further, yet there was a small group from RIR 121, which sat like a small island amidst the enemy swarms three kilometers to the north by Blécourt.

Little is known about the events that had taken place by RIR 121 on 1 October 1918 as few men returned to the rear at the end of the fighting. What is known is that at 5.00 a.m., heavy drum fire began to fall upon the regimental position in a strength that had apparently surpassed anything ever experienced before. Dense masses of enemy infantry attacked close behind the rolling fire but not against the front of the II/R121. Then the enemy suddenly appeared on both flanks of the II Battalion after he had apparently broken through the line of the neighboring Prussian regiment.

During the fighting, part of the enemy force had turned off to the south, struck the weak remnants of RIR 121 in the position and attacked them in the flank and rear. Part of the regiment, presumably under the leadership of the battalion commanders *Hauptmann* Klaus and *Oberleutnant der Reserve* Stark, both missing since the fighting, defended a completely isolated position in a sunken road south of Blécourt, the entire day. This was known from reports by infantry flights that flew over the position numerous times and observed German troops occupying this locality and still fighting behind the enemy front line.

The two officers were last seen fighting against superior enemy strength amidst their men with pistols in their hands. Unfortunately it was not possible to rescue the handful of men from RIR 121. After speaking to the few survivors of the regiment was it later determined that the small group of men fought on until evening and it was not until they had run out of ammunition, were they overpowered by the enemy.

Following the destruction of the II and III/R121 the enemy continued to advance and quickly overwhelmed the I/R121 that consisted of 30 men that were lying further to the rear. Individual men from the regiment were able to strike through to the rear, but only a handful of those who had been in the positions at the start of the day. The enemy attack became brought to a stop through artillery fire that fired into the advancing columns at close range from Cuvillers. The regimental commander finally assembled all of the men still available in the 26th Reserve Division in Thun-Léveque, including battle orderlies, bearer troops, Other Ranks of the First Line Transport, and placed them at the western edge of Eswars as a security garrison; however, they were not involved in the fighting. When RIR 121 became extracted out of the front, only two weak companies could be formed out of the survivors.

The night of 1 October 1918 had proceeded without any special incidents by IR 180. Then, at 5.00 a.m. the enemy drum fire began upon the sector of IR 180 and the troops connecting to the north. The strong enemy fire lasted until 6.00 a.m. Then it was transferred to the rear at 6.10 a.m., at which point strong machine gun fire was clearly audible in the direction of Tilloy.

However, within a short time the German defensive fire stopped and the enemy infantry could be seen advancing by the northern part of Tilloy and further north of the village. The adversary apparently only met tenacious resistance at the earthworks located east of the village which contained the battle headquarters of the I and II/180. This strongpoint located in a small copse on a dominating rise was under the command of *Hauptmann der Reserve* Mehl, the commander of the II/180. Mehl had developed the location into a strongpoint through the installation of numerous machine guns and by inserting a platoon of two guns from the escort battery 1/43.

The strongpoint then became taken under attack by enemy troops advancing from all sides. Starting from 7.00 a.m. six enemy aircraft circled the position and attacked it from an altitude of 20 up to 30 meters high with machine gun fire and bombs.

This location was still being held at 7.30 a.m. with the machine guns working splendidly and both field guns firing at the enemy at very close range while exposed in the front line. The guns were specially targeted by the six enemy aircraft that also directed the enemy artillery fire against them. During the fighting a German gas shell depot located on the nearby railway line was destroyed by enemy fire the defenders were forced to wear their gas masks when clouds of Blue Cross gas blew across the strongpoint, carried by the wind.

Finally, after the field guns had fired all of their ammunition, the largest part of the machine guns had also run out of ammunition, and the remaining guns had become unserviceable, or destroyed, the strongpoint suddenly came under enemy machine gun fire from the right rear. This new threat forced the defenders to create a front facing north. Under these circumstances the toughly defended position had to be evacuated, and the Other Ranks received orders to withdraw to the sunken road west of Ramillies that was occupied by RIR 99. Only a few of the men going to the rear reached the sunken road, because the terrain they crossed was under very strong machine gun fire coming from three sides.

At 8.45 a.m. *Oberleutnant der Reserve* Teuffel, commander of the I/180, delivered a verbal report over the course of the attack and the current situation. At 9.00 a.m. Abaucourt, Blécourt, Bantigny and Cuvillers that had been occupied by the 22nd Infantry Division, were lost. At 9.15 a.m. the regimental staff of IR 180 transferred its battle headquarters to the embankment east of Escaudoeuvres and sent out an officer with the task to verbally report to the brigade about the current situation and the headquarters change.

The attacks on the morning of the 1st had forced the 26th Reserve Division to curve back the front line held by the II/R119 across the hill northeast of Tilloy to the area west of Ramillies in order to counter the threat of being encompassed from the north. In doing so the division had used up all of the available reserves from IR 180 and RIR 119. Subsequently to the north stood the II and III/R99 in a sunken road west of Ramillies and a gap two kilometers wide had formed between the right wing of RIR 99 and the left wing of the 22nd Infantry Division.

In this critical situation, while the 51st Reserve Infantry Brigade attempted to close the gap by gathering together orderlies, Baggage men from the division train, stragglers and the survivors of RIR 55 held a counterattack from out of the area northeast of Bantigny. This counter thrust completely linked up all units in the possession of the 26th Reserve Division. The counterattack effectively prevented the enemy from taking full advantage of the hole in the German line and subsequently overwhelming the remnants of the 26th Reserve Division.

Every gun in the area that was still capable of firing from the II/RFAR 26 and other batteries located in a position east of the canal, directed their combined fire, mostly in direct fire, on the threatened position. With the enemy infantry approaching the gun positions, everything appeared to be lost. The heaviest enemy fire had fallen on the 2/RFAR 26 since 8.00 a.m., making it almost impossible to operate the guns. Despite the strong fire, shell upon shell shot out of the gun barrels into the enemy ranks that were barely 200 meters in front of the battery. One gun was silenced by a direct hit until nearby *Vizewachtmeister* and *Unteroffiziere* replaced the fallen gunners.

The badly shaken enemy infantry could not withstand the infantry counterattack and the close range artillery support and was forced to yield back over Bantigny–Ervillers in the Blécourt– Tilloy sunken road. The opposing lines now formed an arc projecting in the direction of Eswars and Ramillies, where the enemy troops remained, probably as a result of the heavy losses they had suffered. It was accepted that the enemy yielded more from the concentrated artillery fire than any pressure from the few infantrymen still involved in the fighting.

The enemy attacks continued a short time later and the machine guns assigned to the artillery fired at the enemy advance against the battery flank. Finally, the field guns and machine guns ran out of ammunition, allowing the enemy to penetrate the battery position; only a few gunners were able to escape along with the yielding infantry in the hail of enemy bullets, the others were lying dead or wounded by the guns.

At 12.00 noon the enemy attempted to advance once again out of the Blécourt-Tilloy sunken road with strong forces. The attack broke down entirely in well placed artillery fire. An attack occurring at 1.30 p.m. out of Tilloy as well as several strong advances upon Morenchies also became refused outright despite the heaviest enemy fire and heavy losses among the tenacious defenders from IR 180 and RIR 119.

During the day the adversary had attacked twelve times, during which all of the battalion staff were directly involved in the fighting in the position. Finally, when the fighting had ended, Cambrai was still in German hands. The overall situation was a mass of confusion and conflicting stories about what was occurring along the front. Towards 4.00 p.m. a German counterattack north of Ramillies advanced toward the enemy. When the skirmish line reached Hill 78.4 east of Tilloy and attempted to cross it, German artillery and infantry fire struck their ranks, resulting in shouts of ewilderment, orders, counter-orders and forced the counterattack to hesitate. Finally, he men flooded back to the exit position without having achieved anything.

An enemy machine gun on Hill 78.4 continuously annoyed the reserves located behind Morenchies and stopped any traffic, any movement in the position. *Leutnant der Reserve* Eugen Rettenmaier, commander of the 5/R119, noticed a British soldier looking for shelter behind some cast up earth that could conceal him. Rettenmaier walked over o the hiding place while only carrying a cane and came upon a wounded Canadian oldier and helped to bind his wounds. Afterward, he told the man that 'he would be picked up there afterward!'

Then Rettenmaier ordered the enemy machine gun nest to be taken under constant fire from two heavy machine guns in order to hold down the garrison. He borrowed a machine-pistol from one of his men, took *Kriegsfreiwilliger* Kurt König (5/R119) and *Unteroffizier* Balb with him and sneaked up to the annoying nest. When they were close enough to the enemy nest Rettenmaier waved a handkerchief. The machine guns stopped firing at which time Rettenmaier and his companions leaped into the nest in a long, swift jump. Rettenmaier was astonished to see an enemy soldier, as he described as 'a giant beanpole chap in front of him!' Two of the occupants quickly took cover and laid down; one other man was shot by a pistol that shattered his arm. The other men in the nest raised their hands and Rettenmaier brought back six Canadians Highlanders and three captured Lewis Guns back to the battalion, without suffering any losses.

RIR 119 had held most of the regimental position until now but time was rapidly running out for the few men still standing as the losses were heavy. The majority of the 8/R119 was missing, the 11/R119 numbered only seven men and was merged into the 10/R119. The other companies had lost 25-33 percent of their previously existing weak strength leaving the companies with the battle strength of 20-30 men each. The restless enemy was still sitting on the nearby hill and a catastrophe was feared when he attacked again following a period of fresh drum fire.

The few men left in RIR 119 were on their own; there were no supports or reserves and there was no chance of being relieved. The hole punched through the German line in the north was devouring all available reserves. So the small handful of troops waited through the night to see what the following day would bring.

During the night another enemy nest located inside the German lines in an earthwork southeast of Cuvillers was attacked, where approximately 50 Canadian soldiers became captured. During this action *Leutnant* Schwab, leader of the 1/RFAR 26, drew special attention to his actions here. On the evening of 1 October 1918 the line ran from Blécourt *Hohlweg* to Tilloy hill northeast of Tilloy to the railroad causeway southeast of Tilloy.

Up until the afternoon the staffs of the three battalions whose units were totally dispersed, were located with the regimental staff. The brigade becomes notified about the situation and a plea was made to extract the regiment in order to assemble the survivors and reform the ranks. At 8.00 p.m. the long awaited order arrived, to march to Avesnes le Sec and to assemble there. When the survivors of IR 180 arrived at Avesnes le Sec an attempt was made to evaluate the losses. It was found that for the most part no one knew what had happened to the majority of the men.

Eight *Unteroffiziere* and Other Ranks were known to have been killed; three officer and 53 Other Ranks were reported wounded; nine officers (*Leutnants der Reserve* Völte Einsele, Katz, Schütze, Stier, Frey, Schweizer, Schmid, Erh., Schultheiss) and 142 Othe Ranks were missing. The remnants of IR 180 could then barely form a single weal company.

During the night the German artillery batteries covered the enemy approach route under strong disturbance fire and towards morning made held fire raids with the neigh boring division on the suspected support areas of the enemy. The attack expected on th following day did not take place; it was suspected that the Canadians were exhauste from the recent fighting.

The performance of the 'Iron 26th Reserve Division' was given high praise in th army report of 1st October 1918:

> The British placed fierce attacks on both sides of Cambrai the entire day. On the afternoon a newly inserted Canadian division temporarily succeeded in thrusting forward north past Cambrai on Ramillies. Under the leadership of *Generalleutnant* von Fritsch the especially proven Württemberg 26th RD threw the enemy back again upon Tilloy in the fighting between Arras and Cambrai. Therefore south of Cambrai we have completely held our positions against the numerous onrushes by the enemy.[2]

Commanding General XVIII Army Corps *Generalleutnant* von Etzel also sent a congratulatory message to the 26th Reserve Division. The *Oberbefehlshaber* of the 17th Army *General der Infanterie* Otto von Below sent a telegraph to the King of Württemberg, praising the work of the division.

The overall consensus was that the enemy had become exhausted from the recent attacks and needed time to recover. Some men in the 26th Reserve Division even went so far as to believe that if three fresh divisions were available, the British could be thrown back in an attack.

While the enemy may have been exhausted from the recent fighting, it was no different in the German units. On 2 October 1918 the remnants of IR 180 that had been assembled during the night were distributed into a half battalion consisting of two companies, with one machine gun platoon attached to each company. One of the companies was created out of handful of Other Ranks from the I/180, the other company was formed by combining the few survivors of the II and III/180. *Oberleutnant der Reserve* Teuffel was assigned to command the half battalion. The two companies consisted of one company commander, two platoon leaders, six Unteroffiziere and 48 men along with four light machine guns. The total combat strength of IR 180 at this time was 115 officers and men.

The losses in the 26th Reserve Division were heavy, especially in battle proven leaders. The extreme efforts by the Other Ranks in the hard days of fighting had sorely tested the strength of the men yet the mood of the troops was still reported to be excellent. If the men were in an excellent mood or not, there were simply too few of them left in the division to truly make a difference in the final days of the war. Even of all of the losses could be replaced, the division would only be fully manned with men who had no training or very little training behind them and as such would be considered almost useless.

The night to 2 October 1918 proceeded quietly. The regimental commander of RIR 99 disbanded the I/R99 and divided the remnants into the companies of the III/R99. Then, the regiment became ordered to capture a nearby hill. At 3.00 p.m., after three hours of artillery preparation, the two battalions of the regiment advanced in waves 200 meters apart. The attack met considerable opposition, particularly at the right wing. Under the personal leadership of *Hauptmann* Leiling the 11/R99 captured a British machine gun nest and 12 prisoners. Unfortunately this outstanding officer as well as *Leutnant der Reserve* Lamprecht, were killed during the fighting. Leiling was the officer who had become so well-known for the underground defenses by Beaumont-Hamel and Beaucourt and who had the *Leiling Schlucht* named after him. During the fighting by RIR 99 no connection could be established with the regiments on the right or on the left of the regiment, not even when the hill was stormed. As a result, constant flanking fire came from the right. In the evening hours enemy drum fire caused particularly strong losses at the right wing, so that the companies had to withdraw into the main opposition line after the fire had eased up somewhat. Only a few sentries from each company and an infantry group with one light machine gun were left behind on the hill.

On 2 October 1918 the remnants of the I and III/R121 became reorganized into one company each and then moved to Naves as the brigade reserve and remained there until the relief of the division in the night of 6/7 October 1918. The losses suffered by RIR 121 during the battle by Cambrai amounted to two Officers (*Leutnants* Rimmele and Mayer), 40 *Unteroffiziere* and Other Ranks killed; 13 officers, 195 *Unteroffiziere* and Other Ranks wounded, five officers, 215 *Unteroffiziere* and Other Ranks missing. On the morning of the 2nd the 220th Infantry Division took over the command of the northern half of the sector of the 26th Reserve Division.

Enemy drum fire was directed on the men of RIR 119 on 3 October 1918, alternating the entire day with fire raids on the advance routes to Morenchies and the battle zone. British pilots flew overhead undisturbed and everywhere one looked there were British observation balloons rising into the sky. The men of RIR 119 were lying in the open without protection against the night frost, and the extreme tension from the constant observation of the front line and the heavy enemy fire had badly weakened the opposition power of the companies.

After a quiet night heavy artillery fire was placed on the sector of RIR 99 at 5.00 a.m. on 3 October 1918, however the enemy infantry did not attack. In the morning two companies from RIR 25 were sent forward to reinforce the sector of the regiment, they would remain for two days. The additional reinforcements allowed the regiment to establish connections with the forward pickets of the neighboring regiments on the right and on the left. The rest of the day and the following night proceeded quietly.

The headquarters staff of the 26th Reserve Division knew that something had to be done to relieve the situation before the entire division simply vanished. The division had sent several requests to Group Headquarters pleading to be relieved, each time in vain. Finally, all requests or appeals had to stop due to the precarious situation facing the German forces. The 26th Reserve Division could apparently still play a role in the defense of Cambrai despite having a combat strength of an early war infantry company. The division was severely depleted even further when the Half Battalion/180 had become transported on motor lorries to the western exit of Naves and to the west of the village as the brigade reserve at 3.30 a.m. on the 3rd.

On 4 October 1918 the Army Group praised the efforts of the men of RIR 119:

> In continuous heavy fighting up to now the Württemberg RIR 119 under the command of *Oberstleutnant* Schäfer held its position at Tilloy–Morenchies for the fifth day. Encircled numerous times, attacked twelve times in one day. It has thrown back the enemy who was replaced numerous times over and over in constant fighting and counterthrusts. The battalion staff has stood in the actual fighting many times. The troops have had no rest day and night. That Cambrai is still in German hands today is thanks to this regiment. However, its losses are also correspondingly high.[3]

Finally, the order arrived, relieving RIR 119 through units of RIR 25. However the regiment was not destined to be sent to the rear to rest, instead it was to meet another major enemy attack on the north of the Schelde canal. No additional regiments were moved forward to the exposed position, which the Swabians from RIR 119 had held in the heaviest fighting. Now, only weak outposts protected the positions in Morenchies.

In the night of 4/5 October 1918 the companies from RIR 119 left the position in dispersed order, and did not assemble once more until the men were in Naves. Apparently the British did not resume attacks or even send patrols against the former position of RIR 119 until four days later when the former regimental position became the main opposition line.

Losses continued among the men left behind. On 4 October 1918, during a strong bombardment of the rear terrain, the regimental battle headquarters of RIR 99 that had been transferred to a simple farmer's house in Thun Levêque received a direct hit. The regimental commander was killed along with an orderly while an officer's servant was severely wounded. Nowhere was safe as long as the British dominated the countryside.

At 9.00 p.m. on 6 October 1918, the remnants of RIR 121 marched 25 kilometers to Noyelles and on the following day marched 17 kilometers to Lallaing, northeast of Douai. Just as the regiment arrived in Lallaing several British aircraft flew overhead and dropped bombs on the column resulting in the loss of six horses killed. RIR 121 remained in this area until the 16th and during this time worked on the third position, the *Wotan Stellung*.

On 7 October 1918 the remainder of the 26th Reserve Division was relieved by the 10th *Ersatz* Division and the moved into the area west of Valenciennes. IR 180 had also been relieved of duty by Naves and arrived back again in the division association at this time. Despite the numerous fire raids by Naves, the losses of the Half Battalion/180 were considered moderate. During the entire time the regiment was outside of the division the losses amounted to one Officer, 15 *Unteroffiziere* and Other Ranks wounded. While moderate in numbers, these losses were the equivalent of 10 percent of the regimental combat strength. The division had suffered grievous losses in the fighting around

Cambrai. 71 officers and 1,360 men had been killed, wounded or missing, of which even officers and 180 men belonged to the artillery units assigned to the division.

Accommodation by Valenciennes was not very pleasant. There were constant aircraft attacks and continuous bombardments by long range enemy artillery which did not allow the men to relax. News then arrived that the division was to be transferred to the I Bavarian Reserve Corps in the area east of Douai; the new division headquarters would be located in Lallaing.

While the majority of the infantry of the 26th Reserve Division had been relieved and moved to different parts of the front the artillery batteries of the division remained in the positions north of Cambrai until 8 October 1918, all the time lying under strong fire. However, no major enemy attack took place and it appeared that the attack strength of the Canadians had been broken. Finally, the batteries were relieved and the guns were withdrawn from the battlefield. The relief of the last parts of RIR 119 and RFAR 26 did not become completed until the night from 8/9 October 1918, after having been deployed on a major battle front for almost two weeks.

The brief period of time that RIR 99 had been attached to the 26th Reserve Division again had come to an end. On the 8th the brigade received orders to go back behind the Sensee-Schelde canal. The 5/R99 secured the line up to the Paillencourt-Thun Levêque sunken road. The front line of the Canal position directly south of Estrun up to the hill at the northern edge of Jwuy became occupied on the right with Company Krieg (the remnants of the I/R99), and on the left by the II/R99. In the rear stood the III/R99 as the reserve under *Oberleutnant der Reserve* Andres.

The regimental staff moved its battle headquarters into le Pav, d'Hordain, and shortly afterward it was ordered to move to Lieu-St. Amand. These villages all came under strong enemy artillery fire. Four heavy machine guns from Sharpshooter Detachment 46 were placed in possession of the regiment and the guns reinforced the front in the Paillencourt-Thun Levêque sunken road sunken road and further to the east. From reports received from RIR 55 the enemy had reached Paillencourt at 5.00 p.m. A half hour later he attacked Thun Levêque, where the British were repulsed. However, the enemy had been able to penetrate the German positions at the right wing of the 5/R99.

Once in the new sector, the 26th Reserve Division much needed replacement arrived and were distributed equally among the existing companies of IR 180 and all three battalions were restored. The replacements, one *Vizefeldwebel*, 12 *Unteroffiziere*, 124 Other Ranks and 27 Machine Gun *Schützen* nearly doubled the size of the regiment.

The lead elements of RIR 119 received billets in Roost-Warendin, north of Douai, which had been evacuated by the inhabitants on 7 October 1918. All along the march route the men watched the wretched migration of fleeing or evacuating civilians. In Roost the occupants had supposedly destroyed or rendered unserviceable everything that was not riveted or nailed down before their departure. Rumors of a major retreat to prepared positions had been spreading through the ranks and were soon confirmed. Gigantic explosions took place in the coal region of Northern France, which had been ordered by the High Command. Anything of possible value to the enemy was being destroyed, much the same way as in Operation Alberich on the Somme in early 1917:

> The deep penetration by the British at Cambrai had clearly allowed General Headquarters to recognize that the old, trustworthy divisions of the Somme and Flanders battles were no longer numerous. The young replacements, who had spent the hardest year of the war at home and getting high income and who now had almost become abruptly thrown into the fire storm of the gigantic material battle, proved to be bad. Many were morally depraved, without any sense of duty and honor; he refused to fight, ran in mobs over to the enemy and concerned themselves not about the death of the faithful elders, who in heroic sense of duty withstood the enemy. More than once the Swabians had been witnesses to the unworthy drama that German divisions gave up their positions almost without any opposition and let themselves be taken prisoner in crowds. Still there are many good divisions; however there were too few for the long front and they ended up for the worse in the continuously new requirements and were merged together. RIR 119.[4]

The Allied breakthrough on the Flanders front, the loss of Cambrai that followed on 10 October 1918 and the unfavorable fighting at the Aisne and Maas in the zone of the 5th German Army, as well as the deteriorating political situation in Germany, forced the OHL to order a withdrawal along the entire western front. Strict orders were issued that no structures should be burned down, especially the senseless and pointless destruction of entire villages. The OHL issued orders that with every withdrawal into a new position a rearguard of two up to three battalions under a regimental commander were to be left behind. These regimental commanders would also become subordinate to the artillery and act as a rearguard. In the night from 10/11 October 1918, while heavy fighting flared up in Flanders and by St. Quentin, the positions west of Douai became evacuated and a withdrawal was ordered to the Deule canal.

On 11 October 1918 the 26th Reserve Division became inserted in the canal position in and on both sides of Douai with RIR 119 and IR 180 in the front line. In the darkness of night the surviving batteries of RFAR 26 went into position to support the infantry. The enemy pressed closely behind the retreating German divisions but it did not come to any significant fighting by the canal position. On 12 October 1918 the 26th Reserve Division took on the command in the canal sector, on the right was the 187th Infantry Division, on the left the 22nd Infantry Division. Division Headquarters was in Marchiennes.

This was the start of a long drawn out battle of movement with the German armies withdrawing under fire. The German troops no longer thought about victory, but instead about an acceptable peace. Even this notion was a fantasy as the German armies crumbled with each step to the rear. There had been some talk that despite the enemy's overwhelming superior strength there had been no critical breakthrough of the German lines. While this was correct, the German Army of late 1918 had already lost far too many of the best troops. The replacements were considered useless in most situations, in poor health from privations at home and still worse, were contaminated with anti-war propaganda and Bolshevism.

The men of the 26th Reserve Division, despite the heaviest losses, still considered themselves to be among the best divisions. Many recalled the words of General

Ludendorff: 'Württemberg had only good divisions,' and the Swabians were proud that they had held firm until the last, bitter end. However, these concepts did not take into account that the number of fighters in the 26th Reserve Division was dreadfully small, the horses could no longer move any distance and could barely pull unloaded wagons let alone all of the supplies the division required. Materials and supplies arrived sporadically placing even more strain on both men and horses. Every soldier had been informed about the overall situation facing the army. When looking around the men saw only a sad, dejected picture. Shirkers and unrestrained marauders moved among the supply trains during the evacuation. The orders, to break off from contact with the enemy and move to the rear and take up positions supposedly designed to preserve troop strength didn't come as a surprise.

IR 180 was assigned a sector in the Canal position of Douai where the regiment relieved IR 82. The III/180 became the Battle Battalion on the canal the western edge of Douai; the I/180 was designated as the support battalion in Douai and the II/180 as the rest battalion, which was positioned at the eastern edge of Douai, and later in Le Marais de Sin, east of Douai with the regimental headquarters.

The enemy was apparently unaware of the new takeover of the position and had left the men alone for the most part. Then, at 10.15 a.m., British patrols were observed before the front line, and at 11.00 a.m. the enemy advanced in three waves against the sector of the 9th and 10/180. The enemy skirmishers worked forward to within 1,000 meters of the canal. In the afternoon the enemy lines approached even closer to the canal and were within 400 meters of the opposite bank where they dug in. During the enemy advances, the regimental machine guns fired into the opposing ranks and reportedly inflicted considerable losses on the enemy, however this could not be confirmed. Once the British had prepared positions the opposing artillery started to shell Douai, the Canal position and in particular the pickets by which the 9/180 suffered two men killed and two men wounded and a light machine gun became unserviceable.

The battalions from IR 180 were provided with substantial accommodations which provided protection against the British shells. Most of the III/180 was housed in two concrete dugouts, one mined dugout and the casement of the fortress, far better protection than the men had been used to. A smaller number occupied recesses in the canal embankment, the rest in cellars, about 100 meters distant from the canal. The KTK occupied a mined dugout that had several exits about 300 meters east of the canal. The I/180 was distributed in the area of Porte de Valenciennes in houses, whose cellars offered moderate protection during bombardments. The BTK was about 100 meters west of Porte de Valenciennes in a former military hospital together with the 3/180. The II/180 was accommodated in Le Marais de Sin, in houses that were quite scattered apart. The battalion commander was about 150 meters directly west from the regimental battle headquarters which was in a farmstead at the eastern edge of the house group of Le Marais de Sin.

Later, RIR 119 relieved IR 180 from the positions in Douai. The men made note that the city of Douai, with its churches and spires, had until recently been deep inside the military district. Now it was defended as the front line. The city had already suffered considerable damage from the British artillery fire; entire houses lay in ruins, others

Left: Oberleutnant Frhr. Von Mühlen, RFAR 26 (*Das Württembergisches Reserve-Feldartillerie-Regiment Nr.26 im Weltkrieg 1914-1918*)
Right: Leutnant der Reserve Hugo Wendler, RFAR 26 (*Das Württembergisches Reserve-Feldartillerie-Regiment Nr.26 im Weltkrieg 1914-1918*)

were badly damaged. The windows were missing in numerous street cars; telephone and telegraph wires hung down from the poles; the civilian population had only become evacuated a short time earlier.

The regiment found numerous places for the support battalion and the rest battalion in the abandoned suburbs. However, it was not the elegance of the above ground quarters the men craved, instead it was the security provided by the cellar vaults. Officer patrols were still sent into the Outpost zone and they shortly ran into British patrols advancing from Cuincy toward the regimental front. Additional enemy patrols were observed during the day and the opposing artillery continued to be annoying.

On 13 October 1918 the enemy artillery fire became even more active by Douai, however the enemy infantry showed no inclination to advance. Following the orders issued by the OHL regarding the manner in which each withdrawal was to be handled, the 26th Reserve Division began its withdrawal on 14 October 1918 to the *Hagen Stellung.*

Even as the situation grew ominous and the end of the war appeared imminent, promotions and transfers still occurred. On the 15th the regimental commander of IR 180 separated from the regiment because of his posting to Army Group Herzog Albrecht as Inspector of Field Recruit Depots. Until the new commander, Major Reich, a former battalion commander in *Füsilier* Regiment 122, *Hauptmann* von Raben would take over the leadership of the regiment.

On the evening of 16 October 1918 the companies of RIR 121 received quarters in Bred and the farmsteads surrounding the village, only the outposts remained in he position for protection of the regiment. The withdrawal continued without a pause n the night to the 17th into the *Wotan III Stellung*. The Hagen Front and *Wotan III Stellung* were intermediate positions between the *Wotan-Siegfried* and *Hermann-Hunding Stellung*. Simultaneously with the movement into the *Wotan III Stellung*, the rearguard became withdrawn from Douai. Only officer patrols remained behind to observe the enemy.

On 16 October 1918 the retreat continued and IR 180 was able to disengage from the enemy without incident at 11.00 p.m. The regiment marched via the *Wotan III Stellung* in an easterly direction until reaching Tilloy west of St. Amand, where the men stopped and occupied billets for the night. The I/180 and the II/180 remained with the rearguard and were subordinate to RIR 121.

Four officer patrols still remained by the canal up to 3.00 a.m., when the galleries as well as the railroad bridge at the exit of Douai to Wazieres and to Sin le Noble became blown up by the *pioniers*. The British did not follow after but still bombarded the old position.

RIR 119 abandoned the position that the men had expected to hold off enemy attacks with almost no effort. The men were moved from one rearguard position to the next, all with names such as the *Hagen Stellung* and the *Wotan Stellung*, which according to the men of RIR 119 existed out of a line on a map and the beginning of a few obstacles. With the arrival at each 'defensive' position the troops found it necessary to start entrenching in order to create some sort of cover. On 18 October 1918 the enemy finally attacked, especially in the south. Officer patrols had been sent out in front of the position when they were suddenly recalled in accordance with orders before being cut off by the advancing enemy.

The French inhabitants of Flines had supposedly given enemy pilots signals by placing French flags on all of the houses in anticipation of the arrival of their countrymen after the Germans had left. *Leutnant der Reserve* Jetter from the III/R119 who had watched the flags being set out from a distance, decided to go back into the village again with his patrol and tear down an enemy flag right under the eyes of the advancing British bugle corps. While Jetter was busy avoiding capture following his actions heavy shells from the German artillery started to fall on the roads and houses of Flines which scattered the enemy troops and ruined the celebrations of the French civilians. On the evening of the 18th the enemy pressed forward and reoccupied Flines.

On the same evening IR 180 along with the I/R119 occupied a rearguard position west of St. Amand in the line Western edge of Rosult-La Vallee on the St. Amand-Orchies road. The II/180 and one battalion from RIR 119 arrived in this rearguard position at 3.00 a.m. and now the entire sector was divided into two regimental sectors: RIR 119 on the right, IR 180 on the left. The former rearguard regiment, RIR 121, had been extracted in the morning of 19 October 1918.

The withdrawal continued that night with the II and III/R119 marching to St. Amand, where they arrived early in the morning of the 19th. Unfortunately they did not remain here long: in the evening alarm orders were shouted in the *Sehnen Stellung* northwest of Château l'Abbaye, while the I/R119 was held back one more day in the rearguard position at Bouvignies. Enemy patrols did not appear in front of the *Wotan*

III Stellung until 19 October 1918 after the bulk of the division had already evacuated the position and had gone back into the *Hermann Stellung*.

Shortly after midnight on 19 October 1918 RIR 121 marched via Marchiennes to St. Amand, where the men were allowed to sleep the entire day and on the evening marched further to the *Hermann Stellung* behind the Schelde north of Vieux-Condé. The *Hermann Stellung* had been explored and marked out, however it was still not developed; it too existed more or less only on paper. Only weak rearguards remained in front of the enemy for protection and the *Hermann Stellung* became protected by outposts.

In the meantime the companies of RIR 121 received a few new replacements and were accommodated in the villages of Hergnies, Etinsart and Mansart directly north of Vieux-Condé on the Schelde canal. Over the next days the position was explored, patrols were sent into the foreground, advance sentry posts were set up and the men worked on the extension of the position.

Whilst the *Hermann Stellung* was only a geographical line on paper; the sector of the 26th Reserve Division was formed along the river Schelde with its numerous canals. Essentially the course of the German position was on the eastern shore; only at individual positions were they on the raised west bank of the river. The proper extension of the position demanded too much manpower, which the division no longer had.

The I/R119 did not follow the rest of the division until the night of 19/20 October 1918 and moved to Peruwelz. At the same time the officer patrols of the I/R119 had small skirmishes with the enemy following after. While the *Sehnen Stellung* was only a geographical line; it was the high waters of the Schelde Canal between Thun and Bouridon that offered an effective obstacle.

The men quickly took position and awaited the inevitable arrival of the enemy. The British behaved quietly in the first days. Then enemy troops were observed in the houses of Château l'Abbaye, otherwise nothing else occurred before the regimental front. The enemy was severely pressing against the II Bavarian Army Corps positioned to the south and advanced swiftly. The neighboring II/R119 at Bouridon was thereby forced to bend its wing back and form a block to the south.

On 21 October 1918 the enemy occupied St. Amand and was only detained by individual patrols of the division. In the afternoon III/180 was transferred to Grimaumez, and was therefore now on the Belgian border. The first line transport moved over to Peruwelz, and therefore had already crossed onto Belgian soil. It was here that the new commander arrived, Major Reich, and he took over command of the regiment. The British continued to follow the German withdrawal and on the 22nd the first enemy shells started to fall on the regiment.

The days in Peruwelz were uneventful at first. It was a lovely small Belgian border town with resplendent Villas owned by rich industrialists, beautiful gardens and parks, and offered good quarters for the exhausted regiments to relax in. The Belgian population was aloof, but not hostile. Although the front line was only a few kilometers away the British apparently intended to spare the friendly town. Neither pilots nor artillery disturbed the relaxation of the regiments in the first days. It was not until after some time when the enemy artillery began to place short fire raids in the evening and after hours on the main traffic routes, without inflicting many losses to the troops. Only a few Belgian inhabitants became victims of the bombardments.

On 23 October 1918 enemy infantry made an appearance in front of the sector of the 26th Reserve Division. On this day IR 180 took over half of the sector of RIR 121 because that regiment had to occupy the sector of the 22nd Infantry Division that had been forced to withdraw. With each passing day the situation grew more threatening. Soon the delicate juggling act of moving troops around the battlefield could no longer be possible, there were too few men left.

In the night from 23 to 24 October 1918 the *Sehnen Stellung* outpost zone of the main opposition line on the Schelde became the *Hermann Stellung*. The 5th, 6th and 10/R119 remained as the outpost garrison, while the remainder of the regiment was assembled in Peruwelz and became the division reserve.

The British were already pressing after on the following day. This time strong enemy forces advanced out of a nearby wood in the south and attacked the flank of the division. *Leutnant der Reserve* Rettenmaier threw the reserve platoon of the 5/R119 against the attackers and held them back. Part of the 7/R119 were sent up to help. However between the reserve platoon and the 5/R119 on the canal a large hole opened through which the British had penetrated. The 5/R119 was forced to take its right wing back for protection.

The enemy also attacked across the canal over a bridge that had not been completely destroyed by the *pioniers* against the 6/R119, however the attack was repulsed. With the enemy penetration of the line, the canal position could be rolled up from the south and nothing could stop this from happening, despite Rettenmaier and his men only giving up a few meters of terrain to the enemy. The 6/R119 had to go back slowly under the increasing enemy pressure. Further attacks also caused the 10/R119 to evacuate the main opposition line, when all previous attacks against the company had failed. Finally, the hard pressed companies of RIR 119 became relieved through IR 180. During the fighting *Vizefeldwebel* Herterich drew particular attention to himself through courageous and prudent behavior.

About 8.30 a.m. the enemy also attacked the outpost garrison of IR 180 with strong forces supported by artillery and aircraft and pressed the outposts back from one opposition nest to another opposition nest, during which the British suffered considerable losses through machine gun fire. The enemy eventually reached the eastern edge of the raised railroad, while the sentries from IR 180 were still on the La Boucaulde–Bruille road and attempted to prevent the enemy from penetrating into Bruille. The companies of the outpost garrison then moved back on the main opposition line about 10 a.m. from the pressure of the superior enemy strength with the exception of a few sentries who remained west of the Schelde. Of the three light *Minenwerfer* in the position two could be brought back to the rear and one became blown up.

After midday the sentries of the I and II Battalions west of the Schelde were pressed further back. The enemy reached the river with patrols and expelled the sentries of the I/180 from the eastern bank of the Schelde. In the afternoon the battle battalions were reorganized, each battalion placed two companies in the main opposition line along the canal and one company as the reserve in the vicinity of the KTK. The front line companies were then: 6th, 7th, 1st and 2/180. These companies occupied the eastern bank of the Schelde with strong infantry and machine gun posts. The II/180 was behind the front with the 10/180 as the regimental reserve, positioned at Château de Biez, east of Vergne.

In the evening the enemy was about 700-800 meters distant from the Schelde by the III/180 and at the eastern edge of Bruille in front of the I/180. The pontoon bridge lying in the sector of the I/180 which had crossed the Schelde from Bruille to Hergnies had already been blown up in the morning. The other bridge crossings were destroyed in the night by the *pioniers*. Losses in the regiment were small but represented a major portion of the combat strength still left to IR 180: I/180 four men wounded, two men missing. II/180 one man killed, 23 men wounded, one officer and four men missing.

In the days following the enemy artillery was reinforced more and more and in addition to scattered fire on the Schelde and the Canal position, the British also placed strong fire upon the German battery positions and approach routes, especially at night and at dusk. It was not until 27 October 1918 when the enemy outposts pushed forward until they were approximately 200 to 300 meters from the western bank of the Schelde. The enemy only advanced slowly because of the open terrain leading up to the river which did not offer any cover. The German artillery covered the open areas, the enemy approach routes from the rear and batteries with heavy fire.

Early on the 28th the enemy succeeded in crossing over a tributary of the Schelde and reached an island by the eastern shore of the river. A counter thrust planned by RIR 121 accompanied by artillery and *Minenwerfer* was successful and brought back one officer and 20 men from the 8th English Division as prisoners. According to statements from the prisoners the crossing was part of an attempt to cross the Schelde by the entire division. Most of the artillery fire from both sides concentrated on the crossing and the counterattack and the rest of the front remained quiet. The British made no other attempts to cross the river following the failure of this initial thrust.

The problems facing the division from this period were bluntly laid out in a report written by an officer of the 26th Reserve Division to the general commanding the I Bavarian Reserve Corps:

> To the general commanding I Bavarian Reserve Corps the subsequent consideration is submitted with the plea that senior headquarters should be informed: The 26th Reserve Division consists of troops, which until now have performed exquisitely. Nevertheless the recent battles make it clear that the current fighting value of the infantry is very deficient.
>
> Although physical exhaustion because of the heavy major fighting and a lack of subsequent rest time, as well as the economic and political situation at home exerts an unmistakable impression on the mood and view of duty by the Other Ranks, rather, this is justified in the extraordinary lack of leadership and in the attitude and training of the usually equally bad replacements that follow after.
>
> Since the beginning of the spring offensive RIR 121 had suffered losses of 110 officers and 3,216 men, received replacements of 28 officers and 2,150 men. IR 180 had losses of 119 officers and 3,074 men, as well as receiving replacements of 20 officers and 1,550 men.

> It is without further clarity that the faulty positions alone, particularly by officers, almost prevented any organized duty activities. Furthermore however, still comes the great inexperience that forced by necessity to make company leaders from young *Leutnants*. If, for example, a young infantry platoon leader must became appointed as the company leader of a Machine Gun Coy, so the large fighting strength of such a company of course could not be taken advantage of.
>
> In general the cohesion and the trust between leader and men within the company is lacking, because the time needed to integrate the replacements and to wield them together as a single unit has been lacking.
>
> In spite of outstanding bravery of the officers and a large number of men most companies however are no longer a fighting unit, but instead many times a mob rolled together that possess neither the knowledge of their own weapons, or still have any notion of modern independent combat leadership and instinctive cooperation.
>
> At the time the battalion leaders almost everywhere had to personally position their sentries if they wanted to have a certain guarantee for their appropriateness.
>
> In the present state of the troops there is not much to start with. The regiments, particularly RIR 121 and IR 180 were burned out. The good reputation of the division remained intact, so their fighting strength must certainly be increased. It is a concern that the immediate transfer of further officers and the opportunity for undisturbed training time so that the companies could at least work together reasonably again and to get them in hand, is imperative. With RIR 119 the situation is somewhat better however the officer shortage here has also become very large.
>
> If this front remains quiet, then the employment of officer replacements for training of the rest battalion should be moderately allowed to be increased, however, if it come to fighting or if the division is employed in major fighting again without previous training, it is my dutiful discretion to anticipate a breakdown of parts of the regiments with the most considerable probability.
>
> I might especially still bring forth that according to reports from two regimental commanders the use of the troops at night during any further withdrawal is out of the question. First of all the influence of the officers is quite lacking here. I do not believe that their appearances have any further influence on all of the good assets; it is however high time that the troops are disciplined in a severe training period again after the replenishment of officers. It should also not be overlooked, the attitude of the current Other Rank replacements at present is first of all is not at the old level, morally and militarily ... [5]

Despite the lack of any further enemy attacks or attempts to cross the Schelde, the enemy skirmish line continued to advance. In the following days the enemy could not be prevented from becoming firmly established at the opposite bank of the canal, so that only this waterway separated the positions on both sides.

On 29 October 1918 RIR 121 received a detachment of replacements from home that allowed the regiment to form three understrength battalions once again. On 30 October IR 180 received 390 replacements and 10 men previously in the regiment who had recuperated from their wounds, all of which became distributed to the battalions, respectively for specialized weapons teams including the light *Minenwerfer* and the MG 08/15 light machine gun crews.

On 31 October 1918 the British successfully became firmly established on the north-east shore of the Schelde, between the river and canal. The canal levee was then breached and the outpost zone was under water more and more, because the Schelde slowly rose from the daily downpours.

Strong rain continued to fall in the first days of November. As a result of the heavy rain the water level of the Schelde climbed to such an extent that a large part of the outpost zone had become flooded and almost all of the sentries located by the river had to be sent back to the main opposition line while other sentries had become isolated due to the quickly rising water. In the night the water level dropped slightly so that at individual places the sentries could become inserted into the outpost zone once again. With this natural barrier the position of the entire division seemed secure and the morale of the troops increased noticeably.

The three regiments of the division held the line with their diminished numbers with one company of each battalion in the outpost zone. The remainder occupied the main opposition line and reserve areas. The *Minenwerfer* were positioned to provide support for the infantry and at least three light 7.6cm *Minenwerfer* from IR 180 were solely utilized in an anti-tank role.

Up until 5 November 1918 the enemy infantry behaved quietly while the opposing artillery scattered the canal position with shrapnel only occasionally and the German battery positions at Grimaumez and Rengies and the advance roads received only weak bombardments. It almost seemed as if the opposing artillery had been withdrawn. Enemy pilots, the bane of the infantryman's existence, did not appear overhead because of the constant rain of the past few days. Overall losses in the 26th Reserve Division were exceptionally low. IR 180 reported only one man wounded on the 5th.

Then, without warning or explanation the orders came to evacuate the *Hermann Stellung* and to withdraw into the *Antwerp–Maas Stellung*. What the men did not know was that nearby sectors of the front had already been abandoned and this left the position of the 26th Reserve Division and several nearby divisions in a precarious position. If the divisions remained where they were, was only a matter of time before they would be surrounded and overwhelmed by the enemy.

On 5 November 1918, two battalions of RIR 119 were released at Hergnies, while the I/R119 moved to Peruwelz again. The I Battalion had barely arrived in the village when it became alarmed on the following day, loaded into motor lorries with the regimental staff at the market place and transported southward to Thulin. While in Thulin the regimental staff and I/R119 met up with the II/R121. The two battalions then formed a combined regiment under the leadership of the regimental staff of RIR 119 and were given the responsibility to protect the withdrawal of the 187th Infantry Brigade against attacks by the enemy; the 187th Brigade had been forced back and was in danger of being destroyed. The companies of the composite regiment were positioned to intercept any enemy advance and immediately sent patrols out towards the enemy positions.

On the following day the enemy continued to behave quietly. The only difference was that the artillery was very active against the canal position, and especially against the German batteries at Grimaumez, Folquin and the approach roads. The village of Peruwelz even received a few shells again. The enemy pilots were still idle because of bad weather as it rained often during the day, at times quite heavily.

The staff of RIR 119 with the I/R119 and II/R121 were transported on the morning of the 6th by motor lorries into Valenciennes and vicinity. The remaining units of the 26th Reserve Division occupied the division sector as best they could with the loss of the two battalions. At 7.00 a.m. on 7 November 1918 the II/180, Staff of RIR 121 and the reserve battalion I/R121 marched to Stambruges. The command over the fighting battalion, the III/R121, was taken on by IR 180 at daybreak.

The I/180 and II/R119 marched from their billets at 9.00 a.m. to Bauffe and after arriving there were placed under the command of Major Hartenstein from RFAR 26. The Staff of IR 180, III/180, III/R119, III/R121, Staff of *Fuss* Artillery 59, 1st, 3rd, 6th, 7/RFAR 26, 3/59 and 6/*Pioneer* 13 formed the rearguard from the *Hermann* up to the X *Stellung*. The 6/*Pioneer* 13 reported to IR 180 only about demolition activity, likewise the 4/*Pioneer* 13 that took care of the demolition activity between the *Hermann* II and X *Stellung*. Starting from 7.00 a.m. the rearguard acted independently.

At 1.30 p.m. the First Line Transport of the Regimental staff and the battalions in Peruwelz and Trieu, with the exception of combat vehicles and the Field kitchens, were marched to Gages southeast of Ath. At 4.00 p.m. the battle headquarters of IR 180 became transferred to Peruwelz and quartered in the former brigade staff quarters.

On the evening of 7 November 1918 the division order arrived to begin the withdrawal to the A-M (Antwerp-Maas) *Stellung*. The rearguard positions were the *Hermann II Stellung*, the X *Stellung*, the Y *Stellung* and the T *Stellung*. Everything was made ready for the move. The staff of the 26th Reserve Division went back to Cambron–Castean. Detachment from the enemy was carried out without interference, probably as a result of the bad weather; the division sector then became taken over by the 208th Infantry Division.

The enemy had apparently not observed anything despite the numerous explosions set off by the *pioniers* during the withdrawal preparations and behaved unusually quiet. The enemy artillery continued the usual disturbance fire on the main opposition line and the battery positions, while the German artillery and *Minenwerfer* replied in kind. The German withdrawal was aided greatly by the poor weather that prevented enemy aircraft from flying and even provided protection from observation balloons.

The remaining parts of the First line transport located in Quevaucamps marched off at 9.00 a.m. under *Leutnant der Landwehr* Loës to Eigen-Brackel, where they rested for the night. On the night of 7/8 November 1918 the transport continued on to Chièvres. On the 7th RIR 121 began the march into the *Antwerp–Maas Stellung*. Once detached from the enemy, the regiment marched eastward to Hal, southwest of Brussels, where the first news of the Armistice became known. In addition to this welcome news, further reports of unrest in Brussels also arrived. Part of the regiment was then transported on automobiles to the environs of Brussels in order to protect a corps provisions office located there against being plundered by local civilians or army deserters. Under the current circumstances the supplies at this location were urgently required by the troops still in the field.

Enemy troops first became active on 7 November 1918 as patrols appeared advancing toward the German positions. These patrols were moving cautiously and when the composite regiment under the command of RIR 119 opened fire, the patrols quickly came to a halt. Apparently there were no indications whatever that these patrols were going to advance upon the German position and in the evening the enemy moved back. The composite regiment was then able to leave the positions without losses and without the enemy following.

At 1.00 a.m. on 8 November 1918 the position battalions of IR 180 evacuated the *Hermann Stellung*, leaving behind one officer patrol with the strength of one officer and 15 men armed with one light machine gun as well as two *Radfahrer* from each battalion. Shortly following the evacuation the bridges over the canal were blown up by the *pionier*s after which the officer patrol was given orders to arrive in the Y *Stellung* in the night of 9/10 November 1918.

The battalions moved into the former billets of IR 180 and rested until daybreak: the III/R119 in Peruwelz, the III/180 in Mont de Peruwelz and the III/R121 in Bonsecourts. At daybreak the battalions marched to the rear along with the III/180, going to Quievremont, two kilometers northeast of Grosage, while the III/R121 marched to Rue de Bois, two kilometers east of Grosage.

The British patrols did not cross over the Schelde until the afternoons of 8 November 1918. At noon telephone orders from brigade arrived in Grosage and at 1.30 p.m. written orders followed that the 26th Reserve Division was becoming extracted out of the front of the I Bavarian Reserve Corps and being moved to the XV Reserve Corps. The orders regarding the occupation of the Y *Stellung* through Detachment Hartenstein subsequently did not come to execution.

The march into the *Antwerp-Maas Stellung* went smoothly; however, the men were noticeably fatigued from the march to the XL Reserve Corps because of the especially long distance needed to be crossed by the division in order to reach the new sector. At the end of the day the 26th Reserve Division headquarters was in Graty.

The III/R119 with the 3rd and 7/RFAR 26 and 3rd *Fuss* Artillery 59 under *Hauptmann* Zettler occupied the *Hermann II Stellung* east of Peruwelz, while RIR 121, as the rear guard, occupied the X *Stellung* that proceeded east of the Belveil-Sirault road, and the II/180 proceeded west of Grosage. The regimental staff moved to the rear at 8.00 a.m. and by 9.00 a.m. was in Blaton, and at 12.00 noon in Grosage.

The II/180 became released to Quievremont and subordinate to the commander of IR 180 again and marched in the course of the afternoon to Cambron-Casteau, where it received billets. The I/180 was released to Brugelette and subordinate to the regiment again. Detachment Reich marched after a short pause in Quievremont upon the direct route to Brugelette respectively Cambron-Casteau. The regimental staff received billets in the château in Cambron-Casteau, the III Battalion in Brugelette.

The officer patrols of the right and left neighboring divisions had already gone back by this time and in order for the officer patrol of IR 180 to avoid the possibility of becoming cut off and captured, it also withdrew and arrived safely in the rear by 3.00 p.m. The patrol reported that the enemy had continued to shell the evacuated artillery positions the entire night with heavy caliber shells and that the first British troops did not cross over the Schelde using pontoon bridges until at 10.00 a.m.

There was no longer any clear line of defenses and units did not know where friendly troops were located or where the enemy had possibly advanced. Under these circumstances a rearguard was formed to protect the billets as well as providing sentries to watch over the camp during the night. The withdrawal continued on the following morning when the First Line Transport of IR 180 and the infantry moved to Steenkerke.

8 November 1918 had been the start of the general retreat of the 26th Reserve Division. On the morning of the 8th the III/R119 followed the marching columns and occupied the *Hermann II Stellung* east of Peruwelz, on the following day the retreat continued to the Antwerp-Maas line; the march route was the large road from Tournai–Hal to Brussels. While there was no contact with the enemy infantry, the columns were constantly annoyed by enemy aircraft that had taken to the skies following a period of good weather. Over the next few days enemy pilots covered all of the march routes with bombs, 'as if they desired to vent their fury on the columns in the last minutes.' This was particularly upsetting as the men knew that the war could end at any moment. Fortunately only the III/R119 suffered minor losses from the air attacks.

On the afternoon of 9 November 1918 the regimental staff and the battalions of IR 180 as well as the III/R119 marched on March Route 3 to Steenkerke, with the III/R119 marching to Thoricourt, where the different units arrived between 6.00 p.m. and 9.00 p.m. The housing provided to the men was considered to be poor; mass quarters in houses where there was insufficient room for all of the men and equipment. Fortunately the weather was very good, clear, and quite cold at night. Enemy pilots attacked the column in the following afternoon with machine guns and bombs as the men moved north.

On the evening of the 9th the 26th Reserve Division arrived in Hal, 12 kilometers southwest of Brussels where the division headquarters was set up. Wild rumors about a revolution in Germany and the collapse of the government spread quickly. News also arrived that a Red revolution had taken place in Brussels where the revolutionaries were celebrating with immense orgies, and soldier councils had assumed command of the city. All of this news was extremely upsetting to men who were accustomed to army discipline and it all seemed so foreign to them when the stories spread through the regiments and took on even greater intensity as they spread from man to man.

On the morning of 10 November 1918 the division commander traveled down to see the commanding general of the *Antwerp–Maas Stellung* in order to discuss the possible deployment of the division. Then, in the evening, the message arrived from the OHL that the Supreme Commander, Kaiser Wilhelm, had resigned from his position and left the country. What effect this would have on the events taking place could only be guessed at. To the troops in the field this news was taken as a clear indication that the war was at an end. The morale and the discipline of the fighting troops, while shaken from this news and recent unsettling events, still resisted all revolutionary encouragements; the demand to form soldier councils was the strongest among individual rear area formations that had not seen any fighting during the war.

At 10.00 a.m. on 10 November 1918 IR 180 marched via Rebecq-Rognon-Saintes to Beert, where after arriving between 3.00 and 5.00 p.m. the men were provided with housing in the village and the surrounding farmsteads. While en route enemy aircraft were very active again against the column on the road leading to Enghien.

Armistice

On the morning of 11 November 1918 the regiments of the 26th Reserve Division were made ready to be deployed in the *Antwerp-Maas Stellung*. The division staff had quickly settled into the new sector assigned to it, with the headquarters located in Linkebeek.

At 11.00 a.m. on 11 November 1918 reports arrived from headquarters of the XXXX Reserve Corps that in according to orders from OHL all hostilities would be suspended starting from 11.45 a.m. (Keep in mind, the German time was one hour earlier than British time so this would translate as 10.45 a.m. for the British). The conclusion of the Armistice with the Entente finally became known; while there was still nothing known of the specific conditions of the Armistice. Corps orders stated that the return march home was to begin on 13 November 1918. The 11th and the following day would be used to prepare for this march.

On 11 November 1918 IR 180 was still located Beert when orders arrived from brigade headquarters at 11.00 a.m. that the Armistice was signed and would take affect at 12.00 noon. Any Officer patrols were immediately recalled to the outpost zone, while the situation facing the rest of the regiment remained unchanged. A roll call was held in the battalions in the afternoon, during which the regimental commander mentions that the Other Ranks should preserve order and discipline, so that the departure and the transportation home could proceed quickly and smoothly.

News of the Armistice reached the other units of the division at the same time; the war was finally over. One of the last units to be informed of the Armistice was RFAR 26, where the regiment learned of the news at 11.55 a.m.

Soon, more news began to arrive about the turmoil at home; it seemed that everything was suddenly falling apart at the front and in the rear at the same time. All of this news came unexpectedly and the mood of the men was conflicted; however no one showed any desire to be directed by the soldier's council.

Apparently the bond that had been created between the officers and the men in the fighting had been stronger than many knew and there was mutual trust between both sides. The regiments remained close, disciplined units, where everyone worked together for the well-being of the whole. Then more details became known of the Armistice and the conditions that had been dictated. All unnecessary vehicles and horses were left behind for the local population. Entrenching tools were sold to the civilian population and all unnecessary ammunition, especially hand grenades was to be destroyed.

12 November 1918 was the last day to make arrangements before the withdrawal home would begin. Everything needed to be prepared if the journey to Germany could be accomplished in an orderly fashion and in accordance with the strict timeframe dictated under the conditions of the Armistice. On this day the II/180 was accommodated in Trop, Muisen and Saintes. Sentries and patrols were still in the position to observe the enemy and to help guide 2,700 Italian and 260 British prisoners of war to the village of Bierk, where they would be turned over to the Allies.

On 13 November the 26th Reserve Division formed columns at Linkebeek where a division order was given out to the men. According to orders, the German troops would be divided into five groups in order to accommodate all of the different support and rear echelon units that would accompany the division. The different columns would range from eight up to 12 kilometers in length.

The route to be taken by the 26th Reserve Division would lead south of Brussels, then past Löwen, further through Thienen via Lüttich, Herbestal to Cologne. The enemy had provided clear instructions of when the occupied areas of Belgium and France would be evacuated. Any failure to comply would result in the stragglers being taken prisoner.

On 13 November 1918 IR 180 arrived in the assembly area of the division, east of Hal. At 11.00 a.m. the regiment marched off and in a short time the battalions had reached their first destinations: Buisingen, Neerdorp and Buisingen Château. The different battalions arrived in the quarters between 2.00 and 4.00 p.m. and were assigned local billets. The orders containing the route to be followed through Belgium for the next few days came in the evening. The 26th Reserve Division travelled on Route II, on which seven divisions with their assigned columns and other formations also marched. The route would lead the divisions through numerous small villages until they finally reached Lüttich. IR 180 belonged to March Group 2 and formed part of Sub-Group Reich along with the II/RFAR 26 and *Feldlazarett* 505.

The journey home for the men of the 26th Reserve Division officially began at 11.00 a.m. on 14 November 1918 and on this day the area southwest of Löwen was reached. IR 180 began the evacuation movement at 9.30 a.m., when March Group 2 assembled on the Beersel-Droogebosch road with the head of the column in Droogebosch.

The men began to march at 12.00 noon and at first there were numerous delays associated with the movement of such large numbers of men and equipment. Finally, after several long halts, the men finally moved through Ouderghem, Tervaeren, Leefdael, Neerische to Loonbeck and Frankenberg, where Sub-Group Reich received accommodations. The regimental staff arrived at 8.00 p.m. and the remaining parts of the regiment a few hours later. The men had marched 25 kilometers on the first day, quite a feat considering the condition of the men and horses was not the best. Fortunately the weather was good, which made marching easier. When the men received billets they were jammed into mass quarters that were not in the best condition, still they had a roof over their heads.

On 15 November 1918 the 26th Reserve Division started the march at 9.00 a.m. by way of Neerische, Wart, Löwen, Bantersen, Vertryk to Willebringen and reached the area of Thienen (Tirlemont). Upon arriving there the first signs of trouble had appeared when several Army and Line of Communication formations had started to withdraw on their own initiative. In order to ensure a smooth journey home, these units had to become integrated into the columns of the division.

During the day the route being followed had to be changed slightly and there was a detour through Löwen, because the road assigned to one of the other columns was not passable for vehicles and there was too much congestion on the other routes. The troops arrived at the billeting area between 5.00 p.m. on the 15th and 1.00 a.m. on the 16th. The billets were still mass quarters but at least they were in better condition than the previous night. The division had made approximately 25 kilometers for the day in consistently cold weather.

In order to meet the Allied deadline for the evacuation of France and Belgium there was no time to rest. At 8.00 a.m. on 16 November 1918 the units were assembled

233 light machine guns turned over to the Allies according to Paragraph 4 of the Armistice. (Lawrence Stallings)

and marched off by way of Camptich, Tirlemont, Gussenhoven, Landen, Gingelon, Montenacken to Corswarem, near Truyen where the men received billets for the night. The division marched an impressive 40 kilometers in very cold weather but dry weather and arrived in Corswarem between 6.00 and 8.00 p.m.

On 17 November 1918 the 26th Reserve Division reached the area west of Lüttich. Because of the long distance marched on the previous day the men and horses were very tired and as a result, the departure from Corswarem did not take place until 12.30 p.m. The columns marched via Warenne, Lamine, Momalle, Fooz to Awans, a total distance of about 20 kilometers. After arriving in Awans most of the men were provided with billets while the II/180 became sent to Lüttich to act as a guard for stores of provisions that were needed by the different columns if the timetable was to be met.

18 November 1918 was the first day of rest for the tired men and horses. Because of the arrival of colder weather the majority of the horses received winter shoes on this day that should help them in the long journey home. While most of the men were allowed to rest, the 11/180 was given another special assignment to guard Bakery Columns 85 and 86 until the morning of 19 November 1918. The weather continued to become colder and towards the end of the 18th a light snow began to fall.

The Red Soldier's council had taken charge of the cities of Brussels and Löwen and had already eagerly distributed all of the food stocks from the Line of Communication depots, which was very shortsighted as now there was a shortage of rations for men and horses in these places. It was a different story in Lüttich where good order had been maintained. The Line of Communication formations had taken charge of the supplies that were meant for the use of the twenty seven divisions that were marching on three different routes simultaneously through Lüttich, and were prepared to distribute them as the units arrived. Red posters were taped up on poles at every street corners of Lüttich:

> The march through Lüttich must take place in an orderly manner. Concerning this I need every decent Officer and man. All officers coming through without any direct use must therefore immediately report to me.
>
> Signed: Schneider, *Hauptmann* on the General Staff and Chairperson of the Soldier's Council in Lüttich.[6]

On 19 November 1918 the division marched through Lüttich. The journey through the large city was carried out without incident thanks to the good order and organization of *Hauptmann* Schneider. This was fortunate as the strong gradient of the road east of Lüttich made heavy demands on the horses which were not in the best condition to begin with. One item that was quite evident was that when the men marched through the city every house and building was decorated with Belgian flags from top to bottom. On the evening of the 19th the division reached the area of Hervé after marching 25 kilometers. Most of the men were billeted in houses with the local population while the horses had to remain in the open in light drizzle.

It was expected that on the following day the German border would become crossed. There were concerns among the troops as to just how the men would be received in Germany; would the population rejoice because of the red flags carried by some of the units, or would they be received in silence and fear? The troops from IR 180 that had been assigned to guard duty a few days earlier rejoined Group 2 after being relieved by an infantry detachment from the division following behind 26th Reserve Division.

In addition to the national flags that covered every building in Belgium, so many in some cases, one could barely see the houses for the flags there was clear evidence that the German authorities had been less than effective during the war. Everywhere the men looked they could see windows that were decorated with brass and copper appliances, a sign of contempt of the German authorities, who in four years had not been able to find these items and confiscate them for the war effort.

When the 26th Reserve Division approached Herbestal on 20 November 1918, black-white-red flags could be seen everywhere, from the largest towns to the smallest villages and on the smallest houses. The quarters assigned to the men were extremely cramped as a result of the close proximity of several columns; every spare space was filled with troops. Despite this overcrowding the reception of the men by the German Rhine population was very friendly and open. By the end of the day the area of Astenet, five kilometers northeast of Herbestal, was reached.

On 20 November 1918 the I/180 marched to Herbestal at 7.00 a.m. to take over the Herbestal-Hergenrath railway guard, while the rest of the regiment marched at 5.30 p.m. via Battice to Herbestal where the infantry arrived about 11.00 p.m. while the baggage column did not arrive until 6.00 a.m. the following morning. As the men crossed over into Germany the route was lined with bright red-white flags of the

Rhineland and everyone in the columns were happy that they no longer had to see the 'venomous and scornful faces of the Belgians.'

The 26th Reserve Division reached the area of Stolberg on 21 November 1918 where IR 180 left the column at 12.30 p.m. and travelled via Lontzen, Wallhorn, Ober Forstbach to Cornelimünster where it arrived between 6.00 and 10.00 p.m. IR 180 still had numerous military duties to perform and in the evening the III/180 had to take on guarding a food train, otherwise there was a good chance the contents would be looted in a very brief time. The III/R119 was also detached from RIR 119 from 21-23 November 1918 in order to protect the railway by Eschweiler-Düren.

On 22 November 1918 the 26th Reserve Division reached the area of Düren where the troops were quartered in schools, halls of inns and in local factories as well as in civilian homes. The III/180 was able to rejoin the column after being relieved by a battalion from the 6th Infantry Division. On the 23rd the 26th Reserve Division began the march at 10.30 a.m. via Düren, Sindorf to Horrem and the area of Schlenderhan, 20 kilometers west of Cologne, arriving in the early evening. The division marched between 30-35 kilometers in cold and dry weather and the men were quite happy to finally stop for the night.

24 November 1918 was a day of rest, or at least it was until 9.00 a.m., when IR 180 had to vacate Horrem and received new billets in Quadrat and Königsdorf. Once there, the regiment was given decent quarters and the men took full advantage of the time allotted to rest.

On the 25th the 26th Reserve Division came up in front of the gates of Cologne, the first major city the men had reached in Germany and the route across the Rhine. The bridge the men needed to cross the Rhine was already packed with troops from other columns so the river would not be crossed on this day and the men were provided with mass quarters for the night by the Soldier Council, however the local population had other ideas and rushed about looking for alternative quarters for the men, and the largest part of the regiments found quarters in the homes of local citizens. The residents of Cologne provided a warm and friendly reception for the men as they marched through the garland and flower decorated city.

On 25 November 1918 IR 180 marched at 9 a.m. from Königsdorf via Mingersdorf to Ehrenfeld where it arrived at 12.00 noon. The entire regiment was accommodated in a local school, in halls that were warm and comfortable and which were large enough to hold 50 men each. IR 180 remained in Ehrenfeld on the next day where the men could bathe in the city baths in Neptune Place.

On the 26th RIR 119 went via Deutz, Schlebusch, Burscheid, Platz bei Remscheid to Schwelm. The Swabians became enthusiastically and heartily received everywhere they went. The local people offered the men everything they had in order to entertain them, especially in Schwelm, in the suburbs of Barmen, where the regiment waited several days before being transported away.

On 27 November 1918 the 26th Reserve Division finally marched through Cologne while flying the black-red and black-white-red flags and came into the area of Burscheid. The crossing over the Rhine on the Hohenzollern Bridge was carried out without any disruption, in spite of the fact that two divisions marched next to one another over each

Cramped quarters: Men of the 26th Reserve Division. (Author's collection)

bridge simultaneously. While passing Fortress Cologne the 26th Reserve Division took a number of artillery pieces from the fortifications on orders from the new German government. From Cologne, the column moved further north into the Westphalian coal region in the area of Remscheid and Lüttinghausen.

At 7.30 a.m. on 27 November 1918 IR 180 left Ehrenfeld and marched to Cologne and eventually reached the parishes of Deutz, Mühlheim, Dünnwald and Schleebusch at noon and the men were provided with comfortable billets. Other parts of the 26th Reserve Division did not reach their scheduled destination by Remscheid until the early morning hours of 28 November 1918. The column had marched 18 kilometers on this day with some difficulty through very hilly terrain. The weather in the morning was dry and cold, and in the afternoon it began to rain. Morale among the men rose when it became known that after of a few day of rest the regiments would be sent home by transport trains; the end of the long journey was in sight.

At 7.00 a.m. on 28 November 1918 IR 180 completed the march to Remscheid where the regiment arrived at 6.00 p.m. after being delayed mainly by the large gradients. The length of the route travelled by the regiment was about 38 kilometers. Fortunately the billets were good, part of the men sleeping in mass quarters and schools, part in local homes. The weather continued to vary with fog in the morning and rain by midday.

On 29 November 1918 the 26th Reserve Division was in the area of Schwelm, where it would remain for the next few days. A few of the units were still scattered along the march route and after a short time, began to arrive at the division assembly area. IR 180 marched at 6.30 a.m. by way of Ronsdorf, Barmen Ost and eventually to Schwelm after a journey of 30 kilometers in dull, cloudy weather. Once the regiment arrived there in

Crossing the Hohenzollern Bridge in Cologne. (*Das Reserve-Infanterie-Regiment Nr. 111 im Weltkrieg 1914 bis 1918*)

the early afternoon the men were provided with good housing. The regiments were later joined by RFAR 26, now the full division was assembled once more.

Because the regiments would become transported by rail over the next few days the time spent waiting became used to spruce up uniforms and attempt to restore the equipment to good working order. Despite the situation facing the men, of having to face defeat following years of fighting, they still wanted to present the best possible appearance when they arrived home.

On 2 December 1918 the units of the 26th Reserve Division were transported to Stuttgart, Ulm, Gmünd and Tubingen from the embarkation railway station Schwelm-Loh, where the men would be demobilized and allowed to return home. It had taken a number of days before enough transport trains could be located that would be needed to transport all of the men and their equipment, at least three trains being needed for each unit. With each passing day, as trains departed, the division slowly shrank in size.

On 2 December 1918 the III/180 departed at 9.00 p.m. along with half of the *Minenwerfer* Company. On the 3rd the II/180 and the other half of the *Minenwerfer* Company departed at 2.30 p.m. followed by the regimental staff and the I/180, which departed at 10.00 p.m. The journey went through towns and villages including Mannheim, Bruchsal, Bietigheim, Untertürkheim toward Tübingen where the trains came to a stop at Gmünd.

The three battalions of IR 180 slowly made the final journey towards home. It must have been agonizing for some to almost be within reach of their loved ones as the trains moved slowly through the region. The III/180 arrived in Tübingen at 11.00 a.m. on 4 December 1918, the II/180 arrived in Gmünd at 8.00 a.m. on the 5th and the regimental staff and I/180 arrived in Tübingen at 11.00 a.m. on 5 December 1918:

> The reception given to the men of IR 180 corresponded to the seriousness of the time, unpretentious and simple, but no less warm was the reception of the authorities and inhabitants of both locations and they had on this occasion also greeted the brave 180er with the warmest feelings, the highest respect and gratefulness, because their unswerving tenacity in the adherence to their positions during the defense and the daring following attacks, how altogether the excellent resolution of all their work while that reached the duration of the war is to thank them that the enemy was kept away from our borders and that the home remained spared from the horror of war.[7]

However, the first signs of the concept that the army had not really been defeated in the war, almost a precursor for the 'stabbed in the back' theory that soon took root, had begun to appear, as it did in the 1921 regimental history of IR 180:

> Undefeated by the enemy, the regiment returns back and every 180er can hold his head up high, his fellow citizens look them openly in the face, because he has done his duty for the Fatherland in full measure with respect and nobody has the right, to make any accusation against the army about the end of the war.
>
> The mighty German army, the pride of Germania, the education place for the ever increasing youth in manliness, obedience, faithfulness, order and patriotism, free of any partisanship that looked frightening to the foreign countries, who are envious and jealous of this brazen shield and defense of the German people, when after it has afforded victorious opposition from enemies in the war of a world, until he dissolves into his smallest atoms and only belongs today to history. However his spirit will live on, because he sits firmly rooted with the people, and if the entire people shout from their deepest soul for freedom and deliverance from servitude, then will an army being emerge also again that now sustains an epitaph that in no manner is to become on the proficiency and steadiness for their well-being and benefit, to the recovery and rise of the German people. Then every 180er will tell to his sons and grandsons, what great things the regiment had afforded in this World War and that their descendants are worthy to their ancestors and that all in this regiment could take part in the heroic deeds.[8]

On 4 and 5 December the three battalions of RIR 121 arrived in Gmünd, where they became greeted at the railway station by *Oberbürgermeister* Möhler and enthusiastically received by the local population. The greatest part of the officers and Other Ranks were demobilized over the next few days, only the staff and the Orderly Room personnel still had work to perform completing all of the paperwork associated with demobilization. This lasted until February 1919, when the last men were processed and the regiment no longer officially existed.

On the same days RIR 119 embarked in Schwelm and arrived in Stuttgart on 6 and 7 December 1918. At 10.00 a.m. on the 7th the regiment made its entry into the city in well-ordered march columns, moving along a route that was decorated and draped with flags as if the city was celebrating the homecoming of a victorious army. The troops were triumphantly and enthusiastically greeted by the local population. At the Neckartor it became greeted in the name of the government through *Oberst* Ströhlin. In front of the town hall there was a formal reception by the representatives of the government including Minister Kiene and the officers and men thanked with a sincere, touching speech. It was a memorable moment, when the regiment marched past its commander at the King's Gate in a robust parade march, the last parade march of the regiment; two days following the discharges began.

The remaining personnel of 26th Reserve Division traveled home on 7 December 1918. The division staff made the journey on the 6th and arrived in Stuttgart on 8 December 1918. RFAR 26 was transported home on 6 December 1918 and in the course of the next two days the batteries arrived in Ulm. For the process of demobilization the I and III/RFAR 26 were accommodated in and by Blaubeuren, the II/RFAR 26 in and by Herrlingen. The final dissolution of RFAR 26 took place on 12 December 1918 where Major Hartenstein, who commanded the regiment under difficult circumstances in 1917-1918, issued the following parting order:

> After a glorious, almost 4 1/2 year existence the regiment now becomes disbanded. For two years I had the privilege to command the regiment, and I will be filled with pride in my later life anytime I look back at this time. If the regiment had so many beautiful and rich successes to record, it is because of the devotion of every individual to thank, and everyone can look back with gratification on this time. I want to say a hearty farewell to all who belonged to the regiment and wish them everything good for the future.
>
> Signed: Hartenstein.[9]

Notes

1. Klaus, op. cit., p. 113.
2. Stühmke, op. cit., p. 82.
3. Gerster, op. cit., p. 127.
4. Gerster, op. cit., p. 128.
5. Stühmke, op. cit., pp. 84-86.
6. Stühmke, op. cit., p. 88.
7. Vischer, op. cit., p. 157.
8. IBID.
9. Klaus, op. cit., p. 115.

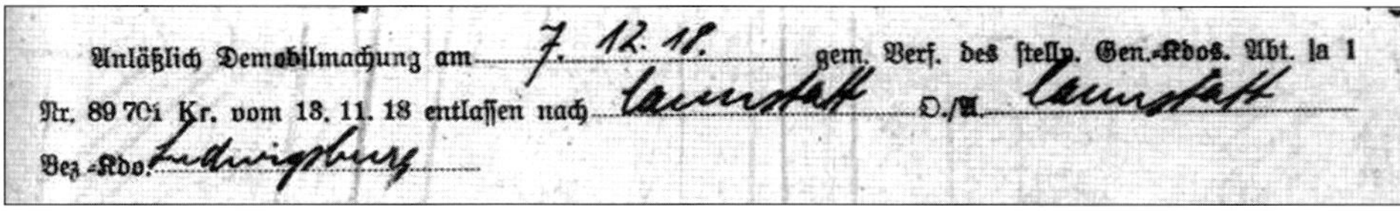
Anläßlich Demobilmachung am 7.12.18 gem. Verf. des stellv. Gen.-Kdos. Abt. Ia 1
Nr. 89 701 Kr. vom 18. 11. 18 entlassen nach Cannstatt O./A. Cannstatt
Bez.-Kdo. Ludwigsburg

Discharge slip issued to *Ersatz Reservist* Anton Dressler, 1/R121. (Landesarchiv Baden-Württemberg, Hauptstaatsarchiv Stuttgart)

Arrival of RIR 119 in Stuttgart, 7 December 1918, (Source: Author's collection)

Arrival of RIR 119 in Stuttgart, 7 December 1918, (Author's collection)

Arrival of RIR 119 in Stuttgart, 7 December 1918, (Author's collection)

Arrival of RIR 119 in Stuttgart, 7 December 1918, (Author's collection)

Arrival of RIR 119 in Stuttgart, 7 December 1918, (Author's collection)

Arrival of RIR 119 in Stuttgart, 7 December 1918, (*Die Württemberger im Weltkriege*)

10

XIV Reserve Corps

Post-War Years

The events on the Western Front as experienced by the men of XIV Reserve Corps have been discussed in detail in four volumes of this series. What subsequently happened to corps' veterans in the months and years following the First World War is chronicled below.

The rumors of civil unrest in Germany that had reached the troops at the end of October and early November had far reaching effects on the lives of every citizen of Germany, whether at home or still in the field in the army. These early events would later become known as the German revolution or *Novemberrevolution*, when the old Imperial government was transformed into a republic during the last month of the war.

The revolutionary period lasted from November 1918 through August 1919 when a new republic was created, which later became known as the Weimar Republic. While the army in the field was disintegrating in the final months of the war, the tensions being felt at home were rising to a breaking point as a result of famine brought on by the Allied blockade, the recent news from the war, which was all bad, and the impact of the millions of men already killed, wounded or missing.

Actually, the seeds of discontent that led to the collapse of the German government had their roots as far back as the start of the war in August 1914. While the various German political parties had virtually joined together in support of the war the tensions that appeared shortly afterward only increased in size and scope until there was little of the early war unity left by 1918.

Following the Russian revolution, tens of thousands of disaffected workers in Germany went on strike, which only caused more unrest and conflict between the government and the civilian population. The rising death rates at home, primarily from malnutrition and the increasing size of the daily *Verlustlisten* only increased the unrest throughout the country.

While the men of the XIV Reserve Corps were being urged to hold out against the ever increasing enemy pressure in the final months of the fighting, as far back 29 September 1918 the Supreme Army Command informed the Kaiser and the Imperial

Chancellor, Count Georg von Hertling, at the army Headquarters in Spa that the military situation was hopeless. General Ludendorff went as far as stating that he could not guarantee to hold the front for another 24 hours.

The situation facing the Army High Command was real and the fact that the end of the fighting would not come until 11 November 1918 was more of luck than anything else. Ludendorff was especially concerned that his army, the pride of Imperial Germany before 1914, would not bear the brunt of the responsibility attached for losing the war.

Ludendorff wanted to force blame on the democratic parties and parliament in order to save face for the army for the imminent capitulation and subsequent consequences thereby creating the 'stab in the back' theory. A theory that supported a false premise that certain victory was turned to defeat as a result of the revolutionaries in Germany forcing an end of the war.

The concept of the stab in the back theory was embraced by many at the highest levels of the army in order to deflect any blame for the imminent loss of the war and transfer the blame on the political parties who were pressing for peace; anything to save the reputation of the army. Support for the concept that the government and the various political parties were the cause of the loss of the war and the immense loss of life that accompanied the heavy fighting grew among the soldiers at the front, many of whom had become very disillusioned and felt betrayed by the very government that had sent them to war.

Much of the disillusion, both at home and at the front, was the result of years of deception by the Supreme Army Command, which had disseminated false information to the army and the public for most of the war, primarily to reduce the negative impact that the true situation facing Germany might have on morale. When the collapse started in late 1918 the negative impact of the news on Germans was amplified, as most had no idea of the dire situation facing the country. While the initial deceptions might have lessened overall discontent between 1914 and 1918, it actually amplified the disaster facing Germany in late 1918 far beyond what it might have been if the people and the army had been kept informed of the true progress of the war all those years.

By October 1918 it was very evident to all that the end of the war was only a matter of time, just how long was not known, but it was accepted that it would be a matter of weeks and not months or years. The overall dissatisfaction of the war that had taken hold of the German population was only intensified even further by a single action that demonstrated just how out of touch the German military was with the actual situation.

On 24 October 1918, a naval order was issued that would send most of the *Kaiserliche Marine's* capital warships out in a last great attack. Unlike the army, the navy had seen little action since the Sea Battle of Jutland in 1916. For more than two years the ships had been kept close to home in the different naval ports where the sailors were idle much of the time. Boredom, increasingly poor rations and too much free time had a negative effect on the men. When this final order was issued it was not received with enthusiasm.

Many of the sailors simply did not want to risk their lives so close to the end of the war and also thought that if such an attack was made that it could effectively put an end to any peace talks. The question then arose as to what could be done to prevent the attack from happening. As the squadrons of warships steamed out of port on their way to the final sea action groups of sailors on several capital warships suddenly refused to obey orders, some even sabotaged portions of their ships, something not seen before in the Imperial Navy.

There were few mutineers and the revolt was put down quickly, however the attack was called off as the officers felt they could not rely upon the loyalty of the crews. While the warships returned to their berths, the ringleaders had been arrested and confined. What the officers did not know what that there was a plan to release the mutineers. The disorder came to a head on 3 November 1918 when large groups of sailors made demands that their comrades who were in confinement should be freed, the war was to end and the rations being issued were to be improved.

The protesters were met with force and as a result of clashes with military police units seven were killed and 29 were severely wounded. Some of the demonstrators had returned fire once the police had started shooting. While the protesters and military police dispersed following the initial clash the riot grew in size as more and more sailors joined the protest and in the end it grew to a general revolt.

On 4 November 1918 the troubles in the naval ports spread and as a result the first soldier's councils were formed. The sailors who had been imprisoned following the mutiny were released and when government troops arrived at Kiel with orders to quell the riot they either joined the revolt or returned to their barracks. By the evening of the 4th Kiel was in the hands of 40,000 mutineers, Wilhelmshaven came under the control of mutineers two days later; the collapse of Germany was at hand.

Late on the 4th and the next days the sailors sent committees throughout Germany spreading the revolt. A worker's and soldier's council forced the abdication of Ludwig III, the King of Bavaria. The uprising spread quickly and became rampant throughout the country, culminating in the proclamation of a Republic on 9 November 1918, which resulted in the demand, that Kaiser Wilhelm abdicate; the country was literally unraveling within days of the initial spark.

Turmoil and confusion reigned with the different parties vying for power including the Marxist Spartacist organization. Finally, with the abdication of the emperor and the Kaiser leaving the country, there was no hope of continuing the war and the demands by the Allies for an Armistice and the stringent requirements it contained were accepted and would take effect at the 11th hour of 11 November 1918; the war was effectively over. By 23 November 1918 the rulers of all German states had abdicated. There was little else done, other than remove the heads of state. All other aspects of the government remained intact.

During this time of unrest in the days immediately following the end of the Great War a number of para-military units were formed that were called the *Freikorps*. These organizations were made up mostly of men who had served in the army and navy during the war as a result of the deteriorating political situation in Germany between the different factions and a perceived threat from Bolshevik forces in the east.

One such *Freikorps*, the 1st *Gardelandeschützen Abteilung*, was formed between 1 and 8 December 1918 and primarily from men who had belonged to the 2nd Guard Reserve Division, the same division that had defended Gommécourt on 1 July 1916 and that had fought alongside the 26th Reserve Division in the final years of the war. This

Freikorps unit was under the command of a former General Staff Officer from the division, *Rittmeister von* Neufville.[1]

The *Freikorps* became involved in the fighting in the east against the Bolsheviks as well as helping to put down the German Revolution and the Marxist Spartacist uprising on 14-15 January 1919.

Elections for the new Weimar National Assembly were finally held on 19 January 1919 and the revolution ended when the Weimar Constitution was adopted on 11 August 1919. Before this constitution came into effect, civil unrest and armed uprisings spread across Germany. There was fighting in many German cities at the end of December 1918. In January 1919 clashes between the different political groups left 156 people dead in Berlin.

The uprisings were perceived as a threat to the existence of the German state and were met with brutal force by the army and the *Freikorps* units. By the end of March approximately 1,200 people had been killed, many of whom were bystanders that were not taking part in the fighting on either side. Even after the formation of the Weimar Republic in August 1919, clashes continued, government takeovers were attempted, including the 1923 Nazi Beer Hall Putsch, which failed.

While I have no direct information regarding the men of the XIV Reserve Corps being involved in any of the rioting or participating in the different *Freikorps* units there is always the chance that some did. Whether they were involved or not, the constant turmoil following the end of the war and the collapse of the monarchy was a time of great stress and worry for every German. During this same time the Allied blockade continued, which only added to the misery of the general population. To all who lived through this time it must have appeared that the world was coming to an end with the fall of empires, the overthrow of royal families and the rise of communism.

The men of the XIV Reserve Corps that had managed to survive the war and were now home had to face the constant political turmoil that flared up across Germany while trying to return to a normal life. While much of the fighting took place in Berlin and the surrounding areas, Bavaria and other parts of Germany also felt the pain of civil unrest.

To make matters worse, Germany started to go through a period of hyperinflation within a year of the war ending. Germany had financed the war through borrowing, which had slowly reduced the value of the Mark as the war progressed. The Treaty of Versailles that was eventually signed on 28 June 1919 only accelerated the decline of the Mark's value. At the end of 1919 the exchange rate was just more than 32 paper Marks were the equivalent of $1.00. In 1921 this ratio increased to 330 paper Marks to $1.00.

Reparations that were part of the treaty called for payment in gold and foreign currency plus 26 percent of foreign exports. As the value of the Mark dropped several attempts were made to stabilize the currency but all failed; by December 1922 the ratio was 800 paper Marks to $1.00.

In addition to the civil and political unrest there were other events that occurred, which aroused the hatred of the German population; enemy occupation of parts of Germany and finally the complete takeover of German territory by a foreign power. Following the Armistice the Rhineland was occupied by Allied troops. In 1920 the Saar was separated from the Rhine Province by the French and held until a plebiscite in 1935.

The areas of Eupen and Malmedy were turned over to the control of Belgium. French troops then took full control over the entire area of the Rhineland. The military occupations were undertaken primarily to ensure that Germany made good on the repayment of the war debt as outlined in the Versailles Treaty. By taking over mineral rich and industrial centers of Germany the Allies could force repayment by literally taking the resources from the land.

Civil and political unrest only increased as foreign troops occupied parts of Germany and this lead to even more inflation in Germany. By 1923 the ratio was 4,210,500,000,000 Marks to $1.00. There was a plan put into place in 1923 when new currency was issued, eliminating twelve zeros and as a result the currency began to stabilize; this was successful primarily because the new currency was backed by hard assets, mostly mineral and agricultural resources. In 1924 a new law allowed each old paper one trillion Mark note to be exchanged for one new Reichsmark.

The Weimar Republic would remain in existence until 1933 despite all of the seemingly overwhelming odds it had faced when formed. Once the new constitution was written and adopted on 11 August 1919 the fledgling government had to deal with the revolutions, hyperinflation, political extremists on the right and left and the Allies and the Treaty of Versailles. Then, the worldwide depression of 1929 hit Germany harder than most countries due to the perceived instability of the government.

In 1930 President Hindenburg took over emergency powers to bolster the existing administration. During the Great depression the overall situation grew worse with a policy of deflation, which led to a surge in unemployment. These circumstances eventually led to the appointment of Adolf Hitler as Chancellor of a coalition government. At that time the National Socialist Party held only three cabinet seats out of eleven.

However, despite these seemingly overwhelming obstacles, the Weimar Republic managed to reform the currency, unify tax policies and the railway system and eliminated most of the requirements of the Treaty of Versailles in its short time in existence. For many reasons, Germany only repaid a portion of the war reparations that had been laid down by the treaty.

In the end the issue of war guilt, the stab in the back theory and the loss of power and prestige by the old ruling class with constant pressure on the republic lead to its instability and eventual takeover by the Nazi Party in 1933. One are of contention was the borders of Germany. While the western borders were acceptable to the republic, the eastern border with the Polish Corridor that cut off a portion of the country from the whole and the loss of the city of Danzig remained a major issue.

Before the republic collapsed it should also be noted that Germany never fully disarmed. In the years between the two world wars Germany managed to bypass the treaty provisions regarding the military through a secret agreement with Russia where German troops were trained inside Russia. New tactics and weapons continued to be developed and when the Nazi Party assumed control in 1933 the country already had a head start on fully rearming the country.

Adolf Hitler and the Nazi Party moved quickly once in a position of power. The Reichstag fire of 27 February 1933, the product of a so-called Communist revolution, led to the Reichstag Fire Decree that with one signature wiped out most constitutional civil liberties.

The Enabling Act of 1933 then allowed Hitler as Chancellor to govern by decree and without the legislature. The republic was gone, a democratically elected legislature was disbanded and a single party state was formed.

Among Acts put into place in weeks following power grab was to remove anyone who was Jewish from the Civil Service with the exception of any Jewish soldier who had served at the front in the Great War, an exception that had been demanded by President Hindenburg. When Hindenburg died on 2 August 1934, Hitler quickly moved to consolidate the office of president and Chancellor and assumed control over the German government. Trade unions were banned, controls placed over newspapers, outlawed political parties and anyone of the Jewish faith were quickly eliminated from Civil Service positions whether veterans or not.

This was the beginning of an almost unprecedented period of rule by terror that had huge consequences for the people of Germany as well as the rest of the world and would only end in the destruction of the Third Reich. Before that occurred, there was the rise and rearming of Nazi Germany that led to the Second World War, 1939-1945, which was a true global war. Yet despite the destruction of Nazi Germany in late 1945 and the defeat of Japan several months later the effects of this turbulent period in world history are still with us to this day.

How all of this fit into the lives of the men of the XIV Reserve Corps and more will be discussed in the next section. With the returning troops and the end of the fighting came a period of time where the larger social and political upheavals occurred in the background while the men who returned attempted to fit back in to society. This could prove to be a difficult transition as for many the years fighting on the western and eastern fronts had consumed every aspect of their lives.

An uncertain future now faced the survivors of the XIV Reserve Corps, as it did all other soldiers who were returning to a home that was far different than the one they had left. Everything they had once known had changed. Facing an uncertain future is never a pleasant experience but there was little anyone could do but live through this time period as best as possible.

Amidst the social and political upheaval that faced the German population following the end of the Great War was a matter that impacted tens of thousands of families in the most personal manner possible; what had become of their family members who had simply been listed as *Vermisst* (missing) on one of the numerous *Verlustlisten* published during the war. At the end of 1918 there were 14,698 officers and 846,692 enlisted men, a total of 861,390 German soldiers, officially listed as missing. The families of these men had been living in hope that they would eventually be found alive in an Allied prisoner of war camp, hospital or simply been listed as missing through an error. These hopes faded only slightly over time as the weeks, months and years of the war passed. Then, when the fighting was over and the troops started to return home it soon became evident that their loved ones were never coming home.

Great efforts were made to account for these men by the German civil bureaucracy. Official inquiries were made, casualty lists were scanned over and over again and returning prisoners of war were interviewed for the knowledge of their comrades listed as missing. Anything and everything possible was done to provide closure to the thousands of families across the country.

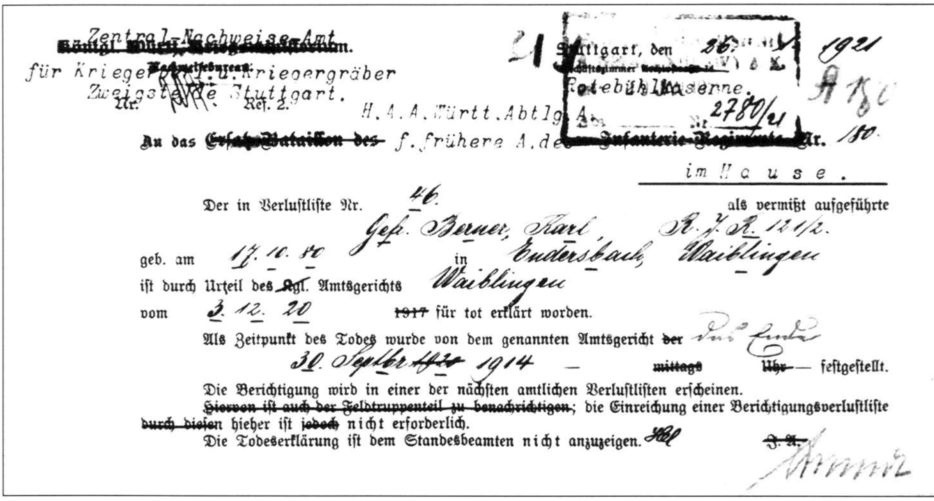

Zentral-Nachweise-Amt ~~Königl. Württ. Kriegsministerium.~~
für Kriegerverluste u. Kriegergräber
Zweigstelle Stuttgart.
Nr. Ref. 2.
H.A.A. Württ. Abtlg. A.

Stuttgart, den 26. 1921
Rotebühlkaserne.
Nr. 2780/21

An das ~~Ersatz-Bataillon des~~ f. frühere A.d. ~~Infanterie-Regiments~~ Nr. 180.
im Hause.

Der in Verlustliste Nr. 46. als vermißt aufgeführte
Gefr. Berner, Karl R.I.R. 121/2.
geb. am 17.10.90 in Endersbach, Waiblingen
ist durch Urteil des ~~Kgl.~~ Amtsgerichts Waiblingen
vom 3.12.20 ~~1917~~ für tot erklärt worden.
Als Zeitpunkt des Todes wurde von dem genannten Amtsgericht ~~der~~ das Ende
30. Septbr. ~~1920~~ 1914 — ~~mittags~~ ~~Uhr~~ — festgestellt.
Die Berichtigung wird in einer der nächsten amtlichen Verlustlisten erscheinen.
~~Hiervon ist auch der Feldtruppenteil zu benachrichtigen~~; die Einreichung einer Berichtigungsverlustliste ~~durch diesen~~ hieher ist ~~jedoch~~ nicht erforderlich.
Die Todeserklärung ist dem Standesbeamten nicht anzuzeigen.

MIA since 30 September 1914. Declared dead 3 December 1920. (Landesarchiv Baden-Württemberg, Hauptstaatsarchiv Stuttgart)

Often word about a missing friend or loved one came from the men who had returned from the war who had firsthand knowledge of the fate of the missing man. However, as many of the returning veterans discovered, the meeting with the family of a missing man could be very traumatizing for both parties.

For one man, Hans Ludwig from RIR 120, his first such experience proved to be his last. While trying to find civilian clothes that would fit he had gone into the local town to shop.

> As long as I was in town I decided to go to a friend's office where he worked with his father as a law apprentice before he enlisted. It was difficult for me to find the place but eventually I saw the office shield and went in, not realizing that it had been raining and I was soaking wet. I gave the receptionist my name and asked to see my friend Otto. I must have looked terrible. All out of breath, soaking wet, cloth clinging to my bones, a living skeleton. She looked at me in such a way that I was ashamed for sitting in a nice chair soaking it through with my wet clothing and I got up and was standing when she went into the private office and after a while she came out and asked me to follow her into the big room where Otto senior just sat in his chair, staring at me if I was a ghost. The old gentleman had aged and his hands were shaking. I had to repeat my name several times and then suddenly he remembered me, most likely as the guy who always was in scrapes with his son. Tears were running down his face and I knew that something was wrong. When a lawyer cries then there is real trouble and there was. Otto Jr. was killed in Russia soon after I was taken prisoner and after hostilities were supposed to have stopped. He had been dead for three years, there was not even a grave; he was just missing. As was the habit then and I think is still to the day, the living quarters

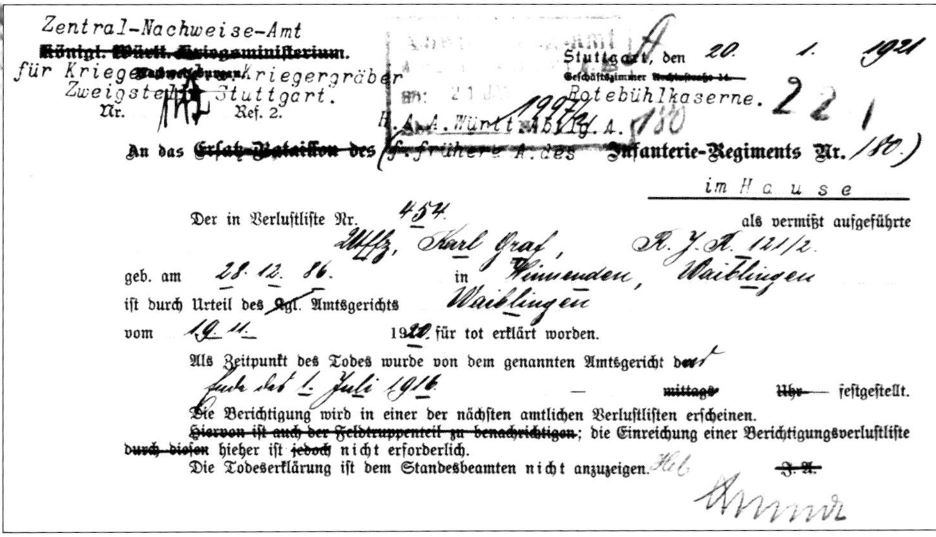
Zentral-Nachweise-Amt
~~Königl. Württ. Kriegsministerium.~~
für Kriegerverluste u. Kriegergräber
Zweigstelle Stuttgart.
Nr. Ref. 2.
Stuttgart, den 20. 1. 1921
Geschäftszimmer Rotebühlkaserne.
An das ~~Ersatz-Bataillon des~~ Infanterie-Regiments Nr. 180
im Hause
Der in Verlustliste Nr. 454 als vermißt aufgeführte
Uffz. Karl Graf, R.J.R. 121/2.
geb. am 28. 12. 86. in Winnenden, Waiblingen
ist durch Urteil des ~~Kgl.~~ Amtsgerichts Waiblingen
vom 19. 11. 1920 für tot erklärt worden.
Als Zeitpunkt des Todes wurde von dem genannten Amtsgericht der
1. Juli 1916 — ~~mittags~~ ~~Uhr~~ festgestellt.
Die Berichtigung wird in einer der nächsten amtlichen Verlustlisten erscheinen.
~~Hiervon ist auch der Feldtruppenteil zu benachrichtigen~~; die Einreichung einer Berichtigungsverlustliste ~~durch diesen~~ hieher ist ~~jedoch~~ nicht erforderlich.
Die Todeserklärung ist dem Standesbeamten nicht anzuzeigen.

MIA since 1 July 1916. Declared dead 19 November 1920. (Landesarchiv Baden-Württemberg, Hauptstaatsarchiv Stuttgart)

> of professional people were right behind their office rooms and Otto senior took me there and told the housekeeper to get me dried out and replace what had been ruined by the rain and also gave me a raincoat. Later on he came back and we talked until late at night and I felt that I had to tell him before it became embarrassing that I was going to sleep on the floor and why and that is just what I did. The next morning I went home and made up my mind to forget all about those many visits I had planned to make with all the families of the men of my company who were still listed as missing but were actually dead, killed on that June 7th, 1917, 3 and 1/2 years ago. I don't think that I could have lived through so many cases if one was so much.[2]

The level of effort to have a missing man declared to be dead officially was quite involved and required sufficient proof to have such a decision made. This level of proof is evident in the effort to determine the fate of *Ersatz Reservist* Karl Reil, 2nd Company, 6th Bavarian Reserve Regiment who was involved in the fighting on 1 July 1916 near Curlu and never heard from again. In this instance, his father, Sebastian Reil, a baker from Waldau, proceeded to file documents that would officially pronounce his son dead:

> Court Administrator Vohenhas. *Amtrichter* Remy declares the following in the matter concerning the notice for the purpose of the declaration of the death of the Baker's son Karl Reil of Waldau who was missing in the war. Decision: Reil, Karl, born on 24 September 1893 in Waldau, the son of a baker from there, formerly *Ersatz Reservist* of the 2nd Company, Reserve Infantry Regiment 6 is confirmed to be dead. The time of his death is determined to be 1st July 1916 at 12 o'clock at

night. The burden of the expense of the proposition filed falls on the estate of the missing man.

Findings and reasons: Born on 24 September 1893 in Waldau, the baker's son Karl Reil from there, was an *Ersatz Reservist* in the war, in the 2nd Company Bavarian Reserve Regiment Nr. 6, he became missing since the battle at Curlu on 1st July 1916, in which he was involved.

On 17 February 1919 the father of the missing, Baker Sebastian Reil in Waldau, has, according to the protocol under the signature of the court clerk in his official capacity of the court filed the proposition, to declare his son dead.

On 17 February 1919 the municipality administration of Waldau has confirmed that no news of any sort has been received by the municipality about the existence of Karl Reil since 30 June 1916.

The *Nachweisebüro* of the Ministry for Military Affairs in Munich has reported under the inquiry of 7 March 1919, that *Ersatz Reservist* Reil, since the fighting by Curlu from the 1st of July 1916, by which he had been involved, became missing, that he was not present in the prisoner of war lists and that since the day he was reported missing no news about him has been received by the *Nachweisebüro*. The knowledge of his name became transmitted under the act of the State enacted on 14 March 1919.

On the aforementioned application of Sebastian Reil, to which the position that he, as the father of the missing was shown to be legitimate, enacted the signed judgment for the last known residence under the notice of 19 March 1919 which through posting on the court notice board and the municipality public notice board in Waldau was made well known. The terms of the notice were obeyed; on the date of 2nd May current.

The proposition placed on the aforementioned father Reil, to perform the terms of the notice. No date has been set today to announce the decision through a public session. 955 Z.B.O.

No news has been obtained of the life of *Ersatz Reservist* Reil to suspend the enactment of the judgment of the court. The reason for the declaration of death from the required facts became on reason of the previously mentioned attestations as completely proven, that *Ersatz Reservist* Reil had participated in the battle by Curlu on 1st July 1916 and since then was missing.

It was such that after the material and formal requirements the judgment that was enacted is to be issued, how it occurred under the establishment of the time of death on 1st July 1916 at 12 o'clock at night and the expenses are set over to the estate. Affirmed on 4th July 1919.[3]

Similar efforts were made across Germany, especially in the first years following the end of the war, and the time and resources utilized for these inquiries reached a staggering amount. Once the requirements for proof had been made an official document was issued that established the exact date of death. This document could then be used by the families to obtain possible benefits from the government as a result of the soldier being deceased.

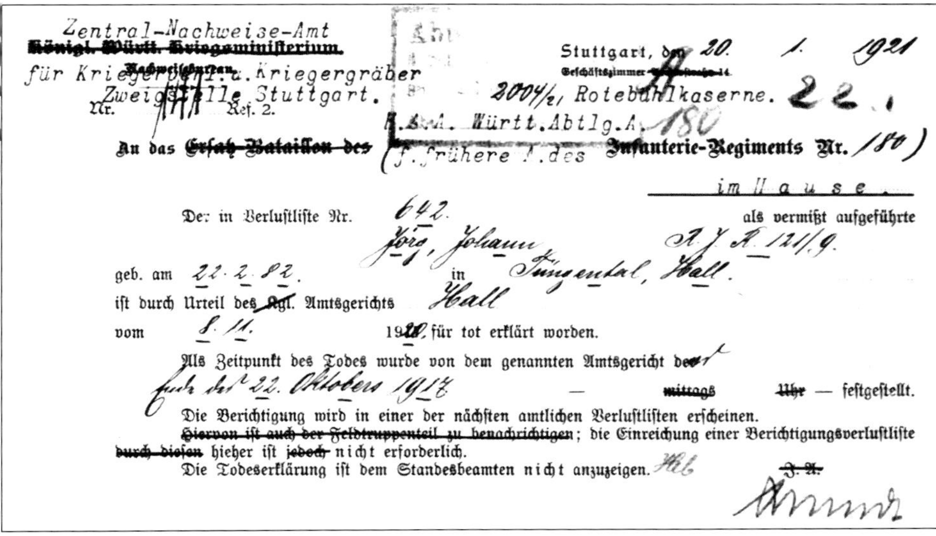

Zentral-Nachweise-Amt
~~Königl. Württ. Kriegsministerium.~~
für Kriegerverl. u. Kriegergräber
Zweigstelle Stuttgart.
Nr. 2004/21 Ref. 2.

Stuttgart, den 20. 1. 1921
Geschäftszimmer
Rotebühlkaserne. 22.

An das ~~Ersatz-Bataillon des~~ Abw.A. Württ. Abtlg. A. 180 (f. frühere A. des Infanterie-Regiments Nr. 180)

im Hause.

Der in Verlustliste Nr. 642 als vermißt aufgeführte
Jörg, Johann R. I. R. 121/9.
geb. am 22. 2. 82. in Jungenthal, Hall.
ist durch Urteil des ~~Kgl.~~ Amtsgerichts Hall
vom 8. 11. 1920 für tot erklärt worden.

Als Zeitpunkt des Todes wurde von dem genannten Amtsgericht der Ende des 22. Oktobers 1917 — ~~mittags~~ ~~Uhr~~ — festgestellt.

Die Berichtigung wird in einer der nächsten amtlichen Verlustlisten erscheinen.
~~Hiervon ist auch der Feldtruppenteil zu benachrichtigen~~; die Einreichung einer Berichtigungsverlustliste ~~durch diesen~~ hieher ist ~~jedoch~~ nicht erforderlich.
Die Todeserklärung ist dem Standesbeamten nicht anzuzeigen.

~~J. A.~~

MIA since 22 October 1917. Declared dead 8 November 1920. (Landesarchiv Baden-Württemberg, Hauptstaatsarchiv Stuttgart)

Officially, the process of accounting for the numerous missing men continued until the end of 1933, fifteen years after the end of the war. By this time, the total number of official missing soldiers was 974,977 officers and men. The highest number of missing soldiers had been 1,080, 255 at the end of 1919 once the confusion that existed in the last months of the war had been thoroughly examined, and the final reports had been obtained and reviewed. From the end of 1919 to the end of 1933 the numbers of missing fluctuated at times but were eventually being reduced as new information was being obtained about the fate of these men.

Nevertheless, the families would have to live with the knowledge that their loved ones had simply disappeared. Some would know the fate of their family members through letters and accounts related by their comrades; at least they knew their fate. Others, the majority of the missing, had simply disappeared from existence. One minute they were alive and the next they were simply gone. Some remained buried in collapsed dugouts and tunnels such as those recently discovered during road construction in Alsace where the remains of 21 soldiers from the 6/94 were discovered during a construction project. Others simply lay where they fell; buried in a farmer's field where crops grow over what had been trenches and battlefields during the war. The remains of these soldiers are being recovered even today during building projects and archaeological digs. When found, every effort is being used to give these men an identity and if possible to notify surviving family members.

While thousands of men returned home in November and December 1918 during the withdrawal from France and Belgium, others were not as fortunate. These were the prisoners of war, thousands of men who had been captured during the war and despite the Armistice and the withdrawal of the German armies; these men remained behind the barbed wire enclosures, in some cases for nearly two years following the Armistice:

Meanwhile three years had passed in the country, and we were still behind the entanglements. The prison camps we were in during this time changed every now and then. Approximately one year we were behind the front, the last two years found us in the French port of Le Havre. There we had a relative humane camp, with large barracks we built ourselves, our own electric lights, canteen and bowling alley. Furthermore our own orchestra and prisoner choir, whereby we could forget our monotonous and sad life slightly. Two particularly sad and black days I do not want to be allowed to forget:

First of all, the day of the complete breaking of the German front. How this day has made us front soldiers mad! So we would like to help our poor Fatherland, however we were defenseless and without weapons! This day was an unparalleled celebration by the British, and it almost broke our German hearts. We had however wished our troops the victory that we craved from the first day of the World War – and now this defeat and conditions of the Armistice, you could almost cry!

The other black day was when we had to look at three dear comrades in the grave, the comrades Jäck, Blattmann and Paul Birk. The death of the latter was especially close to me; after all he was a countryman of mine and the only other Konstanzer in the entire prison camp. Comrades Jäck and Birk succumbed to the malignant influenza, Blattmann died from blood poisoning. The deceased comrades lie buried at the cemetery St. Marie in Le Havre.

In the meantime 15 July 1919 had arrived. It was a Sunday, when we were told of the order to leave our old camp and once again to go traveling. It was no joy for us however; we waited a long time for the homecoming. At 11.30 in the morning we became embarked and not until after three days did we arrive in our new home, in Hollebeke in Flanders. Our camp was entirely primitive. At our arrival it consisted of a leveled site that was surrounded with entanglements. We brought our tents from Le Havre, kitchen, washing facilities, latrines, louse institutes and combustion stoves we built first in the course of that time. The most important part of our work was to look for old war materials in the terrain, which in part lay around in masses. Many a hare became caught there in the wide terrain during the work and cooked in camp.

The food was not exactly the best. It didn't become uncommon before that at midday we only got gruel with raisins. Meat was something normally rarely seen, instead it was frequently herring. Some days there was even no bread, and we had to be content with hard biscuits. The cooking and drinking water we got with the small railway, the wash water we got ourselves out of the many surrounding shell holes. The canteen that had provided such good service to us in Le Havre, did not work at all at first and one often did not like how much less his sorely earned 5.40 Francs per month was worth. Furthermore great dissatisfaction came over the long postponement of the repatriation. It was no wonder that the man attempted to strike several times, however they failed by the force of the British every time, now the most restless minds attempted to play tricks on the British in different ways: They wanted to run away! Approximately twelve men stealthily fled away from the work within three to four weeks. A few succeeded, the others became caught about half way, brought back to the company and punished with arrest. Three men in the night before the final order for our repatriation came, escaped and happily made it home. I helped them through the entanglements.

On 26th August the message for our repatriation arrived in the camp. And right, on the same day therefore, the order to march off came. The long-awaited day had come, what a feeling of joy, the relief and hope that moved there in the hearts of the prisoners. How suddenly the good mood hit us. And how grateful we were towards God, who was so kind and merciful to us, leading us through the three heavy years of patience in captivity.

At 8 a.m. on 30th August, the company marched with the exception of 24 men that were from the Rheinischen area, to Wytschaete, where we were embarked. We traveled first of all until to Meteren, from there we had a half hour of marching, until we came to the Concentration camp. There began the exchange. We were still cooped up in that very primitive camp for 18 days. It was lucky for us that the weather during these days was always beautiful and warm. Our men were so sullen and unsatisfied again that they no longer wanted to carry out the smallest work. However, the longing for home had become too strong at the end.

Finally, at 4 o'clock a.m. on 18th September the signal sounded in the camp for the breakup and for the journey home. Everything was already ready to march for two days. So in a few minutes the entire company was quick and ready at the assembly places ready for payment. About 6 o'clock in the morning we moved into our platoon, in order to travel to the long-awaited home. Our journey went via Armentiéres, Lille, Charleroi, and soon we were in Herbesthal, where we heard the first German voices. At 5 o'clock in the evening we were in Düren. There we received the first gifts.

Our further journey through German lands resembled a triumphant journey. Everywhere we became joyfully greeted and entertained. Before Cologne the rejoicing of the population was very hearty. People stood on the roofs and balconies and waved at us with handkerchiefs and sheets, to greet us. In Cologne that was occupied by the British, the English accompanying Other Ranks left us. Before we traveled further, they didn't want to leave us before singing an English parting-song to us. We were finally completely free! In Munster i W. the regimental band was at the railway station to greet us. A general held a speech, the effect was excellent. And so it was at each larger station. We were all perplexed – we had not expected anything like this. It was a joy to be allowed to travel through the home like this, greeted and cheered everywhere.

It was late in the evening when we arrived high in the north, in the *Münsterlager*. There we were still thoroughly deloused, received new clothing and our wages, which were not too meager. After two days we traveled like newborns to the dear home, which already long anticipated us.

However, God was still heartily thanked, who preserved and guarded us in all the war and prisoner years, and brought us back safely again to our loved ones. Otto Hengel, 9th Company, RIR 111.[4]

10.07.1919
Dear Johanna! Today I was surprised by the mail with your packet from August 25, have thanks for that! Although I am sorry if you repeatedly dismisses as good things, but they do indeed taste exquisite. Our return home received an unfortunate delay by the local 9-day railway strike, when it really takes place, no one can predict. My main wish is of course to come home at least before Christmas, before the time of wet and cold coats us anew here and throws us back into a mood of despair. Right now we have beautiful autumn days, the trees slowly torn golden and it is just a pity that the night frost has already destroyed many of our flowers that we had planted and tended next to our huts. The evening time, now the most unpleasant for us, because the illumination in part fails, in part it is deficient, but I also fear for you so often. And once the long winter evenings were always extra nice if you could sit at the family table so cozy. May this time to come back soon, may she rest and our home and bring prosperity. In the local strike England had also come close to the brink of civil war, it spits all over the world. Where first gathers together inwardly, has come up, and we have this opportunity. In the hope that I may soon contribute my little bit, I greet you with all my heart.
Your faithful cousin Albert [Reihling].[5]

Whilst many of the veterans of the Great War continued their lives as best they could, for some, the stress and uncertainty was simply too much. Many veterans decided that an entirely new life was needed, one that would hopefully be free of unrest, hardship and political turmoil. For these men the final destination would be the United States. Many had relatives who had already emigrated to the United States in the decades before the war and at least had some idea of what they could expect. For others it did not matter if they had connections to the United States, they simply knew that their lives could be better if they left Germany.

Among these men was Emil Goebelbecker, RIR 109, who, after surviving a prisoner of war camp decided that he was going to move to the U.S. where he lived until his death many decades later. Hans Ludwig, RIR 120 was also among the men who came to the United States and made a new life for himself. For one man, Johann Kacmarzik, formerly in the Machine Gun Company od RIR 109, emigrating to the U.S. may have made a great difference in healing the internal wounds from fighting in the war. Johann had been one of the few men in the XIV Reserve Corps who had served throughout the entire war and survived unharmed. However, the events he witnessed and participated in were horrendous and in coming to the U.S. he found some peace and stability in his life.

Johann and his wife Anna traveled to the United States in 1922 and like many other emigrants, they had family already in the United States, Anna's sister and husband, Gertrude and Richard Boehm who sponsored Johann and Anna. Johann eventually found work as a fireman in a coal mine owned by Anheuser Busch. His love of animals, especially after what he witnessed to the regimental mules and horses during the war, played a part in his life after the war. He would purchase mules that had worked in the mines their entire lives and were considered to be unfit for work. Johann led these mules to his home with blindfolds as they had never seen the light of day. He cared for these animals and brought them back to health and used them to plow the ground for his garden. It was not difficult work and Johann, or John as he became called, had a great affection for these animals who were able to live out their remaining years in comfortable surroundings, almost part of the family, especially one mule named Barney. Johann (John) lived until 1960 when he passed away.

Shortly after the end of the war, the first of numerous regimental histories were printed that provided a history of the regiment during the war. Some of these appeared in the early 1920s, and the books continued to appear into the 1940s during another world-wide conflict. While not every unit produced such an account, large numbers did. These were mostly written by officers and men who had served in the regiment and the stories were drawn from official records, diaries and letters from the

Johann and Anna Kacmarzik, RIR 109 (Jason Coad)

Machine Gun Company R.I.R. 109 from Johann Kacmarzik. He had a special affinity for the horses during the war and especially for mules and horses while he lived in th U.S. after the war. (Jason Coad)

members of the regiment. The books were illustrated with photographs taken by the men during the war and can often be seen today in the form of photographic postcards.

Most of the regimental histories were considered attempts to portray the experiences of the men who had fought and suffered in the World War. However, these volumes only provide a brief glimpse into the momentous events of the war, they could only describe a limited number of stories and accounts due to a lack of space. It was a means to preserve the deeds and memories of the men who served together and maintain the bonds that had formed during the war and until the last man in the regiment had died. The deeds recorded in the books merely represented the obscure and unnamed men, who faithfully performed their duty, suffered wounds and death and would have been forgotten otherwise.

The regimental history of RIR 109, published in 1931, speaks of the returning soldiers:

> Not decorated with laurels and with the joy of the victor on the lips of the brave men that returned home. However out of the shining eyes of the front-fighter, who crossed over his threshold again and that which sprang from his heart, spoke of the proud awareness of the brave man: I have preserved you, my house, my fatherland with the actions of my life.[6]

Or in the history of RIR 111 that was published in 1938:

> The battalions had therefore come back to the Baden cities, out of which they had moved into the field in August 1914. Only very few with the regiment had experienced the day of the marching out and the day of the return. Many, only all too many, that since August 1914 had worn the number 111 on the shoulder, altogether no longer returned home. They rest on the numerous battlefields of the western front, from the Vosges in the south to the north of France. The commemoration of them lives further in the hearts of the comrades, and so that therefore remains the badischen Reserve Infantry Regiment Nr. 111 that disbanded in the December day of 1918, an honorary remembrance preserved. The end of the War was different than the energy and sacrifices of the German army and so that also RIR 111 had deserved. The German soldiers however remained proud of the awareness of having done his duty for the Fatherland and home up to the most extreme. *He returns home undefeated out of the field.* [Author's Italics] We know today that the victims had not been brought in vain, and that out of the bloody seed that in four long heavy years of fighting had sowed, a new, joyous future, a united Germany should arise. The generation of the front fighter has with their spirit created the Third Reich. The memory of the great events of the World War does not hold back the spirit, so that a defense ready German youth can continue the work that the war generation had begun under untold victims.[7]

While researching materials for this series of books, one main source of information was the published regimental history. However, when using these sources an author needs to be aware of when it was published and the political situation that existed at that time

Great War veterans, circa 1930's. (Author's collection)

in history. You need to be aware of certain attitudes and descriptions, flowery rhetoric extolling the Nazi Party as this could taint the accuracy of the material presented. Generally it is not too difficult to recognize the bluster and bluff in the narrative and separate it from the presentation of the events that actually did take place between 1914-1918:

> The war was over; what came were hardship, desperation and finally chaos. A "revolution" without character and leadership, without ideas and answers, however full of phrases and theories to make you happy shattered with the shameful dictates of Versailles about the wager, was there still an Ethos in the German people. Once again the Germans made their history. Millions of Germans were ready, to erase their peoples name, if an international human paradise made it happy for them. However they did the arithmetic without the front warrior. He knew about the meaning of the defeat. And therefore Germany would survive the collapse, when countless of its dwellers were also mentally corrupted and had died. A people with that unheard of performance in the World War could not go under. With the first appalling grey working day after the Great War began the new show for the soldiers…
>
> Years passed. Years of aimlessness, disappointments, programs and parties. The Front soldiers actions created on the consciousness of the nation, the heroic expression it was and had to become again. What remained however, that seemed to be given, to work on the formation of a new German people, when out of their ranks the immense leadership personality of Adolf Hitler who carried out the only true and essentially German revolution. In two splendid spring days, the 21st of March 1933 and the 16th March 1935 the new people's defense of the Germans marched under the pardoned leadership of the unfamiliar Gefreiten out of the Great War to his first triumphant victory. Now would the old front fighters of 1914 see their war history finished, after they finally have their 'Miracle of the Marne.'[8]

I have also come across obvious anti-Semitic references in regimental accounts published in the early 1920s, long before the rise of the Nazi Party. This only emphasizes how rampant anti-Semitism was in German society before the rise of Hitler. In part it was always present in German society and in part it was encouraged with the increasingly popular myth of the German army having been stabbed in the back by communists, Jews and other groups which did not support Germany during the war and were demonized as being the reason Germany lost the war.

The Nazi Party under Adolf Hitler in the 1930s and the subsequent outbreak of WWII had a particularly horrible impact on numerous religious and ethnic groups inside Germany as well as in the occupied countries. Many of the people in these groups faced organized extermination or at the very least were used as slave labor in German factories, a fate that was extermination at a slower rate than being executed or gassed as so many were. Of these groups, the population of Germany and the occupied countries that were of the Jewish religion were particularly at risk.

Of the 12,000,000 people who died in the Nazi concentration camps in the 1930s and 40s, 6,000,000, or half, were of the Jewish faith. Of these millions of victims who died during the Second World War there were men who had served Germany faithfully in WWI. Apparently nothing could help these men as they were taken away and sent to the concentration camps. No level of protest, no display of service records and medals could save these men who had fought for the Kaiser.

There are no words that can properly describe the horrors of this period in time for the millions of people who were exterminated overall and for the Jewish veterans of the Great War in particular. It seemed as if these veterans had been betrayed twice over; once by simply being Jewish, and once for having their record of faithful service to their country erased.

After years of research into this series, I looked for any details on the lives and experiences of the men of the XIV Reserve Corps. Part of this research delved into the issue of the Jewish soldiers, primarily because of the events of the Nazi period. While I had some references to these soldiers, including one book, '*Kriegs Tagebuch eines Juden* by Julius Marx, who was an officer in RIR 120, and the list of Jewish war dead that can be found in the book, *Die Judischen Gefallenen des Deutschen Heeres, der Deutschen Marine und der Deutschen Schutztruppen,* 1914-1918, there was no other direct evidence of the post-war lives of these men.

Then I was fortunate to make the acquaintance of Rod Otey who resides in London, England. Rod and I met through a mutual friend following a local event from the series 'Who do you think you are', sponsored by Ancestry.com. Rod was making inquiries into the history of several of his relatives who had served in the German Army in WWI and who were of the Jewish faith. Our mutual friend passed along the inquiry to me and I was able to provide some details on several of Rod's relatives. Over the next months we exchanged details on his family members that will be presented below. What the reader will see is a record of service and sacrifice, no different than any German family at this time in history in some aspect, yet in at least one facet far more as of the men who served from Rod's family, every one became a casualty during the war, something that not every family experienced.

Kameradengrab in Lens Sallaumilles. (Rod Otey)

Rod's paternal grandfather was one of six siblings, four boys and two girls, While Rod's grandfather was too young to serve in the war, his three older brothers did. The first brother is Arthur Moses. He was born on 3 August 1892 in Glan-Münchweiler, joined the German army on 7 April 1915 as a *Landsturmmann* and was eventually sent to the 5th Bavarian Infantry Regiment, which he joined on 10 July 1915. His service record indicated that he served with the regiment in Flanders from 10 July 1915 to 21 October 1915 when the regiment was moved to another part of the front, in French Flanders.

Arthur served at this location from 23 October until 3 November 1915 when he was killed by an artillery shell at 7.30 a.m. Arthur's final resting place is located in the *Kameradengrab* in Lens Sallaumilles. His remains had been moved from another location in the late 1920s as was common at many locations in France following the war.

The second family member was Ludwig Moses. Ludwig was born on 10 April 1901 and did not serve in the war. Ludwig eventually married a woman named Martha Heilbronn and they had one daughter, Edith. I do not have any specific details on his life but in the early 1940s Edith was sent to the U.S. where she arrived on 22 September 1941. Her mother and father were not as fortunate as Martha died in Auschwitz and Ludwig ended up in Buchenwald. Ludwig did manage to survive the Second World War and eventually returned to Glan-Münchweiler. Unfortunately he died in 1947 as a result of severe injuries he received while in the concentration camp. Of the six siblings, only Ludwig, Karl and one sister survived to see the end of World War II.

The service record and subsequent history of the next brother can be used as an example of what the Jewish veterans of the Kaiser's army faced during the rise of the Nazi Party in the 1930s. He was *Gefreiter* Wilhelm Moses, No. 1203, 2nd Company, 12th Bavarian Infantry Regiment.

According to his *Stammrolle* entry he was of the Jewish faith and his occupation was a clerk or shop assistant. He was single when he joined the army in 1914. The following details were taken from his *Stammrolle* entries:

1 October 1914 sent to I *Ersatz* Battalion 22nd Bavarian Infantry Regiment *Rekruit* Depot II
19 November 1914 sent to I *Ersatz* Battalion 22nd Bavarian Infantry Regiment 3rd Company
3 December 1914 sent to 22nd Bavarian Infantry Regiment in the field
6 December 1914 sent by train to 7th Company, 22nd Bavarian Infantry
13 December 1914 assigned to 1st Machine Gun Company 22nd Bavarian Infantry Regiment
6 December to 14 December 1914 involved in the fighting in French Flanders.
15 December 1914 to 26 December 1914 in position warfare by Ypres.
29 December 1914 involved in fighting at the *Eckhof* east of St. Eloi, wounded on left lower thigh by an infantry projectile
29 December 1914 to 31 January 1915 in Field Hospital 4, II Bavarian Army Corps
1 February 1915 to 14 February 1915 battle by St. Eloi
15 February 1915 to 14 March 1915 position warfare by Ypres
14 March 1915 to 15 March 1915 fighting on the *Lehmhügel* (Clay Hill) south of St. Eloi
16 March 1915 to 30 March 1915 position warfare by Ypres
In April 1915 the 22nd Bavarian IR was sent to become part of the newly formed 11th Bavarian Division located in the Carpathian Mountains in Galicia
25 April 1915 transferred to 7th Company, 22nd Bavarian IR
1 May 1915 to 4 May 1915 Battle of Gorlicze Tarnow
4 May 1915 to 8 May 1915 pursuit fighting in the Battle of Tarnow
8 May 1915 wounded in the right knee and calf by an infantry projectile in the pursuit fighting in the Battle of Tarnow
9 May 1915 to 5 August 1915 in Reserve Hospital Landeshut
6 August 1915 to 9 January 1916 in *Heimat* (Home) *Lazarett* Glan–Münchweiler
10 January 1916 transferred to *Gendarme* Company I *Ersatz* Battalion 22nd Bavarian IR
19 September 1916 transferred to *Rekruit* Depot 2nd Bavarian Infantry Division, 6th Company, in the field
19 June 1917 awarded the Iron Cross 2nd Class
28 June 1917 promoted to rank of *Gefreiter*
5 July 1917 transferred to 12th Bavarian Infantry Regiment, 2nd Bavarian Infantry Division
From 18 September 1917 transferred to 2nd Company 12th Bavarian IR, designated as 'g.v.' [Suitable for garrison duty]
18 September 1917 to 9 October 1917 defensive battle by Verdun
From 16 October 1917 transferred to division staff as assistant clerk/orderly
9 November 1917 to 18 November 1917 position warfare in Upper Alsace
21 November 1917 to 16 January 1918 position warfare in front of Verdun
17 January 1918 to 24 March 1918 preparation for the Great Battle in France (Spring Offensive)

25 March 1918 to 8 May 1918 German offensives, in particular: 1 April 1918 to 8 May 1918 fighting between the Somme and Avre
27 April 1918 to 1 May 1918 in Field Hospital 6 suffering from an illness with fever, then transported by medical train to Germany and on 4 May 1918 in the Reserve Hospital Bad Naunheim, *Abteilung* G, Aubers Hotel
2 August 1918 to *Ersatz* Battalion 12th Bavarian IR.

The details of his service record after August 1918 are difficult to read as the original *Stammrolle* entry has faded with time. It is known that he survived the Great War and was eventually discharged from service. According to family history, Wilhelm returned to Glan-Münchweiler where he lived with his family.

In the late 1930s the German police arrived at Wilhelm's house in order to arrest him for being Jewish. In this instance, when the police saw that he was a decorated veteran from the Great War they left the house without Wilhelm and his family. However, once the Second World War started, the police returned to his home, arrested both Wilhelm and his wife who were eventually sent to the Buchenwald Concentration Camp where they were both killed. It did not matter that he had served his country on the Western and Eastern fronts for four years, was wounded twice, awarded the Iron Cross II Class and promoted to *Gefreiter*. All of this was simply ignored by the German authorities who only saw him as a Jew who was slated for a concentration camp.

On Rod's Grandmother's side, everyone was born in Krefeld. The first was Leopold de Beer, he was born on 9 September 1883 and joined the German Army where he was placed with Infantry Regiment 159, in the 3rd Company. Leopold served with his regiment until sometime in late 1914 when he was slightly wounded in action. His wound was reported on 27 October 1914 when published in the *Verlustlisten*. Leopold returned to his regiment and by 1916 he was involved in the fighting at Verdun.

In the *Verlustlisten* of 11 May 1916 he was listed as being slightly wounded. His wounds were far worse than first reported and in the *Verlustlisten* of 20 May 1916 he was reported to have died in Bavarian Reserve *Sanitäts* Company 21. He apparently died on 14 April 1916 and was buried near the medical company. His body was never located after the war and his name appears on the war memorial located in the Jewish cemetery in Krefeld.

His last message sent home was written on 12 April 1916 and reached the *Feldpost*, where it was postmarked on the day he died:

> *Wehrmann* de Beer 14. Reserve Division IR159 3. Komp
> 12th April 1916
>
> My Dear!
> I received your dear letter from the 6th the day before yesterday, but I had no opportunity to write an answer. I have also not got any mail in a few days. Now it is back to the old way. I was very pleased with the letter and entirely satisfied with its substance. I feel exactly as Ida about letter writing. Even with the best intentions I cannot get any paper, so I limit myself only to cards. Hopefully that is enough

Krefeld Jewish War Memorial. (Rod Otey)

> for you. I was pleased from the contents of the letter to hear that you are all well and can likewise be informed by me. I received a card from Bruno at the same time and he is once again completely comfortable at home. No wonder, it would be the same way for me as well. Now for today the warmest greetings to all, your Leopold.
> *Wehrmann* de Beer, 14th Reserve Division, IR 159, 3rd Comp.

Leopold's brother, Walter de Beer, born on 10 October 1888, also served in the army, in fact he was in the 1st Company, Reserve Infantry Regiment 99, 26th Reserve Division, XIV Reserve Corps. This was an unexpected coincidence as I had always been looking for soldiers that had a connection with the XIV Reserve Corps and this information was only recently discovered. There is little information regarding Walter other than he had been wounded and spent time in Reserve *Lazarette* Beuthen in October 1915. Walter served on the Somme until sometime in April 1916 when he was captured by the British, probably during a raid, and he spent part of the war in a Prisoner of War on Corsica. In the *Verlustlisten* dated 13 August 1918 he was reported as a returned prisoner of war. He was probably released as a result of serious wounds he received when captured or a severe illness.

The de Beer family was fully integrated into Krefeld society where there were a number of Jewish families. Rod's great-grandmother could see how bad the situation was becoming for Jewish families in Germany in the late 1930s and knew that is was not going to get any better in 1938. Life for the Jewish members of the population had been growing worse each year since 1933.

In order to have an emergency plan on hand, Rod's great-grandmother had been sending money over the border to Holland by courier, not only for her family but for other local Jewish families as well as having already obtained visas in order to travel to Chile. The courier was eventually arrested and one day the Gestapo came knocking on the de Beer door. The Gestapo detained Rod's great-grandmother for several days and it looked as if their plans of escaping to Chile were getting very slim. The Gestapo was apparently after Walter and he was forced to go into hiding.

Walter de Beer (Rod Otey)

In a stroke of good luck the family managed to have Rod's great-grandmother set free and the family was given one week to leave Germany for good with only 10 Marks in their possession. Even this small amount was sufficient and the great-grandfather his wife and daughter managed to reach a boat in Hamburg and made it safely to Chile where part of the family remains to this day. Walter de Beer unfortunately died in Chile in 1944, but at least he and his family had managed to leave the horrors of the Holocaust behind them.

The third brother was Bruno de Beer, who was born on 22 May 1887. He served in the army but there are no details of his service available other than a photo of him at a military hospital, Reserve *Lazarette* Forbach in which his hands are bandaged. Sometime in the late 1930s or early 1940s Bruno was deported to the Dachau Concentration camp and later moved to the Izbica Ghetto where he was murdered in 1942.

The final family member is Karl Weisner who was born on 19 October 1896. Karl was reported to have been wounded on 27 September 1914 and apparently he survived the Great War. In 1939 he immigrated to Cuba, where all traces of him have disappeared. Unfortunately Karl's wife and children all perished during the Holocaust. Rod does know that Karl was wounded and that he apparently lost several fingers in 1914. Following the end of the Great War he had a shop at Breite *Strasse* 39 in Krefeld and Rod's grandmother remembers avoiding the shop because she was scared of his hand.

Of the six known members of Rod's family that served during 1914-1918, two were killed during the war; four were wounded and of these two were killed in Concentration Camps during WWII. Considering that of every member of Rod's family that served in the war was a casualty at some point in their service there are probably few families on either side of the conflict where every serving member suffered death or wounds.

It was a sad chapter in history when an entire religion, including men, who saw themselves as Germans first and Jewish second, could be treated so brutally. It is something that needs to be remembered and kept in the public eye so that it never happens again to any group of people due to their religion, colour, ethnic background, or for any reason. I would like to thank Rod Otey for sharing his family history with me and allowing me to use it in this book.

XIV Reserve Corps Jewish War Dead

Name	DOB	Birthplace	Unit	Date of death
Adler, Arnold	18-Nov-1886	Weikersheim	2/R40	19-Aug-14
Apfel, Ludwig	8-Jun-1896	Mannheim	8/R111	03-Jun-18
Aronson, Viktor	9-Sep-1891	Colmar	5/R119	27-Jun-16
Bloch, Max	7-Dec-1896	Sulzburg	9/180	26-Sep-16
Block, Max	21-Oct-1896	Endingen	11/R109	22-Jun-17
Borchardt, Gustav	25-Oct-1882	Bernburg	6/R111	05-May-17
Cohen, Moses Wolf	10-Jan-1876	Neustadt-gödens	11/R111	18-Feb-18
Cohn, Robert Moritz	13-Feb-1888	Hamburg	4/R111	12-May-18
Freudenthal, Hugo	26-Nov-1885	Theilheim	5/R119	22-Aug-17
Gideon, Julius	24-Jul-1886	Rexingen	2/180	01-Apr-15
Gutmann, Julius	20-Apr-1878	Uffenheim	11/R109	31-Aug-18
Haas, Ferdinand	31-Dec-1886	Bödigheim	3/R40	26-Aug-14
Haas, Siegmund	1-Apr-1898	Neudenau	5/R121	26-Jul-18
Heim, Dietmar	19-Nov-1896	Müllheim	2/R110	14-Aug-17
Heinsfurter, Willi	11-Nov-1896	Crailsheim	11/R121	26-Jul-16
Henle, Josef	24-Jun-1890	Lehrensteinsfeld	7/R119	29-Sep-16
Hess, Emil	4-Jun-1880	Malsch	7/R110	01-Nov-18
Hirsch, Milton	14-Jan-1889	Göppingen	8/180	30-Nov-14
Hirschfield, Moritz	25-Jun-1890	Talheim	3/R119	18-Aug-17
Hochberger, Sigmund	5-Dec-1876	Stuttgart	9/R119	06-Aug-17
Jesse, Fritz	17-Sep-1887	Warburg	2/R99	01-Jul-16
Jordan, Eugen	8-Nov-1888	Freudenthal	3MG/R121	02-Apr-16
Joseph, Friedrich	10-Oct-1896	Neu Isenburg	2/R111	04-Jun-18
Kahn, Moritz	26-Dec-1884	Külsheim	6/R110	01-Jul-16
Kander, Heinrich	2-Apr-1881	Hüffenhardt	Co. Ganter/R111	06-May-17
Kaufmann, Nathan	13-Jan-1881	Baiertal	9/R109	01-Jul-16
Klein, Hermann	22-Apr-1884	Waldau	11/R109	10-Jan-20
Lauchheimer, Fritz	13-Nov-1894	Esslingen	2/180	18-Aug-17
Ledermann, Felix	25-Sep-1879	Menzingen	1MG/R119	01-May-18
Levistein, Berthold	25-May-1881	Ettenheim	12/R109	23-Nov-15
Levy, Edmund	7-Jul-1890	Illingen	2MG/R121	01-Oct-18
Levy, Eugen	30-Sep-1888	Albersweiler	1/R111	01-Jul-16
Lipschütz, Felix	1-Sep-1896	Prenzlau	3/R111	09-Oct-16
Löwenstein, Max	10-Apr-1896	Stuttgart	6/RFAR 26	20-May-17
Manasse, Isidor	1-Oct-1887	Talheim	Ersatz Bn/R121	16-Oct-18
Marx, Bernhard	30-Aug-1879	Schriesheim	11/R109	01-Jul-16
Metzger, Hermann	9-Apr-1889	Rappenau	1MG/R110	23-Aug-18
Moos, Dr. Ernst	12-Aug-1878	Hechingen	5/180	22-Apr-18
Morgenthau, Simon	31-Mar-1880	Ludwigshafen	R111	13-Jun-19

Name	DOB	Birthplace	Unit	Date of death
Moritz, Isak Levi	3-Apr-1884	Buttenhausen	8/180	26-Aug-17
Müller, Adolf	10-Feb-1893	Stuttgart	5/R119	21-Aug-17
Müller, Maximilian	9-Jan-1878	Lodz	5/R99	03-Nov-14
Oppenheimer, Max	12-Aug-1887	Gemmingen	10/R109	10-Jan-20
Pressburger, Max	15-Nov-1895	Nürtingen	4/R119	22-Aug-16
Reichert, Arthur	19-Mar-1898	Berwangen	8/R111	20-May-17
Rohrbach, Simon	23-Feb-1886	Heidenheim	7/R109	30-Sep-14
Rosenfelder, Max	25-Jan-1891	München	7/R110	04-Sep-14
Rotheimer, Simon	15-Apr-1888	Gondelsheim	5/R109	12-Jun-15
Rothschild, Theodor	22-Jul-1896	Stuttgart	R119	29-Jun-16
Rotschild, Karl	16-Jul-1878	Randegg	5/R111	07-Jun-16
Scharff, Ludwig	10-Mar-1883	Bruchsal	2/RFAR 29	19-Jul-15
Scheuer, Moritz	21-May-1885	Heilbronn	8/R121	24-Mar-18
Schmelzer, Eugen	14-Nov-1887	Lambsheim	5/R111	20-Aug-14
Stahl, Josua Josef	16-Jun-1884	Flehingen	11/R109	22-Aug-14
Stein, Maximilian	18-Sep-1885	Grosseicholzheim	4/R40	11-May-15
Stern, Benjamin	27-Mar-1881	Gissigheim	11/R109	01-Jul-16
Stern, Philip	23-Mar-1884	Schwanfeld	10/R109	18-Jan-17
Türkheimer, Albert	19-Dec-1896	Hockenheim	7/R109	04-Nov-18
Walter, Siegfried	23-May-1886	Schwegenheim	11/R109	01-Jul-16
Wbernheim, Wilhelm	9-Mar-1888	Wangen	MGSST/R111	01-Jul-16
Weil, Ludwig	24-Sep-1888	Mergentheim	8/R110	14-Oct-16
Weiss, Fritz	21-Aug-1895	Mannheim	6/R111	01-Jul-16
Winter, Paul	5-Dec-1890	Gelsenkirchen	R110	03-Jul-16
Wolff, Gaston	29-Jul-1887	Zabern	1/R40	29-Aug-14
Wolfsberg, Gerhard	28-Apr-1895	Hamburg	3/R109	17-Apr-18
Wollrauch, David	24-Sep-1889	Mannheim	3/R110	12-Apr-15

By the 1930s the Great War was being remembered through the numerous regimental associations that had formed in the previous decade. The men who had been members of the different regiments would get together in order to maintain friendships and to remember the fallen and reminisce about the events of the war. These groups were also the impetus for the erection of monuments to the fallen from each regiment that formed a central meeting place for future reunions. One of the first reunions to be held by former members of the XIV Reserve Corps was by the members of RIR 111:

Celebration pamphlet
for the Reunion Celebration
To those who belonged to the former Res. Inf. Regt. 111
Guest of Honor:
Comrade Oskar Daubmann, Endingen
In the Capital Karlsruhe
Saturday, the 3rd, Sunday, the 4th, and Monday, the 5th of September 1932
Celebration sequence!
Saturday, the 3rd of September 1932
Afternoon 14.00 hours: Rendezvous of the celebration participants in the hall of the main railway station Karlsruhe

14.10 hours: Arrival of Comrade Oskar Daubmann and greeting of the same. Lining up in front of the railway station and march off with the musical accompaniment in the lead to the Hotel Lutz at the old railway station.
20.00 hours: Celebration banquet at the Celebration room: Halle 1. Address: Herr Enggesser former Leutnant and company leader RIR 111. Friendly get together.

Sunday, the 4th of September 1932

Morning 10.00 hours: Rendezvous at the monument to the fallen at the cemetery. Celebration religious service. Celebration preacher: Herr Pfarrer Geiger from Büchenbronn, former Leutnant and regimental adjutant of Res. Inf. Regt. 111.
Afternoon 14.00 hours: Lining up to the celebration train at the Mühlburgertor. Train through the city to the celebration place. Welcoming the guests by Herrn Hauptlehrer Rupp, former Leutnant and company leader VII/RIR 111. Speech and welcoming Comrade Oskar Daubmann by Herrn Enggesser, former Leutnant and company leader RIR 111. Friendly get together.

Monday, 5th September 1932

Morning 9.30 hours Rendezvous at the celebration place. Tour of the city.
Afternoon 17.00 hours: City. Celebration hall at the Stresemann Square: Talk by Comrade Oskar Daubmann. Subject: My experience in a French prisoner camp. Further details about this in the advertisement part and in the daily newspaper.
Afternoon 19.30 hours Rendezvous at the celebration place. Friendly get together. Conclusion.

Just a few years later, on the 20th Anniversary of the Battle of the Somme, the 26th Reserve Division veterans also prepared for a major reunion of the former members of the division:

Guide for the Meeting of the 26th Reserve Division, 5 July 1936

Information Locations:
Here quarters were issued, event badges, commemoratives, and postcards
Saturday, July 4, 12 to 20 hours,
Sunday, July 5, 7-10 hours:
Hauptbahnhöf,
Westbahnhöf.
Office of the Reunion Committee: Alleen *Strasse* (Gaststatte 'New Railway Station'), also:

IR 180: Alleen *Strasse* 9, 'Alleen Café',
RIR 119: Alleen *Strasse* 2, 'Pelican',
RIR 120: Alleen *Strasse* 9, 'Alleen Café',
RIR 121: Schiller *Strasse* 23, 'Württemberger Hof'
RFA 26 and 27: Alleen *Strasse* 7, 'Lederhof'
Pioneers: Eberhard *Strasse* 49, 'Schellmann', Hirsch *Strasse* 14, 'Hirschbräu'.

For all other formations, the information center is in the business rooms of the Reunion Committee: Alleen *Strasse* 6 (Gaststatte 'New Railway Station').

Comrades who arrive on July 5 at 9 o'clock and later in Stuttgart on special trains go from the station in the private train to the barracks. Further details will be announced on the train. Guides will be available at the station.

Saturday, July 4, 1936

17.00 hours: rehearsal of the ceremony in the city hall for Sunday afternoon.
Admission for members of the *Wehrmacht* and accommodation owners is free; all other spectators must possess the festival badge (Price 50 *Pfennig*). Barracks open at 15.00 hours.
17.00 hours: Laying a wreath at the memorial shrine in the New Castle by His Excellency *General der Infantry Frhr. Von* Soden in the presence of the Regimental Commanders.
17.30 hours: Forest Cemetery, wreath at Division Monument and at the grave of His Excellency von Fritsch. Delegations of the regiments and formations of the 26th Reserve Division with the participation of the choir composed of the 2nd IR 13 (led by Choirmaster Zimmermann).
19.00 hours: City Garden Hall. Welcome address by His Excellency General der Infantry Frhr. Von Soden. Joint meal with the guests of honor, the officers of the Tradition troops and officers, doctors, officials with delegations from non-commissioned officers and men of the 26th Reserve Division. Music: String Orchestra of the Kyffhäuser chapel.
23.30 hours: City Hall:
Welcome evening.
In charge: Comrade Wicke (RIR 119).

Contributors:
Kyffhäuser Chapel (headed by Music Director Benning).Hohner Harmonica Orchestra (provided by the company Hohner, Trossingen,).
Manager: Herrn Schrittenhelm.
Entertainment interlude, donated by the city of Stuttgart.

Admission for members of the Wehrmacht and Accommodation owners free, all other participants must possess a reunion badge (Price 50 Pfennig). Ticket sales: 19.30 hours.

Sunday, July 5, 1936

8.00 until 9.15 o'clock: Assembling of the members of the Division: infantry, pioneers and cyclists: Feuersee and Johannes *Strasse*.
Mounted troops, artillery, divisional staff, medical units, columns, Trains, Weimar *Strasse*.
9.00 a.m.: Severely war injured with tickets for busses at the gas station between the main railway station and Reichs Railway office and in the Weimar Strasse between Herzog and Gutenberg *Strasse*. A carriage is awaiting the arrival of the last special train at the main station.
9.30 until 10.00 a.m.: Kasernenhof: Unified entry of regiments and formations for deployment places in the barracks.
Honour Guard barracks entrance deployment from 10.00 and 10.10 a.m., formation march in.
10.10 a.m.: Entry of the Honor Stormers.
10.15 a.m.: Entry of the guard of honor with the flags of the Division.
10.15 until 10.25 a.m.: Guard of fronts through His Excellency *General of Infantry Frhr. Von* Soden, *General of Infantry Frhr.* Seutter von Giżycko, *General-Leutenant* Geyer and Reich Governor Murr.
10.30 Clock: Field Church Service.
Music: Dutch Thanksgiving. Address: City Dean Dr. Lempp (Field Division clergyman).
Music: 'I had a comrade.'
Prayer: Pastor Gentner (Field Division clergyman).
Music and joint singing: 'Now thank we all our God', 1st verse.
Welcome by the Vorst Zenden the festival committee: Comrade Rueff.

Speeches by:
His Excellency *General of Infantry Frhr. Von* Soden,
Reich Governor Murr,
Lieutenant General Geyer,
Mayor Dr. Strölin.

11.15 a.m.: March to the New *Schloss*.

Guests of honor in the car driving in front of the procession into the castle courtyard. Holders of VIP tickets take the entrance at the Adolf Hitler *Strasse* through the southern *Schloss Kügel*. March past our division commander His Excellency General of Infantry Frhr. Von Soden and flags.

12.00 until 14.00 o'clock: The regiments and formations eating together (locale see last page).

14.30 o'clock: Closed march from the eateries (IR 180 Upper installations beside the theaters to the city hall).

Anyone not in possession of honor cards (input for this in the Werder Strasse), must march in closed train with his regiment and his formation.

15.45 o'clock:

Ceremony in the town hall

Musical piece.

Address: His Excellency *General der Infantry Frhr. Von* Soden

Musical piece.

Gymnastic performances by the *Wehrmacht*: 2nd IR. 13.

Fanfare march. 'We hold the fort'

Dramatic poem with tableaux from the war experience of the 26th Reserve Division.

Design: Comrade Rueff.

Text: Comrade Elwenspoek.

Pictures: Comrade Pilz.

Speakers: Junker comrade.

1st Image: The flag of the II/180 in Markirch (August 1914).

2nd ": Storm on the *Granathof*, R120 and Pioniers (Jan 1915).

3rd ": The Battle for the *Heidenkopf*, R121 (July 1 1916).

4th ": The Battle for Thiepval, IR 180 (26th September 1916).

5th ": Great Battle in *Houthoulster Wald*, R119 (Oct 1917).

6th ": Artillery saves the Battle of Vis-en-Artois, RFA 26 (august 1918).

In honor of the memory of our fallen comrades, the festivities end with the joint singing of 'Good Comrades'.

Large tattoo: Played by 5 military music corps and 2 marching bands under the direction of Music Director Langer. Deutschland and Horst Wessel played at the end are sung together.

7.45 Clock: Meeting point lookout on the Burgholzhof. Tram: 5, 15, 16 Prague tavern, 12 and 22 Hallschlag,

8.00 until 9.00 clock: battle pictures of the *Wehrmacht*. Followed by a tour of the new barracks.

Fixed schedule.

Bruno de Beer, first row, far right. (Rod Otey)

Saturday 4th July 1936

17.30 hours wreath-laying ceremony in the forest cemetery. Officers and delegations of regimental associations are at the division monument at 17.15 hours.

19.00 hours meeting of the officers and officials with representatives of the regimental associations in the garrison mess, Rotebühl barracks. Communal meal.

20.30 hours welcome evening for the comrades who have already arrived in the town hall. Music and photo presentations. Places are provided for family members in the gallery. These have to purchase a festival badge at the price of 50 Pfennig.

Sunday, July 5, 1936

9 o'clock assembly of festival subscribers.

9.15 o'clock march to barracks.

10 clock beginning of the ceremonies. Field church service. Speeches.

11.15 march on König Strasse to the New Castle. March past our Division Commander His Excellency General der Infantry Frhr. Von Soden. March to the dining locations.

14.45 unified march of regiments and formations to the city hall.

15.45 hours ceremony in the town hall. Large military concert with a large tattoo. Tableaux vivants, gymnastic demonstrations by the Wehrmacht.

Monday, July 6, 1936

7.45, the comrades gather at the Burgholzhof, Lookout tower (tram stop Prague tavern, line 5, 15, 16 or tram stop Hallschlag, line 12 and 22). Combat pictures of the Armed Forces, followed by a tour of the new barracks.

General fixed rules.

Payments and helpdesks.

Payments to postal check account Stuttgart Nr. 44237 of the bill Tzschöckell Council, Stuttgart, Alexanderstrasse 7b. Receiving agencies from Saturday, July 4, 1936, 12 o'clock on from the main and Westbahnhof (Quarters payment).

The festival badge must be worn visibly by all festival participants. Participation in these events is not permitted without a physical badge. Adult family members can, as far as the space would be enough to attend the ceremony in the barracks square (access to the parade ground through the lower gate at Reithaus). The places for the spectators are particularly dependent. All spectators must also use to acquire and a festival badge. Price 50 *Pfennig*. Under no circumstances it is permissible for females to march or parade ground. The collection of all fixed subscriber is entirely at the specified assembly points (see map). Additions to barrack are banned for individuals (exceptions: special guests, family members of fallen comrades and viewers with festival badges).

Officers, Unteroffiziere and Other Ranks move by their company (battery, formation).

Smoking is prohibited during the marches and of course also during the open parade ground.

On arrival at the barracks each Party Participant must necessarily remain in his place.

In the march of the disabled (injured in war, & c.) held by cars only those comrades who are registered in good time and received a similar certificate can be transported.

During the period of regimental and division reunions into the late 1930s there was an underlying rumble of events that would have a devastating effect on the German nation and its people. War was about to break out once again in September 1939 and would last nearly six years before the world returned to a relatively peaceful state.

When war did return in 1939 many of the men who had served in the XIV Reserve Corps were considered to be too old for military service. However, for some of the younger members of the corps as well as officers that had remained in the army during the inter-war years, they would also see active service on many fronts during

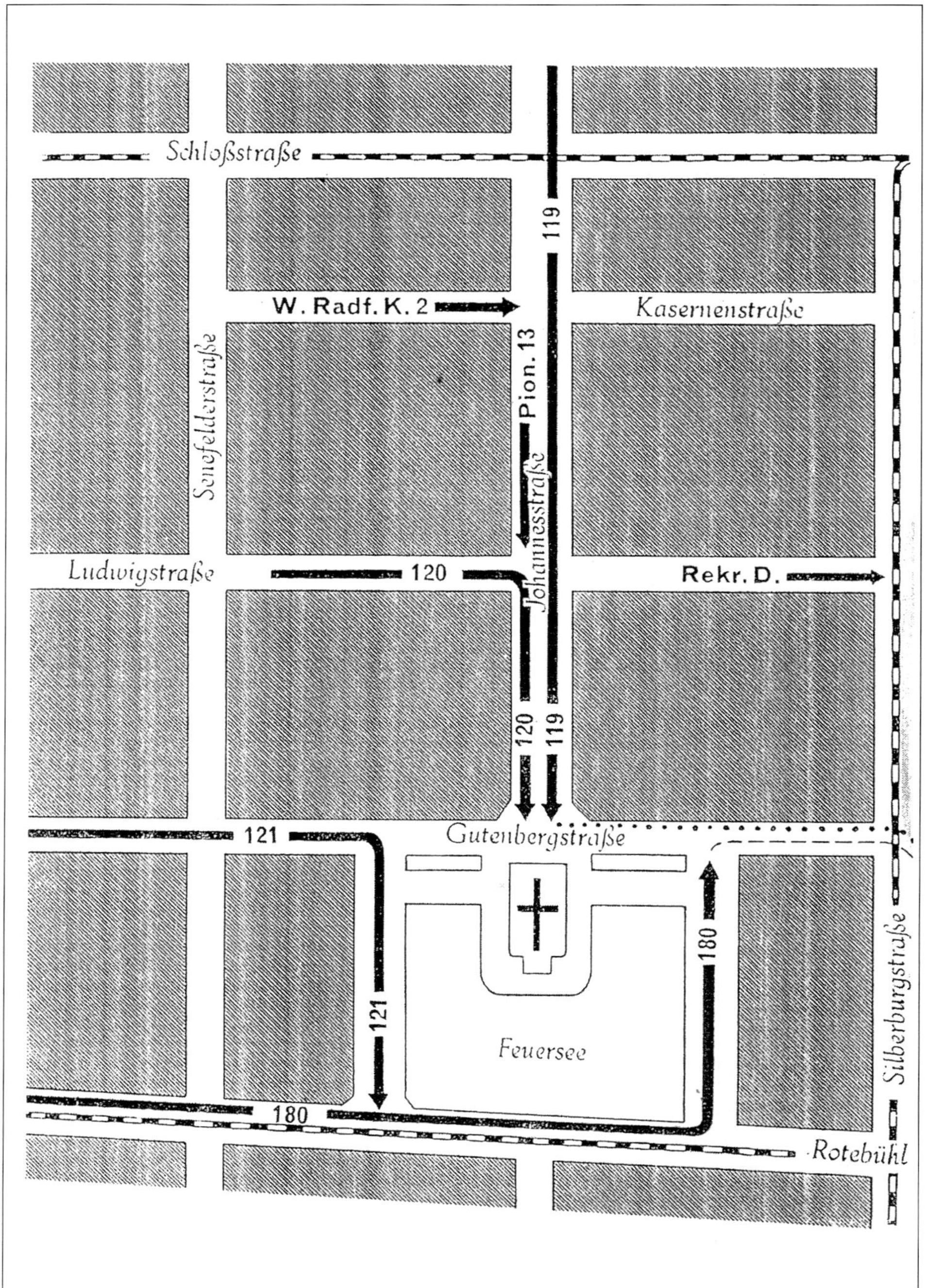

Parade route of the 26th Reserve Division.

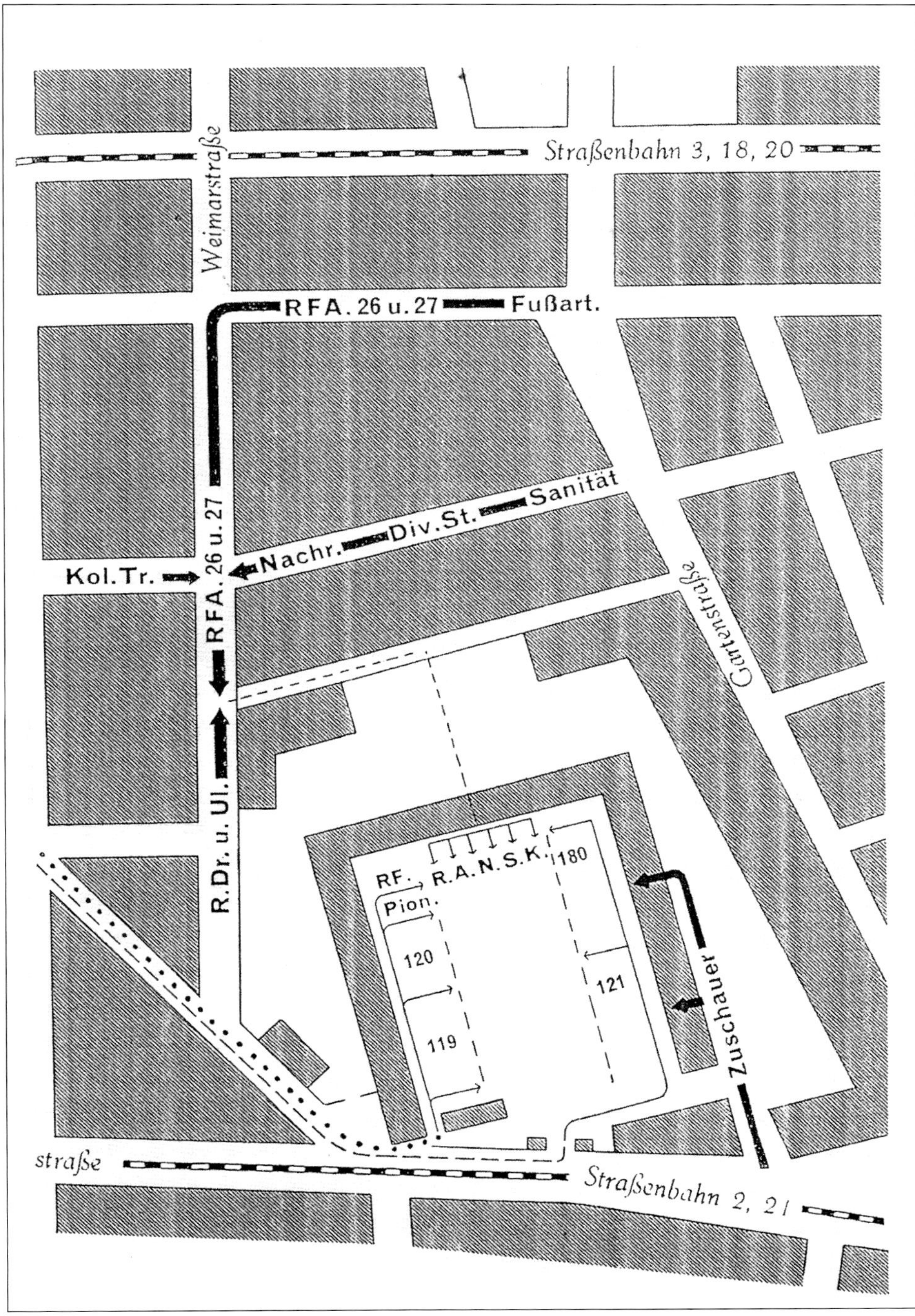
Weimarstraße
Straßenbahn 3, 18, 20
RFA. 26 u. 27
Fußart.
Sanität
Div. St.
Nachr.
Kol. Tr.
RFA. 26 u. 27
Gartenstraße
R. Dr. u. Ul.
R. A. N. S. K.
180
RF.
Pion.
120
121
119
Zuschauer
straße
Straßenbahn 2, 21

Veterans of the 26th Reserve Division, 1936. (Author's collection)

Durch ein tragisches Geschick verlor ich am 14. 8. 44 in Folge des letzt. Fliegerangriffes am 9. 8. 44 auf Karlsruhe mein. innigstgeliebt., herzensg. Mann, d. glückl., treusorg. Vater seines Kindes, mein. lieben Sohn, uns. braven Schwiegersohn, Schwager, Onkel und Neffe

Otto Würz

Revier-O.-Wachtm. d. Poliz.-Reserve, Weltkriegsteilnehmer 14—18, mit viel. Auszeichnungen, im Alter von 48 J.

Karlsruhe, den 17. August 1944.

In tief. Schmerz: Frau Berta Würz geb. Rüger u. Kind Christa; Mutter: Berta Würz, Witwe, und alle Anverwandten.

Beerdigung: Freitag, 18. Aug. 1944, 8.30 Uhr, auf dem Ehrenfriedhof.

Death notice for Otto Wurz: formerly in the 6/R109. (Author's collection)

the six year conflict. While many veterans did not serve in the military again, they were active as air raid wardens, civil defense workers and at the very end of the conflict they were drafted into the *Volksbund* and given a variety of weapons in order to resist against the Allied advance into Germany. Of these men, I only know the fate of one man, Police Reservist Otto Wurz, who was called into military service at the outbreak of WWII only to be discharged a short time later. He then served in the Police Reserve as an air raid warden and served until he was killed in an air raid in August 1944 in Karlsruhe.

It appears that reunions were held infrequently at best before the Second World War and in the case of the 26th Reserve Division the first one held was in 1936 and the next one did not take place until 1956, two decades later.

Stuttgart, January 1956

To all comrades of the former 26th Reserve Division

On Sunday, 1 July 1956, the comrades of the 26th Reserve Division meet after a twenty-year-old break for a reunion celebration in Stuttgart. In this year also falls the 100th anniversary of the birthday of our former division commander Frhr. von Soden. We want to find ourselves together at 11 o'clock in the morning on 1 July, for a simple celebration in front of the monument created by him in the Forest Cemetery in Stuttgart and remember our dead comrades. There will be an informal gathering of the individual troop units in the afternoon.

All comrades are asked to pass this message on and if necessary to request further copies of this flyer from one of the comrades specified below and the supposed number and if possible the names of the participants in that location, if necessary to also communicate to further places.

So that the necessary preparations can be made in time, it is necessary that these reports are presented in the form of lists at the latest up to 15 April 1956. Please note the date.

If each comrade contributes his share to it, this meeting will most beautifully reaffirm our old comradeship again.

Please report further! Stuttgart, April 1956.

Comrade Meeting of the 26th Reserve Division

As already reported by the press special news edition the meeting of the comrades of the former division is on 1 July this year in Stuttgart. The 100th anniversary of the birthday of both our division commanders, General *Freiherr* von Soden and *von* Fritsch, 40th return of the anniversary of the Battle of the Somme, 20th return of the anniversary of the last comrades meeting.

Memorial plaque of the 26th Reserve Division in the Stuttgart *Waldfriedhof* Military Cemetery. (*Die Württemberger im Weltkriege*)

Preparation and transportation of the stone monument for the war dead of RIR 110. (. (*Reserve-Infanterie-Regiment Nr. 110 im Weltkrieg 1914-1918*)

The undersigned specified the following program:

10.30 am: Meeting place at the entrance of the Forest Cemetery in Stuttgart, arranged according to regiments.

10.45 am: March in conjunction with music to the cenotaph.

11.00 am: Laying a wreath at the grave of the second division commander General von Fritsch and at the cenotaph in front of the plaque of the 26th Reserve Division.

11.30 am: Still there, a welcoming address and remembrance speech by our Comrade Minister Gammertsfelder from Weinsberg.

12.00 noon: return to the city into the designated restaurants, where a simple lunch can be taken; a comradely gathering.

The meeting will take place in any weather. The comrades are also asked to bring along the survivors of fallen or comrades of the 26th Reserve Division who died to this meeting and to communicate directly or about their numbers that are participating to the signatory representatives up to 30 May 1956 under the indication of the head count (necessary for boarding).

The completed monument to the war dead of RIR 110 in Pfingsten, Baden, 1933. (*Reserve-Infanterie-Regiment Nr. 110 im Weltkrieg 1914-1918*)

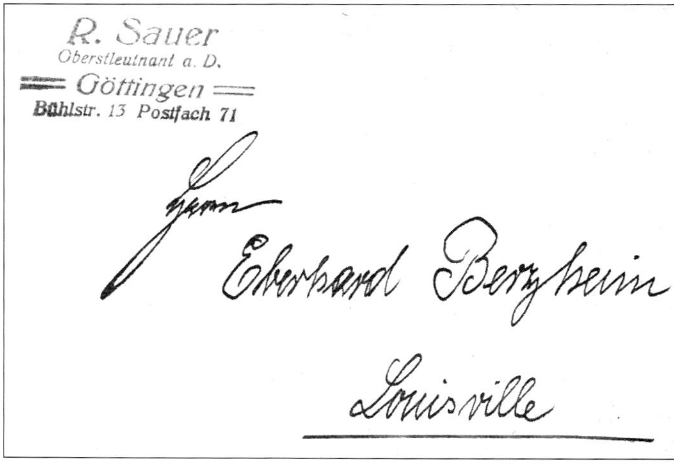

Letter sent to a veteran of R.I.R. 99 from Oberstleutnant Sauer. I should note that the postcard sent by then Major Sauer was the catalyst for the creation of this series of books. (Author's collection)

Vergessen Sie nicht, diesen Bestellzettel noch heute in den nächsten Briefkasten zu werfen oder Ihrem Briefträger zu übergeben!

Hiermit bestelle ich bei der Postanstalt die Monatsschrift des Reichsbundes ehemaliger 99er e. V. (Sitz Düsseldorf)

„Der gute Kamerad"

(Postverlagsanstalt Düsseldorf)

Vor- und Zuname: ....

Ort, Straße und Hausnummer: ....

Postanstalt: ....

(„Der gute Kamerad" kostet, durch die Post bezogen, 0,60 RM. vierteljährlich zuzüglich Bestellgeld.)

An invitation to subscribe to the Veteran's Newsletter for R.I.R. 99 . (Author's collection)

The reunions continued to be held at fairly regular intervals as long as there any veterans left in the various regiments. Year after year there were fewer and fewer familiar faces as many of the men died from old age. Still, even in 1968 there were quite a few survivors of the two division still alive. In IR 180 an address booklet was produced that provided the names and addresses of all surviving members of the regiment.

From the message attached to the address book it is evident that the survivors of IR 180 were holding regular meetings each October. Just when this stopped or when the other regimental or division meeting stopped is not known. All that is certain at this time is that every veteran of the XIV Reserve Corps has passed away from old age or illness and no one is left to commemorate their time in service during the Great War. From the length of time these regiments held reunions it is evident that the events of 1914-1918 played a very large part in their lives.

By presenting this history of the XIV Reserve it was my intent to restore its proper place in history, to ensure that the men who served in the corps, their families and their experiences would remain in the public eye, or at least in the eyes of those who read these books. Almost as a fitting end to the story can be seen in the accompanying illustrations of a card mailed to a former member of RIR 99 which advertised the regimental paper, *'Der gute Kamerad'*, published monthly for a very reasonable price. This advertisement was sent by *Oberstleutnant* a.D. R Sauer, from Göttingen. It was found in the map sleeve of the regimental history of RIR 99 after I purchased the book. It is the same man who sent the original postcard of the British prisoners captured in a trench raid by Thiepval in May 1916 that led to the series being written in the first place. A fitting end to the story it seems.

Ehem. 10. (württ.) Inf.-Reg. Nr. 180

Am Sonntag, den 8. Juni 1958, findet eine

Wiedersehensfeier

der Kameraden zur 60jährigen Gründung des Regiments statt.

9.45 vorm. Treffpunkt am Denkmal des Regiments,
11.00 Uhr vorm. Festakt im Schillersaal des Museums.

Die Kameraden des früheren Regiments, insbesondere die Angehörigen der gefallenen und gestorbenen Kameraden, sowie die Einwohnerschaft von Tübingen werden zu der Feier herzlich eingeladen.

Tübingen, den 5. Juni 1958
Ortsgruppe der ehemaligen 180er

1958 IR 180 reunion notice. (Author's collection)

Various post-war veteran's pins. (Author's collection)

Notes

1. The 1st *Gardelandesschützen Abteilung* consisted of one company of volunteers each from RIR 77 and RIR 91; one platoon from RIR 55, volunteers from RIR 15; one squadron of *Jäger zu Pferde* 13; one battery from RFAR 20; volunteers from Infantry Division 185, a Cavalry Machine Gun *Abteilung* and a *Kraftfahrzeug Kolonnen* for a total of 30 officers, 600 Other Ranks, 300 horses and 75 motor vehicles. Eventually this *Freikorps* unit became part of the post-war 100,000 man German Army as part of IR 17.
2. Ludwig, Hans, Red Blood – Red Ink, p.170.
3. *Stammrolle* records for Karl Reil, 6th Bavarian Reserve Regiment, Archives in Munich.
4. Bachelin, op. cit., pp. 361-363.
5. Feldpost letters of Albert Reihling.
6. Frisch, op. cit., p. 291.
7. Klaus, op. cit., p. 226.
8. Gallion, op. cit., pp. 336-367.

Appendix I

Statistical details of a sample regiment of XIV Reserve Corps

Reserve Infantry Regiment 121

All throughout the volumes that comprise this series of books on the XIV Reserve Corps I have attempted to provide the reader with as much detail as possible on the actual soldiers who served in the corps during the war. Movements of armies and divisions, while useful in certain situations, do not provide any insight into the people who make up the armies. This is one reason why I tried to use as many photographs, illustrations and personal letters of the men who served in the XIV Reserve Corps. The following series of charts will provide the reader with a detailed look at the makeup of one reserve regiment, RIR 121.

Deaths according to rank

Officers	**Field Regt.**	**Ersatz Bn.**	**Other Ranks**	**Field Regt.**	**Ersatz Bn.**
Stab Offizier	1		*Off. Stellvertreter*	5	
Hauptmann	6		*Feldwebel*	4	
Oberleutnant	5		*Vizefeldwebel*	47	
Leutnant	63		Sergeant	32	
Sanitäts Offizier	1		*Unteroffiziere*	165	1
Oberzahlmeister		1	*Mannschaften*	1,990	76
Totals	76	1	Totals	2,243	77

Cause of death

Cause	Officers	Other Ranks
Infantry projectile*	44	786
Artillery projectiles	22	921
Artillery-Burying	4	48
Mine	1	101
Hand grenade		46
Aircraft bomb		12
Gas	1	36
Bayonet thrust		8
Fatal accident		5
Definitely missing	3	246
Sickness Field Regt.	1	42
Sickness Ersatz Bn.	1	69
Totals	77	2,320
*Includes: Machine guns, pistols, rifle grenades		

Occupations of the men who were killed

Officers		**Other Ranks**	
Active Officer	8	Agriculture & wine making	902
Judicial positions	6	Tradesman	739
Teacher positions	11	Industry	370
Business position	13	Civil Servant	119
Govt. employee	10	Shopkeeper	109
Rail & Postal Service	5	Student	26
Banking	2	Open appointment	8
Finance	2	Domestic servant	38
Open appointment	5	Active *Unteroffiziere*	8
Student	11	Unknown	1
Agriculture & horticulture	2		
Architect	2		
Total	77	Total	2,320

Family status

Officers		Other Ranks	
Married	25	Married	661
Single	52	Single	1,656
		Widower	2
		Divorced	1

Year of birth of officers and Other Ranks killed

Officers		Other Ranks	
1860	1	1874	3
1866	1	1875	1
1875	1	1876	13
1876	2	1877	13
1877	3	1878	47
1878	3	1879	47
1879	2	1880	59
1880	1	1881	58
1881	2	1882	82
1882	3	1883	115
1883	3	1884	135
1884	8	1885	136
1885	3	1886	129
1886	1	1887	153
1887	5	1888	157
1888	5	1889	74
1889	1	1890	81
1890	3	1891	58
1891	6	1892	53
1892	5	1893	111
1893	5	1894	160
1894	5	1895	116
1895	6	1896	118
1896	3	1897	176
1897	2	1898	115
		1899	96
		1900	12
		Total	2320

Age at time of death

Officers		Other Ranks	
20	1	16	1
21	3	17	8
22	8	18	62
23	3	19	184
24	6	20	217
25	9	21	182
26	3	22	134
27	4	23	111
28	4	24	81
29	7	25	74
30	3	26	134
31	6	27	139
32	2	28	135
33	1	29	150
34	3	30	128
35	3	31	116
36	4	32	90
37	2	33	74
38	2	34	78
39-41		35	69
42	1	36	30
43-47		37	43
48	1	38	34
54 (Ersatz Bn.)	1	39	21
		40	13
		41	10
		42	1
		43	1
Total	77	Total	2,320

The oldest officer to die in the regiment was Major and Battalion commander Andersch, III/R121 who was 43 years, four months old at the time of his death. The youngest officer to die was *Leutnant der Reserve* Schlösser, 5/R121 who was 20 years, one month old at the time of his death.

The oldest Other Rank to die in the field regiment was *Landsturmmann* Reinhold Rall who was 41 years 11 months old at the time of his death. The youngest Other Rank to die was *Kriegsfreiwillige* Konrad Knupfer, 1/R121, who was 16 years 10 months old when he was killed on 1 July 1916.

Appendix II

Overall German casualties of the Great War & Casualties relating to the XIV Reserve Corps (26th and 28th Reserve Divisions)

When the armies of Europe set off for war in August 1914 no one could have anticipated how long the war would last and how immense an area of the globe would eventually become involved in the fighting. There had been no precedent for the scale of the fighting, which occurred on three continents as well as across the seas and oceans that cover the earth.

At the same time, no one could have foreseen the immense loss of life that came about as a result of the war, with millions upon millions dead and so many more wounded or simply missing as if they just disappeared from the face of the earth. The war tore apart societies, tumbled governments and empires and brought about changes to the world that reverberate to this day.

There have been recent discussions among historians and enthusiasts regarding the casualty numbers from the Great War, especially in regard to Germany's losses where there are several opinions of the number of war dead that range from 2,000,000 up to 4,000,000 men. I belong to the group that believes the Germans lost approximately 2,000,000 war dead between 1914 and 1918 and it is in this vein that I am presenting the following information. I will leave the argument over the disputed number to another time.

If there was anything that could be counted upon during the Great War it was the dedication of the German bureaucratic system in compiling statistics of every aspect of German life, or in this instance, death. The records that had been maintained during the war included the ten day casualty reports filed by every unit within the German Army. These reports, called the 10 *tägigen Truppenkrankenrapporten* listed men who had become casualties in the fighting, suffered accidents, illnesses and even suicides.

There were additional reports such as the *Monatskrankenrapport, Fünftägige Meldung*, and others that chronicled the day to day events of the troops.

Following the end of the war the statistical records were used as the basis to create books that provided specific details of the losses suffered in the war in a series called *Sanitätsbericht über das Deutsche Heer (Deutsches Feld und Besatzungsheer) im Weltkriege 1914/18*. Volume 3 of this series deals specifically with the losses suffered by the German Army in combat as well as by illness during the war.

The books were part of a massive government research program during the Weimar Republic and the main purpose of the work was to provide detailed information that could be used in the event of a similar conflict in the future. It was completed and printed in 1934, just after the rise of the Nazi government under Adolf Hitler, but it was produced by retired officers and public officials that had served in the Imperial Army and in the new German Republic.

At the end of 1918 the official records showed that the German Army had suffered 6,586,234 officers and men killed, wounded, captured and missing. Despite the overall efficiency of the bureaucracy, not every record had been recovered from the final months of the war as a result of the collapse of the army and the reporting structure. The work being done on the *Sanitätsbericht* to compile and review the statistical information continued well after the war was over and the review was completed at the end of 1933 and used to reflect the losses as uncovered by the commission. The total losses in the war as counted at the end of 1933 came to 7,091,515 officers and men. The total fatalities in the army as well as in the *Kriegsmarine* and former colonies came to 1,936,897. In 1933 the number of men reported as prisoners or missing came to 974,977 and of this number it was estimated that at least 100,000 men should be considered killed as no details had been received on them since the time they went missing. This meant that the official German fatalities came to 2,036,897 officers and men, a devastating number for any country at that time.

The losses suffered by the two divisions of the XIV Reserve Corps, the 26th and 28th Reserve Divisions, formed part of the overall statistical detail of the German losses and while only a small part of the total, the casualties suffered by these divisions does provide the reader with some idea of the losses suffered throughout the different units in the German Army.

The 26th Reserve Division reported the following casualties:

	Officers	**Other Ranks**
Killed	446	13,994
Wounded	947	33,257
Total	1,393	47,251

In the case of the 26th Reserve Division there were statistical sources that provided further detail of the losses down to the level of individual units that formed part of the division. Before anyone tries to add up the loss numbers that will follow and compare them with the losses shown above I can save people the trouble; they do not add up. The losses that follow represent a major portion of the overall division losses but they do not include every unit inside the 26th Reserve Division and therefore the total is lower than the chart above.

Unit	Killed		Wounded	
	Officers	Other Ranks	Officers	Other Ranks
RIR 119	73	2,216	160	5,735
RIR 120*	93	3,398	176	7,897
RIR 121[a]	72	2,294	137	5,913
IR 180	110	3,065	182	6,225
Recruit Depot	1	136	2	404
Reserve Drag.	1	33	4	67
RFAR 26	14	351	48	1,057
RFAR 27	12	326	41	869
4&6 *Pioniers*	7	193	18	492
MW 226	3	93	9	199
Fernsprech Abt.	0	7	0	7
Totals	386	12,046	777	28,865
*Left the division March 1915.				

I have not been able to identify the losses suffered by the 28th Reserve Division other than the number of men killed in the infantry regiments; RIR 109, RIR 110 and RIR 111.

Regiment	Officers and Other Ranks killed
RIR 109	64 officers 2,761 Other Ranks
RIR 110	63 officers 2,399 Other Ranks
RIR 111	81 officers 2,105 Other Ranks
Total	208 officers 7,264 Other Ranks

The troops that were attached to the division including the two *Jäger* Battalions, artillery, medical, supply, etc. would materially increase the number of men killed. If the same ratios applied to the men killed as opposed to the men wounded when there are statistics, then it is likely that the three infantry regiments lost about 17,412 men were wounded in the war, approximately 2.33 men wounded for every 1 man killed.

Regardless if the exact figures remain unknown known individual units, the overall losses suffered by the men of the XIV Reserve Corps reflect the intensity of the fighting that the corps experienced in the Great War.

Appendix III

'Red Ink – Red Blood', the Manuscript of Hans Ludwig, RIR 120

Following the release of volume one of this series, *The Other Side of the Wire*, I have received a number of inquiries regarding one of the people prominently appearing in the initial part of that book, Hans Ludwig, a soldier in RIR 120 whose experiences by La Boisselle in 1914 and early 1915 provided a personal insight into the intense fighting surrounding that small village. Many of the inquiries involved questions as to what ever happened to Hans in the later years of the war. While I cannot provide the complete manuscript for this volume, I can provide a capsule history on what happened to Hans Ludwig in the Great War.

When Hans Ludwig and RIR 120 were sent to the 58th Infantry Division in early 1915, the men were re-equipped, given new uniforms, weapons, and other much needed equipment and all of the regiments and units forming the new division were brought up to full strength once again with an influx of new recruits.

Throughout the initial training phase of the new division, it was an open secret that the men were being trained to be used in the upcoming offensive in Russia. However, instead of Russia, the division was sent to Arras, much to the discomfort to the newer men as they had hoped to avoid the fighting for as long as possible. For the older, experienced soldiers, they knew all too well what was in store for them. The 58th Infantry Division would eventually fight at Givenchy by Vimy Ridge. During this time, Ludwig was promoted to the rank of *Vizefeldwebel* and after a period off heavy fighting the division was finally sent to Russia, where it fought by Vilna.

Later in 1916 the division returned to the west from Russia and was sent to Avocourt by Verdun. Following a period of fighting by Verdun the division was sent to the Champagne by Rheims and then to the Somme in September where it fought against the French. In November 1916 the division and RIR 120 were positioned by Miraumont. Then, following a period of rest the division was sent to the Verdun front while RIR 120 left the division and was transferred to the 204th Infantry Division and was positioned by the hamlet of America near Hill 60 where it remained into 1917.

As a *Vizefeldwebel*, Ludwig was now in charge of a platoon in the 3/R120 and spent his time in rotation by Hill 60 until 7 June 1917. This was the day he was captured and then spent the next three years as a POW; he finally returned to Germany on 17 October 1920.

The description of the events that took place on 7 June 1917 experienced by *Vizefeldwebel* Hans Ludwig deserves to be presented in his own words:

> On June 6, 1917, I received orders to relieve Platoon #3 of Company #6 in the Saubucht early on June 7th. No further orders were given. I could select the time myself but had to be in the line by three a.m. I spent the whole day wondering how I could get out with a minimum of loss and talked this over with my sergeants and corporals. I always considered this above everything else, which accounted for the fact that my men would follow me blindly. I could also depend on them. The English artillery usually quieted down between eight and ten p.m., probably this was their supper time but on this day there was no let-up. Midnight was the latest hour for me to depart but I was going to hang on until then as it could not get any worse.
>
> Around eleven o'clock the whole front suddenly went dead. Everything was quiet. I took advantage of this, even if I could only reach the entrance to the Bulgaria trench. That was the only one I could use if I wanted to reach the Saubucht. I chased my men down into the valley in groups, where a sergeant was to assemble them behind the ruins of a house. About half a mile to the right was the entrance to the trench, but even though everything sounded quiet on top of the hill I saw now that the shells were dropping at that point at regular intervals, always four shells and four shrapnel arriving together. This looked bad and I changed my mind about going there as my losses would have been terrific. One load must have done heavy damage. Loud yells went through the night and I later learned that our second platoon had been wiped out to the last man.
>
> One look along the trench was enough for me. It was covered with high explosives its entire length as far as I could see. I took the only way remaining, and started right ahead in the open, depending on the dark night and my usual good luck. I had never gone this way before; in fact I had never bothered looking at the maps of this territory. But I would rather get lost for an hour than get my men killed off in the Bulgaria trench. We passed artillery positions, and fell into shell holes just thrown out by mines aimed at the guns. It is a funny feeling to walk on through the night knowing that 60 men are following when I was not sure myself what was coming. When I reached the second defense and the KTK, I found the latter destroyed by a heavy one with a deferred action. The shell had drilled underneath the concrete walls and the following explosion had smashed the whole staff against the ceiling, killing them all, including our doctor. We had to use the trenches now as machine gun and sniper bullets were too numerous to be disregarded. The trench was in very bad condition. Sometimes twenty to thirty yards would be levelled. Everything was quiet, far too quiet to suit me.
>
> Very few whizz bangs whistled past. I called out for a corporal who was an old-timer like myself. Word had passed from man to man and when he came up to me

I asked him if he knew what this meant. He just nodded and said nothing. He had lost the left index finger at Verdun and used to scare people by placing the stump against his nose which made it appear as if he had his whole finger up his nose. He would not live to see daylight. When we reached the trenches of the company district everything was still quiet. I went to the dugout of the officer in charge to find out if anyone else had arrived ahead of me. No, nobody was there as yet. But as long as I was here he packed up and went back. His company was not more than 25 men strong. I asked if he wanted something to eat as I knew the food carriers had not gotten through for the past few nights. He just said, 'who in hell wants to eat here?'

Cold sweat broke out on my face when I saw the man in charge of the Saubucht trenches, who was an old friend. Once I belonged to this company myself. He climbed out of a hole, stared at me with feverish eyes, took my canteen, emptied it out, turned around and walked back without saying a word. He was shell shocked, but still strong enough to keep from acting like a maniac. My company commander came up with the bad news that the Second Platoon was wiped out and that the First Platoon consisted of not more than five men who were on their way up. I thanked my stars that I had not followed the Bulgaria trench.

These heavy losses forced me to divide my men and place them at points to which they were not accustomed. Some dropped off as they went on duty and soon everybody was asleep. I wondered how I could arrange for them to get some rest. I went back to a dugout to take off the linen jacket which I wore over my blouse to protect the uniform but it was getting too hot to wear it. I hardly had it off when all hell broke loose. I just managed to slam my helmet on, and hang the belt with the pistol loosely around my waist, when in came a ton of earth closing the exit, smashing everything to pieces. Up on top was an air hole facing the Saubucht about a foot square and through that I squeezed, blinded by the explosions of phosphorous shells, coming down by the thousands. Next I pulled out my orderly and the corporal I had mentioned before. The three of us were standing there against the wall of the pill box with shells actually raining down on us. Then in front of us an enormous flame shot skywards. We heard nothing as we were too close to the explosion, but the air pressure threw us far away. Hill 60 had been blown up and other explosions all along the line to the south kept the ground shaking for many minutes. Debris began to fall down and something hit me on the helmet which knocked me cold for a while. Again I was glad that I had picked the steel helmet in place of the cap which I usually wore in the trenches. It was still night but everything was lit up by the explosions of the phosphorous shells. They looked pretty but were very dangerous as a drop of the liquid they were throwing around was enough to put a man out of commission. My orderly got splashed on the chest and passed away shortly afterwards. Nothing could be done to help him.

My leg and back hurt as if they had been broken in a thousand places. Finally I managed to sit up, facing back toward the second lines. The corporal crawled over. He looked terrible. The force of the explosion had thrown him face first and blood was streaming down. He showed me where someone was crawling around on top of the trenches and dugouts of the second line which were unoccupied as far as I knew. I realized they must be Englishmen as the Second Platoon, which was to occupy that trench, had never reached this spot and was wiped out. There must have been hundreds of Tommies. My corporal raised his rifle, pulled the trigger, and sank back with a bullet hole through his head. This left me all alone... I knew I could get down to the Saubucht and that down there I was reasonably safe. First I picked off the bird who had killed my corporal. He was standing on top of a pill box not more than 30 yards away, raising his rifle to take aim at me. I laid down and he dropped his rifle, stretching his neck. Then he raised his rifle again but before he had it halfway up he pitched down head first.

The journey down to the Saubucht about 300 feet away was painful enough as my spine was dislocated and both my legs were in bad shape. I crawled the entire distance, biting on my lips as I went. Once down there I was surprised to see two of my machine guns spitting bullets into the advancing lines of Englishmen, who could only advance slowly through the swamps. First I had the ladder-like pathway on which I had come blown up with hand grenades, burning my bridges behind me. Then I posted two men on the other side which connected to the one time Hill 60, now a huge crater. About 15 men from my platoon and some from Regiment 414 were down here. If I could hold this line for an hour or two I was sure to be relieved by a counter attack. I knew such was coming as my regiment had never lost any ground without fighting to the last for it. We were at the end of the English drive, which extended here south to Armentieres along what was known as the Wytschaete bend.

Not more than half a mile to the right near Double Hill 60 and the new Ash Wednesday trench, the German lines held and we could hear our machine guns pumping lead over there. This was the reason we were not troubled by anybody from the right which would have been the weakest spot as the few scattered remnants of the pill boxes in my district would have offered nice cover for advancing snipers.

We ourselves had two heavy machine guns with us and if we could hang on for only a few hours we certainly would be liberated. The counter-attack which we expected came, but too late to save us. The English tried several times to take us from the front. This was easy for us as they could hardly move in the mud through which they could only advance very slowly. There were no shell holes for them to take cover in. sometimes we saw them sink down to their knees and they must have known that their case was hopeless. Next we had to chase away a few snipers who had found their way to the right where I had come down. They did not reach the valley however. I moved one machine gun over to face them and they were gone. The machine gun back in position again, I was anxiously watching the remains of Hill 60. I was not disappointed as there the British now began to put up light and heavy machine guns in the crater left by the explosion. They were about 20 feet higher than we were, but we did not think of giving up. We knew we could expect no mercy as we had been ruthless enough ourselves. Empty cartridges piled up alongside the two guns and dead Tommies piled up in front of us.

There was nothing going on out front just then and we covered the edge of the crater. Another frontal attack forced me to move the guns back into the old position again which left two men near Hill 60 alone to hold off the English with hand grenades. Four of my men were killed there and others were killed and wounded by snipers. The rising sun found five men alive including myself. One machine gun was dead, the other jammed. While repairing this gun I was too anxious to clear it away. I pulled hard on the remover and got caught. I turned the gun over to a sergeant who fired a few shots and then was dead and I had to take his place. My spine nearly drove me crazy and every machine gunner knows that the back has to do a lot of work, nearly more than the two thumbs which press the triggers. One slow move from left to right, one cartridge belt used up and another frontal attack has been stopped. All I was thinking about was July the first. A corporal whom I had never seen before and who belonged to another regiment was feeding the gun and a young kid in the trenches for the first time took care of the empty belt shooting out from the gun. Another young kid was over at the south side of the trench near Hill 60, heaving hand grenades at the English who still tried to get their machine guns started at us. That was all until two more men drifted in who had been closed in a dugout and had dug their way out. They went over to help the kid with the hand grenades.

Suddenly a strange noise mixed with the others. An English scout plane dove down and the pilot threw out hand grenades, waving at us as he passed. The hand grenades fell far away and I figured out that he was gone when again he dove down from the rear not more than 20 feet high, spraying us with his machine guns. Bullets hit all around and the corporal was wounded in the shoulder. I raised my gun a little and held right into the big target. At the same time a shrapnel exploded near him. The machine bucked like a bronco and I pulled in my neck as I expected him to fall right back at me but the momentum of his flight was too great. He was carried more than 500 yards further and there piled up into a heap of kindling wood. Another airplane went down alongside of him, hit by one of their own shells.

One of the new men near Hill 60 had been wounded in the leg by the airplane and he crawled over now taking the place of the corporal, who could do nothing with his shoulder wound. The other man who had come with him was dead, so again the young kid was over there all alone. God, what a fight he put up! He must have been a wonder and this his first time in the trenches. He had come from home a few days after I returned from furlough. My wounded feeder told me that sometimes the kid would stand right up to make sure he did not miss and so I was not at all surprised when the English got too strong for the man. He pulled the wire from a hand grenade and put the grenade into the right spot, blowing himself to pieces and taking about five English machine gunners along to keep him company on his trip across the River Styx. There should have been four of us left now but there were only three as the kid taking care of the empty belt was dead. He had received at least ten bullets from the airplane. In another frontal attack, the belt jammed. I reached over to pull it straight and then the lights went out.

> When I came to I saw an English officer turn me over like a bag of salt, using his feet, not his hands. The game was up. I tried to get up but I could not. English stretcher bearers came up and when they put me on a stretcher I asked them to dress the wounds of the corporal first who was losing too much blood. They shook their heads and when they turned around to climb up the incline to Hill 60 I saw my corporal dead with my pistol in his hand. He must have shot to the last. The only two left were the man with the wound in his leg and myself.[1]

This was the start of Hans Ludwig's time as a PoW. He was severely wounded in several places, especially his legs and there was a brief discussion by the initial treating doctors when possible amputation was discussed. Fortunately for Hans, both legs were saved.

The ordeal he had already suffered in the fighting was not quite over. After being placed in an ambulance and during the transport to the rear the ambulance came under German fire. The ambulance was struck and Hans was thrown clear of the vehicle. Men in nearby dugouts rushed over to help and placed Hans into another ambulance. The man below Hans in the ambulance had been killed, both of the attendants had been wounded and a small dog, apparently their pet, had also been killed. Hans Ludwig also survived this trip and was sent to England for treatment and then placement in a PoW camp.

After a long time as a prisoner, the time for his release finally arrived. Considering that he had survived three years of fighting you might expect that the trip home would be the easiest part of his ordeal, however this was not to be.

On the trip home, he and his companions were the target of rage by the local Belgian population as the repatriation train travelled through the countryside. Belgian farmers would fire shotguns at the passing trains, more in anger than anything else. Even though being struck by this fire was remote, it was still very unpleasant for the returning soldiers. Once the train reached Germany, there were no further shooting incidents, only indifference on the part of the local population. There were no cheering crowds or any type of warm welcome. The local population had already experienced unrest and upheaval following the end of the war and was coping with extreme hardships over the shortages of food, heating fuel, basics such as medicines, the start of hyperinflation and massive unemployment. Faced with these issues and others of a similar nature the people had no time for a few returning prisoners.

Just before reaching Frankfurt the train started to accelerate and sway from side to side as it careened down the tracks toward the city. The first attempts to engage the brakes failed and it was not until the conductor realized that the air hose had separated and then fixed the problem did the train stop. The train stopped so suddenly that everyone on board was violently thrown forward and many people were injured as a result.

While awaiting the next train at the station and watching the injured being taken away in ambulances Hans and his companion decided to get something to eat. The meal they were able to obtain was of poor quality as well as inadequate in size. Following this meager meal the two men were approached by two well-dressed men who spoke poor German and who asked if they had enough to eat. When they replied, 'no', the two men took them to a good restaurant nearby and ordered a large meal. However, the waiter said that all of the food was gone and he could not provide the meals. One of the men then gave the waiter a U.S. $1 bill, and within a short time they were all enjoying a good meal.

The two strangers turned out to be members of the American Consulate in Geneva, Switzerland and were travelling there when they saw Ludwig and his associate and figured they were returning PoW's and they decided to help the rather gaunt looking soldiers.

When Ludwig finally returned home, he was not recognized by friends or family, not even by his dog Pascha. His father missed his return as he was out in the countryside trying to find food for the family. At night Hans tried to sleep in a feather bed but after falling asleep quickly he woke up a short time later feeling pain and agony everywhere in his body, as if he had been beaten and trussed up. He sat on the floor and in a short while felt better and decided to sleep on the floor and had a good night's sleep. Hans pointed out that the hips on both sides were like leather and 'I could stick a pin into them without feeling it.' It would be quite some time before he was able to sleep in a soft bed again after so many years of sleeping on hard surfaces and in poor weather conditions.

It was not too many months before Hans Ludwig decided to emigrate to the United States for a better life. He already had experienced the difficulty in finding work as there were so few jobs and so many people looking for work. After being away from home for six years he had no true skills that would land him a good position. Fortunately he already had an uncle who was operating a dry cleaning establishment on West 49th Street in in New York City so he would have someone to help him when he immigrated to the United States.

Upon his arrival at Ellis Island Hans Ludwig still appeared gaunt and far older than his years as a result of the war. He passed by one cousin on Ellis Island and another at the pier by Battery Park without being recognized as he made his way toward his uncle's business. Upon arrival his uncle was quite surprised to see him standing there and his first words were, 'How in hell did you get here?' Hans explained his long journey to his uncle and from that date forward he liked the U.S. He started a family after his arrival and it is thanks to them, especially Brian Ludwig that I have been able to share some of the experiences of Hans Ludwig in the Great War.

Notes

1. Ludwig, Hans, 'Red Ink – Red Blood', unpublished manuscript.

Bibliography

Unpublished Sources

Correspondence

Feldpost letters of Oberleutnant Erwin Boy RIR 111

Feldpost letters of Leutnant der Reserve Albert Reihling, 4 /R119

Feldpost letters of Chr. Gerber, 8/R119

Feldpost letters of Unteroffizier Otto Nuding, IR 180 2nd Comp. 26 Res. Div. 14 RAK,

Ludwig, Hans, Red Blood-Red Ink, manuscript, n.d.

Regimental Stammrolle Books

Kriegsstammrollen, 1914-1918. Bavarian State Archives. Department IV, War Archive, Munich.

Bavarian RIR 6

Kriegsstammrollen M468, Infantry Regiment 180, Württemberg Hauptstaatsarchiv, Stuttgart

Kriegsstammrollen M476, Reserve Infantry Regiment 119, Württemberg Hauptstaatsarchiv, Stuttgart

Kriegsstammrollen M478, Reserve Infantry Regiment 121, Württemberg Hauptstaatsarchiv, Stuttgart

Kriegsstammrollen M527, Reserve Feld Artillerie Regiment 26, Württemberg Hauptstaatsarchiv, Stuttgart

Kriegsstammrollen M528, Reserve Feld Artillerie Regiment 27, Württemberg Hauptstaatsarchiv, Stuttgart

Kriegsstammrollen M595, Vermisstenkartei I, Württemberg Hauptstaatsarchiv, Stuttgart

Kriegsstammrollen M596, Vermisstenkartei II, Württemberg Hauptstaatsarchiv, Stuttgart

Kriegsstammrollen M597, Vermisstenkartei III, Württemberg Hauptstaatsarchiv, Stuttgart

Kriegsstammrollen Generallandesarchiv Karlsruhe Nr. 2431, RIR 109

Kriegsstammrollen Generallandesarchiv Karlsruhe Nr. 2543, RIR 110

Kriegsstammrollen Generallandesarchiv Karlsruhe Nr. 2638, RIR 109

Official War Diaries

Australian War Diaries, Australian War Memorial, Canberra
Canadian War Diaries, Library and Archives Canada, Ottawa

Printed Sources (Books & Articles)

Anon, *Deutsche Verlustlisten*, (1916-1919), Berlin, 1914-1919

Anon, *Die 26. Reserve Division 1914-1918,* Stuttgart, 1920

Anon, *Ehrenbuch der Stadt Karlsruhe 1914-1918*, Karlsruhe, 1930

Anon, *Festschrift zur Wiedersehens-Feier der Angehörigen des ehem. Res. Inf. Regts. 111*, Karlsruhe, 1932

Anon, *Illustrierte Geschichte des Weltkrieges 1914/18*, Band 5-9, Stuttgart, n.d.

Anon, *Kriegstagbuch aus Schwaben*, Stuttgart, 1914-1919

Bachelin, Major Eduard, *Das Reserve-Infanterie-Regiment Nr. 111 im Weltkrieg 1914 bis 1918,* Karlsruhe, 1938

Bayerisches Kriegsarchiv, *Die Bayern im Grossen Krieg 1914-1918,* München, 1923

Delmensingen, *General der Artillerie* Konrad Kraft von & Feeser, Generalmajor a.D.

Friedrichfranz, *Das Bayernbuch vom Weltkriege 1914-1918,* Stuttgart, 1930

Edmonds, Brigadier-General Sir James E., *History of the Great War. Military Operations France and Belgium 1918. March-April: Continuation of the German Offensives,* London, 19

Ehrler, Hans Heinrich, *Ehrenbuch der Gefallenen Stuttgarts 1914-1918,* Stuttgart, 1925

Fabeck, Hans von, *Im Orkan der Sommeschlacht. Ein Abschnitt aus der Kriegsgeschichte des Reserve-Infanterie-Regiment Nr. 99,* Berlin, 1930

Frisch, Georg, *Das Reserve-Infanterie-Regiment Nr. 109 im Weltkrieg 1914 bis 1918,* Karlsruhe, 1931

Führen, Franz, *Lehrer im Krieg*, Berlin, 1932

Gallion, Leutnant der Reserve W., *Das Reserve-Infanterie-Regiment 40 im Weltkrieg,* Karlsruhe an Rhein, 1936

General Staff, *Handbook of the German Army in War, January 1917,* Wakefield, 1973

Gerster, Matthäus, *Das Württembergische Reserve-Infanterie-Regiment Nr. 119 im Weltkrieg 1914-1918,* Stuttgart, 1920

Gerster, Matthäus, *Treffen der 26.R.D. am 5 Juli 1936,* Stuttgart, 1936

[Greiner & Vulpius], *Reserve-Infanterie-Regiment Nr. 110 im Weltkrieg 1914-1918,* Karlsruhe, 1934

Holtz, Hauptmann Freiherr Georg vom, *Das Württembergische Reserve-Infanterie-Regiment Nr. 121 im Weltkrieg 1914-1918,* Stuttgart, 1921

Jäger, Herbert, *German Artillery of World War One,* Marlborough, 2001

Kameradschaftsbund, *Ehrentafel Res. Inf. Regt. 119,* n.d.

Klaus, Major a.D. Justizrat Max, *Das Württembergisches Reserve-Feldartillerie-Regiment Nr. 26 im Weltkrieg 1914-1918,* Stuttgart, 1929

Knies, Oberstleutnant L., *Das Württembergishe Pionier Bataillon Nr. 13 im Weltkrieg 1914-1918,* Stuttgart, 1937

Kölbig, Kurt Siegfried, Kuhn, Hans-Karl, *Gedanken an der Westfront 1914-1917. Das Tagesbuch des Leutnants der Reserve Karl August Zwiffelhoffer,* Nyon, 2007

Korps Buchhandlung, *Der Schützengraben, Feldzeitung des XIV Reservekorps (1915-1917),* Bapaume, 1915-1917

Korpsverlagsbuchhandlung, *An der Somme,* Bapaume, 1917

Korpsverlagsbuchhandlung, *Zwischen Arras und Péronne,* Bapaume, 1916

Kühl, Hermann von, *Der Weltkrieg 1914-1918,* Berlin 1933

Kümmel, Leutnant d.Res. a.D. Studienrat Dr. Phil., *Reserve-Infanterie-Regiment Nr. 91 im Weltkriege 1914-1918,* Oldenburg, 1926

Lutz, Ralph Haswell, Fall of the German Empire 1914-1918, Stanford, California, 1932

Lutz, Ralph Haswell, *The Causes of the German Collapse in 1918*, Stanford, California, 1934

Merkatz, Friedrich von, *Unterrichtsbuch für die Maschinengewehr-Kompagnien Gerät 08,* Berlin 1918

Moos, Leutnant d. R. a.D. Ernst, *Das Württembergische Res.-Feld-Artillerie Regiment Nr.27 im Weltkrieg 1916-1918,* Stuttgart, 1925

Moser, Generalleutnant Otto von, *Die Württemberger im Weltkriege,* Stuttgart, 1938

Müller, Major d.R. Paul, Fabeck, Oberst a.D. Hans von & Riesel, Oberstleutnant a.D. Richard, *Geschichte des Reserve-Infanterie-Regiment Nr. 99,* Zeulenroda, 1936

Müller-Loebnitz, Oberstleutnant Wilhelm, *Die Badener im Weltkrieg,* Karlsruhe, 1935

Offiziersverein des I.R. 180, *Totenbuch des 10.Württembergischen Infanterie-Regiment Nr. 180. Namentliches Verzeichnis der im Weltkrieg 1914-1918 gefallenen Offiziere, Unteroffiziere und Mannschaften,* Stuttgart, 1936

Reichskriegsministerium, *Der Weltkrieg 1914 bis 1918. Die Militärischen Operationen zu Lande, Zehnter Band,* Berlin, 1936

Reichskriegsministerium, *Der Weltkrieg 1914 bis 1918. Die Militärischen Operationen zu Lande, Elfter Band,* Berlin, 1938

Reichskriegsministerium, *Der Weltkrieg 1914 bis 1918. Die Militärischen Operationen zu Lande, Zwölfter Band,* Berlin, 1939

Reichskriegsministerium, *Der Weltkrieg 1914 bis 1918. Die Militärischen Operationen zu Lande, Dreizehnter Band,* Berlin, 1942

Reichskriegsministerium, *Der Weltkrieg 1914 bis 1918. Die Militärischen Operationen zu Lande, Vierzehnter Band,* Berlin, 1944

Reichskriegsministerium, *Der Weltkrieg 1914 bis 1918. Die Militärischen Operationen zu Lande, Beilagen zum Vierzehnter Band, Die Kriegführung an der Westfront im Jahre 1918* Berlin, 1944

Silbereisen, Leutnant der Reserve, Ehrler, Landsturmmann Hans Heinrich, Eisenmann, Landsturmmann Alexander & Schulze-Etzel, Gefreiten Theodor, *Schwäbische Kunde aus den grossen Krieg,* Stuttgart, 1918

Stallings, Lawrence, *The First World War, a Photographic History,* New York, 1933

Stühmke, General der Infanterie a.D., *Die 26.(Württembergische) Reserve-Division im Weltkrieg 1914-1918,* Stuttgart, 1935
Vischer, Oberstleutnant Alfred, *Das 10. Württembergische Infanterie-Regiment Nr. 180 im Weltkrieg 1914-1918,* Stuttgart, 1921
Volksbund Deutsche Kriegsgräberfürsorge e.V., *Deutsche Kriegsgräber, Am Rande der Strasse, Frankreich, Belgien, Luxemburg und Niederlande,* Kassel, n.d.
Wissmann, Oberst von, *Das Reserve-Infanterie-Regiment Nr. 55 im Weltkrieg,* Berlin, n.d.
Wohlenberg, Oberleutnant d.R. a.D. Rektor Alfred, *Das Reserve-Infanterie-Regiment Nr. 77 im Weltkriege 1914-18,* Hildesheim, 1931

Newspapers

Freiburger Zeitung
New York Times Mid-week War Pictorial Extra